Historical Dictionary
of
Togo

AFRICAN HISTORICAL DICTIONARIES
Edited by Jon Woronoff

1. *Cameroon,* by Victor T. LeVine and Roger P. Nye. 1974. Out of print. See No. 48.
2. *The Congo,* 2nd ed., by Virginia Thompson and Richard Adloff. 1984.
3. *Swaziland,* by John J. Grotpeter. 1975.
4. *The Gambia,* 2nd ed., by Harry A. Gailey. 1987.
5. *Botswana,* by Richard P. Stevens. 1975. Out of print. See No. 44.
6. *Somalia,* by Margaret F. Castagno. 1975.
7. *Benin [Dahomey],* 2nd ed., by Samuel Decalo. 1987. Out of print. See No. 61.
8. *Burundi,* by Warren Weinstein. 1976.
9. *Togo,* 3rd ed., by Samuel Decalo. 1996.
10. *Lesotho,* by Gordon Haliburton. 1977.
11. *Mali,* 2nd ed., by Pascal James Imperato. 1986.
12. *Sierra Leone,* by Cyril Patrick Foray. 1977.
13. *Chad,* 2nd ed., by Samuel Decalo. 1987.
14. *Upper Volta,* by Daniel Miles McFarland. 1978.
15. *Tanzania,* by Laura S. Kurtz. 1978.
16. *Guinea,* 3rd ed., by Thomas O'Toole with Ibrahima Bah-Lalya. 1995.
17. *Sudan,* by John Voll. 1978. Out of print. See No. 53.
18. *Rhodesia/Zimbabwe,* by R. Kent Rasmussen. 1979. Out of print. See No. 46.
19. *Zambia,* by John J. Grotpeter. 1979.
20. *Niger,* 2nd ed., by Samuel Decalo. 1989.
21. *Equatorial Guinea,* 2nd ed., by Max Liniger-Goumaz. 1988.
22. *Guinea-Bissau,* 2nd ed., by Richard Lobban and Joshua Forrest. 1988.
23. *Senegal,* by Lucie G. Colvin. 1981. Out of print. See No. 65.
24. *Morocco,* by William Spencer. 1980.
25. *Malawi,* by Cynthia A. Crosby. 1980. Out of print. See No. 54.
26. *Angola,* by Phyllis Martin. 1980. Out of print. See No. 52.
27. *The Central African Republic,* by Pierre Kalck. 1980. Out of print. See No. 51.
28. *Algeria,* by Alf Andrew Heggoy. 1981. Out of print. See No. 66.
29. *Kenya,* by Bethwell A. Ogot. 1981.
30. *Gabon,* by David E. Gardinier. 1981. Out of print. See No. 58.
31. *Mauritania,* by Alfred G. Gerteiny. 1981. Out of print. See No. 68.

64. *Uganda,* by M. Louise Pirouet. 1995.
65. *Senegal,* 2nd ed., by Andrew F. Clark and Lucie Colvin Phillips. 1994.
66. *Algeria,* 2nd ed., by Phillip Chiviges Naylor and Alf Andrew Heggoy. 1994.
67. *Egypt,* by Arthur Goldschmidt, Jr. 1994.
68. *Mauritania,* by Anthony G. Pazzanita. 1996.
69. *The Congo,* 3rd ed., by Samuel Decalo. 1996.

HISTORICAL DICTIONARY
OF
TOGO

Third Edition

by
SAMUEL DECALO

African Historical Dictionaries, No. 9

The Scarecrow Press, Inc.
Lanham, Md., & London

SCARECROW PRESS, INC.

Published in the United States of America
by Scarecrow Press, Inc.
4720 Boston Way
Lanham, Maryland 20706

4 Pleydell Gardens, Folkestone
Kent CT20 2DN, England

British Cataloguing-in-Publication Information Available

Library of Congress Cataloging-in-Publication Data

Decalo, Samuel.
Historical dictionary of Togo / by Samuel Decalo.
p.   cm. — (African historical dictionaries)
1. Togo—History—Dictionaries.   2. Togo—Bibliography.
I. Title.   II. Series.
DT582.5.D4   1996   996.81′003—dc20   95-44920   CIP

ISBN 0-81083073-6 (cloth : alk. paper)

The author wishes to acknowledge the generous financial support of the University Research Committee of the University of Natal, without which this third edition could not have been completed.

This book is dedicated to
ROMA, RUTH, AND NIV

Contents

Editor's Foreword

On a continent littered with political and economic failures, Togo's are among the most disappointing. Under German occupation, it was styled the "model colony." Under French colonization, it made modest economic progress, and its educated youth found jobs throughout the metropolis. The beginnings of the new independent state were also promising, although ethnic friction and political instability soon set in. When General Eyadema took power after a coup d'etat in 1967 there was still some room for hope. More than a quarter of a century later he is still there, and every trace of hope has faded after repeated demonstrations, disturbances, and false democratizations.

This is the third edition of the *Historical Dictionary of Togo;* it is also the saddest. It traces the downward path of this unfortunate state and it includes entries on the whole cast of characters, the more sinister regularly winning out over the more credible. It also provides the necessary background entries on Togo's history, politics, foreign relations, economy, society, geography, and ethnic diversity. Yet no matter how negative, it does show that there are positive elements and tenuous hopes for a better future. For those who want to know more about Togo, it also offers an amazingly extensive and comprehensive bibliography.

This third edition was written by the author of the first two editions, Samuel Decalo. Professor Decalo, who has taught at the University of Natal and the University of Florida among others, remains one of the leading authorities on French-speaking Africa and also military regimes. His books include *Coups and Army Rule in Africa* and *Psychoses of Power: Personal Dictatorship in Africa* as well as the Benin, Chad, and Niger *Historical Dictionaries*. Like the others, this greatly updated and expanded edition will quickly become a privileged source of information.

Jon Woronoff
Series Editor

TRANSPORT AND COMMUNICATIONS

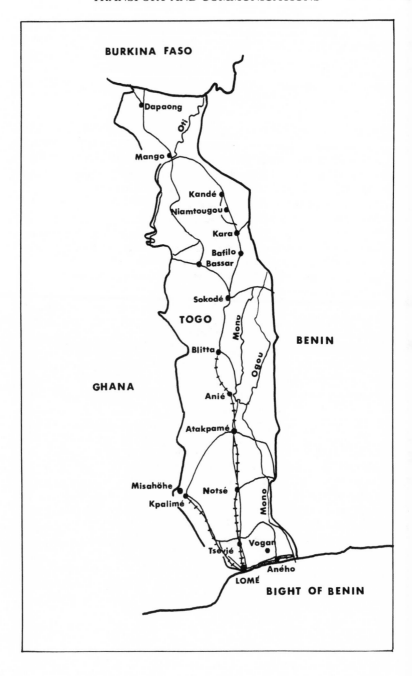

ADMINISTRATIVE DIVISIONS

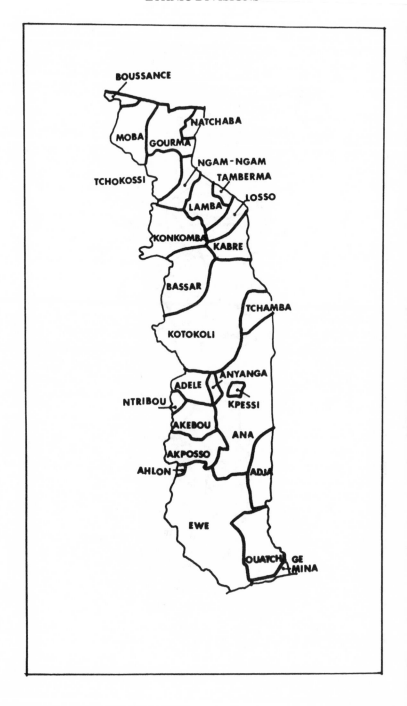

A Note on Spelling

Many of the names of Togo's ethnic groups are spelled differently in English and in French. In most cases the variations are easy to recognize as with Gurma-Gourma, Kotokoli-Cotocoli, Chokossi-Tyokossi, Ehvé-Ewe, Watchi-Ouatchi and Cabrais-Kabré. Any decision as to which form of spelling to use in this dictionary would of necessity have to be arbitrary, especially since many authors writing in English use the French spelling, while some (fewer) French authors utilize the English version. The procedure in this dictionary has been, therefore, to use the most common form of spelling in the literature (usually the French) while cross-listing other variants for the convenience of the reader.

With respect to the personal names of Togolese personalities, it should be noted that the cultural authenticity drives of the early 1970's resulted in numerous adoptions of ethnic names and the discarding of Christian ones. At the same time a number of towns also reverted to a more phonetic transliteration of their original (pre-colonial) name. A good example of this is the "renaming" of Aného (instead of Anécho) and Notsé, instead of the colonial Nuatja.

These changes have caused and, surprisingly, still cause considerable confusion. In general place-name changes have *not* been acknowledged abroad, at least if judged by the prevalence of old forms of spelling in atlases and reference works appearing decades after the official changes. At the same time, Togolese have tended to use their Christian and ethnic names interchangeably to suit various conditions. Thus, a certain minister might be known under one set of names at home and prefer to be known (and hence be addressed) by a completely different given name abroad. In this dictionary all place names are recorded with cross-references to old variants, while biographical listings record contemporary given names with "old" variants noted in parentheses.

Abbreviations and Acronyms

ADR	Alliance de Democrates pour le Renouveau
AEC	All-Ewe Conference
AEF	Afrique Equatoriale Française
AJMT	Association de la Jeunesse Musulmane du Togo
ALT	Assemblée Legislative du Togo
AN	Assemblée Nationale
ANT	Assemblée Nationale du Togo
AOF	Afrique Occidentale Française
ART	Assemblée Représentative du Togo
ATD	Alliance Togolaise pour la Démocratie
ATP	Agence Togolaise du Presse
ATT	Assemblée Territoriale du Togo
BALTEX	Banque Arabe-Libyenne Togolaise du Commerce Extérieur
BCEAO	Banque Centrale des Etats de l'Afrique de l'Ouest
BIAO	Banque Internationale pour l'Afrique du Togo
BTCI	Banque Togolaise pour le Commerce et l'Industrie
BTD	Banque Togolaise de Développement
Bund	Bund der Deutschen Togoländer
CAF	Collectif d'Associations des Femmes
CAR	Comité d'Action pour le Renouveau
CATC	Confédération Africaine des Travailleurs Croyants
CATR	Comité d'Action contre le Tribalisme et le Racisme
CCCE	Caisse Centrale de Coopération Economique
CCFOM	Caisse Centrale de la France Outre Mer
CCTT	Congrès des Chefs Traditionnels du Togo
CDC	Caisse des Dépots et Consignations
CDP	Convention Démocratique Panafricain
CDPA	Convention Démocratique
CEB	Compagnie Electrique du Bénin
CEET	Compagnie Energie Electrique du Togo
CERK	Centre d'Etudes et de Recherches de Kara
CFA	Communauté Financière Africaine
CFAF	Communauté Financière Africaine francs
CFT	Chemin de Fer du Togo

CIGB	La Cartonnerie-Imprimerie Générale du Bénin
CIMAO	Ciments de l'Afrique de l'Ouest
CIMTOGO	Ciments du Togo
CNCA	Caisse Nationale de Crédit Agricole
CNDH	Commission Nationale pour le Droits de l'Homme
CNP	Conseil National de Patronat
CNSS	Caisse Nationale de Securité Sociale
CNTT	Confédération Nationale des Travailleurs du Togo
COD	Collectif d'Opposition Démocratique
COD2	Collectif d'Opposition Démocratique 2
CONGAT	Conseil des Organismes Non-gouvernementaux en Activité au Togo
COTOMIB	Compagnie Togolaise des Mines du Bénin
CRN	Comité de Réconciliation Nationale
CSI	Collectif Syndicale Independant
CSTT	Confédération Syndicale des Travailleurs du Togo
CTM	Compagnie Togolaise Maritime
CTMB	Compagnie Togolaise des Mines du Bénin
CTR	Comité Togolaise de Résistance
CUT	Comité de l'Unité Togolaise
ECOWAS	Economic Community of West African States
EDF	European Development Fund
EDITOGO	Establissement National des Editions du Togo
EEC	European Economic Community
EEC	Ewe Evangelical Church
EET	Eglise Evangélique du Togo
ENA	Ecole Nationale d'Administration
EPC	Ewe Presbyterian Church
EUA	Ewe Unionist Association
FAC	Fonds d'Aide et de Coopération
FAO	Food and Agricultural Organization
FAR	Front des Associations pour le Renouveau
FCSP	Fonds Commun des Sociétés de Prévoyance
FEANF	Fédération des Etudiants de l'Afrique Noire en France
FED	Fonds Européen de Développement
FIDES	Fonds d'Investissement pour le Développement Economique et Social des Territoires d'Outre Mer
FIR	Forces d'Intervention Rapide
FNLT	Front National de Libération du Togo
FOD	Front d'Opposition Démocratique
FORS 93	Force de Reconciliation et Securité
FP	Front Patriotique des Peuples Africaines
FPSNT	Front Populaire de Salut National du Togo
GITO	Groupement Interprofessionel des Enterprises du Togo
GMC	Générale de Matieres Colorantes

GRAD	Groupe de Reflexion et d'Action des Jeunes pour la Démocratie
GSP	Groupe Social Pan-Africain
GTFT	Groupement du Théâtre et du Folklore Togolais
HCR	Haut Conseil de la République
IESB	Institut d'Enseignement Supérieur du Bénin
IFAN	Institut Français d'Afrique Noire
IMF	International Monetary Fund
INARES	Institut National de Recherches Scientifiques
INFAL	Institut National de Formation Agricole de Lomé
INITO	Initiative Togolaise
INPT	Institut National des Plantes à Tubercules
INSE	Institut National de Science de l'Education
INTSHU	Institut Togolais des Sciences Humaines
IOTO	Industrie Oléagineaux du Togo
IPN	Institut Pedagogique National
IRAT	Institut de Recherches Agronomiques Tropicales
IRCC	Institut de Recherche du Cacao et du Café
IRCTE	Institut de Recherches du Coton et des Textiles Exotiques
IRHO	Institut de Recherches pour les Huiles et Oléagineaux
IRTO	Institut de Recherches du Togo
ITOCY	Industrie Togolaise du Cycle et du Cyclomoteur
ITP	Industrie Togolaise des Plastiques
ITT	Industrie Textile Togolaise
JPA	Jeunesse Pionnière Agricole
JRPT	Jeunesse du Rassemblement du Peuple Togolais
LTDH	Ligue Togolaise du Droit d'Homme
MELD	Mouvement Etudiant de Lutte pour la Démocratie
MNU	Mouvement Nationaliste pour l'Unité
MO-5	Mouvement d'Octobre 5
MONESTO	Mouvement National des Etudiants et Stagiaires Togolais
MPT	Mouvement Populaire Togolais
MRN	Mouvement de Régroupement National
MTD	Mouvement Togolaise Démocratique
MTP	La Manufacture Togolaise des Plastiques
NIOTO	Nouvelle Industrie Oleagineaux du Togo
OAU	Organization of African Unity
OCAM	Organisation Commune Africaine et Malgache
OCAMM	Organisation Commune Africaine, Malgache et Mauritienne
ODEF	Office National de Développement et Exploitation des Ressources Forestières
ONADEC	Office National du Développement de l'Elevage

ONAF	Office National des Abattoirs Frigorifiques
ONP	Office National des Pêches
OPAT	Office des Produits Agricoles du Togo
ORPV	Office Régionale pour la Population des Produits Vivriers
OTP	Office Togolais des Phosphates
OTTD	Organisation Togolaise des Travailleurs Démocratiques
PAD	Parti d'Action pour le Développement
PCT	Parti Communiste Togolais
PDR	Parti Démocratique de Renouveau
PDU	Parti des Démocrates pour l'Unité
PPT	Parti Progrèssiste Togolais
PRDD	Parti Populaire pour la Démocratie et le Développement du Togo
PRSB	Parti de la Révolution Socialiste du Bénin
PSD	Parti Social-Démocrate
PSP	Parti Socialiste Pan-Africain
PSRT	Parti Socialiste Révolutionnaire du Togo
PTP	Parti Togolais du Progrès
PUT	Parti de l'Unité Togolaise
RIAT	Regiment Inter-Arme Togolais
RPT	Rassemblement du Peuple Togolais
RTNM	Radiodiffusion Télévision de la Nouvelle Marché
SALINTO	Société des Salines du Togo
SATAL	Société Agricole Togolaise Arabe Libyenne
SCIMPEXTO	Syndicat des Commerçants Importeurs de la République Togolaise
SEPT	Syndicat des Enseignants Protestants du Togo
SGG-Togo	Société Générale du Golfe du Guinée-Togo
SGMT	Société Générale des Minoteries du Togo
SIP	Sociétés Indigènes de Prévoyance
SIPAL	Société Industrielle de Preparations Alimentaires
SMRT	Sociétés Mutuelles Rurales Togolaises
SNIT	Société Nationale d'Investissement et Fond Annexes du Togo
SNS	Société Nationale de Siderurgie
SOLITO	Parti Sociale-Liberale du Togo
SOAEM-Togo	Société Ouest Africaine d'Enterprise Maritimes du Togo
SONACOM	Société Nationale de Commerce
SONAD	Société Nationale de Développement
SONAM	Société Nationale Maritime
SONAPH	Société Nationale pour le Développement de la Palmeraie et les Huileries

SOPROLAIT	Société de Produits Laitiers du Togo Sociétés
SORAD	Sociétés Régionales de Développement et d'Aménagement
SOTEHPA	Société Togolaise d'Extraction d'Huile de Palme
SOTEXIM	Société Togolaise d'Exportation et d'Importation
SOTEXMA	Société Togolaise d'Exploitation du Materiel Fruitière
SOTOCO	Société Togolaise du Coton
SOTODAS	Société Togolaise et Danoise Savons
SOTOMA	Société Togolaise de Marbrerie
SOTONAM	Société Nationale Maritime
SOTOPROMER	Société Togolaise des Produits du Mer
SPAR	Sociétés Publiques d'Action Rurale
SRCC	Société Nationale pour la Rénovation et le Développement de la Cacaoyère et de la Caféière Togolaises
SSRC	Société Sucrière de la Région Centrale
STAB	Société Togolaise des Attapulgites et Bentonite
STALPECHE	Société Togolo-Arabe-Libyienne de Pêche
STB	Société Togolaise de Boissons
STH	Société Togolaise de l'Hôtellerie
STH	Société Togolaise des Hydrocarbures
STS	Société Togolaise de Siderurgie
STSL	Société Togolaise de Stockage de Lomé
Togobund	Bund der Deutschen Togoländer
TOGOFRUIT	Société Togolaise pour le Développement de Culture Fruitière
TOGOGRAIN	Office National des Produits Vivriers
TOGOPROM	Société Togolaise de Promotion pour le Développement
TOGOROUTE	Société Nationale de Transports Routiers
TOGOTABAC	Régie Togolaise des Tabacs
TOGOTEX	Compagnie Togolaise des Textiles
TOLIMO	National Movement for the Liberation of Western Togoland
UCPN	Union des Chefs et des Populations du Nord
UCTT	Union des Chefs Traditionnels du Togo
UDPT	Union Démocratique des Peuples Togolais
UMOA	Union Monétaire de l'Ouest Afrique
UMT	Union Musulmane du Togo
UNCTT	Union Nationale des Chefs Traditionnels du Togo
UNELCO	Union Electrique Coloniale
UNESCO	United Nations Educational, Scientific and Cultural Organization
UNETO	Union Nationale des Etudiants Togolais
UNFT	Union Nationale des Femmes du Togo

UNJT	Union Nationale de la Jeunesse Togolaise
UNTT	Union Nationale des Travailleurs Togolais
UT	Unité Togolaise
UTB	Union Togolaise de Banque
UTD	Union Togolaise pour la Démocratie
UTR	Union Togolaise pour la Renouveau
ZAAP	Zones d'Amenagement Agricole Planifié
ZFTE	Zone Franche de Transformation pour l'Exploitation

Recent Political Chronology

July 4, 1884	German Protectorate Treaty with Chief Mlapa III of Togo
Aug. 8, 1914	Anglo-French invasion of Togo
July 10, 1919	Anglo-French partition of Togo under League of Nations mandates
Dec. 13, 1946	Anglo-French Trusteeship over Togo ratified by the United Nations
Feb. 6, 1952	Double Electoral College System abolished
May 9, 1956	Plebiscite in British Togoland; territory opts to merge with the Gold Coast
Oct. 28, 1956	Following a referendum, France establishes the Autonomous Republic of Togo under leadership of Nicolas Grunitzky
April 17, 1958	U.N.-supervised elections bring Sylvanus Olympio to power
April 27, 1960	Proclamation of Independence
Jan. 13, 1963	Coup d'état of the demobilized veterans
May 5, 1963	New constitution and Grunitzky administration set up
Nov. 19, 1966	Adossama and Malou resign from the cabinet, precipitating major governmental crisis
Nov. 21, 1966	Lomé uprising against Grunitzky regime
Jan. 13, 1967	Coup d'état of General Eyadema
Jan. 14, 1967	National Reconciliation Committee created under Kleber Dadjo
April 14, 1967	General Eyadema gathers all powers and sets up his administration
May 12, 1967	All political parties banned
Aug.–Nov. 1969	Erection of the Rassemblement du Peuple Togolais
Aug. 8, 1970	Attempted coup sponsored by self-exiled leader Nöe Kutuklui
Aug. 1971	RPT abolishes position of Secretary General in favor of a collegiate Political Bureau
Jan. 9, 1972	National Referendum on the continued leadership of General Eyadema

April 26– 28, 1972	OCAM Summit meeting in Lomé
Jan. 24, 1974	General Eyadema's plane crashes near Lama Kara. Shortly after, the nationalization of COTOMIB is announced.
Sept. 17, 1974	RPT drive against "imported names" as part of the authenticity policy of General Eyadema
Jan. 13, 1975	Abolition of the unpopular head tax
Jan. 13, 1976	Controversial irredentist ad placed in London *Times* calling for the restoration of Togo's precolonial boundaries
Nov. 30, 1976	RPT Congress "rejects" a return to civilian rule, and modifies Government and party structures
Feb. 1, 1977	Cabinet reshuffle results in Eyadema remaining the only military officer in the government. Massive intensification of the Cult of Personality in Togo
Oct. 1977	Mercenary assassination plot against Eyadema thwarted
Nov. 1978	Core "Brazilian" families, including the Olympio and de Souza ones implicated in the 1977 plot
Aug. 26, 1979	Trial commences of the ten main conspirators of 1977
Dec. 30, 1979	Election of Togo's first National Assembly since 1967 under a new Constitution with Eyadema as president of the Third Republic
June 16, 1980	Inauguration of the last segment of the paved North-South axis
Nov. 27, 1982	Major economic stress brings about the reimposition of a five percent solidarity tax on all salaries
Dec. 3–4, 1982	RPT Congress examining the bloated, inefficient, corrupt parastatal sector recommends the dissolution of several companies and the placing on probation of others.
June 1984	Rescheduling of Togo's large ($812 million) international debt
Sept. 13, 1984	Major cabinet reshuffle
Dec. 1984	Privatization of the steel industry
Mar. 24, 1985	High turnout for Togo's second legislative elections under Eyadema
Mar. 29, 1985	Colonel Koffi Kongo dies while under house arrest
Aug.– Sept. 1985	Series of bomb explosions in downtown Lomé
July 1986	Complex coup attempt against Eyadema.
Sept. 23, 1986	Armed plot against Eyadema from across Ghana. France dispatches 250 soldiers to stabilize the situation.
Dec. 23, 1986	Eyadema re-elected to another seven year term by 99.85 percent of the population.

Oct. 5, 1990	Violent demonstration calling for Eyadema's resignation or overthrow erupts in Lomé. Numerous dead and wounded. Eyadema concedes liberalization and multipartyism.
Mar. 12, 1991	Civil unrest continues; clashes between students and army.
Apr. 18, 1991	Brutal Bé Lagoon massacres take place in Lomé's outskirts. Eyadema's elite units responsible.
June 6, 1991	Tens of thousands demonstrate for a National Conference and declare an "indefinite strike" when Eyadema seems to renege on his political liberalization promise. Eyadema capitulates on June 12th.
June 20, 1991	Memory of Sylvanus Olympio rehabilitated.
July 6, 1991	Gilchrist Olympio returns to Togo from exile and is greeted by thousands of supporters. Other opposition exiles also return.
July 8, 1991	National Conference convenes, to last fifty-two days: it lambasts Eyadema and the armed forces, declares its sovereignty, dissolves existing National Assembly and RPT party, and abrogates the 1980 Constitution.
Aug. 23, 1991	Revelations that 900 billion CFAF have been embezzled under the Eyadema regime, one third by Eyadema himself.
Aug. 26, 1991	National Conference selects a transitional government (Haut Conseil de la République) under Kokou Koffigoh pending elections in June 1992.
Oct. 1, 1991	Troops seize Radio Lomé to call on Eyadema to dissolve the transitional government.
Oct. 8, 1991	Another violent military rebellion in Lomé.
Nov. 28, 1991	Troops again seize Radio Lomé.
Dec. 3, 1991	Troops move in strength into Lomé, kidnap Koffigoh, and demand changes in his HCR government. Koffigoh agrees on a government of national unity including RPT ministers, which is set up on December 31st.
Dec. 15, 1991	Troops again seize Radio Lomé, demanding the dissolution of the HCR and an end to the defamation of Eyadema and of Northerners.
Mar. 25, 1992	Hundreds of heavily armed policemen go on a rampage in Lomé over non-payment of salaries for up to nine months.
Apr. 9, 1992	Troops re-occupy Radio Lomé.
Apr. 16, 1992	HCR amends the constitution to prevent both Koffigoh and Eyadema from running for the Presidency.

May 5, 1992	Olympio's campaigning motorcade ambushed in North Togo by army units under the command of Eyadema's son. The wounded Olympio is evacuated to Paris.
May 9, 1992	Southern Togo paralyzed by a general strike.
Oct. 22, 1992	Army storms the National Assembly over the confiscating of RPT party funds. Party leaders beaten up.
Oct. 26, 1992	Unlimited general strike erupts in southern Togo, tapering off in May 1993 at a cost of sixty billion CFAF. Up to one third of Lomé's population eventually flees to Ghana.
Feb. 9, 1993	Reconciliation talks at Colmar, France fail.
Mar. 25, 1993	Intra-military attempt on Eyadema's life fails with the death of several key senior officers.
June 17, 1993	Talks commence in Ouagadougou to break impasse on election dates.
July 24, 1993	Another of Eyadema's opponents shot in downtown Lomé: attempted assassination of another takes place on Aug. 17, 1993.
Aug. 24, 1993	After Olympio is disqualified on a technicality, most opposition leaders boycott the Presidential elections. Eyadema elected in a 35 percent poll, and "inaugurated" the next month.
Feb. 6, 14, 1994	Parliamentary elections take place, boycotted by Olympio's and affiliated parties. Yao Agboyibor's CAR party emerges the largest party, narrowly trailed by the RPT.
Apr. 1, 1994	Eyadema appoints Edem Kodjo, who had only won seven seats as Prime Minister. Kodjo forms a coalition with the RPT and a few smaller parties.

Introduction

The Country and Its People

Togo is a small state in West Africa with an area of 56,000 square kilometers (21,620 square miles), extending from a narrow 32-mile Gulf of Guinea coastline to a point 320 miles inland. Nestled between Benin to the east and Ghana to the west, Togo—which occupies two thirds of the territory of the original German colony of the same name—has a northern border with Burkina Faso, providing the latter country with an access to the sea.

Togo is composed of six natural geographical regions stretching from (1) sandy beaches, estuaries, and inland lagoons (the biggest being Lac Togo) to (2) the barre-soil Ouatchi plateaus in the immediate hinterland, followed by (3) the higher Mono tableland (highest altitude, 1,500 feet) drained by the Mono River and its tributaries and (4) the Chaine du Togo mountains that dissect the country in a southwest-northeast direction and are part of a range beginning with Benin's Atakora mountains and ending in Ghana's Akwapim hills. Togo's highest altitude is found here at Pic Baumann (986 meters, or 3,235 feet). The country's two other regions are (5) the northern sandstone Oti plateau (drained by the Oti, a tributary of the Volta river) and (6) the northwestern granite regions in the vicinity of Dapaong.

The country is, in general, more heavily wooded than neighboring Benin, though grasslands are predominant vegetation. The highest rainfall—seventy inches a year—falls at Kpalimé, 120 kilometers in the interior, with the coast essentially dry, recording an average of twenty-five to thirty-five inches of rainfall per year. The north has one rainy season between April and July (forty-five inches per year), while in the south there are two rainy seasons—from April to July and from October through November.

Togo's population of 3.85 million (1994 estimate) is composed of between eighteen and thirty ethnic groups (depending upon the classification used), of which two of the most important are the Ewe (and other Adja-related groups) in the south (encompassing 44 percent of the people) and the Kabré and related ethnic groups (27 percent) in the north. Prior to the colonial intrusion the various groups had little contact with

1

each other except in cases of contiguous territorial occupation. State formation was retarded, with most entities (apart from two small kingdoms in the north) being decentralized groupings of villages under military pressure from both the Ashanti in the Gold Coast and the Dahomey kingdom to the east. Thus, from the colonial point of view the region was a power vacuum, a weak neutral zone between the territory of the two other strong West African states.

As elsewhere in West Africa, the coastal elements and groups immediately to their rear developed socioeconomically at a much earlier date and at a much faster pace than insular groups in the interior. In Togo the Ewe (composed of some 120 clans and subclans), Mina, and other related groups were the first to experience contact with Europeans and to adjust to the changing socioeconomic context. They rapidly seized modern venues for upward social and economic mobility, a fact that brought on its heels their political and administrative ascendance during the colonial and postcolonial eras. The northern populations, by contrast, opposed the colonial intrusion, fought the penetration of their territory, and were in turn kept isolated and undeveloped by the German and, to a lesser extent, the subsequent French administration. The different reactions to modern influences and colonial rule and the growing socioeconomic disparities between northern and southern ethnic groups created interethnic hostility and mutual resentment that contributed to the growth of regionalism and the rise of antagonistic regional political parties in the pre-independence era.

The Economy

The Togolese economy underwent three periods of rapid growth: the first during the German colonial era (followed by stagnation between 1920 and 1940), the second after the end of the Second World War, and the third sparked by the temporary (1974) boom in global phosphate prices. During the colonial era, German efforts to transform their new possession into a model self-sufficient colony (*Musterkolonie*) brought economic advances in its wake in the southern part of the territory. There a plantation economy developed that resulted in steadily increasing exports of coffee, cocoa, palm products, and cotton, and that benefited from the construction of Togo's three railway lines. During this period Togo surged ahead in the spread of education, which in 1914 covered nine percent of school-age children, a ratio not achieved by Senegal, for example, until 1938. (By 1990 fully 72% of children attended primary school, 24 percent going on to secondary school.)

Following the Anglo-French partition of the colony, Togo entered a period of stagnation aggravated by the global economic crash of the 1920's and 1930's. Average GDP growth during these twenty years was barely 1.5 percent per year, and as late as 1949 Togo's volume of exports was much the same as during the German era. After the end of the Second World War, the economy started to improve as a result of investments by the French FIDES program, and in the mid-sixties new state funds became available as the country's phosphate industry came of age. In 1974 a massive but temporary global price increase for phosphates quadrupled State revenues from them and ushered in the country's third period of economic expansion.

Togo's main cash crops are cocoa and coffee (grown in the humid hilly Kpalimé area, snug against the Ghana border), palm nuts, and cotton, the latter strongly expanded in the 1980's. In the past, these four commodities accounted for up to two thirds of the country's export earnings, with maize, millet, cassava (manioc), and sweet potatoes being grown for local consumption.

Apart from tourism—the country's third-largest foreign exchange earner, astutely courted and booming in the late 1970's, in severe decline with the societal turmoil of the 1990's—phosphate exports have been the key to much of the vibrance of the Togolese economy. From some of the richest deposits in the world, conveniently located near the coast, heavy exports of phosphate ore (especially after COTOMIB was nationalized in 1974) and by-products stabilized what would otherwise have been a very shaky agrarian economy. Though other mineral deposits abound, they are mostly found in quantities too small or too distant from the coast to be commercially exploitable due to the massive infrastructure outlays necessary. (The Aveta limestone quarries are an exception.)

Fueled by a short-lived boom in global phosphate prices and heavy French and German largess in the 1970's, the Togolese economy underwent its latest and most serious bout of transformation and expansion. Dozens of parastatal and joint enterprises, plants, corporations, and ventures were mounted, sharply setting off Togo from neighboring Benin. Coupled with a liberal investment code, a balanced developmental policy leading for the first time to attention to the transformation of the neglected North, and a blind eye to the smuggling activities to/from Ghana and Benin carried out by Lomé's marketwomen and other entrepreneurs, Togo presented the image of a stable, albeit military, state, satisfying group demands while developmentally forging ahead.

What was referred to as the "Togolese economic miracle" collapsed rapidly by the early 1980's. Massive corruption and administrative incompetence had seeped in during this period of economic growth. Indeed, in the inevitable post-mortem of the deficitory State sector—erected in the 1970s and closed down, restructured, or privatized at bargain basement prices in the 1980s and 1990s—it was discovered that at times enterprises were authorized by cabinet members solely for the anticipated (10 percent) kickbacks from contractors. Some senior officials were in due course purged for corruption, but most were merely shuffled to less sensitive posts where they continued their personal misdemeanors. The activities of the Presidency, in any case, were not scrutinized until the remarkable revelations attending the attempt at democratization that came with the convening of the National Conference in 1991.

As long as the economy was booming, such profligate policies could continue, though at a heavy cost to the economy, but the moment the phosphate prices normalized, the parastatal sector became a major drag on socioeconomic development. Togo's imminent bankruptcy was recognized at the 1982 RPT Congress and the slow, costly, and humiliating process of liquidating, restructuring, or privatizing much of the State sector commenced. At the same time, both party and cabinet underwent a facelift under global donor pressures (especially by France and Germany) which reflected a reluctance to funnel additional aid to personal pockets. *The Guardian*'s August 21, 1979 issue best summarized the ethos in Lomé: "The whole administration has become so corrupt that it has fallen into anarchy; in the choice of investments profitability has ceased to matter. All that matters is the percentage rakeoff."

Despite a decade of efforts at trimming the parastatals, the process was not yet complete in 1994, since in some fields buyers simply could not be found, while in others the government would not accept the low bids tendered. However, the stunning financial turnaround of several privatized enterprises, commencing operations without previous redundant labor, costly layers of State administrators and consultants (sinecure posts), or exorbitant expenses, suggests that most of the State sector need not close down under lock and key.

The fiscal austerities triggered by the need to downsize the bloated Togolese economy and civil service and control the staggering national debt (at one time among the highest in the world on a per capita basis), coupled with the fact that Eyadema's unpopular military regime now possessed few sources of patronage with which to glue itself to power, destabilized the political system. This process was accelerated by domestic pressures for democratization in the 1990s and the continental "winds of change" in Africa. Within a decade, one of West Africa's "economic miracles" had become the region's "sick man": a country referred to as "the Switzerland of Africa" in the early 1970s came to be equated with Zaire—the continental epitome of corruption, mismanagement, and dictatorial rule—and Eyadema, like Mobutu, came to be referred to as one of Africa's dinosaurs whose time had long past gone.

Historical Background

The first Europeans to see the Togolese coast were the Portuguese navigators Joao de Santarem and Pedro Escobar, travelling from 1471 to

1473. In the nineteenth century the coastal region between Accra and Lagos rapidly became an area of contention among a number of colonial powers, including France, Great Britain, and Germany. (Previously the Danes were quite active in the western part of the coastal littoral, but they withdrew from the area with the sale of Keta to Britain in 1850.) The main town in the region was Aného (at the time better known as Petit Popo), a small Mina slave-port in which factors of various nationalities were established. The town never became a preferred port of call because of the alleged "bad disposition" and sharp 'middleman' practices by local traders, as well as the more plentiful supply of slaves available at Ouidah (Benin) and along the Gold Coast.

The territory obtained its name from the small coastal village of Togo (To=water, Go=coast) where on July 4, 1884, German Imperial Commissioner Gustav Nachtigal signed the first protectorate agreement with Chief Mlapa III. The push inland from the coast was slow and punctuated by the resistance of the indigenous population, especially in the north. Still, resistance was feeble compared to the opposition that France and Britain encountered in neighboring Dahomey and Gold Coast, where military campaigns had to be mounted. Germany's slow expansion inland resulted in the frustration of one prime imperial goal—attaining a bridgehead on the Niger river. The colony's definitive borders were fixed in a number of conferences with the other colonial powers and ratified in the Treaty of Paris of 1897.

Although the German colonial era was brief (lasting thirty years, until August 1914) and was very authoritarian, it was during this period that the basis for much of Togo's infrastructure was laid. A good road system was developed, Lomé's breakwaters and wharf were constructed, and, just prior to the outbreak of the First World War, a third of the territory's railroads was completed (later to be extended by the French), greatly facilitating the movement of cash crops to the coast. The parallel expansion of Togo's agriculture made the colony the first in West Africa to balance its own budget (1906). Despite such advances and similar efforts toward education, the harshness of the German administration led to considerable opposition, Ewe migration to the Gold Coast, and a welcome to Allied troops when the World War broke out.

The conquest of Togo in 1914 by an Anglo-French force was the first Allied victory in the war, taking only eighteen days. After the end of the war, the two occupying powers were given League of Nations mandates over the partitioned territory (see 127). The division of the Ewe by the Gold Coast and British and French Togoland was the root of the so-called Ewe "problem" that emerged to occupy the attention of the United Nations Trusteeship Council after World War II. The nationalist aspirations of the Ewe translated into several unification movements in the Gold Coast and French Togo, one of which was the *Comité de l'Unité Togolaise* of Sylvanus Olympio, Togo's future president.

The Ewe goal of unification within the borders of one political entity was not attained. Failure was due to a variety of factors: mutual Anglo-French suspicions as to each other's colonial ambitions, divergent decolonization policies within their respective trusteeship territories, inter-clan jealousies among the Ewe, and personality clashes among their leaders. With the approaching independence of Ghana, Britain informed the United Nations that she could no longer maintain her duties in British Togoland (that had been administered from the Gold Coast). Consequently, a plebiscite on the future of the territory was held in 1956, with the majority of the population (though not the Ewe) opting for unification with the soon-to-be independent Ghana. France, suspicious of Britain's intentions and fearful of the pan-African pull of Kwame Nkrumah, resisted pressures to conduct a similar plebiscite. Instead, French Togo moved towards independence under the conservative pro-French Nicolas Grunitzky after a referendum in which the French administration supported such separatism, helped by a CUT boycott. Grunitzky's rise was fuelled by the alliance of his PTP with a UCPN composed of northern chiefly elements, dislodging the CUT—with active French support—from its early dominant political position in the territory (1945–1951). His Autonomous Republic (1956–58) collapsed, however, and his political allies were humiliatingly defeated in 1958 when a UN-supervised vote brought a dramatic CUT/Olympio victory.

The next few years saw the entrenchment of the CUT, which set out to settle old scores. As power become centralized in the hands of CUT militants, Togo became more and more authoritarian. Less than two years after independence a single party state was declared. In the process, some of Olympio's closest original associates (especially of the Juvento, the CUT's former youth wing) ended up in prison under harsh conditions, while scores of others went into self-exile in Ghana.

Olympio's leadership was characterized by a drive to set Togo on an internationally nonaligned course, one requisite of which was fiscal independence from France. A financial conservative who strove (and succeeded) to balance Togo's budget utilizing local resources, Olympio's plethora of new taxes and austerity measures antagonized many groups (including the Ewe) that had previously supported the CUT. His friction with Nkrumah led to the closure of the border with Ghana, hurting the livelihood of Lomé's traders, while his clash with Lomé's Archbishop alienated him from a segment of the Ewe intellectual elite. Finally, his austerity policies and anti-military stances led to the 1963 ex-servicemen confrontation and coup and his own cold-blooded murder by Eyadema.

The 1963 coup set off a wave of disapproval from other African states (this was West Africa's first coup, and Olympio's murder was traumatic to other leaders) that was barely soothed by the putschists' handover of power to Grunitzky and Antoine Méatchi and the May elections in which

Togo's resurrected parties united to form a joint electoral list. From the outset, the new regime was not popular with the masses: in the north, feelings ran in favor of a Méatchi presidency (he was Grunitzky's Vice President), while in the south the new government was seen as identical to the one turned out of office in 1958. Indeed, the regime was to become paralyzed by a tug-of-war for supremacy between the two leaders at the helm. In addition, relations with Ghana remained poor, continuing to adversely affect local trade; the economy was weak and sapped by new expenditures for an army that had been tripled in size to accommodate the authors of the 1963 coup.

Grunitzky was also the target of several plots sponsored by opposition members still in exile and from within his own cabinet. The most serious of these erupted in November 1966 when, after a cabinet crisis, massive popular demonstrations (sponsored by Nöe Kutuklui, self-styled political heir to Olympio) occurred in the capital, calling for the ouster of Grunitzky and the establishment of a PUT government. (The CUT's name had been slightly changed in 1962.) The upheaval was quelled by the army after hours of deliberation by the officer corps (authors of the 1963 coup) as to the merits of supporting the regime. Their decision was that they could not allow the government to be ousted, and troops were ordered to disperse the southern demonstrators. Two months later, however, on the fourth anniversary of Olympio's murder, the army moved in to dismiss the Grunitzky regime. After a brief military interregnum Eyadema moved into the vacuum to establish his own authoritarian regime that remained in office until forced to symbolically democratize in 1991.

The Eyadema Era

Eyadema's years in power fall into five distinct phases: the period to 1969, during which he was acutely aware of his extralegal status in a hostile Ewe environment and strove to project an image of "honest broker" abetted by stage-managed spontaneous demonstrations in his favor and the period from 1969 to 1980, during which, aided by increased state revenues from booming phosphate exports and a generally improved economy, the regime felt secure enough to move towards a controlled dialogue with allies within a newly created party, the *Rassemblement du Peuple Togolais*. Still, it did not feel secure enough and developed an ubiquitous Cult of Personality of grotesque proportions—a continuation of earlier efforts to orchestrate support for the regime.

Paradoxically, much of the relaxed style in Lomé in the 1970's, the early stability of the regime, and even some of the favorable accolades heaped on it, could be attributed to Eyadema's early surprisingly astute leadership of both armed forces and the country in general. In much of

Africa a military intrusion in politics presaged the erosion of the army's chain of command and further military upheavals. This did not immediately occur in the Togolese army, which witnessed only a few minor plots stemming from an unresolved power clash between Eyadema and Bodjollé (leader of the 1963 veterans). Indeed, the Army's chain of command during this period was kept largely intact through judicious promotions, constraints against the involvement of too many officers in political or civilian posts, and a low-keyed effort at keeping military self-aggrandizement within limited bounds.

Notwithstanding its later record and some brutal overreactions, in its early years the regime was relatively "forgiving" to opposition activity and open to the infusion of new talent at the highest reaches of the political hierarchy, including the cabinet. Thus, the loyalty that was denied Eyadema because of his northern, military, and non-intellectual credentials and his role in the murder of Olympio was gained through a pragmatic, easygoing political style, liberal economic policies, and the political cultivation of outstanding Mina and Ewe technocrats. Benefitting from increasing state revenues as Togo's phosphate industry (fifth largest in the world) came of age, the regime was able to accelerate development in the south, commence the first serious and large-scale efforts at the socioeconomic modernization of the north, and construct major public works projects throughout the country (paving the entire north-south road artery, a major urban renovation of Lomé, etc.), while keeping the civil service and armed forces happy with increased budgetary allocations. It was the short-lived 1974 spurt in phosphate royalties that tripped the regime into a frenzy of public spending, the price for which was austerity at a time of rising expectations and multiple demands which lead to the harshness of Eyadema's latter years.

The late 1970s and 1980s see the beginning of a short third "era," marked on the one hand by Eyadema's claim to permanence in office as Togo was granted (on January 1, 1980) a constitution, legislature, and (uniparty) elections which allegedly constitutionalized and civilianized Eyadema's rule, and, on the other hand, by the erosion of the Togolese economic dream as the costs of the etatist error had to be paid. Eyadema's early easygoing style also came to an end. Not only had the acutely upwardly-mobile and educated southern Togolese become too sophisticated to be swayed by the stifling personality cult and incredible political mythology that had been built up to prop the credentials of the unlettered *Le Guide* (who allegedly even had aspirations to be nominated for a Nobel Peace Prize in the mid-1990s), but Eyadema also became increasingly more heavy-handed and authoritarian. His early astute appointments gave way to the nomination of sycophants, incompetents, personal cronies, family members (especially in command of key units in the armed forces), and individuals out to siphon the benefits of office in full.

Northerners and military officers strutted as if in conquered territory. High officials caught embezzling State funds were forgiven their transgressions and shifted to less lucrative pastures in the public sector. Abuses of human rights increased, until the country came to be judged by some as having Africa's worst human rights record. As any visitor to the country at this time could visibly see, by the early 1980s the infrastructural transformation of the country was matched by a heavy increase in repression, decline in civic zeal and public spirit, and the onset of chronic corruption and nepotism. So bad was the regime's image abroad that in 1981 Eyadema had to hire a Washington-based public relations firm to boost up his image by commissioned articles and books and by the offer of free holidays in Togo to assorted public influentials.

A fourth period emerges directly in the mid-1980s with the collapse of the economy due to its mismanagement and persistent, increasingly violent efforts, primarily by Southerners (including Gilchrist Olympio, one of Sylvanus Olympio's sons), to permanently dislodge Eyadema from office. With development funds drying up, sinecure posts becoming increasingly difficult to locate, corruption and mismanagement of the State sector bankrupting the economy, and popular grievances building up, the social glue that had kept society together slowly dissolved, and political instability again became a fact of life. During this period most of the systematic and brutal abuses of human rights took place: arbitrary and mass arrests, imprisonment without trial, torture, and liquidation while in prison.

A fifth period is the unstable era since 1990, when the economic crisis, global winds of change, and external donors forced Eyadema to convene a National Conference that promptly declared itself sovereign. Though originally appearing to be consigned to the dustbin of history, Eyadema was aided by a French hands-off policy and used his loyalist northern army to terrorize society into submission, clawing his way back to power in 1993. Referring to this period, when one third of Lomé's population fled to Ghana during a paralyzing 18-month strike and riots and societal tumult in the south (costing the economy 200 billion CFAF), the Economist Intelligence Unit noted (*Togo, Niger, Benin, Burkia: Country Report,* no. 1 (1993): 10) "only the absence of weapons in the hands of the opposition is preventing a full scale civil war . . . Eyadema's mainly Kabré army is operating as an army of occupation in the center and south of the country."

Notwithstanding the resolutions of a euphoric National Conference, no doubt feeling it was writing history when it stripped him of executive power, denied him the right to run for office again, banned the RPT and expelled it from its headquarters, and publicly revealed (though accounts had previously been published overseas) sordid details of brute murder and crass corruption by him and his close associates (as former lieutenants "cleansed" themselves by revealing all in public), Eyadema remained serene in the Presidential Palace. It was interim Prime Minister Koffigoh (1991–1994) who was at risk, humiliated by troops who three times seized Lomé's radio station to lambast him and his interim government, mounted several attempted coups, stormed the National Assembly, and finally kidnapped him for a confrontation with Eyadema that led to a coalition of "National Unity" with the RPT. Members of the interim government were assaulted, murdered, or intimidated right up to the much-flawed legislative and presidential elections of 1993 and 1994. In particular, Gilchrist Olympio, Eyadema's prime nemesis and contender for the political throne, was ambushed by the military (led by Eyadema's son) while campaigning in central Togo and was later disqualified from the Presidential elections on a technicality, a fact that led to his boycotting the subsequent parliamentary elections.

The result of "democratization" in Togo was Eyadema's re-election in August 1993 in a contest boycotted by all serious candidates. Voters turned out primarily in the North, and most international observers (including President Carter) withdrew from monitoring the irrelevant event. Olympio, back in self-exile in Paris, redoubled his efforts to oust Eyadema by force, with assaults reaching right into the Presidential house at the Tokoin barracks. The legislative elections of February 1994 were also marked by intimidation and violence by the army, though they were ultimately certified fair. The RPT emerged as Togo's second largest party, though now clearly a regionalist northern formation. With Gilchrist Olympio's party out of the race, the southern vote split among several contenders (one estimate has it that sixty-six political parties were certified at one stage or another) with the predominantly southern CAR of Yao Agboyibor (a lawyer, and prime catalyst of the National Conference) emerging as the country's largest party. Edem Kodjo, an Ewe leader from Kpalimé, came third (after the RPT) with barely seven seats. Koffigoh, thoroughly discredited by his cooperation with Eyadema, barely secured his own seat in the Assembly.

Indicating he had no intention of being relegated to the sidelines, Eyadema stunned the country on April 22, 1994 by appointing Edem Kodjo as Prime Minister, leading to the formation of the current coalition between Kodjo's UTD and the RPT (as well as a few minor parties). The regime cannot be regarded as stable, however. One of the major political forces in the country—the former CUT Ewe and their leader, Olympio—are disenfranchised; the largest party, the CAR, is in the opposition; and the presidency was stolen by brute force by a minority (roughly 35 percent) regional vote. Democracy increasingly seems to sprout from the barrel of the gun and not from the ballot box.

The implications are not too pleasant for either Eyadema, his cohorts, or the Kabré in general. In neighboring Benin, for example, where a similar (though Marxist) northern military autocracy had reigned supreme for seventeen years, General Kérékou accepted democratization and his own eclipse, ushering in Africa's fairest elections to date, seeing his sins of omission and commission forgiven by a National Conference willing to put the past to rest and proceed with the reconstruction of an equally ravaged economy. Consequently, in Benin there has been no mass retribution, and the slow healing process has commenced. Togo is probably not destined to follow this route. Far too much brutality and too many individual murders have occurred since 1990, and continue to occur, to allow a future smooth political transition to Ewe leadership. The recent sentencing (May 1994) of an editor in Lomé to four years' imprisonment for questioning the probity of African leaders including Eyadema, thus "insulting the Head of State" (*West Africa* May 16, 1994), is the best testimonial to how little has really changed in Togo.

The Dictionary

A

ABAGLO, EUGENE ANTOINE, 1937– . Director of Taxes. Born in
Tsévié on December 29, 1937, Abaglo was educated locally and studied law in France. He obtained degrees from Aix-en-Provence (1961)
and Paris (1965), returning to Lomé to become Director of Economics in the Ministry of Finance in January 1966. He served concurrently
as a government administrator on the board of BCEAO. In 1967 he
was reassigned to other duties in the same ministry, most recently as
Director of Taxes.

ABALO, ALFA. Minister of Defense since May 1994 in the RPT-UTD
coalition government under Prime Minister Edem Kodjo.

ABALO, CELESTIN. Dramatologist whose only work, *Kalian,* met
with critical acclaim when first presented in Lomé in 1964. Nothing is
known of the author, whose name may indeed be a pseudonym.

ABALO, JOSEPH FIRMIN FENENOU, 1918–1968. Former popular
President of **Juvento** and cabinet minister. Born in 1918 in Okou in
the Plateaux region, Abalo was educated in Togo and worked for a few
years as a Catholic instructor (1934–36) before becoming a customs
official (1936–52). A militant pan-Africanist espousing the unification
of all **Ewe** including those in Ghana, Abalo was elected to the Territorial Assembly as **CUT** delegate from the Akposso district shortly
before Juvento—the CUT's young wing—broke off to become an independent party. He served in the Assembly between 1958 and 1961
and in the latter year was the assembly's secretary. A top leader of Juvento, Abalo was imprisoned without trial in 1962 as President Olympio cracked down on opposition parties. Freed after the 1963 coup
d'etat, Abalo became Secretary General of his party and in 1964 its
President. In that year he was also brought into President **Grunitzky's**

Bold type indicates a cross-referenced entry.

13

four-cornered cabinet coalition as Minister of Rural Economy. When the alliance foundered late in 1966 Abalo was dropped from the cabinet. He died a short time later in a car accident.

ABDOULAYE, SANI (EL HADJI), 1873–1970. The venerable Imam of the **Chokossi** of Sansanné-Mango, mostly responsible for the heavy Islamic proselytizing in the region in the 1930s and 1940s. Born in 1873, the son of Mama Sani, the tenth Imam of Sansanné-Mango, Abdoulaye was involved in his youth in trade in cattle between Atakpamé, Kpalimé, and Kumasi (Ghana). His breadth of Koranic knowledge spread far and wide, however, and when he was nominated Imam he renounced trade to concentrate on his religious duties. After his death at age ninety-seven, his son, Al Haji Yaya, was invested Imam (in 1973), but he fell afoul of General Eyadema when he got involved in a political conflict and was deposed by Eyadema.

ABDOULAYE, SOULEMANE, 1947– . Economist and senior civil servant. Born in 1947 in north Togo and trained at home and in France in Economics, Abdoulaye returned to Lomé to be appointed Inspector of Taxes. He was later promoted to Director General of Taxes of Togo and in 1981 Director of Personnel. Since 1984, Abdoulaye has been a Technical Adviser in the Ministry of Economic Affairs and Finance.

ABOTCHI, DEKOU. Journalist. The author of various articles in the cultural review *Timbo,* as well as a play, Abotchi is a journalist working with the Ministry of Press and Culture in Lomé.

ABOTCHI, KOFFI N'KOLEY. Former cabinet minister. A leader of the post-1990 **PDU** political party, Abotchi joined the Transitional government of Prime Minister Koffigoh on September 7, 1991 as Minister of Rural Development and the Environment. He retained his portfolio after the creation of a coalition with the **RPT** party but was dropped from the government in February 1993.

ABOULAYE, MASHOUDOU, 1953– . Mathematician. Born in 1953 in north Togo, and trained in France in Mathematics and Statistics (1976) and in the United States in Applied Statistics, Computer Sciences (1982), and Economics and Econometrics (1983), Aboulaye returned to Togo to join the Ministry of the Plan to assume the post of Head of the Division of Scientific Studies and Research, a position he still holds.

ACOUTEY ECOUE, THEODORE, 1921– . Lawyer and former Magistrate. In February 1967 Acoutey Ecoué became, in rapid succession, Deputy President, then President, of Togo's Appeals Court, concurrent with his position as President of the Supreme Court's administrative chamber. He has been in retirement since the 1980's.

ADABA, KODZO PAIL, 1941– . Electrical engineer and administrator. Born in 1941 and trained in Electrical Engineering, Adaba served between 1974 and 1975 as Area Maintenance Supervisor and Administrator with the Communauté Electrique de Bénin in Lomé. He then served as Regional Engineer at the petroleum refinery in Lomé, before being tapped to become Chief Electrical Engineer of CEB from 1977 to 1980. In 1982 Adaba, who has written several scientific publications, was appointed Planning Engineer of the corporation.

ADANI, IFE. Political leader who set up the **ATD** party with the emergence of multi-partyism in Togo in 1991. The party was basically aligned behind **Gilchrist Olympio,** though Adani pursued an independent line. Adani was one of only two leaders to run in the August 1993 Presidential election that most southern leaders boycotted. In the contest, won by General Eyadema, Adani received only 1.87% of the popular vote.

ADDRA, TAMATA COMLAVI (Grégoire), 1938– . Economist. Born March 12, 1938 and educated abroad, Addra worked as a civil administrator at Lomé Port before obtaining degrees in Economics (University of Dakar) and Statistics (University of Warsaw) in the mid-1960's. He was then appointed head of a division in the Ministry of Commerce, Industry, and the Plan and Professor at the University of Benin. In 1982 he became Head of Development Planning in the Ministry of the Plan and Deputy Director of the National Plan of Togo.

ADELEYE, ADEKEKE GEORGES, 1944– . Economist. Born in 1944 and educated abroad in Economics (with a specialized diploma in Customs Economics), Adeleye returned home to work with Togo's Customs Division. In 1983 he was appointed department head in Customs headquarters in Lomé.

ADEWUI, KIDJANDA ROBERT (COLONEL). Former Commander of the Second Motorized Battalion. A little known **Kotokoli** from Bafilo, Adewui was one of the Sergeants in the French colonial armies demobilized in 1962. Promoted to Lieutenant, and then Captain, his control of the central arms depot in 1967 guaranteed the success of Eyadema's coup d'etat of that year. Arrogant and ruthless in public and private life, Adewui was promoted to Major in January 1970 and Lieutenant Colonel in 1975. The regime's number two man, Adewui was planning to announce he had succeeded Eyadema at the time of the **Sarakawa** air accident, when Eyadema emerged unscathed from it. Possibly because of his alacrity, he was shortly to be stripped of operational command over the second battalion, though the official reason was that his private trucking and trading empires (Lomé-Lama Kara) were taking up most of his time. Supremely confident of his status in the military elite, Adewui was personally involved in the July 1975 murder of a political prisoner, Major Paul Comlan, on the orders of General Eyadema. Despite the furor aroused by this action, Adewui was retired from the army with full honors on October 12, 1976. He remains an important commercial figure in Togo.

ADJA. Important ethnic group in southern Benin and Togo. According to tradition, the Adja are a **Yoruba** branch that migrated from Oyo (in Nigeria) in the thirteenth century, eventually settling in **Tado** and later in **Notsé.** Following the Notsé dispersal in 1720, one branch moved mainly southward (the "western" Adja) to become the **Ewe** of today, while other segments crossed from Tado and Notsé into areas currently in Benin to found the Allada kingdom. Figures for Togo's Adja vary, since they are frequently lumped together with the **Ewe** or **Ouatchi,** but are estimated at around 30,000. Togo's Adja are found mostly in the Aného and Atakpamé areas. The Adja language is the basis of all languages between the Volta and Ouémé rivers and especially of the Ouatchi, **Evegbe,** Vodun, Kpessi, Fongbé (spoken by the Fon and Mahi), and Guin (spoken among the Mina along the coast). *See also* EWE.

ADJANGBA, MESSAH K. 1932– . University instructor. Born on October 25, 1932 and educated in the United States (M.Sc.) and France obtaining a doctorate in Physics, Adjangba teaches Physical Chemistry at the University of Benin in Lomé.

ADJARALA. Location on the **Mono River** roughly 100 kilometers from **Nangbeto,** viewed as the site for a possible second dam to provide additional electricity for Benin and Togo. Feasibility studies commenced in 1988, with the possible dam augmenting the **CEB**'s local electricity production to 58 percent of its needs.

ADJETEY-BAHUN, ADJEVI TEVI NYAKPOGBE, 1920– . Early key civil administrator. Born in Lomé on December 27, 1920 and educated largely in Togo and via correspondence courses (France 1956–58; United States 1962), Adjetey-Bahun was originally a teacher (1939–43) before becoming a clerk in the Administration and Finance department of colonial Togo (1943–55). In 1955 he obtained his first major promotion to Assistant Head, Personnel; in 1958 he became Deputy Director of Personnel and the Civil Service, and the next year he assumed the Ministry's top administrative post. After the 1963 coup d'état he was shunted aside to head the newly created National School of Administration, during which time he wrote several texts on the Togolese civil service and taught French. Retired from the civil service in 1975, Adjetey-Bahun set up a couple of trading companies, one of which he still heads.

ADJOVI, METONOU DO-KOKOU (JACQUES). One of Togo's poets, and a history teacher by profession. Adjovi's work, that stresses legends and history, has appeared in several collections.

ADJOVI, SOSSAVI-AKANSOMON (MICHEL), 1941– . Pharmacist. Born in 1941 in Atakpamé, Adjovi was educated in his hometown and in Lomé before proceeding to the United States where he studied at Temple University in Philadelphia. He returned to Togo in 1969 and, rapidly promoted to the post of Chief Pharmacist of Kara, became director of Togopharma, the Togolese state pharmaceutics company until the latter went bankrupt in the early 1980s.

ADMINISTRATIVE ORGANIZATION. Until independence, Togo was administratively divided into a number of cercles which were in turn further subdivided. Just prior to independence there were ten cercles: Lomé, Anécho, Atakpamé, Bassari, Dapango, Lama Kara, Mango, Sokodé, Tsévié, and Kluoto. Except for the latter, each cercle had its administrative capital in the town of the same name; Kluoto's capital was in Palimé. In the post-independence administrative reorganization, four regions were created, encompassing **circonscriptions,** or districts, each headed by a chef de circonscription. A fifth economic region (La Kara) was carved out of the Centrale and Savanes regions in the mid-1960s and subsequent creation of new districts raised the latter's number to twenty-one. Togo also had seven communes, or urban circonscriptions (districts). The country's current administrative breakdown until the June 11, 1981 reorganization was: (1) Maritime Region: encompassing the communes of Lomé, Aného, and Tsévié and composed of the districts (circonscriptions) of Lomé, Aného, Tsévié, Vagan, and Tabligbo. (2) Plateaux Region: including the communes of Kpalimé and Atakpamé and the districts of Kluoto, Atakpamé, Akposso, and Notsé. (3) Centrale Region: including the communes of Bassari and Sokodé and the districts of Sokodé, Bafilo, Bassari, Sotouboua, Badou (1974), and Tchamba (1975). (4) La Kara Region: including the districts of Lama Kara, Niamtougou, Pagouda, and Kandé. (5) Savanes Region: including the districts of Dapango and Mango. During the colonial period, many of the cercles had a **Conseil de Notables;** these were transformed in 1946 into **Conseils de Circonscriptions.** The latter—whose range of authority changed over the years—included representatives of the most important families, clans, and ethnic groups in the district. The Conseils de Circonscription (District Council) continued to exist after independence until banned following the 1967 coup d'etat. In 1973 they reappeared under the name of Delegations Speciales, with restricted powers. (For details on these administrative structures or the various regions, circonscriptions, or communes, see the individual entries.) On June 11, 1981, Decree 81/9 changed, for the third time, the administrative organization of Togo. The country was now divided into five regions, each with several prefectures. The reorganization also saw La Kara becoming a major political division at the expense of the Savanes region. The new administrative division of Togo now consists of five regions: (1) Region Maritime: encompassing the prefectures of Golfe, des Lacs, Yoto, Vo, and Zio. Its headquarters remains Lomé. (2) Region des Plateaux: includes the prefectures of Ogou, Kloto, Amou, Wawa, and Haho, with headquarters in Atakpamé. (3) Region du Centre: encompassing the prefectures of Tchaoudjo, Sotouboua, and Nyala with headquarters in Sokodé. (4) Region de la Kara: including the prefectures of Kozah, Binah, Doufelgou, la Keran, Assoli, and Bassar and headquartered in Kara. (5) Region des Savanes: including the prefectures of Oti and Tone, with headquarters in Dapaong. The twenty-one prefectures with their headquarters and previous circonscription appellation are:

Former Circonscription	Current Prefecture	Headquarters
Amlamé	Amou	Amlamé
Aného	des Lacs	Aného
Atakpamé	Ogou	Atakpamé
Badou	Wawa	Badou
Bafilo	Assoli	Bafilo
Bassari	Bassar	Bassar
Dapango	Toné	Dapaong
Kandé	Keran	Kandé
Kluoto	Kloto	Kpalimé
Lama Kara	Kozah	Kara
Lomé	du Golf	Lomé
Mango	Oti	Sansanné Mango
Niamtougou	Doufelgou	Niamtougou
Notsé	Haho	Notsé
Pagouda	Binah	Pagouda
Sokodé	Tchaoudio	Sokodé
Sotouboua	Sotouboua	Sotouboua
Tabligbo	Yoto	Tabligbo
Tchamba	Nyala	Tchamba
Tsévié	Zio	Tsévié
Vogan	Vo	Vogan

The following previous *postes administratives* became, with the reorganization, sous-prefectures with the following names and headquarters:

Former Poste Administratif	Current Sous-prefecture	Headquarters
Agou	Agou	Agou-Gadzépé
Blitta	Blitta	Blitta
Dayes	Danyi	Danyi-Apéyémé
Elavagnon	Est Mono	Elavagnon
Guérin-Kouka	Dankpen	Guérin-Kouka
Kévé	Avé	Kévé
Mandouri	Kpendjal	Mandouri
Tandoauré	Tandjouaré	Tandjouaré
Tohoun	Moyen-Mono	Tohoun

ADODO, YAOVI, 1942– . Former Foreign Minister and old Eyadema crony. An Ewe born in Lomé in 1942 and educated in France and the United States (UCLA) in Law, Public Administration, and Political Science, Adodo briefly taught at Bordeaux before returning to Togo with his American wife to become the principal private secretary of the Presidential Office and Director of Cooperation. In 1981 he was dispatched as Ambassador to Belgium, The Netherlands, Luxembourg, and the EEC, to return to Togo in 1984 as Minister of Planning and Industry. In 1987 he was shifted to the position of Minister of Foreign Affairs, a post he held until the multiparty reforms when his overly close links to Eyadema brought his eclipse and reassignment to Ambassadorial duties overseas.

ADOGNON, KOFFI, 1942– . Statistician. Born in 1942 and educated abroad in Statistics and Demography, Adognon returned to Togo to assume the post of Director of Statistics in the Ministry of Finance, a position he still holds.

ADOSSA. Traditional annual **Kotokoli** celebrations, known also as Yeke-Yeke. Their significance is that they unite all Kotokoli, animists, Muslims, and Christians at a time when religion has produced internal schisms in the community. Celebrated on the birth of the Prophet—and hence a religious feast as well to those who are Muslim—the Adossa is actually the continuation of the pre-Muslim animist Tchaoudjo festivities. Contemporarily, the Adossa is composed of both religious celebrations of the Prophet's birth and a series of violent and vivid dances (depicting decapitation of prisoners) in honor of the Semassé Kotokoli warriors of the past.

ADOSSAMA, PIERRE ADAM, 1929– . Former cabinet minister and indirectly a precipitant of the 1967 coup d'etat that toppled the Grunitzky regime. Born to a Kabré family in Lomé on September 12, 1929, Adossama was educated locally (including at the Togolese School of Administration) and abroad at the School of Meteorology in St. Cyr, France (1956–57). Having worked originally as a teacher in a Catholic mission (1945–49), Adossama spent the next nine years (to 1958) as radio operator, telegraphist, and meteorologist. An early member of Sylvanus Olympio's **Comité de l'Unité Togolaise** (CUT), Adossama became attaché (1958–59) at the Ministry of Education and served as cabinet director of the Minister of Economic Affairs after the Olympio regime's rise to power in 1958. Following Olympio's assassination in 1963, Adossama headed a wing of the CUT that urged cooperation with the successor Grunitzky administration. In the four-cornered coalition the latter established, Adossama served first as Minister of Education (May 1963–January 1966) and then as Minister of Labor and the Civil Service (January–November 1966). Increasingly disgruntled with the indecisiveness and malleability of Grunitzky and the perennial tug-of-war between the latter and Vice President **Antoine Méatchi,** Adossama resigned from the cabinet on November 19, 1966, precipitating the November 21, 1966 PUT upheaval in Lomé. See COUP (ATTEMPTED) OF 1966. Following the January 1967 coup d'etat, Adossama was appointed Secretary General of the **Comité de Réconciliation Nationale** with special responsibilities in foreign affairs. After touring Francophone Africa to explain the causes of the military takeover and to gain international legitimacy for it, Adossama returned home to become Minister of State in charge of rural economy in the Eyadema regime (1967–69). In 1969 Adossama left the cabinet to become technical expert with the International Labor Organization in Geneva. Upon his return to Lomé in 1971 he joined the Ministry of Economic Affairs as the Minister's Chef de Cabinet while also secretary of the Association of Togolese Cultural Exchanges. He has been in retirement for several years.

ADOTEVI, ADOVI JOHN-BOSCO, 1934– . Journalist and author. Adotevi was born in Lomé on March 29, 1934 and was educated at home and in France, obtaining advanced degrees in Public Law and in English Literature. He then joined the weekly *Afrique Nouvelle* in Dakar, Senegal, serving as its prime correspondent until the paper closed down in the 1970s. He has also been a journalist for Dakar's *Le Soleil* and *Voix d'Afrique,* as well as teaching in a Dakar school.

ADZEVODU. Important term in Ewe/Mina society, referring to protective vodu against sorcery.

ADZOMADA, KOFFI (JACQUES). Pastor of the Ewe Evangelical Church and longtime President of the Academie de la Langue Ewe. In the latter, he has been influential both in translating many works into the Ewe language and in popularizing the language as a major lingua franca with its own literature, journals, and newspapers.

AFAN, HUENUMADJI, 1947– . Professor of Literature. Born in 1947 and holding a doctorate in Letters and specialization in Black African Theatre, Afan teaches literature at the University of Benin in Lomé. He is also the author of several plays.

AFANTCHAO, KOKOU LUCAS. Minister of Tourism, Crafts, and Small and Medium-Sized Enterprises in the transitional government between December 1991 and September 1992.

AFFO, ISSA. Minister of Technical and Professional Training in the transitional government between December 1991 and September 1992.

AFLAO. The Ghanaian-Togolese border checkpoint, at the village of the same name on the coastal road. Virtually a suburb of Lomé, barely two kilometers away, Aflao is both a center of smuggling between the two countries and of Togolese intellegence-gathering on subversive movements in Ghana.

AFOTCHE (also, AFOTCHEGNON). Legendary late seventeenth- and early eighteenth-century Ewe leader who founded **Notsé** after the trek from **Tado** becoming the first king of the Notsé dynasty. Afotche was the father of **Agokoli.** *See* NOTSE, AGOKOLI.

AFRIQUE OCCIDENTALE FRANCAISE (AOF). French West Africa— one of France's two colonial African federations—that encompassed the territories of Ivory Coast, Niger, Upper Volta, Mauritania, Senegal, French Soudan, Guinea, and Dahomey. Established between 1895 and 1904, after the Second World War the AOF was headed by a Governor-General in Dakar, Senegal, who was responsible to the Minister of Colonies in Paris. The Governor-General was assisted in Dakar by a Council of Government possessing consultative powers and composed of five delegates from each of the federated territories. Each colony also had its own Governor responsible to the Governor-General in Dakar and a territorial assembly with initially limited powers. Togo, being a trusteeship territory, was not part of France's AOF (except for a brief period between the two World Wars), though in many respects its evolution paralleled that of France's colonial empire. In the constitution of the **French Union,** Togo was allocated the status of **associated territory,** which was different from the overseas territory status of most of France's colonies. Togo did not send delegates to the AOF Council in Dakar, though it did elect delegates to the French National Assembly in Paris, as did France's colonies. In 1955 the proclamation of the birth of the **Autonomous Republic of Togo**—under pressure from the United Nations Trusteeship Council—and the creation of a legislative assembly with wide powers, was, however, a major deviation from standard AOF administrative evolution. For the list of governors, *see* FRENCH WEST AFRICA—GOVERNORS OF.

AGBA, KONDI CHARLES, 1948– . Veterinarian. Born on August 26, 1948 and educated in Lomé (B.Sc., 1968) and abroad in Veterinary Sciences (University of Dakar doctorate, 1975), Agba currently serves as Head of the Anatomical Section of the Veterinary School in Dakar, Senegal.

AGBEKA, BENJAMIN KOMLAN MENSAH. Minister of Communications. Agbeka joined the third Transitional government of Prime Minister Koffigoh in September 1992 as Minister of Communications as an RPT appointee and was dismissed the next month on the grounds of lack of solidarity with the government and refusal to follow government policy. He refused to leave his Ministry, and under RPT pressure he retained his post and was reappointed in the fourth Koffigoh government in February 1993. In February 1994 his house in Lomé was bombed by anti-Eyadema elements.

AGBEKO, KOFI, 1948– . Agronomist. Born on December 14, 1948 and educated at the University of Toulouse where he obtained a doctorate in Pedology-Microbiology, Agbeko is currently a teacher at the Higher School of Agronomy at the University of Benin.

AGBEMEGNAN, JEAN, 1914– . Former Minister of Trade and Industry. Born in Lomé on May 19, 1914, Agbemegnan was educated locally at the Catholic Mission (1920–34). After a few years as an instructor in the Mission, he joined the customs service (1937), eventually rising to be its director. An early member of the **Comité de l'Unité Togolaise** and its youth wing, **Juvento,** Agbemegnan became Juvento Minister of Trade and Industry in President Grunitzky's coalition government (1963–67). He retired from politics after the 1967 coup d'état.

AGBENON, ASSIONGBON, 1937– . Diplomat. Born in 1937 and educated at the International Institute of Public Administration in Paris,

Agbenon was posted in 1976 as Ambassador to West Germany. He was later shifted to the United Kingdom to represent Togo and in 1989 became Ambassador to Belgium and the EEC.

AGBENOU, KOMLAN, 1957– . Journalist, educator, and poet. Born in 1957 in Tchekpo-Dedekpoe, Agbenou attended a journalism course in Belgium after secondary school, and after a short sojourn in Togo he relocated to Mali where he teaches French in a secondary school. He is the author of a number of poems.

AGBETIAFA, KOMLAN (MICHEL), 1930– . Former Minister of Interior and General Eyadema crony. Born in Baguida in northern Togo and a schoolteacher by profession, Agbetiafa taught for several years in Togo (including at Pya's where he was Eyadema's teacher in primary school, the sole reason for his subsequent political promotion) and Burkina Faso. He has also been a School Inspector and a soccer referee. Shortly after the 1963 coup d'etat, Agbetiafa became director of Primary Education (1965–75) and in December 1979 was elected to the National Assembly where he quickly rose to become second Vice President and a member of the RPT Politburo. In 1982 he was appointed Minister of Primary and Secondary Education by Eyadema; in 1984 he was shifted to Minister of National Education, and in 1987 he was appointed Minister of Interior, serving in that post until 1989.

AGBETRA, AISSAH. Former Minister of Health, Social Affairs, and Women's Affairs. General Eyadema's cousin, Dr. Agbetra joined the cabinet in 1982 as Minister of Higher Education and Scientific Research, was reassigned in 1984, and left the cabinet in 1988.

AGBLEMAGNON, FERDINAND N'SOUGAN, 1929– . Well-known sociologist and UNESCO official. Born in Ahépé in the Tsévié area on May 30, 1929 to a family of simple cultivators, Agblemagnon left home at the age of ten to obtain an education in Aného and Lomé. A brilliant student, he was given the option of continuing his studies either at the prestigious **Ecole William Ponty** in Dakar, Senegal or at the Ecole Technique Superièure in Bamako, Mali. Agblemagnon chose the latter and later studied at Grenoble and the Sorbonne (1951–56), obtaining degrees in philosophy, African studies, and ethnology. In 1956 he was admitted to the prestigious CNRS. Agblemagnon has published extensively on African ethnology and oral traditions and has lectured in the United States, Canada, Scandinavia, Poland, and Lebanon. Since 1964 Agblemagnon has been working in Paris with UNESCO and lecturing at the Sorbonne's Ecole Pratique des Hautes Etudes. He has been chairman of UNESCO's subgroup on education in Africa (1962–64), Visiting Professor in several universities including those of Montreal and Mexico, Vice-Chairman of UNESCO's Committee of Experts on Educational Planning, as well as Togo's representative to UNESCO.

AGBO, TOSSOU (AUGUSTIN), 1908–1980. Early CUT militant and prominent Mina influential from Aného. Born in 1908 in Agouégan and a popular tailor by profession, Agbo descended from an influential Brazilian family. He was an early CUT militant and financial contributor and served as the party's National Assembly deputy from Aného between 1958 and 1963. He retired from party life after the 1963 coup.

AGBO, YAO, 1948– . Former diplomat and cabinet minister. Born in Ahlon-Tinipé in the Kloto region on August 19, 1948 and educated at home and in France, Agbo worked with the Ministry of the Economy and Finance and then the Ministry of Foreign Affairs. In 1979 he was appointed Ambassador to China and Japan, returning to Lomé in 1982 to join Eyadema's cabinet as Secretary of State in charge of Industry and Parastatal Companies. In 1984 he was appointed Minister of Youth, Sports, and Culture but was dropped from the cabinet in 1987 and reappointed to his former Ambassadorship to China and Korea.

AGBOBLI, FRANCIS. Leader of the Parti Socialiste Pan-Africain that in late 1993 joined with two other small groups to form the **Groupe Social Pan-Africain** to boycott the 1994 legislative elections.

AGBOBLI, JOACHIM ATSUTSE. Minister of Communications and Culture since May 1994 in the RPT-UTD coalition government of Prime Minister Edem Kodjo. A journalist by profession, Agbobli, who is an Ewe, was in 1991 appointed Head of the government's Commission de Défense et de Securité aimed at serving as a buffer between the aggressive marauding army of Eyadema and the forces of the south. Close to Edem Kodjo, he was brought into the latter's cabinet when Kodjo was named Prime Minister by General Eyadema.

AGBODAN, MAVOR TETEY, 1938– . Educator. Born on September 29, 1938 and educated abroad (where he secured a diploma in Master of Ceremonies), Agbodan teaches financial administration in the School of Administration of the University of Benin.

AGBODJAN, GEORGES COMBEVI. Cabinet Minister. An independent, Agbodjan entered the third Transitional government of Prime Minister Kottigah in September 1992 as Secretary of State in charge of Elections and was retained in the next transitional government of February 1993 as Minister of Territorial Administration and Security.

AGBODJAN, LABITE EYRAM, 1947– . Agricultural economist. Born in Lomé in 1947, Agbodjan was educated in Economics and Agriculture at the University of Abidjan, in France, and at the Texas Technical University in Waco (M.Sc., 1982) before returning to Lomé. There he joined the Ministry of the Plan, where he has remained, working on various agrarian development projects.

AGBODRAFO. Original Ewe name of Porto Seguro, known to tourists for its lake and water sports, but to Ewe especially for its sacred forest—off-limits to tourists—where sacred stone ceremonies are practiced in September.

AGBOGBOME. Popular name for Notsé, meaning "within the gates" in Evegbe. See NOTSE.

AGBOGBOME FESTIVAL see HOGBETSOTSO; NOTSE

AGBOYIBOR, YAO, 1943– . Important moderate political leader who currently heads Togo's largest party, the CAR, that is the official opposition to the UTD-RPT coalition government. A lawyer by training, Agboyibor was picked by General Eyadema in mid-1988 to head the semiofficial **Comité Nationale pour le Droits d'Homme** (CNDH), aimed solely at deflecting increasing global attacks on Togo for its human rights violations (torture of political prisoners). Elected to the National Assembly in 1990, he participated in the revolt that ushered in the **National Conference** that whittled down Eyadema's executive powers. He resigned from the CNDH in October 1990 after the latter took no concrete stand on the killings by the military of that month and became President of the **Comité d'Action Contre le Tribalisme et le Racisme** which was formally set up in January 1991. On May 1, 1991 he inaugurated a new political party—the **Comité d'Action pour le Renouveau** (CAR), which in the 1994 legislative elections gained thirty-six of the Assembly seats, becoming Togo's largest political formation. Notwithstanding this, Eyadema—who brutally intimidated his opposition with his loyal army in order to be elected President—chose **Edem Kodjo** as his Prime Minister, an effort to split his southern opposition.

AGENCE TOGOLAISE DU PRESSE (ATP). State press agency set up in 1975 and attached to the Ministry of Information. It is specifically charged with covering local events throughout the country and is headed by Tschatisa Amah.

AGNAGAN. Small ethnic sliver of around 5,000 people, mostly animist and non-indigenous to the country. They are found along border valleys of Western Togo.

AGOKOLI. Legendary king of **Notsé** whose excesses sparked the Ewe dispersal to the south. Agokoli was the second king of Notsé, succeeding his father Afotché, founder of the dynasty. He ruled during the first decades of the eighteenth century. During his reign, ritual sacrifices were made of **Akposso** children, leading to the migration of an important segment of the latter tribe to Savalou in Benin. Agokoli's brutal excesses, haughty mannerisms, and autocratic rule (including the insistence on the building of earthen walls around Notsé) led to the **Adja**-Ewe dispersal in 1720, when an important part of the population deserted him. The painful memory of his rule contributed to the Ewe's future distaste of monarchical government; the Notsé dispersal is a major Ewe celebration annually commemorated in the **Hogbetsotso** festival. *See also* NOTSE; EWE.

AGOPOME, PROSPER, 1926– . Administrator. Born in Lomé on April 26, 1926 and an accountant (1943–1958), he was appointed Head of Supplies with the Togolese railroad Lomé Port station in 1958. With independence in 1960, Agopomé was appointed head of the Bassari district, returning to Lomé in 1963 as head of the Secretariat of Fiscal Control at the Ministry of Finance and the Economy. He was retired from the civil service in 1976.

AGOUE. Small coastal village across the border in Benin from which many of Togo's elite **Brazilians** trace their origins, including former president Sylvanus Olympio. Agoué was the site of the first chapel along the coast, built by the Brazilian Venessa de Jesus in 1835. Prior to independence, Agoué was the site of the proposed joint Togo-Dahomey deep-water port aimed at replacing the primitive facilities in Cotonou and Lomé. Benin's decision to modernize the port of Cotonou put to an end Agoué's developmental hopes and shortly after German funds were pledged for the modernization of Lomé. With the eclipse of the Brazilians' influence in both countries, Agoué lost importance: only during funerals is its original status visible, as thousands of mourners flock in from as far as Nigeria and Ghana.

AHLIN, BERNARD MATHIAS KOUAVI, 1902– . Early pharmacist. Born in Aného on January 27, 1902 and educated in Togo, Benin, and Ecole William Ponty in Senegal, he studied pharmacology at Dakar Medical School, obtaining his degree in 1929. He then worked for several years in Dakar, Porto Novo, and Niamey (Niger). He is the author of a number of collections of oral traditions.

AHLONKO, DOVI. Barrister at Lomé's Court of Appeals and successor to **Yao Agboyibor** as Head of the **CNDH.**

AHMED, IDRISSOU (EL HADJ), 1903–1973. One of Togo's leading theologians. Born in 1903 in Kpalimé to the first Yoruba family to settle in the local **zongo,** Ahmed studied the Koran and Arabic zealously and made the pilgrimage to Mecca in 1948—the first from Kpalimé to do so. After his return to Togo he acquired fame as a pious scholar and was in demand for various religious services. He was also very successful in private commerce. Utilizing a personal Yoruba network, he became the major cattle trader in the area. His death in 1973 opened a wide rift in the Muslim community, pitching the Yoruba and Hausa (his prime supporters) against the Kotokoli and Chamba, embittering inter-Muslim relations.

AHODIKPE, SALOMON. Long-time Mayor of Aného.

AHOULAN. Small Ewe-speaking coastal group estimated at 30,000 people, the Ahoulan are found mostly along the Togo-Ghana border region where they engage in fishing. Their scattered huts along the beaches are highly picturesque and constitute one of Togo's major tourist sights.

AHYI, PAUL. Well-known Togolese sculptor and artist in great demand. Ahyi studied art at the Paris Ecole des Beaux Arts and is currently an art instructor at the Lycée de Tokoin in Lomé. From time to time he is commissioned by the government, as when charged with decorating the Conseil de l'Entente villas and several other public buildings.

AIDAM, GEORGES KWAO. Secretary of State for Security and Territorial Administration in charge of Elections during December 1991 and September 1992.

AIR TOGO. Founded in Lomé in 1963, Togo's small national airline owns several small planes and has scheduled flights to Sansanné-Mango, Sokodé, Dapaong, and Lagos, the latter its only international link. For other foreign services Togo relies upon Air Afrique—Francophone Africa's regional airline.

AIRFIELDS. Togo has only one international-class airfield, at Lomé, whose original 3,000-meter runway (accommodating only small jets) was expanded in the 1980's. Traffic at the airport is low, however, as many tourists prefer to make the scenic Accra-Lomé-Cotonou-Lagos circuit by road. Despite high hopes in the 1960's, Lomé continues to be regarded by tourists as an intermediate stop, and they arrive or depart on their international journeys at Accra and/or Lagos. Lomé airport processed 5,989 tons of freight in 1981, a figure that actually declined in subsequent years (e.g., a low of 3,796 tons in 1987), though the number of passengers has gone up significantly from the 147,514 of 1981 to 213,378 in 1989 (with a high of 255,745 in 1985). The recent tumult in the country has dramatically decreased tourism, however. Apart from the Lomé airfield, there are three other major ones in the country, at Sokodé, Sansanné-Mango, and Dapaong, plus several other smaller strips that can accommodate small propeller planes. Pilot studies have explored the possibility of building international airports in Niamtougou (or Kara) in the north, but lack of foreign interest and Togo's precarious fiscal situation has prevented any serious action on this.

AITHNARD, AHLONKOBA (MRS.). President of the **Union Nationale de Femmes de Togo** (UNFT), the powerful pressure group that includes much of the country's trading elite. In February 1990 Mrs. Aithnard was brought into the cabinet as Minister of Social Affairs with special responsibility for women's affairs.

AITHSON, MESSAN. Early radical political leader. *See* Juvento.

AJAVON, AYIVI MAWUKO, 1931– . Teacher, diplomat, and former cabinet Minister. Born in Glékové (Kloto) on February 21, 1931 and educated at home and in France as a teacher, Ajavon first taught and served as Headmaster at the Lycée Tokoin in Lomé (1962–71). He then moved to the Ministry of Education as its Director (1972–77) and in 1978 was appointed Ambassador to Britain by General Eyadema. He returned to Lomé in 1982 to join Eyadema's cabinet as Minister of Justice and in 1986 was appointed Minister of Industry. It was Ajavon who suggested, and saw to fruition, Lomé's Industrial Free Zone, the first in Africa, that was inaugurated with great fanfare in 1989. Ajavon lost his position in the cabinet as soon as Eyadema's grip over the country loosened, and he was reassigned as Technical Counsellor in his own Ministry. Between 1991 and 1993 he was a member of the Haut Conseil de la République.

AJAVON, HENRI, 1906–1980. Educator and former administrator. Born in Aného on September 25, 1906, Ajavon was educated locally and at the prestigious Ecole William Ponty in Senegal, returning home to engage in education. He served as teacher and then school director (authoring several books and plays) until Sylvanus Olympio's rise to power in 1958, when he was appointed Cabinet Director of the Ministry of Education, a position he held until the 1963 coup d'état. After the coup he returned to teaching, retiring in 1970.

AJAVON, OSWALD AYIKOE. Former powerful Secretary General of the **Comité de l'Unité Togolaise** and Director of Information under both President Grunitzky and General Eyadema. Member of a prominent Aného family and a top leader of the CUT under Sylvanus Olympio, Ajavon did not renounce hopes of a CUT comeback after Olympio's assassination and the rise of the Grunitzky regime. On November 21, 1966—while serving as Grunitzky's director of information—Ajavon led a special civilian commando unit that invaded government installations and issued the call for the overthrow of the regime over the radio. *See* COUP (ATTEMPTED) OF 1966. The attempt failed, and Ajavon was imprisoned for his role in it. He was freed in January 1967, when the army seized power from Grunitzky but was rearrested barely eleven months later for calling for another revolt in his subversive Mina-language newsletter *Kurie,* which was promptly banned. Eventually making his peace with Eyadema, Ajavon was reinstated as Director of Information (his old post), which he held until 1972. Since then he has been involved in commercial printing activities.

AJAVON, ROBERT, 1910– . Physician and politician. Born on April 10, 1910 in Lomé, Ajavon was educated locally and won one of the first six scholarships of Governor Bonnecarrere for medical studies in France. Combining a political career with his medical work, he was elected Togo's deputy to the French National Assembly in 1952. At the completion of his term (1956), Ajavon was elected to Togo's assembly, serving as its president between 1956 and 1958. A bitter and ambitious arch-rival of Sylvanus Olympio, the latter's comeback locked Ajavon out of public life until after the 1963 coup, when Ajavon was reelected to the national assembly (1963–67) and served as president of the Committee on Defence and Foreign Affairs (1963–64). In August 1964, Dr. Ajavon was named Togo's ambassador to the United States and Canada and permanent representative to the United Nations, positions he held until June 1967. Retiring from public life, Ajavon opened a clinic in Ivory Coast and, in 1974, one in Lomé, where he practiced medicine until 1985. His continued political importance was attested to by the fact that in mid-1987 General Eyadema met with him and other former PTP leaders as part of his drive to secure support from all segments of the country.

AKAKPO, AMOUZOUVI MAURICE. Head of the Department of History at the University of Benin and author of numerous historical studies.

AKAKPO, ANDRE, 1913–1967. Eminent biologist and Togo's first Ambassador to the United States and the United Nations. Born on June 21, 1913 in Aného, Akakpo was educated locally and studied in France on one of the first six scholarships of Governor Bonnecarrere. Working and teaching locally and abroad, Dr. Akakpo built a name for himself. An important member of the **Comité de l'Unité Togolaise,** he entered political life in the 1950's and was elected to the assembly in 1958, serving as his party's parliamentary head. In 1959 he was also elected Deputy Mayor of Lomé. Following independence, Akakpo was named Ambassador to the United States and the United Nations, serving in these capacities until August 1964. He died a few years later.

AKAKPO, ASSIBA, 1958– . Journalist and poet. Born on November 16, 1958 in Lomé, Akakpo proceeded to Yaoundé, Cameroun to study journalism after secondary schooling. Currently with the Togolese broadcasting company, Akakpo has written a number of poems, winning third prize in the 1986 International Poetry Festival.

AKAKPO, AYAYI JUSTIN, 1945– . Veterinarian. Born on August 8, 1945, Akakpo was trained in Veterinary Medicine at the University of Dakar Medical School (1976), the Institut Pasteur in Paris, and University of Claude Bernard (Lyon), obtaining his doctorate and specializing in microbiology. Akakpo returned to teach at the University of Dakar, becoming full Professor in 1988. He is the author of some thirty-two scientific papers and has delivered fifteen conference papers.

AKAKPO, KOKOE 1948– . Home economist. Born in Sokodé on March 18, 1948 and educated wholly in Togo, Akakpo currently serves as Head of Applied Nutrition with CONGAT in Lomé.

AKAKPO-AHIANYO, ANANI KUMA (SAMUEL), 1937– . Former Minister of Foreign Affairs and Eyadema crony. An Ewe born on December 12, 1937 in Tsévié, Akakpo-Ahianyo was educated in Lomé and in 1960 proceeded to Paris to study agricultural economics and rural sociology, acquiring a degree in the latter in 1965. He subsequently earned a Ph.D. in the same field (1971) and was appointed Director General of the Institut National de la Recherche Scientifique. An ambitious person seeking a political career, Akakpo-Ahianyo's fawning and praise for Eyadema gained him appointment as Permanent Secretary of Rural Development in 1975. The same year he was also made RPT councillor from Lomé and member of the Central Committee of the Party. In 1977 he was dispatched to Peking as Ambassador to China and North Korea, but by July 1978 he was back in Lomé to take over the Ministry of Foreign Affairs, replacing Edem Kodjo who had been appointed OAU Secretary General. One of Eyadema's most ardent supporters in the 1980's, Akakpo-Ahianyo was dropped from the cabinet in September 1984 after six years as Togo's Foreign Minister. In the 1980's he wrote a number of poems inspired by the "glory" of North Korean Marxism.

AKAKPO-TYPAMM, PAUL, 1916– . Poet. Born in Hlandé in the Lac prefecture on October 14, 1916, Akakpo-Typamm was educated in Kpalimé where he concluded primary studies and entered the civil administration working for the Togolese railroads. He completed his secondary education to become a teacher. Akakpo-Typamm is regarded as one of Togo's foremost poets. His work has appeared in various publications, both at home and abroad, and he has recently published a collection, *Rhymes et Cadences,* in Paris.

AKAKPOVIE, KAGNI GABRIEL. Minister of Justice since May 1994 in the RPT-UTD coalition government headed by Prime Minister Edem Kodjo.

AKEBOU. Small ethnic group (est. 18,500 in 1990) normally not affiliated to any larger ethnicity, found nearly exclusively mixed with the Akposso in the Plateaux region.

AKITANI, EMMANUEL, 1930– . Senior mining engineer. Born on July 18, 1930 in Aného, Akitani was educated in France and obtained degrees in Mathematics and Engineering. He worked in Senegal for a while before returning to Togo as Deputy Director of Geology and Mines in Lomé (1961–62) and administrative head of the Compagnie Togolaise des Mines de Benin shortly after. Since 1962, he has also been Director General of the Bureau National de Recherches Minières du Togo and Director of Mines and Geology in the Ministry of Public Works, retiring in 1990.

AKOU, MARTIN, 1913–1970. Togo's first Deputy to the French National Assembly. Born on September 25, 1913 in Lomé to Pastor Akou, who had played an important role in developing the **Ewe Evangelical Church.** After primary education, Akou accompanied Mission Inspector Stoevesaudt to Germany where he continued his education in Westheim, in Basel (Switzerland), and in France, completing his medical studies after the end of World War II. In 1946, running as the candidate of the Comité de l'Unité Togolaise, Dr. Akou beat **Nicolas Grunitzky** and became Togo's first Deputy to France's National Assembly. During this tenure in Paris (1946–51), he was affiliated with the Independents d'Outre Mer parliamentary group, though less out of ideological sympathy than to conform to parliamentary practice of joining a recognized faction. An isolationist and conservative, Akou kept away from the various interterritorial groupings then developing both in the French National Assembly and in Africa, establishing the pattern of Togolese "noninvolvement" in Francophone Africa's affairs. Dr. Akou was defeated in his 1951 reelection bid by his old foe, Grunitzky, who benefited from the French Administration's support. Following his defeat, Dr. Akou retired from political life and re-established his medical practice in Ghana until his death in 1970.

AKOUETE, PAULIN, 1907– . Trade union leader and key politician and cabinet minister in the Olympio era. Born in Grand Popo (Benin) in 1907, Akoueté was trained for a civil service career. He rapidly became absorbed in trade union affairs, rising to be Secretary General of the Union des Syndicats Confédérés du Togo (which was affiliated with the militant interterritorial UGTAN) and later president of the **Union Nationale des Travailleurs Togolais,** Togo's biggest and most influential union movement. An important member of Sylvanus Olympio's Comité de l'Unité Togolaise party by virtue of his control of the UNTT, Akoueté was Deputy in the Territorial Assembly from March 1952 to June 1955 and from April 1959 to April 1961. In May 1958 Akoueté became Minister of Labor, Social Affairs, and the Civil Service, and in May 1960 he was named Minister of Justice as well, holding both positions until 1963. A powerful prop for Olympio's increasingly heavy-handed administration, Akoueté fled into exile following the 1963 coup d'etat and did not return to Togo until April 1971. He has since been in retirement.

AKOUETE-AKUE, EDJENE, 1947– . Administrator. Born in 1947 and educated at home and in France in Law and Public Administration, on his return home Akoueté-Akué joined the Ministry of the Plan and rose to become department head of its Research division. He is the author of two books on Togo.

AKPEME. Initiation ceremony of young (fourteen to eighteen years old) Kabré girls, lasting a full week and symbolizing the attainment of maturity. Conducted on a sacred hill, the traditional ceremony—very prevalent in Kabré society—prepares the girls for womanhood and motherhood. It takes place in mid-July. The male equivalent of this ceremony is the **Evala.**

AKPO, GNADI (LT. COLONEL), 1947–1993. Former Commander of the Presidential Guard and a close Eyadema aide-de-camp. Succeeding to his command in 1992, Akpo died defending Eyadema during the assault on the latter at the Tokoin barracks in 1993.

AKPOSSO. Mountain ethnic group found in the Akposso district of the Plateaux region, west of Atakpamé, and also across the border in Ghana. In Evegbe their name means "equal to panthers" (Akpo=panthers; esso=equal). Estimated in 1990 to number around 60,000, the Akposso were chased to their mountain habitat by Ashanti and Ewe raids. The Ashanti-Akposso wars of 1869–1873, in particular, resulted in fully one third of the Akposso being either killed or driven into slavery to Kumasi. After the Ashanti defeat at the hands of Sir Wolseley in 1874, the Akposso started descending from their mountain retreats to reoccupy their foothill villages, a process further encouraged by the pacification of the area by the German administration of Togo. The Akposso had also suffered during the reign of King **Agokoli** of Notsé in the eighteenth century. Currently the Akposso cultivate coffee and cocoa farms twenty, thirty, or even one hundred kms. away from their mountain villages, descending to the plains only at harvest time and returning to the hills in March. Known for their rebellious and anarchic spirit, the Akposso have no superior chiefs or king. The Akposso district used to be one of four such subdivisions in the Plateaux region and had its administrative headquarters in Amlamé, with an estimated population of 180,000 and several cocoa-coffee cooperatives. In 1972 the district was divided to form a Badou circonscription, for ethnic reasons, and in the 1981 reorganization of Togolese administrative units the Akposso district was renamed the prefecture of Amou, though retaining its Amlamé headquarters.

AKPOSSO-BENA RANCH. Joint German-Togolese experimental ranch involved in improving cattle, pig, and rabbit stock in the country. *See also* CENTRE D'ELEVAGE D'AVETONOU.

AKROUA WATERFALLS. Scenic series of cascades and pools of a river emerging from a source, found near Badou in the Plateaux region.

AKUAVI. Periodical, in French, issued in Lomé by the RPT Women's branch. It is edited by Nabedé Pala.

ALADJI, VICTOR, 1941– . Author and poet. An Ewe born in Hang-nigba near Palimé, Aladji completed his studies in Journalism at the University of Lille in France and returned to Togo to join the staff of Radio-Togo. He is the author of several published novels and currently teaches at the National University of Benin in Lomé.

ALASSOUNOUMA, BOUMBERA. Foreign Minister of Togo. A former Ambassador to France, and close friend of General Eyadema, Alassounouma was appointed Foreign Minister in May 1994 in the UTD-RPT coalition government of newly appointed Prime Minister Edem Kodjo.

ALEDJO see FAILLE D'ALEDJO.

ALIDOU DJAFALO, MENVEYINOYU (ALBERT), Colonel, 1922– . Former powerful head of Togo's gendarmerie (police), Minister of Public Health, key officer in the armed forces, and Togo's number two man. Born in Lama Kara on February 3, 1922 to a Kabré family, Alidou Djafalo joined the militia in 1942, serving in postings in Bassari, Atakpamé, and Aného. On June 22, 1956 he commanded the platoon that carried out the massacre of Kabre in Pya that fifteen years later would be commemorated by General Eyadema. In 1961 he attended a police officers' school in Melun, France, having been promoted from the ranks by President Olympio. Following completion of the course he was appointed Commander of the Garde Togolaise units in the north (1962–63). After the 1963 coup d'état, Alidou Djafalo was promoted to Captain and Commander of the mobile police force. In 1965 he became a Major and head of the gendarmerie. In 1970 he was promoted to Lieutenant Colonel. One of General Eyadema's closest friends and most trusted lieutenants, Alidou Djafalo became a key man in the new military regime set up after the 1967 coup d'etat. A member of the **Comité de Reconciliation Nationale** set up after the coup, Alidou Djafalo served as Minister of Public Health, at the same time also being a member of the Political Bureau of the **Rassemblement du Peuple Togolais** since the party was created. A strong and hard personality, Alidou Djafalo was the most important support of the Eyadema regime and was literally the last military officer to be dropped from President Eyadema's cabinet with the civilianization of that body in the 1970's. He was retired from the armed forces in 1982.

ALIPUI, KOMLAN, 1936– . International administrator and former technocrat cabinet Minister. An Ewe born in Anou Oblo near Kpalimé in 1936, Alipui was educated at home and in France where he obtained a doctorate in Economics from the University of Rennes

(1973). After his studies he joined the International Monetary Fund and later worked with BCEAO, the central bank of Francophone West Africa in Dakar. In 1984 he heeded General Eyadema's request to return home, take over the Ministry of Finance and the Economy, and help put Togo on the direction demanded by the World Bank. Though he brought a technocratic input to this effort, the massive corruption of the Eyadema regime, including that of his Ministers, neutralized his impact, and his tenure merged with the wave of democratization and violence that reached Togo in 1990. By 1991 Alipui, who had participated in the National Convention committee investigating corruption, had left the cabinet to return to Dakar.

ALL-EWE CONFERENCE (AEC). Organization set up in the Gold Coast on June 9, 1946 to campaign for the unification of all segments of the Ewe population under British tutelage. A merger of several previous groups, including the Ewe Unionist Association of **Daniel A. Chapman,** who was elected Secretary General of the All-Ewe Conference, the organization—claiming to represent all Ewe clans—had only moderate support in French Togoland. There its most prominent members were the **Brazilian Augustino De Souza** and some twenty customary chiefs. Sylvanus Olympio, the political leader of French Togo's Ewe, was campaigning for his own Comité de l'Unité Togolaise party and had an ambivalent attitude toward the AEC and its goals. In late 1948 and early 1949 the AEC suffered major splits in its ranks as a result of incipient resentments against the organization's **Anlo**-Ewe leadership, resentments having their origins in the "treason" of the Anlo clan during the Ashanti-Ewe wars of 1868–1871. *See* ANLO. Though the All-Ewe Conference has long since disappeared, its goals and concerns are very much alive on both sides of the Togo-Ghana border, complicating amicable relations between the two countries. *See also* TOLIMO.

ALLASSOUNOUMA, BOUMBERA, 1942– . Former Minister of Higher Education and Scientific Research. Born in 1942 in Niamtougou and a Lasso (an affiliate Kabre group), Allassounouma studied in schools in Kara and Sokodé before gaining a scholarship to travel to France and study psychology at the University of Caen. He later continued in labor studies in Paris. He returned to Togo in 1970 and worked with the National Pedagogical Institute. In 1973 he was appointed its Director and five years later joined Eyadema's cabinet as Minister of Labor and the Civil Service. Six months later he was reassigned to the Ministry of Education. In July 1980, the ministry was split into two sections and Allassounouma assumed responsibility for Higher Education. (The ministry was further split in 1982.) He was dropped from the cabinet in the September 1982 shuffle and reassigned to the Ministry of Education as senior technical consultant. In August 1983 he was appointed Ambassador to China, and in 1987 he returned to Lomé as senior consultant in the Ministry of Foreign Affairs.

ALLIANCE DE DEMOCRATES POUR LE RENOUVEAU (ADR). Zarifou Ayéwa's political party in the 1990's. The party, especially strong in Ayéwa's ethnic region, was joined by two other regional formations to create the Groupe Social Pan-Africain that boycotted the 1994 legislative elections. Earlier, in 1990 Zarifou set up the **Alliance Togolaise pour la Démocratie**.

ALLIANCE TOGOLAISE POUR LA DEMOCRATIE (ATD) *see* ALLIANCE DE DEMOCRATES POUR LE RENOUVEAU (ADR).

ALMEIDA, AYITE. Prominent **Brazilian** lawyer with chambers in downtown Lomé.

ALMEIDA, AYIVI GAMELE D'. Former High Commissioner of Tourism. Succeeding to the post in 1979 after a career within the department, d'Almeida acquired the distinction of being the longest lasting of such Commissioners. Most of his predecessors had been purged for embezzlement or corruption while in office. He was dropped from the post in 1986 and left the civil service.

ALMEIDA, JEAN-JULIEN D'. A medical doctor who was formerly Director General of Public Health, Inspector General of Medical Services, and head of the Smallpox division, d'Almeida is currently in retirement from public life and has a private practice in downtown Lomé.

ALMEIDA, SILIVI KOKOE D', 1950– . Educator. Born in 1950 in Bobo-Dioulasso (Burkina Faso) to a prominent **Brazilian** family from Togo, d'Almeida studied at schools in Benin and Togo, and for her higher education she studied at the University of Benin in Lomé, obtaining a Master's degree in History. She teaches History in a Lomé secondary school and has written a number of books on the colonial administration.

ALOME *see* LOME.

ALOU, KPATCHA ALABA M., 1949– . Educator. Born in 1949 in Pya-Kioude in northern Togo and educated in Lomé and Sokodé,

Alou travelled to Yaoundé where he studied Protestant theology and to Bordeaux where he obtained his doctorate. He currently teaches Philosophy at the Protestant College of Lomé where he is also Deputy-Director and Chaplain.

AMAIZO, BASILE FOLI, 1927– . Former head of the Stockbreeding Services of Togo. Born in Kpalimé on August 27, 1927 and trained in Toulouse as a veterinarian, Amaizo headed Togo's Stockbreeding Services between 1963 and 1987 when he retired and represented Togo in various veterinarian conferences abroad.

AMAIZO, DOVI (LOUIS), 1939– . International civil servant and social scientist. Born in Kpalimé on August 17, 1939, Amaizo was educated locally and proceeded to the universities of Rome and Ghana before finally arriving at the University of Wisconsin, and later Montreal, where he obtained a degree in African Studies. He served as Information Officer with the United Nations in New York and later in Lomé (1965–66). Between 1966 and 1970, he was attached to the United Nations office in Addis Ababa, and in 1970 he became administrative officer for the FAO in Rome. In 1974 he shifted to Geneva, where he has been since.

AMAKUE, GEORGES see APEDO-AMAH, GEORGES AMAKUE DOHUE.

AMEDEGNATO, AMOUSSOUVI VIGNIKO (FERDINAND), 1930– . Former cabinet minister. Born in Agouégan on May 30, 1934 and a teacher by profession, Amedegnato served as Education Inspector and Director of Primary Education between 1959 and 1965. In 1965 he was appointed Director of Youth and Sports, and after the 1967 coup he was shifted to head primary education in the Kloto district. In 1980 he was brought into Eyadema's cabinet as Minister of Information, later of Education. He turned out to be one of Eyadema's less successful choices and was soon dropped in 1981 and reassigned his old duties in the Ministry of Education. In 1990 he went into retirement.

AMEDOME, ABRA (MRS.), 1933– . Former cabinet minister. A vocal RPT militant, aggressive merchant/entrepreneur, unionist, and president (1975–1987) of the **Union Nationale des Femmes du Togo** (UNFT), the popular Mrs. Amedomé was brought into Eyadema's cabinet as Minister of Social Affairs in charge of women's interest, to attract support from the merchant-queens of Lomé. Of Ewe origin, she was dropped in September 1982 in favor of Mrs. Shefti Meatchi, a Northerner, wife of the former Vice President under Nicolas

Grunitzky—a fact that caused discontent in Lomé. Mrs. Amedomé studied pharmacology at Lyon and Montpellier (1955–60) and worked as a pharmacist in Lomé prior to her appointment to the cabinet.

AMEDZOFE. "Place of origin" in Ewe. *See* NOTSE.

AMEFIA, YAO JOSEPH. Former Minister of Equipment and Mines in the transitional government between September 7, 1991 and September 1992. Amefia was a victim of an attempted assassination in downtown Lomé on August 17, 1992.

AMEGA, ATSU-KOFFI (LOUIS), 1932– . Former Minister of Foreign Affairs, international administrator, and long-term President of the Supreme Court. Born on March 22, 1932 in Lomé, Amega moved to Congo/Brazzaville with his family and was later educated there and in France, obtaining a law degree. While in Paris he took an active part in the various African students' organizations and served as President of the Congolese Students' Association (1957–58) and deputy secretary of the militant Federation des Etudiants de l'Afrique Noire en France (FEANF). Upon the completion of his studies, Amega returned to Brazzaville and joined the State Procurer's (Attorney's) Office while also teaching at Brazzaville's Law School (1961–62). In 1963 he was appointed Technical Councillor and Director of Political and Legal Affairs of OCAMC and in 1964 President of Brazzaville's Court of Appeals. Earlier, between 1962 and 1963, he had been President of the Brazzaville Tribunal and Judge on the Court of Appeals. He returned permanently to his native Togo after Massemba-Debat's rise to power in Congo shifted the political climate to the left. He was appointed Vice President of the Lomé Court in 1964 and in 1967 became advisor to the Supreme Court. In 1970 he was appointed to the **Cour de Sûreté de l'Etat** that tried the August 1970 plotters. In January 1972 Amega was brought into the cabinet as Minister of Rural Economy, a position he occupied until August 1973. He was appointed to head the Supreme Court after he left the cabinet and held that post for nine years until his nomination on December 24, 1981 as Togo's Ambassador to the United Nations. In September 1984, he was repatriated to Lomé and assumed the Ministry of Foreign Affairs. He has been a member of the Political Bureau of Eyadema's Rassemblement du Peuple Togolais, since the latter's inception. In the cabinet changes of March 1987 Amega was returned to his old post as President of the Supreme Court, where he strongly supported Eyadema by rejecting various efforts in 1990 to challenge the single-party system in Togo. Because of this, Amega's own position became untenable after multipartyism was ultimately institutionalized, there were calls for his replacement, and he was indeed retired in 1992.

AMEGANVI, CLAUDE. Radical trade unionist, who since the liberalizations of 1990 has set up his own independent trade union, the Trotskyite Organisation Togolaise des Travailleurs Démocratiques (OTTD) that has been gaining members from the old union confederation set up by Eyadema. Ameganvi was a member of the 1991–93 Haut Conseil de la République.

AMEGBLEAME, SIMON. Academic. After completing his studies at Center for African Studies in Bordeaux, Amegbléame returned to Lomé to teach at the University of Benin. In 1975 he compiled the most definitive bibliography of literature written in the Evegbé vernacular.

AMEGBOH, GBEGNON (JOSEPH), 1937– . One-time *eminence grise* of the Eyadema regime. Born on March 19, 1937 at Zalivé and educated in History, Amegboh joined the Ministry of Information in 1975 as a journalist and producer, later director, and still later its Secretary-General. There he wrote a number of laudatory studies of historical African leaders, ranging from Rabah (Chad) to Béhanzin (Benin). In 1981 he came to the attention of **Laclé,** then the regime's second most powerful man, and was appointed Minister of Information, Posts, and Telecommunications. In 1984 he joined the Presidential Office as Minister-Delegate to the President and as Laclé's deputy was secretary for the Lomé branch of the RPT. It was in the latter capacity that he acquired his immense influence as the regime's prime tactician and aide, directing day-to-day operations as General Eyadema became more reclusive. He has remained one of Eyadema's main assistants.

AMEGEE, KODGO YAHWONON, 1942– . Agronomist. Born on September 21, 1942 in Lomé, Amegee was educated at home and abroad, completing his degrees (1968, 1971) in Belgium. He currently teaches at the University of Benin.

AMEGEE, KOFFI GROLO, 1945– . Veterinarian. Born on September 14, 1945 and educated at home and at Alfort in Veterinary Medicine, Amegee earned his doctorate in 1973 and returned to teach at the University of Benin's School of Agronomy.

AMEGEE, LOUIS, 1903–1976. Administrator. Born in Lomé on March 28, 1903, Amegee started off as a simple accountant before becoming head clerk of the French firm SCOA (1929–60). He was elected to Lomé's municipal council as a CUT member in 1954 and remained a councillor until the assassination of President Sylvanus Olympio and the collapse of the regime. After independence Amegee was also appointed Director of the Alokoegbe State Mills (1960–65), and he has also been on a variety of administrative boards, including those of the

National Lottery, the Savings Bank, and the **Office des Produits Agricoles du Togo.** Since May 1959 Amegee was also treasurer of the Chamber of Commerce. He went into retirement in 1969.

AMEGEE, PAUL ANANI, 1913– . Veterinarian, administrator, and former cabinet minister. Born in Lomé on August 21, 1913, Amegee was educated locally and abroad, specializing in Veterinary Medicine. He has occupied a variety of posts in Lomé (1937–41), Sansanné-Mango (1941–43), and Sokodé (1943–1951), becoming Director of Stockbreeding Services in northern Togo (1951–54) in 1951, and Deputy Head of the National Bureau (1954–58). In June 1958 he was selected to head the ministerial cabinet of **Namoro Karamoko,** and in June 1959 Amegee was himself appointed Minister of Public Works, Transport and Telecommunications in Sylvanus Olympio's government. He retained his ministry until the coup d'état of 1963, at which time he was shifted back to administrative-technical duties until his retirement in 1973. He practiced medicine in a veterinary clinic in Lomé until 1982.

AMEGEE, YAO, 1948– . Director of the Benin University's School of Agronomy. Born in 1948 and trained at the University of Dakar in Veterinary Science, Amegee returned to Togo in 1974.

AMEGIE, MAWULIKPLIM YAO (GENERAL), 1948–1993. Eyadema's military right-hand man. Amegie came into prominence in August 1980, when with **Colonel Assila's** resignation on the grounds of ill health, he assumed the post of Deputy Chief-of-Staff of the Togolese armed forces. Prior to that, Amegie had been Assila's deputy and commander of the elite Third Battalion, based in Kara. In December 1988 Amegie joined the cabinet as Minister of Interior, providing the steel fist blunting the first pressures for democratization. With the January 1989 disgrace of **Kpotivi Tevi Dzidzogbe Laclé,** Eyadema's main civilian ally, Amegie temporarily took over the former's duties as Minister of Justice as well. The National Convention in 1990 stripped Eyadema of much of his executive powers: Amegie, too powerful to be completely eliminated, inherited the Defense portfolio which he used to issue diatribes against the new government, the illegality of its activities, and the possibility of civil war if the vilification and eclipse of Eyadema continued. As the tug-of-war between Prime Minister Koffigoh and President Eyadema continued, Amegie assumed the role of Eyadema's Minister of Defense, even as Koffigoh appointed another Minister in charge of Security to his cabinet. General Amegie died in defense of Eyadema in the 1993 assault on the latter's domicile in the Tokoin barracks.

AMEGNINOU, PAUL (Captain). Former Head of the Brigades de Vigilance of the gendarmerie, a unit set up by General Eyadema in the late 1970's to monitor security in the Lomé area. Personally responsible to Eyadema, Amegninou used to prepare weekly intelligence reports on the mood of the capital and potential sources of opposition. His quasi-absolute authority in a region adjacent to the Ghanaian border led him to engage in drug trafficking for which he was dismissed from the armed forces in 1984. Alternate reports suggest that his drug activities—common among officers along the frontier—were but the official excuse in an internal settling of accounts in the gendarmerie.

AMELA, HILLA-LAOBE, 1947– . Academic. Born in 1947 in Aného and educated locally and in Paris, Amela has a Ph.D. in Classics. He is currently head of the Department of Modern Literature at the University of Benin in Lomé and has published several volumes of poetry.

AMELA, YAO AMELAVI. Minister of Education and Scientific Resources between May 1991 and 1993.

AMELETE, TOYETOM. Journalist. Editor-in-Chief of the governmental daily *La Nouvelle Marché* until June 1987 when Amelété was appointed Deputy General-Manager of the national publishing house, Editogo.

AMENYAH, PAUL. Director General of the Bank of Togo since 1968. Prior to this, Amenyah had been Director General of Credit du Togo.

AMENYEDZI, AMEGEE, 1946– . Author. Born in Assahun on January 26, 1946. Although enrolled in a seminary in Tekoin, Amenyedzi renounced his vows in 1968 and became a teacher instead. Since 1973 he has been attached to the Ministry of Culture. He is the author of three plays.

AMETOZIM, PIERRE. Poet. A teacher by profession, Ametozim has contributed poems to various literary journals and reviews and is known for concentrating on social issues.

AMEVOR, KWAMI (ROBERT), 1937– . Educator and administrator. Born on November 30, 1937 in Amlame. A teacher by profession, Amevor has been attached to the office of the Minister of National Education in a variety of policymaking capacities since 1967.

AMITIE 77. Joint Franco-Togolese military exercises held in the Atakpamé region from November 24th to 25th, 1977. Touted at the time as reflecting France's military commitment to the survival of the Eyadema regime, the exercises were militarily viewed in French circles as a near disaster, attesting to the poor condition of the Togolese army.

AMLAME. Administrative headquarters of the prefecture of Amou, formerly known as the prefecture of Amlamé and, prior to that, the circonscription of Akposso. A small village south of the Atakpamé-Badou axis, Amlamé is the capital of the Akposso ethnic group. *See also* AKPOSSO.

AMORIN, AYAO TAVIO, 1958–1992. Leader of the Parti Socialiste Pan-Africain (PSP), assassinated by the Togolese military on July 23, 1992. Born on November 20, 1958 in Lomé and educated in Catholic schools, Amorin pursued his higher studies in Mathematics and Physics at the University of Poitiers, continuing his postgraduate studies in Computer Science. During his stay in France he had contacts with the French Communist Party and thus developed his radical leanings. In 1989 he moved to Cote d'Ivoire as a computer consultant, but as soon as preparations for a National Conference commenced in Togo, he returned home and was appointed to the Haut Conseil de la République setting up his radical PSP party. He was shot while walking in downtown Lomé in broad daylight and flown to Paris where he died. His death sparked massive riots in Lomé.

AMOU. Part of the former Akposso circonscription (later renamed Amlamé circonscription) that was renamed Amou in the 1981 administrative reorganization of Togo. The new prefecture encompasses the core of Akposso country and retains its headquarters in Amlamé. *See also* AKPOSSO.

AMOUSSOU, COMLANVI LUE, 1941– . International administrator. Born in 1941 and educated in Journalism and Postal Law in France, on his return to Lomé Amoussou was appointed Postal Inspector with the Ministry of Posts. In 1978 he became Chief Inspector, and a few years later he was appointed as head of the Press and Public Relations section of the Francophonic UAPT organization based in Brazzaville.

AMOUZOU, AKOSSOU. Former Minister of Primary and Secondary Education. Brought into the cabinet in May 1981, Amouzou, who is Ouatchi, was previously the Director of the cabinet of the Minister of Foreign Trade. He left the cabinet in 1984.

AMOUZOU, JACQUES. Presidential hopeful. One of only two candidates to declare their Presidential candidacies in the August 1993 elections when all the other opposition leaders pulled out in the contest against Eyadema. In the election Amouzou received 1.64% of the popular vote.

ANA. Small group—not to be confused with the **Ané**—living in Atakpamé (in the Gnagna and Djama quarters) midway between Atakpamé and Sokodé along the Togo-Benin border. The Ana are seen as the most western extension of the **Yoruba** group. They trace their origin to Ife (Nigeria) and speak an Ife-Yoruba dialect. Their history has been one of perennial strife, warfare, and vassalage to the powerful Dahomey kingdom to the east. There are an estimated 60,000 Ane, some twenty percent of whom are post-independence Muslim converts.

ANAGOKOME. The Yoruba Moslem **zongo** quarter of Lomé, one of the oldest parts of the capital. Initially populated exclusively by **Brazilian** Yoruba from the Benin coastal town of **Agoué,** who came to join their Portuguese employer Octaviano Olympio. Erecting a small mosque in 1882 (Lomé's first), the area grew in size as newcomers flocked to the new center that also traded in slaves. Anagokomé became the commercial hub of the growing capital of Togo. With independence, its prime "downtown" location attracted urban renewal efforts and in 1975–77 it was razed to the ground and its population relocated to **Togblekopé** in the suburbs.

ANANI, DAGBA. Former High Commissioner of Foreign Affairs, imprisoned in September 1985 in connection with the bombs in downtown Lomé and released in a mid-1986 amnesty.

ANANI, JEAN KOUASSI. Interim Minister of National Education and Scientific Research in the second Transitional government of Prime Minister Kottigah between September 1991 and September 1992.

ANANI, MAWUGBA. Lawyer and Magistrate, who briefly replaced Mawuko Ajavon as Minister of Justice in May 1986.

ANANI KPONTON, THEODORE. Statistician. Trained in Economics and Mathematics, Anani Kponton was appointed to the post of Deputy-Director of National Accounts (1968) on his return from France. In 1969 he was promoted to Director of Statistics and National Accounts.

ANE. Founding ethnic group of Aného. Not to be confused with the **Ana,** the Ané founded Aného between the years 1663 and 1690, having migrated to the area from El Mina (Ghana) under the leadership of a Fanti prince named Quam-Dessou. The Ané eventually adopted the **Ouatchi** dialect and are known, together with the nearby **Ga,** as **Mina,** a reference to their original home in El Mina. Together, the Ga and Ané number around 90,000 and are found only in the coastal areas, especially in the vicinity of Aného.

ANECHO *see* ANEHO.

ANEDEGNATA, VIGNITO. Since 1990, the Secretary-General of the RPT, now essentially the political vehicle of the Kabré.

ANEHO (also, Anécho). Lovely historic coastal town, former capital of both German and French Togo and intellectual center of Togo. Also known in the colonial era as Petit Popo (Little Popo) and as Anécho (until 1974). Aného is twenty-seven miles east of Lomé near the Benin border. The town was an important slaveport and commercial entrepot, and, as Togo's intellectual center (i.e., hometown of a large percentage of the country's intellectuals and senior bureaucrats), it is directly comparable with Ouidah, further east along the coast in Benin. Founded by **Ané** refugees from El Mina (now in Ghana) who were escaping perennial Ashanti assaults, the name Aného means, in Ouatchi dialect, "the home [ho] of the Ané." The town was established around 1663–90; just prior to this, in 1663 or 1687, a **Ga** group from the Accra region installed itself nearby at Glidji (a zongo village of considerable historical importance), and both ethnic groups have been referred to as Mina, an allusion to their point of origin. The two main clan-families in the area, the **Lawsons** and the Adjigo, have historically claimed original possession of the land and hence title of Superior Chief. The Adjigo clan's claims have usually been recognized; in 1961, however, the traditional "post" was abolished with the concurrence of both clans. The last "Chief" of Aného was **Ata Quam-Dessou XIII** who reigned between 1922 and his death in 1977.

With the establishment of Glidji and the first communities of Aného, other families and clans from the Accra area gravitated to the quieter atmosphere of Aného, which also attracted **Brazilian** settlement, eventually becoming the biggest coastal center in Togo. (The ancestors of the Ajavon, Tekoé, Wilson, Akoué, Lawson, de Silveira, d'Almeida, and De Souza families settled in Aného during this period.) The town became a loosely held tributary of the Allada kingdom in Benin and a slaveport, trading especially with the Danes, Dutch, and British. The port never developed, however, into a major competitor to the bigger centers of the slave trade (such as Ouidah) because of the smaller volume of slaves available and the alleged sharp practices of the Mina middlemen. For some time the Dutch were very active in Aného, building one of the first trading compounds in 1772, their influence radiating out of Christianborg (Accra). Control of much of the trade then gravitated into the hands of the Da Souza family (*see* DA SOUZA, FRANCISCO FELIX) and later French, German, and Portuguese companies established themselves in the area. The Aného area was also the scene of early missionary drives, including those of the **Moravian Brothers,** under **Jacob Protten,** and the Methodists, under Thomas Birch Freeman. Thus, at the time of the German occupation Aného had been in close contact with Europeans for over two centuries. Briefly the capital of the new German colony (1885–1887) and interim capital of the French segment of Togo prior to the definitive Anglo-French partition (1914–20), Aného's importance rapidly declined with the onset of colonial rule. In 1937, for example, only nine ships called at this historic port, most trade gravitating to the new administrative capital, Lomé. Currently, the town is Togo's eighth largest urban center with 24,000 inhabitants, constantly losing ground to other expanding urban centers in the interior or to Lomé, barely a half-hour drive away. In 1972, for example, when Aného had less than today's population, it was Togo's fifth largest center, and in 1960—again with roughly the same population—it was Togo's second town after Lomé. Nevertheless, Aného remains one of Togo's intellectual centers, with a large percentage of the country's elite coming from families originating there. Glidji, an Aného suburb, currently has a population of 1,500.

The Aného circonscription, with administrative headquarters in the town of Aného, encompasses a population of 150,000. It was renamed Prefecture des Lacs in the June 1981 administrative reorganization of the country. Most of the inhabitants are of Mina, Ewe, or Ouatchi ethnicity. Most hold to ancestral beliefs, though the town has a considerable Christian minority. The district is of great historic and tourist interest. Apart from the old colonial and precolonial relics in Aného proper and the town's delightful setting between the river and the Ocean, the region boasts **Porto Seguro** on **Lac Togo** and the latter's aquatic center and popular Le Lac hotel-restaurant. Nearby also is Togo's phosphate port of Kpémé and, across the lake, the phosphate deposits that give Togo much of its relative prosperity.

ANKRAH, DAVID, 1915– . Educator. Born in Aného on September 15, 1915. A graduate of William Ponty school in Senegal, Ankrah served in a variety of teaching positions during the colonial era. After independence, he was appointed Director of the cabinet of the Minister of Education, serving for two years until the 1963 coup d'etat. He then reverted to teaching duties before retirement.

ANLO. Important Ewe clan residing along the coast between the Volta river (Ghana) and the Togo-Ghana border. Known to their neighbors as the Awuna, the Anlo trace their origins to the historic **Notsé** dispersal during which one of their chiefs, exhausted from the trek, could march no longer ('me nlo' = I am going to rest.) The clan's capital is Anloga; they number around 7,000 and speak the Anlo dialect. An upwardly mobile group, the Anlo have attracted hostility and envy consequent to their prominent status among the other Ewe clans. Several Anlo Ewe were also prominent in the **All-Ewe Conference** that collapsed because of anti-Anlo sentiments, which coalesced with residual resentments over the Anlo alliance with the Ashanti—perennial enemies of the Ewe—in the late 1800's, in opposition to the other Ewe clans.

ANNO (also, ANOUFOU) *see* CHOKOSSI.

ANTHONY, YAO SYLVANUS, 1943– . Economist. Born in Lomé on July 1, 1943, Anthony was trained locally and at the University of Dijon (1963–68) in development Economics. He also obtained specialized training in banking. Since 1969 he has been Credit Director of the Banque Togolaise de Developpment, as well as serving as trustee and government appointee on the board of several parastatal companies.

APALOO, JACQUES. President of the Supreme Court of Togo since 1991. Apaloo is a member of the Parti Démocratique de l'Unité (PDU) party.

APEDO, EMMANUEL. President of the Supreme Court.

APEDO-AMAH, AYAYI TOGOATA, 1952– . Dramatologist. Born on January 28, 1952 and educated locally and abroad, Apedo-Amah specialized in Fine Arts (Theatre) in which he received his doctorate in 1979. He served between 1991 and 1993 on the Haut Conseil de la République and currently teaches in the University of Benin.

APEDO-AMAH, GEORGES AMAKUE DOHUE, 1914– . Former Speaker of Togo's National Assembly, Ambassador to Nigeria, and Minister of Foreign Affairs. Born to a prominent Aného family on August 21, 1914, Apedo-Amah was educated locally and abroad and joined the French colonial administration in the 1930's. He served in a variety of important positions including that of Secretary to the French High Commissioner in Lomé. In April 1946 he joined the pro-administration and conservative **Parti Togolais du Progrès,** the party of Nicolas Grunitzky and Dr. Pedro Olympio, that was actively supported by the French administration and whose members at the time were mostly civil service officials and pro-French dignitaries. At the time, Apedo-Amah was also director of **Le Togo Français,** the administration's official periodical. In 1952 he was sent to the United Nations to participate with the French delegation and, following the establishment of the **Autonomous Republic,** Apedo-Amah was named councillor of education, youth, and sport and later Minister of Finance in Grunitzky's 1956–58 government. After the UN-supervised elections that turned out the Grunitzky regime and brought Sylvanus Olympio to power, Apedo-Amah left the country and worked first in France and then in Belgium with the European Economic Community. He returned to Lomé after the coup of 1963 to become Foreign Minister in Nicolas Grunitzky's 1963–67 government. His highly conservative policies proved to be unpopular among the urban population in the south, but Grunitzky was unwilling to lose his old ally and resisted efforts to displace Apedo-Amah. Rapidly, the latter came to be viewed as the epitome of the stolidness of the Grunitzky regime and one of the targets of both the November 1966 Lomé upheaval—*see* COUP (ATTEMPTED) OF 1966—and the 1967 military coup d'etat. After the 1967 coup, despite Apedo-Amah's flair for efficient administration and extensive contacts abroad (where he was widely appreciated), he was replaced as Foreign Minister. Together with Grunitzky, Apedo-Amah relocated to the Ivory Coast where they both had commercial interests. A few years after Grunitzky's death in a car accident in Cote d'Ivoire, Apedo-Amah returned to Togo and in mid-1973 was appointed Ambassador to Nigeria. After a number of other administrative appointments he was elected Deputy to the National Assembly in the 1980 elections and Speaker of the House, posts he occupied until 1987.

AQUEREBURU, SAMUEL 1905–1975. Educator, former cabinet minister, and former Secretary General of the **Mouvement Populaire Togolais.** Born in Aného on October 17, 1905, Aquereburu was educated locally at Benin's Ecole Victor Ballot and at the prestigious Ecole William Ponty in Senegal. In 1930 he continued his education at the pedagogical academy of Aix-en-Provence, France and returned to Togo where he worked as an educator and school inspector, eventually setting up his own school, of which he was Principal until 1963. A founding member of the conservative, pro-French **Parti Togolais du Progrès,** he was in the faction that rejected Grunitzky's leadership of the party and opted out in 1955 to form the Mouvement Populaire Togolais (under ousted leader Dr. Pedro Olympio) of which he became Secretary General. *See* POLITICAL PARTIES.

After Sylvanus Olympio's assassination in 1963, Aquereburu joined the four-cornered coalition of Nicolas Grunitzky and became MPT Minister of Labor, Transportation, and the Posts, a position he held until November 1966. Following the 1967 coup, Aquereburu retired from public life.

ARMED FORCES. Togo's armed forces, the majority Kabré from the North and many from General Eyadema's home village, Pya, have for long been the latter's main, and since the 1990s, sole means of maintaining his office. Since the onset of the multiparty era (1991) they have also been the main force destabilizing the country, murdering individual political leaders, carrying out massacres and other atrocities, and in general intimidating the government of the day.

Many of the senior officers of the armed forces (some of whom have been or are now being retired) are non-commissioned officer veterans of France's colonial armies that were demobilized in 1962. They were integrated, with officer rank, into the Togolese army after the 1963 coup. The current junior and middle rank officers are recruits since that event, heavily drawn from the Kabré ethnic group. Scattered remnants also remain of the Garde Nationale, Togo's minuscule army prior to the 1963 coup. Specialized units have been erected to cater to Eyadema's unique security needs.

Since the 1963 coup the size of the armed forces increased nearly tenfold but both the rank-and-file and the officer corps have remained heavily dominated (eighty percent) by Northerners, especially **Kabré.** Originally this was due to the fact that only these groups were attracted by the career possibilities inherent in military life during the colonial era. Since Togo was not a French colony but a trusteeship territory, France was prohibited from active recruitment within its confines. This presented no problem to northern youth wishing to enlist; they merely crossed the border into Dahomey and (usually) presented themselves at the Djougou recruitment center as Dahomeans. During the German colonial era, Northerners had also joined the German Polizeitruppe in large numbers and hence there was an established tradition in the north of participation in European security forces. On the eve of World War I, for example, there were over 1,500 indigenous personnel in the Polizeitruppe, the majority being Kabré, Bassari, Kotokoli, and Dagomba. Under French rule, the local militia, the Garde Cercle, was also heavily staffed by Northerners, who after independence became the nucleus for the Garde Nationale.

After the 1963 coup d'état—sparked by the desire of demobilized northern veterans to be integrated into an expanded Togolese army—the armed forces were tripled in size with the integration of the veterans, and selective recruitment drives were mounted to assure the continued northern composition of the armed forces. Togo's main recruitment and training camp is in the Kabre heartland, at Kara (ex-Lama Kara), which is also the base of the powerful Third Battalion. Army Headquarters are at the Tokoin base in the suburbs of Lomé, where General Eyadema maintains his residence, shunning the more vulnerable Presidential Palace at night.

The Togolese armed forces saw three periods of rapid expansion. Right after the 1963 coup d'état there was an immediate doubling (and eventual tripling) of the force, with the integration into the hitherto minute army of the veterans of the French colonial armies (including Eyadema, Assila, Bodjollé, and Alidou-Djafalo—all NCO's hitherto). Between 1963 and 1967, defense expenditures increased by 350 percent, an increase surpassing that in all African countries save Uganda. By 1967 Togo's defense allocations as a percentage of the national budget placed Togo in tenth rank among thirty-two African states, while, in terms of absolute increase in personnel, Togo led the continent.

The second period of rapid expansion commenced in 1972, when the Third Battalion was erected, and was accelerated by the boom of revenues of 1974–75 (*see* PHOSPHATES) that led to the recruitment of a Fourth Battalion as well. Defense expenditures for 1975, for example, were sixty percent higher than those in 1974. Though State revenues fell as the phosphate boom collapsed, defense expenditures were not cut; however, the inability of the regime to provide adequate "perks" of office to its military cohorts led to the immersion of many officers in various commercial enterprises, at times in direct competition with civilians.

The third period of rapid increase in the armed forces took place in the late 1980s as Eyadema augmented the force in face of mounting pressures to depose him. The current precise size of the Togolese armed forces is difficult to ascertain, due to widely disparate data tendered by equally reliable soruces. The military did go up from a force of 3,250 in 1980 to 4,500 in 1984 and 6,650 in 1988. The latter figure was composed of an army of 5,100, a Presidential Guard of 800, and a gendarmerie of 750. Structurally organized into five battalions, the bulk of the force is found in two motorized infantry battalions and three infantry battalions. Their combined armor includes fifty armored cars and several tanks. There are engineering, signals, and headquarters units and three paracommando companies. The Navy and Air Force were reduced in strength in the 1980s due to the high cost of materiel and maintenance. The Navy currently numbers less than fifty men and two patrol craft (originally five boats and a force of 200) while the air force was pared down to sixty men and five Magisters (usually training jets) and an assortment of eighteen planes, many grounded. The original three helicopters in service have allegedly been recently augmented to five. There is also a paramilitary force of 1,400 men stationed mostly in the countryside, that might have been greatly augmented, giving rise to the disparity in figures about the military. However, since several current estimates put the armed forces at 13,600 men, the increase would have had to be phenomenal.

The Togolese armed forces have been commanded by **Colonel Kleber Dadjo, Major Emmanuel Bodjollé,** and General Gnassingbe Eyadema. Between 1975 and 1980, the Deputy Chief of Staff and *de facto* commander was **Colonel James Dedum Ayaovi Assila,** who resigned in 1980 on grounds of health, to be succeeded by General Yao Mawulikplim Amegie and in 1992 by Colonel Bassabi Bonfoh.

The Togolese armed forces remained, until the 1980s, largely cohesive and immune to the internal unrest afflicting their compatriots in neighboring Benin, because of their ethnic unity (most troops are from the North) and the tight control exercised over the force by their commanders. The latter, either promoted to officerhood after the coup of 1963 or recruited after that of 1967, are keenly aware that they sustain one of their own in office in a country where the center of gravity is in the South. Moreover, the army is pampered, officers are allowed to develop personal commercial empires, corruption is tolerated, and a military life is a lucrative option for northerners without employment prospects elsewhere in the economy.

Notwithstanding this, there has been some unrest and a number of upheavals within the armed forces. The early instances of unrest can be traced to a continuation of the Bodjollé-Eyadema tug-of-war and to intra-northern gripes about the Kabré monopoly over military careers, which was the root of the 1969 mutiny of Moba officers, news of which only leaked out in 1972. In all instances the regime dealt harshly with unrest and increased recruitment of Kabre personnel specifically from Pya and Kara, deemed more loyal than Kabre and/or Moba from Bodjollé's Kouméa district.

Starting in the late 1970s, however, more serious instances of unrest began to rock the Togolese military, as pockets of southern officers started plotting the overthrow of Eyadema. An early example of this was the 1977 plot of **Brazilians.** Eyadema's reaction to these signs of opposition was to strengthen his *personal* control apparatus — the Presidential Guard, recruited from one quarter of his home village, Pya and in 1986 commanded by his own son, Lt. Ernest Gnassingbé (estimated at between 800 to 1,600 men), and after 1992 by his second cousin Colonel D. T. Gnassingbé. Another presidential relative, Major Yoma Djoua, was appointed Commander of the Brigade Pigeon, the Political Police, and later implicated in a variety of atrocities on behest of the regime. Two parallel intelligence-gathering hierarchies of spies compete in ferreting out opposition in the army or society at large, including at the Aflao border with Ghana. *See* BRIGADE DE VIGILANCE; BRIGADE DE RECHERCHE.

Starting in 1990 and following his humiliation by the National Conference, moreover, Eyadema moved on a counter-offensive: using relatives in command of segments of the armed forces, and especially the Presidential Guard, he brutalized and terrorized the various budding political movements that sought to supplant him and his RPT, until by 1993 he was firmly back in power. There is little doubt that Togo's armed forces regard themselves solely loyal to General Eyadema, and no act of theirs occurs without his sanction. This will pose problems for the current Prime Minister, Edem Kodjo, who rules in alliance with the Kabré (i.e., Eyadema-beholden) RPT party. It will pose serious problems in the future if the Ewe parties coalesce to capture political power or try to remove Eyadema himself from office.

AROUNA, MAMA, 1928– . Former northern CUT leader, born in Sokodé in 1928 and educated locally. Arouna joined the administration and in 1958 was elected to the Togolese assembly as CUT deputy. He remained in the assembly until the 1963 coup d'etat, serving as Secretary of the assembly's Central Bureau from 1959 until 1963. Following the 1963 coup, Arouna's political career came to an end, and he has since been involved mostly with administrative duties.

ASAFOHENE. Traditional nominal sovereign of the Ewe **dou,** who, together with the unit's chiefs, notables, and elders, possesses decision-making powers. The term comes from the Ashanti and means 'military commander.' In the absence of widescale wars among the Ewe the Asafohene became territorial chiefs. *See* DOU.

ASSEMBLEE LEGISLATIVE DU TOGO (ALT). In 1955 a statute created the Autonomous Republic of Togo, changing the powers and name of the local assembly from **Assemblée Territoriale du Togo** to Assemblée Legislative du Togo. The statute constituted a major deviation from French colonial and administrative precedent and gave the ALT much wider powers than then prevailing in the AOF or AEF colonies. The two years of the Autonomous republic and the ALT were marked by the executive and legislative control of **Nicolas Grunitzky,** who was strongly sustained in power by the local French administration. In 1958 power shifted dramatically to **Sylvanus Olympio** and his **Comité de l'Unité Togolaise,** and the assembly's name was changed to **Chambre de Deputes.**

ASSEMBLEE NATIONALE DU TOGO (ANT), 1961–1967. The name of the legislative body established in April 1961 to replace the

Chambre de Deputes that functioned between 1958 and 1961 and had itself replaced the previous **Assemblée Legislative du Togo.** The ANT's membership was composed of fifty-one deputies, all supporters of the **Comité de l'Unité Togolaise** of **Sylvanus Olympio** as a result of electoral manipulation and the intimidation of opposition parties. The President of the ANT was the old President of the Chambre de Deputes, **Jonathan Savi de Tové,** with **Fio Agbano II** as Vice President. The assembly was dissolved in the aftermath of the 1963 coup, and the new assembly under Grunitzky's leadership—also called ANT—was composed of a four-cornered coalition of Togo's main parties (the PUT, Juvento, MPT, and UDPT), with each party having an equal number (fourteen) of deputies under the presidency of **Barthelemy Lambony.** See POLITICAL PARTIES; LISTE NATIONALE DE L'UNITE ET RECONCILIATION. The assembly was dissolved following the 1967 coup d'etat of General Eyadema, and new elections were promised for a new assembly. This promise was rescinded shortly thereafter, and Togo did not have a legislative body for thirteen years, until the new 1980 body. See ASSEMBLEE NATIONALE DU TOGO, II (ANT II).

ASSEMBLEE NATIONALE DU TOGO (ANT II). First national assembly of Togo since the 1967 coup d'etat. Installed on January 13, 1980 with sixty-seven members elected on the single slate of the Rassemblement du Peuple Togolaise (RPT), the Assembly was convened for five years. Its first speaker (president) was **Georges Apedo-Amah.** New elections for an enlarged seventy-seven-seat Assembly were held in 1985 and in 1990. In 1991 the convening of a **National Conference** ushered in competitive multiparty politics and gave rise to the non-elected **Haut Conseil de la République** that acted as interim legislature. A new Assemblée Nationale finally emerged after the much-postponed legislative elections of February 1994, with an array of parties represented, the CAR party the largest with thirty-six seats, followed by the RPT (thirty-five) and Prime Minister **Kodjo's** UTD with seven. Several parties, however, had boycotted the elections, including Gilchrist Olympio's.

ASSEMBLEE REPRESENTATIVE DU TOGO (ART). Deliberative body established on October 25, 1946, with powers similar to those granted the Conseils Generaux set up by France in her African colonies. Composed of thirty members, six elected by the first electoral college and twenty-four by the second (*see* DOUBLE ELECTORAL COLLEGE), the assembly had the authority to discuss taxation, customs duties, the organization of the public services, and similar matters. Meeting twice a year, the ART was highly politicized from the outset, with the **Comité de l'Unité Togolaise** of **Sylvanus**

Olympio in a dominant position and with Olympio as its president. In 1952 the assembly's name was changed to **Assemblée Territoriale du Togo,** and power shifted to Nicolas Grunitzky, who was strongly supported by the local French administration.

ASSEMBLEE TERRITORIALE DU TOGO (ATT). Successor to the **Assemblée Representative du Togo,** the ATT was established in 1952 with enlarged powers and with delegates elected for the first time under a single electoral college. *See* DOUBLE ELECTORAL COLLEGE. The enlarged electorate and active French support for northern and conservative political groupings shattered the former legislative supremacy of **Sylvanus Olympio** and his **Comité de l'Unité Togolaise.** In 1955 an **Autonomous Republic** of Togo was established and the ATT was transformed into the **Assemblée Legislative du Togo.**

ASSIGNON, KODJO V., 1950– . Administrator. Educated in Chemistry, Biology, and Agronomy, Assignon completed his studies in 1976 and joined the Ministry of Planning and Industry. Steadily promoted, he has been involved since 1976 in mounting feasibility studies of the various development projects proposed in that ministry.

ASSIH, AGOSSOYE, (Captain). Former Director of the Gendarmerie Nationale and the son of the chief of Pya-bas, the quarter in the northern village in which General Eyadema was born. Assih was seen as ultra-loyal to Eyadema and was rapidly promoted in the gendarmerie and was appointed Colonel and Head of the gendarmerie over the head of **Major Paul Comlan.** In early 1987, however, it was discovered that he was involved in the massive embezzlement at the **CNCA** for which he was reduced in rank to Captain and dismissed from the gendarmerie in April 1987. His replacement was Major Walla Sinzing Akawélou, General Eyadema's brother-in-law.

ASSIH-AISSAH, ASHIRA, 1952– . Ethnologist. Born in north Togo on March 2, 1952, Assih-Aissah was educated at home and abroad in Ethnology. Between 1978 and 1986 she studied at the University of Bordeaux, where she obtained her doctorate. Since 1987 she has been teaching at the National University of Benin in Lomé.

ASSILA, DEDUM AYAOVI (JAMES) (Colonel), 1932–1982. Former Chief of Staff of the Togolese armed forces, member of the original "troika" that seized power in 1963, and former Minister of Interior. Born in Notsé in 1932 of Ewe origin, Assila joined the French armed forces in 1951, serving in Indochina (1954–56) and Algeria (1956–57). After military courses in France (until 1962), Assila was repatriated to Togo and was a member of the inner clique that sponsored the 1963 coup that resulted in President Olympio's assassination. Promoted to Captain in the aftermath of the coup, and to Major in 1965, Assila was a key man in the **Comité de Réconciliation Nationale** established in the aftermath of the 1967 coup. Deputy Chief of Staff and commander of one of Togo's two infantry battalions, Assila was brought into General Eyadema's government as Minister of Interior, and in January 1970 he was promoted to Lieutenant Colonel, becoming the second-ranking officer in the Togolese armed forces. Already suffering from a critical kidney ailment, Assila spent the next two years in a Paris sanatorium, though he was retained officially in both the government and army hierarchy. In February 1972 he was finally dropped from the government. Originally not expected to live much longer, Assila returned to Togo in 1972 (with a kidney machine) and slowly assumed his military (though not ministerial) duties. He was promoted and appointed Chief of Staff in 1975 but resigned from military duties in August 1980 due to inability to perform those duties. He died under mysterious conditions in 1982, according to some sources, poisoned on Eyadema's orders.

ASSIMILATION POLICY. An underlying theoretical tenet of French colonial policy in Africa, which assumed the slow cultural assimilation of colonial populations. The status of assimilé or **evolué** was granted to colonial subjects who acquired the accoutrements of French civilization—i.e. language, dress, customs, education, religion, etc.—or who had served with distinction either in the French colonial armies or in the colonial civil service. The status conferred the right to petition for French citizenship, a process so complex that in the entire AOF only 2,000 Africans acquired it. Advantages of being classified as an evolué and attaining citizenship included voting rights, subjection to French civil and penal codes (instead of customary law), and freedom from the **indigenat** code or **corvée** labor. The basic assumption of the assimilation policy was the unquestioned superiority of French culture and its suitability for all populations. When this tenet proved to be idealistic and the end result unattainable, colonial policy shifted to the concept of "association"—the development of close cultural, economic, and political cooperation between France and her overseas territories. The assimilation policy was applied in Togo as in France's other colonies in Africa. *See also* INDIGENAT.

ASSIMILE *see* ASSIMILATION POLICY

ASSOCIATED TERRITORY. Togo's status within the **French Union,** as specified in the French constitution of October 1946. *See* FRENCH UNION.

ASSOCIATION DE LA JEUNESSE MUSULMANE DU TOGO (AJMT). Precursor of the **Union Musulman du Togo** (UMT). Formed in 1960 in Lomé by a very small number of individuals, many of whom were Ewe (among whom Islam is nearly nonexistent) and some Yoruba and Kotokoli. Among them were Kassim Mensah (Ewe), Belly El Fouti (the Fulani who was to become Togo's prime theologian), and Mama Fousseni. With the success of their efforts to expand the organizational base of Islam in Togo, the UMT was created to replace the AMT. *See also* UNION MUSULMAN DU TOGO.

ASSOCIATION POUR LA PROMOTION DE L'ETAT DE DROIT. Pressure group, linked with various international civic rights movements, set up in 1991 by the lawyer Djovi Gally to promote civil and human rights in Togo.

ASSOLI. New name for the former circonscription of Bafilo. The prefecture d'Assoli is now in the region of Kara (and not, as formerly, in Centrale), though its administrative headquarters remains in the town of Bafilo. *See also* BAFILO.

ASSOR, MAURICE. Former highly influential business consultant and financial manger to Eyadema. Of Moroccan origin and normally resident in Paris where he has a major trading empire, Assor was the inevitable middleman in all trade transactions with Togo until 1990, solely due to his personal connection to Eyadema. Until then he was sought out by all foreign businessmen for his ability to smooth out any problems and secure the necessary permits (from Paris, and in exchange for a kickback). Assor also had an unofficial monopoly over all Togolese imports and most non-ore exports. He was Togo's purchasing agent in Paris (in particular for SONACOM) and marketing agent for OPAT and OTP. He has been the intermediary for many loans granted to Togo and has handled Eyadema's growing business investments, helping him spirit some 80 billion CFAF out of the country. Assor's Paris organization is known as the Groupe Assor. With the opening up of political space in 1990 Assor's name was increasingly mentioned in the National Conference in connection with Eyadema's shady deals and governmental corruption, and in March 1991 he fled the country, severing his link with Togo and Eyadema.

ASSOUMA, ABDOUDOU. Former Minister-delegate for the Armed Forces. One of Eyadema's closest associates, Assouma's appointment was virtually forced upon hapless Prime Minister Koffigoh on December 30, 1991 after the incidents between the government and the armed forces still loyal to Eyadema. At the time it was rationalized that having the Defense portfolio controlled by "one of their own" would keep the military ruly. In fact, Assouma very much acted to camouflage what was transpiring in the armed forces and to deflect criticisms against them. He was summarily dropped from his post in June 1992, when he left a cabinet meeting gruffly, the latter having just criticized the Army and Eyadema for the attempted assassination of **Gilchrist Olympio.** He is retained as an Eyadema assistant in the Presidential office.

ATAKPAH, OGUKI, 1914–1976. Former Bishop of Atakpamé who attained a measure of notoriety by speaking out against Eyadema's economic policies and the mismanagement of the parastatal sector. Equating nationalization (especially of COTOMIB) with theft and rejecting as quasi-sacrilege the authenticity policy of doing away with Christian given names, Atakpah brought the wrath of the regime upon himself. Despite the fact that he comes from the important Yoruba chiefly lineage that founded Atakpamé, Atakpah was arrested and removed from office — a fact that the Church reluctantly had to accept.

ATAKPAME. Important town, administrative headquarters of the **Plateaux** region and of the Ogou prefecture within it. It was originally settled by Ewe elements — still found in the Voudun quarter — in the nineteenth century and by a **Yoruba** clan that was chased there a few years later by Dahomean forces. (The town is named after the leader of the clan, Chief Atakpa.) The settlement rapidly grew as a commercial center as it straddled the traditional trade route from Aného to Paratao (the Kotokoli capital) that linked up in **Sokodé** with the east-west caravans connecting Salaga with Gomba territory. *See* CARAVAN ROUTES.

Renowned also as a "refugee" town and a hotbed of anti-Dahomean sentiments, Atakpamé suffered from periodic heavy Dahomean assaults. (*See* ATAKPAME WARS.) During the colonial era the region witnessed a major immigration of land-hungry **Kabré** peasants from the north, encouraged by the French administration. Currently the town of Atakpamé is a growing center of 30,000 people (1992) and thus Togo's fourth-largest urban concentration, after Lomé, Sokodé, and Kpalimé. The administrative capital of the relatively prosperous Plateaux region, Atakpamé is connected with the south by paved roads and the railroad (at the Agbonou juncture).

The Atakpamé district (renamed the Prefecture de l'Ogou in June 1981) covers a population of 120,000 people and such centers as Blitta (the railroad's northern terminal and railtruck transshipment center for the north-south axis), Dadja (where the Industrie Textile Togolaise factory is located), and Anié (an important market town thirty kilometers away).

ATAKPAME WARS. Series of assaults against the town and region of **Atakpamé** by invading armies from the kingdom of Dahomey to the east. The first major attack took place during the reign of Dahomey's King Adandozan (1797–1818) and was repulsed. The second attack, under King Ghézo, was spearheaded by Dahomey's dreaded Amazon units and resulted in the total destruction of Atakpamé (1840) and the dispersal of its population. Populated by refugees from Dahomey (Yoruba, Adja, Mahi, Fon, etc.) who made the town a hotbed of anti-Dahomean rebellion, Atakpamé was again invaded during the reign of King Glélé (1859–1889), when some of the biggest assaults took place (in 1860, 1877, and 1880). In the latter instance, the town was again completely razed prior to the withdrawal of Dahomean troops.

ATAYI, SOLOMON, 1891–1970. Educator, former cabinet minister and Secretary General of the **Mouvement Populaire Togolaise.** Born in Aného on February 12, 1891, Atayi was educated locally and in Dakar, Senegal (1910–13). He worked most of his life as a teacher, first in Benin (Porto Novo, Ouidah, Savé, Abomey, Ketou, and Djougou) and then in Togo in Sokodé, Kpalimé and Lomé (1920–1951). A member of the conservative **Parti Togolais du Progrès** founded by Nicolas Grunitzky and Dr. Pedro Olympio, Atayi joined Dr. Olympio, when the latter was expelled from the PTP in 1955, and helped set up the new MPT party of which he became Secretary General. Following the 1963 coup d'etat, Atayi joined President Grunitzky's four-cornered coalition and became MPT Minister of Rural Economy (January–May 1963) and later Minister of Information (1963–1966). After being dropped from the cabinet late in 1966, Atayi went into retirement.

ATIKPO, YAO TETE SAMUEL MAWUSSEY. Leader of the small post-1991 SOLITO political party and Minister of Equipment and Mines. Atikpo joined the third Transitional government, a coalition with General Eyadema's RPT party, on September 14, 1992 and was retained in the same ministry on February 14, 1993.

ATIPEDE, MARC, 1912–1970. Physician, politician, and former critic of the Eyadema regime. Born in Kpadapé on March 12, 1912, Atipedé was educated locally and at the prestigious Ecole William Ponty in Dakar, following which he completed medical studies at Dakar's School of Medicine. A popular doctor in the south, Atipedé joined Sylvanus Olympio's Comité de l'Unité Togolaise and in 1961 was elected to the national assembly from the Kluoto region. Following the assassination of Olympio, Atipedé withdrew from political life. In August 1970 he was arrested for alleged complicity in an anti-

Eyadema plot—*see* COUP (ATTEMPTED) OF 1970. Sentenced to twenty years' imprisonment, his death while in prison was announced shortly after. It was widely assumed in Lomé at the time, and confirmed in 1990, that his death had not been due to natural causes.

ATIVON, KODJO LOL, 1944– . Rural water resources administrator. Born in Aného in 1944 and educated in Water Engineering in France, Ativon worked for several years (1975–77) with the Department of Hydrology and Energy in Lomé, and was Head of its Southern subdivision, before moving to Burkina Faso where he has been Head of the Department of Urban Water Services. He has been dispatched on consultantships to several other African states, notably to Mali, Benin, Cote d'Ivoire and Congo.

ATOHOUN, CELESTIN. Prominent southern politician. Atohoun served during the Olympio years as the powerful Director of the cabinet of the Minister of Labour and Civil Service. Shunted aside during the Grunitzky era, he was one of a number of southern leaders who strenuously opposed the 1967 Eyadema takeover, and he was arrested after the coup. Released only two years later in 1970, Atohoun made his peace with the regime and was retained in the civil service until his retirement.

ATSOU, JEAN. Head of the Division of Public Works in the Ministry of Public Works, Mines, and Transport. Trained as a civil engineer, Atsou has progressively been promoted from Deputy Head to Head of Construction Projects in the south, to his current post.

ATSOU, JULIEN. Young poet-playwright, widely acclaimed for his first two works: *Agokoli: Cruauté ou Devoir* (questioning the negative image of King Agokoli) and *L'Abomination de la Desolation*.

ATTIGNON, HERMANN, 1933– . Educator and administrator. Born in 1933 in the Aného region and educated locally and abroad, Attignon has long been an instructor of Geography and History at Lomé's Tokoin Lycée. He is the author of several standard texts on Togolese History and Geography as well as numerous articles. Onetime Secretary General of the Ministry of National Education, he is currently director of the Bilingual Multinational Training Institute, **Village du Bénin** in Lomé.

AUTHENTICITY. Series of policies aimed at the indigenization of Togo's social, cultural, and economic life. Cautiously introduced in 1972 and codified in 1974 as official policy by the **RPT** (influenced by Zaire's Mobutu), the policy has included the renaming of streets and towns (e.g. Anécho to Aného), the declaration of new national holidays (Journée Commemorative des Martyrs de Pya), marginally more nationalist economic and foreign policies, and the rejection of Christian first names in favor of indigenous ones. The policy was implemented remarkably smoothly and was quite popular with most elements of the educated elites (the prime target, after all, of the "indigenization" of names). There were clashes, however, quite sharp, with the Catholic church that chose to regard as quasi-sacrilege the de-Christianization of given names. Outside Togo, the changes—many now two decades old—have still not been fully integrated in standard reference works or maps, causing a measure of confusion for the uninitiated.

AUTONOMOUS REPUBLIC. The two-year period (1956–58) of full internal autonomy of the administration of Nicolas Grunitzky. The Autonomous Republic of Togo was declared following a plebiscite boycotted by the **Comité de l'Unité Togolaise** of Sylvanus Olympio and resulted in the dominance of Olympio's rival, who had been strongly supported by the French administration. At the time, none of France's colonial territories possessed the internal autonomy and legislative powers granted to Togo.

AVETONOU. Important experimental and agricultural farm. Part of the various technical cooperation accords of West Germany signed in 1964. The station is some 100 kilometers from Lomé, in the Kloto prefecture.

AWESSO, ALPHONSE, 1937– . Journalist. Born in 1937 in Bohou, Awesso was educated at home and in Lille, France, where he studied Journalism. Upon his return to Togo he worked as a teacher, journalist, and consultant to the Ministry of Information. In July 1967, he was appointed Director of Information, reverting to his previous consultantship duties and Journalism in 1974.

AWUME, AGBI (Pastor). Pastor of the Evangelical Church of Togo, elected as its new moderator in 1990 but denied the post by General Eyadema who forced the election of his own brother-in-law. *See* TOULEASSI, KOKOU.

AWUNA *see* ANLO.

AWUTE, DODZI KWASI PASCAL, 1937– . Agricultural engineer. Born on May 16, 1937, in Kpalimé, Awuté was educated at home and then proceeded to France to continue his higher education. In 1963 he was also at Utah State University, University of Wisconsin, and the University of Puerto Rico, returning to Montpellier and Toulouse for the conclusion of his studies. On his return to Togo he assumed a variety of key posts including Deputy Director of SEMNORD in Dapaong (1961–62), director of the East Mono modernization project (1962–63), and head of the Lama Kara Agricultural District (1964–65). In April 1967 he was appointed Deputy Director of Togo's Agricultural Services in Lomé, and in 1970 he was appointed Director of Studies at the National School of Agriculture at Toré Kpalimé. Since 1975 he has been director of the Agronomic Research Center at Lomé.

AYAKOU, MADJI KODJO (Major). Gendarmerie officer and former prefect of Tchamba. Following the series of bomb explosions in Lomé in August–September 1985, Ayakou was appointed head of the National Police.

AYASSOU, KOSSIVI V., 1947– . Educator. Born on August 3, 1947 and educated in Statistics in France, Ayassou teaches in the School of Economics and Administration at the National University of Benin in Lomé.

AYEVA, DERMAN. Health official and former Kotokoli political leader. Born in Sokodé to a branch of the royal family (and brother of **Uro Issifou Ayéva,** Superior Chief of the Sokodé Kotokoli), Ayéva worked as a health official in the north before entering politics. A founding member of the northern **Union des Chefs et des Populations du Nord,** he was instrumental in organizing the superior chiefs and notables in central and northern Togo against the predominance of coastal political parties and politicians in local political life. Elected Deputy to the territorial assembly, Ayéva became President of the assembly after the CUT boycott of the 1952 elections. He made a tactical alliance with the conservative pro-administration **Parti Togolais du Progrès** and sided with Nicolas Grunitzky at the time of the internal PTP schism that led to the establishment of the **Mouvement Populaire Togolais** in 1955. Following the CUT's rise to power in 1958, Ayéva's fortunes declined and his party crumbled. In 1961 a one party system was established and all opposition parties were banned. Ayéva made a brief comeback following the 1963 coup d'etat but has not been a key figure in Togolese politics since. He currently resides in retirement in Sokodé.

AYEVA, ISSIFOU, URO OF THE KOTOKOLI. Appointed **Uro** in 1949 despite his origins from Koma and not Paratao, the traditional village from which Kotokoli Uro are chosen. A modern individual, well-versed in French and a transporter by occupation, Ayéva's brother had been President of the Territorial Assembly.

AYEVA, ZAKARI. One of General Eyadema's last ministers prior to the liberalizations of 1991. A member of the Sokodé royal family, Ayéva joined Eyadema's cabinet in 1988 as Minister of Telecommunications, leaving it in February 1990.

AYEVA, ZARIFOU, 1942– . Economist, former cabinet minister and current political leader of the Kotokoli. Born in Sokodé in 1942, of the Kotokoli royal family as his name attests, Ayéva was educated locally and in Atakpamé before proceeding to Mons (Belgium) to study Economics. He majored in Industrial Economics and returned to Togo in 1969. He originally joined a private company (Société Générale du Golfe du Guinée) as Sales Manager and Director of Accounting and in 1975 moved to head the parastatal steel company **SNS** as Deputy Director General. From this post, he rapidly moved into the cabinet as Minister of Commerce and Transport (January 1978). He was shifted to head the Ministry of Information in November 1978 and dropped from the cabinet altogether in March 1979, allegedly on the grounds of excess corruption. With the onset of multi-partyism in 1991, Ayéva created a number of political groupings (*see* ALLIANCE TOGO-LAISE POUR LA DEMOCRATIE) to further the interests of his region, ethnic groups, and his own political ambitions. Because of his "deserting" Eyadema after for so long benefitting from high office under him, one of his houses in Sokodé was destroyed on January 9, 1992 by the armed forces. A member of the Haut Conseil de la République between 1991 and 1993, in late 1993 his Alliance des Démocrates pour le Rénouveau joined with two other parties to form the **Groupe Sociale Pan-Africaine** to boycott the elections.

AYIGBE. Pejorative term used in Ghana and among non-Ewe elements to refer to the Ewe, Mina, and Fon. The term translates as "Ayi refused" and refers to leaders of the **Ga** and **Ané** clans—who founded Glidji and Aného—who refused to return a stool (symbol of authority) that they brought with them (stole?) from the Accra region in the late seventeenth century at the time of the establishment of the two Togolese centers. The stool is still jealously guarded in a hut near Glidji. *See also* GA; MINA; ANEHO.

AYIVOR, SIMON. Former director of tourism. A top administrator of the Société Togolaise d'Hotellerie, Ayivor was selected to head the Division of Tourism in 1972, a post with a very high turnover. A year later, in October 1972, he too was arrested and sentenced to eight years in prison for corruption and mismanagement. He was paroled before the end of his term and has since been involved in private commercial activities.

AYIZAN. The "bean festival" among the Ewe of the Tsévié area. Essentially, an agrarian celebration that takes place in August.

B

BABELEME, SYLVAIN, 1926– . Instructor, former Minister of Education and ambassador to Ghana. Born in Kabou in the north on May 26, 1926, Babélémé was educated locally and at the prestigious Ecole William Ponty in Dakar. After training for an educational career, Babélémé served in a variety of postings, especially in Bassar and Sokodé (1960–67). In April 1967, he was brought into General Eyadema's government as Minister of Education, and in February 1970 he was dispatched as Togo's Ambassador to Ghana. He served in Accra until 1973 and has since continued his teaching activities.

BADOU. Important Kotokoli commercial center, eighty kilometers west of Atakpamé near the Ghana border. Situated in a coffee/cocoa growing region, it is also a major center of smuggling of produce from Ghana into Togo, with a very large nonindigenous resident trading minority established to cater to the needs of smugglers. (Many of these are Hausa or Yoruba from Benin.) The nearby Akroua waterfalls have brought to Badou a measure of tourist traffic as well, though the center had been previously largely unknown abroad. Badou, originally in the circonscription of Akposso, was set up as a separate administrative unit under its own name in the 1972 administrative reorganization of Togo and renamed the prefecture of Wawa in a similar reorganization in 1981. The prefecture's headquarters are in the town of Badou.

BAFILO. **Kotokoli** town of 12,000 people (tenth largest in Togo) in the mountainous region of northern Togo, fifty-three kilometers from Sokodé, and a center of important weaving of *kante* cloth on hand-carved looms. The town's name comes from the European corruption of K'Gbafoulou, the name of a fetishist, and was founded three centuries ago at the time of religious wars along the border with Burkina Faso and the arrival into Togo of the **Temba.** The town was annually raided toward the end of the eighteenth century by **Chokossi** armies. Bafilo, by 1980 Togo's ninth largest town, was also the administrative headquarters of a district with the same name, formerly part of the **Centrale** region. In the 1981 administrative reorganization of the country, the district was renamed the prefecture d'Assoli (with headquarters unchanged in Bafilo) and was attached to the Region de la Kara. In 1990 it was estimated that the district had 38,000 people. *See also* KOTOKOLI.

BAGNAH, OGAMO (JOSEPH). Former cabinet minister. A civil administrator by profession, Bagnah served in a variety of senior positions until 1973. In September of that year he was brought into Eyadema's cabinet as Minister of Interior. Though highly regarded prior to his appointment, he did not survive long in that key post and was shunted aside to head the Ministry of Rural Deveopment in March 1975. Appointed Director General of OPAT in 1977, he was also shifted to head the new Ministry of State-Run Companies. The new post was created consequent to increasing concern about the huge deficits piled up by potentially profitable state companies. Bagnah's views on how to solve the problem clashed, however, with vested interests in the regime, and those of Eyadema, and he was eased out of the cabinet via a terminal two-year appointment as Minister of Tourism in March 1980. He was reassigned to the Ministry of Interior as senior technical consultant in September 1982, a sinecure post.

BAHRI, MOHAMMED. Tunisian national, intermittently resident in Lomé, and until 1990 the de facto intermediary between the government of Togo (and General Eyadema specifically) and Arab risk capital in the Gulf area. He has been instrumental in bringing Arab money into the Togolese economy.

BAKOBOSSO, NORBERT. A gendarme, relative of **Major Bodjollé,** who attained notoriety on April 24, 1967 when his shot at General Eyadema from point-blank range was deflected by a notebook in the latter's shirt pocket. The attempted assassination was part of the Bodjollé-Eyadema tug-of-war of the early years of military rule in Togo. Sentenced to death, Bakobosso was paroled a few years later.

BALA, ISSIFU (EL HADJ). Important trader in the northern town of Dapaong. A devout Muslim who made the pilgrimage in the 1950's, Bala is of Hausa origins. Born locally, he utilized his ethnic contacts to establish a commercial network reaching into neighboring Benin, Ghana, and Burkina Faso. He has a small fleet of trucks serving the entire north and owns one of the two oil stations in town.

BANGANA, ISSAKA, 1947– . Deputy-Director of the School of Agronomy at the University of Benin in Lomé. Born in 1947 and educated in France, where he obtained a doctorate in Nutritional Science (University of Dijon, 1973), Bangana returned to teach in Togo, reaching his current post in 1986.

BANKS. Until the pro-democracy disturbances of 1990 and the violence and political and economic decay attending General Eyadema's refusal to sanction his eclipse, Togo had developed into a budding regional banking center, as especially attested to by the 1988 opening in Lomé of the Head Office of the ECO Bank. The following banks and/or credit agencies operate in Togo:

Bank of Credit and Commerce International Overseas Limited (BCCI)
Banque Commerciale du Ghana
Banque Internationale pour l'Afrique Occidentale (BIAO)
Banque Libano-Togolaise (BLT)
Banque Togolaise pour le Commerce et l'Industrie (BTCI)
Banque Togolaise de Devéloppement (BTD)
Caisse Nationale de Credit Agricole (CNCA)
Ecobank Transnational Incorporated
Ecobank-Togo
Société Interafricaine de Banques (SIAB)
Société Nationale d'Investissement et Fonds Annexes (SNI & FA)
Société Togolaise de Credit Automobile (STCA)
Union Togolaise de Banque (UTB)

BANQUE ARABE-LIBYENNE TOGOLAISE DU COMMERCE EXTERIEUR (BALTEX). Joint Togolese-Libyan bank (with 50 percent equity on the part of each partner) set up in 1975 and active since January 1977. The bank doubled its working capital by the end of its first year and pumped some $5.6 million into Togolese developmental projects. It has financed the building of a banking center in Lomé, the expansion of COTOMIB facilities, and in funding the various joint companies set up by Togo and Libya under their accords of technical cooperation. In 1991 the bank's name was changed to Société Interafricaine de Banques (SIAB), though with the same partners and equity. Its president is Barry-Moussa Barque.

BANQUE CENTRALE DES ETATS DE L'AFRIQUE DE L'QUEST (BCEAO). Francophone Africa's central bank for the former AOF colonies and Togo. (There is a separate structure for the AEF—French Equatorial Africa—and Cameroun.) The bank has branches in all member states and was established in its current form in 1958. The BCEAO had its headquarters in Paris, though in response to African pressures (spearheaded *inter alia* by Togo), it relocated to Dakar, Senegal, late in 1974. The Togolese branch is headed by Yao Messan Aho.

BANQUE INTERNATIONALE POUR L'AFRIQUE AU TOGO (BIAO). The formerly BOAO-Togo integrated with the Meridien group to form the popularly called "Meridien-BIAO." The Meridien group owns sixty percent of equity and private Togolese interests 40 percent. Its President is Kossi Paass.

BANQUE TOGOLAISE DE DEVELOPPEMENT (BTD). State bank created on December 12, 1966 to succeed the former **Credit du Togo** that had been in existence since 1957. The earlier bank's agricultural loan operations (which constituted the bulk of its activities) were transferred to the newly created **Caisse Nationale de Credit Agricole,** while the BTD was charged with the development and encouragement of small and medium-size enterprises of a nonagricultural nature through the grant of low interest loans. The BTD was set up with 400 million CFA francs (later increased to 1,000 million) of capital under the directorship of **Sandani Bawa Mankoubi.** By September 1990 the total amount of loans made was just over two billion CFA francs. Its director is Napo Kakaye with Kokuvi Dogbé as president. The state's original 60 percent share of equity has recently been reduced to 43.26 percent; the BCEAO has 20 percent, the BOAD 13.38 percent, with the rest owned by the CCCE, CNSS, and others.

BANQUE TOGOLAISE POUR LE COMMERCE ET L'INDUSTRIE (BTCI). Commercial bank set up with Togolese state capital in 1974. Capitalized at 450 million CFAF and with headquarters in Lomé, the government's original 35 percent share in its operations has been passed on to parastatals such as OPAT, OTP, CNSS, and SNIT. Its General Director is from the French Banque Nationale de Paris, that holds 23.77 percent of shares.

BARANDO, JEAN-MARIE, 1937– . Diplomat. Born in 1937 in Siou-Birou, Namtougou, and educated in Benin (at the Ouidah Seminary) and Togo, Barando joined the Togolese Statistical Office in 1962. With the rise of the Eyadema regime in 1967 Barando's fortunes suddenly improved. He was appointed interim director of the Ministry of Finance cabinet and between 1967 and 1969 served as prefect of Bafilo and Aného. In 1969 he was appointed Ambassador to France, returning to Togo in 1974 to continue his career in the civil administration.

BARIBA. Northern ethnic group found preponderantly in Benin, elements of which (about 7,000 in number) also reside in Togo. The remnants of a cavalry expeditionary force sent from Kouandé and Nikki (in Benin) in the nineteenth century, Togo's Bariba are found mostly in the Cambolé (Dapaong) area.

BARNABO, NANGBOB (RAPHAEL), 1943– . Until the 1990 upheavals Secretary General of Togo's trade union movement, the **Conféderation Nationale des Travailleurs du Togo,** Director of the National Social Security Fund, and Vice President of the National Assembly. Born in Nano on April 20, 1943, Barnabo worked as a bank clerk while improving his education. Already an energetic young trade union leader, he was nominated in 1968 to represent labor on the **Conseil Economique et Social.** In 1973 he was President Eyadema's choice to head the newly formed national trade union. Signifying satisfaction with his able leadership in keeping Togo's labor under tight control, Barnabo—a member of the RPT Lomé Committee—was nominated as the party's choice for one of the Lomé seats at the 1979 national elections, was re-elected in the subsequent elections to chair two of the National Assembly's committees, and was elected Vice President of the Assembly. In December 1988 it came to light that he had been receiving two salaries all along, one from the Togolese Banking Union, eroding his hold over the rank and file unionists.

BARQUE, BARRY-MOUSSA. Long the able Muslim Kotokoli manager of the Autonomous Port of Lomé, Barque was appointed Minister of Public Works, Mines, and Energy in March 1979. He joined the RPT Politburo a few years later. He remained in these posts until the 1990 liberalizations, steadily acquiring power and influence. By the early 1980's he was widely regarded as the "brains" behind the Eyadema presidency. With power came temptation, and at the time of the 1990 National Convention he was implicated in massive corruption scandals in his ministry. Notwithstanding this, he was appointed President of the Société Interafricaine de Banques (SIAB).

BASSAR. The former circonscription of Bassari, until 1981 part of the Centrale region, now one of six prefectures in the Region de la Kara. The prefecture remains headquartered in the town of Bassar (ex-Bassari). It was in this district that new phosphate reserves were discovered in 1983. *See also* BASSARI.

BASSARI. Ethnic group found mostly northwest of Sokodé and in neighboring Ghana. Also, name of a town and a district formerly in the Centrale region. Their number currently estimated at around 38,000, the Bassari inhabit the area around Mount Bassari and get their name from the deity Bassar that resides on the mountain. Some of the population also calls itself Bi-Tchambé ('the metal-workers'), though this is an example of identification with their prime occupation in the pre-colonial era. (They are often lumped together with **Chamba** and are not to be confused with similarly named groups in Cameroun, nor with the Bassari along the Guinea-Senegal border.) The Bassari speak a language which, together with Konkomba, Moba, and Gurma, is grouped in the paragurma language family. In their villages live large numbers of assimilated non-Bassari elements, especially Guang, Mossi, and Gurma, as well as Ashanti. They have never had a centralized state or internal cohesion, if only because of their intense heterogeneity. In the pre-colonial era the Bassari were renowned metallurgists, and both their weapons and their alliance were highly prized. In general sedentary and not involved in much warfare the Bassari suffered from repeated **Dagomba** attacks late in the nineteenth century, the last one occurring in 1873. Many escaped from Ghana into Togo to avoid these persecutions. The colonial intrusion broke the Bassari's quasi-monopoly over metallurgy, forcing them to shift to agricultural work on their poor soils or to join the German police force.

The town of Bassari (in 1981 renamed Bassar) is sixty-one km. from Sokodé and is the main Bassari concentration. It is Togo's seventh-largest town but is experiencing major growth. Its estimated population is subject to controversy, with numbers as diverse as 18,000 and 22,500 being cited. The district of Bassari was one of six such subdivisions within the Centrale region. In the 1981 administrative reorganizations, Bassari was renamed the prefecture of Bassar and was detached from the Centrale region and included in the much expanded Region de la Kara. The town remains the headquarters of the prefecture, though Kara is now the administrative headquarters of the region in which it belongs. In 1983 potentially important phosphate ore was discovered in the district, that if exploited could transform the economy of the entire region.

BATAMMARIBA *see* TAMBERMA and SOMBA.

BATA-TOGO. One of a series of shoe factories found throughout Africa. Capitalized with 180 million CFAF, of which twenty-five percent is state money and the rest from the BATA parent group, the company has been active in Lomé since 1968. Employing over 120 workers, the general prosperity of Togo in the 1970's boosted sales to 1.1 million pairs of shoes in 1978, worth 938 million CFAF. The company had the capacity of producing 1,000 pairs daily and with modest adjustments, up to 6,000 daily—much more than the Togolese economy could ever absorb. In the 1980's, reflecting Togo's moribund economy, the company encountered a decline in sales and closed down.

BE (Ewe clan) *see* NOTSE.

BE. Eastern side of downtown Lomé, home to a large number of Ewe fetish priests who use the surrounding wooded areas for worship. The market near the tourist Hotel de la Paix is essentially a fetish supplies market.

BE LAGOON MASSACRES. An April 1990 brutal massacre by elite units of the Togolese armed forces (allegedly under the personal command of Eyadema's son) of an unknown number of defenseless Ewe youth, whose bodies were dumped into the Bé Lagoon. The killings took place shortly after General Eyadema had conceded multi-party-ism and ushered in a prolonged period (1990–1993) of non-stop pressure in southern districts to eliminate his dictatorship in the country.

BEDOU, BENOIT, 1920– . Administrator, key RPT militant, and former cabinet minister. Born in Porto Novo, Benin of Togolese parents on April 2, 1920, Bedou was educated in Benin and at the prestigious Ecole William Ponty in Dakar, Senegal, graduating in 1940. For the next twenty years he served with the French colonial administration in Senegal, eventually becoming head of the **AOF** federation's Finance Services. After a brief study trip to the United States in 1961, Bedou returned permanently to Togo and was appointed Deputy Director of Finances (January–July 1961) and then Director of Finances in the Sylvanus Olympio administration. He held this position, despite the 1963 coup d'état, until December 1966, at which time he was promoted to head the Finance and Economics Ministry in the last weeks of the Grunitzky administration. A member of the interim **Comité de Reconciliation Nationale** with responsibilities for Finance and Economics, Bedou was shunted aside following the establishment of the Eyadema regime in April 1967 and was reassigned his old position of Director of Finances and of the Budget in the Ministry of Finance. He has also served on the administrative boards of the Union Togolaise du Banque and of the **Compagnie Togolaise des Mines du Bénin.** Assistant Secretary General of the **Rassemblement du Peuple Togolais** under **Edem Kodjo,** he was retained on the Political Bureau (with responsibilities for Finance) following the abolition of the positions of Secretary General and his deputies. He remained in the key leadership role of the party until the mid-1980s.

BEKOUTARE, KANAOUA. Head Librarian of the **Bibliotheque Nationale.**

BELLY EL FOUTI, MOHAMED, 1920– . One of Togo's most renowned Muslim theologians, popularly known in the Lomé **zongo** where he resides as Mallam Bello. A Fulani born in Accra, Ghana on December 6, 1920 to Senegalese grandparent emigres to Nigeria, Belly El Fouti attended koranic schools in Accra and then went to study religion in Kano (North Nigeria) in 1936. On his return to Accra in 1941, he set up his own Arab language koranic school; in 1952 he initiated a new religious political party—The Muslim Reformation Party—and in 1956 he established a new Anglo-Arab school attached to the Accra central mosque. He erred politically by aligning his party to Nkrumah's opposition and had to flee Ghana after the Convention Peoples' Party rose to power, settling down in Lomé in October 1958. Vowing never again to mix religion with politics, he first set up a school for adults in Lomé in 1959 and worked on propagating the faith and on writing religious treatises. He has written thirty-odd of these in Arabic alone (most published in Egypt and Tunisia) and numerous others in English and African languages. Mallam Bello was a founding member of the **UMT** and served as its treasurer. Ousted from the body, together with its President, after prolonged allegations of autocratic internal rule, he ultimately made peace with the rank and file of the Muslim community and was accorded a leadership role in 1976 through membership in the UMT's Research Council. Mallam Bello has made the pilgrimage to Mecca over a dozen times.

BENA DEVELOPMENT. Experimental cattle-rearing farm in the tsetse-free Badou plateau, supplying the Marox-Afrique butchery in Lomé. The ranch is under joint German-Togolese management.

BENGALI. Site, in North Togo, of major iron ore deposits intermittently considered for possible exploitation. Estimates of the deposits range around 1,000 million tons. The high costs of exploitation and evacuation of the ore, or concentrate, have worked against the early exploitation of the reserves.

BENIN INSTITUTE OF HIGHER EDUCATION *see* INSTITUT D'ENSEIGNEMENT SUPERIEUR DU BENIN.

BESSERUNGSIEDLUNGEN. German-sponsored "improvement" villages, set up in southern Togo, especially in the vicinity of Notsé and Atakpamé, in order to alleviate acute land pressure in the northern (mostly Kabre) areas, while developing virgin lands in the south. After the surrender of the colony to French forces, the policy of resettling Kabre youth in the south continued. Often, the new settlements were nothing more than penal colonies, though they did provide an answer to the need of land-starved peasants from the north. Today, largely as a result of these colonial policies, there are over 100,000 Kabre outside the core La Kara region, with more migrating southward yearly.

BIBLIOTHEQUE NATIONALE. Togo's national library, administered by **INTSHU.** The library is the repository of government publications and pre- and post-independence documentation. Created in 1969 in

Lomé, and currently administered by Kanaoua Bekoutare, the Library possesses some 8,000 publications, 60 periodicals and a variety of other items.

BINAH, PREFECTURE DU. Small prefecture with administrative head-quarters in the village of Pagouda in the La Kara region. Until the June 1981 administrative reorganization of Togo, the prefecture was known as the circonscription de Pagouda. It is a tiny, north-south sliver of rolling countryside of great beauty (and showing acute signs of soil erosion) dotted with palm trees (though far from the coast) along the Benin border.

BINUMBA *see* GURMA.

BIOVA, SESHIE. Since mid-1987 editor-in-chief of the Togolese News Agency. He assumed his post upon the death of the former director, Ama Tsa Tize.

BISMARCKBURG. Established by Dr. Wolf, the explorer, in 1888, the post, in the Adélé mountains, was an important jumping-off point for explorations of the region during the German colonial era.

BLITTA. Small but important village in the Sotouboua prefecture, just south of the town of Sotouboua, that is also the administrative head-quarters of the prefecture. Apart from being a marketing center, Blitta is the terminus of the railroad from the south and a major transship-ment center for goods going on to Burkina Faso and Niger. Formerly designated as a mere poste administratif, Blitta became a subprefec-ture under the new June 1981 reorganization of Togo.

BODJOLLE, EMMANUEL, 1928– . Retired former Chief of Staff of the Togolese armed forces during part of Grunitzky's presidency. Born in 1928 in Kouméa of Kabré-Moba origins, Bodjollé enlisted in the French colonial army in 1948 and served in Indochina and North Africa. Demobilized and repatriated to Togo in 1962 with the rank of Sergeant, Bodjollé was the leader of the ex-soldiers who petitioned President Sylvanus Olympio to be integrated into an expanded To-golese army. At the time of the 1963 coup d'etat, Bodjollé played an ambiguous role, unwilling to join the mutiny, and according to one ac-count forewarning the regime of the impending assault. Though Bod-jollé did not participate in the confrontation with Olympio, after the coup he was sought by the putschists (and especially by Eyadema and Chango, who did not know what to do next) and was promoted to of-ficer rank (Captain) to became commander of the new battalion formed from the ex-veterans. (*See* COUP OF 1963.) Briefly Chief of Staff under Grunitzky (and again promoted, to Major) Bodjollé was eased out of his position in the Army in 1964 by Eyadema, by then confident enough to assume the leadership of the armed forces. In order to prevent a split of loyalties in the armed forces, Bodjollé was ordered to return to his home village. In March 1965 he was partly rehabilitated and appointed Director of the military cabinet of President Grunitzky, who trusted him more than Eyadema. In August of the same year he was arrested for plotting a comeback, storing arms, and building up a personal following loyal only to him in the army. (Most of the personnel involved were Moba.) After Eyadema's rise to power in 1967 Bodjollé was again arrested and sentenced to twenty-six months in prison for illegal possession of a gun. While awaiting sentencing, one of his relatives (**Norbert Bakobosso**) tried to assassinate Eyadema (April 14, 1967), who miraculously escaped unharmed when the bullet was deflected by a notebook in his shirt pocket. In November 1967, Bodjollé was released from prison following petitions from Kouméa village elders who guaranteed that he would be under their personal surveillance in Kouméa and would never leave the village confines. Eyadema has not been able to trust Kabré personnel from the Kouméa district/clan since this incident, and this explains the overwhelming presence of Kabré from Pya and Kara in the Armed Forces.

BODJONA, HODABALO, 1940– . Former Minister of Public Health and Social Affairs. Born in Kodjoné-Haut in the La Kara region, Bodjona was educated at the Lycée Bonnécarrére in Lomé before proceeding to the University of Dakar to study Medicine and Pharmacology. On his return to Togo in 1961, he became Chief Pharmacist at the Sokodé Hospital (1966–67) and at the University Hospital Center in Lomé (1967–70). For seven years Director General of Togopharma, in January 1977 he was appointed Eyadema's Minister of Public Health. He was retained in that post until 1984 when he returned to medical practice in Lomé.

BOKO, MENSAVI. Dramatologist who won second place in the Harmattan literary competition for his *Isabebelle* in 1969.

BOKONOU. Diviner of the **Fa** in southern Togo. Among the northern ethnic groups, the corresponding title is Teo (Kabré), Djiba (Moba), Ouboua (Bassari, Konkomba), etc. Sorcery, witchcraft, and magic are still extremely prevalent in Togo, especially among the coastal populations.

BOMB EXPLOSIONS OF 1985. Series of mysterious bomb explosions in downtown Lomé a month after the liquidation of Colonel Kongo and some others in August 1985. A wave of arrests followed, including several university professors, intellectuals, and engineers, though most were released in due course. A second series of bombings later exploded at the building best symbolic of Eyadema's reign, the RPT party headquarters, as well as at the headquarters of SONACOM, the State trading company (plundered by the regime) and the Hotel du 2 Fevrier. Later more bombs exploded at the main market and at the headquarters of the Social Security Fund, and a bomb was found at the airport.

BONFOH, BASSABI (General). Chief of Staff of the Togolese armed forces, formerly commander of the Second Battalion. A Kabre from Pagouda, Bonfoh was steadily promoted by Eyadema, being regarded as trustworthy. He was appointed General and Chief of Staff in 1991.

BONIN, ANDOCH NUTEPE, 1939– . One of General Eyadema's sharpest critics. Born on October 12, 1939 in Sansanné-Mango to a distinguished teacher from the South, Bonin served as an interpreter at various international conferences. He remained in Accra until 1975 due to the repression in Togo, returning to Lomé that year to set up a translation agency. Between 1979 and 1982 he joined the Eyadema regime as the latter's aide and interpreter but resigned to flee to Paris. There he wrote the highly critical book *Le Togo du Sergeant au Général*. Because it underscored the ludicrous brutality of the Eyadema regime, exposing some of Eyadema's personal vagaries and idiosyncrasies and reminding readers of the lengthy early liquidations that can be laid at Eyadema's door (starting with the 1963 murder of Sylvanus Olympio), Bonin became one of Eyadema's most hated enemies. Bonin risked liquidation by returning to Lomé at the time of the liberalizations in 1990 to join the National Conference. Though promptly arrested, he was released at the insistence of the National Convention. As Eyadema slowly won in his tug-of-war with the National Assembly, Bonin returned to Paris, aware he was a marked man.

BONNECARRERE, AUGUSTE FRANCOIS NARCISSE DOMINIQUE PAUL, 1875–1966. Former Governor of Togo after whom a number of structures are named, in Togo as well as elsewhere. Born in Tarbes (in the Pyrenees) on October 29, 1875 and educated in Law, Bonnecarrere served for ten years as Governor of Togo, between January 30, 1922 and December 27, 1931. He later also served in Cameroun.

BOUKARI, ABDOU KARIM. Veterinary inspector and head of the Fisheries Service since May 1967. Boukari has been government delegate on the board of the Caisse Nationale du Credit Agricole and technical consultant in the Ministry of Rural Economy.

BOUKPESSI, PAYADOWA. Cabinet minister. Boukpessi joined the first interim cabinet of Prime Minister Kottigah in September 1991 as Minister of Commerce and Transport and was retained through the next two governments, though in the third he was shifted to the Ministry of Industry and State Companies. Boukpessi is a leader of the UTD party.

BOURAIMA, INOUSSSA TRAORE, 1945– . Former Minister of the Environment and Tourism. Born on February 10, 1945 and educated in the natural sciences (Agronomy) at the University of Dakar (1971) and Marseilles (1973) where he obtained a degree in Ecology, Bouraima returned to Togo to teach Zoology and Ecology at the University of Benin in Lomé. Active politically, during the post-1990 liberalization in Togo he was integrated into the interim government (May 1991) as the RPT Minister of Defence and was reappointed in the following interim government of February 1993.

BRASSERIE DE LA KARA. New plant, inaugurated in January 1982 after the investment of 2,300 million CFAF. Employing 125 workers, the plant has a capacity of 200,000 hectoliters of beer and 50,000 of other beverages per year. Owned and operated by the Lomé-based **Brasserie du Bénin,** recently privatized and renamed Brasserie BB de Lomé, the Kara-based plant was widely heralded as attesting to the economic coming of age of the former neglected north.

BRASSERIE DU BENIN. Highly successful joint company set up in Lomé in 1964 and in due course greatly expanding to employ 523 workers. Originally capitalized at 375 million CFAF (increased to one billion by 1984 and 2.5 billion in 1988) with a twenty-five percent state participation (increased to forty percent), the bulk of the original investment capital came from Hamburg, Germany. With the privatization drive of the 1990, the state equity has been reduced back to twenty-five percent and the company renamed Brasserie BB Lomé. The company produces an array of beverages, including a highly successful local beer. Experiencing an annual eighteen percent increase in sales between 1973 and 1978 and a turnover of eight billion CFAF in 1981, the company opened up a second plant, in La Kara (*see* BRASSERIE DE LA KARA) in 1982.

BRAZILIANS. Collective name for Togolese and Beninois of mixed Euro-African parentage, formerly exiled or deported Africans, or slaves taken to Brazil who went back to the coastal areas in the nineteenth century. Among the first and most prominent of these families were those of **Da Souza, Olympio, Santos,** and d'Almeida. Most of them settled in communities such as **Aného** or **Agoué,** engaging in trade or other middleman activities. Other elements referred to as Brazilians include Sierra Leoneans or Nigerians who settled in Aného, such as the ancestors of the **Lawsons** of Togo. Most of them were already Christian, Europeanized, and relatively well educated, factors that enabled them to play an important early role in the evolution of political life in Togo, a role totally disproportionate to their actual numbers. With the extension of the franchise, their political importance rapidly declined, though they long remained in the highest echelons of the civil service and the liberal professions.

BREMEN MISSIONARY SOCIETY. More correctly known as the Norddeutsche Missiongesellschaft, the Bremen Missionary Society was engaged in proselytizing in southern Togo and played an important role in the formation and education of the early coastal elite. Approximately 100 missionaries were dispatched to the Ghanaian-Togolese coastal areas in the forty years preceding official German colonization of Togo, and over half of them perished in the process. One of their main bases was Aného (in the 1850's), and most of Togo's Protestants of the time were known as "Brema," a corruption of the word "Bremen." The high quality of most of the personnel sent to Africa and their strong concentration along the coast has resulted in the paradox that, despite a much longer period of Catholic missionary effort, especially under the French mandate, around fifty percent of Togo's southern elite is Protestant. (*See also* PROTESTANTS.) After World War I and Germany's loss of Togo, the Bremen Missionary Society had to cease operations in the territory. The fact that no major missionary order moved into the vacuum gave birth to the early autonomy of the **Ewe Evangelical Church.**

BRENNER, JACQUES. Former Head of the Foreign Commerce section of the Ministry of Commerce in Lomé and administrator on the board of the Brasserie du Bénin between October 1968 and its privatization in 1990. Brenner is from an important mixed-parentage family.

BRENNER, YVES. Of mixed parentage (a German father and a Togolese mother), Brenner served as Kpalimé's deputy to Togo's Territorial Assembly during Grunitzky's pre-independence administration (1955–58). With Olympio's rise to power, Brenner became press attache at the Ministry of Information, Press, and Radio and between 1967 and 1969, technical consultant in the same ministry. Since 1969 he has occupied a number of similar posts, including government representative on CIMTOGO. Brenner is currently in retirement.

BRIGADE DE RECHERCHE. Part of General Eyadema's personal security apparatus. Headed by one of his half-brothers, Captain Amouzou Koffi, the Brigade gathers information on potential sources of political opposition to the regime both at home and abroad. Not an executive branch of the Togolese Secret Service, it works very closely with the **Brigade de Vigilance.**

BRIGADE DE VIGILANCE. State security organization, long headed by Captain Paul Amegninou, a personal protege of General Eyadema. In charge of monitoring potential subversive activities, specifically in the capital. It duplicates some of the work done by the Sûreté Nationale (that is intensely distrusted by Eyadema, if only because the latter is heavily suffused by southerners) and maintains a network of informants in Lomé, at the Aflao border crossing village, and in Ghana. The Brigades have conducted covert activities (in Ghana and Nigeria) as well.

BRIGADE PIGEON. The political police, implicated in a variety of atrocities on the behest of General Eyadema, commanded by Major Yoma Djoua, a relative of Eyadema.

BULLETIN D'INFORMATION DE L'AGENCE TOGOLAISE DE PRESSE. Weekly newsletter on local events, issued by the Ministry of Information in Lomé.

BUND DER DEUTSCHEN TOGOLANDER (BUND). Pro-German quasi-covert organization set up in 1929 and aided by the German firm *Togo Gesellschaft.* The organization was set up to agitate against French rule in Togo and to press for the return of the territory to Germany. Encompassing mostly southern elites brought up and educated under the previous German administration and displaced in the civil service by Dahomeans (because of their lack of linguistic abilities and unfamiliarity with French administrative practice), the Bund petitioned the League of Nations against the abuses carried out by the French in Togo. In 1939 Governor Montagne expelled known members or sympathizers from the territory; these were either promptly interned in Accra by the British authorities or made their way back to Togo and hid out the duration of the war in the Akposso district. The pro-French **Cercle des Amities Françaises** was created in 1936 in Lomé as a counterorganization to the Bund. Paradoxically, after the end of World War II, the Cercle became—under its new name, **Comité de l'Unité Togolaise**—a militant nationalist organization. *See also* GERMAN ADMINISTRATION.

C

CABRAIS *see* KABRE.

CAISSE CENTRALE DE COOPERATION ECONOMIQUE (CCCE). Official French agency through which French governmental aid to Francophone Africa is channeled, banked, and administered. Successor to the Caisse Centrale de la France d'Outre Mer. In October 1989, in the latest such move, the CCCE cancelled 98 percent of Togo's debt—a total of forty-two billion CFAF—and agreed to finance several new projects for Togo at interest rates of 1.5–2 percent for thirty years with ten years' interest grace.

CAISSE CENTRALE DE LA FRANCE D'OUTRE MER (CCFOM) *see* CAISSE CENTRALE DE COOPERATION ECONOMIQUE.

CAISSE DES DEPOTS ET CONSIGNATIONS (CDC). Official French agency that serves as banker, administrator, and manager of Francophone Africa's pension, national security, and other social welfare programs.

CAISSE NATIONALE DE CREDIT AGRICOLE (CNCA). Established in October 1967, the CNCA provides agricultural credits to farmers and cooperatives implementing projects of agrarian development approved by the regional **Sociétés Regionales de Devéloppement et d'Amenagement.** During its first year of operations, the CNCA distributed 190 million CFA francs in loans. The successor of **Crédit du Togo,** by 1980 it had expanded tremendously and, with sixteen branches, offered 27,200 loans to the value of 3.7 billion CFAF. The CNCA has been the target of several major embezzlements over the years, the largest two in 1981 and in 1987. In the latter instance a total of between 2.7 and 4 billion CFAF were absconded, with Donou Hometowou, the directing manager, sentenced to twenty years' imprisonment and several other employees for lesser periods. Colonel Assih (at the time the second ranking officer) also lost his position in the army in connection with the embezzlement. Currently principal equity in the CNCA is in the hands of the State (36.4%), **BCEAO** 18.2%, and **OPAT** 15.9%.

CAMPOS, BONIFACE DE. Former secretary general of Togo's Chamber of Commerce, Administrator of the Togolese State Hotels Society, and Vice President of the **Conseil Economique et Social.** Campos comes from an old **Brazilian** family.

CARAVAN ROUTES. In the pre-colonial era, several important caravan routes crossed through Togo. The most important of these were the salt trade route to Adda and the kola nut route to Salaga. The principal stops on the east-west caravan routes were: 1) Gomba via Dahomey (Nikki, Parakou, Bassila) to Sokodé and Fasao in Togo and then to Salaga (Ghana); 2) Gomba via Dahomey (Nikki, Djougou) to Sokodé; 3) Gomba via Dahomey (Nikki, Djougou, Birni, Kouandé) to Sansanné-Mango in Togo and on to Gurma country; and 4) Gomba via Dahomey (Nikki, Bouay) to Sansanné-Mango in Togo and on to Salaga. The major north-south route went from Aného on the coast via Atakpamé to Sokodé (which developed into a major transshipment center) and on to Sansanné-Mango.

LA CARTONNERIE-IMPRIMERIE GENERALE DU BENIN (CIGB). Established in 1971 by private Togolese interests in Lomé to produce cartons and paper products. Capitalized with six million CFAF, the CIGB constantly exports up to ten percent of its product to neighboring states.

CATHOLICISM. The first permanent Catholic influences in Togo were through contact with returning **Brazilian** families and the religious services that sprang up to accommodate them. Thus in 1835 a chapel was built in Agoué (just across the current border in Benin) by the Brazilian Venossa de Jesus to cater to the needs of a small but thriving Catholic population, most of whom were Brazilians. In 1842 the Catholic proselytizing in the coastal region was centralized in the hands of the missionaries of the Sacred Heart of Mary, with headquarters in Libreville, Gabon. In 1860 a major reorganization created the apostolic vicariate of Dahomey (with headquarters in the fetishist center of Ouidah), which encompassed the huge region between the Volta and the Niger rivers and from the Atlantic Ocean to the Sudan. Francois Borghero (1830–1892) was placed in charge of Catholic activities in this region, but the Togolese segment always remained an unimportant appendage to the much more important effort in Dahomey. In June 1883 a new apostolic division was created, centered in Agoué and encompassing the area between the Volta river and the Ouemé. Just prior to the total consolidation of German influence in the area, an effort was made to implant a Catholic mission in the interior, at Atakpamé. (The mission was abandoned in 1887 as a result of strong fetishist opposition.) In 1892 German Catholic missionaries supplanted the French societies for the duration of the German colonial era. Their efforts were also concentrated in the south or in the Ewe areas in the interior. Indeed, throughout much of the early colonial period (German as well as French), the civil administration resisted opening the north to either missionaries or to European influences. Only in 1912 were Catholic missionaries allowed to establish themselves in Sokodé. In the south, the Divine Word order established schools, built Lomé's neo-gothic cathedral (1902), and expanded into the coastal hinterland. Following the First World War, the African Missions Society took over from the German order. Togo was declared a separate vicariate in 1914 under the names Lower Volta (1924–1938) and Lomé (1938–1955). Proselytizing in the north still lagged; in 1937 the newly created apostolic prefecture of the north (based in Sokodé) only counted 772 converts serviced by five priests. (The 1960 census listed 23,567 Catholics.) In 1962 the first indigenous archbishop was named, **Robert Dosseh-Anyron,** and a year later the Catholic church counted 232,000 converts (388,000 in 1970) out of an adult population of 894,000 and 108 priests. These figures were a major improvement over those of 1945, when there were only 88,000 converts and 20 priests. *See also* RELIGION. For attendance at Catholic schools *see* EDUCATION.

CENTRALE. One of Togo's administrative regions, with headquarters in Sokodé and a population estimated in 1967 at 420,000. Covering a territory of 16,985 square kilometers, the Centrale region—as it was then constituted—was inhabited by a variety of ethnic groups, including Bassari, Kotokoli, Konkomba, and Kabré. At independence, the region included the circonscriptions of Bafilo, Bassari, Lama Kara, Niamtougou, Pagouda, and Sokodé. Since then the region has been greatly truncated to create the new region of La Kara. In the 1981 administrative reorganization of the country, Centrale encompassed the (newly renamed) prefectures of Sotouboua, Tchaoudjo, and Nyalla, with both a reduction in territory and population. The region grows extensive crops of cotton and peanuts and has seen a spurt of economic development since the rise to power of the regime of General Eyadema. Both Centrale and Sokodé are heavily Muslim, with over 59 percent of the population (1990) professing Islam.

CENTRE D'ELEVAGE D'AVETONOU. Experimental German-Togolese breeding cooperative center established in 1964 and covering some 682 hectares of land, most of which is pasture. Aimed at improving the quality of the Togolese cattle herds, the ranch has imported stock and conducted research into local stockbreeding practice.

CENTRE D'ETUDES ET DE RECHERCHES DE KARA (CERK). Research organization set up in 1967 at Pya (President Eyadema's home village) in the **La Kara** region for the purpose of conducting studies on the culture, history, and socioeconomic potentials of the **Kabré** regions. The center has published several important collections of articles on these topics.

CERCLE. French colonial Africa's basic administrative units. Just prior to independence, Togo had ten cercles: Lomé, Anécho, Atakpamé, Bassari, Dapango, Lama Kara, Mango, Sokodé, Tsévié, and Kluoto, the latter with headquarters in Kpalimé, and the other nine with administrative centers in the towns of the same name. Each cercle had in turn several smaller subdivisions. *See also* ADMINISTRATIVE ORGANIZATION.

CERCLE DES AMITIES FRANCAISES. Pro-French sociocultural organization inaugurated in Lomé on September 5, 1936 to counter residual pro-German sentiments among the coastal elites. (*See* BUND DER DEUTSCHEN TOGOLANDER.) The Cercles des Amities Françaises tried to enlist all Europeans and African assimilés and was under the presidency of local French procurer (attorney) Thebault, with **Sylvanus Olympio** as Vice President. Several years later, Olympio was to transform the Cercle into the nationalist pan-Ewe party, the **Comité de l'Unité Togolaise.**

CESSOU, JEAN-MARIE. First apostolic Vicar of Togo, appointed on March 20, 1923.

CFA FRANC *see* COMMUNAUTE FINANCIERE AFRICAINE (CFA) FRANC.

CHAMBA. Small indigenous ethnic sliver mostly residing in the district of the same name some thirty-five kms. from Sokodé in the Centrale region. Numbering around 24,000, most are Muslim and are closely associated with the **Bassari** and with the Kotokoli whose vassals they once were. Their language is quite distinct, however, from that of any of their neighbors.

CHAMBRE DE COMMERCE, D'AGRICULTURE ET D'INDUSTRIE DU TOGO. Founded in 1921 with headquarters in Lomé, the chamber of commerce is headed by Gbondjide K. Djondo, with Gbemeho A. Alouman as Secretary General. Its membership includes the bulk of the commercial and industrial elite of the country, as well as most expatriate interests.

CHAMBRE DE DEPUTES. Legislative body established in 1958 to replace the **Assemblée Legislative du Togo,** which itself had replaced the **Assemblée Territoriale du Togo.** In 1961 the Chambre de

Deputés changed its name to **Assemblée Nationale du Togo.** The Chambre de Deputés had forty-six members, thirty-four of whom were delegates of Sylvanus Olympio's **Comité de l'Unité Togolaise;** the assembly's president was **Jonathan Savi de Tové.** By 1961 Togo was a de facto one-party state and in 1962 opposition parties were banned.

CHANGO, JANVIER (Colonel). Police commander and former Minister of Justice. One of the Kabre personnel demobilized from France's colonial armies in 1963 (as Sergeant), Chango did not squander his severance pay, as most of the other former troops (including Eyadema), but instead used it to set up a lucrative Lama Kara-Lomé trucking enterprise. After the 1963 coup he was integrated into the police to become commander of the First Group of the National Police, and later Deputy Chief of Staff of Togo's gendarmerie. In August 1969 he was brought into the cabinet as Minister of Justice, serving in that position until February 1974 when, in a cabinet reshuffle, he was returned to military duties.

CHAPMAN NYAHO, DANIEL AHMLING, 1909– . Ghanaian educator, diplomat, and early promoter of the pan-Ewe unification movement. Born in Keta, principal town of the **Anlo** Ewe in the Gold Coast, on July 5, 1909, Chapman was educated at a **Bremen Missionary Society** school in Lomé, at the Gold Coast's Achimota College, and later at Oxford, Columbia, and New York universities. In 1930 he was appointed Instructor at the prestigious Achimota College (1930–1933), becoming Senior Geography Master in 1933 (to 1946). In May 1945 Chapman started issuing the *Ewe Newsletter* which urged the unification of all Ewe territories under British rule. He developed close contacts with other Ewe leaders, including Sylvanus Olympio in French Togo. Under Chapman's leadership, the **All-Ewe Conference** was formed, an organization that was a merger of Chapman's own Ewe Unionist Association and other pan-Ewe groups. The AEC, with Chapman as Secretary General, claimed to represent all the Ewe clans on both sides of the Gold Coast-Togo border, though support for the association was meager in French Togo and restricted to a few top leaders and a handful of customary chiefs. The movement collapsed from within as a result of personality differences, interclan jealousies, and divergent policy preferences of its various leaders. Late in 1946, Chapman himself left the Gold Coast to become an area specialist with the United Nations Secretariat (1946–1954), following which he was appointed Secretary to Prime Minister Nkrumah. As of 1991 he was still alive, in retirement, in Ghana. *See also* ALL-EWE CONFERENCE.

CHEMIN DE FER DU TOGO (CFT). Togo's railroad system. The network was built during the German colonial era and was expanded by the French (1929–1933) to reach Blitta, northwest of Atakpamé. The system has three lines: Lomé-Aného: a total of 45 kms., opened to traffic in 1905 to cater to palm oil exports; Lomé-Kpalimé: a total of 119 kms., opened in 1907 (the "cocoa line"); and Lomé-Tsévié-Notsé-Blitta: a total of 277 kms. The section up to Agbonou was opened in 1911, the line reached Atakpamé (via a spur) in 1913, and following French construction work between 1929 and 1933, reached Blitta, the final terminus. During the 1970s, the line carried less traffic than in the 1950s and 1960s. The Lomé-Aného section no longer carries passengers. In 1972 total passengers amounted to 1,373,000 compared to 1,644,000 in 1968. Major bed improvements, badly needed for decades, and the increase in oil prices in the mid-1970s sharply reversed the attrition in passenger traffic. The figure for 1978 zoomed to 2,286,000, with small increases since. The president of the CFT is Kossi Adorglah.

CHIEFS. Except among some of the northern populations, there are no important paramount or superior chiefs of wide authority in Togo, nor were there established in the territory any truly large or powerful kingdoms, remnants of whose royal families could command strong customary allegiances in the modern era. With few exceptions, most of Togo's chiefs are of the village or clan variety and, especially in the south, have few real powers. The government's relations with the chiefs have vacillated from administration to administration. Under Sylvanus Olympio (1960–1963), chiefs were regarded as a modern-day anachronism; they were discriminated against (with a few prominent exceptions) and their official subsidies were drastically curtailed. The Grunitzky administration (1963–1967) reversed somewhat Olympio's fiscal harshness towards the chiefs and half-heartedly tried to engage the chiefs in periodic consultations. Under Eyadema (1967+), chiefly subsidies were significantly augmented, and the concept of periodic consultations was fully institutionalized in the form of annual conferences. The first such meeting took place on May 12, 1968 in Atakpamé and others have been held since in various towns, including Sokodé, Notsé, and Kara. Not surprisingly, these highly pragmatic policies garnered the Eyadema regime considerable support from Togo's traditional elements, including from Ewe chiefs in the south.

The historical absence in Togo of large kingdoms, or powerful chiefs, (to a considerable extent a consequence of the negative consequences on state-building as a result of the constant military pressures from the kingdom of Dahomey to the East and the Ashanti Federation in the West, who periodically sent assaults at each other that fought it out in Togo) has meant that in the contemporary era the "traditional factor" has been much less prominent in Togolese political life, though it is visible in Kotokoli and Chokossi areas. Traditional elites have played a lesser role, either directly through participation in politics or indirectly through opposition to modern policies, and the modernization of the country has proceeded much more rapidly than elsewhere.

CHOKOSSI. Northern ethnic group found both in Ghana and in the Sansanné-Mango and Dapaong areas of Togo. Prior to the German occupation of Togo, the Chokossi had a small kingdom with its capital in Sansanné-Mango. Of Manding origins, the Chokossi came to northern Togo during the latter part of the eighteenth century, traveling from Cote d'Ivoire via Ghana and Burkina Faso and moving south to Togo as a consequence of internal struggles between the Gurma and the Mamprusi. A warrior clan led by a branch of the royal family of Kong (Cote d'Ivoire), the Chokossi speak the Anoufou (or Tsekohale) language, which is a Baoulé dialect with many Mande expressions, very similar to the Anyi dialect still spoken in Abengourou in Cote d'Ivoire. The Chokossi (in French, Tyokossi or Tchokossi) obtained their name from neighboring tribes (especially the Mamprusi, Dagomba, and Konkombo) and among themselves are known as Anoufou. Their former kingdom's capital (Sansanné-Mango) means in Hausa and Mande "the Anno's warcamp" and attests to the Chokossi's principal occupation in the precolonial era—territorial expansion and warfare on their own behalf or serving as mercenary troops for neighboring ethnic groups. (They themselves call their kingdom and principal town, which was renamed from its original name Kundyuku, N'zara.) At the height of their kingdom, the Chokossi dominated the Moba, Gurma, and Guang (and some Konkomba) and exerted control over Fada N'Gurma (currently in Burkina Faso), all the way south to Sokodé. Their state included the Mande royal clans, Akan subjects (from Ghana), and Muslim Dioula itinerant merchants. Though the Chokossi resisted the German advance into their territory, after being vanquished—and despite sporadic revolts—they joined the German military columns in the subjugation of other areas. The Chokossi's social organization is marked by sharply defined social classes and stratification; it is currently estimated that there are over 30,000 members of the ethnic group in Togo, possibly forty percent of whom are Muslim. Despite their relatively small numbers, the Chokossi have produced such powerful political figures as Nomoro Karamoko (former Minister of Rural Economy), nine former National Assembly deputies, RPT Politburo member Hamadou Guinguina, and over fifty high civil administrators in Lomé or in the administration in the North.

CHOUKROUN, GERMAIN. Director General of the Société Nationale de Commerce (SONACOM). Choukroun comes from a mercantile family and is himself a major Lomé businessman.

CHRISTIANBORG. Danish fort (in what is now Accra, Ghana) established in 1659. From Christianborg, Danish influence radiated along the coast to Anécho (now Aného) in Togo. The Danes were very active in this area until forced out by other European companies, especially after Denmark abolished the slave trade in 1803.

CIMENTS DE L'AFRIQUE DE L'OUEST (CIMAO). One of West Africa's largest and costliest white elephants, the former perennially financially troubled multinational cement and clinker complex. West Africa's largest regional industrial venture, CIMAO tapped rich calcium deposits in several areas, including at Aveta and Tabligbo. The establishment of CIMAO was a prolonged process, though the company ambitiously planned to satisfy the cement needs of most states in the region from Cote d'Ivoire to Nigeria. Paradoxically, despite the participation and initial cooperation in the CIMAO project of most Francophone states in West Africa, each and every one of them was to set up its own national cement plants, undermining the basic rationale behind CIMAO. The company was created in 1968 with one billion CFAF capitalization, though actual construction of the industrial complex only commenced in 1976. Sited in Tabligbo, some eighty kms. northeast of Lomé, CIMAO included a whole township for its workers, an electricity grid, a port terminal, and a port-to-rail link. Phase one of CIMAO's construction cost $316.7 million, nearly half the sum coming from the World Bank. The partners in the venture were Togo, Cote d'Ivoire, France, and Ghana. The plant—that at no time operated at full capacity—was capable of processing 1.2 million tons of cement and could double that figure easily in case of strong international demand.

Massive cost overruns, utter lack of control over expenditures, total administrative mismanagement, high salaries and allowances (for its 567 staff including 12 expatriates), poor accounting practices, and free-for-all embezzlement by all and sundry, brought operations to a standstill in 1981, less than one year after the plant had been inaugurated with great fanfare. CIMAO was at that time officially bankrupt and owed between five and six billion CFAF to various creditors. Since the project had been highly touted as an example of regional (and Anglo-Francophone African) cooperation, each of the state partners felt compelled, reluctantly, to funnel in an additional two billion CFAF to allow the plant to recommence operations. There had always been considerable controversy regarding the merits of the project, especially whether CIMAO could ever be profitable. Most of these criticisms, however, came from abroad and were viewed in Africa as reflecting the chagrin of Western cement makers at the loss of lucrative African markets. The actual problems encountered were not anticipated.

CIMAO all along sold its products to member states at a price higher than locally available imports (despite customs duties on these) and was still unable to make ends meet, recording losses due to high operating costs. (Cost of production were 6.5 times that originally projected; the cost of building the complex was 3 times higher than anticipated.) Running losses were "distributed" among the member states so that never-ending infusions of capital were envisaged. Such new infusions were made in 1982 and 1983, but the drain upon the scarce resources of the states capitalizing it resulted in CIMAO being closed down again in 1984, for an anticipated twenty-nine months— this time to allow a fundamental review of possible cost-cutting measures and due to the acute shortage of electricity consequent to low levels of the Volta dam, supplying Togo with much of its power needs. CIMAO's accumulated debits at that date were estimated at $66.25 million. CIMAO never re-opened: in early 1989 it went into liquidation, with its debt split among the various partner-states.

CIMENTS DU TOGO (CIMTOGO). Mixed Franco-Togolese company in which the state still owns a fifty percent equity, the rest originally invested by Lambert Frères et Cie. and in 1988 transferred to the Norwegian SCANCEM International. CIMTOGO was established on February 20, 1969 with an initial capitalization of fifty million CFAF, later increased to 750 million. The company has steadily increased its profitable operations from the initial 120,000 tons to 300,000 tons (1978), with a turnover of 4,000 million CFAF that year, and again up to 9,700 million CFAF in 1991. Since then production has slowly increased. Employing 134 workers, CIMTOGO has Kwami Brenner as director general. Undeterred by the 1981 establishment of **CIMAO,** CIMTOGO completed a second major expansion program in an effort to aggressively move into the Nigerian market and managed to compete effectively while CIMAO floundered and had to be liquidated.

CIRCONSCRIPTION. Administrative districts that replaced the colonial **cercles** and were themselves replaced by prefectures in the June 1981 administrative reorganization of Togo. Until that date, Togo's circonscriptions had been grouped into four (after 1967, five) regions, though their number had slowly been augmented with the carving up of more cohesive "ethnic" districts. Just prior to the 1981 reorganization, there were twenty-one circonscriptions (for the list, *see* ADMINISTRATIVE ORGANIZATION) and seven urban (or municipal) circonscriptions, called communes. Each circonscription was headed by an appointed chef de circonscription (now prefect) assisted by elected bodies whose names have varied over the years but which included local influentials. These bodies were abolished between 1967 and 1973. When re-established, they were renamed **Delegations Speciales.** *See also* CONSEIL DE NOTABLES: CONSEILS DE CIRCONSCRIPTION.

COCO, DOMINIQUE HOSPICE, 1902– . Leader of a section of the Ewe and former Minister of Finance and one of Sylvanus Olympio's earlier allies in the **Comité de l'Unité Togolaise.** Born in Cotonou, Benin, in 1902, Coco obtained a medical degree and specialized in Surgery. For a number of years he headed the Surgery Department of Lomé hospital. Coco entered political life in the early 1950's and was elected to the Legislative Assembly in 1956, chairing the latter's permanent committee. Following Olympio's rise to power (1958), Coco was appointed Minister of Commerce, Industry, Economy and Planning. In 1960 he was shifted to head the Ministry of Finance and Economic Affairs and remained in that position until the 1963 coup d'etat. Following the coup, Coco returned to medical practice, retiring in 1988. In mid-1987 he was one of the former politicians visited by General Eyadema as part of the latter's attempt to appease the former civilian leaders of Togo. With the advent of multipartyism Coco, his advanced age notwithstanding, felt obliged as the only member of Olympio's CUT executive alive, to set up a political party—the UTR—though aligned behind Olympio's son, Gilchrist.

COCOA. One of Togo's principal export crops. Since cocoa grows well only in rich, humid soil with adequate shelter from the sun, the crop is limited in Togo to the **Kpalimé, Akposso,** Adélé, and Akebou areas. **Coffee** plantations are also found in these areas; the two plants are usually found intermixed. Togo's cocoa is of a high grade, and exports have risen dramatically over the years to 29,368 tons in 1971 and 1972. The highest export earnings from the crop occurred in 1970, when Togo received over 6.3 billion CFA francs. The total crop figures, however, reflect non-Togolese illicitly smuggled cocoa from Ghana where low purchase prices and strict import regulations do not encourage farmers to sell their harvests to their government. It has been estimated that as much as one third of Togo's coffee and cocoa exports may be of non-Togolese origin. Of all the local coffee/cocoa growing areas the Kpalimé region is one of the lushest and hence the richest in terms of per capita incomes. The crop is usually grown on small family farms.

COFFEE. One of Togo's principal export crops. Especially developed by the French administration during the colonial era. Togo's coffee growing region largely coincides with that where **cocoa** is grown; the two crops are usually found intermixed, since the leaves of one provide the shade needed by the other, and both need the same kind of rich, humid soil. Coffee is also grown in the Tsévié and Tabligbo districts. Exports of coffee have gradually increased over the years, reaching their highest value in 1970 when they stood at nearly 2.7 billion CFA francs. A significant percentage of Togo's coffee exports originates from Ghana, where low producers' prices and strict import policies are conducive to the smuggling of crops into Togo and of consumer goods back to Ghana. It has been estimated that as much as (and according to some, more than) one third of Togo's coffee and cocoa exports—the country's main export crops—are of Ghanaian origin, smuggled into Lomé across the porous border. The patrol of these borders has been the Ghanaian government's prime object over the years, and lack of success (due to connivance of Ewe—police and smugglers alike—to evade the dragnets, and Lomé's turning a blind eye to the traffic that contributes so much to its prosperity) has been the prime source of international friction between the two states.

COFFI, EMMANUEL (DR.). Physician and, since 1968, Head of Epidemic Diseases in the Ministry of Public Health.

COLLECTIF D'ASSOCIATIONS DES FEMMES (CAF). New women's association set up in 1990, based predominantly in the South, in opposition to both the regime of General Eyadema and the monopoly exerted by the latter's official women's associations.

COLLECTIF D'OPPOSITION DEMOCRATIQUE (COD). Caucusing group led by **Edem Kodjo** and **Gnininvi** that on June 8, 1991 initialled an agreement with General Eyadema for the convening of a National Conference and respect for the latter's decisions after the massive strikes in southern Togo. COD was challenged a few days later as not being representative of all opposition groups in Togo.

COLLECTIF D'OPPOSITION DEMOCRATIQUE 2 (COD 2). United front of twenty-five opposition groups formed in July 1992 in response to the continued assaults on southern political leaders by military units acting on behest of General Eyadema.

COLLECTIF SYNDICALE INDEPENDANT (CSI). Organization grouping all labor no longer affiliated within the official government trade union that in November 1992 called for an unlimited general strike to resolve the impasse between General Eyadema and Prime Minister Koffigoh. The strike ultimately lasted nine months at the cost of some 42 billion CFAF to the economy, and failed to dislodge Eyadema. The CSI comprises of ten former CNTT affiliates and was later reorganized as the Union Nationale des Syndicats Indépendants du Togo.

COLLEGE POLYTECHNIQUE BRUCE. One of Togo's major vocational schools, located in Lomé.

LE COMBAT. Quarterly publication of the Paris-based opposition **Mouvement Togolais pour la Démocratie,** seeking to overthrow the Eyadema regime.

COMITE CONSTITUTIONNEL. Committee set up in October 1967 to provide Togo with a new constitution, composed of eleven members of the cabinet, five jurists (including **Anani Santos**), three representatives of Togo's religious communities, and ten other members selected for their legal, political, and economic competence, under the chairmanship of President Eyadema. The committee marked time studying several constitutions (including those of France, Cameroun, and the Central African Republic), and on September 1968 it drafted a constitution for Togo. The latter was never promulgated because of Eyadema's decision, ratified by the newly established **Rassemblement du Peuple Togolais,** that the constitutionalization of the regime was premature in light of the persistence of societal cleavages.

COMITE D'ACTION CONTRE LE TRIBALISME ET LE RACISME (CATR). Opposition organ set up by **Yao Agboyibor** on January 1, 1991, including a number of lawyers, civil servants, and teachers, aimed at combating ethnic discrimination in Togo.

COMITE D'ACTION POUR LE RENOUVEAU (CAR). Political party set up on May 1, 1991 by Yao Agboyibor. In September 1992 the CAR joined Eyadema's RPT in a national coalition, receiving three seats in the cabinet. Vigorously competing in the 1994 elections, the first free multi-party elections since Eyadema's seizure of power in 1967, and assisted by an electoral alliance of several smaller groups, the CAR emerged with thirty-six seats as Togo's largest political formations. Notwithstanding this, Eyadema—having succeeded to be re-elected President fraudulently—did not appoint Agboyibor as Prime

Minister but rather, in an attempt to divide his opposition, appointed **Edem Kodjo** whose party had obtained only a minority of the seats.

COMITE DE L'UNITE TOGOLAISE (CUT). One of Africa's first nationalist movements and Togo's foremost party until 1963. The Comité de l'Unité Togolaise evolved from the sociocultural **Cercle des Amities Françaises,** set up by French Commissioner Montagne to counter the pro-German propaganda of the **Bund der Deutschen Togolander** in the years just before the Second World War. The statutes of the CUT were drawn up in 1941, and the movement included a large number of representatives of Togo's various ethnic groups as well as the paramount chiefs of the **Kotokoli, Chokossi,** and **Kabre.** After the war the CUT rapidly came under the total control of the southern **Mina** and **Ewe** elements and was converted into a militantly nationalist pan-Ewe movement and a critic of the French administration in Togo. The party's first President was **Augustino de Souza,** with Sylvanus Olympio as Vice President and **Jonathan Savi de Tové** as Secretary General. In 1946 the CUT succeeded in electing **Martin Akou** to the French National Assembly in a race in which **Nicolas Grunitzky** was the other candidate. The party cooperated with **Daniel Chapman** and his **All-Ewe Conference** in the Gold Coast in the drive to reunify all segments of the Ewe living under different colonial administrations. Within the CUT, a more militant pan-Africanist group coalesced around **Anani Santos** and **Firmin Abalo,** leaders of the CUT's youth wing, **Juvento,** that split from the parent party in 1959. Because of its links with the Gold Coast, pan-Ewe positions, and anti-French petitions to the United Nations, the CUT came to be viewed by the French administration as a pro-British secessionist movement and, accordingly, was administratively discriminated against. The French also encouraged and supported the creation of other political parties, especially the conservative **Parti Togolais du Progrès** of **Pedro Olympio** and Nicolas Grunitzky (Sylvanus Olympio's cousin and brother-in-law, respectively) and later the **Union des Chefs et des Populations du Nord.** This anti-CUT policy and the expansion of the electorate in the early fifties broke the CUT's political ascendance and ushered in the administrations of Nicolas Grunitzky (1952–58). Only after the United Nations-supervised elections of 1958 was the CUT to re-emerge as the dominant political party in Togo. Following independence, the CUT began cracking down on sources of opposition, first through administrative regulations and finally through mass arrests of non-CUT politicians. In 1962 Togo was officially declared a one-party state. In the aftermath of the 1963 coup d'etat, a four-cornered coalition of the existing parties emerged under the presidency of Nicolas Grunitzky. Only one wing of the CUT, now renamed the Parti de l'Unité Togolaise, participated in Grunitzky's administration, the more militant and rigid leaders unwilling to accept Grunitzky's rule or the integration and promotion in the armed forces of Olympio's assassins. (*See* ARMED FORCES; COUP OF 1963.) The latter group was led by **Nöe Kutuklui, Theophile Mally,** and **Oswald Ajavon,** among others. The two wings of the PUT found themselves united following a series of clashes between Grunitzky and his ambitious Vice President, **Antoine Méatchi**—*see* MEATCHI-MAMA CRISIS—a process that led to the November 1966 uprising in Lomé. (*See* COUP [ATTEMPTED] OF 1966.) The latter event inevitably paved the way for the military takeover two months later (*see* COUP OF 1967). Since the coup, all parties (and political activity) have been banned, except for the **Rassemblement du Peuple Togolais,** set up in 1969 by the Eyadema regime. Scattered die-hard PUT loyalists still remain. Most are either in self-imposed exile (the Eyadema regime offered full amnesty a number of times), as is Kutuklui, or sufficiently content with the Eyadema regime not to oppose it actively. Periodically, anti-Eyadema plots have been revealed (as in 1970 and 1977). In most instances, at the core of the conspiracy have been members of the ancient **Brazilian** families that were both at the fulcrum of the CUT and the nationalist movement prior to independence and the prime losers (and currently in exile) consequent to the Eyadema coup d'état.

COMITE DE RECONCILIATION NATIONALE (CRN). Temporary eight-man committee set up after the coup d'etat of 1967 under the chairmanship of **Colonel Kleber Dadjo.** The CRN was disbanded on April 14, 1967, when Colonel Eyadema took over political power. The members of the CRN and their ministerial responsibilities were: Kleber Dadjo (Defense and Foreign Affairs), Barthelemy Lambony (Education), Alex Mivedor (Public Works and Rural Economy), Boukari Djobo (Labor and Social Affairs), Benoit Bedou (Finance and Economics), Alexandre Ohin (Public Health), Benoit Malou (Information), and Paulin Eklou (Commerce, Industry, and Trade). From the point of view of ethnic or political affiliation, the CRN was composed of three southerners and five northerners or one military officer, five PUT members, one independent, and one Juvento member.

COMITE TOGOLAIS DE DEFENSE DES PRISONNIERS POLITIQUES. Paris-based organization set up in 1972 with financial assistance from some of the leading Brazilian families in Togo, aimed at alleviating the plight of political prisoners in Togo.

COMITE TOGOLAISE DE RESISTANCE (CTR). Opposition movement, set up in Paris in December 1992 under the leadership of Isidore Lajo, calling for General Eyadema's resignation or ouster by force as the first priority for all Togolese.

COMLAN, PAUL (Major), 1940–1975. Gendarmerie officer arrested in July 1975 for plotting against the regime of President Eyadema. Of Mina origins, Comlan was arrested due to an alleged connection to a de Souza family conspiracy and liquidated in his cell by Colonel **Kidjana Adewi,** allegedly on Eyadema's orders. Comlan had been Director of National Security (with the rank of Lieutenant) until 1970, at which point he was promoted to Captain and given command of the second group of the gendarmerie. He was promoted again in 1975, just prior to his arrest.

COMMISSION NATIONALE POUR LE DROITS DE L'HOMME (CNDH). Created by the National Assembly at General Eyadema's suggestion in October 1987 in order to deflect international complaints about violations of civic and human rights and political prisoners that had brought in the unwelcome attention of the global press and pressures from external bodies such as Amnesty International. Within the Togo of 1987, the CNDH was supposed to be a lackey of the regime, allegedly assuring no violations of human rights transpired. Composed of thirteen eminent members, two magistrates, one military police, two lawyers, one doctor, one law professor, and a member each of the Red Cross, traditional chiefs, youth, women, and labor, the CNDH was in theory elected by its corporate constituents but in reality appointed by Eyadema. Its chairperson was **Yao Agboyibor.** Until the pressures for liberalization, the CNDH was indeed window dressing and lacked in audacity; after 1990, though it assumed greater pressure on behalf of human rights, its function was completely superceded by the resurgent National Assembly. Agboyibor resigned as its President in 1990 to create the **Comité d'Action contre le Tribalisme et e Racisme** and later his own political party, the **CAR**, campaigning for a return to multipartyism.

COMMUNAUTE FINANCIERE AFRICAINE (CFA) FRANC. Common currency of the Communaute Financiere Africaine, i.e., all former colonial territories of the French West African Federation (AOF) and the French Equatorial African Federation (AEF). Secessions have decimated the ranks of affiliated member states. Guinea never had anything to do with the "colonial" current after independence, and Mali left the community in 1962, though it was to return in 1968 after experiencing fiscal havoc. Both Malagasy and Mauritania left the

CFAF in 1970, though Equatorial Guinea joined the financial community after the overthrow of the Macias Nguema dictatorship. A number of states have expressed discontent off and on with the control from Paris (later Dakar) of basic fiscal policy. Established in 1946 as the Colonies Françaises d'Afrique Franc, the currency's name was changed in 1962. Fully guaranteed by France, the CFA franc is monetarily pegged to the French franc into which it is fully convertible, giving it quasi-hard currency status which is invaluable to member states. By the same token, any devaluations of the French franc translate into an automatic devaluation in all CFAF states, something that rankled many Francophone governments, especially in light of the multiple devaluations of the 1980s. Long artificially pegged at fifty CFA francs to a French Franc—and arguably grossly overvalued at that ratio—shortly after Houphouet-Boigny's death in 1993 the CFAF was devalued by fully 50 percent, causing massive havoc in most Francophone countries.

The adoption of French currency in Togo officially occurred in 1921, but the local population continued using a variety of other currencies into the 1930s. Until 1921 the German mark was the common currency, with British silver shillings extremely popular as well because of the strength of the pound. Austrian silver Maria Theresa dollars were also used for some time, and it was only after strenuous efforts that the French franc became the common currency in Togo. Since 1969 there have been persistent requests from several Francophone countries, including Togo, that fiscal reserves then held in Paris be transferred to Africa and that monetary treaties be modified. The first step in this direction occurred late in 1974 when the central bank of the monetary union, the Banque Centrale des Etats de l'Afrique de l'Ouest moved its headquarters to Dakar, Senegal, and fiscal reserves were localized.

COMPAGNIE DU BENIN. Partly (nineteen percent) state-owned company founded in 1960 in Aného, with a capitalization of 275 million CFA francs. At the time, it was Togo's first "industrial" enterprise and subject of much nationalistic rhetoric. The company manufactures manioc flour and tapioca in its starch factory in Ganavé. It has had serious difficulties in the past, due to irregularities in the supply of raw manioc, and nearly floundered several times in the late 1970s. Its General Director is Datio Guesledji Atsu and its President is A. Amouzou.

COMPAGNIE ELECTRIQUE DU BENIN (CEB). Joint electricity consortium created in 1968 by Benin and Togo. It is charged with promoting the development of electric power in the two neighboring countries. The CEB tries to develop local power and to diversify the sources of supply of the two countries. Togo and Benin still acquire the bulk of their needs from Ghana's Volta River Hydroelectric Authority at Akossomba. CEB's 1977 turnover was 835 million CFAF. It is headquartered in Lomé and has recently built several local electricity producing plants. On January 1, 1988 the Nangbeto dam and hydroelectric complex (thirty-five kms. from Atakpamé) came on line (it was inaugurated May fifth), having been built during the preceding three years with CCCE aid and with the capacity of producing 147 million kilowatts of electricity or fully 30 percent of CEB's needs. Feasibility studies of another dam, at Adjarala, capable of boosting local production to 58 percent of CEB's needs, were recently completed.

COMPAGNIE ENERGIE ELECTRIQUE DU TOGO (CEET). Togo's retail electric company, set up as a state-owned enterprise in 1963, after taking over the colonial installations of UNELCO (Union Eléctrique Coloniale) at Kpémé, at the time the sole hydro-electric station in the country. CEET was capitalized at 627.5 million CFAF. Its local turnover was 2.027 million CFAF in 1977. CEET cooperates with its Béninois counterpart within the joint **CEB;** it purchases its electricity from the latter and is involved essentially in its redistribution, repair, maintenance, and billing operations. CEET has also set up several local generators for the exclusive use of the Togolese economy, including a thermal center of 120 million kilowatts set up in 1976.

COMPAGNIE TOGOLAISE DES MINES DU BENIN (COTOMIB or CTMB). State-owned industrial complex engaged in the extraction and export of phosphates from Togo's coastal deposits. Originally COTOMIB was founded in 1954 as a mixed-economy expatriate-controlled company with capitalization of three billion CFA francs. The Togolese government first acquired a 20 percent interest in COTOMIB in 1957, the other shareholders being a French consortium (42.7%) and a United States group (37.3%). In 1973 Togo increased its share in the company to 35 percent, and on January 24, 1974, COTOMIB was fully nationalized following President Eyadema's allegations that company officials had conspired to assassinate him. (*See* EYADEMA'S PLANE CRASHES.) COTOMIB employs over 2,500 employees, including some 50 expatriates and is by far Togo's largest company and employer. The company extracts ore in Hahotoe and other nearby locations for processing at its Kpémé phosphate factory and harbor, which is situated approximately thirty-five kms. east of Lomé and near Aného. Exports of phosphates, Togo's prime hard currency earner and the underpinning of the economy, have progressed from 500,000 tons in 1961 to over 2.8 million tons in the late 1970's.

Though revenues had been stagnant in the late 1960's, they spurted in the 1970's, reaching an all-time high of over 34.5 billion CFA francs in 1974.

This spurt in revenues was both a boon for the regime and a curse. Assuming that the era of high phosphate prices had arrived, Eyadema embarked on highly ambitious development plans that had to be scrapped only a year later as phosphate prices plunged to near their original levels in 1975. The overexpenditures of 1974 and 1975 and the state companies erected or nationalized at that time were at the root of Togo's economic woes in the 1980's. Prices fell in 1975, allegedly due to dumping practices of Morocco (third global exporter of phosphates, compared to Togo's fifth or sixth rank), while Togo was desperately in need of funds for its Saharan war. Prices remain depressed, and with greater wastage, mismanagement, and embezzlement in COTOMIB in recent years, costs of production have gone up and profitability down. Since nationalization, several new reserves have been discovered, new sites have come into production, and the capacity of CTMB has gone up to over four million tons per year. The constant unrest in the south during the period 1990 to 1994, however, and especially the nine month strike that attempted to dislodge Eyadema, was especially ruinous to the company which managed to produce only half its normal mineral output. *See also* PHOSPHATES.

COMPAGNIE TOGOLAISE DES TEXTILES (TOGOTEX). Textile complex, founded in Kara in 1978 with 1,800 million CFAF in capital, partly (twenty-five percent) state-owned, as part of the drive to industrialize the north. The company soon became deficitory and was closed down for several years. Efforts to sell it as part of Togo's privatization drive met several snags as first Spanish-Korean, then American, bids collapsed. In 1989 the company, together with the **ITT** in the south, were sold at a bargain price to a Hong Kong Chinese entrepreneur and are now known as Togotex International.

COMPAGNIE TOGOLAISE MARITIME (CTM) *see* SOCIETE NATIONALE MARITIME.

COMPLEX PETROLEUM DU LOME (COMPEL). Company set up in 1990 by Shell International and the Togolese government to privatize the Lomé petroleum company administered jointly since 1984 but in liquidation in 1989. Shell is the majority shareholder, having invested over three billion CFAF in the project.

CONFEDERATION AFRICAINE DES TRAVAILLEURS CROYANTS (CATC). Catholic interterritorial trade union federation with branches in most of Francophone Africa. Until the January 1973 forced merger of all Togolese unions into the **Confederation Nationale des Travailleurs du Togo,** the CATC branch in Togo was the 600-member **Confederation Syndicale des Travailleurs du Togo.** The latter has often been referred to as "the CATC" though such usage is incorrect.

CONFEDERATION NATIONALE DES TRAVAILLEURS DU TOGO (CNTT). Former unified (and still largest) trade union organization established in January 1973 under Secretary General **Nangbob (Raphael) Barnabo** following the December 1972 government-sponsored dissolution of all existing trade unions. The two major Togolese unions which merged into the CNTT were the **Union Nationale des Travailleurs Togolais** and the **Confederation Syndicale des Travailleurs du Togo.** The Confederation held its first congress in 1976. Its membership in the late 1980's stood at 70,000, organized in three divisions: public workers, parastatal workers, and private sector workers. The 1991 drive for multipartyism saw the collapse of the CNTT monopoly and the secession of the Collectif des Syndicalistes Independents (CSI) that shortly renamed itself Union Nationale des Syndicats Independants du Togo (UNSIT). The CNTT managed, however, to retain 105,000 members of thirty-three affiliated unions. *See also* TRADE UNIONS.

CONFEDERATION SYNDICALE DES TRAVAILLEURS DU TOGO (CSTT). One of Togo's largest pre-1973 trade unions, though small compared to the front-ranking **Union Nationale des Travailleurs du Togo.** Affiliated with the Catholic interterritorial **Confederation Africaine des Travailleurs Croyants,** the CSTT had 600 members and was led by President Bernard Akakpo. In January 1973 the CSTT was dissolved, as were all other unions, and merged into the unified **Confederation Nationale des Travailleurs du Togo.** *See also* TRADE UNIONS.

CONFERENCE NATIONALE. Togo's National Conference that led to the liberalization of the Eyadema regime and multipartyism, though most of the key planks of the Conference have not been actualized. In March 1990, shortly after student riots, political parties were legalized and the convening of a Conference of National Dialogue was pledged. In April came the **Bé Lagoon massacres** and after the massive demonstrations of June 1991 (triggered by Eyadema's appearing to backtrack on the issue of a conference) the Conference finally took place.

Lasting fifty-two tumultuous days (July 8 to August 26, 1991) with its proceedings relayed by radio and television, during the conference there were many confessions of wrong-doing and revelations of murder, torture, and corruption by former minions of the Eyadema regime. (Eyadema himself was accused of the theft or misappropriation of 900,000 million CFAF [$3 billion] or three times the then Togolese national debt.) Though an attempt was made by the regime to suspend the proceedings on August 23rd—when the Conference declared itself "sovereign"—it ignored Eyadema and elected a nine-month interim HCR government encompassing "all political persuasions" under an interim Prime Minister, **Joseph Kokou Koffigoh,** that was supposed to usher in a new political system.

CONGRES DES CHEFS TRADITIONNELS DU TOGO (CCTT) *see* UNION NATIONALE DES CHEFS TRADITIONNELS DU TOGO (UNCTT); CHIEFS.

CONSEIL DE L'ENTENTE. The Council of the Entente is a regional organization encompassing Cote d'Ivoire, Burkina Faso, Niger, Benin, and Togo. Created on May 29, 1959, under the auspices of Cote d'Ivoire as President Houphouet-Boigny's countermove to the projected Mali Federation. The Council of the Entente provides for freedom of movement across state boundaries, coordination of policies in the fields of judicial, communications, developmental, and economic matters, and a Solidarity Fund aimed at fiscal redistribution of accumulated funds in favor of the weaker member states. Most of the goals of the Entente have not been fulfilled; this is due to the lack of serious interest or total commitment on the part of the member states and the economic inequality between Cote d'Ivoire and the other states. Togo joined the Entente only in June 1966, having kept out of it at first (1960–63) because of President Olympio's desire to avoid international alliances, especially indirect ones, with France. Later (1963–66), Togo was kept out by Vice President Antoine Méatchi's vehement opposition to joining an essentially conservative grouping. Méatchi's opposition was overridden in the final months of the Grunitzky administration, but Togo began to play a serious role in the Entente only in the 1970's.

CONSEIL DES ORGANISMES NON-GOUVERNEMENTAUX EN ACTIVITE AU TOGO (CONGAT). Organization of Togo's private enterprises.

CONSEIL ECONOMIQUE ET SOCIAL. Advisory council on social and economic matters created in Togo in May 1967 but active since March 1968. The council is composed of twenty-five members, divided equally among representatives of the trade unions, industry and commerce, and agriculture with five technocrats and five sociologists/ economists representing the academic and administrative branches. The longest-lasting President of the Conseil Economique et Social has been **Koffi (Gervais) Djondo.** Its membership has included key figures from Togo's social, economic, and political life.

CONSEIL NATIONAL DE PATRONAT (CNP). Togo's major employers' association. The CNP joined in the call for an unlimited strike against the Eyadema regime in 1993.

CONSEILS DE CIRCONSCRIPTIONS. Local advisory councils that in 1946 replaced the **Conseils de Notables.** The Conseils de Circonscriptions were composed of representatives of the most important clans, ethnic groups, and villages in each circonscription, or district. Largely moribund until July 1951, they were then fully institutionalized and given slightly wider powers than the previous Conseils de Notables, including the authority to discuss local budgets and developmental priorities. In 1955 they were granted wider decision-making powers. Some of the councils became highly politicized and that of Lomé and of Kpalimé fell under the political control of Sylvanus Olympio's **Comité de l'Unité Togolaise,** becoming sounding boards for the party.

After independence, the reorganized councils continued functioning until the 1967 coup d'etat, when they were dissolved. They were resurrected in June 1973 under the name **Delegations Speciales,** under tighter central control and with fewer powers. There were twenty-one Delegations Speciales (one for each district) and seven Delegations Municipales for the country's seven municipalities. The Delegations Speciales were originally composed of five or seven members (depending upon the district's population), appointed by presidential decree. *See also* ADMINISTRATIVE ORGANIZATION; DELEGATIONS SPECIALES; CONSEILS DE NOTABLES; CIRCONSCRIPTIONS.

CONSEILS DE NOTABLES. Former local councils assembled at the administrative headquarters of most of Togo's **cercles.** First established by decree on February 17, 1922, and reorganized in 1924 and 1933, the Conseils de Notables were operative in Lomé, Aného, Atakpamé, Kpalimé, Sokodé, Bassar, Kara, and Mango. They were composed of ethnic and village notables elected by two electoral colleges: one of chiefs of cantons and villages and the second of chiefs of urban quarters and clan heads in urban centers. The councils convened at the request of the cercle administration, or every three months, to discuss government activities in the fields of taxation, public works, and the local budget. In 1946 the Conseils de Notables were supplanted by

Conseils de Circonscriptions, which themselves were replaced in 1973 by **Delegations Speciales.** *See also* ADMINISTRATIVE ORGANIZATION; CONSEILS DE CIRCONSCRIPTIONS.

CONSTITUTIONS. Togo adopted a new constitution (its sixth) by referendum on September 27, 1992, replacing another one, ratified in July 1991, that itself abrogated one adopted in December 1979. The latter had been the country's first since the 1967 coup that toppled the regime of President Nicolas Grunitzky. Though a constitutional committee was set up in 1967 (*see* COMITE CONSTITUTIONNEL) to report a draft constitution for the country, it was only in 1979 that the regime felt the need to fully legitimate itself.

Prior to that, the country has had three constitutions: 1) the Constitution (Provisional) of April 23, 1960, providing an interim parliamentary system; 2) the Constitution of April 14, 1961, providing a strong presidential system with most powers in an Executive President, elected for seven years (reelectable), and a weak National Assembly, elected for five years. Several specific issues could be brought to the population for decision via referenda, and, under specific conditions, the executive could acquire vast emergency powers; 3) The Constitution of May 5, 1963, establishing an executive composed of a President elected for five years and a Vice President, a National Assembly with weak powers, and (for the first time) a Supreme Court; 4) The December 30, 1970 Constitution, Togo's fourth, stipulated a uniparty state (under the RPT) led by an Executive President elected for seven years by universal suffrage on the recommendation of the RPT Congress. Re-electable, the President could dissolve the newly created National Assembly, elected for five years from a list of deputies approved by the RPT. Assembly sessions could not by law last more than two months. A Supreme Court was also erected. The constitution was easily modifiable by either the President or the National Assembly, after approval by the party. The constitution was promulgated on January 9, 1980, after being ratified by 99.9 percent of the population in the earlier elections for President of the Republic and National Assembly.

The July 1991 constitution was drafted by a 109-member Constitutional Commission set up in October 1990 to prepare a document anticipating a democratic multiparty system. The Commission completed its work on December 28, 1990 and submitted a Constitution of 110 articles organized under 16 chapters, setting up a dual executive with the Prime Minister accountable to the Presidency and National Assembly, and a Constitutional Council as the ultimate arbiter between the three branches of government. Neither President Eyadema nor interim Prime Minister Koffigoh was entitled to seek the

Presidency. The Constitution was approved by the **Conference Nationale** in July 1991; to further assure that Koffigoh (aged forty-four) was barred from seeking election, in mid-April 1992 the government changed the minimum age from forty to forty-five. A modified version, however, was actually submitted for ratification at the referendum of September 27, 1992 and approved by 98.11% of the vote. The main difference was that the restrictions on who might run were lifted.

CONVENTION DEMOCRATIQUE PANAFRICAIN (CDP). Political party, vehicle of the radical presidential aspirant Professor **Léopold Messan Gnininvi** who in 1991 lost in his bid as interim Prime Minister to Koffigoh by 388 votes to 312.

CORNEVIN, ROBERT, 1919– . Former colonial administrator and foremost scholar of Togolese history. Born on August 28, 1919 in Malesherbes in France, Cornevin was educated at the elitist Ecole Nationale de la France Outre Mer and graduated in 1941. He then served in the Army until 1947 and as a colonial administrator in the Togolese cercles of Atakpamé (1948–53), Bassari (1953), Dapango (1954–55), and Lomé (1955–56). Attached to the French Ministry of Education between 1958 and 1960, Cornevin completed his Ph. D. in African history at the University of Paris, and later that year he joined France's Direction de la Documentation. Between 1961 and 1985 he served as head of the Centre d'Etudes et de Documentation sur l'Afrique et l'Outre Mer, Director of the review *Afrique Contemporaine,* Life-Secretary of the Academie des Sciences d'Outre Mer and a member of various other societies. He wrote over 400 articles on Africa and several books on African history. A number of his publications have dealt with Togo, including several of his books.

CORVEE. Forced labor for purposes of infrastructure building and porterage. The corvée was exacted in Francophone Africa until the end of World War II as part of the **indigenat** code applied to the non-assimilé (*see* ASSIMILATION POLICY) population. Corvée labor also existed under the preceding German administration when, for example, every Togolese male was liable to be called up for twelve days a year. Under both the Germans and the French, the imposition of corvée—frequently arbitrary, beyond the official limits, or by unpopular traditional chiefs—caused civil unrest in sections of the country.

COTOCOLI *see* KOTOKOLI.

COTTON. One of Togo's export cash crops. The Togo Sea Island variety was successfully introduced by the Germans at the beginning of the colonial era; currently, the most important varieties are the Mono and the Allen. Cotton is mostly grown in the central-east part of the country along the border with Benin. West Africa's top cotton producer in 1959 with 9,200 tons, Togo has seen great variations in production over the years. In 1977, for example, production was less than 4,537 tons, while in 1980 the crop was 23,380 tons. Even the latter figure, however, was by 1980 less than ten percent of West Africa's production since the region had made tremendous strides with the crop. Average Togolese yields have gone up and ginning facilities have improved.

COUCHORO, FELIX, 1900–1968. Author. Born in Ouidah, Benin on January 30, 1900, Couchoro attended Ouidah's seminary, following which he taught at several schools in the vicinity (1917–39). In 1939 he settled in Anécho as a commercial agent while at the same time commencing his career as an author in earnest. His support for Sylvanus Olympio and the latter's **Comité de l'Unité Togolaise** resulted in sedition charges against him, and in 1952 he relocated again, this time to Aflao just across the Togolese border in the Gold Coast. He remained there until the rise to power of the Olympio regime in 1958, following which he returned to Lomé and became Director of the Togolese Ministry of Information. Couchoro's first novel (*L'Esclave*) was published in 1930, and his next two books came out in 1941 and 1950. It was essentially in Lomé, however, that he did most of his writing, publishing twelve more books before his death in 1968. His work marked him as one of Africa's first regional writers and Togo's most prolific author. His novels were always written in simple everyday language, understandable to the masses, and dealt with commonplace life and were set in either Benin or Togo.

COUP (ATTEMPTED) OF 1966. Popular uprising in Lomé on November 21, 1966, aimed at unseating the increasingly unpopular and unstable regime of Nicolas Grunitzky and bringing back to power the lieutenants of former President Sylvanus Olympio and his **Parti de l'Unité Togolaise,** successor to the **Comité de l'Unité Togolaise.** The uprising commenced early in the morning with the seizure of the radio station and other public buildings in the city and the appeal over the airwaves—by **Oswald Ajavon**—for massive demonstrations and a march to the presidential house. The uprising took place against the background of the resignation of the last PUT members (*see* MEATCHI-MAMA CRISIS) from Grunitzky's cabinet. Estimates of the crowds that obeyed the appeal for an uprising are unreliable, ranging from 5,000 to 50,000, but the crowds were undoubtedly large and the appeal popular. Various PUT leaders addressed the masses, including **Noe Kutuklui,** self-styled heir-apparent to the Olympio throne. The reaction of the armed forces was muted and ambiguous until early in the afternoon, when they started clearing the crowds. The basic consideration that brought in the military on the side of Grunitzky was the fact that to allow the coup to succeed would have strengthened the PUT and ushered in a PUT-dominated government, several members of which were known to be adamant in their demands that Olympio's assassins (i.e., Eyadema and other ranking officers of the army) be brought to trial. Following the army's belated entry on Grunitzky's side, the latter drastically reshuffled the cabinet, purged and downgraded Vice President Antoine Méatchi, and tried to provide a more assertive leadership. These efforts were to no avail, since the officer corps had already decided that the Grunitzky regime was a liability and would be overthrown on the next anniversary of Olympio's demise. *See also* GRUNITZKY, NICOLAS; COUP OF 1967.

COUP (ATTEMPTED) OF 1970. An anti-Eyadema conspiracy and alleged attempted coup that was averted by infiltration of the plotting group by a government informer and, according to some, agent-provocateur. Planned by **Noe Kutuklui,** self-styled political heir to Sylvanus Olympio, the plot entailed seizure of government installations and a call for an upheaval in the coastal regions against the regime of General Eyadema. The plotters were arrested during the night of August 8, allegedly as they broke up their meeting prior to the actual assault. A total of twenty-seven defendants were brought to trial on November 25 before a specially constituted **Cour de Sûreté de l'Etat,** on which sat the former Interior Ministers of both Sylvanus Olympio and Nicolas Grunitzky. Among the arrested were a large number of non-Togolese (Béninois and Ghanaians) as well as Police Commissioner **Jean-Alexandre Osseyi,** who was in charge of the military aspects of the attempted coup, and former National Assembly deputies Dr. **Marc Atipédé** and **Clement Kolor,** the latter killed when he tried to escape.

Despite open hearings, there is still controversy regarding the facts and the true role of the agent-provocateur (Lolé Mamiyable), since the defense convincingly argued that he had incited the conspiracy. Trial irregularities pointed out by uninvolved lawyer/spectators were dealt with summarily by the disbarment of the lawyers reporting them (and Lucien Olympio, Togo's Supreme Court State's Attorney was purged). A few of the arrested were later liquidated while in prison, though the rest, sentenced to long prison terms, were amnestied in 1972. Kutuklui, who allegedly masterminded the plot from his refuge in Benin, received a twenty-year sentence in absentia; paradoxically, his extradition was not requested at the time. Some defendants who had not been in on the conspiracy—such as **Robert Fiadjoe**, former Mayor of Lomé—were nevertheless tried and given light sentences.

COUP (ATTEMPTED) OF 1977. An October 1977 conspiracy aimed at a takeover of state power. Planned and financed from abroad (including donations from a mysterious Canadian arms dealer) and linked to the "Brazilian" families in Lomé, including the ever-frustrated Olympio family. The plot was thwarted by the British government (that had infiltrated the mercenary group being put together) forewarning Eyadema via the United States Embassy in Lomé. The twenty-odd mercenaries, who had already secreted weapons in Lomé and Aného, consequently aborted the plot due to the increased vigilance of the local security forces. Involved were elements from the United States, United Kingdom, France, and Italy. The full dimensions of the plot did not become clear until much later. At the time, only a few Togolese intellectuals were arrested, seemingly only for the sake of appearances. But by November 23, 1978—over a year later—a number of senior military officers were directly implicated in the 1977 plot that was now seen as a major conspiracy hatched by Olympio-De Souza family members. In August 1979, after a number of political kidnappings in Accra and Lagos by the Togolese secret service, the trial of the 1977 conspirators commenced. Several death-in-absentia sentences were passed, including on Olympio's sons, who were in self-exile abroad. A commuted death sentence was also passed on Major Sanvée, Emmanuel de Souza, Kouassi Savi de Tové, Kouassi de Souza, Abalo de Souza, and others.

COUP (ATTEMPTED) OF 1986. An alleged September 23, 1986 assault from Ghana (with support of the Ghanaian, Burkina Faso, and Libyan authorities) on several installations in Lomé, including General Eyadema's domicile in the Tokoin barracks, the RPT headquarters and the radio station, allegedly to assassinate Eyadema and set up a new government under the interim leadership of Captain Francisco Lawson and **Gilchrist Olympio.** Thirteen people were killed in the assault, and nineteen of the raiders (including Ghanaians) were captured. The reason why what actually transpired (aside from a conspiracy) is shrouded by mystery is that official accounts are riddled by inconsistencies. In reality there were at least two plots, including one earlier in July of the same year. On December 20, 1986, thirteen people were sentenced to death for their role, including Gilchrist Olympio in absentia.

COUPS (ATTEMPTED) OF OCTOBER 1991. Two separate incidents on October 1 and October 8, 1991 in which military elements tried, crudely, to reverse the tide of democratization in Togo. In the first, troops seized Lomé's radio station and broadcast Prime Minister **Koffigoh's** resignation, following which they withdrew, killing a few civilians. In the second incident, a military unit invaded the Hotel Fevrier 2 and demanded a confrontation with Prime Minister Koffigoh (who was actually not there), allegedly to force him to change his policies vis-a-vis General Eyadema. Three senior officers were subsequently arrested for these incidents, including Colonel Gnassingbé, General Eyadema's second cousin and Commander of the Presidential Guard, but not Lieutenant Gnassingbé, Eyadema's son, also seen in one of the incidents. Nothing came out of these arrests.

COUP (ATTEMPTED) OF DECEMBER 1991. A series of events in December during which Prime Minister **Koffigoh** was kidnapped on the dawn of December 3, 1991. The military had first cordoned off Lomé, declared Koffigoh ousted, and called upon General Eyadema to appoint a new Prime Minister. When this did not result in Koffigoh's voluntary resignation, they bombarded his residence and after dozens of soldiers were killed, kidnapped the Prime Minister and brought him to Eyadema. He was released the next day, following which he announced the formation of a new government "of national union" more amenable to Eyadema. The latter act was seen as capitulation by many in the HCR, irretrievably eroding whatever support Koffigoh still retained in that body.

Earlier on November 28, 1991, the radio and TV stations had been seized after the dissolution of the RPT (declared by the HCR) annoyed the military. The HCR rescinded this act to appease the troops, but once again on December 15th they invaded the radio station to demand the dissolution of the **HCR** for slurs on their leader Eyadema.

COUP (ATTEMPTED) OF 1993. Bloody commando attack during the night of March 25, 1993 on the Tokoin military barracks outside Lomé. Two senior officers who died protecting Eyadema were General Mawulikplim Amegie (the force commander) and Colonel Gnandi Akpo. The assault was masterminded by Colonel Koffi Tépé, Deputy Commander of the Togolese Armed Forces (who was summarily killed after the coup failed), reflecting an internal split in the officer corps about Eyadema's running again for the Presidency. After the assault failed, remnants of the 120-man force fled across the border to Benin and Ghana. Amnesty International reports at least an additional twenty summary executions took place.

COUP (ATTEMPTED) OF 1994. A commando raid, involving a force of 100 men, bazookas, and rockets, on several military installations and on

General Eyadema's motorcade. The force, organized by **Gilchrist Olympio** as a response to Eyadema's earlier attempt (in like manner) to liquidate him during his political campaigns in the country, infiltrated Togo from Ghana. Separate units attacked the elite RIAT Adidogomé barracks and Eyadema's motorcade as it pulled up to his residence. Poor intelligence preparation prior to the assault (e.g., lack of clarity about the location of Eyadema's compound), bungling, and sheer bad luck prevented the assault from succeeding. For example, though Eyadema's car was peppered by bullets and fully penetrated by rockets (and his driver was hit), Eyadema himself miraculously survived the assault. There was gunfire in Lomé for four days. Some thirty soldiers of the assaulting force were killed and an additional forty arrested.

COUP OF 1963. The coup d'etat of January 13, 1963 was staged by a clique of demobilized NCOs allegedly acting in the name of several hundred veterans of France's colonial armies who had been repatriated to Togo earlier in 1962 (*see* ARMED FORCES). The veterans, most of whom were northerners and were led by **Etienne Eyadema** and **Emmanuel Bodjollé,** had petitioned President Olympio to be integrated into the small Togolese army. Their request had been supported by several French officers then training the army and by indigenous NCOs and officers, all of whom envisaged an enhanced role and advanced rank in a larger army. When Olympio vetoed a much scaled-down petition asking that only sixty of the best-qualified veterans be recruited, a clique (specifically excluding Bodjollé) retaliated by assaulting Olympio's residence. Confronted by the putschists in the unguarded Presidential residence in the middle of the night, Olympio was shot in cold blood by Eyadema (who allegedly panicked), with the story propagated (to project a more "professional" account) that Olympio had been shot while scaling the United States Embassy gates, seeking asylum.

Following the coup, all former political exiles were invited to return to Togo and power was handed over to Nicolas Grunitzky (as President) and Antoine Méatchi (as Vice President). In reality, the putschists preferred to give Méatchi, also a northerner, the top position, but Grunitzky's refusal to serve under his former minister and French opposition to the abrasive and militant Méatchi tipped the scale in favor of a Grunitzky presidency.

Shortly after, the army's size was tripled with the integration of the unemployed veterans, and several of the ringleaders of the coup were promoted to officer rank. **Bodjollé,** official head of the clique but one who allegedly had played a double role on the night of the coup, was soon purged from the Army, which fell under the control of Eyadema. (For the core clique, *see* INSURRECTIONIST COMMITTEE.) The fact that the coup resulted in the assassination of Olympio has had major repercussions for Togo's political evolution; it has meant that the key officer clique headed by Eyadema (directly responsible for Olympio's death) could not afford to allow an Ewe-led regime to come to power for fear of retribution. When such a possibility arose in 1966—see COUP (ATTEMPTED) OF 1966—the Army moved in and established a military administration. See COUP OF 1967. In like manner, with the partial political liberalization in Lomé bringing **Gilchrist Olympio** as the main political contender for the Presidency, Eyadema, even were he so inclined (which he isn't) has to fear retribution once again if he were to allow his full political eclipse.

COUP OF 1967. The coup d'état of 1967 came on the fourth anniversary of the 1963 coup (January 13), though its stimulus was the **Méatchi-Mama Crisis** and the Lomé upheavals of 1966. *See* COUP (ATTEMPTED) OF 1966. In the November 1966 demonstrations, urban crowds in Lomé demanded the end of the Grunitzky government and the rise of a **PUT** administration. Since the PUT's most prominent plank was the trial of Olympio's assassins (i.e., the senior Army hierarchy who in 1963 were NCOs, and Eyadema specifically), the Army had to side with Grunitzky even though he had become a major liability and was no longer acceptable to the officer corps. The absence of any suitable civilian alternatives sealed Grunitzky's fate and resulted in the decision—as early as November 1966—that a full military takeover would be consummated on the anniversary of the first coup. Following the coup, Grunitzky left the country together with some of his closest political allies (e.g., Apedo-Amah, the former Foreign Minister), and a **Comité de Reconciliation Nationale** was set up under the chairmanship of Colonel **Kleber Dadjo,** the most senior officer in the armed forces, though not a core member of the 1963 veterans' clique. Prompt elections were promised as well as a new constitution. In April 1967 these promises were rescinded by Eyadema, who gathered all executive powers into his hands and set up a mixed military-civilian administration that lasted until he was forced by the demonstrations of 1990 to concede some power.

COUR DE SURETE DE L'ETAT. Special State Security Court set up in September 1970 to try crimes against the internal and external security of the state, starting with the defendants of the August 1970 conspiracy. *See* COUP (ATTEMPTED) OF 1970. In the original trial, the Court—convening in November—was composed of two military officers, the Ministers of Interior under the preceding Olympio and Grunitzky administrations (**Theophile Mally** and **Fousseni Mama,** respectively) and presided over by the president of Lomé's Court of Appeal, **Atsu-Koffi (Louis) Amega.** The Court was reconvened on August 24 and 25, 1979 to try fifteen individuals accused of plotting against Eyadema.

COUR SUPREME. Togo's Supreme Court, officially established in 1961, though not fully operative until the onset of the Grunitzky administration. Its first President was Jean Laloum, President of the Lomé Court of Appeals, followed by Dr. **Valentin Mawupé Vovor** and **Atsu-Koffi (Louis) Amega.** The court has not been very active, and, compared to Benin's Supreme Court for example, has been positively timid on issues requiring strong intervention. Currently, the President of the Court is Jacques Apaloo.

COURIER DU GOLFE. Independent weekly established after freedom of the press was specifically recognized in 1990. Notwithstanding this, its journalists were harassed, intimidated, and arrested on several occasions for writing unsavory articles about General Eyadema. Its Editor Koffi Homawoo was hauled to court on one occasion and the newspaper threatened with the closure of electricity and water unless it ceased publishing lies about Eyadema. The *Courier* managed to outsell the official government newspaper, *La Nouvelle Marché,* though unsubsidized by the State its issues cost ten times more.

CREDIT DU TOGO. State organ created in 1957 to offer credit services to Togo's agricultural cooperatives and farmers and to support, through loans, the creation of small new firms. The bank gave out a total of eight billion CFA francs in loans until its activities were curtailed in December 1966. At that time two state banks were created to replace the Crédit du Togo. The **Caisse Nationale de Crédit Agricole** inherited the agricultural loans operations of Crédit du Togo (which constituted the bulk of that organ's operations) and a new **Banque Togolaise de Développement** was created to encourage more forcefully the creation of new, small, and medium-sized enterprises in Togo.

CREPPY, ARTHUR. Physician and former head of antiepidemic diseases in the Ministry of Public Health. Creppy currently serves as Chief Medical Inspector of Schools. He is based in Lomé.

D

DABLA, EMMANUEL. Painter and designer. Born in the village of Togoville and educated there and in the former British Togoland, Dabla received the professional encouragement and assistance of Jacob Ohin, a prominent Togolese painter. Dabla has exhibited his works domestically (first prize at Togo's 1960 Independence Exposition) and abroad (silver medal at the Tenth Expo-Paris in 1961). He has a salon in Lomé and has, in turn, encouraged other budding Togolese artists.

DADJO, KLEBER (Colonel), 1914–1979. Former head of the **Garde Togolaise,** Minister of Justice, and until his death, Chef de Canton in the north. A Nawde (ethnically close to the Kabre) born in central Togo on August 12, 1914, Dadjo was educated locally and joined the Togolese police in 1933. He served in Togo until 1941 and then joined the Free French Forces. He received training in Accra and later served in Brazzaville, Dakar, and Cotonou. In August 1948 he was posted to Paris and later fought with the French forces in Indochina until 1955. Repatriated to Lomé, Dadjo rose up the ranks to Captain (1957) and to Major and Commander of the Garde Togolaise in 1960.

   In 1963 he supported the demands of the recently demobilized Togolese veterans for integration into the Garde (*see* COUP OF 1963; ARMED FORCES) and assisted in the armed confrontation that resulted in Olympio's assassination. Following the 1963 coup he was promoted to Lieutenant Colonel and, in a reorganization of the Army command in 1965, appointed head of President Grunitzky's military cabinet, a position he held until the coup of 1967. By virtue of his rank and seniority, Dadjo became Chairman of the interim **Comité de Reconciliation Nationale,** set up after the 1967 coup and, after General Eyadema's assumption of executive power in April 1967, Dadjo was brought into the cabinet as Minister of Justice. In 1969 Dadjo was retired from the armed forces and from the cabinet and appointed Chef de Canton in a northern district, a position he held until his death. Despite the succession of top posts he occupied since the original military intrusion in Togo's political life in 1963, Dadjo was never a true member of the inner core of military decision-makers. Separated from the latter (i.e., Eyadema, Assila, Alidou) in terms of age, experience, and training, Dadjo's permanence at the highest ranks of the army was always a reflection of the unwillingness of the young putschists to disrupt the command hierarchy or to purge one who had assisted them in 1963. Major decisions, however, were usually made by the aforementioned trio, though usually with Dadjo's concurrence.

DADZIE, EMILE. Minister of the Economy and Finance since May 1994 in the RPT-UTD coalition government under Prime Minister Edem Kodjo.

DAGADZI, BARNABE. Civil administrator. Trained overseas in Engineering, Dagadzi returned to Togo to work with the Department of Public Works, rapidly becoming its principal engineer. In 1967 he was appointed Deputy-Director of Public Works and Director in 1970. In that year he was nominated President of the Banque Togolaise de Développement by the government, serving in that capacity until his retirement in 1980.

DAGADZI, MASSA (MRS.). Former Akposso minister in charge of relations with the National Assembly. A prominent merchant, unionist, leader of the RPT women's branch and Presidential consort, Mrs. Dagadzi joined Eyadema's cabinet in January 1980 as Secretary of State. Her post was upgraded to full ministerial rank in May 1981. In essence the representative of women in the cabinet, since Eyadema's late 1970s sensitivity to the need of including at least one woman on his cabinet. She was dropped from the cabinet in September 1984, after an embarrassing incident between her husband and General Eyadema.

DAGOMBA. Ethnic group found mostly in Ghana and in what was previously British Togoland. In the middle of the sixteenth century the Dagomba, led by King Na Louro (1554–70), established their capital in Yendi (now in Ghana) after chasing away the original inhabitants, the **Konkomba** into Togo. The German colonization split the Dagomba in half. Yendi fell to German troops in 1884 and became effectively separated from a major segment of the Dagomba who lived under the British administration in the Gold Coast. Following the expulsion of the Germans from Togo in 1914, Yendi and the Togolese Dagomba fell into the territory designated as the British mandate of Togoland, and the plebiscite of 1956 in that area united the Dagomba people within Ghana.

DANSOU, APETI PIERRE, 1938– . Chemist. Born in 1938 and educated in Chemistry, Physics, and Mathematics at home and in France, Dansou returned to Togo to assume the post of Head of Equipment in the Government Offices. In 1984 he was appointed Coordinator of the Development Program for Building and Construction Material Industries. He is the author of numerous studies and reports.

DAPANGO *see* DAPAONG.

DAPAONG. Known as Dapango until the authenticity drives of the 1970s, and also briefly as Dapaon, Dapaong is a northern town some seventy kms. from Sansanné-Mango in the northwest. It is also the former name of a district in the Savanes region. The district is populated by Chokossi and Moba as well as other northern groups, including Mossi from Burkina Faso. During the pre-colonial era, Dapaong was largely under the control of the Chokossi kingdom based in Sansanné-Mango. In the administrative reorganization of Togo in 1981, the name of the district was changed to the prefecture de Tone. The town itself has an estimated population of 7,000 (but according to some estimates as high as 9,000 [making it Togo's eleventh-largest urban center]) and has a **zongo** on its hilly suburbs that contains an important Hausa, Mossi, and Djerma merchant class.

DA SILVA, FRANCISCO OLYMPIO. President Sylvanus Olympio's grandfather and founder of the Olympio family in Togo. A mestizo with some Indian blood, Da Silva emigrated from Brazil to West Africa in the middle of the nineteenth century. He settled in **Agoué** where there was already a bustling **Brazilian** community and a Catholic chapel, dropping the Da Silva part of his name, under which he had been a slave in Brazil.

DA SOUZA, FRANCISCO FELIX, 1760?–1849. Portuguese drifter or political refugee who became an important trader in the Aného area and later official Governor of Ouidah under the aegis of the king of Dahomey. Of humble origins, Da Souza commenced his West African career as a minor trader in a variety of commodities, including slaves and guns. He first installed himself in Aného around 1788, establishing the Ajuda quarter, precursor of the current Adjido quarter. After a dispute over a debt owed to him by Dahomey's King Adandozan, Da Souza was imprisoned in Abomey (Dahomey's capital) and was only released after the intervention of Ghézo, the future king of Dahomey who rose to power with Da Souza's assistance. Elevated to the position of Chacha (chief customs Collector, effectively Governor) of Ouidah, the biggest slaveport on the coast, Da Souza exercised a monopoly over all trade in the region and became enormously wealthy. Fully involved with his duties in Ouidah, Da Souza relegated his authority in Aného to his lieutenant, Akouété Zanklibossou, and his commercial enterprises to his sons. After the slave trade was abolished, the Da Souza interests shifted to palm oil. Francisco Da Souza died in Ouidah in 1849 and received a regal funeral including human sacrifices.

DEDAURE. The **zongo** quarter of Sokodé and one of the original settlements of the Kotokoli in Togo. Dedauré includes the residence of the **Uro** of the Kotokoli.

DE FANTI, KWEKU SIMON. Interim Minister of Trade and Transport, joining the cabinet on February 14, 1993.

DEGOUNE, JEAN YAOVI. Briefly Minister-Delegate to the Presidency in charge of relations with the **HCR** and Head of the League for Human Rights, Degoune was appointed to his post in December 1991 by Eyadema and Prime Minister Koffigoh.

DELEGATIONS SPECIALES *see* CONSEILS DES CIRCONSCRIPTIONS.

DENDI. Found in larger concentrations in neighboring Benin (where they number 38,000), the Dendi are nonindigenous Mende merchants from Songhay (Niger) who migrated through the Niger river valley and settled along the principal pre-colonial caravan routes offering middleman services to long distance traders. The Dendi still speak their own language, a Songhay dialect, and are all Muslim. As they are intermarried with the local Muslim population and largely indistinguishable from them, the size of Togo's Dendi population cannot be estimated.

DERMANE, ALI FREDERIC, 1933– . Former cabinet minister and Ambassador to France. Born of Kotokoli parents in Bafilo in 1933, Dermane, a Catholic, was educated in Alédjo, Yadé, and Lomé, becoming a teacher in 1955. In 1959 he won a bursary for administrative studies and in 1962 was appointed head of the Division of Price Controls in the Ministry of Commerce. Between 1963 and 1965 he was sent abroad (to Paris) for further training. On his return, he was integrated into Eyadema's cabinet as interim Minister of Interior (during Major Assila's convalescence) and of Information between 1969 and 1973. In 1973 he was reassigned to the Ministry of Interior where he served as Secretary General. In 1978 he commenced his diplomatic career through an appointment as Ambassador to Brazil, and in 1980 he was given Togo's top posting, Ambassador to France, a post held until 1986 when he returned to the Foreign Ministry in Lomé.

DE SOUZA, AUGUSTINO, 1877–1960. Powerful early supporter, founder, and first President of the **Comité de l'Unité Togolaise.** Born to an important **Mina Brazilian** family in Porto Seguro in 1877, De Souza pursued a commercial and entrepreneurial career most of his life. In 1903 he joined the Deutsche Togo Gesellschaft and, following the latter's expulsion from Togo in 1914, he set up his own import-export firm. Later, he branched off into the production of palm oil and coconuts, purchasing large tracts near Aného for this purpose. Throughout the years, he prospered and was considered Togo's richest merchant in the pre-independence era. After the Second World War, De Souza became involved in the various movements aiming to unify all Ewe under one colonial administration. Toward this end, he was a liberal contributor to the nascent Comité de l'Unité Togolaise, which he had helped found and of which he was first President (with Olympio at that time serving as Vice President). Indeed it was in De Souza's extensive plantations that the CUT leadership met to map out strategy and tactics. De Souza was also one of the few ardent supporters in French Togo of the **Anlo**-led **All-Ewe Conference** of **Daniel Chapman** in neighboring

Gold Coast. Too old to assume an active role in the CUT struggle vis-à-vis the French administration in Togo, De Souza's support for the movement in its early days was nevertheless invaluable. The De Souza family remains extremely powerful in Togo, and together with the Olympio sons and several other Brazilian elements, forms the core of the anti-Eyadema opposition at home and abroad.

DE SOUZA, EMMANUEL KODJOVI. Entrepreneur and alleged mastermind behind the 1977 attempted coup against the Eyadema regime. A very prosperous timber merchant from the illustrious De Souza Brazilian family, related by blood and marriage to the Olympios and also owning a fleet of taxis in Lomé, De Souza allegedly was also the one who bankrolled the mercenary assault. When the plot failed (*see* COUP [ATTEMPTED] OF 1977) De Souza fled to Accra but was kidnapped by Togolese agents and brought home to stand trial. Sentenced to death, he was released from prison in 1980 as part of Eyadema's clemency on the eve of the constitutionalization of his regime.

DEVELOPMENT PLAN (SIXTH), 1991–95. Completely moribund development plan, originally drawn (as was the fifth) in accord with World Bank and IMF maxims stressing agrarian self-sufficiency, giving the private sector a major role, and diminishing the parastatal sector. As with the case of the Fifth Development Plan (1985–1990) the projected revenues were not forthcoming; more importantly, the constant political turmoil in Togo since 1990 meant that few of the targeted projects could even commence.

DEVELOPMENT PLAN (FOURTH), 1981–85. Originally dubbed the plan of "Grandes Realisations," because of scheduled massive uplifting of the economy, the plan was in shambles and completely outdated even before it was printed. Scheduled investments were cut by one third barely six months into the plan, due to massive shortfalls in anticipated revenues and the reluctance of both private and public capital to invest in Togo. Originally targeting investments at 368.5 billion CFAF (vs. 251 billion in the earlier plan, 145 billion for the second, and merely 75 for the first), the plan had a minimum priority segment of 251 billion in investments (that was not met) and an optional segment of 117.5 billion, most of which was chopped off almost immediately. As the plan originally stood, rural economy would have benefited most with investments of 116 billion CFAF, followed by industrial, artisanal, and commercial projects (98 billion) and infrastructure, urban and transit facilities, and tourist outlays (100.7 billion).

DEVELOPMENT PLAN (THIRD), 1976–1980. Conceived of as a bridge between the preceding two largely ground-breaking and research development plans and the following (fourth) full-fledged development plan. Total investments were targeted at 251 billion CFAF, of which some sixty-nine percent were to come from internal resources (public fifty-nine percent, private nine percent) and thirty-five percent from external donors (thirty-three percent public, two percent private). Industrial projects (seventy billion CFAF), rural development (fifty-six billion), and infrastructure works (forty billion) were the prime sectors of the economy to benefit. The plan had to be scaled down due to falling state revenues, and only some seventy percent of the plan was realized.

DISTRICT *see* CIRCONSCRIPTION

DJABAKU, ALBERT, 1919– . Pharmacist, unionist, and former President of Togo's Chamber of Commerce. Born in Tsévié on July 27, 1919, Djabaku was educated locally and then continued his specialization in Medicine and Serology at the Sorbonne. Upon his return to Togo he became director of Togo's Central Pharmacy (1953–78) and President of the Pharmacists Union. He was also President of Togo's Chamber of Commerce between 1968 and 1977.

DJAFALO, ALBERT ALIDOU *see* ALIDOU DJAFALO, MENVEY-INOYU (COLONEL).

DJAGBA, LAURENT, 1926–1971. Former deputy to the National Assembly from Dapaong and Speaker of the National Assembly during Sylvanus Olympio's presidency. Born in 1926 in Bantamboaré (Dapaong), Djagba was educated locally and joined the colonial administration in the far north. A member and later Secretary General of the civil service union that was affiliated with the interterritorial **Confederation Africaine des Travailleurs Croyants,** Djagba joined the **Comité de l'Unité Togolaise** and was elected as the latter's deputy from Dapaong in 1958. He played a prominent role in the assembly becoming its Speaker [Questor] and serving on the Committee on Foreign Affairs and Defense, the assembly's Central Bureau, and the National Hospital's administrative commission. After the coup d'etat of 1963, Djagba lost his assembly seat and was largely shunted aside. In 1970 he was allegedly involved in the pro-CUT attempted coup and died during torture while in prison early in 1971. *See* COUP (ATTEMPTED) OF 1970. Further details about his death came to light during the debates at the National Conference in 1990.

DJALLA, PALI. Former Minister of Trade and Transport. In 1987 Djalla was appointed Managing Director of **OPAT** in an effort of revitalizing it.

DJITRI *see* LOME.

DJOBO, BOUKARI, 1936– . Former Minister of Finance and President of the Union Togolaise du Banque. Born in Sokodé in the north in 1936, Djobo traces his descent from the superior chief of the Kotokoli at the time of the German conquest. He was educated locally and studied law in Dakar, Senegal, and in Bordeaux and Paris. In 1960 he returned to Togo and was appointed Director of the International Aid section of the Planning Department in the Ministry of Finance. Following Olympio's assassination in 1963 Djobo—who though a northerner had joined the **Comité de l'Unité Togolaise**—was appointed head of the Togolese delegation to the eighteenth session of the United Nations General Assembly. In June 1964 he was brought back by President Nicolas Grunitzky to continue serving in the Planning Department and to become Chairman of the Union Togolaise du Banque. In January 1966, he was promoted into the cabinet as Minister of Finance and Economics. He was briefly dropped from the cabinet on December 23, 1966 in the aftermath of a major cabinet reshuffle, occasioned by the ongoing tug-of-war between Grunitzky and Antoine Méatchi, but was reinstated after the 1967 coup d'état as a member of the **Comité de Reconciliation Nationale,** with responsibility over Finance. Following General Eyadema's military takeover in April of the same year, Djobo became Minister of Finance again and held the position until early 1969. Also a former Director of the Office de Commercialisation des Produits Agricoles du Togo (OPAT), Djobo continued to serve as President of the Union Togolaise du Banque and a noncabinet advisor on economic affairs.

DJOMEDA, FERDINAND KODJO. Civil administrator who has occupied a number of posts as government delegate to parastatal bodies, including President of the Compagnie du Benin and President of SOTEHPA. He is permanently attached to the Ministry of Commerce and Industry.

DJONDO, KOFFI (GERVAIS), 1937– . Former Minister of State Companies, banker, influential member of the Political Bureau of the **Rassemblement du Peuple Togolais,** and influential President of the **Counseil Economique et Social.** Born in Aného on July 4, 1937 and educated at the University of Paris, Djondo started his career as a labor inspector and eventually became Director of Togo's Caisse de Compensation, des Prestations Familiales et des Accidents du Travail. In 1968 he was named President of the Conseil Economique et Social. An early member of Togo's single party, the RPT, Djondo was an influential leader in the latter's Political Bureau (in charge of social affairs), while his wife was the president of the RPT's women's wing, the **Union Nationale des Femmes du Togo;** she is also very prominent in the country's textile wholesale trade. Djondo has been President of Togo's Chamber of Commerce since 1977 and Secretary General of the Société Commerciale de l'Afrique Occidentale. In September 1984 he was brought into Eyadema's cabinet as Minister of State Companies, charged with privatizing the State sector, a position he held until May 1991.

DJOUA, YOMA NARCISSE (MAJOR). An Eyadema relative and staunchly loyal commander of the **Brigade Pigeon** Forces d'Intervention Rapide (FIR), essentially as a political police. A Kabré from Eyadema's home area, Yoma was rapidly promoted and in 1980 assigned administrative duties as Prefect of Oti. There for six long years he ruled supreme and with a harsh hand, triggering numerous complaints about his arrogant behavior. He was particularly attacked for brutally enforcing the ban keeping the local population out of the newly created Oti Hunting Preserve that was frequented by General Eyadema himself. After 1986 he joined the Presidential Guard where he was notorious for his zeal in interrogating political prisoners. It was Yoma and his units that seized the National Assembly in October 1992 in support of Eyadema during the tug-of-war between Eyadema and interim Prime Minister Kottigah.

DOGBE, GODWIN KOUASSI. 1910–1978. Senior administrative officer. Born in Lomé on August 23, 1910, Dogbé joined the civil service in 1928 and remained in it until his death in 1978. On May 23, 1958 he was appointed Director of the cabinet of Anani Santos, the Minister of Justice. When Santos was purged, Dogbé was reappointed to serve in a similar role in the cabinet of Paul Anani Amegée, the Minister of Public Health (June 1959). He remained in a senior capacity in the administration until his retirement and death.

DOGBE, YVES-EMMANUEL, 1939– . Educator and Togo's foremost poet. Born in Lomé on May 10, 1939, Dogbé studied locally and in Ghana, after which he taught in several Béninois schools while publishing articles, poems, and fables in local newspapers. During the 1970s, Dogbée resided mostly in Paris and soon started publishing volumes of fables and poems through his own publishing company (Akpagnon). In 1977 while in Lomé he was arrested for criticizing the

Eyadema regime's economic policies and returned to Paris where he resided until 1991, when with most exiles he returned to Togo. His stature as Togo's greatest living writer remains unchallenged.

DOGBEH, RICHARD, 1932– . Educator, poet, and author, of Beninois origin but currently established in Togo. Born in Cotonou, Benin, on December 31, 1932, Dogbeh was educated locally, in Cote d'Ivoire, and in Senegal. His brilliant school record enabled him in 1954 to continue his studies in several French Universities where he was also involved in the militant students' movement the **Fédération des Etudiants de l'Afrique Noire en France,** a branch of which he headed. After his return to Benin he became Cabinet Director of the Minister of National Education (until 1966) and later head of the National Pedagogic Institute in Porto Novo. He has served briefly as head of the French section of the Ghanaian Academy of Sciences' Africa Encyclopedia project and since 1968 has been associated with UNESCO. In 1969 he established himself in Togo, teaching in a high school in Atakpamé and at the University of Benin in Lomé. He has published several novels and collections of poems that have received international acclaim and has written articles for local and French newspapers.

DOGO KOUDJOLOU, MEGBENEWE (Henri), 1938– . Former extremely influential Minister of Planning, Trade and Industry and former Assistant Secretary General of the **Rassemblement du Peuple Togolais.** Of Kabré origins, Dogo was born in Pagouda in the north in 1938 and entered the civil service after obtaining a law degree abroad. He has served as administrator with the Togolese Development Bank, Togo's representative to the African Development Bank, and Director of Research on the Plan at the Ministry of Commerce, Industry and Tourism. In 1969 Dogo was a founding member of the RPT party and was named Assistant Secretary General under **Edem Kodjo.** When the party was reorganized a year later and the position of Secretary General was abolished, Dogo became a member of the party's Political Bureau. Considered one of the key northern technocrats in Eyadema's regime and a personal crony of the president, Dogo joined the cabinet in 1972 as Secretary of State for Trade, Planning and Industry and in February 1974 was promoted to full ministerial rank. He has also been Director of the **Société Togolaise de Marbrerie et de Materiaux,** Togo's state marble corporation, and served on numerous other parastatal boards. One of the longest-tenured of Eyadema's cabinet ministers, Dogo was finally summarily dismissed in September 1982 under intense pressure from international financial circles demanding an end to corruption and inefficiency in Togo's parastatal sector prior to any further financing so urgently requested by the regime. In January

Dogo was also purged from the RPT on the grounds of corruption and inefficiency, especially during his tenure at the head of BALTEX. Briefly Advisor to Eyadema, Dogo was appointed Deputy Managing Director of Air Afrique in 1985. Immensely rich by now, Dogo briefly bounced back into the cabinet in February 1990 as Minister of Rural Development before the multiparty liberalization swept him out.

DOH, ALBERT, 1908–1988. Former CUT deputy to the National Assembly and Treasurer of the CUT parliamentary group. Born in 1908 in Agbouvé in the south, Doh was educated locally and was engaged in commercial activities until the late 1940's when he joined the **Comité de l'Unité Togolaise.** With the rise of the Olympio regime, Doh was elected to the National Assembly from Notsé (1958) and remained a deputy until the 1963 coup d'etat. The parliamentary party's Treasurer and member of the Assembly's Finance and Economics Committee until the demise of the Olympio regime, Doh was engaged in commercial activities since 1963.

DOH BRUCE, LAURIA. Important textile merchant, dominating the retail trade in Lomé. Doh Bruce is also President of the Association des Revendeuses de Tissus and member of the local Conseil Economique et Social.

DO KOKOU, JACQUES METONOU, 1949– . Cinematographer. Born in Lomé in 1949 and educated both at home and in France, Do Kokou produced the acclaimed film *Kouami* and has also published some poetry.

DONOU, AYI (CAPTAIN). One of General Eyadema's half-brothers and commander of the presidential guard, the key unit assuring the personal safety of the President. The 1,200 man North Korean-trained unit is assisted by two intelligence services (*see* BRIGADE . . .) both of which are also headed by trusted Eyadema relatives. Captain Donou himself is much feared in Lomé as a ruthless, swaggering officer.

DOSSEH, KOUASSI. Senior administrative officer. Togo's Director of Customs and also Director of OPAT.

DOSSEH-ANYRON, ROBERT CASIMIR (ARCHBISHOP OF LOME). Appointed Archbishop in 1962, replacing **Joseph Strebler,** Dosseh-Anyron became the first indigenous Togolese to occupy that post. Previously, he had served in Lomé's archdiocese.

DOU. Term designating the specific Ewe clan of origin and its traditional territory. A dou may encompass several thousand people and has its own particular mythology of origin, history, and leadership.

DOUBLE ELECTORAL COLLEGE. Electoral system that existed for some time in the French colonial territories under which representatives were elected by two separate electoral colleges. One college was composed of metropolitan citizens and local **assimilés** or **evolués,** while the second was composed of African subjects satisfying certain lower criteria for membership. The system drastically overrepresented the French community in each colony and, among the native population, restricted the franchise to local elites. Used also in territories placed under France's mandate, in Togo the first electoral college included only 1,500 voters who elected twenty percent of the deputies in the first postwar territorial assembly (six of the thirty members). The double electoral college was abolished in Togo in February 1952, earlier than in France's other African territories.

DOUFELGOU, PREFECTURE DE. The former circonscription of Niamtougou, with administrative headquarters in the village of the same name, just north of Kara (ex-Lama Kara) and the core Kabré prefecture of Kozah. The administrative designation and name change occurred with the June 1981 reorganization of Togo.

DOUMEGAWO. An assembly of all the representatives of the noble families that, together with the **fiohawo,** exercises power among the Ewe.

DOUNYAH, PAUL KOUASSI. Former Minister. Dounyah joined the September 1991 interim government as Minister of Labor and the Civil Service as a representative of the PAD party. He was retained in the subsequent 1992 coalition government with the RPT but was dropped from the cabinet in February 1993.

DOVI, AHLONKO. Head of the **Commission Nationale pour le Droits de l'Homme.** In 1991 he supervised the publication of a report accusing the Togolese armed forces of causing thousands of deaths in the 1980s, including a systematic burning of witches.

DZABA, KOUGBLENOU. Briefly Minister of Communications and Culture in the interim 1991 government.

DZO. Symbol of fire in Ewe magic rituals.

E

ECOBANK-TOGO. West Africa's first offshore bank, bankrolled with forty-five million dollars by the sixteen-member **ECOWAS** and established in mid-1988 with Headquarters in Lomé. The bulk of the bank's equity comes from its parent company (Ecobank Transnational) that is privately held. Only five percent is local money from private investors.

ECOLE NATIONALE D'ADMINISTRATION (ENA). Advanced School of Administration for middle-echelon officials and candidates for administrative careers. The school's intake is only 50 of the 300-odd potentially acceptable candidates, out of a total of some 800 annual applicants. The staff is composed of full-time instructors (five, headed by Law Professor Messan Accoutey) and part-timers including a large number of senior government officials who participate in the program. Students take normal courses as well as participate in internships. Once they complete their course of studies, they are, in principle, ready for senior administrative duty.

ECOLE WILLIAM PONTY. Prestigious lycée on Gorée island just off Dakar, Senegal (after 1938 at Sebikotané, a suburb of Rufisque), to which the cream of Francophone Africa's elite were usually admitted, to be practically guaranteed a high level civil service appointment upon completion of studies or entrance to French universities. Among Togolese educated at the Ecole William Ponty were Henri Ajavon, Samuel Aquereburu, Dr. Marc Atipédé, Sylvain Babélémé, Benoit Bédou, Emmanuel Gagli, Fousseni Mama, and Bruno Savi de Tové.

ECONOMIC COMMUNITY OF WEST AFRICA (ECOWAS). International community of sixteen French- and English-speaking states aimed at creating a vast common market stretching from Mauritania to Nigeria and including 150 million people. The headquarters of the organization is in Lagos. Officially founded in 1978 but traces its origins to the Niamey ECA meeting of 1965 and the 1975 ECOWAS treaty. ECOWAS includes Togo (with Eyadema as president in 1980 and 1981).

EDE, GASTON. Deputy, elected on the **CAR** party list in the February 1994 elections, shortly after which he was murdered by the Togolese security forces.

EDEE, MAWULI AGBEKO, 1939– . Educator. Born in 1939 and earned a doctorate in Physics (specializing in Optics and Acoustics) from the University of Besançon, Edee teaches at the University of Benin in Lomé.

EDITOGO *see* Etablissement National des Editions du Togo.

EDOH, KOFFI, 1939– . Former Minister of Technical Education. Born in 1939 in Amou-Oblo and educated in Togo, France, and in the United States (University of Arizona) in Physics, Edoh first joined the University of Benin teaching Physics, concurrently Director of Studies at the Lomé Protestant College. In September 1984 he was appointed Minister of Technical Education by General Eyadema, a post he held until 1988.

EDUCATION. Togo is one of Africa's most highly-educated states, in part because of avid interest in education among southern groups (Ewe, Mina, and, to a lesser extent, the Ouatchi) and partly because of the early presence of missionary schools along the coast. Since most early educational drives (private or public) were concentrated in the south, school enrollment figures were until recently unevenly spread throughout the country. Only with the rise of the northern Eyadema regime was a serious effort mounted to bridge the educational gap between the north and the south. In the 1971–72 school year, for example, ninety-nine percent of school-age children in Lomé attended school, compared to eighteen percent in Sansanné-Mango in the far north. Though the imbalance still remains, by the late 1980s the latter percentage had gone up to thirty-six percent, a major achievement.

Missionary schools have been at the forefront in promoting rapid educational advances in the south. Only in 1956 did public education surpass private education in enrollment, with more of the latter in the south and public education concentrated in the north, but, even in 1982 mission schools continued to educate fully fifty percent of Togo's pupils. The progress of education in Togo is clearly visible if one notes that in 1921 there were only thirteen public schools with 1,242 students and nineteen private institutions with 4,063 students. At independence (the 1960–61 school year) primary school figures stood at 52,816 students enrolled in public schools and 41,318 in private ones, for a grand total of 94,134. To this figure should be added 3,485 students attending secondary or technical schools, both public and private. By 1966 Togo was ranked sixth in Africa in terms of secondary school enrollment per 10,000 population and third in Africa in terms of number of girls in primary school as a percentage of total primary enrollment. The 1982–83 school year commenced with nearly 700,000 students for a seventy-one percent scholarization rate, an extremely high one, and with twenty-five percent of the national budget going for education. In a separate development, indigenous languages were introduced for the first time in primary schools in 1978 (after a trial run in two districts in 1975), though the policy was more popular in the south, where Ewe was a lingua franca anyhow, than in the north where the "imposition" of Kabré was seen by many as cultural colonialism. The figures for the 1982–83 school year were:

Level	Teachers	Students	Schools
Primary	9,800	500,200	2,300
Junior	3,440	110,890	279
Secondary	638	21,400	52
Technical	451	7,500	27
Higher	427	4,500	1

The number of schools in the country thus tripled from 934 in 1971–72 to over 2,600 in 1982–83. In light of these massive increases subsequent advances in the following decade were modest: by 1991 the number of schools stood at over 2,750, of which thirty-six were new secondary schools. In the 1980s technical schools received major new financial assistance, greatly increasing student attendance, though by the late 1980s financial conditions caused a slow-down in the projected quadrupling of this sector of public education. (Togo has six state and twenty-one private technical schools in the country.) Student registration at the local Université du Togo also zoomed up in the 1980s, in part as the regime gave more scholarships for (cheaper) study at this University than in France. In the 1990–1991 school year (just before the massive unrest that was to distort statistics for two years) there were over 8,250 students at the University. The 1990–91 budget for education consumed 13,911 billion CFAF, though the percentage of the budget going for education halved from 23 percent to 12 percent as resources were shifted to other more pressing areas.

EDUCATIONAL REFORM OF 1975. A restructuring of school curriculum and introduction of two "national" languages, Kabre in La Kara and Ewe in Notsé. The original plan, already modified, was that eventually French language instruction (though not French language) would be completely phased out of the Togolese school system. The educational reform also provided for universal free education for children between the ages of two and fifteen, programs of continuing education, and automatic class promotion of all children irrespective of school performance.

EFE EKPE. New Year festival among the **Mina** and affiliated ethnic groups, during which seers perceive whether or not the coming year will be a good one. The festival includes costumed demonstrations. Occurring in September, the pageant also symbolically purifies all Mina in honor of the new year.

EGLISE EVANGELIQUE DU TOGO (EET). The only major completely indigenously staffed church in West Africa, the EET has existed since the 1920s. The roots of the Evangelical Church of Togo are imbedded in the 1847 entry into West Africa (via Accra) of the **Bremen Missionary Society** that eventually made the Ewe the prime focus of their activities. After the Ashanti wars in the Gold Coast (1865–74), the Society greatly expanded its efforts among the Ewe, though it was expelled from Togo with Germany's loss of the colony. The United Free Church of Scotland was invited by the British administration to British Togoland to replace the activities of the Bremen Society. Shortage of manpower, however, resulted in a policy stressing the utilization of indigenous staff as much as possible, leading eventually to the autonomous spirit of the local church. In 1927 the church opted for the name Ewe Presbyterian Church. In the French mandate of Togo the Ewe church proclaimed its independence after the end of World War I, and it has been autonomous since, despite the entry into the territory of the Société des Missions de Paris in 1929. In 1954 the church in British Togo changed its name to the Evangelical Presbyterian Church (to satisfy non-Ewe elements) while in 1957 the French Togo branch changed its name to Eglise Evangélique du Togo. In 1960 the latter had twenty-eight pastors, baptized 15,668 children, and counted as adherents fully 20,000 of Togo's 37,000 Protestants. Paradoxically, the Church's percentage of Protestants was higher in the north (640 of Kara's 775 Protestants, for example) than in either the Ewe areas of **Kloto**—11,000 of 19,500 Protestants—or Lomé, where it claimed to have the allegiance of 1,700 of the 3,226 Protestants. The Church operates some fifty schools (sixteen each in the Kloto and Anou prefectures), with 8,382 pupils. One of the Church's most celebrated pastors is **Ayi Houenou Hunlédé,** former Foreign Minister of Togo, who was ordained after stepping down from the cabinet.

EHE, N'SOUWODJI KAO. Executive Director of the Union Togolaise de Banque and briefly Minister of Trade and Transport. Ehe joined Eyadema's cabinet in March 1987 but was dismissed on December 21, 1988 for fiscal mispropriety when it was discovered he had continued to receive two salaries, one from his former employer. He then rejoined the UTB.

EHLAN, DOGBEVI BADAGBO. Head of the National Sanitary Service of Togo and Secretary General of the Association of Sanitary Educators of Africa since the 1970s.

EHOUE. Small ethnic group, part of the Agni-Tchi constellation, found exclusively in the Mono region in the vicinity of Atakpamé-Notsé-Tchoum. Their numbers are estimated at 36,000.

EKLO, YAO KUNALE (MICHEL). Former Minister of Interior and representative to the United Nations. Director of the Political Affairs Department at Togo's Ministry of Foreign Affairs between August 1968 and 1970, Eklo was dispatched in mid-1970 to become Economic Counselor at Togo's Embassy in Paris. In August 1971 he was appointed Togo's permanent representative to the United Nations, and two years later he was repatriated and brought into the cabinet as Secretary of State in charge of information. In February 1974 he was promoted to full ministerial rank, and in March 1975 he was shifted to the key position as Minister of Interior, though he was dropped from the cabinet altogether in February 1977. Eklo has been retained in his powerbase in Eyadema's political party, the RPT, being the latter's administrative secretary for nearly two decades. Eklo is one of Eyadema's prime cronies.

EKLOU, PAULIN, 1928– . Economist and former cabinet minister. Born on February 19, 1928 to an Ewe family in the Kpalimé area, Eklou was educated locally and in France where, after secondary schooling, he continued his studies at the University of Montpellier (1950–52) and at the National Institute of Economic and Financial Studies, graduating in 1957. He continued his practical training at the Central Bank in Paris and then in Brazzaville (Congo), Cotonou (Benin), and at the United Nations. Upon his return to Togo in 1962, he was appointed Director of Togo's Economic Planning Department by President Sylvanus Olympio. He continued serving in this capacity under the successor regime of Nicolas Grunitzky until November 1966. A former prominent member of Olympio's **Comité de l'Unité Togolaise,** Eklou was involved in the November 1966 conspiracy to topple Grunitzky— *see* COUP (ATTEMPTED) OF 1966—and was consequently arrested and imprisoned in Sansanné-Mango in the far north until the 1967 coup d'état. In the aftermath of the coup he was brought into the interim **Comité de Reconciliation Nationale** with responsibilities in the fields of commerce and industry. Following General Eyadema's assumption of full powers in April 1967, Eklou was brought into the latter's cabinet as Minister of Commerce and Industry and became a key member of the newly formed **Conseil Economique et Social.** In 1969 he was shifted to head the Ministry of Rural Economy, holding this position until January 1972. At that date Eklou was dropped from the cabinet and reassigned as technical counselor attached to Ministry of Economics and Finance. He then served for several years as President of CIMTOGO before entering retirement.

EKOH, FRANCIS. Deputy Chairman of the **HCR.**

EKPEMOG. Colloquial Ewe word referring to the unruly irregular southern pro-civilian government militia that sprang up to support Prime Minister Koffigoh's government in August 1991 against intimidation and/or assault by the Togolese armed forces supportive of the continued dictatorship of General Eyadema. The word comes from "Ekpe" which is "stone" (their sole weapons) in Ewe and "mog" from the ECOWAS peace-keeping force in Liberia.

ELECTIONS OF APRIL 1958. The elections of April 1958 were crucial for two reasons. First, being United Nations-supervised they ended the era of active gerrymandering, intimidation, and discrimination by the local French administration against the **Comité de l'Unité Togolaise** and in favor of northern and conservative political formations and thus allowed for a true reflection of the balance of political power in the territory. Secondly, the outcome of the elections shattered the complacent and pro-French **Autonomous Republic** administration of Nicolas Grunitzky and his **Parti Togolais du Progres,** brought about the CUT government of Sylvanus Olympio, and paved the way for independence. The elections were under the supervision of a Haitian administrator and a team of United Nations-appointed personnel. The various parties competed for forty-six seats equally apportioned between the north and the south of the country. The PTP hardly campaigned before the elections, being overly confident of its electoral power. Yet the results were a clearcut victory for the southern CUT, which had been in the political wilderness since 1952. The 1958 elections brought out 317,669 voters of a registered electorate of 489,519, who voted in the following manner:

Party	Votes	Seats
CUT	191,220	29
UCPN	56,517	10
PTP	40,569	3
Independents	22,611	4

ELECTIONS OF DECEMBER 1979. The elections of December 1979 were the first since independence and were held under the constitution that set up the Third Republic. There were in essence three votes: for the presidency, the uniparty National Assembly, and as ratification of the constitution itself. The official turnout was 98 percent, of which 99.9 percent ratified the constitution, the National Assembly list, and the choice of Eyadema as president.

ELECTIONS OF 1985. The elections of March 24, 1985, the second under the Eyadema regime, were marked by a high (seventy-nine percent) turnout and greater competition for the sixty-six seats. Though all candidates ran under the banner of the single party, the RPT, multiple candidacies were allowed and a total 131 individuals contested the available seats. Only twenty-two incumbents were re-elected, and the new National Assembly had a lower average age than the previous one.

ELECTIONS OF 1990. The elections of March 18, 1990 for the seventy-seven seats in the National Assembly took place against the rising tide for multipartyism. In the first round on March 4th, sixty-nine seats were filled, the remaining being filled in the second round on March 18th. A total of 1.3 million voters participated in the elections and 188 candidates (with as many as six in some constituencies) ran for office.

ELECTIONS OF 1993–94. Two elections took place in 1993–94: the flawed 1993 Presidential elections in which Eyadema intimidated and barred real competitors, on the basis of which he was "re-elected," and the first multiparty elections since Eyadema's seizure of power finally took place on February 6 and 20, 1994, postponed several times due to violence, attempted coups, massive union strikes, and intimidation by the Togolese armed forces.

Despite a measure of intimidation and irregularities in several districts, the parliamentary elections were seen by most foreign monitors and observers as basically fair. The largest number of seats (thirty-six) was won by the southern **Comité d'Action pour le Renouveau** (CAR) coalition of **Yao Agboyibor,** followed by Eyadema's **RPT** with thirty-five seats (all in the North), both trailed by the Union Togolaise pour la Démocratie with seven and the Union pour la Justice et la Démocratie (UJD) with two. The much discredited interim Prime Minister Koffigoh did not align himself with any party and won his own seat in the second round. After the resignation of Koffigoh's transitional government of national unity, Eyadema appointed Edem Kodjo of the minority UTD as his new Prime Minister in an effort to further split the southern vote, deeply divided by Kodjo's being unwilling to form an electoral alliance with the CAR.

In the Presidential elections of August 25, 1993, General Eyadema ran against himself, as international observers pulled out of the country in order not to provide any legitimacy to a non-event. All but two minor independent candidates (Ife Adani who got 1.87% of the vote and Jacques Amouzou who obtained 1.64%) boycotted the election after Eyadema engineered the disqualification of **Gilchrist Olympio.** The turnout was just 39.5% of the electorate.

EL LOKO, 1950– . Well-known Togolese sculptor, residing abroad. Born in 1950 in Pedakondji, El Loko studied textile design in Accra, Ghana before entering the German State Academy of Art at

Dusseldorf to study under Joseph Beuys. He returned to Togo for a few years, but disenchanted by conditions in his home country, he returned to Germany to live in Duisburg. He has had major exhibitions (since 1972) in galleries in Germany, Poland, Denmark, Sweden, Switzerland, and the United States, as well as in Africa.

ESPOIR DE LA NATION TOGOLAISE. Quasi-monthly socio-cultural publication issued by Togo's official publishing house, the Etablissement National des Editions du Togo, under the auspices of the Ministry of Information and the directorship of M. Awesso. The journal's circulation is around 5,000.

ESSO, SILITOKO. General Director of **Television Togolaise.**

ETABLISSEMENT NATIONAL DES EDITIONS DU TOGO (EDI-TOGO). Established in 1961 as a public corporation to prepare and issue the publication needs of the Ministry of Education, the Information Services, and other government agencies. One of EDITOGO's prime responsibilities since 1962 has been the publication of Togo's daily newspaper, *Togo Presse* (renamed *La Nouvelle Marche*), and subsequently a variety of government-sponsored monthlies. Operating at all times at a significant deficit, EDITOGO receives sizable government subsidies. Total government investments to EDITOGO amount to 500 million CFAF; its turnover in 1989 was 645 million CFAF and it employed 420 workers.

ETUDES TOGOLAISES. Very valuable academic series of reports, studies, and collections of oral history and linguistics, issued at irregular intervals by the **Institut Togolais des Sciences Humaines.** The Institute was established in 1960, and the first issue of *Etudes Togolaises* was published in December 1965.

EUROPEAN DEVELOPMENT FUND (EDF) *see* FONDS EUROPEEN DE DEVELOPPEMENT.

EUROPEAN ECONOMIC COMMUNITY (EEC). Consequent to the Yaoundé convention of 1963 and 1969, Togo has been an associate member of the EEC, receiving preferential tariff treatment for her commodity exports and partaking of the community's technical assistance fund, the Fonds Europeen de Développement.

EVALA. Traditional wrestling bouts and other exhibitions of martial arts and prowess practiced among the Kabré of the North. The custom is aimed at inculcating into youth a fighting spirit and testing their physical and moral strength. The bouts are divided according to age, from eight to thirty years, but the main festivities center around those coming of age—the eighteen year olds. There is an equivalent ceremony for females, the Akéma. In recent years the Evala has been further built up by ethnic elders as a force to keep Kabré youth united. General Eyadema has elevated the Evala ceremonies to the status of a quasi-public holiday: annually going to his native village, Pya, for two weeks, he is usually accompanied by virtually all the influential Kabré politicians in Lomé, bringing government and administration to a standstill. The local television station also offers two hours of the wrestling on a daily basis, causing deep resentment in the south.

EVEGBE. The Ewe language, as called by the Ewe. The language has many dialects: three are the Anlo, spoken by the **Anlo** Ewe of Ghana; the Mina (or Gé) spoken by Togo's **Mina** in Aného; and Ouatchi, the dialect of the Ouatchi along the coast and in Atakpamé. (*See* ADJA; EWE.) There is a considerable amount of vernacular literature (especially in the Anlo dialect) including religious tracts, translations of the Bible, and educational material. Many important scholars have analyzed Evegbé, including the noted linguist Dr. Diedrich Westermann, who compiled the seminal *Die Ewe-Stamme.* The language is spoken by over one million people in southern Togo, southwest Benin, and southeast Ghana and is understood by considerably more, being part of the Kwa language family of which the closely related Fon and Adja (of Benin) are also members.

EVEIL DU TRAVAILLEURS TOGOLAIS, Publication of the CGTT trade union confederation.

EVOLUE *see* ASSIMILATION POLICY; INDIGENAT.

EWE. A group of **Adja** clans living in southeastern Ghana, southwest Benin, and southern Togo and speaking a variety of dialects of the **Evegbé** languages. The total number of Adja in Togo, Benin, and Ghana is estimated at over 1,250,000. As do some other neighboring ethnic groups, the Ewe trace their origins to Oyo (in Nigeria), from which they migrated in the thirteenth century via Ketou (Benin) to **Tado** and then to **Notsé.** *See* ADJA. Early in the seventeenth century, the Ewe dispersed from Notsé as a consequence of the brutalities of their king, **Agokoli,** several groups swinging back to Benin to found the Allada kingdom (and later that of Dahomey), the others moving mostly to the south. The latter never developed a centralized state structure, supposedly because of their experience with authoritarian rule under Agokoli. Essentially peaceful, the Ewe remained instead a series of clans of origin, or **dou,** and subclans (approximately 120) bound to each other by temporary alliances. Chiefly authority has usually been weak and mostly ceremonial with popular councils or assemblies, **fiahawo,** playing a more important role. Referring to this decentralized form of authority along the Togolese coast, early European charts carried the designation "**Mina** Republics" for the area between the Gold Coast's Ashanti and Dahomey (now Benin). In 1993 Togo's Ewe were estimated at approximately 650,000 and were concentrated mostly in the Tsevié and Kloto regions, but to them should be added the very closely related **Ouatchi**—numbering 210,000—**Adja** and other coastal groups. Attempts to bring about the unification of all Ewe clans under one colonial administration sparked the creation of several pan-Ewe movements in both the Gold Coast (*see* ALL-EWE CONFERENCE) and in French Togo. (*See* COMITE DE L'UNITE TOGOLAISE.) The Ewe "problem" (referring to the division of the Ewe among several colonial administrations in British Togo, French Togo, and the Gold Coast with small minorities also in Dahomey) preoccupied the Trusteeship Council of the United Nations in the 1940s and 1950s; the issue was not resolved as the Ewe are still divided by the Ghana-Togo border. Ewe pan-nationalism has not abated since independence and was even lauded (for both pragmatic and nationalistic reasons) by President Eyadema, a northerner, who in the 1970s had in his cabinet several officials specifically charged with exploiting this issue in relations vis à vis Ghana. On January 13, 1976, for example, the government published an ad in the London *Times* calling for a "restoration" of Togo's pre-colonial borders—a direct challenge to Ghana. The regime also supported irredentist ("Liberation") movements on both sides of the border, though their activities often escalated beyond the control of Lomé.

The Ewe were quick to profit from the various avenues of upward mobility that presented themselves with the advent of colonial rule, especially education. During the German **Musterkolonie** era, the Ewe were regarded as the future administrators of German Africa; the subsequent French administration also heavily utilized skilled and educated Ewe personnel at all levels of the colonial civil service, both in Togo and in other French colonies. The gross disparity between all social indicators in the south and those of the north contributed to interethnic strife in Togo and the grudges harbored in the north against the more advanced and domineering coastal elements. The CUT's political dominance between 1958 and 1963 further exacerbated these tensions, which the subsequent Grunitzky administration (1963–67) did little to alleviate. Only with the rise of the regime of General Eyadema has the pro-southern bias been corrected, though the top echelons of Eyadema's pre-1990 RPT party, administration, and civil service were heavily staffed with Ewe, Mina, and other coastal elements. Extremely few Ewe (0.1%) are Muslim: most are either still animist or (increasingly) Christian.

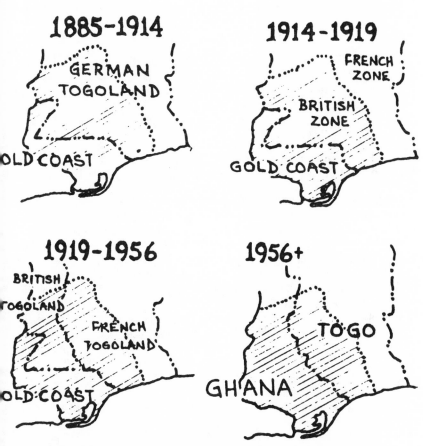

SKETCH MAP OF PARTITIONS OF THE EWE (adapted from J. S. Coleman, *Togoland*, New York, 1956).

EWE EVANGELICAL CHURCH (EEC) *see* EGLISE EVANGELIQUE DU TOGO.

EWE PRESBYTERIAN CHURCH (EPC) *see* EGLISE EVANGELIQUE DU TOGO.

EWE UNIONIST ASSOCIATION (EUA) *see* CHAPMAN, DANIEL; ALL-EWE CONFERENCE.

EWOMSAN, KOKOU MAWUENA (DIEUDONNE), 1954– . Educator. Born in Agomé-Koutoukpa on July 30, 1954, Ewomsan was educated in Atakpamé and Lomé and then studied Philosophy and Social Science at the University of Benin. A founding member of the Togolese Society of Men of Letters, Ewomsan is the author of numerous poems and currently teaches Philosophy in a Lomé school.

EXPORT PROCESSING ZONE *see* ZONE FRANCHE DE TRANSFORMATION POUR L'EXPLOITATION (ZFTE).

EYADEMA, GNASSINGBE (ETIENNE) (GENERAL), 1937– . De facto President of Togo since 1967, Chief of Staff of the Togolese armed forces, and President of the **Rassemblement du Peuple Togolais.** Born in Pya (near Kara) on December 26, 1937 to Kabré parents, Eyadema (whose real name is Gnassingbé, Eyadema being a Kabré term self-chosen *after* he killed Olympio, connoting "courage") barely completed six years of primary schooling before enlisting in the French colonial forces at the age of sixteen. He saw action in Indochina (1953–55) and Algeria (1956–61), following which he was stationed in Dahomey and Niger before being repatriated to Lomé in 1962 with NCO rank. A member of the core group of veterans that petitioned President Sylvanus Olympio for their integration into an enlarged Togolese Army, Eyadema assumed the mantle of leadership on the eve of the 1963 coup d'etat when his compatriot Emmanuel Bodjollé, the official leader, refused to mount the assault against Olympio. *See* BODJOLLE, EMMANUEL; COUP OF 1963; ARMED FORCES. During that assault Eyadema cold-bloodedly killed the hapless Olympio and fabricated evidence to suggest the latter was killed while trying to seek refuge at the American Embassy. (Since the uprising against his rule in 1990 some less complimentary accounts of the events of 1963 have been published.)

After the coup d'état all the key NCO veterans joined the Army and were promoted to the officer corps. Eyadema became a First Lieutenant in 1963 and moved up the ranks under the Grunitzky administration to Captain (1963), Major (1964), and Lieutenant Colonel (1965), becoming a General after his coup d'etat of 1967. In the meantime, a tug-of-war between Eyadema and Bodjollé was resolved with

Bodjollé's purge and imprisonment and Eyadema's assumption of the command of the armed forces. In the November 1966 popular uprising against Grunitzky—*see* COUP (ATTEMPTED) OF 1966—Eyadema supported the incumbent administration out of apprehensions that any new regime would be dominated by **PUT** militants that would demand his purge and trial for Olympio's assassination. Grunitzky's unpopularity and increasingly unstable hold over the country, however, indicated that a change of leadership was imminent, and in the absence of any suitable alternative candidates, the decision was taken by the officer corps (as early as November 1966) that the army would assume power on the anniversary of the first coup d'état. Following the coup, Colonel **Kleber Dadjo** was placed in charge of an interim **Comité de Reconciliation Nationale** and in April 1967—citing the country's sharp ethnic cleavages and the difficulties of getting Togo's politicians to cooperate—Eyadema took over executive power and set up his first cabinet. The date of the two coups (January 13) was subsequently declared a public holiday, much to the consternation of southern elements who viewed this as glorification of Olympio's assassination. *See* JOURNEE DE LIBERATION NATIONALE.

Until 1969, when the **Rassemblement du Peuple Togolais** was set up, Eyadema's style in office reflected his insecurity as a northern leader ruling a country whose largest elites were from the south. Having originally declared that his regime would be an interim one, and that he had no political ambitions and merely wished to alleviate the worst of the social cleavages before turning over power to competent civilian politicians, Eyadema openly courted influential southern groups (such as Lomé's powerful marketwomen, trade unions, etc.) while periodically orchestrating "popular" demonstrations in favor of his remaining in office. Though the National Assembly and existing political parties were banned, a **Comité Constitutionnel** was set up to hammer out a new constitution for Togo, although the proposed draft was rejected by the newly created RPT national party on the grounds that the constitutionalization of the country was still premature in light of continuing ethnic friction. By 1969, the regime, fiscally bolstered by increased phosphate revenues and grudgingly popular in the south because of its laxness on smuggling activities with Ghana, declared its permanence by "popular demand." A plebiscite (1972) later confirmed that Eyadema's popularity in the north was matched at least by the unwillingness of sizable elements in the south to see an end to his (economically) beneficial administration, despite his northern origin, military credentials, and role in the Olympio assassination. Since 1969 and 1970, Eyadema's regime has appeared more secure and comfortable in office, with Eyadema himself projecting the image of a truly national, and civilian, leader.

General Eyadema's success at the helm of the nation during his *early* years in office was due to his total command of the largely northern armed forces, a very liberal import-export code (that resulted in profitable smuggling activities to/from Ghana and cheap prices domestically), increased governmental revenues for the expanding civil service, and development projects (flowing into the treasury from the progressively nationalized phosphate industry), as well as to his own open administration, pragmatic leadership, and astute top echelon appointments to the cabinet and civil service. Surrounded by innovative technocrats and intellectuals with relative autonomy in their spheres of competence, Togo has moved out of its previous isolationism while forging ahead for the first time in the modernization of its northern regions. Since 1972 the country has pursued a more aggressive domestic and foreign policy (*see* AUTHENTICITY; COTOMIB) both of which have proved relatively popular to the more militant coastal elites. The armed forces were relatively unobtrusive (though always vigilant) in daily life and only moderately involved in either politics or administration. On the other hand, the Army's corporate needs have traditionally been the first to be satisfied, averting the gripes and grudges that have developed in many other armies on the continent. Signifying his intent to remain at the apex of power for the foreseeable future, in 1980 Eyadema engineered the adoption of a new constitution and holding of elections—the country's first in sixteen years, following this up by other elections in 1985 and 1990.

Much of the early favorable image of the Eyadema reign was to change in the late 1970s as public finances decayed due to the mounting official corruption and the massive State splurges of 1974 resting on erroneous assessments that global prices for phosphates would remain high. The regime had, however, mounted a large number of very costly projects—some of which had to be scrapped altogether, many in midstream—that began piling up debts and deficits that could not be met. Eyadema tarried before calling an end to public spending, again assuming phosphate prices would rebound. (They actually brought a fiscal bonanza for only one year!) By the mid-1970s corruption had seeped in, having previously been held at bay. Northern pride in "their" leader, Eyadema's vanity, and North Korean advice led to the emergence of an extremely oppressive cult of personality, reminiscent of Stalinist Russia: references to Eyadema became more laudatory; statues in his likeness began to permeate all parts of Togo; his "collected speeches" were published in a three-volume collection; and there were even leaks that he was hoping to be nominated for a Nobel Peace Prize. Early astute cabinet and administrative appointments gave way to the nomination of opportunistic and corrupt "yes men," cronies, relatives, and friends who were neither reined in nor disciplined, leading in 1984 to a World Bank decision not to help Togo with structural adjustment unless several key individuals were removed from positions where they had access to fiscal infusions.

All of these progressively disenchanted the Ewe South which suffered more from the country's economic problems and, never fully granting Eyadema legitimacy, began to be drawn behind opposition candidates, including Olympio's self-exiled sons in Paris. Eyadema's response to his loss of legitimacy was an increased reliance on brute force. What began as a string of arrests of political opponents and military officers in the mid-to-late 1970s ushered in routine reliance on torture and liquidation in prison of anyone who opposed the regime or conspired against it, a process accelerating as conditions in Togo plummeted and opposition mounted. Amnesty International has documented many of these abuses of human rights that included even brutalization and killing of students who merely vocally opposed the regime.

By the late 1980s the regime was reeling from mismanagement and corruption and was fiscally bankrupt to boot. As structural adjustments were implemented, a large number of denationalizations of the country's State companies took place. (Symbolizing the effectiveness of good management in reversing deficits, the former deficitory national steel mills—for long closed under lock and key—turned in a profit within *one* month of coming under private control.) Then the pro-democracy movement suddenly reached Togo, forcing a much-rattled Eyadema to concede the convening of a National Conference that proceeded to strip him of all powers, called for his demise, decreed the dissolution of the RPT party, and documented the civic and economic abuses of his reign, including his ill-gotten wealth (eighty billion CFAF) and brutalization of aides who annoy him.

Eyadema was not to be dislodged from power easily, however. Entrenched in the Presidential Palace he retaliated through his command of the armed forces—though claiming they were acting outside his control on behalf of the "nation." Numerous individual killings, several crass massacres, attempted assassinations on important political opposition figures (who returned to Togo to campaign in the now officially "open" political system), assaults on the National Conference, the National Assembly, and Radio-Togo (forced to broadcast Northern demands), and even the kidnap of interim Prime Minister Koffigoh indicated Eyadema did not intend to resign. Indeed an eighteen-month near-total strike in southern towns (that devastated the economy and has been likened to civil war without weapons) failed to dislodge the dictator.

Ultimately, a battle-weary Koffigoh was forced to consent to Eyadema and the RPT's participation in the much postponed elections, scrapping original legislation (and constitutional provisions) barring the two. Eyadema, using brute intimidation and electoral technicalities succeeded to disqualify his main competitor (Gilchrist Olympio), leading to the withdrawal from the Presidential race of most viable candidates, resulting in Eyadema's "re-election" in 1993 with ninety-three percent of the vote of at the most a thirty-nine percent poll. Eyadema's actions brought about a boycott of the subsequent parliamentary elections by Gilchrist Olympio and several other southern parties that worked to Eyadema's advantage. Using similar intimidation and much violence by his armed forces he was able to get the north to vote cohesively behind his RPT in the 1994 elections, with the party ending up second in size in the Assembly. In April 1994 he then nominated the leader of a minor moderate (Ewe) party, Edem Kodjo, as Prime Minister (in a coalition government between the latter's UTD, the RPT, and some small parties), assuring his immunity from parliamentary assaults.

The regime, however, remains utterly discredited internationally, though the country is too weary from the strife of 1990–1993 to continue the struggle against the Eyadema dictatorship. The main opposition—Gilchrist Olympio—is again underground, engineering violent assaults against Eyadema, as happened in 1994 (*see* COUP [ATTEMPTED] OF 1994). Inside the country Yao Agboyibor, leader of the country's largest party (CAR) and denied the right to form a government, is biding his time in opposition, as Kodjo—just like Koffigoh before him—discredits himself by association with Eyadema. Civil society continues its disengagement and passive resistance to the regime in Lomé.

EYADEMA FOUNDATION. Formally established on March 3, 1977 with the financial backing of the German Hans Seidel Foundation and the personal support of Eyadema's friend Franz Joseph Strauss. The Foundation involves itself in projects of job training and adult literacy in the countryside.

EYADEMA'S PLANE CRASHES. Two crashes within the space of one year, involving President Eyadema's planes, allegedly aimed at his assassination by disgruntled French officials of **COTOMIB**. The first crash involved Eyadema's DC-3 plane that force-landed on January 24, 1974 in the Kara area, resulting in Eyadema's injury and the death of the French pilot and three passengers. The second crash occurred in January 1975, shortly after Eyadema took possession of a new jet. The plane crashed after flying Niger's President Kouantché back to Niamey following Eyadema's mediation efforts in the border crisis between Upper Volta (now Burkina Faso) and Mali. Killed were its

American pilot and two crew members. Shortly after the 1974 crash, the French officials of COTOMIB were denounced for their role in the affair, and it was revealed that the company had earlier tried to bribe Eyadema with 1.5 million CFA francs to prevent the nationalization of Togo's phosphate industry. COTOMIB was then nationalized with a great deal of fanfare and the date (January 24) was declared a national holiday. *See* JOURNEE NATIONALE DE LIBERATION ECONOMIQUE. The site of the first crash (Sarakawa) was kept intact, improved, and became a veritable national shrine, part of the grotesque Eyadema Personality Cult to which youth (mostly Kabré) came in droves to "re-dedicate" themselves to selfless service to Togo's development. In Lomé a Sarakawa Hotel was built, and the myth of the invincibility of Togo's *Le Guide* was expounded.

F

FA. Ewe word referring to destiny as dictated by the spirits and gods. Fa can be foreseen by the **bokonou,** who are still highly respected in the southern and central Togolese villages. There are a large number of ways to divine fate, one common way being through the manipulation and examination of sixteen palm kernels on a rectangular board. Divination procedures (different) also exist in non-Ewe areas.

FAILLE D'ALEDJO. A narrow cut through solid rock cliffs through which Togo's main north-south highway passes in the northern part of the country. Actually a minor curiosity, the cut is touted as a major Togolese tourist attraction.

FANTOGNON, FRANOIS XAVIER KOKOU, 1934– . Senior civil administrator and water engineer. Born in Atakpamé on December 21, 1934 and educated abroad as a hydraulic engineer. Fantognon joined the Ministry of Public Works in 1960 and was appointed head of the Southern Hydraulic Subdivision of Togo (1960–66). After a series of advanced courses in Germany, Fantognon became (in 1967) head of the Togolese Water Service.

FARE, KPANDA GINGUITCHA. Former cabinet minister. Fare was appointed Minister of the Environment in the interim December 1992 cabinet as an RPT delegate balancing a largely southern cabinet after Kottigah's concessions to Eyadema following his kidnapping. He resigned on orders from Eyadema in July 1992 in protest over the cabinet's linking the latter's son with the attempted assassination of Gilchrist Olympio, then campaigning in central Togo.

FAZAO FOREST RESERVE. The Forest de Fazao is found in the Plateaux region and is a heavily wooded area of significant tourist interest. It links up with the Reserve de Koué and stretches from Bassar to Blitta, parallel to (but not abutting) the Ghana border.

FEDERATION DES ETUDIANTS DE L'AFRIQUE NOIRE EN FRANCE (FEANF). Militant union of Francophone Africa's students in France, with branches in most university cities. Several of Togo's current intellectuals and professionals played a role in FEANF during their student days, including **Louis Amega, Richard Dogbéh,** and **Noe Kutuklui.**

FETISHISTS. Priests of the various fetish cults, **bokonou** of the **fa,** and venerators of spirits and other deities. Still very prevalent in Togo (where two thirds of the population have animist religious beliefs) in the non-Muslim areas of the south and center, where an association of fetishists meets annually in a quasi-convention. Two of the most important fetish ritual shrines are in Doumé (Benin) and Shiari (Ghana). Every seven years there is a pilgrimage to the latter site where the chief fetishist of Atakpamé is invested.

FIADJOE, ROBERT EDMOND, 1919– . Physician and former Deputy Mayor of Lomé. Born in Lomé on October 31, 1919, Fiadjoe was educated locally and abroad (obtaining a degree in Medicine), following which he worked as resident physician at Lomé's National Hospital. A member of the **Comité de l'Unité Togolaise,** Fiadjoe entered political life in the early 1950s and served as Deputy Mayor of Lomé between 1959 and 1962. In 1961 he was elected to the National Assembly where he served as Vice President of the Defense and Foreign Affairs Committee. Returning to medical practice after the coup that brought down the Olympio regime, Dr. Fiadjoe was arrested in 1970 for alleged involvement in the attempted coup of that year. *See* COUP (ATTEMPTED) OF 1970. Amnestied early in 1971, Fiadjoe immediately enrolled in the **Rassemblement du Peuple Togolais** to indicate his support for the Eyadema regime. Despite advanced age he remained Chief Physician at Lomé Polyclinique until finally retiring in 1987.

FIGAN, YAOVI SESSE, 1946– . Agronomist. Born in 1946 and educated abroad in Agronomy, Figan has been the long-serving director of Research at Lomé's SOTED. He is the author of several works on Togo's indigenous fruits and their possible exploitation.

FIO AGBANO II, 1898–1973. Former superior chief of **Glidji** and important early political supporter of the **Comité de l'Unité Togolaise.**

Born in Glidji on June 24, 1898 to a chiefly family, Fio Agbano's support for the CUT was an important aid to the party's rapid assumption of political leadership in the south and part of the traditional network of allegiances hammered out by Sylvanus Olympio. With the rise of the latter's government in 1958, Fio Agbano was elected to the National Assembly and served there until the coup d'état of 1963. The permanent Vice President of the Assembly, Fio Agbano was also Vice President of the Committee on Justice, Legislation, Institutional, and Administrative Affairs. Largely shunted aside after the coup, Fio Agbano was a member of Togo's Chamber of Commerce before his death in 1973.

FIOHAWO. Assembly of chiefs and notables of an Ewe **dou** that, together with the nominal sovereign the **Asafohene,** exercises traditional authority over the **dou.**

FOFONA, SAIBOU DERMANE. Administrator and former cabinet minister. Fofona joined General Eyadema's cabinet in September 1973 as Minister of Rural Development after a career as an administrator based in the north (Kandé). In March 1975 Fofona was dropped from the cabinet and assumed administrative-technical duties in his previous ministry.

FOLI BEBE, KING (c.1694–1733) OF GLIDJI. Data on the legendary founder of the Glidji kingdom (see Aného) is very contradictory, but he succeeded Ofory around 1694 (hence being the second King of the dynasty) and is regarded as the true founder of the small kingdom.

FOLIGAN, JEAN. A teacher by profession, Foligan has been Director of the Centre Pedagogique National since 1966 and a senior official in the Ministry of Education.

FOLKA 80. Major cultural festival held in Lomé in April 1980. The program gathered the various ethnic groups of the country in a pageant of dance and folklore throughout the streets of the capital Lomé. The richness and diversity of the Togolese ethnic fabric and culture was dramatically visible in the carnival-style festivities.

FON. Neighboring Benin's major ethnic group, founding core of the ancient Dahomey Kingdom that periodically ravaged the Atakpamé area in Togo. (*See* ATAKPAME WARS.) Some 25,000 Fon are found in Togo along the southern border areas. They are mostly farmers.

FON-MAHI. Collective name in Togo for two separate ethnic groups found mostly in Benin, elements of which were chased into Togo and settled in the Atakpamé region that became a place of refuge for anti-Dahomean forces. Both the **Fon** (the actual dominant group in the former Dahomey kingdom) and the Mah (traditionally raided for slaves by the latter) settled in Togo around the year 1854 after migrating from the Allada and Savalou regions respectively. They have conserved their language, customs, and beliefs, the Mahi also retaining traditional allegiance to the Savalou royal family. Together they number around 35,000 and are found in small groups, mostly in the south.

FONDS AFRICAIN DE SOLIDARITE (FAS). The African Solidarity Fund was set up in 1976 by France and fifteen former colonies in Africa, aimed at alleviating fiscal pressures upon member states caused by the oil crisis, while also deepening Franco-African economic ties.

FONDS COMMUN DES SOCIETES DE PREVOYANCE (FCSP) *see* SOCIETE INDIGENE DE PREVOYANCE.

FONDS D'AIDE ET DE COOPERATION (FAC). French development fund dispensing financial and technical assistance to former colonial territories. The FAC is the successor, after the decolonization of the French empire, of the **Fonds d'Investissement pour le Devéloppement Economique et Social des Territoires d'Outre Mer.** The fund has allocated to Togo an average of 660 million CFA francs per year since its creation in 1959, a total of 10 billion CFA francs between 1959 and 1973, and 16 billion CFA francs since. It is under FAC auspices that French *coopérants* come to Togo. Before the rioting of 1990–93 there were a total of 318 such personnel in Togo, fully 161 of whom were teachers, and 50 technicians in various Togolese ministries.

FONDS D'INVESTISSEMENT POUR LE DEVELOPPEMENT ECONOMIQUE ET SOCIAL DES TERRITOIRES D'OUTRE MER (FIDES). Precursor of the contemporary **Fonds d'Aide et de Cooperation.** French development fund that dispensed financial and technical assistance to overseas colonies and associated territories. In the ten years from 1947 to 1957, over 750 million dollars were allocated to French West Africa, though only a small proportion of this reached Togo.

FONDS EUROPEEN DE DEVELOPPEMENT (FED). The European Development Fund is an agency of the European Economic Community with which most of Africa is linked via the Yaounde treaties of 1963 and 1969. The FED allocates the Community's financial and technical assistance to member and associated states. Togo has received important credits from the FED for a variety of projects, including the paving of its entire north-south road axis.

FORCE DE RECONCILIATION ET SECURITE (FORS 93). Special security force of gendarmes, police, and prefectural guards—but not military troops—set up in February 1993 to assure peace during the 1993 elections in Togo, demanded by the various opposition candidates (feeling threatened by Eyadema's troops) as a precondition for participating in the election. The force grew to 3,500 men by June 1993, part of its budget picked up by various foreign donors.

FORCES D'INTERVENTION RAPIDE (FIR). Elite mostly Northern 200-man paracommando force with high mobility and superior firepower that is one of General Eyadema's main military props vis-à-vis society. The FIR is under the command of Major Yoma Narcisse Djoua and was behind much of the societal repression and brutalities of 1991–93.

FORUM HEBDO. Independent weekly that emerged after the 1990 relaxation of freedom of the press. The paper, that has a press run of around 3,000, has reported a variety of murderous government acts that might otherwise have gone unreported: a good example being the casual mowing down of protesting villagers by troops at Bena, 250 kms. north of Lomé. The paper's entire press-run of January 1991 was confiscated by Eyadema for daring to print pictures of that atrocity, the regime claiming this was an attempt to incite rebellion in Togo.

FOSSE AUX LIONS. The Foret de la Fosse aux Lions is a small national forest just southwest of Dapaong in the far north of the country.

FOURN, KIKI. Former Mayor of Lomé. Coming from a prominent early political family, Fourn was imprisoned by General Eyadema between 1982 and 1984.

FRANC ZONE. Monetary transaction association formed by most of the territories previously ruled by France, including the **Communauté Financiere Africaine.** National or regional currencies (such as the CFA franc) are pegged to the French franc and are freely convertible and transferable within the Franc Zone, which is under French fiscal control.

FREITAS, HORATIO GBENON. Former cabinet minister. A leader of the post-1990 UTR party, Freitas (who comes from an important **Brazilian** Aného family) was brought into the interim Koffigoh government on September 7, 1991 as Minister of Youth, Sports and Leisure and was retained in the third transitional government, an alliance with the RPT. He was dropped from the cabinet of the next government on February 1993.

FREITAS, PAULIN JACINTO, 1909– . Educator, administrator, and former Minister of Foreign Affairs. Born in Lomé on December 3, 1909 to an important Aného family of **Brazilian** origins, Freitas was educated in Senegal and returned to Togo to work as a teacher. An active member and leader of the **Comité de l'Unité Togolaise** since its inception, Freitas was dismissed from his teaching post by the French administration for his political involvements. In 1946 he was elected on the CUT ticket as deputy to the Assemblée Representative, and he served on the various Assemblies between 1946 and 1955 and again between 1958 and 1961. With the rise of Olympio's government in 1958, Freitas moved into the cabinet, first as Minister of State in charge of Interior, Press and Information (1958–60) and then as Minister of Foreign Affairs (1960–63). Since 1963 he has not been active politically, serving with the World Health Organization in Brazzaville until his retirement in 1974. In 1987 General Eyadema, seeking partial reconciliation with southern leaders, met with the aging Freitas in a much publicized visit.

FRENCH ADMINISTRATION. On August 8, 1914, French troops moved into Togo from Dahomey (now Benin) and occupied Aného, Porto Seguro, and Togoville. Lomé was occupied the next day, and the German colonial presence in the territory was virtually over eighteen days later. Simultaneously with the French assault, British troops were brought in by sea from the Gold Coast. The colony was subsequently divided into British and French spheres of occupation, with the former smaller in size but containing Lomé, the rich cocoa/coffee producing areas, and the larger segment of Togo's railroads. Following the end of the war, the Allies redrew their spheres of occupation (with France assuming control of Lomé and the railroads) and were granted mandates over what were called British and French Togoland. In actual fact, the administration of the two (class B) mandates was no different from that of the other colonial possessions of the two metropolitan powers. Freedom of religion was guaranteed, but military recruitr. ..t was prohibited. *See* ARMED FORCES for the repercussion of the latter on the evolution of Togo.

Except for a brief period between the two World Wars, French Togo was not part of the **French West Africa** federation. The territory's governor was directly responsible to the Minister of Overseas France in Paris and not to the **AOF** Governor-General in Dakar, Senegal. Administratively, France's rule over Togo falls into four periods: (a) between 1914 and 1922 the era of direct military occupation during and following World War I; (b) from 1922 to 1934 a period of autonomy of the French administration in Togo from the AOF administration in Senegal; (c) between 1934 and 1936 the "personal union" of French Togo with the neighboring French colony of Dahomey, for reasons of budgetary austerity. This was discontinued in 1936 as it was not viewed favorably by the League of Nations; (d) from 1936 to 1945 the gradual de facto assimilation of French Togo into the AOF federation for administrative reasons.

During the entire period of French rule, the local administration was markedly stable, Governors or High Commissioners remained in office for longer tenures than in the neighboring French colonies, and the Africanization of the civil service was rapid. In 1932, for example, fully 599 of the 863 colonial officials were Togolese, and a ratio of over seventy-three percent indigenous staff was the norm. With the end of World War II and the establishment of the United Nations, Togo's status was changed to that of a Trusteeship Territory with France and Britain entrusted with the socio-economic and political development of their charges. In 1945 also, the **French Union** was created, and Togo was given representation in the French National Assembly. (Originally Dahomey and Togo shared one deputy, but in 1946 each territory was allocated a separate representative.) Within the Union, Togo was classified as an Associated Territory to distinguish her from France's colonies.

Under the Trusteeship Council's provisions, petitions could be heard against the Administering Powers, and much of the Council's time was spent on various petitions regarding the "Ewe question" (i.e., the pan-Ewe unification movement *see* ALL-EWE CONFERENCE), France's maladministration of her Trusteeship Territory (presented by various CUT leaders, including Sylvanus Olympio), and the very slow progress toward self-government. In 1955 France accelerated the move toward autonomy in French Togo by passing statutes that created the **Autonomous Republic of Togo.** Though the degree of internal autonomy granted to the resultant administration of **Nicolas Grunitzky** was unequalled at the time in any of France's overseas possessions, the statute was sharply criticized for its arbitrariness, continuation of the pro-French and unrepresentative regime of Grunitzky, and reflection of a lack of coordination of French policy with that of British Togo. Indeed, since the mid-1940s when the previously favored Comité de l'Unité Togolaise of Sylvanus Olympio had become a militant pan-Ewe movement with links with Ewe leaders in British Togo and the Gold Coast, the French administration had fostered the rise of alternate political formations in Togo. The CUT was viewed not so much as pan-Ewe as anti-French, a Trojan horse for British influences, and the eventual annex of the weaker French Togo into the Gold Coast (together with British Togo). The latter view seemed substantiated when the 1956 plebiscite in British Togo (*see* PLEBISCITE OF 1956) resulted in a three to two vote in favor of merger with the Gold Coast. Hence the French resistance to a similar plebiscite in French Togo and the separate evolution of the French Trusteeship territory. Two years later France was forced to accede to United Nation-supervised elections that shattered the political control of the pro-French conservative puppet-parties and led to the rise of the CUT and Olympio administration. Political differences between the latter and the new government of Ghana assured that pan-Ewe unification aspirations could not be realized upon independence in 1960.

FRENCH UNION. Structure established under the French constitution of October 1946, allowing a measure of representation in the decision-making process to French colonial territories in Paris. The French Union was composed of metropolitan France and her overseas territories, which were classified as Overseas Territories, Overseas Departments, Associated Territories, Protectorates, and Associated States. The mainland African colonies fell under the Overseas Territories heading, while Togo was classified as an Associated Territory.

The Union had a President (the President of France), a High Council, and an Assembly in which deputies from the various territories participated. The new provisions also provided for African representation in the two houses of the French Parliament and in the Economic Council. In 1945 one Deputy was allocated to Togo and Dahomey together (Dahomey's Sourou Migan Apithy was elected); in 1946 each territory received a separate Deputy.

FRENCH WEST AFRICA *see* AFRIQUE OCCIDENTALE FRANCAISE (AOF)

FRENCH WEST AFRICA (AOF), GOVERNORS (1895–1959).

1895–1900	J. B. Chandié
1900–02	N. E. Ballay
1902–08	E. N. Roumé
1908–16	W. Merlaud-Ponty
1916–17	M. F. Clozel
1917–18	J. van Vollenhoven
1918–19	G. L. Anjoulvant
1919–23	M. H. Merlin
1923–30	J. G. Cardé
1930–36	J. Brevié

1936–40	J. M. de Coppet
1940	L. H. Cayla
1940–43	P. F. Boisson
1943–46	P. C. Cournarie
1946–48	R. V. Barthès
1948–51	P. L. Bechard
1951–56	B. Cornut-Gentille
1956–58	G. Cusin
1958–59	P. A. Messmer

FRONT DES ASSOCIATIONS POUR LE RENOUVEAU (FAR). Broadly-based southern anti-Eyadema political front set up on March 15, 1991 in opposition to the regime, calling *inter alia* for the demise of Eyadema, dismissal of brutal Minister of Interior and Security General Yao Mawlikplimi, political amnesty, and competitive free elections. The FAR was headed by **Yao Agboyibor** as President of the group and Kokou Koffigoh as Vice President. It dissolved itself on April 12, 1991 when five of its twelve constituent groups set up political parties following their legalization that month. In due course the structural successor to the FAR was the **Front d'Opposition Démocratique.**

FRONT D'OPPOSITION DEMOCRATIQUE (FOD). Successor to the former **FAR.** A broad anti-Eyadema front of ten political parties (now legalized) set up in May 1991 to form a common front against the regime. The FOD negotiated the convening of a **National Conference** in June and was subsequently transformed to the Collective d'Opposition Démocratique (COD).

FRONT NATIONAL DE LIBERATION DU TOGO (FNLT). Opposition group that sprang up in the 1970s, representing an alleged military approach to General Eyadema's usurpation of power and supported by the exiled **Colonel Merlaud Lawson** in Paris. The FNLT was essentially moribund, though from time to time it did issue bulletins calling for the overthrow of Eyadema or reporting on conditions in Togo.

FRONT PATRIOTIQUE (FP). October 1992 Electoral pact between eight southern political parties, headed by **Yao Agboyibor** of the CAR party and **Edem Kodjo** of the UTD, in preparation for the 1993 legislative elections, postponed to 1994. Despite the electoral pact that stipulated a united front to assure RPT strength be kept at bay, the opportunistic Kodjo bolted the alliance after the elections (in which he gained only seven seats) when offered the post of Prime Minister by

Eyadema, thus joining the RPT in an (coalition) alliance against the CAR.

FRONT POPULAIRE DE SALUT NATIONAL DU TOGO (FPSNT). Largely moribund opposition party, based in France and in Ghana, calling for the demise of the Eyadema regime in the 1980s.

FULANI. A mostly Muslim people numbering over ten million, scattered throughout West Africa and found especially in northern Nigeria, Mali, Niger, Guinea, and Cameroun. Comparatively few Fulani made their way into Togo, and the majority there (estimated at 35,000) are to be found in northern urban and rural districts where they are frequently called Similsi. Most of Togo's Fulani (also known in French as Fulbe or Peul) are concentrated in the Dapaong and Sansanné-Mango areas. Over eighty percent of them live in the Savanes and central regions where they are involved in herding of cattle; they arrived in Togo from Mossi areas, now Burkina Faso in the north. Other groups came to Togo from Benin (to Sokodé and then south to Atakpamé or north to Dapaong). The *lamido* (chief) of the latter branch is of direct descent from Othman Dan Fodio, the great nineteenth-century Fulani leader. Togo's Fulani are, as elsewhere, mostly Muslim and pastoralists. Their religion is less puritanical, zealous, or proselytizing than elsewhere, however, and Togo was only minimally affected by the great religious battles and Fulani wars of conquest in the nineteenth century.

G

GA. Small segment of a Gold Coast ethnic group found in the Aného area. Led by two brothers, Foli Bebe and Hemazro, the migrating clan left the Accra area in 1663 (or 1687) and founded Glidji. They brought with them a stool (which allegedly they had stolen) that is still zealously guarded in the neighboring village of Zowla. The alleged theft of the stool resulted in the use of the pejorative name Ayigbé for the Ewe, Mina, and Ga, an epithet still used in the Accra region. Shortly after the foundation of Glidji, Ané refugees from the Gold Coast also migrated to the same area and founded Aného. The Ané and Ga are collectively known as **Mina,** a reference to their specific point of origin, El Mina in the Gold Coast. They have adopted the **Ouatchi** Evegbé dialect of their new home and added Ga words to it. Together the two groups number around 90,000 people. *See also* ANEHO; MINA; ANE. The Ga in Togo are also often referred to as Guin; as such they should not be confused with the Gun of Goun of neighboring Benin, of completely different origin.

GABA, KWADJO ZOKHEVO (LAURENT). Former cabinet minister and director of Togo's Société Nationale d'Investissement du Togo. A civil administrator by profession, Gaba became Deputy Director of Togo's Office of the National Budget in 1968. In 1972 he was brought into President Eyadema's cabinet as Secretary of State for Public Works but held this position for only sixteen months. In August 1973 he was shifted to head the SNIT. Accused, together with some other officials, of corruption and embezzlement during his tenure as head of SNIT, he was tried and imprisoned.

GABA, LEON. Senior tax inspector. Alternately in charge of tax inspections in the North and in the South, Gaba has also served as Chief Accountant of the Lotterie Nationale (since 1968) and has been on the commission charged with eliminating all indirect taxes in the country.

GADO, SOULEYMANE. Briefly Minister of Telecommunications in February 1990 before the onset of the several Transitional governments.

GAGLI, KODJO (EMMANUEL), 1915– . Physician, **Juvento** leader, and former cabinet minister. Born in Atakpamé on December 22, 1915, Gagli was educated locally and at the elitist Ecole William Ponty in Senegal. He returned to Togo in 1938 and for the next fifteen years worked in various clinics, completing his medical education between 1954 and 1956 at Dakar's Hospital, Bordeaux, and Paris. In 1960 he again returned to Togo and was appointed (by Sylvanus Olympio) administrator of the country's health services and later (1962) Chief Medical Officer in Dapaong. An active member of Juvento (and the party's Vice President in the mid-1960s), Dr. Gagli was elected to the National Assembly in May 1963, after the rise of the Grunitzky administration. He served as the assembly's Deputy Vice President (1965), Vice President (1966), President of the Institutional Committee (1963–64), and Vice President of the Assembly's Bureau (1965–66). In 1965 and 1966 he was also municipal councilor of Kpalimé and, following the **Méatchi-Mama clash,** he was briefly brought into the cabinet as Minister of Health and Justice (November–December 1966) and then Minister of Health (December 1966–January 1967). He was a member of the **Comité Constitutionnel** that was set up after the 1967 coup d'etat. Between 1968 and 1984 (when he went into retirement) Gagli has been Co-Director of Togo's National Hygienic Institute and Chief Medical Officer of the Traumatology Clinic.

GALLY, DJOVI. Lawyer and civic leader. Formerly an RPT member and close to General Eyadema, Gally changed sides in 1991 and set up a pro-democracy movement, the Association pour la Promotion de l'Etat de Droit.

GAM, H. BENOIT, 1931– . Until recently Director of the civil service. Born in Grand Popo on September 18, 1931 and trained for an administrative career in Paris (IHEOM), Gam joined the Ministry of Labor, Social Affairs, and Civil Service in 1960 as Deputy Director of the civil service. In 1968 he was promoted to the headship and was in charge of all the country's civil servants until his retirement in 1990.

GAME SU. Monthly publication issued by the Ministries of Education and of Social Affairs. Set up in 1972 to reach an audience normally totally outside readership circulation in the deep "outback" rural areas. It has been remarkably successful with an extremely high (for Togo) readership of 8,000 and a strong reader feedback, an indication that it was satisfying a felt need.

GARDE TOGOLAISE *see* ARMED FORCES.

GARTNER, OTTO AUGUSTIN, 1933– . Civil engineer. Born in Lomé on August 28, 1933 and educated at home and abroad in mathematics and engineering, Gartner has been, since 1968, head of Petroleum Services in the Ministry of Public Works, Mines and Transportation, based in Lomé.

GASSOU, ERNEST ANANI, 1931– . Former Minister of Rural Development, former Director of the **Société Nationale pour le Développement de la Palmeraie et les Huileries,** and former Deputy Secretary General of the CUT parliamentary party. An Ewe born in Bobo-Ahlon on October 21, 1931, Gassou was trained as an agricultural engineer. A CUT militant in his youth, Gassou was elected to the National Assembly (from Kloto) in 1958 and remained a deputy until the 1963 coup d'état. In the assembly, he rose to be Deputy Secretary General of the CUT parlimentary party. Following the coup, Gassou was involved in several plots against the Grunitzky regime. In 1967 he was appointed Deputy Director of the Agricultural Services; in 1968, director of the Palm plantations section of the Ministry of Agriculture; and a few years later, director of SONAPH. In 1978 Gassou was again brought into the cabinet as Minister of Rural Development, a post he held until 1984.

GAYIBOR, NICOUE L. Prolific author and important Professor of History at the National University of Benin in Lomé. Gayibor has written several books on the history of various parts, mostly in the south, of

Togo (e.g. Glidji/Aného), based upon oral history that is fast disappearing in the country.

GAZARO, WERE. Pro-Koffigoh cabinet minister. Mrs. Gazaro joined the interim government of **Koffigoh** as Minister of Social Welfare and National Solidarity in December 1991 and was reappointed through the third interim government of 1993.

GBATI, KOMLAN. Briefly Minister of Labor and Civil Service (March–June 1980), Gbati was arrested while in office in connection with the sale of examination answers to civil service and school tests. It was later revealed that this practice had been going on for four years. He was released from prison in mid-1981, having served one year of his three-year sentence.

GBEDEMAH, SATI YAWO G., 1942– . Educator. Born in 1942 at the Tové Mission in Zio where he completed primary studies, attended other schools in Lomé and Sokodé. He then proceeded to the University of Aix-en-Provence obtaining degrees in History in 1971. He has taught at several secondary schools in Togo, serving also as Director of the Protestant schools of Kpalimé (1972–74) and of Lomé (1974–1979).

GBEGBENI, NANAMALE (ROBERT), 1933– . Former Minister of Labor, Civil Service, and Justice. Born in 1933 of Bassari/Konkomba origins in Koudjudjou, Gbegbeni was educated locally and worked as an educator in northern Togo before entering political life. One of the earlier members of the northern and conservative **Union des Chefs et des Populations du Nord** and later its Vice President, Gbegbeni switched allegiances in the mid-1950s, joined the **Comité de l'Unité Togolaise** and in 1955 was elected CUT deputy from Bassar (1955–1961). He was re-elected on the CUT ticket again in 1961 and participated in the electoral coalition forged after Olympio's assassination. Following the 1967 coup d'état Gbegbeni was appointed Cabinet Director of the Minister of Labor, Social Affairs, and Civil Service and, in August 1969, he was brought into Eyadema's cabinet as Minister of Commerce, Industry, and Tourism. In January 1972 Gbegbeni was reassigned to head the Ministry of Labor and the Civil Service, adding the Justice portfolio in February 1974. A hardworking and able administrator, Gbegbeni's responsibilities in the Eyadema regime steadily grew. He has also been a member of the Political Bureau of the **Rassemblement du Peuple Togolais** since 1971. In 1979 he was dropped from the cabinet to provide space for new blood but was retained as a senior administrator in the ministry.

GENDARMERIE NATIONALE. In Togo, as in most of Francophone Africa, the gendarmerie [police force] is an integral part of the country's armed forces, though maintaining a separate command hierarchy, facilities, recruitment policies, and duties. For a long time, the top hierarchy of the gendarmerie included Colonel **Menveyinoyu (Albert) Alidou Djafalo** as the force Commander and General Eyadema's most trusted lieutenant, with Lieutenant Colonel **Janvier Chango** as his deputy. With these two disappearing from the force in the mid-1970s the role of Ewe and/or Mina officers has declined, though the force is less solidly dominated by northern elements. In 1988 it was estimated that roughly sixty percent of the rank and file were Kotokoli and Kabré. *See also* ARMED FORCES.

GENERALE DES MATIERES COLORANTES (GMC) *see* LOME INDUSTRIAL ZONE.

GEOMANCY. A form of divination through the study of signs traced on the ground, part of the **Fa** cult so prevalent in Togo and Benin. It is in particular linked to the Yoruba of the region.

GERMAN ADMINISTRATION. The German administration of Togo lasted a total of thirty-one years, from July 1884 until the end of August 1914, when Anglo-French troops occupied the territory. (*See* FRENCH ADMINISTRATION.) Germany's official penetration of the area began in 1882, when German traders established themselves in Aného with a guarantee of freedom of trade. (German religious and commercial contacts had, of course, been in existence for at least seventy-five years prior to this; *see* BREMEN MISSIONARY SOCIETY, for example.) An imbroglio involving the ambitious pro-British **Lawson** family—a member of whom had declared himself sovereign and appealed for British military assistance from Lagos, Nigeria—resulted in the dispatch of the German ship *Sophie* to protect German interests in Aného. Following a classic show of force, the 1882 freedom of trade treaty was reaffirmed, but further incidents resulted in the arrest of William Lawson (at the time a British subject), whose ambitions had sparked the unrest, and his transportation to Germany. The abducted Togolese returned to Aného in July 1884 aboard the *Mowe* that was bringing **Gustav Nachtigal** to Africa to establish the formal colonial presence of Germany in the area. (At the time it was essentially Nachtigal and domestic public opinion that expanded the German colonial empire, since Bismarck was very lukewarm on the issue, preferring to see France enmeshed abroad and in the process forgetting Alsace-Lorraine.)

On July 4, 1884 a treaty was signed with the chief of the minute coastal village of Togo and, on the basis of this, the German flag was raised over the area, it was renamed the German colony of Togo, and the German penetration-occupation of the coastal and hinterland areas commenced. Competing French claims on parts of Togo (especially the areas around Aného) were resolved by the Convention of Berlin (December 24, 1885), when Germany renounced territory east of a line between **Petit Popo** and Agoué—that became part of French Dahomey (now Benin)—in exchange for French recognition of German Togo, including Porto Seguro where France had had important commercial interests. The western borders were negotiated with Britain and resolved on July 14 and 28, 1886 and signed in the Treaty of Zanzibar in 1890, with the definitive borders sanctified in the Treaty of Paris, 1897. Though both France and Britain were blocked in their northward expansion from their coastal enclaves (by the Dahomey kingdom and the Ashanti, respectively), Germany, encountering only sparse opposition in the absence of strong local kingdoms, did not exploit this advantage and never reached the Niger River, a prime colonial goal.

The German era in Togo falls into two periods: (1) the years of pacification and occupation, to 1900, and (2) the Musterkolonie period of intense development until Germany's loss of the colony with the start of World War I. Togo's capital was originally Bagida; in 1887 it was shifted to Sébé (an Aného suburb), and in 1897 Lomé, a small village, became the capital. The concerted push into the hinterland began only in 1893, though by 1899 the entire territory was fully occupied. The extension of German control in the north was relatively smooth, with only a few sporadic uprisings (*see* INSURRECTIONS OF 1897 AND 1898). Despite scattered opposition to German rule by their own clans, northern elements, especially Kotokoli, Chokossi, and Djerma, joined as auxiliary troops in the conquest of the north and quelled disturbances among the Somba, Moba, and Konkomba. Thirty-five police columns had to be dispatched on punitive and/or pacification missions between 1897 and 1901, though none of the disturbances was considered very threatening. In the south, physical occupation was not a problem either, though the German administration was faced with the problem of imposing their mastery over Mina, Ewe, and Ouatchi populations accustomed to dealing with Europeans as equals. The latter problem was resolved with the decision to grant the southern elements a privileged status within the German administration and to train them for similar second echelon duty in Germany's other colonial territories in Africa.

During the second part of the German era in Togo, the country was divided into five administrative units in the south (called *Bezirksamter*) and three northern *Stationsbezirke,* which were in turn subdivided into

Unterbezirken. (There was little real difference administratively between the *Bezirksamter* and the *Stationsbezirke.*) The northern units were virtually closed to all Europeans in order to "protect" the natives (ordinances of September 20, 1907 and October 5, 1907) and a strong pro-Muslim bias was practiced. Only in 1912 were Christian missions granted privileges in the north (Protestant in Yendi, currently in Ghana; Catholic in Sokodé). In the south, the beginnings of a well-developed economic and administrative infrastructure were laid in the years prior to World War I in an effort to transform Togo into a model colony (Musterkolonie). The German administration even boasted a powerful radio station in Kamina which could communicate directly with Berlin and with German cruisers in the Atlantic Ocean.

Germany's special affinity for Togo had all along been a function of the fact that the territory had been the only colony that had been self-sufficient from the outset and did not require any special fiscal outlays. Also, being unsuitable for colonization, it avoided the native-settler friction that developed elsewhere, embittering race relations. With the beginning of World War I an effort was made by the German Governor to keep the region a neutral one so as to prevent Africans from observing Europeans fighting each other; moreover, German forces in the colony were minimal. The proposal was rejected by the Allies and on August 8, 1914, French troops moved into Togo from Dahomey while British troops were ferried over from Accra. On August 26 the Kamina radio station fell, and with it collapsed the German administration in the territory. The conquest of Togo was the first Allied success in the war. Paradoxically, despite many harsh aspects of German colonial rule and indeed, its brevity, many Togolese fondly remembered this era and in the interwar years petitioned the League of Nations for the return of Togo to Germany, and, during World War II, there was considerable pro-German sentiment in the Colony, especially after the early collapse of France in 1940 (*see* BUND DER DEUTSCHEN TOGOLANDER). France had major difficulties in imposing her currency in her new mandate (*see* FRENCH ADMINISTRATION) with the German mark and the Austrian Maria Theresa dollar circulating freely until the mid-1930s. German nostalgia for their former Musterkolonie did not fail after World War II either; West Germany has allocated the independent Togo significant credits, especially for the port of Lomé, and remains a major source of technical assistance for Togo. Many Germans currently work in Togo, joint companies are common, and Togolese students routinely go to German universities. The sentimental links between the former metropole and the former colony were attested to when Germany's last colonial Governor, **Adolf Friedrich zu Mecklemburg,** attended the 1960 independence celebrations. *See also* GOVERNORS OF TOGO, GERMAN.

GHAN, AYICOE, 1945– . Television producer. Born in Treichville (Cote d'Ivoire) on November 4, 1945, Ghan was educated in Kpalimé, following which he proceeded to France to obtain training in audio-visual technology at Bry-sur-Marne, as well as a degree in Humanities. On his return to Togo he assumed duties with Togo Television and is currently in charge of its production division. He is also the author of numerous poems, some recently published.

GHANA-TOGO FRICTION. The state of relations between Togo and Ghana during the 1950s and 1960s vacillated from overt hostility to cool aloofness, until the overthrow of President Nkrumah in Ghana and the rise of General Eyadema in Togo. At the root of this friction were the differential forms of reaction of the various Ewe clans to the pan-Ewe unification movement during the colonial era. In the mid-1950s, major splits developed between the **Anlo**-Ewe in the Gold Coast and those in British Togoland and between the latter and the Ewe in French Togoland, over the question of whether pan-Ewe sentiments should focus upon unification of the Ewe people within the about-to-emerge Ghana or within an independent Togo state. Similarly, after the issue was "settled" in British Togoland consequent to the referendum that resulted in the merger of the latter with Ghana (*see* PLEBISCITE OF 1956), the residual ethnic pull of Togo upon Ghana's Ewe constituted a threat to the pan-African aspirations of Nkrumah. Relations between the two countries further deteriorated as a result of President Sylvanus Olympio's statement that part of the former British Togoland (now in Ghana) should be reunited with Togo, the 1956 referendum notwithstanding, and by Nkrumah's threatening speech in which he stated that Togo would soon become just another region in an expanded Ghana. Subsequent to this, the Ghana-Togo border was closed in an effort to apply economic pressure to Togo and to make Olympio more pliable. Between 1960 and 1963 a number of border skirmishes erupted between the two states, and Nkrumah gave refuge in Accra to dissident Togolese elements aiming at the overthrow of Olympio. After the assassination of Olympio—originally suspected to be Nkrumah's handwork—relations between Ghana and Togo slightly improved (Vice President Antoine Méatchi had been a refugee in Accra and was known to be a pan-Africanist), though shortly afterwards the mutual border was once again closed, much to the economic detriment of Lomé's merchants and traders. The Lagos-Accra trade was also disrupted by President Grunitzky's retaliation against transit trade to Ghana. In July 1965 the border was reopened, although relations between the two countries did not seriously improve until the late 1960s. Amicable relations then prevailed between Togo and Ghana.

In the 1970s, relations once again plummeted as continued massive smuggling along the joint Ghana-Togo border hurt Ghana's economy. At the same time, the Togolese government's official support of **TOLIMO,** an irredentist Ewe movement in Ghana, and high-level Togolese contacts with Ewe leaders in Ghana started directly to threaten the stability of the Accra regime. In 1977 Lomé even declared the need to re-examine the results of the 1956 plebiscite with a view to reunifying the various populations on both sides of the border within an expanded Togolese state. This was in a sense a declaration of support for Ewe irredentism in Ghana, and it embittered Ghana-Togo relations again. Several years later, in 1981, a series of other incidents again enflamed tensions between the two countries. Togolese **Konkomba** crossed into Ghana to join their brethren there who were on a rampage against the Nanumba, never forgiven for their 1956 vote to integrate northern Togo with Ghana. Some 1,500 casualties resulted from this orgy of ethnic fighting. A year later, with the 1981 incidents still fresh in Ghanaian minds, Ghana closed her border with Togo unilaterally, claiming that overflights over the sensitive smuggling border routes were themselves official smuggling efforts.

In 1983 the border was again closed, on Ghana's initiative, stranding hundreds of thousands of refugees recently expelled from Nigeria. Relations between Ghana and Togo continued to be uneasy during much of Jerry Rawlings's tenure as Ghanaian head of state, but due primarily to Accra's harboring of (and according to Eyadema, even abetting) elements trying to overthrow the dictatorship in Lomé. On at least five occasions (including in the 1990s) armed groups are known to have crossed to Togo from Ghana to plot or to actually assault Eyadema. Though Ghana has on numerous occasions stated that it did not sanction such activities, directly or indirectly Togolese opposition elements have used Ghana as safe haven en route to missions against Eyadema. Ghana has also been a safe haven for populations fleeing unrest at home. During the period of the non-stop southern total strike against Eyadema in 1991 and 1992 fully one third of the population of Lomé fled across the border to Ghana, as did many inhabitants of central and north Togo prior to the 1993 parliamentary elections when the army and RPT thugs hounded all potential sources of opposition to the Kasbre party.

GLIDJI. Very important historical suburban village four kilometers from Aného, north of the lagoon, of much greater traditional import than its small size and decrepit setting might indicate. Currently containing barely 1,500 people, and never much larger, Glidji was founded in the latter part of the seventeenth century (possibly as early as 1663) by Ga elements from the Gold Coast coastal areas shortly before Ané refugees settled Aného. (But the precise history, which would give primacy to one group over another, is hotly disputed by both groups.) Glidji is regarded as both the **zongo** of Aného and a venerated ancient quarter of the historic town. Many influential southern leaders and families (Ajavons; Lawsons) trace their descent from Glidji and/or Aného. Glidji has a sizable Hausa minority. *See* GA; ANE; ANEHO.

GLIME. "In the Walls" in Ewe. Popular name for **Notsé.**

GNAMEY, BENOIT MENSAH, 1938– . Journalist and poet. Born in Lomé on April 6, 1938, Gnamey moved into journalism after a brief stint as a teacher. He is well-known, working for Radio-Lomé, specializing in Literature and Sports, but is equally known for his two novels, serialized by *Togo-Presse,* and for his poetry, some of which has been published at home and abroad.

GNASSINGBE, DONOU TOYI ERNEST (COLONEL). Eyadema's eldest son and Commander of the Presidential Guard. Both he and his Guard were implicated in a variety of crimes and massacres such as the bloody **Bé Lagoon massacre** and in liquidations, assaults on government buildings, etc., including on the motorcade of **Gilchrist Olympio** in 1992. He was killed during one of these sorties in December 1992.

GNASSINGBE, ETIENNE. Actual name of General Eyadema, who took on the Kabré "Eyadema" term that signifies bravery after his murder of President Olympio in 1963.

GNEHOU, GASTON-CHARLES (CAPTAIN), 1950–1977. President Eyadema's brother-in-law. According to one official version, Gnehou was involved in a murky plot against the regime, leading to his arrest and death in prison. In actual fact Gnehou, about whom little is known, was gunned down by security personnel outside the tourist-filled Hotel de la Paix in Lomé and was then taken to the Tokoin Army Hospital where he was tortured and finally liquidated. His crime was apparently confronting and coming to blows with Eyadema over the latter's rape of the wife of one of his uncles.

GNEMENYA, KOMLAVI DOMETO. Former cabinet minister. Previously an Assistant Director of the CNCA, Gnemenya joined the cabinet in March 1987 as Minister of Youth, Information and Sports but was dismissed twenty months later, in December 1988.

GNININVI, LEOPOLD MESSAN. Political leader and presidential aspirant. Originally Professor of Physics at the University in Lomé, and a Marxist-Leninist-turned Social Democrat, Gnininvi set up a political party for his aspirations in 1990, the Convention Démocratique Panafricaine. In his bid against Koffigoh for leadership in the interim government he lost by 312 votes to 388, primarily because Gilchrist Olympio did not support him. His political candidacy was viewed with concern by both France and the United States.

GNRONFOUM, TOSSEH KOKOUVI, 1937– . Former Minister of Rural Development. Born in Lomé on October 6, 1937 and originally trained for a teaching career, Gnronfoum went to a forestry school in Cote d'Ivoire, following which he was dispatched to Barres, France (1961–63) and Nancy (1964–66). Upon his return home he served in rapid succession as Togo's Deputy Head of Water and Forests and director of **ODEF.** In January 1977 he joined the cabinet as Minister of Rural Development. The successive failures of Togo's agricultural development efforts brought about his dismissal from the cabinet in September 1982.

GOGUE, TCHABOURE AYME, 1947– . Economist and former minister. Born in 1947 and educated in Economics overseas, including in Canada, Gogue taught for several years at the University of Montreal (1973–1976) before returning to the University of Benin where he was to rise to Dean of the Faculty. Gogue has been the author of several books. With the liberalization in Togo in the 1990's he co-founded the ADDI party and joined the September 1991 interim government of Koffigoh as Minister of Planning and Territorial Development. He was shifted to head Education and Scientific Research in the next government of September 1992 but was dropped from the third government's cabinet in September 1993.

GOLFE, PREFECTURE DU. The former circonscription of Lomé, one of the five in the Maritime region renamed in the administrative reorganization of 1981. The prefecture's headquarters remains in Lomé. *See also* LOME.

GOURMA *see* GURMA.

GOVERNORS OF TOGO, FRENCH (INCLUDING HIGH COMMISSIONERS).

Fourn	March–April 1917
Woelfel	April 1917–Jan. 1922
Sasias	Jan. 1922
Bonnecarrere	Jan. 1922–Dec. 1931
DeGuise	Dec. 1931–Oct. 1933
Pêtre	Oct. 1933–April 1934
Bourgine	April 1934–Oct. 1935

Geismer	Nov. 1935–Oct. 1936
Montagné	Nov. 1936–March 1941
Delpech	March 1941–Feb. 1942
deSaint Alary	1942
Saliceti	1942–1943
Mercadier	1943–1944
Noutary	1944–1948
Cédile	1948–1951
Digo	1951–1952
Péchoux	1953–1954
Bérard	1955–1957
Spénale	1957–1960

GOVERNORS OF TOGO, GERMAN. Apart from **Gustav Nachtigal,** who was dispatched in 1884 on certain specific missions to the area, and Heinrich Randad, de facto but only interim governor, the following served as governors of German Togo.

Ernst von Falkenthal	1886–1889
Jesko von Putkammer	1889–1895
August Köhler	1895–1902
Waldemar Horn	1902–1903
Julius, Graf Zech auf Neuhofen	1904–1910
Edmund Brückner	1911–1912
Adolf Friedrich zu Mecklemburg	1912–1914

GREEN REVOLUTION (1977). A program for self-sufficiency in food-stuffs, formally launched by President Eyadema in 1977. While the program was not successful, it did bring about a degree of self-reliance for basic staples. The program relied on a variety of incentives to stimulate both production and more efficient marketing of produce. The program included government outlays for the development of animal resources, building forest reserves, diversifying crop planting and production, and expansion of such basic staples as cereals, fruits, and vegetables. Government subsidies for fertilizers and insecticides were increased. The program came under severe fiscal cuts during the 1981–82 RPT scrutiny of state enterprises.

GROUP ASSOR. Powerful Paris-based marketing and purchasing agency that controlled much of Togo's import/export trade prior to 1990, as well as General Eyadema's personal financial transactions and investments. *See* ASSOR, MAURICE.

GROUPE DE REFLEXION ET D'ACTION DES JEUNES POUR LA DEMOCRATIE (GRAD). Youth and student group that sprang up in

1990 to press for democracy, multipartyism, and an end to the Eyadema dictatorship.

GROUPE SOCIAL PAN-AFRICAIN (GSP). Electoral coalition including Gnininvi's CDP, Ayeva's Alliance du Democrates pour le Renouveau (ADR), and Agbobli's Parti Socialiste Pan-Africain (PSP), formed late in 1993 pledging to boycott the 1994 legislative elections.

GROUPEMENT DU THEATRE ET DU FOLKLORE TOGOLAIS (GTFT). Founded in Lomé in 1962 by the Cultural Affairs Department, the GTFT sponsors many cultural activities at home and abroad, though it is best known for its African Ballet ensemble.

GROUPEMENT INTERPROFESSIONNEL DES ENTERPRISES DU TOGO (GITO). Employers' association with headquarters in Lomé. It is headed by Clarence Olympio.

GRUNITZKY, GILBERT YVES, 1932– . Former Secretary General of the Ministry of Interior. Born on April 6, 1932 in Atakpamé, Grunitzky was educated locally and in France, where he obtained a law degree. In 1961 he joined the Togolese civil service as Deputy Inspector of the Maritime region and, following the collapse of the Olympio regime in 1963, was appointed Secretary General of the Ministry of Interior (1963–1966). In 1965 he also became Director of the Caisse de Compensation des Prestations Familiales et Accidents du Travail, serving in the position until 1968. Since 1968 Grunitzky has been mostly living abroad, especially in Cote d'Ivoire.

GRUNITZKY, NICOLAS, 1913–1969. Engineer, political leader, and former President of Togo. Born in Atakpamé on April 5, 1913 to a Polish officer in the German armed forces in Togo and his wife of the Atakpamé nobility, Grunitzky was also Sylvanus Olympio's brother-in-law and hence also indirectly related to Dr. Pedro Olympio. Indeed, much of the history of the evolution of politics in Togo has been a tug-of-war between the three above-named politicians. Grunitzky was educated locally and abroad (receiving one of the first scholarships ever granted to a Togolese), studying Mathematics and obtaining an Engineering degree (1937). Upon his return to Togo, Grunitzky joined the civil service as a public works engineer with the Chemin de Fer du Togo and in 1949 started his own transportation company. (Later, in exile in the Ivory Coast, he was to establish a similar enterprise.) An active Gaullist underground member during World War II in Vichy-controlled Togo, Grunitzky was strongly supported after the war in his bid to be elected Togo's Deputy to the French National Assembly. Despite the support of many of Togo's pro-French evolués and French civil servants, Grunitzky was defeated in his first effort in 1946 by Dr. **Martin Akou,** who ran under the aegis of Sylvanus Olympio's Comité de l'Unité Togolaise. His second bid was successful, for by then the balance had swung against the CUT, and Grunitzky beat the incumbent Akou and represented Togo between 1951 and 1958. A founding member of the conservative **Parti Togolais du Progrès,** which also included Dr. **Pedro Olympio,** Grunitzky's political career nearly came to an abrupt end in 1952 after his electoral defeat in his own home district for a seat in Togo's territorial assembly, when Ewe, Kpessi, and Kabré voters alike rejected his candidacy. Temporarily expelled from the PTP party, Grunitzky made a comeback by utilizing his Paris platform and French administration supporters. In the process, Dr. Pedro Olympio was expelled from the PTP and, taking with him the less conservative members, set up the **Mouvement Populaire Togolais.** Benefiting from the administration's apprehension regarding the CUT and its pan-Ewe policies, Grunitzky finally entered the Togolese assembly in 1955 and became Prime Minister of the **Autonomous Republic** of 1956–1958, hammering out a tactical alliance with emerging northern political parties also being supported (against the CUT) by the French administration. Grunitzky was dislodged from power by the United Nations-supervised elections of 1958, in which his PTP party obtained only three seats (out of forty-six) and got barely a fifth of the votes the CUT polled (*see* ELECTIONS OF 1958). His electoral ally the northern Union des Chefs et des Populations du Nord was also trounced in the same elections, which saw the re-emergence of a strong CUT government under Sylvanus Olympio. Grunitzky remained in Togo until 1961, merging his party with the UCPN to form the **Union Démocratique des Peuples Togolaises.** In 1961 he relocated to the Ivory Coast with some of his pre-1958 colleagues and returned to Lomé only after the 1963 coup d'état at the request of the Insurrectionist Committee. Originally slated to become Vice President under **Antoine Méatchi,** who was favored by the putschists, Grunitzky refused to serve under his young former minister, and French pressure tipped the balance in favor of a reversal of their respective positions.

A four-cornered coalition was forged between the resurrected parties (all except the CUT had been hounded until 1961 and banned in 1962), each receiving an equal number of assembly seats and a number of cabinet portfolios. The second Grunitzky administration was very much a rerun of his pre-independence conservative policies, indecisive rule, and familiar cabinet appointees, all of which had been defeated and rejected in 1958 during Togo's only honest election. Grunitzky's four years in power were also marked by a continuous tug-of-war between him and his aggressive, ambitious, and more militant Vice President (who actively connived in 1966 to topple Grunitzky), intense fiscal pressures necessitated by the tripling of Togo's armed forces (a condition virtually imposed by the 1963 putschists), economic unrest in the south aggravated by the closed border with Ghana (*see* GHANA-TOGO FRICTION), and continuous plotting against the regime by a militant wing of the renamed CUT which refused to cooperate with Grunitzky or to accept the presence of Olympio's assassins at the helm of the armed forces. The regime was also unpopular in the south because of its timid and conservative domestic and foreign policies.

The contradictions inherent in the Grunitzky regime came to a head with the **Méatchi-Mama crisis**—in which Grunitzky felt forced to downgrade Minister of Interior **Mama** when Mama clashed with Vice President Méatchi over a Méatchi-sponsored drive to unseat Grunitzky—and led to the resignation of the remaining PUT ministers from the cabinet and then the Lomé upheavals (*see* COUP [ATTEMPTED] OF 1966). Though the army belatedly moved in to prevent the collapse of the Grunitzky regime, he was toppled on the fourth anniversary of the first coup d'etat (*see* COUP OF 1967). Following the coup, Grunitzky left Togo with some of his associates (notably his Foreign Minister, Apedo-Amah) and relocated to the Ivory Coast where he had business interests. He died in a Paris hospital on September 27, 1969 after being injured in a car accident in the Ivory Coast. During the National Conference of 1991 there was mention of his complicity in Grunitzky's death among the various allegations made against General Eyadema. In 1984 Grunitzky's youngest daughter married Cote d'Ivoire's President Houphouet-Boigny.

GRUNITZKY, YAO (OTTO HANS), 1934– . Former Ambassador to the United States. Born in Atakpamé on December 13, 1934, and a nephew of Nicolas Grunitzky, the former President of the republic, Yao Grunitzky was educated in Atakpamé and Lomé before proceeding to Bordeaux where he studied Law. Between 1959 and 1961, he also studied Finance and treasury activities at the Ecole Nationale du Tresor in Paris and, upon his return to Lomé, served in the National Treasury.

In 1962 he was appointed Treasury Inspector and later, head of the Expenditures Division. In November 1964 he was appointed Director of the Budget, holding this post until after the collapse of the Grunitzky regime. Shunted aside during much of the Eyadema regime, Grunitzky served briefly as Minister of Finance and the Economy (September– November 1978) but was dropped for mismanagement of fiscal resources and other improprieties. Earlier, he had held the post of Director of Studies at the Togo National School of Administration and other technical posts in the Ministry of Finance. He was appointed Ambassador to the United States in 1980 and stayed in that post through 1983.

GUENOU, AMKOKOEWO, 1948– . Educator. Born in Tsévié on September 14, 1948 and educated both in Scotland and at the University of Benin, Guénou teaches French in a Lomé lycée and is also a published poet.

GUENOU, TOUSSAINT COSSY. A teacher by profession, Guenou is an aspiring young poet whose work has already been published abroad.

GUIDE, LE. "The Guide"—popular reference to General Eyadema, part of the pervasive Cult of Personality in Togo.

GU-KUNOU, EMMANUEL. Educator and critic of General Eyadema. Gu-Kunou was a Professor of Geography at the University of Benin and one of Eyadema's arch-critics. In August 1985 he was arrested for suspicion of complicity in the mysterious bombs that exploded in downtown Lomé that month. Both he and members of his family were severely tortured in prison and figured prominently in Amnesty International's efforts to safeguard basic civic and human rights in Togo.

GUMEDZE, MAWUENA YAWOVI, 1947– . Agronomist. Born in 1947 and trained in Agronomy in Belgium, Gumedzé teaches at the Agronomy School of the National University of Benin and is also in charge of the ESA Agro-Pedagogical Farm in Lomé.

GURMA (ALSO, GOURMA). Ethnic group of around 90,000 found mostly between Mossi areas and the Niger River in the Burkina Faso but also in small concentrations further south. In Togo, Gurma elements are to be found in Sansanné-Mango and in Dapaong. Calling themselves binumba, Togo's Gurma emigrated from the Fada N'Gurma area in Burkina Faso consequent to famines and wars and have assimilated local customs and language, though remaining mostly animist.

H

HABYE. Purification rites with rich magical symbolism, practiced by the Kabré every five years in November. The last rites took place in 1990.

HAHO, PREFECTURE DU. The former circonscription du Nuatja, renamed in the June 1981 administrative reorganization. Its headquarters remains in Notsé (ex-Nuatja). *See* NOTSE.

HALIDOU, ADAM AKARAWATO. Long the President of the Union Musulmane du Togo. Halidou was appointed to succeed Kassim Mensah in August 1976. Of Chamba origins, and widely respected for his piety and Koranic learning, Halidou is a postal inspector in civil life. He had been involved in the UMT from the outset and was the unanimous choice of the nominating committee in 1976.

HAUSA. A Muslim people numbering over twenty million (1993 estimate) and found mostly in northern Nigeria and southern Niger and in small concentrations as traders throughout West and Equatorial Africa. They speak Hausa, which belongs to the Chadic group of the Hamito-Semitic languages and is infused with Arabic words because of Islamic influences. Estimates of Togo's Hausa community vary widely, from 10,000 to 20,000, with over half in Lomé proper and the rest in the various **zongo** in the North. A very important mercantile and religious group throughout Africa, Togo's Hausa have been the prime transmitters and propagators of Islam in the country.

HAUTE CONSEIL DE LA REPUBLIQUE (HCR). Transitional government replacing the 1990 Eyadema-controlled Assemblée Nationale after the conclusion of the National Conference in August 1991. It was presided over by Bishop Kpodzra and had the specific function of ratifying a new constitution leading to multi-party elections. The HCR was constantly harassed and bullied by Eyadema and his loyalist army, and many of its edicts were ignored. Ultimately, after Koffigoh was abducted and confronted with an ultimatum by Eyadema, the HCR conceded the creation of a government of National unity with the RPT, also allowing Eyadema to run for the 1993 Presidential elections. The HCR gave way in 1994 to the new National Assembly elected in February and a coalition government (with the RPT) headed by **Edem Kodjo.**

HEALTH FACILITIES. Constantly expanding, Togo has an elaborate system of health facilities for a country its size. Obviously the best facilities are in Lomé and the south; however, since General Eyadema's seizure of power in 1967, massive strides have been achieved in the north as well. By the early 1980s the La Kara region, Eyadema's own, had facilities virtually equal to those in the south. The center and far north of the country, however, lags behind these two regions. In 1990 the entire country had 21 hospitals, 317 dispensaries (crude clinics in most villages), 2 leprosariums, 17 maternity clinics, and centers with 10 operating theatres. There were also 168 doctors, 20 pharmacists, 7 dental surgeons, 304 midwives, 101 technical lab officials, and over 1,000 nurses for the country's total of 3,600 hospital beds.

HODO. Togo's first cargo ship, object of much nationalistic fervor at the time of its formal launching. *Hodo,* launched on December 10, 1978 in Flensburg, West Germany, weighs 7,000 tons. It connects French (especially Rouen) ports and West African ports and is the flagship of the CTM. The line added another cargo ship in 1980.

HOGBETSOTSO. Popular festival in southern Togo and several areas in southeast Ghana and southwest Benin, commemorating the exodus of the Ewe ancestors from **Notsé** and **King Agokoli's** brutal rule. Held annually (around September) at Notsé or other Ewe centers, the festival is a very lively affair and draws a large number of visitors from all over the region. The festival is known by a wide variety of names, all alluding to the historic Ewe dispersal or to Agokoli's rule.

HOMAWOO, KOFFI. Publisher of the independent and widely-read **Courier du Golfe** set up following the declaration of freedom of the press in 1990. Both the newspaper, its reporters, and Homawoo have been intermittently harassed and/or brutalized by the Eyadema regime. In January 1991 the newspaper was brought to court for publishing "false charges" against the regime.

HOMETOWOU, DONOU. Managing director of the CNCA, arrested and imprisoned for twenty years in 1988 for mismanagement of the company and embezzlement of over 2.5 billion CFAF. Two other employees received nine and ten year sentences. Earlier, in 1987, five other individuals were sentenced to between six and ten years for similar offenses. *See also* CNCA.

HOTEL DU PARTI. Ambitious thirty-two-floor RPT party headquarters, construction of which commenced in 1976. Prior to that, the party HQ was at the Maison du Parti where they shared offices with the municipality and other government services. The Togolese regime spared no effort to assure that the RPT edifice would be a modern one, capable of serving international conferences in style. During the heyday of the National Conference and early **HCR** edicts the Hotel du Parti was technically "taken back" from the RPT, with the latter evicted from its premises. Like many of the HCR edicts, these had to be rescinded.

HOTEL SARAKAWA. One of Lomé's modern hotels, named after General Eyadema's airplane crash in **Sarakawa** and landscaped in somewhat unusual manner to reflect that event. As with many of the city's new hotels, massive kickbacks were received by General Eyadema and other government officials, boosting the hotel's actual construction costs from 4.4 billion CFAF to 7.2 billion CFAF.

HOTEL 2 FEVRIER. Luxury hotel in downtown Lomé, a veritable white elephant allegedly constructed solely due to the thirty-five percent kickback of construction costs to General Eyadema. Due to its exorbitant price structure, when there are no official State conferences and/or OAU or other summit meetings, very few of the hotel's 362 rooms are occupied.

HOUENASSOU, KAHOHONOU. Entrepreneur. A graduate of the Bonnécarrére secondary school and business school, Houenassou was invited to visit the United States on a cultural exchange program and was much impressed by marketing methods in the West. Opening a modern, American-style supermarket in Lomé, he attained virtually instant success.

HUILERIES DU BENIN. Company originally established in 1970 in Cacaveli to extract oil from groundnuts. It was set up with twenty-two million CFAF in capitalization, 22.7 percent of which came from **OPAT.** The first plant came into operation in 1972 but encountered immense operational problems: it could not acquire an adequate supply of peanuts for processing purposes because its cost-structure required offering producer prices considerably lower than open market prices. Drought also afflicted West Africa, right down to coastal areas, decimating groundnut harvests. More importantly, Togo, even in the best of times, had never produced enough groundnuts to provide the factory with more than a three-month supply of raw material. The company went bankrupt in 1976, when it could not pay its bills, but was not allowed to collapse. It was purchased by OPAT in January 1979 and continued operating at a deficit, employing seventy workers and working at forty percent of capacity. It was again closed in 1990, and its future is in doubt.

HUNLEDE, AYI HOUENOU (JOACHIM), 1925– . Former key Minister of Foreign Affairs in President Eyadema's cabinet. Born on February 2, 1925 to an important Aného family, Hunlédé was educated locally and at the Lycée Victor Bauot in Porto Novo (Benin), Dabou Teacher's Training College (Cote d'Ivoire), and at the University of Montpellier in France, where he obtained a degree in Law in 1952. Between 1952 and 1956 Hunlédé worked as Deputy Inspector of Education in north Togo and as a teacher at Atakpamé, following which he returned to Paris to study at the prestigious Ecole Nationale de la France Outre-Mer (1956–58). When he returned to Togo for the second time, he became Deputy Mayor of Lomé (1958) and, later, Mayor of Tsévié. In 1960 President Olympio appointed him Togo's first Ambassador to France and Great Britain; he was later accredited also to the European

Economic Community. In September 1965 he was repatriated and appointed High Commissioner for Planning in the Grunitzky administration. By now widely respected as a diplomat and an efficient administrator, Hunlédé became General Eyadema's first Foreign Minister in April 1967. He was increasingly given total autonomy in determining Togo's foreign posture, even when his views went against General Eyadema's original feelings (as when Hunlédé recommended the break with Taiwan and the recognition of China). An astute politician and a widely respected individual, Hunléde became General Eyadema's most successful cabinet appointee. Under his guidance Togo steered a generally pro-French foreign policy while at the same time giving expression to Togo's vital national interests and Africa's changing circumstances. It was under Hunlédé's leadership that Togo began to play a modest role in intra-African affairs after the long period of quasi-isolationism under Olympio and Grunitzky. Late in 1976, Hunlédé resigned from his various political positions, retired from public life, and commenced a period of relative seclusion that resulted in his being ordained a pastor of the Ewe Evangelical Church in September 1977. He currently lives on a modest experimental farm northwest of Lomé.

I

IMAGE DU TOGO. Monthly publication produced in Lomé with a circulation of 2,000, stressing local and national Togolese developments.

INAWISSI, NAYE THEOPHILE, 1953– . Educator and author. Born on December 20, 1953 in Borada, Ghana of Togolese origins, Inawissi was educated locally and at the Saint Paul Seminary in Atakpamé. Trained as a teacher and currently teaching History and Geography at a school in Bouaké in Cote d'Ivoire, Inawissi has published several volumes of poetry and non-fiction that have gained him literary recognition.

INDIGENAT. Civil status established in 1924 (though de facto since 1887) restricting the civil rights of the indigenous populations that had not attained the status of **evolué** or **assimilé.** Restrictions in civil and political liberties included the obligation to perform **corvée** labor, including porterage and the legal jurisdiction under customary law in the presence of a French administrator. The indigenat code, with its gross abuses and frequent arbitrary application, was one of the greatest sources of friction in colonial Africa until it was abolished in the aftermath of World War II. *See also* ASSIMILATION POLICY.

INDUSTRIE OLEAGINEAUX DU TOGO (IOTO). Cottonseed oil processing company. Deficitory as many of Togo's state-initiated ventures, in 1987 the French company CFDT—that has a stake in many cotton industries in other African countries—agreed to take over a majority (fifty-one percent) equity in IOTO, thus saving it from closure. The new company, renamed Nouvelle Industrie des Oléagineaux de Togo (NIOTO) (fifty-one percent owned by CFDT and forty-nine percent by private Togolese industries) under the directorship of Anani Ernest Gassou, dismissed some forty percent of existing workers and shortly later started turning profits.

INDUSTRIE TEXTILE TOGOLAISE (ITT). One of Togo's first industrial companies, originally a mixed German-Togolese enterprise engaged in spinning, weaving, and printing textiles. Established in 1962 at Dadja in a cotton growing area in the Plateaux region, with the Togolese government holding twenty-five percent of the shares and German interests sixty-four percent. Capitalized at 300 million CFA francs, augmented later to 540 million CFAF, and employing 1,300 workers, ITT commenced operations in its factory in 1966. In 1970 it produced 2.4 million meters of printed textiles of all kinds, and by 1975 the output had gone up to 20 million meters. The ITT bought its cotton from **OPAT,** exporting part of its products to neighboring states. An additional plant was constructed in Kara with a capacity of over 3,000 tons of textiles, aimed exclusively at foreign markets. In the mid-1980s the Togolese government tried to privatize its textile industry—ITT and Togotex (Compagnie Togolaise de Textiles)—but was offered very low bids. The latter was actually closed down. The two plants were finally sold in 1989 to a Chinese entrepreneur from Hong Kong for barely $10 million.

INDUSTRIE TOGOLAISE DES PLASTIQUES (ITP). Joint company set up in 1980 by the Togolese government, the Danish company DAOPLAST, and the Swiss PROMATEC. The company had also had financial backing from the Danish Fund for Cooperation and Development. Inaugurated in January 1981, the Lomé-based company produced an array of plastic tubes and other items. The Togolese government acquired ninety percent of the shares in the company in due course but ran it into the ground, and it had to close down as insupportable deficits were pile up. In late 1986 the company was privatized with German, Dutch, Danish, and private Togolese investors moving in, and it re-opened in January 1987 with increased capitalization.

INDUSTRIE TOGOLAISE DU CYCLE ET DU CYCLOMOTEUR (ITOCY). Founded in Lomé in 1972, ITOCY produces a variety of bicycles. Employing some sixty workers, in the 1980s it was producing

4,800 Vespa scooters and 6,500 bicycles, for a turnover of over 258 million CFAF. It is capitalized at 140 million CFAF with the government having a thirty percent share in the enterprise.

INITIATIVE TOGOLAISE (INITO). Trucking company. Established in 1959 and currently capitalized with 25 million CFAF, INITO undertakes 109 million CFAF of business per year, employing some eighty workers.

INSTITUT ARABE DE KLOTO. One of the first and major examples of Arab cultural aid to Togo. In recognition of Kpalimé's importance as an Islamic center, Arab funds were donated for the establishment of a large koranic school in 1969. In 1971 it enrolled 600 students, taught by a team of Egyptian and Togolese instructors. Since then the number of students has been augmented and the staff localized.

INSTITUT DE RECHERCHE DU CACAO ET DU CAFE (IRCC). Established in Kpalimé, the core coffee/cacao producing region, the IRCC aims at furthering the production of robust coffee and cacao harvests. In 1985 it branched its experimental research into the production of fruits, especially bananas, guavas, mangos, and citrus.

INSTITUT DE RECHERCHES AGRONOMIQUES TROPICALES (IRAT). Experimental agricultural institute with headquarters in Lomé and land and farms in the countryside. IRAT is a major player in the drive to improve seeds and crops and to promote greater use of the proper kinds of fertilizers. IRAT cooperates closely with **SOTOCO** and **IRCTE.**

INSTITUT DE RECHERCHES DU COTON ET DES TEXTILES EXOTIQUES (IRCTE). Experimental research station at Anié-Kolokopé. IRCTE cultivates, perfects, and distributes cottonseed to farmers. It also undertakes basic research and experimentation with insecticides. IRCTE is closely linked to **SOTOCO.**

INSTITUT DE RECHERCHES DU TOGO (IRTO). Branch of the French Office de la Recherche Scientifique et Technique d'Outre Mer (ORSTOM) that was established in 1949 with the function of coordinating and publishing research and scientific data. IRTO has published a large number of very valuable monographs.

INSTITUT DE RECHERCHES POUR LES HUILES ET L'OLEAGINEUX (IRHO). Experimental farm station and research institute that develops and distributes seeds for Togo's farmers.

INSTITUT D'ENSEIGNEMENT SUPERIEUR DU BENIN. Joint Togolese-Beninois institute of higher studies in existence between 1965 and 1970. The school had a Humanities division in Lomé and a Sciences division in Porto Novo, Benin. Benin's 1970 decision to establish a Humanities section in Abomey-Calavi, as part of the new University of Benin, brought an end to the joint institute and led to Togo's establishment of its own Université du Bénin in Lomé.

INSTITUT FRANCAIS D'AFRIQUE NOIRE (IFAN). Research and documentation center set up in Lomé in 1945 as part of a network of IFAN centers throughout Francophone Africa. In 1960 the Institute's name was changed to **Institut Togolais des Sciences Humaines.** Prior to the establishment of IFAN, Togo possessed only a Service de Documentation Generale.

INSTITUT NATIONAL DE FORMATION AGRICOLE DE LOME (INFAL). Agricultural training institute founded in Lomé in 1979 and aimed at promoting a host of training and modernization projects in the countryside. Its first projects were initiated only in 1981, financed by the United Nations Development Fund and the World Bank.

INSTITUT NATIONAL DE RECHERCHES SCIENTIFIQUES (INARES). Organization created in 1965 under direction of M. Voule and attached directly to the presidency, entrusted with the control, supervision, and centralization of all research conducted in Togo in the pure and applied sciences. It is currently part of the University of Benin.

INSTITUT NATIONAL DE SCIENCE DE L'EDUCATION (INSE). Teachers College set up in 1972 in Lomé to satisfy the country's enhanced need for elementary and secondary teachers. A number of very valuable historical monographs were published by INSE.

INSTITUT NATIONAL DES PLANTES A TUBERCULES (INPT). State organ set up in August 1976 but operational only in 1979. It was mandated to promote the planting and marketing of crops such as potatoes, manioc, and igname.

INSTITUT PEDAGOGIQUE NATIONAL (IPN). Lomé Teachers Training School, increasingly involved in retraining existing teachers and lifting national standards of education.

INSTITUT TOGOLAIS DES SCIENCES HUMAINES (INTSHU). Post-1960 name for the local **IFAN** research center in Lomé. Originally headed by Gabriel Kwaovi Johnson, with departments of Anthropology, Archaeology, Prehistory, History, Geography, Sociology, and Linguistics, INTSHU also maintains a museum, a library, and a documentation center. Since 1965 it has published the research periodical *Etudes Togolaises* at regular intervals and other monographs. In 1972 it was formally affiliated with the new University of Benin. Some of its publications, in the fields of Demographics and Oral History, are invaluable.

INSURRECTIONIST COMMITTEE. Formal name adopted by the core clique of army veterans that brought about the coup d'etat of 1963 and the transition to the Grunitzky-Méatchi administration. Members of the Committee—all having promoted themselves to officer rank—included Lieutenants Etienne Eyadema, James Assila, Robert Alidou Djafalou, and Ayité.

INSURRECTIONS OF 1897 AND 1898. Revolt of the **Konkomba** ethnic group in northern Togo, occasioned by the brutalities of the nervous commander of a German column that opened fire at a Konkomba gathering at Binaparba market, killing seventy-nine men, women, and children. The column, led by Dr. Gruner, was subsequently encircled at Bapuré, a relief column (composed of **Chokossi** mercenaries) was blocked and ambushed, and a general Konkomba revolt commenced. The disturbance lasted from May 1897 to March 1898, during which time (in January 1898) a **Kabré** revolt also occurred. The Konkomba had to be suppressed again in February and March 1923 and in 1935 and 1936, when they refused to pay taxes.

ISLAM. Still a minority religion in Togo, Islam has been steadily gaining converts. Islam was introduced in the region by the **Chokossi** clans that settled in the **Sansanné-Mango** region in the latter part of the eighteenth century. (Prior to that the Muslim beliefs of Togo's **Hausa** and **Fulani** had had only a minimal influence upon the animist beliefs of the majority.) Active—and occasionally violent—Chokossi proselytizing and their intermarriage with the Moba and the Gurma spread the religion. The Kotokoli of Bafilo and Bassar also slowly converted to Islam, straddling as they did trade routes that carried Muslim influences, including the kola caravan routes between Salaga (Ghana) and Djerma and Hausa country. At times bitter religious wars erupted between clans of the same tribe that had been proselytized in different manners. The German administration had a great deal of admiration for Islam and encouraged its spread in north Togo, closing the region (until 1912) to Christian missionaries.

It is estimated that approximately 260,000 Muslims currently reside in Togo, though this figure is probably an underestimate. (Some scholars suggest that a figure closer to fifteen to eighteen percent of the population would be more accurate.) Lomé has a large and well-organized, though factionalized, mostly Hausa-Fulani Muslim community. The principal centers of Islam in Togo are Kpalimé, Sokodé, and Lomé. The most Islamized groups in the country are the Chokossi, Bassari, and Kotokoli; such smaller groups as the Fulani and Hausa, nonindigenous to the area, are, of course, even more Islamized. The 1970 census showed that 43.6 percent of the Centrale region, 11.5 percent of Savanes, 8.2 percent of Plateaux, 4.3 percent of La Kara, and 2.7 percent of the Maritime region were Muslim. The Centrale, therefore, with 130,412 Muslims, had at the time over 57 percent of Togo's total Muslim population. Over 47 percent of Togo's Muslims were Kotokoli, virtually all of whom were Muslim. (For relative percentages, see the table below.)

Of the various Muslim sects prevalent in Islam, until recently the Tarbiya was largely unknown in Togo. The Tidjaniya is by far the dominant sect, though by the 1980s some small Muslim sects were beginning to sprout. Indeed, by the late 1980s and in the 1990s Togo's Muslims were increasingly coming under the sway of various Muslim marabouts from Senegal and Mali. The only Tarbiya lodge (an offshoot of the Tidjaniya) exists in Sokodé, supported by dissident Kotokoli. The Quadriya sect is also nearly nonexistent and supported by only a few in Bafilo (mostly Bassari) and in Lomé by some of the merchant Yoruba. Though a distinct minority, Togo's Muslims outnumber the country's Protestants and wield much more influence, both individually and collectively. Togo's Muslim community received a major boost in prestige and a very noticeable increase in political clout with the creation of the Muslim Union of Togo, which also undertook a variety of educational functions. Organized religious life among the Muslims of Togo has, however, been highly factionalized with recriminations of various kinds constantly erupting. Several leaders of the **UMT**—that has slowly become government-controlled—have been ousted from office for "dictatorial" policies, and the political leadership of Togo has had to intervene to impose peace in the community. **Fousseni Mama,** former Minister of Interior under President Grunitzky, was for considerable time the President of Togo's Muslim community. More recently General Eyadema has tried to bring Togo's Muslims behind him by promoting one of their leaders, the Kotokoli (but not very influential) **Barry Moussa Barque** as one of his closer lieutenants. *See also* RELIGION; UNION MUSULMANE DU TOGO.

TOGO'S ETHNIC GROUPS: LEVELS OF ISLAMIZATION

Ethnicity	% Muslim
Hausa	98
Chamba	97
Kotokoli	93
Bassila	92.5
Fulani	80.2
Yoruba	76.4
Nago	74
Mossi	55.4
Chokossi	37
Yanga	29.5
Ana	20
Tamberma	17.3
Bassari	15
Gurma	3.6
Kpessi	2.5
Kabre	1.5
Agnagan	1.4
Others	Below 1

ISSA, SAMA. Former Minister of Justice, Labor and the Civil Service. Issa acquired notoriety for being suspended from office without pay for two months for being consistently late to work. Appointed in February 1977—and one of Eyadema's least successful appointees—Issa was dismissed from office exactly a year later.

J

JEUNESSE DU NORD TOGO. Youth wing of the northern **Union des Chefs et des Populations du Nord** party. The youth organization was poorly organized and barely more than a paper structure except in a few isolated areas.

JEUNESSE DU RASSEMBLEMENT DU PEUPLE TOGOLAIS (JRPT). General Eyadema's RPT party youth wing. The JRPT was established following a Constituent Congress on February 27 and 28, 1970, as the youth wing of the **Rassemblement du Peuple Togolais.** In December 1971 all existing youth movements were dissolved, and their membership merged into the JRPT. Very much a control mechanism, the JRPT was never very popular or influential in southern regions. With the onset of the pro-democracy disturbances in 1990 the JRPT rapidly became merely the youth wing of the northern RPT.

JEUNESSE PIONNIERE AGRICOLE (JPA). Youth structures, initially set up with Israeli technical assistance in the mid-1960s, aimed at syphoning unemployed rural youth, training them in modern agricultural technology, and resettling them on virgin fields. The program was continued after Togo's break with Israel in 1973. It involved the training of groups of 100 to 300 young people for two years at a central farm, following which they were resettled to form cooperatives. A main farm-school was at Glidji, near Aného, with other settlements in Notsé, Togodo, Atakpamé, Sansanné-Mango, Kara, and Sotouboua. The program was, compared to other countries that embarked on similar ventures with Israeli aid (including neighboring Benin), moderately successful. This was largely due to the fact that for large numbers of the population (and especially among the **Kabré** in the north) agriculture remains a viable option, and traditional pulls are not overly high. On the other hand, the program was compromised by the departure of the Israeli instructors in 1973 (when Togo reluctantly ruptured diplomatic relations to conform with the Arab boycott) and by low financial and infrastructure commitments on the part of the state.

JOHNSON, AMPAH GUMALON, 1930– . Rector of the University of Benin in Lomé. Born in 1930 in Aného, Johnson completed secondary school at the Academy of Poitiers and continued higher studies in Mathematics and Natural Sciences at the University of Poitiers (1952–59). For some time a Fellow at the prestigious French C.N.R.S. (1956–60), he later joined the faculty of the University of Abidjan as Reader in Zoology. He was recalled from Cote d'Ivoire in 1968 to become the founding Chancellor of the new National University in Togo. He is a respected scholar and member of various learned societies, though his subservience to Eyadema was intensely disliked in the University.

JOHNSON, KUKOVI BENYI (GABRIEL POLYCARPE), 1924– . Former Minister of Information. Born in Lomé in 1924 and educated locally at Dakar and in France where he studied Journalism, Johnson joined the staff of *Togo-Presse* becoming in due time the director general of Editogo. In March 1975 he was co-opted into the Eyadema cabinet as Secretary of State in charge of Information, Posts, and Communications. In 1976 he mounted a brief propaganda campaign (at Eyadema's behest) calling for the return to Togo of the territories "lost" to it in the 1956 plebiscite to Ghana. The campaign, and Johnson's powerful links with Libya, brought Togo-Ghana relations to a nadir and much bitter acrimony. Though originally politically close to Eyadema, Johnson was dropped from the cabinet in 1978 and left for self-exile in Paris the next year, declaring his opposition to his former leader. Notwithstanding this, he was invited back by the beleaguered Eyadema in 1987 and was assigned to the Presidency with responsibility for missions and diplomatic reporting. Constantly rumored to be re-appointed to a major cabinet post, Johnson briefly re-emerged in the political spotlight in February 1990 when he was named to his old post as Minister of Information. After the liberalizations of 1990 he lost his post due to being too close to his former master, Eyadema.

JOHNSON, RAYMOND MESSANVI, 1925– . Psychiatrist. Born on June 29, 1925 and obtaining his MD from the University of Paris in 1961, Johnson specialized in Psychiatry and Psychoanalysis, obtaining his certification from the University of Dakar in 1978. Returning to Lomé he joined the University of Benin where he still teaches, at the same time heading the Psychiatry Division at Lomé Hospital. A WHO-designated Mental Health Expert, Johnson is the author of numerous acclaimed books and articles.

JOHNSON-ADJAMAGBO, BRIGITTE, 1958– . A popular teacher by profession Mrs. Johnson-Adjamagbo was appointed Minister of Social Welfare, National Solidarity, and Human Rights in the interim government of Prime Minister Koffigoh, serving for exactly three months from September 26, 1991.

JOURNAL OFFICIEL DE LA REPUBLIQUE DU TOGO. Edited by Editogo, the official government gazette of Togo appears every two weeks and lists all laws, administrative decrees, and ordinances. Once published, these acquire the status of law.

JOURNEE COMMEMORATIVE DES MARTYRS DE PYA. National holiday declared in 1972 commemorating a bloody clash at Pya (General Eyadema's home village) between French forces and a group of Kabré on June 21, 1957. The date of June 21 has been elevated to the status of a national holiday as part of Eyadema's **authenticity** drive, though it gained only slow and minimal acceptance, even in the north.

JOURNEE DE LIBERATION NATIONALE. National Liberation Day commemorating the "liberation" of Togo from civilian rule by Togo's armed forces. Since both of Togo's coups occurred on the same day (January 13), the national holiday also commemorates former President Olympio's assassination, a fact that rankles many in the south. The holiday was abolished by the HCR in 1991.

JOURNEE NATIONALE DE LIBERATION ECONOMIQUE. National Economic Liberation Day (January 24) celebrates Togo's nationalization of the important phosphate industry, **COTOMIB.** The nationalization was announced shortly after President Eyadema revealed an alleged attempt on his life (*see* EYADEMA'S PLANE

CRASHES) that formed part of the government's **authenticity** and Cult of Personality drives.

JUVENTO (ALSO JUVENTOS TOGO). Also known under its original, but largely unused, founding name, Mouvement de la Jeunesse Togolaise. Established in September 1961 as a youth movement and as the more radical youth wing of the **Comité de l'Unité Togolaise** of Sylvanus Olympio. Its leadership has included **Anani Santos,** Messan Aithson, **André Kuevidjen,** and Secretary General **Firmin Abalo.** Juvento was separated from the parent CUT in its more firm anti-French posture, pan-Africanist views (many of its leaders were quasi-Nkrumahists), and more adamant position on the pan-Ewe movement. Juvento suffered several splits, the most important of which was caused by Messan Aithson who, having built the movement, wished to see it become the local branch of the militant interterritorial Rassemblement Démocratique Africain. In 1954 Aithson resigned from Juvento, carrying with him some of the more militant members, while Ben Apaloo (who died in a car crash in 1964) assumed the leadership of the truncated movement. Juvento broke away from the CUT in July 1959 over Olympio's conservative policies. Prior to the April 1961 elections, the party made a tactical alliance with the northern-based opposition, the **Union Démocratique des Peuples Togolais,** forming the **Mouvement Nationaliste Togolaise-Juvento.** The formation was disqualified, however, as Olympio cracked down on sources of organized opposition, and, after the discovery of an alleged plot, Juvento itself was banned (in January 1962), and Togo became a de facto one party state. Most of the party's leaders were arrested (including the aging Santos) and imprisoned under harsh conditions in Sansanné-Mango in the far north. Following the 1963 coup d'état Juvento, now led by President Firmin Abalo, Vice Presidents Idrissou Touré and **Emmanuel Gagli,** and Secretary General **Gregoire Kouessan,** joined President Grunitzky's four-cornered coalition that remained in office until the 1967 coup d'état. With the rise of the Eyadema regime all parties, including Juvento, were banned.

K

KABASSEMA, MBA HANKPADE. Former Director-General of the Office Togolais des Phosphates. He was arrested in April 1981 for massive embezzlement of funds and sentenced to life imprisonment, though he was released in 1984. At the time of the National Conference in 1991 Kabassema publicly revealed that General Eyadema had amassed a personal fortune of eighty billion CFAF through kickbacks and high percentages from construction projects.

KABOU. Important pre-colonial market town on the main Salaga (Ghana)-to-Kano (Nigeria) kola nut caravan route. Kabou is in the Bassari prefecture in the La Kara region.

KABRE (ALSO CABRAIS, KABYE). Mountain ethnic group estimated in 1993 to number over 350,000 and together with certain closely affiliated peoples roughly twenty-four percent of the population. The Kabre live mostly in the north (in the La Kara and Centrale regions), though as a result of migrations in search of land (encouraged as early as during the German and French eras), concentrations are also found in the vicinity of Atakpamé in the Plateaux region. Tilling volcanic soil in the north, which suffers from water erosion, and practicing crop rotation, the Kabre collective construction of stone embankments led the scholar Frobenius to nickname them Africa's Steinbauer (''stone-peasants''). The Kabre are relatively cohesive as an ethnic group, possess chiefs with wider powers than their equivalents among southern ethnic groups, and are still mostly animist. Up to the seventeenth century the Kabre were spread over a much wider territory—up to Djougou (in Benin), for example. Invasions and expansion of such ethnic groups as the **Bariba** forced the Kabre back to their core mountain retreats around Kara and Sokodé, where their population density is extremely high. Many have become assimilated with the **Kotokoli**.

The origin of the southern Kabre was the German administration's creation of "improvement villages" (Besserungsiedlungen) in 1909 near Notsé and Atakpamé. The French continued the practice of enticing Kabre elements to unoccupied land in the south, though some of the original settlements were more like penal colonies for road construction. There are currently estimated to be over 100,000 Kabre in the Plateaux, and more are migrating south in search of better land.

The Kabre (in French originally Cabrais, and more recently in recent official usage, Kabyé), call themselves Lan-mba (''of the forests''), transformed by the first Germans into Lama. The name "Kabré" is probably a corruption of the Hausa term kafiri, or pagans. There are several Kabre subgroups, notably the Logba, Lamba (69,000 strong), and Losso (the latter cultivating palm plantations found between Kara and the Benin border). In the absence of any effort on the part of either the German or French colonial administration to develop the north and under acute land pressure, many Kabre have in the past enlisted in either the police force or in the French colonial armies for duty abroad. Their repatriation shortly after Togo's independence and their integration into the much expanded Togolese army after the 1963 coup d'etat (which they triggered) has resulted in the domination of the armed forces of today by Kabre. (*See* ARMED FORCES.)

With the rise of the regime of General Eyadema (who is a Kabre) in 1967, the first concerted and significant efforts have been made to modernize and revitalize the northern regions of Togo and in particular the Kabre areas. The creation in the mid-1960s of the region of La Kara was a first step in the direction of defining the limits of the depressed Kabre areas prior to the creation of specific structures charged with socio-economic modernization. The process was greatly accelerated in the 1970s, with the result that the north has been virtually transformed, both socially and economically, in less than twenty years.

KABYE. Increasingly the more commonly-used name, especially in French, in referring to the Kabre ethnic group. (In the 1960s the name Cabrais was also used.)

KAMBAKATE. One of the royal Mande clans of the Chokossi. The earliest to arrive in Togo, the Kambakaté traditionally appoint the Imam of all the Chokossi from its learned men. The ethnic clan also has several other privileges and priorities in rites. *See also* CHOKOSSI.

KANDE. Small town in the northeast of Togo, north of Niamtougou. Formerly administrative center of a circonscription with the same name, in the June 1981 administrative reorganization the district was renamed the prefecture de la Keran with headquarters retained in Kandé.

KARA. Main urban center of the **La Kara** region and, until 1981, name of one of the latter's districts. Lama Kara first became a separate **cercle** in 1951 because of **Kabre** fears that they were losing economic and political power to the **Kotokoli** of the Sokodé region. In the mid-1960s the Kabre's special status was further confirmed by the carving of the **La Kara** region out of the Centrale and Savanes regions. The Lama Kara district had an estimated population of 140,000 in 1991; the town itself estimated at 25,000, making it Togo's fifth largest. (Other estimates put its population as approaching Sokodé's.) Kara (formerly Lama Kara) has been totally transformed in recent years, as indeed has the entire La Kara region, today linked via paved roads to Sokodé in the south and to Burkina Faso in the north. Within the town is the main training camp of the Togolese armed forces, the headquarters of the Third and Fourth Battalions. The town has some industry, major public buildings, futuristic hotels (where it previously had merely a camp), and an aggressive, self-confident citizenry. In the 1981 administrative reorganization Kara became the administrative headquarters of a much expanded La Kara region stretching from

Ghana to Benin, encompassing six new prefectures. Kara is also the headquarters of the Kozah prefecture within the La Kara region.

KARAMOKO, NAMORO, 1912– . Former Minister of Agriculture and prominent Muslim leader, one of the very few attracted to the Quadriya sect. Born in 1912 in Sansanné-Mango in the far north of Togo and educated in a Koranic school, Karamoko was an educator before being appointed Minister of Agriculture by President Olympio. A northern Chokossi of royal origins, Karamoko was one of a few northerners that reached positions of prominence in the Olympio regime. He served as Minister of Agriculture until Olympio's demise in 1963, following which he returned to instruction and administrative duties at his former ministry. Elected Vice President of the **Union Musulmane du Togo** in 1970, he was also unanimously appointed Imam of the Chokossi community of Lomé. Retired since 1972, Karamoko participated in the National Conference in 1991 and briefly served as its temporary Chairman, in due course ceding the post to Bishop Kpodzro.

KARAMON-KPIN, SALIFOU (EL HADJ), 1915– . Current Imam of Sansanné-Mango and a key leader of Togo's Chokossi community. Born in Sansanné-Mango in 1915 of the requisite Kambakaté lineage (*see* KAMBAKATE) and of royal blood, Karamon-Kpin studied in koranic schools and taught in several across the border in Ghana. He made the pilgrimage to Mecca in 1965 and on his return to Togo became the lieutenant of the then current Imam, **Abdoulaye Sani**. When the latter died in 1970, Karamon-Kpin was the unanimous choice to succeed him.

KARIM, ABOU BOUKARI. Little-known political prisoner. Arrested for activities against the Eyadema regime, Karim acquired a measure of notoriety upon his release from prison in 1978 because he vindicated Amnesty International's early claims that Togo had a habit of political imprisonment without trial. Karim himself had been detained without trial between 1971 and 1978.

KATO KOAKOU, ATA, 1947– . Engineer. Born in 1947 and educated in France in Physics and Mathematics, Kato Koakou has worked with the Industrial and Artisanal division of the Ministry of Industry since 1978 as Head of Division.

KAZARO, MATTI TASSOU, 1948– . Educator at the University of Benin and published poet.

KEKE, MICHEL, 1933– . Diplomat. Born in Atakpamé on September 14, 1933, Keké was educated locally and in France, where he graduated with a doctorate in the Classics. After teaching for two years at a French lycée (1961–63), he joined the Togolese Embassy in Paris as Cultural Attaché (1963–68). In May 1968 he was appointed first councilor at Togo's Embassy to the United States, and in 1971 he became the Deputy Secretary General of the Francophonic Association. He returned to Washington in 1974 as Ambassador to the United States. His diplomatic career was cut short in 1978, when he was recalled from his post to become councilor at the Ministry of Foreign Affairs.

KEKEH, BIYEMI (Mrs.). Magistrate. First woman appointee to Eyadema's cabinet. Mrs. Kekeh joined the cabinet in February 1977 as Secretary of State for Health, Women's, and Social Affairs. She was promoted to full ministerial rank in November 1978 and sat on a host of committees dealing specifically with children. Mrs. Kekeh was born in Lomé on May 31, 1932 and was educated locally at the Lycée Bonnecarrere, at Lyon University in France (1953–57), and at Paris University (1957–60), acquiring Law degrees. After a brief course of studies at the National School of Overseas Studies in Paris in 1960, Mrs. Kekeh returned to Lomé and was appointed to serve as Magistrate in Lomé. There she set up a Children's Jurisdiction Division. Between 1963 and 1972 she served in Cote d'Ivoire in a similar capacity. Upon her return to Lomé in 1972 she was appointed Vice President, later President, of the Lomé Court of Appeals from which she was promoted into Eyadema's cabinet in 1977.

KEKEH, JEAN. Well-known lawyer and educator. A member of the RPT Politburo since 1971, in charge of youth and culture, Kékéh's political career was cut short by the rise of sentiment against Eyadema, and he now practices Law in Lomé.

KELIH, SANWO, 1941– . Teachers. Born in Lomé in 1941 and educated at home and in France. Kelih completed his higher education in Paris in Philosophy. He currently teaches in a Lomé lycée and is the author of a number of poems.

KENKOU, KOSSI GNANRI, 1943– . Born on January 31, 1943 and educated at the University of Paris where he obtained a doctorate in Sociology in 1973, Kenkou specialized in rural development. He currently teaches at the University of Benin's School of Agronomy, and has published research on the urbanization of the city of Lomé.

KERAN, PREFECTURE DE LA. Formerly the circonscription de Kandé with administrative headquarters in the village of the same name in the La Kara region. The 1981 administrative reorganization changed both the name of the district and the administrative nomenclature.

KERIM, ABDOUL AZIZ, 1936– . Educator and civil administrator. Born in Kabou on March 14, 1936 and trained as a teacher, Kerim taught in a Sokodé public school between 1957 and 1961. Since 1961 he has been attached to several ministries in Lomé, either as a technical consultant (1961–67) or in a senior administrative capacity as Director of the minister's internal cabinet (1967–83). Until 1991 Director of the cabinet of the Minister of Rural Economy, in that year he was reassigned to head an administrative division in that ministry.

KERIM, BOUKARI, 1938–1979. Former political prisoner. A physician and previously an activist in the Union Nationale des Etudiants Togolais and member of the former PTP-UCPN political party, Kèrim was arrested by the Eyadema regime in 1970 and kept in jail without trial for 8 years. He died shortly after being released in 1979.

KERIM, LASSISSIDIKENI, 1936– . Born in Kabou in the Bassar area on March 14, 1936, Kerim was educated locally and in Sokodé and trained for a teaching career. In 1970 he was appointed Director of cabinet of the Minister of Civil Service and later filled a similar post for the Minister of Planning. In 1975 he was appointed head of the Administrative District of Lomé and in January 1977 joined the Eyadema cabinet as Minister of National Education and Scientific Research. In August 1978 Kerim was shifted to head the Ministry of Labor. He was dropped from the cabinet in 1981 and reassigned to duties in the Ministry of Planning. An RPT Politburo member since 1972, Kerim, who is of Konkomba ethnic origin, was in charge of coordinating with and supporting the irredentist **TOLIMO** movement calling for a reunification of all Ewe on both sides of the Ghana-Togo border.

KETA FORT *see* PRINDSENSTEEN.

KETEHOULI, BOONA AHOULON JATA. Civic activist, Ketehouli was elected Vice President of the **National Conference** on July 13, 1991. He then served briefly in the first transitional government of Koffigoh as Minister of Communications and Culture during the period September to December 1991.

KETEVI, PELAGNON ADODO, 1942– . Agronomist. Born on July 9, 1942 and educated in Paris and Toulouse in Agronomy, Ketevi teaches Biochemistry at the Agronomy School of the University of Benin.

KLOTO (FORMERLY KLUOTO). Important hilly prefecture in the Plateaux region snuggled against the Ghanaian border some 120 kilometers north of Lomé. Kloto's administrative capital and biggest town is the bustling and expanding **Kpalimé**. The area is one of the main centers of Togo's cocoa and coffee plantations, and, consequently, the district's 100,000 population (many of whom are Ewe) have a relatively higher income. The Ewe arrived in this region following the **Notsé** dispersal in 1720. Coffee and cocoa were introduced during German colonial rule and missionaries were active among the Ewe from an early date. (The Bremen Missionary Society, for example, was established there in 1847). Kloto is second after Lomé in terms of school enrollment (seventy-five percent) and scores high on other socio-economic indicators. Several important experimental farms and agricultural schools in the area exist, including the Centre de Formations Professionelle Agricole de Tové, the Ecole Nationale d'Agriculture, and the Ferme Experimentale de Tové.

KLUOTO. Former name of the **Kloto** prefecture, renamed in the June 1981 reorganization.

KODJO, EDEM (EDOUARD), 1938– . Prime Minister of Togo, former Secretary General of the Organization of African Unity (OAU), Minister of Finance and Economy, and Secretary General of the **Rassemblement du Peuple Togolais**. Born in Sokodé on May 23, 1938, Kodjo was educated locally and in France, where he studied economics in Rennes and Paris. After a few years as an administrator with the Office de Radiodiffusion Télevision Française (1964–67), Kodjo returned to Togo and began his meteoric rise in the government of President Eyadema. In July 1967 he was named Secretary General of the Ministry of Finance and government representative on the **Comité Constitutionnel**. An able and hardworking administrator, Kodjo was two years later appointed Secretary General of the nascent Rassemblement du Peuple Togolais political party set up to legitimate Eyadema's regime. Ambitious and upwardly mobile, Kodjo lost his post in 1971 when a collegiate Political Bureau was created to avoid too large a concentration of power in the Secretary General's hands. Kodjo was retained in the bureau with responsibilities over finance and in 1972 was appointed Director of the **Société Nationale d'Investissement**. In 1973 he was brought into the cabinet as Minister of Finance and also became Governor of the International Monetary Fund (IMF) regional office. In August 1976 Kodjo was appointed Foreign Minister but barely left his mark on Togolese foreign policy before being asked to accept nomination as Secretary General of the Organization of African Unity. Despite several brilliant years at the head of that organization, Kodjo's leadership stumbled over the twin issues of the admission to the OAU of the Western Sahara government (fighting for independence vis-à-vis Morocco, an important founding member of the OAU and influential faction leader) and the civil war in Chad. Indeed, by 1982 Kodjo's own government had disowned him (since his views were contrary to those in Lomé) while important other factions were also opposed to his continued leadership. He finally stepped down from the OAU position in late 1983. Relations between Kodjo and General Eyadema had by then plummeted so much that, prior to that year's election of a new Secretary General, Togo had formally announced it would withdraw from the organization if Kodjo was given a second term.

Kodjo then joined the Sorbonne where, according to all accounts, he was an outstanding instructor and published a number of books. He returned to Lomé in 1987 and as the Eyadema regime began to unravel joined in the National Conference of 1991, setting up a political party for his aspirations. Among the various politicians in Lomé he was at the time France's choice by far, but his years under Eyadema tainted his credentials among many Ewe who tended to support former President Olympio's son, Gilchrist Olympio. Kodjo's unwillingness to join forces with both Agboyibor and Olympio split the Ewe vote and facilitated Eyadema's clawing his way back to a re-election victory on the back of his loyal military. In the legislative elections Kodjo's UTD party only received a minority of seats (seven) to Agboyibor's thirty-six, but in appointing Kodjo Prime Minister in 1994 Eyadema surprised all observers, part of a ploy to further split southern Ewe allegiances.

KODJO, EMANUEL G. BRUCE, 1918– . Early educator and youth leader. Born in Aného on May 20, 1918, Kodjo was educated locally before being sent off to Germany where he studied European and African languages. Upon his return to Togo, he was appointed to the Colonial Archives because of his command of German. He remained pro-German throughout his life and assisted in various societies and movements established in Togo that eulogized the German colonial past. Kodjo was also involved in youth movements and was responsible for the organization of Togo's youth, being its head through 1958. He also served on the governing council of the World Association of Youth.

KODJO, MENSAH AGBEYOME. Former cabinet minister. An Ewe leader reconciled to Eyadema's rule, Kodjo was long Commercial Director of the national trading company SONOCOM. He first joined the cabinet in December 1988 as Minister of Youth, Culture, and Education but lost his post as political liberalization swept Togo in 1991.

However, he was named as the RPT choice for a ministership in the interim coalition cabinet of Koffigoh and was appointed Minister of Security and Territorial Administration in September 1992. He was dismissed by Koffigoh in November for not following cabinet directives (he was very much an Eyadema loyalist) but refused to resign, and indeed threatened to arrest Koffigoh himself. The crisis was eventually resolved, and Kodjo left the cabinet in February 1993.

KODJOVI, AKANYI-AWUNYO, 1939– . Until recently, Ambassador to the United Nations. Born in Tsévié of Ewe ethnic origin, Kodjovi studied to be an educator and taught for several years in a Lomé school. With approaching independence, he attended the Togo School of Public Administration and in 1960 was attached to the Ministry of Interior. In 1965 he pursued further specialized studies and in 1967 was named Prefect of the Tabligbo district. In 1970 he was shifted to head the Lomé Administrative District, and in 1975 he was named Prefect of the Dapaong area. In March 1975, after only a few months in his last posting, Kodjovi was returned to Lomé to become High Commissioner for Tourism, and in September 1976 he was nominated Ambassador to the United Nations. He served in that capacity until March 1980, when he was repatriated and joined the cabinet as Minister of Justice, serving until September 1982.

KODJOVIAKOPE. In the Anlo dialect of Ewe "little Kodjo's village," a suburb of Lomé squeezed between the latter and the Ghana border town of Aflao. It is a prosperous town of 80,000 people and the acknowledged center of Togo-Ghana legal trade and smuggling. Within it reside a polyglot of nationalities from all over Africa as well as pockets of Indians and Lebanese. The town is West Africa's major foreign currency market, entrepot for precious stones, market drugs from Benin and Nigeria and documentation from all over Africa. Foreign passports, for example, were easily obtainable there in 1993 at very reasonable prices, from 160,000 CFAF for a Senegalese one to 280,000 for an American one.

KOFFI, AMOUZOU (Major). Head of the **Brigade de Recherche**. Koffi is President Eyadema's half-brother and is entrusted with security and intelligence duties in the Lomé area.

KOFFIGOH, BASILE YVES. Briefly Minister of Health and Population in the Koffigoh interim government between December 1991 and September 1992.

KOFFIGOH, JOSEPH KOKOU, 1948– . Much-discredited former Prime Minister of Togo. An Ewe born in 1948 in Kpélé Dafo near Kpalimé,

Koffigoh studied in the Kloto region and at the Lycée Bonnecarrere, majoring in Philosophy. He then went to the University of Abidjan but was expelled for leading a student demonstration against the 1970 mercenary assault on Guinea. He next attended the University of Poitiers, studying Law and continuing his affiliation with **FEANF**. Identified as an opponent of General Eyadema's dictatorship (though his brother, Koffi Mathieu, had served as Minister of Youth and Sports), Koffigoh's scholarship was rescinded by Togo, and he had to work in hotels and bistros to make ends meet.

On his return to Togo Koffigoh practiced Law, working with such distinguished lawyers as Kutuklui, Kouassigah, and Agboyibor and played a leading role in setting up the Togo Bar Association in 1980, being elected its President in June 1990. In 1990 he also formed the League for Human Rights after a similar Eyadema-sponsored group proved too timid. He participated in the National Conference of 1991 and was elected one of its two Vice Presidents and on August 26, 1991 was elected interim Prime Minister over the popular but radical alternative candidate **Léopold Messan Gnininvi** by a vote of 388 to 312, largely due to **Gilchrist Olympio's** support. Koffigoh headed three interim governments until presidential and legislative elections took place in 1994. In 1994 Eyadema—having brutally intimidated his opposition to be fraudulently elected President—selected **Edem Kodjo** as his new Prime Minister. Earlier, in the legislative elections, Koffigoh's lack of popularity was poignantly evident when not only was he unable to forge a political party to support him, but he even did not win his own district until the second round run-off election.

During his tenure as Prime Minister Koffigoh was tested many times and found wanting. Though his regime was constantly assaulted by an army loyal to Eyadema, and he was once kidnapped and brought to Eyadema for a confrontation, Koffigoh was both too weak and ambitious and neither stood up to Eyadema nor resigned his post, ultimately capitulating in creating a government of national unity, and making it possible for Eyadema to run for the Presidency. In the legislative elections of 1994 he was personally elected to the new National Assembly (only after a run-off vote) but with no political party behind him.

KOKOU, ABOLO. Trained as an educator, Kokou has been the Principal of the prestigious Atakpamé secondary school since 1966.

KOKOU TORKO, EMMANUEL, 1926– . Tax collector and accountant. Born in Lomé or April 28, 1926 and a graduate of the IHEPES and the Paris Tax School, Kokou Torko was appointed head of tax collections of the northern division. He later served in a similar capacity within the central division. Since 1968 he has been head of prepaid assessments in the ministry's tax department.

KOLANI, YANDAM. Young published Togolese author.

KOLOR, CLEMENT, 1929–1970. Former CUT deputy and party militant killed in the 1970 anti-Eyadema attempted coup. Born in Anié on April 7, 1929 and a merchant by profession, Kolor was elected to the National Assembly from Atakpamé in 1958 and became Secretary of the Committee on Finances and the Economy. He served in the Assembly until Olympio's demise in 1963, following which he was involved in several plots against the subsequent regimes of Grunitzky and Eyadema. He was arrested in August 1970 in connection with the famous conspiracy of that month—*see* COUP (ATTEMPTED) OF 1970. He died, allegedly, when he jumped out of the window of the police station in an attempt to regain freedom; alternatively, he was tortured to death in prison.

KOMLAN, ADEKOLE KOFFI, 1953– . Engineer. Born in 1953 and educated at the University of Montreal in Canada, Komlan returned to Lomé to work as an Engineer (1981–85) with the Ministry of the Plan and Industry before relocating to Ibadan in Nigeria where he has been working with the African Regional Center for Engineering Design and Manufacturing.

KOMLAVI, YAO. Former cabinet minister. Though an Ewe, Komlavi has been an Eyadema supporter and was for long Prefect of Lomé. In March 1987 he was appointed Minister of the Environment and Tourism, and in May 1991 replaced General Mawulikplimi as Minister of Security and Territorial Administration. Briefly dropped from the cabinet after the **National Conference**, he was reappointed as a RPT minister in the cabinet of December 30, 1991, again as Minister of Security serving until September 1992.

KONGO, KOFFI (RAINHILL) (COLONEL), 1936–1985. Former commander of Togo's First Battalion, head of Military Intelligence and Inspector General of the armed forces. A Mina born abroad (in Cameroun), who joined the colonial armies to be demobilized in 1962 with the rank of Corporal, Kongo was one of the principal architects of the coup d'état of 1963. Promoted to officer rank (Lieutenant) after the coup, Kongo attended France's St. Cyr Officers School (the only Togolese officer to do so up to 1969) and was one of Togo's most polished and dashing officers. After the 1967 coup in which General Eyadema seized power, Kongo was dispatched to several countries (including Ghana) to explain the reasons for the coup, and he was appointed Secretary of **Kleber Dadjo**'s **Comité de Réconciliation Nationale**. In March 1970 Kongo was promoted to Major and later that year was a member of the **Cour de Sureté** that tried the August 1970 plotters. One of Togo's best-known military officers, promoted to Lieutenant Colonel in 1978 and to Colonel in 1981, Kongo was the most senior officer in the armed forces after Eyadema. His possible political ambitions (he was one of only a few officers not to be granted senior cabinet rank initially) was assuaged by a series of high ranking military appointments, the latest of which was that of Inspector General of the armed forces. In 1985 the regime announced he had died after a heart attack; later, stories circulated that he was executed for the embarrassingly mediocre performance of Togoleses units in joint maneuvers with French troops, a story contradicted by French sources that stress that he was actually complimented for the Togolese performance. His wife claimed he had been poisoned by the regime. In reality Kongo was arrested on February 27th, tortured, and executed for a suspected plot against Eyadema.

KONKOMBA. Animist ethnic group found in northern Togo and Ghana. In Togo the Konkomba are especially concentrated along the Oti river, a tributary of the Volta, north of **Bassar** and between the areas occupied by the Moba and the Chokossi. Estimates vary widely, the median being 35,000. The Konkomba call themselves kpunkpamba or kpakpamba and speak a Gurma dialect of the Voltaic group of languages. They live in clans that are not united into centralized structures and because of this have been vanquished numerous times in the past by neighboring ethnic groups. They have also suffered from deep interclan fissures that have sapped their collective strength and resulted in protracted interclan fights. In their villages are found large numbers of Bu-Kombong, better known as Gangan. The Konkomba were displaced in the middle of the sixteenth century by the **Dagomba**, who set up their capital, Yendi, on former Konkomba territory. In the latter part of the eighteenth century the Konkomba were again displaced (to the west) by the **Chokossi**, who had just arrived from Cote d'Ivoire via Ghana and Burkina Faso. Plagued by incessant interclan vendettas and in general rebellious, the Konkomba staged uprisings against both the French and the Germans in 1897 and 1898 (*see* INSURRECTIONS OF 1897 and 1898), February to March 1923, and 1935 and 1936). In 1981 the Togolese Konkomba—who had never forgiven their Nanumba neighbors in the former British Togo for voting in the 1956 plebiscite for union with Ghana—moved in large numbers across the border to join interethnic fighting in that country. Hundreds of Nanumba died in this serious incident. Konkomba unrest also took place more recently, in 1994.

KORTHO, SAMON (ALPHONSE). Former powerful Minister of Rural Administration and key Eyadema lieutenant. A civil administrator by profession, Kortho worked as administrator in the Bobo areas in Burkina Faso prior to independence. He then returned to Lomé and occupied a variety of high level positions as administrator in the Lomé district. In 1971 he was appointed to the Political Bureau of the **Rassemblement du Peuple Togolais** in charge of Press and Propaganda. A hard-working, very efficient, and ambitious individual, Kortho was brought into Eyadema's cabinet in March 1975 as Minister of Rural Equipment. He possessed more power and influence than his cabinet portfolio suggested, and he slowly become a permanent fixture of the Eyadema regime. In March 1987 he was dropped from the cabinet to be promoted permanent Director of the RPT party.

KOTIPOU, GNAGNENENIM BITHO. Civil administrator. Formerly Prefect in the Far North, in May 1986 Kotipou was appointed Minister of the Civil Service, a position he held for eighteen months before reverting to senior administrative duties in the civil administration.

KOTOKOLI. A confederation of chiefdoms of **Gurma** origin that settled in the Sokodé area in the seventeenth and eighteenth centuries and one of the most Islamized in Togo (93 percent). Estimated in 1993 at over 150,000, the Kotokoli (also Cotocoli and similar variants) speak the Tem language and are more properly known as the Temba. They have a paramount chief (Uro) who resides in the Dedauré quarter of Sokodé. Their popular name, Kotokoli, comes from the **Dendi** koto kolim, which means "they give and take back," a reference to the Djougou merchant's annoyance at alleged Kotokoli sharp practices in trade. The name is also used for non-Temba of Muslim faith who speak Tem, except for the **Fulani** and **Hausa**.

The Kotokoli came to Togo from Burkina Faso in two major waves establishing seven royal villages (Kouma, Tchadabe, Kadambara, Paratao, Birmi, Yalouwo, and Pangalam) from which subsequent paramount chiefs have always been chosen by rotation. In the middle of the nineteenth century, Kotokoli country was swept by Muslim influences (some via the Chokossi to the north) that disrupted the cohesion of the ethnic group, causing religious cleavages and wars. Exacerbating this was the fact that in 1880 Uro Djobo III, whose attempt to monopolize the trade in salt, arms, and slaves was rejected by the chiefs of the other villages, invited German assistance to rid his territory of Muslim Chokossi mercenaries supporting his enemies. The Germans helped establish his dynasty over all the Kotokoli. Notwithstanding their original resistance to Islam, the current Uro is Muslim, as are most of the Kotokoli, though they retain pre-Islamic practices, the best-known being the aggressive four-day Adossa ceremonies. Their principal town (now suffused with other ethnic groups) is Sokodé, a Dendi word meaning "to close," a reference to the barriers that were placed on the main routes to the town in the past. The Kotokoli are often lumped together with the **Chamba** who, however, differ from them quite significantly. The first political leaders of the Kotokoli were **Derman Ayéva**, brother of **Issifou Ayéva**, fourteenth Uro, and **Mama Fousséni**, but over 50 percent of the Kotokoli crossed ethnic lines in the Olympio era to support the CUT over their "own" UDPT party. Currently the Kotokoli are organized behind **Zarifou Ayéva** also of the royal family as his name signifies.

KOTOKOLI, UROS OF.
As with all King lists there is considerable dispute about both the sequencing and precise dates of the early Uros of the Kotokoli.

Ogoro Dam	c. 1700
Bang-Na	
Takpara	
Akoriko	
Kura	
Djobo Sémo	
Tcha Djobo	?–1901
Tcha Godému	1902–1911
Buraima	1912–1923
Anyoro	1924–1948
Issfou Ayéva	1949–1980

KOUASSI, KWAM. Ambassador to the United Nations since June 1985.

KOUAVI, HIPPOLYTE, –1967. Former Vice President of Togo. During the debates in the National Conference, where many of the crimes of the Eyadema regime came out into the open, it was revealed in July 1991 that Kouavi had been tortured to death after the 1967 coup.

KOUESSAN, GREGOIRE. Former Secretary General of the militant **Juvento** political party. In March 1967 Kouessan was sentenced to imprisonment for ten months for illegal possession of weapons but was pardoned in September of the same year. He left the country shortly after and has not been involved in political activities since.

KOZAH. The core Kabré prefecture with headquarters in the town of Kara (ex-Lama Kara) that is also the administrative center of the expanded La Kara region. Prior to the 1981 administrative reorganization of Togo, Kozah was known as the circonscription of Lama Kara.

KPALIME (formerly known as PALIME). Administrative headquarters of the lush and hilly cocoa/coffee growing district of Kloto in the Plateaux region. The town of 35,000 (which reverted to its authentic indigenous spelling in the mid-1970s as part of an authenticity campaign), is Togo's third largest after Lomé and Sokodé (and just ahead of Atakpamé, capital of the Plateaux). It is named after one of the Ewe clans that migrated to the region in the aftermath of the historic Notsé dispersal of 1720. About 120 kilometers north of Lomé, Kpalimé is connected to the north and south with excellent paved roads and is also serviced by the railroad. The town lies in the rolling hills at an altitude of 800 feet and has a cool and humid climate; nine kilometers away is the administrative headquarters, at the historic German outpost of **Misahohe**.

KPALIME CONGRESS, 1971. Important Congress of the **Rassemblement du Peuple Togolais** held in **Kpalimé**, November 12 to 14, 1971. Among the various resolutions of the Congress were the "rejection" of plans to constitutionalize the Eyadema regime (the time was not yet ripe), the call for a plebiscite on General Eyadema's continued rule (thus legitimatizing the regime), a call for continued military involvement in the political life of the nation, and the abolition of the party's top executive positions (Secretary General and deputies) in favor of a collegiate Political Bureau. The Congress also urged the erection of a women's and a youth wing, recommended the unification of the trade union movement, and took several foreign policy stands, including the recognition of China.

KPEME. Togo's main phosphate exporting port, twenty-five kilometers from the actual mines and not far from Aného on the main Lomé-Aného highway. The port has a 1,200-meter wharf for bulkloading of phosphates and is connected with the inland mines by a twenty-two-kilometer railroad and a 750-meter bridge over the Porto Seguro (Lac Togo) lagoon. Expansions and improvements have recently been undertaken to increase both the capacity and efficiency of the port.

KPENDJAL *see* MANDOURI.

KPESSI. Ethnic sliver of a larger grouping, currently residing in the vicinity of Sokodé. Originally part of the Ashanti Federation, the Kpessi became assimilated with the Ewe and adopted the latter's language. In 1752 they attacked and briefly conquered Kumasi (Ghana). When ultimately defeated in that battle, they retreated eastward, later becoming vassals of the Dahomean kingdom. Their main village, Kpessi, was at one time an important caravan stop. Estimates of the number of Kpessi in Togo vary since it is difficult today to distinguish them from the Ewe population; some 6,000 of them are known to reside in the Sokodé area.

KPESSOSSO. Goun-Mina festival of the New Year, held in mid-August in the Aného area.

KPETIGO, ELIAS KWASSIVI. Former cabinet minister. An efficient Ewe administrator with an eye for detail, Kpetigo was a Treasury Inspector before he came to Eyadema's attention. In September 1979 he was appointed Minister of Commerce and Transport and nine months later shifted to head the Ministry of Industry and State Companies. He was reassigned duties within that ministry when dropped from the cabinet in September 1982. Kpetigo re-emerged in politics with the liberalizations of the 1990's when he joined Koffigoh's interim government in September 1991 as UTD Minister of the Economy and Finance, leaving it in February 1993.

KPODZRO, FANOKO HYACINTHE PHILIPPE, 1930– . Bishop of Atakpamé and Chairperson of the National Conference that liberalized the Togolese political system. Kpodzro succeeded **Oguki Atakpah** in May 1976 as Bishop of Atakpamé, despite General Eyadema's objections to his nomination and orders to RPT militants to disrupt his investiture. Kpodzro's consecration was consequently moved to Lomé's cathedral, but a riot ensued as the services were disrupted and scuffling broke out. The Pope formally lodged a protest with the Togolese authorities over the incident, but the Togo government retorted that Kpodzro and the Church had been interfering in Togolese internal civil matters. The entire incident, finally soothed, arose over Kpodzro's opposition to the "authenticity" drives in Togo, at one time reiterating that the dropping of Christian given names was tantamount to deserting the Church. An old foe of Eyadema and military rule, Kpodzro was instrumental in guiding to fruition the opposition to Eyadema that led to the convening of the National Conference where Kpodzro was elected Chairperson. In many ways it was his voice of moderation that swayed the Conference, and later the interim **HCR**, from avoiding overly confrontational stances with Eyadema.

KPOMASSIE, TETE-MICHEL. Educator and author. Kpomassie attained a measure of renown when he became the first Togolese to visit Greenland and write about his travels. Born in Atoéta (near Aného), Kpomassie studied in Dakar, Marseilles, and Copenhagen before his visit to Greenland.

KPONTON, HUBERT KOFFI MENSAH, 1905–1982. Born to Aného's chiefly family on November 3, 1905 and the first Togolese to study at Ecole William Ponty, Kponton was secretary of Dr. **Martin Akou,** Togo's First Deputy to Paris. A man of stunning artistic talents,

Kponton invented a musical instrument, taught music at the University, and established in his home compound what became the Musée Kponton, a collection of music instruments and art bequeathed to the state.

KPONTON, MENSAH KOFFI. Member of an illustrious local family, Kponton is a young Togolese poet, some of whose work has recently been published.

KPONTON QUAM DESSOU, EMMANUEL KOKO, 1903–1968. Towering political figure, former Mayor of Aného, CUT militant, and former President of the CUT parliamentary party. Born in Aného to the founding family of the historic town on October 13, 1903, Kponton Quam Dessou worked for many years with the Societé Nationale de Développement before being elected to the National Assembly in 1958. A year later he became Mayor of Aného, remaining in these two positions until the coup d'état of 1963. In the National Assembly he was the powerful President of the CUT parliamentary party as well as President of the Foreign Affairs and Defense Committee and, in 1961, President of the Economic Committee of the Joint Euro-African Parliamentary Session in Strasbourg, France. An extremely influential CUT leader under Olympio, a powerful political broker among the Mina in Aného, and one of the best-known traditional southern leaders in Togo, Kponton Quam Dessou was virtually unknown outside his country until the 1980's when his biography and oral history of Aného was published in Lomé.

KPOSTRA, GERSON VICTOR, 1918–1965. Former cabinet minister. Born in Amou Ablo (Akposso district) on May 20, 1918, Kpostra was educated locally and at the Ecole William Ponty in Dakar and later continued his medical studies at Dakar University. Upon his return to Togo, he worked as head of the Hygienic Services in Lomé until 1958, while being a militant of the **Comité de l'Unité Togolaise** and later of **Juvento**. In May 1958 he was elected Deputy from Kpalimé and shortly after was appointed Minister of Health under President Olympio. He held this portfolio until 1963 despite the crackdown in 1961 and 1962 on former Juvento leaders. After the 1963 coup, Dr. Kpostra left the country to serve with the World Health Organization. He died two years later in a traffic accident in Brazzaville.

KPOTA DAM. A dam on the Sio river at Kpota, some eleven kilometers west of Tsévié. Built with Chinese technical assistance (5,000 million CFAF and approximately sixty Chinese technicians), the dam took two years to build and offers opportunities for rice cultivation in flooded lowlands in the area.

KPOTOGBEY, MESSUAVI K., 1943–. Director of Personnel at the Ministry of Foreign Affairs. Born in 1943 and educated in France in the Social Sciences, Humanities, and Public Administration, Kpotogbey returned to Togo to become First Director of Economic Matters at the Foreign Ministry (1978–80), following which he assumed his current duties. He has also been Chargé d'Affaires for one year (1984 to 1985) at the Togolese Embassy in Accra.

KUDZU, MICHEL WAGBENOXEVI. Minister of Health. Kudzu joined the third interim government of Prime Minister Koffigoh as Minister of Health and the Population on September 14, 1992 and was reappointed in 1993. He is a militant in the UTD political party.

KUEVIDJEN, ANDRE, 1926– . Former Minister of Justice and **Juvento** leader. Born in Aného on December 14, 1926 and trained in Mathematics, Kuevidjen worked as a school teacher between 1961 and 1963, being at the same time one of Juvento's leaders. Following the 1963 coup d'état, he joined the four-cornered coalition of President Grunitzky and served as Minister of Justice (1963–67). He has not been involved in politics since the rise of the Eyadema regime, but in July 1977—while Director of the National Institute of Scientific Research—he was imprisoned for voicing criticism of Eyadema's economic policies.

KUTUKLUI, NOE, 1923–1988. One time leading opponent of the Eyadema regime and former Minister of Labor and Deputy Secretary General of the **Comité de l'Unité Togolaise**. Born in Aného on December 2, 1923 to a poor Mina family, Kutuklui was educated locally and then in Dakar, at Caen University, and at the University of Paris, where he obtained a degree in Law. While in Paris he became active in student movements and was elected President of the militant **Federation des Etudiants de l'Afrique Noire en France**. Returning to Togo in 1958, Kutuklui rapidly rose within the party hierarchy of the CUT and, in the party Congress of October 1962, was elected Deputy Secretary General. Very close to President Sylvanus Olympio during the latter's last two years, Kutuklui assumed CUT leadership after the 1963 coup d'etat, though other contenders might have had a better claim. Appointed interim Minister of Labor immediately after the coup, Kutuklui was arrested in April 1963 for plotting against the regime he had just joined. Released in November 1965, Kutuklui was the prime instigator of the November 1966 Lomé upheaval that would have toppled President Grunitzky had the army not belatedly intervened. *See* COUP (ATTEMPTED) OF 1966. The principal fiery orator at the massive demonstrations, Kutuklui fled to asylum in Benin after the failure of the uprising. He was the only major Togolese personality to refuse to return to Lomé under the various amnesties issued by the Eyadema regime. He was in part distrustful of the latter, whom he regarded as an assassin that should be expelled from Togo, and in part unwilling to compromise his radical socialist credentials by association with the various lukewarm governments in Lomé. Though it was doubtful whether he really had a significant following in Togo, Kutuklui was behind at least five known early plots to topple Grunitzky and Eyadema, the last being the anti-Eyadema 1970 conspiracy. *See* COUP (ATTEMPTED) OF 1970. In exile in Cotonou for some time, where he was under the personal protection of the presidency and free to practice Law, Kutuklui was forced to leave Benin in 1972 since his presence was beginning to cause problems with Togo. He practiced Law in Senegal and Mauritania and in due time relocated to Canada and developed his law practice in Montreal (where he died in 1988).

KUTUKLUI AFFAIR. The so-called "Affaire-Kutuklui" rocked the unstable Presidential Council of Benin in 1972. **Nöe Kutuklui**, political heir of Sylvanus Olympio and leading opponent of the Eyadema regime, had been the sponsor of several anti-Eyadema plots while in exile in Cotonou, barely a two-hour drive from Lomé. Following the latest conspiracy (August 1970), Kutuklui's expulsion from Benin was requested by the Eyadema government. Despite Kutuklui's popularity in Cotonou and his links with various Béninois politicians, President Maga signed the orders and was then faced with the embarrassing situation of Kutuklui's disappearance (aided by Colonel Alphonse Alley and other friends) even as major pro-Kutuklui demonstrations rocked the coastal cities. After the Béninois coup d'etat of 1972, Kutuklui returned to Cotonou but eventually had to relocate more permanently to Senegal/Mauritania, and in due time to Canada where he practiced law until his death in 1988.

L

LAC TOGO. Small lake near the Togo-Benin border, immediately behind the coastal region and opening into the Atlantic Ocean at the mouth of the **Mono** river. The lake's normally salt waters are greatly sweetened at times by the inflow of river waters at the height of the rainy season. The lake separates Togo's phosphate mines from the phosphate port of **Kpémé** and a 750-meter bridge has been constructed to transport the ore over the lake. **Porto Seguro**, fifteen kilometers from Aného and near Kpémé, has a popular aquatic sports center, yachting club, and hotel-restaurant that draws many Togolese and tourists, especially on weekends. Porto Seguro has a very important **zongo** with a large Djerma population and is the site of important fetish ceremonies in its sacred forests. *See* AGBODRAFO.

LACLE, KPOTIVI TEVI DZIDZOGBE (THEODORE), 1934– . Former powerful Minister of Interior, close Eyadema lieutenant and confidant, and the regime's number two man. A southerner born in Agou in November 1934 and educated in the Catholic mission school on the plantation where he was born and at College Saint Joseph in Lomé, Laclé was a journalist with little prospect for advancement until he joined Eyadema's presidential office staff. A former editor with Radio Togo, he served as Public Relations Officer and later Director of cabinet of the presidency. He served in that role for ten years, becoming a member of the RPT Central Committee (1971) and delegate to the Lomé RPT Committee (1969). In February 1977 his long and loyal service to Eyadema was rewarded by an appointment to executive duties as Minister of Interior; he served in that capacity for ten years, to be shifted to head the Ministry of Justice only in 1987, allegedly due to ill-health. Laclé was dismissed from the cabinet in 1989 when his increasingly brazen corruption (the true reason for his demotion) could no longer be tolerated. In 1989 he was placed on trial for various misdeeds including a fifteen million CFAF lottery swindle.

LACS, PREFECTURE DES. The former circonscription d'Aného and one of five such units in the Maritime region. Its headquarters remains in Aného. *See also* ANEHO.

LAJO, ISIDORE. Head of the Comité Togolaise de la Résistance (CTR) set up by several opposition groups in December 1992 to resist political intimidation by General Eyadema.

LA KARA. Northern region with administrative headquarters in **Lama Kara**, renamed Kara in the 1981 administrative organization of the country, and encompassing until 1981 the circonscriptions (i.e., districts) of Lama Kara, Kandé, Niamtougou, and Pagouda. It was carved out of former parts of the larger Centrale and Savanes regions in the mid-1960's in order to delineate the core **Kabre** areas prior to a major drive for their socio-economic modernization and development. La Kara had an estimated population (1971) of 253,000 and it encompasses 4,955 square kilometers. Since the 1967 coup d'état that brought to power a Kabré-led administration, La Kara has seen major advances in health services, education, and agrarian development that have virtually transformed the region, as massive construction efforts have transformed the administrative and tourist infrastructure. In the

1981 reorganization of the Togolese administrative structure, the region was significantly expanded (entrenching earlier developments) by the addition of lands previously in the Centrale region, currently including the Bassar district in the west as well. The reorganization created a major political division stretching across Togo from east to west out of La Kara, rather than being a small enclave snuggled against the Benin border and now including six prefectures—Kozah, Binah, Dufelgou, Keran, Assoli, and Bassar.

LAMA KARA *see* KARA.

LAMBA. Northern ethnic group, nearly all of whom live in the Kandé region. *See* KABRE.

LAMBONY, BARTHELEMY, 1937–1974. Former cabinet minister. Lambony was born in Nandoga in the Dapaong district to Moba parents on December 16, 1937. Educated locally and in France, Lambony was a graduate of the Ecole Nationale de la France Outre Mer (ENFOM) and the universities of Bordeaux and Paris, where he obtained a degree in Law. Upon his return to Lomé, Lambony joined the Olympio administration. A member of the **Juvento** party, Lambony was President Grunitzky's interim Minister of Education prior to the 1963 elections in which he was elected to the National Assembly. There he became the Assembly's President for the duration of the Grunitzky administration (1963–67). A strong and ambitious personality, who at one time thought of supplanting Grunitzky of whom he was contemptuous, Lambony was brought into the **Comité de Reconciliation Nationale** following the 1967 coup d'état and given responsibility over the Education portfolio. With the rise of the Eyadema regime in April 1967, he was brought into the cabinet as Minister of Information. In 1969 he was moved to head the Ministry of Labor and Social Affairs, and in 1972 he replaced the ailing Colonel **Assila**—whose responsibilities he had already assumed in an interim capacity—as Minister of Interior. In August 1973 Lambony was dropped from the cabinet and attached to the presidential office. He had been a member of the Political Bureau of the **Rassemblement du Peuple Togolais** since its inception.

LARE, AUGUSTIN NAMPOUGUIM, 1937– . Diplomat. Born in Bidjenga-Kpantogou in 1937 and educated in Law in Paris and Geneva. Laré served for six months as Director of Political Affairs in the Foreign Ministry (1967–68) before being sent abroad as First Secretary at the Embassy of Togo to the United Nations. In 1974 he returned to Lomé and assumed duties in the Division of Political and International Affairs, rising to be division head.

LASSEY, SEWOA GA JAMES, 1935– . Civil administrator. Born in 1935 and trained in administration at the Institut des Hautes Etudes d'Outre Mer in Paris, Lassey returned to Togo to become a Labor Inspector (1970–73), Head, Unskilled Personnel at the Labor Inspectorate (1973), personnel officer at **OTP** from 1973 to 1977 and since then Head of Administration at OTP.

LAWANI, GREGOIRE ESSOHANAM. Minister of Youth, Sports, and Leisure in the fourth transitional government of Prime Minister **Koffigoh**. Lawani is an ecologist.

LAWSON, ASSION G., 1939– . Agronomist. Born on May 2, 1939 and trained in Agronomy at the University of Toulouse (graduating in 1968) and in Entomology at the University of Paris (1976), Lawson currently teaches at the School of Agronomy at the University of Benin.

LAWSON, BENI. Former attaché at the Togolese Embassy in Paris and a former Lomé businessman. Beni Lawson is a member of the Lawson family of Aného and hence tied by family relations to the opposition to the Eyadema regime. He is also the brother of Lieutenant Colonel Merlaud Lawson, leader of one of the Paris-based opposition groups involved in several of the plots against Eyadema. In 1979 Lawson was abducted by Togolese security service agents in Accra and spirited into Togo to stand trial for the 1977 attempted coup. He was later released, since he was found innocent. He currently resides in Accra and Paris.

LAWSON, BOEVI-MAWUSSI, 1936– . Banker. Born in Aného on January 18, 1936, Lawson was educated locally at the Lycée Bonnecarrére and later secured professional Banking training (1957–59). In 1959 he joined the Banque Centrale de l'Afrique de l'Ouest and became the bank's Section Chief (1960–65), Manager (1965–67), Deputy Director (1967–73), Agency Director (1973–75), and National Director for Togo operations (since 1975). Lawson is apolitical.

LAWSON, LATEVI-ATCHO (ELLIOTT), 1948– . Diplomat. Born in Lomé on September 9, 1948, Lawson was educated locally and then studied English at the University of Bordeaux (until 1972). During his last year of studies he obtained training in Diplomacy in Geneva.

Upon his return to Lomé, he became Assistant Director of the Department of International Organizations and Conferences and later Assistant Director of the Political Department in the Ministry of Foreign Affairs (1972–74). In April 1974 he was appointed councilor at the Togolese Mission to the United Nations, and in 1979 he was reassigned to the EEC mission in Brussels.

LAWSON, MERLAUD (LIEUTENANT COLONEL). Former high ranking army officer implicated in the 1977 attempted mercenary assault on Eyadema. Prior to his conspiracy, Lawson was Deputy Quartermaster of the armed forces as well as Director of Direct Tax Contributions in the Office of Taxes. Regarded as somewhat of an Eyadema protégé, Lawson was a key element in the 1977 affair and promptly fled to asylum in Paris when the attempt failed to set up the Paris-based anti-Eyadema Front National de Liberation du Togo (FNLT) that offered an armed alternative to replace Eyadema.

LAWSON FAMILY. One of the important Aného families, members of which are found in all branches of Togolese life, and until 1961 when by mutual agreement the title was abolished, contenders with the Adjigo clan for the title Superior Chief of Aného. One of the founders of the family was "King" George Lawson, a Fanti from Accra (Gold Coast) who had been a steward on a slave ship before settling in Aného in 1812 and engaging in trade in slaves and other commodities. Involved in a local power struggle, he styled himself "King of Glidji." He died in 1883 and was succeeded by his son G. A. Lawson and another son who came to Aného from Lagos, both of whom acted as customs collectors for the infant chief of Glidji. Strongly pro-British, the Lawsons opposed the expanding German influence in the area and appealed for British assistance from Lagos. In retaliation, the Germans abducted several members of the household and shipped them off aboard the *Sophie*. (*See* GERMAN ADMINISTRATION.) They returned to Aného aboard the *Mowe*, together with **Gustav Nachtigal**, who set up the German colony of Togo. Descendants of the family have since served in a variety of public positions and in the liberal professions. They include Lieutenant Francisco Lawson, a St. Cyr graduate and Deputy Head of the Army's (minute) Engineering Corps; Lieutenant Colonel Eugene Lawson of the gendarmerie; Major Merlaud Lawson, former Deputy Intendant of the armed forces and Director of Direct Tax Contributions; Samuel Lawson in the Ministry of Agriculture; Felix Lawson, the former Deputy and President of the Assembly's Interior Affairs Committee (1963–67); Georges Lawson, the Deputy Procuror (attorney) of Togo; Christian Lawson, head of the Geology Department of the Ministry of Public Works; Amen Lawson, former Medical Inspector and Director of the National Hospital; and **Latevi-Atcho Lawson**, former councilor at Togo's Mission to the United Nations. Being part of the "Brazilian" elite, several of the Lawson family (but according to government sources the entire "clan") have been accomplices in the various anti-Eyadema plots and attempted coups, together with other Brazilian families like the Olympios and the De Souzas.

LAWSON-AHLUIVI, FOGAN, 1950– . Civil administrator. Born on July 18, 1950 in Lomé and educated at Lomé and Notsé, Lawson-Ahluivi attended the Ceramic Pottery Polytechnical School in Lomé before becoming head of a division in the Togo's Office National de la Pharmacie. He is also a published poet.

LEAGUE OF NATIONS MANDATE. Following the Anglo-French invasion of German Togo, the British held the rich cocoa lands of Kloto, the Dagomba capital of Yendi, the three railroads, and Lomé, with the French occupying the rest of the colony. On May 7, 1919, the Supreme Allied Council declared that the League of Nations would assume ultimate responsibility for Togo (and other such territories). On July 10, 1919, there was a new Anglo-French partition of Togo, with France retaining the bulk of her former sphere and gaining the Kloto region, Lomé, and the railroads. The British kept the former German station at Ho (in Kloto) and the Dagomba and northern regions. The two segments of the former German colony were designated class B mandates of the League of Nations and under Article 119 of the Treaty of Versailles, Germany renounced future claims to its former colonial possessions. After the end of World War II, the two mandates became United Nations trusteeship territories under the same administering powers.

LIBYA. Like most African states, Togo was the target of a concerted Libyan diplomatic and financial effort in the early 1970s, aimed at displacing the strong Israeli presence in the country until that date. With the break in relations with Israel in the aftermath of the 1973 Middle East War, several treaties between Libya and Togo were signed and a number of joint companies in a variety of areas were announced. Other treaties, including ones of military cooperation, were signed in 1975 and 1976. Culminating these contacts was the state visit to Tripoli of President Eyadema in February 1976 and Qaddafi's later visit to Lomé. Despite a profusion of contacts and treaties, relations have not been smooth. Muslim and/or Islamic cultural projects have been financed or completed with much greater alacrity than projects in the purely economic domain. Funds have been only grudgingly granted, original schedules have been completely ignored, and there have been numerous complaints of Libyan interference in local affairs, either directly via the cultural organizations created or contacts maintained or through the various joint companies set up. In the 1980s there have also been complaints of Libyan involvement in conspiracies against the regime.

LIGUE TOGOLAISE DU DROIT D'HOMME (LTDH). Human rights organization set up in 1991 as an independent counter-balance to the Eyadema-sponsored CNDH.

LISSA. Creator of the universe according to Ewe mythology, the pantheon of which includes about 600 gods. Mahou is the wife of Lissa. Still widely venerated in Ewe society, traditional beliefs include veneration of a particular animal by each clan; the animal embodies the spirit of a clan ancestor.

LISTE NATIONALE DE L'UNITE ET RECONCILIATION. Unified electoral list of Togo's four major political parties that was submitted to the electorate in the May 7, 1963, elections, following the assassination of President Sylvanus Olympio. The Liste included fifty-six candidates for office, equally apportioned among the **Mouvement Populaire Togolais, Juvento, Parti de l'Unité Togolaise**, and **Union Democratique des Populations Togolaises** under the leadership of the latter's **Nicolas Grunitzky** and **Antoine Méatchi**. At the elections, the Liste obtained 568,893 votes out of the 582,309 cast, with the total number of registered voters standing at 639,523, and members on the Liste became the deputies of the Assemblée Nationale.

LE LIVRE VERT. "The Green Book"—much touted condensed version of the RPT manifesto and economic program, published by Editogo and widely distributed among the population in the mid-1970s. Since the collapse of the Togolese economy in the 1980s nothing much has been heard about the document.

LOGBA. Northern ethnic group. *See* KABRE.

LOI CADRE. The "Enabling" Act passed by the French National Assembly in June 1956. The law expanded the legislative powers of the territorial assemblies in each of France's colonies at the expense of the two French African federations, gave all overseas territories local autonomy, made suffrage universal, and established a single electoral college in each one (*see* DOUBLE ELECTORAL COLLEGE). In the case of Togo (which was not a colony but a trusteeship territory), the double electoral college had already been abolished in February 1952, and the territorial assembly already had powers that assemblies in France's colonies did not yet possess; the Loi Cadre essentially gave Togo total internal autonomy.

LOME. Togo's capital, largest city, rapidly growing nerve center of the modern economy, and administrative headquarters of the Maritime region. Most of Lomé's 1994 population of 450,000 (up from 360,000 in 1984 and 140,000 in 1971) is composed of southern elements (Mina, Ewe, and Ouatchi), though the city has sizable Hausa trading communities and other ethnic groups as well, including many foreigners, both European and the African.

Lomé has been the capital of Togo since 1897 when German Governor Koehler (whose tomb is in the city cemetery) shifted the capital from Aného to the small village of Alomé, settled in the eighteenth century by Ewe and Ouatchi arriving from Notsé. After its designation as capital considerable Mina traders relocated there from Aného and Porto Seguro. One of Lomé's original quarters was its **zongo**, founded in 1884 by Hausa from Salaga—the latter the biggest trade entrepot in the region and terminus of an important caravan artery. The *zongo* remained populated by Hausa and Yoruba merchants and their slaves and attracted other communities, notably Kotokoli, coming to benefit from the commercial activities and employment prospects offered by Octaviano Olympio, who relocated at the same time to the budding "village" from the Brazilian town of **Agoué** in Benin. In many ways Olympio was the "founder" of Lomé. *See also* ANAGOKOME. On the eastern side of town is the Amoutive traditional quarter, home of descendants of Djitri, founder of Alomé. In a colorful ceremony in April the current Chief, in full customary dress, surrounded by Court officials, displays the thrones of his predecessors.

In 1911 Lomé (whose name comes from one of the Ewe clans involved in the historic Notsé dispersal of 1720) had a population of 36,000, the true population explosion occurring essentially after independence and in particular in the past decade. The city is currently rapidly expanding inland, to the north, being blocked on two sides by the Ghanaian border (two kilometers from the center of the city) and the Atlantic Ocean. Lack of orderly city planning in its early days and uncontrolled expansion since independence badly scarred downtown Lomé, presenting major obstacles to urban planners. Only in the mid-1970s were major renovation projects for the center of the city announced. Since 1970 the city has been graced by a steady stream of new modernistic buildings, including the **Maison du Peuple** and half a dozen major new hotels—the **OCAM** village, Presidential Palace, etc.—the cumulative effect being to make Lomé look much more modern than, say, Cotonou in Benin. In the eastern outskirts is the Free Port, constantly being expanded due to Lomé's booming trade and transit role vis-à-vis the landlocked countries to the interior, and the Tokoin military barracks and the new university are located in the north. During the tumultuous events of 1992 and 1993 that pitched General Eyadema and his personalist army against society, over one third of the population of Lomé fled across the border to Ghana, and much of the town's economic activity ground to a halt.

There are two main paved roads connecting Lomé with the interior, and the capital is equidistant—in terms of driving time along the very scenic coastal highway—from Cotonou and Accra in Benin and Ghana respectively, two hours away. Lomé is also the administrative headquarters of the prefecture du Golfe (ex-circonscription du Lomé) covering the suburban villages and encompassing some 72,000 people. It is one of five such subdivisions in the Maritime region.

LOME INCIDENTS OF 1933. A series of popular demonstrations and administrative counterreprisals consequent to a period of general economic downswing and malaise. The incidents arose over petitions handed to the Lomé police headquarters by local district and cantonal chiefs requesting that new taxes on market stalls be withdrawn. A dozen such new taxes had been announced during the preceding year as the French administration tried to raise funds in an effort at fiscal self-sufficiency at a time when the economy had become stagnant during the worldwide Great Depression. (Exports in 1934 were barely thirty-three percent of those in 1929.) The haughty French administration reacted to the petitions by arresting two of the chiefs, in general viewing the incident as a pro-British ploy rather than as a sign of economic malaise. The same afternoon, a crowd of 3,000 Africans marched through the streets demanding the release of their leaders, and a general strike was declared. Though the prisoners were released that evening, the crowds did not disperse and demonstrations continued the next day. Several buildings were set on fire, including the home of **Jonathan Savi de Tové**, Secretary of the Lomé **Conseil de Notables,** regarded a lackey of the administration. As tension increased, Lomé's European population was issued firearms, and troops were brought in from the Ivory Coast. These troops commenced a veritable rampage that extended into the neighboring countryside. Fourteen Togolese were sentenced to death, and scores were imprisoned or fined for such minor infractions as travel without permits (sentences of up to five years were handed out for such offenses). Numerous villagers were killed and women raped during the counterreprisals, and reporters and photographers from Dahomey (covering the events) were imprisoned. The entire press run of *L'Etoile du Dahomey,* which published an account of the atrocities, was confiscated by the French administration in that colony.

LOME INDUSTRIAL FREE ZONE. Major initiative conceived in October 1989 to revitalize the Togolese economy with USAID initiative and the Overseas Investment Corporation. Conceived of as a private enterprise zone governed by a special liberal investment code that would spur industrial relocations from outside the country, the first enterprise to establish itself in the Zone was the subsidiary of the French Compagnie Générale des Matieres Colorantes (GMC), specializing in packing pharmaceuticals, chemicals, and agro-food products, that came in September 1990. An additional nineteen companies had applied and been approved for relocation to the Zone, the site for which had been developed with 800 million CFAF, most from the GMC group. Most did not relocate per schedule, and some actually abandoned participation, due to the political demonstrations that shortly were to rock Lomé and were to last for eighteen months.

LOOKY, L. ZAKARY, 1905– . Former CUT militant. Born in 1905 in the vicinity of Pagouda in the north, Looky worked as a public works surveyor before joining the Comité de l'Unité Togolaise and becoming immersed in political activities. He served as President of the **Conseil de Circonscription** of Pagouda in 1959 and was the Treasurer (1946–52) and Regional Director (1952–61) of the CUT in Kara. Elected Deputy to the Assemblée Representative in 1946, he served as Vice President of the Assembly before losing his seat in 1951 to a non-CUT delegate. With the rise of the Olympio regime, Looky once again was elected from Kara (1961–63) and was Vice President of the CUT parliamentary party and a member of the Committee on Finance and the Economy. Following the 1963 coup d'etat, Looky moved out of political life into retirement.

LOSSO. Northern animist ethnic group found in the Kara, Niamitougou, and Sansanné-Mango areas and also, as a result of land pressures, in the vicinity of Atakpamé. Frequently lumped together with the **Kabré**, the Losso number around 98,000 people. In the north they cultivate isolated palm plantations.

LOSSOU, PAULIN KODJO. Deputy Secretary of the Mouvement Togolais pour la Démocratie political party, behind the September 1986 coup d'etat attempt against General Eyadema. Lossou was in self-exile in Paris since 1972, organizing anti-Eyadema activities. After the 1986 coup attempt he was served deportation orders by Paris that wished to send him to Argentina. His appeal was in the courts when the Togolese secret service mounted both an assassination attempt (in Paris) and a kidnap attempt.

LOUMIOU, AHMED (EL HADJ), 1905– . Religious leader and educator. Born in Lomé in 1905 of devout Hausa parents originating from Sokoto (Nigeria), Loumiou studied the Koran under a succession of religious instructors and made the pilgrimage to Mecca in 1945. Earlier he had set up a school of his own (in 1942) in the Lomé zongo—the first such school in Lomé. A highly respected member of the Muslim community, he continued his teaching until 1987.

LUDO see SOCIETE INDUSTRIELLE DE PREPARATION ALIMENTAIRES (SIPAL).

M

MADEIROS, CARLOS DE, 1921– . Medical inspector. Born in Lomé in 1921 and educated abroad as a physician. Madeiros served as Director of the Hospital Center in Lomé until 1968. He was simultaneously head of the School for Lab Technicians and Nursing Staff. Since 1968 he has been in private practice in Lomé.

MADJRI, DOVI JOHN, 1940– . Journalist and author. Born in 1940 near Lomé to Catholic parents, Madjri was educated in Cameroun and Burkina Faso specializing in adult education and Social Psychology. On his return to Lomé he secured a post with the Catholic weekly *Présence Chrétienne,* moving to become its Deputy Editor and later Editor. In 1971 he left for Vogan in charge of the latter's Social Center and in 1973 became involved in trade union activities as well. He is the author of several acclaimed books, including a detailed overview of Togolese literature.

MAHOU. Wife of **Lissa,** creator of the world in the Ewe pantheon.

MAISON DE L'UNITE see MAISON DU PEUPLE.

MAISON DU PEUPLE. Imposing modernistic building inaugurated in Lomé on the occasion of the 1972 OCAM summit meeting. Built at the cost of 8.5 million dollars on the Place de l'Indépendance, the structure boasts a 17,000 square mile 3,000 seat conference hall (at the time reputed the third largest in the world after that of Brasilia and Los Angeles), which is of a unique architectural design. The Maison du Peuple was until 1990 the national headquarters of the **Rassemblement du Peuple Togolais** and also houses the National Archives, libraries, an exposition gallery, and a museum. The building's facade is of marble (from Togolese quarries), and some of the interior decorations were designed by Togolese artists. In July 1991, as multipartyism reached Togo and both Eyadema and the RPT seemed destined for the dustbin of history, the **National Conference** both renamed the building (to Maison de l'Unité) and disbanded the RPT, evicting it from the building. The RPT, however, was not to be disbanded and retained premises in the building.

MALLAM BELLO *see* BELLY EL FOUTI, MOHAMED.

MALLY, THEOPHILE, 1913–1973. Former powerful Minister of Interior under President Sylvanus Olympio. Born to an Akposso family in Gobé-Admiabra in 1913, Mally was a farmer until he joined the **Comité de l'Unité Togolaise** in the mid-1940s. In 1959 he became the President of the Executive Committee of the Akposso **Conseil de Circonscription** and joined Olympio's cabinet in May 1960 as Minister of Interior, Press, and Information (to January 1962). From the latter date until Olympio's assassination in 1963, Mally concentrated on his duties as Minister of Interior, dropping the other portfolios. Following the establishment of a one party state, Mally was instrumental in tracking down and imprisoning most of the leaders of the opposition parties in Togo, becoming one of the most hated and feared men in the country. He did not fall into the dragnet set for Olympio's ministers at the time of the 1963 coup d'etat and escaped to Nigeria. He later also lived in Guinea. From abroad he directed several plots against the successor Grunitzky government, vying with **Noe Kutuklui** for the leadership of the CUT party. In 1967 he heeded the amnesty call of General Eyadema, made his peace with the new regime, and returned to Togo. Not fully trusted and still resented by many he had previously persecuted, Mally was appointed to various secondary positions in the Eyadema government. In 1970 he was a member of the **Cour de Sûreté** that tried the plotters of the August attempted coup. Not heard of for some time, in March 1973 it was tersely announced that he had died in prison after being imprisoned on February 28 for passing a bad check.

MALOU, YAYA (BENOIT), 1932– . Former Minister of Education. A cousin of President Eyadema, the Kabré Malou was born in Pya in the vicinity of Kara in 1932. Educated in the missionary school and then at a Protestant secondary school in Lomé (1947–53), Malou spent his early years teaching in the north in Atakpamé and in Lomé. In 1958 he entered the Police Training School of the then Mali Federation in Dakar, Senegal, returning to Togo in 1960 to serve with the National

Security forces in Lomé, Atakpamé, and Sokodé (1960–63). Following the 1963 coup d'etat, Malou was appointed Assistant Director of the Sûreté, and in 1965 he attended a specialized course in France. After General Eyadema's assumption of control over the armed forces in 1965, Malou was brought into President Grunitzky's cabinet as Minister of Education. (He had previously served very briefly as interim Minister of Interior.) In November 1966, totally disgruntled with Grunitzky's leadership style and the continuous Grunitzky-Méatchi tug-of-war in the cabinet, Malou—together with **Pierre Adossama**—resigned from the government, precipitating the **Kutuklui**-led uprising in Lomé. *See* COUP (ATTEMPTED) OF 1966. Briefly arrested by Grunitzky for his role in the attempted coup, Malou was a member of the interim **Comité de Reconciliation Nationale** set up after the coup of 1967 and was brought into Eyadema's cabinet (as Minister of Civil Service, Works, and Social Affairs) after the latter's assumption of full power in April 1967. In August 1969 Malou was shifted to head the Ministry of Education. A key personal confidant of President Eyadema, Malou held a great deal of prestige in the regime, though not power, his longevity in the cabinet and family relationship to Eyadema notwithstanding. He has also been a member of the **Rassemblement du Peuple Togolais** from its inception. His former political and personal connections could not save him in 1979, when he was dropped from the cabinet for feathering his nest too liberally. He was appointed Director of the National Police Training College. In January 1983 he was summarily dropped from his college appointment and all political posts (including the Politburo), allegedly for "improperly executing his duties." His purge was one of several demanded by the international community when faced with Togolese demands for a fiscal bailout in the 1980s and rampant corruption at the highest circles of the government and party.

MAMA, FOUSSENI, 1924– . Former Minister of Interior under President Grunitzky. Born in 1924 in Sokodé, Mama's political fortunes have been largely intertwined with Grunitzky's. Trained as a school teacher locally and at the prestigious Ecole William Ponty in Senegal, Mama worked as an educator for eight years before being elected to the territorial assembly as **UCPN** deputy and cooperated with Nicolas Grunitzky's **Parti Togolais du Progrès.** He sat in the assembly until 1956; between 1953 and 1956 he was also Togo's councilor of the Council at the **French Union.** In 1956 he was brought into Grunitzky's government as Minister of State in charge of Public Works and just prior to the collapse of the government was promoted to head the Ministry of Interior. Locked out of power during the Olympio era (1958–63), Mama was recalled to the cabinet with the establishment of the new Grunitzky administration following the 1963 coup d'etat. One of the pillars of the regime and Grunitzky's most loyal ally, Mama was Minister of Interior between October 1963 and November 1966. In November he bitterly clashed with Vice President Méatchi over the latter's attempts to undermine the Grunitzky administration (*see* MEATCHI-MAMA CRISIS) in the aftermath of which he was forced to accept a temporary demotion (to become Minister of Education) in order to avert a major crisis between the two leaders of the Togolese executive. His demotion, which was the last straw for the PUT ministers in the cabinet who were chafing at Grunitzky's lack of decisiveness in resolving his friction with Méatchi, led to a full-blown governmental crisis and the Lomé uprising that nearly toppled the regime. *See* COUP (ATTEMPTED) OF 1966. After the 1967 coup d'etat, Mama revolved in the outer perimeters of political power in Togo, serving as Director of the Ecole Nationale d'Administration, training entry and middle level civil servants. A Kotokoli Muslim who has made the pilgrimage to Mecca, he assisted with the creation of the UMT in 1963. In 1970 he sat—as a former Minister of Interior—on the Cour de Sûreté that tried the August 1970 plotters and has been a member of the Political Bureau of the **Rassemblement du Peuple Togolais** in charge of political affairs. Mama was especially important to Eyadema because of his constructive role, at various stages, during the intensive schisms within the Togolese Muslim community. In 1970 he was virtually forced to take over the Presidency of the community after the ouster of the former President and Treasurer due to their autocratic mannerisms. Mama was reconfirmed in his office a year later but stepped down in 1972 in favor of Kassim Mensah, retaining honorary presidency status (granted to all former Presidents), but he again had to mediate sharp cleavages internal to the community in succeeding years. He is currently in retirement.

MAMAH, FOUSSENI, 1951– . Diplomat. Born in Sansanné-Mango in 1951, Mamah was educated in West Germany at the University of Saar and the University of Frankfurt, obtaining a Ph.D. in Ethnology. After a brief stint in Lomé as the Deputy Head of the Eyadema Foundation and the Institute of Political Studies, Mamah was appointed Ambassador to Germany.

MAMIYABLE, LOLE *see* COUP (ATTEMPTED) OF 1970.

MANDOURI. Small village near the Benin border in the extreme northeast of Togo. Formerly a poste administratif, it was designated seat of a sousprefecture in 1981, that of Kpéndjal within the Tone prefecture.

MANGO *see* SANSANNE-MANGO.

MANKOUBI, SANDANI BAWA, 1938– . Economist, banking administrator, and Administrative Director of the Economy in the Ministry of Economics and Finance. A Moba born near Sansanné-Mango in the north on September 29, 1938, Mankoubi obtained his professional training in Law and Economics at the University of Paris. Upon his return to Togo, he was appointed Deputy Governor of the African Development Bank (1964–67) and administrator of the Union Togolaise du Banque (1964+). Since 1968 he has been Director-General of the **Banque Togolaise de Devéloppement,** a member of the **Conseil Economique et Social,** and, since 1978, Director of the Economy in the Ministry of Economics and Finance. With the political liberalizations of the 1990s, Mankoubi has been head of the UTR political party, aligned with Gilchrist Olympio.

MANUFACTURE TOGOLAISE DES PLASTIQUES (MTP). Company created in 1970 to manufacture shopping bags and other plastic products. Capitalized with ten million CFAF the company had a turnover of 36.7 million CFAF in 1979. It produces sixty to seventy tons of bags and has a capacity of manufacturing one hundred tons. Some fifteen percent of its products are routinely exported to neighboring states.

MARITIME. One of Togo's regions, with headquarters in Lomé and encompassing the prefectures of Golfe, Lacs, Vo, Yoto, and Zio (ex-Lomé, Aného, Tabligbo, Tsévié, and Vogan) and the urban communes of Lomé, Aného, and Tsévié. The region covers 6,100 square kilometers and included, in 1990, an estimated 824,000 people, mostly Ewe in the west and north, Mina in the south and east, and Ouatchi in the east and north. The Maritime is an area of great density (110 persons per square kilometer) and is Togo's most socially, economically, and politically developed region. The country's most important resource, **phosphates,** is found in the Maritime, as well as most industry and commercial enterprises. The region is dissected by the fully paved and scenic coastal highway that connects Lagos with Accra via Porto Novo, Cotonou, Ouidah, Aného, and Lomé and is linked with the noncoastal areas by railroads and paved roads.

MARO. Strangers' quarters in northern Togo. Also known as wangara and zongo.

MAROIX, JEAN EUGENE PIERRE, 1867–1942. French colonial officer. Born in Teret on March 4, 1867, Maroix was commissioned in

1893 and served in Madagascar, Senegal, and elsewhere before being sent to suppress the Holli revolt in Dahomey (now Benin). He later transferred his battalion to Savé by rail and marched overland into German Togo, conquering the Kamina radio station, an act that led to the German surrender of the colony to France. Named Commander of Togo in 1915, Maroix later saw action in several other countries and died in Nice in 1942.

MATHEY, DOSSEVI APOSSAN. President of the Comité National des Foires et Expositions. Prior to this appointment Mathey had served as High Commissioner of Tourism.

MAWUPE VOVOR, VALENTIN *see* VOVOR, VALENTIN.

MAWUSSI, EDIGBO EKELE. Former minister. A leader of the post-1990 **CAR** political party, Mawussi was briefly Minister of Environment and Tourism in Prime Minister Koffigoh's third Transitional government between September 14, 1992 and February 1993.

MAWUSSI, EPIPHANE AYI, MAWUPE, 1935– . International administrator and one time diplomat. Born on January 1, 1935, Mawussi was educated locally and at the West Africa College in Accra, following which he attended a variety of universities, including Northwestern Polytechnic (London), London School of Economics, and the University of Paris, specializing in Economics and Banking. An intern (1961–64) at the National Bank of Paris, Mawussi became a staff member of the bank in 1964 and in 1965 joined the International Bank for Reconstruction and Development in Washington, D.C., serving as an Economic Analyst of Third World Development Banks and as a Loan Officer. He resigned from IBRD in 1969 to join the Kez International company, a Montreal-based engineering advisory corporation. In 1970 he was appointed Ambassador to the United States, but his tenure was equally brief, lasting a few months, following which he disappeared from both financial and public scenes.

MEATCHI, ANTOINE IDRISSOU, 1925–1984. Former Vice President of Togo. Born in Lama Kara to a branch of the Sokodé royal family on September 23, 1925, Méatchi was educated locally and abroad in Bamako, Mali, and France (1942–53) in the field of Tropical Agriculture. Upon his return to Togo, he joined the civil service and was appointed Deputy Head of Agricultural Services, Director of the Tové Farm School, and Head of the Kloto Agricultural Promotion Project, all in the southern part of the country. A member of various northern conservative coalitions of chiefs and nobility supported by the French administration against the Ewe **Comité de l'Unité Togolaise,** Méatchi was selected by Nicolas Grunizky to serve as his Minister of Agriculture (1956) and Finance (1957) in the latter's **Autonomous Republic** administration. After the United Nations-supervised elections that toppled the Grunitzky regime, Méatchi was elected to the National Assembly from Pagouda in the north. With Grunitzky's withdrawal from politics and relocation to Cote d'Ivoire, Méatchi became the de facto leader of their joint party, the **Union Démocratique des Peuples Togolais,** which was a merger of Méatchi's **Union des Chefs et des Populations du Nord** and Grunitzky's **Parti Togolais du Progrès.** In the 1961 elections Méatchi lost his parliamentary seat, was accused of plotting against the regime and arrested. Because of an administrative error in Kara (where he was being detained), he was able to slip across the border to Djougou, Benin and from there made his way to Accra where he remained in exile until the 1963 coup d'etat. While in Accra he briefly headed the notorious Ghanaian Bureau of African Affairs, becoming a militant. After the assassination of Olympio, Méatchi promptly came back to Lomé to claim the presidency. At the time, the inexperienced **Insurrectionist Committee** undoubtedly preferred to see a government formed by Méatchi, a northerner like themselves, over one by Grunitzky, who was also recalled from exile. France's opposition to Méatchi, and Grunitzky's unwillingness to serve under his former minister, tipped the balance against Méatchi, and a split executive government emerged with Grunitzky as President and Méatchi as Vice President, in charge also of the portfolios of Finance, Economy, and Planning. The constitutional arrangement was a disaster from the outset, for it threw together two mismatched personalities with contrary ideologies and styles of operation. The cautious and conservative Grunitzky clashed daily with the militant, ambitious, and abrasive Méatchi, whom he could not purge without causing a major governmental crisis. The continuous friction between the two men, Grunitzky's indecisiveness, and Méatchi's attempts to undermine his competitor led to the famous **Méatchi-Mama crisis,** the **attempted coup of November 1966** and, inevitably, to the coup d'etat of 1967. After the November 1966 crisis, Méatchi was purged when Grunitzky passed a constitutional amendment abolishing the vice presidency; Méatchi was temporarily assigned to head the Ministry of Public Works on December 23, 1966, three weeks before the coup d'etat. Following the collapse of the Grunitzky government, many observers assumed that Méatchi would be elevated to power by the northern clique in the Army. Méatchi had, however, lost his credibility and support in the Army and was not even included in the new cabinet of General Eyadema. Instead he was reappointed to his old professional post as Director of Togo's Agricultural Services, serving in that capacity until 1978. For the next four years engaged in private commercial activity, in 1982 Méatchi was ignominiously arrested and jailed for massive corruption during his long tenure as Director of Agriculture. His purge was specifically demanded by French financial circles unwilling to pump additional funds into the ailing Togolese economy only to have them drained into the pockets of individuals such as Méatchi. Paradoxically, at the same time Méatchi's wife was elected to the National Assembly (in 1979) and served on Eyadema's cabinet. Imprisoned in the distant Sansanné-Mango prison under harsh conditions, according to Amnesty International Méatchi for all practical purposes had been "executed" by torture, maltreatment, and starvation, dying in prison in March 1984 and not of a heart attack in 1987 as the Eyadema regime originally maintained. Reliable sources have also claimed that Méatchi was imprisoned less for his misdeeds than because he remained a threat to Eyadema's increasingly beleaguered status in Lomé.

MEATCHI, SHEFFI (Mrs.). Former Secretary of State at the Ministry of Public Health, in charge of Social and Women's Affairs. Mrs. Méatchi, who was **Antoine Méatchi's** wife, retained her governmental post despite her husband's arrest in 1982 for embezzlement while head of OPAT. She was also elected Deputy to the National Assembly in 1979 and sat on several committees of the assembly. She was dropped from the cabinet in September 1984.

MEATCHI-MAMA CRISIS (1966). Major cabinet crisis in November 1966 that led to the resignation of the last PUT delegates and ushered in the attempted coup of November 21, 1966. The crisis took place against the backdrop of the ongoing tug-of-war between President Grunitzky and Vice President **Antoine Méatchi** and the long history of hostility between Méatchi and Grunitzky's loyal Minister of Interior, **Fousseni Mama.** During Grunitzky's absence in Paris, Mama informed the cabinet that his security forces had discovered that the anti-Grunitzky leaflets being distributed in Lomé were the handiwork of Méatchi. The latter immediately retaliated by suspending Mama from the cabinet, and only after Grunitzky's hurried return from Paris was a semblance of order established, with Mama downgraded to the Ministry of Education. Grunitzky's actions and unwillingness to purge Méatchi constituted the last straw for the PUT members in his cabinet who had been urging their more militant colleagues to cooperate with the Grunitzky regime. The day after they resigned from the cabinet, the country was rocked by the Lomé upheaval—*see* COUP (ATTEMPTED) OF 1966—and, less than two months later, civilian rule came to an end in Togo.

MECKLEMBURG, ADOLF FRIEDRICH ZU, 1873–1969. Last German Governor (1912–14) of Togo, prior to the surrender of the colony to French forces in 1914. Related to the Duke of Orleans, Mecklemburg was born in Schwerin on October 10, 1873. He participated in several expeditions in Central Africa and wrote two books on his travels. At age eighty-six, he returned to Togo in 1960 to celebrate the country's independence. He died in his Holstein castle on August 6, 1969.

MEDEIROS, VICTOR DE, 1932– . Diplomat and Secretary General of the Foreign Ministry. Born in Lomé on March 3, 1932, Medeiros was educated locally and abroad at the universities of Strasbourg and Grenoble and at the Geneva Graduate Institute of International Studies. Upon his return to Lomé, Medeiros was appointed Director of the Department of Political Affairs and International Organizations in the Foreign Ministry (1963), and in 1966 he was sent to the United States as Councilor at the Togolese Embassy. In 1968 he was reassigned to the Paris Embassy as First Councilor and Cultural Chargé d'Affaires, and in 1974 he became Secretary General of the Ministry of Foreign Affairs in Lomé. He is currently technical consultant with the Ministry in Lomé.

MEDERSA DE LOME. Comprehensive religious (Muslim) school in Lomé. Constructed in 1965 with funds from Saudi Arabia, the Medersa was the first such school in Togo. In its first year, it enrolled 286 pupils, 150 of whom joined its primary section, with ten percent of the total student body coming from neighboring countries. Staffed originally by Egyptian teachers, over the years the student body has expanded, and the teachers have been localized. In 1983, for example, there were 423 students in the Medersa (fifteen percent from abroad) and the staff nearly all Togolese. Tuition is free, and there are cooperative arrangements with the University of Al Azhar in Cairo.

MEMENE, SEYI (COLONEL). Secretary of State to the Ministry of Interior in charge of Security since May 1994. Méméne joined the RPT-UDT coalition cabinet of Prime Minister Edem Kodjo as an RPT member. Just prior to this appointment he had been Director-General of the National Police. Between 1986 and 1989 he had been Eyadema's loyal Head of Security Services after a period as Director of Customs. In 1989 Méméne was implicated in the embezzlement of 500 million CFAF of funds connected with arms contracts and served two years in jail. He was rehabilitated in June 1991 to become Director of Eyadema's military cabinet before his further promotion.

MENSAH, KASSIM. Former Ambassador and Muslim leader. Mensah is a Muslim dignitary of Ewe origins (an extremely rare occurrence) who played a central role in helping create the Union Musulmane du Togo in 1963. He served as the UMT's Secretary General between 1963 and 1970. In the latter year, he was elected the association's Vice President, and in 1972 he became President. During his presidency the very same charges he had leveled at prior executives (authoritarian leadership) were leveled against him; he was ousted from the association in 1976 and a year later dispatched by President Eyadema to serve as Ambassador to Libya.

MENSAH, TOUSSAINT DIDEROT. Young Togolese author.

MERCENARY AFFAIR see COUP (ATTEMPTED) OF OCTOBER 1977.

MESSAVUSSA, HERMANN, 1932– . Former Magistrate and political leader. Born in Aného on May 14, 1932 and a graduate of the University of Montpellier, Messavussa was an early leader of the Juvento party. He became apolitical in the 1960's and served as Magistrate in the Lomé lower courts (1961–63), Minister of Commerce and Industry (1963), and Judge on the Lomé Court of Appeals until his recent retirement.

METHODISTS. The oldest major Protestant proselytizing group still established in Togo. Commencing consistent activities along the coast in the middle of the nineteenth century under Thomas Birch Freeman and Thomas Joseph Marshall, the Methodist Church was especially established in Nigeria and Benin and limited its activities in Togo to the Mina and other coastal groups around Aného. There the Church was assisted in its efforts by the **Lawson family,** which had family links with Freetown, Sierra Leone, then home base of the Methodist Church. In March 1888 Pastor Bryan Roe established himself in Aného and greatly expanded the Church's educational and evangelical work. In 1930 the Methodist regional headquarters was shifted from Ahého to Cotonou, Benin—still subordinate to Lagos, Nigeria—though in 1957 a special district was created for efforts in the Lomé-Aného area. At that date the Church counted 3,447 registered converts (with many more informal members) served by five pastors; there were also three schools (two in Aného and one in Lomé) with 727 pupils. The Church suffered heavy attrition in membership as a result of the rise of the Prophet Harris movement in Cote d'Ivoire. Nevertheless, many of Aného's intellectuals (and hence a significant percentage of Togo's elite) are still members of the Methodist Church. The continued importance of the Church in Togo was attested to when, on January 20, 1970, the founding stone was laid for the new Methodist University in Aného, built with Dutch assistance. *See also* RELIGION; PROTESTANTS.

MIGRANT LABOR. Seasonal migration of labor is a common fact of life in West Africa. Up to 100,000 workers, mostly Ewe, seasonally migrate to Ghana as farm labor. Many also gravitate to Abidjan, the magnet of French-speaking Africa.

MIKEM, KUETE DOMETO, 1948– . Economist and administrator. Born in 1948 and educated at the University of Amiens and Paris in Economics, Mikem served for a few years with Credit Lyonais in charge of overseas banking before going to Burkina Faso to teach at the University of Ouagadougou.

MINA. Collective name used to denote the **Ga** and **Ané** elements from El Mina (Gold Coast) that migrated to the Aného vicinity in the middle of the seventeenth century. The two groups founded **Glidji** and Aného. They adopted the Ouatchi Ewe dialect, adding to it traces of Ga. The Mina are estimated at around 130,000 and are found along the coast from Lomé to Ouidah in Benin, most residing in the immediate vicinity of Aného and Porto Seguro. They form a very important percentage of Togo's commercial, intellectual, and political elite, their relatively small number notwithstanding. *See also* GA; ANE.

MINA REPUBLIC. Term used by European cartographers and missionaries in the pre-colonial era to denote the decentralized polities along the Aného coast and its hinterland. The entities so referred were not always **Mina** nor exactly republican in political organization.

MISAHOHE. Former German outpost on the Kpandu road, nine kilometers from **Kpalimé** in the Kloto prefecture. Currently it is the residence of the Kloto chef-de-circonscription and a tourist attraction because of its picturesque site at an altitude of 1,500 feet—dominated by the 2,900-foot Mela Kloto with its summit quinquina plantations—and relics of the bygone German era.

MIVEDOR, AYITE GACHIM (ALEX), 1927– . Former Minister of Public Works, permanent Director of the RPT party, and for long the de-facto number two civilian leader in the Eyadema regime. He was born in Aného to Mina parents on March 2, 1917 and educated locally and at technical colleges in Bamako, Mali (1943–47), Paris, and

Toulouse (1947–55), graduating as an Electrical and Hydraulic Engineer. He then joined the Bamako Water Services, returning to Togo in 1958 to become head of the Electrical and Water Services division of the Ministry of Public Works (1958–66). A member of the militant Mali Youth Association while in Bamako (1956–58), Mivedor joined the **Comité de l'Unité Togolaise** of Sylvanus Olympio in Lomé and in 1966 supported the **Nöe Kutuklui** attempted coup d'etat—*see* COUP (ATTEMPTED) OF 1966. After the collapse of the attempted takeover, Mivedor fled to Mali and only came back at General Eyadema's invitation after the 1967 coup. He was then appointed to the **Comité de Reconciliation Nationale** with responsibilities for public works, later becoming the permanent Deputy Director of the RPT Politburo. After the establishment of Eyadema's government in April of the same year, Mivedor was confirmed as Minister of Mines, Energy, and Hydraulic Resources (later also of Public Works), a post he held until dropped from the cabinet in March 1979. He was retained in the RPT, with growing difficulty, until January 1983 when he too was purged—like so many of the Eyadema "first team"—for corruption, embezzlement, and mismanagement of resources. His eclipse was not due to any revulsion with his acts within the government but due to insistence from abroad that a basic purge be carried out prior to any new development funds being committed. A detested figure in the south, his house was burned to the ground during the demonstrations calling for a National Conference in June 1991.

MLAPA III. Chief of the village of Togo, with whom Germany signed a protectorate treaty on July 5, 1884, giving them control over the coastal areas and eventually leading to the creation of the colony of Togo.

MOBA. Indigenous mountain ethnic groups living on the richer lands in the northern Dapaong area. Small Moba groups also reside in Kara, Sansanné-Mango, and Lomé. One of Togo's more homogenous ethnic groups, the Moba speak a Gurma dialect that is strongly influenced by the More language of Burkina Faso's Mossi people. Their total number has been estimated at around 110,000. A tightly-knit people, the Moba remain under the control of chiefs even in urban settings, who can send petty offenders or criminals back to their home villages as punishment, even from the anonymity of Lomé. (Of note is that **Bodjollé,** who challenged General Eyadema in the 1960s, was released by Eyadema without hesitation to his home village, with the pledge of his village elders that he would not leave its confines.) During the Olympio era the Moba supported the CUT and were rewarded with two of their kinsmen, Martin Sankaredja and Karamoko Namoro, being appointed to the cabinet. In the multi-party era of the 1990's the Moba have continued this support for Ewe leaders, standing behind Gilchrist Olympio's political aspirations, rather than the northerner Eyadema.

MONGOYA, SEGNON K. 1953– . Author. Born in Lomé on October 21, 1953 and educated in Catholic schools, Mongoya has published several collections of folktales while holding a clerical post.

MONO RIVER. A 350-mile long river originating northeast of Sokodé and emptying in Grand Popo in the Gulf of Guinea. The river's last 100 miles are navigable and form part of the Togo-Benin border. Among the Mono's tributaries are the Ogou, Ofe, and Anié.

MONO RIVER PROJECT. Joint Bénino-Togolese cooperation in developing the resources of the Mono river. In 1978 an agreement was reached to build a hydroelectric dam at Nangbeto (on their joint border) with a capacity of 130 million kilowatts, reducing both countries' dependence upon Ghanaian electricity. Other dams, upstream of Nangbeto, have also since been commenced, under a master plan developed by United Nations Development Plan and the World Bank.

MORAVIAN BROTHERS. Offshoot of the Unitas Fratrum (Unity of Brethren), the Protestant sect in Bohemia and Moravia that split from the Ultraquists in 1467 and after persecution became the origin of the Moravian Church and the Evangelical Czech Brethren Church. Under the leadership of Count Nikolaus von Zinzerdorf, the Moravian Brothers sponsored a number of early missionary efforts in Africa, including that of Huckuf and Jacob Protten in 1768 and 1770. Most of the efforts were unsuccessful due to fetishist opposition, hassles with commanders of the European forts and factories along the coasts, and the ravages of diseases. *See* PROTTEN, JACOB.

MOSSI. Dominant Burkina Faso ethnic group. Small numbers of Mossi are found in Togo in the Dapaong area and further south as migrant labor. Most are farmers. There are an estimated 10,000 Mossi in Togo.

MOUVEMENT DE LA JEUNESSE TOGOLAISE. Official founding name of the radical youth wing of Sylvanus Olympio's Comité de l'Unité Togolaise. *See* JUVENTO.

MOUVEMENT DE REGROUPEMENT NATIONAL (MRN). Predecessor of the **Rassemblement du Peuple Togolais** (RPT), declared in 1969 as the new single party of Togo. The MRN's constituent congress was held November 28 through 30, 1969, by which time the MRN's official name had been changed to the RPT.

MOUVEMENT D'OCTOBRE 5 (MO-5). Ad-hoc name for the youth movement that sprang up in 1990 to resist by all means the continuation of the Eyadema dictatorship. It is named after the date of the first anti-Eyadema demonstrations in 1990 and has been at the forefront of all demonstrations and riots in Lomé.

MOUVEMENT ETUDIANT DE LUTTE POUR LA DEMOCRATIE (MELD). Organization set up in 1990 among students to act as a pressure group for a return to multi-partyism in Togo. It has been involved in all the anti-Eyadema demonstrations and riots in Lomé since 1990.

MOUVEMENT NATIONAL DES ETUDIANTS ET STAGIAIRES TOGOLAIS (MONESTO). Successor to UNETO, following the latter's dissolution in October 1977 under charges of subversion against the Eyadema regime. MONESTO was the sole union of Togo's student body until the liberalizations of 1990.

MOUVEMENT NATIONALISTE POUR L'UNITE (MNU). Political party, formed in October 1992 and headed by Koffitse Adzrako, claiming that imperialists were at the root of Togo's problems.

MOUVEMENT NATIONALISTE TOGOLAIS-JUVENTO. Electoral alliance between the militant **Juvento** party and the **Union Démocratique des Peuples Togolais,** formed to contest the April 1961 elections in opposition to Sylvanus Olympio's **Comité de l'Unité Togolaise.** The formation was disqualified, however, for allegedly not placing the required deposits on time. Its leaders were arrested shortly thereafter for an alleged plot, and Togo became a de facto one party state.

MOUVEMENT POPULAIRE TOGOLAIS (MPT). Political party founded by Dr. **Pedro Olympio** and his supporters after the 1951–1954 leadership struggle in the **Parti Togolais du Progrès,** in which Olympio lost out to Nicolas Grunitzky and was expelled. (The intraparty friction went back to 1951 when Olympio forces, dissatisfied with Grunitzky's overly conservative posture, expelled him.) When established, the MPT became Togo's fourth major party, after the CUT, PTP, and UCPN. *See* POLITICAL PARTIES. Starting in 1961, Sylvanus Olympio began to eliminate sources of organized opposition, and the MPT and other parties were in due course dissolved. Following the 1963 coup d'etat, the MPT was resurrected under the leadership of **Samuel Aquereburu** and participated in the four-cornered electoral and cabinet coalition of

Nicolas Grunitzky that lasted until the second coup in 1967. With the rise of the administration of General Eyadema all political parties, including the MPT, were banned.

MOUVEMENT TOGOLAISE POUR LA DEMOCRATIE (MTD). Former Paris-based anti-Eyadema "liberation" movement. Supported by Brazilian elements, both in Togo and in exile in France, the MTD was founded by the Olympio sons in 1977 and led by Gilchrist Olympio. The MTD claimed responsibility for the 1977 attempted coup in Togo. By 1985, however, the MTD was no longer under Gilchrist Olympio's control.

MUSTERKOLONIE *see* GERMAN ADMINISTRATION.

N

NABEDE, PAKAI ALEXANDRE, 1930– . Vice Chancellor of the University of Benin. Born in Kara in 1930, educated locally at Sokodé and at the Académie de Toulouse in Chemistry and Biology, Nabédé continued with medical studies in Toulouse and Morocco (1952–60). He obtained his M.D. in 1960 and served as a physician in Morocco before returning to Togo in 1961 to become Chief Medical Officer of the Dapaong district. A year later he was reassigned to Lomé and served in a wide variety of capacities, specializing further during several study trips abroad. Since 1973 he has been Director of the National Medical Auxiliaries' School and, since 1975, Vice Chancellor of the University of Benin.

NACHTIGAL, GUSTAV, 1834–1885. German explorer, colonial administrator, and author. Better known for his extensive explorations in Central Africa from 1869 to 1875—about which he wrote his classic *Sahara and Sudan*—Nachtigal played a key role in the expansion of the German Colonial empire in West Africa by virtue of being the Imperial Commissioner that formally annexed Togo, Cameroun, and Luderitzland (Southwest Africa) in 1885. As far as Togo is concerned, Nachtigal—at that time consul in Tunis (from 1882 on), following his Central African exploits—was dispatched to West Africa to protect and expand the threatened German interests in the area, especially in Togo where elements of the **Lawson family** were appealing for British protection. *See* GERMAN ADMINISTRATION. Nachtigal arrived off the Togolese coast on board the *Mowe* gunboat with Aného hostages previously taken (*see* LAWSON FAMILY). On July 4 he raised the German flag over Bagida (which became the temporary capital of German Togo) and later signed a treaty with Chief Mlapa of the small lagoon village of Togo that became the basis for the creation of German Togo. On July 6 he named a Provisional Governor (an Aného French trader) to serve until von Falkenthal's arrival, and sailed off to Cameroun.

NAGO. Small ethnic group of some 10,000 people, most of whom are Muslim. They reside in much larger numbers in neighboring Benin, from where they migrated in the eighteenth and nineteenth centuries. Found mostly in the Maritime region, they serve mostly as wharf porters at the Lomé Autonomous Port or as merchants in Lomé. Scattered groups are also found further north in Togo's other urban centers.

NANA BENZ. Popular nickname for the women traders along the coast from Accra to Lagos and especially in Lomé. These are highly successful businesswomen, as the "Benz" (from Mercedes Benz) signifies, who are indeed frequently driven around in their Mercedes Benz vehicles—the ultimate symbol of success in West Africa. Frequently they have attained their wealth from trading in fabrics, there being incredible profits, for example, in retailing in Lomé's *grande marché*. The origins of the word "nana" are not established, though "na" means mother and therefore signifies respect.

NANGBETO. Site, thirty-five kilometers from Atakpamé, of a dam that regularizes the flow of the Mono river, irrigates 43,000 hectares of land, and generates 147 million kilowatts or 30 percent of the electricity need of the joint Togo-Benin **CEB** thus reducing dependence on Ghanaian electricity supplies. Construction on the dam, much delayed, began in 1984 and was completed in 1988 when it was inaugurated. The project included 147 kilometers of high tension lines carrying electricity to the national grid, and a dike 450 meters long and 50 meters at its highest point, creating a lake of 180 square kilometers. The cost of the dam—thirty-four million CFAF—was less than originally anticipated.

NAPO, NYANDI SEYBOU (ALEXIS), 1939. Former Minister of Labor and the Civil Service. Born in 1939 in Kabou-Tinalende (near Bassar) and of Bassari ethnic origins, Napo was educated locally and in Paris at the Institut des Hautes Etudes d'Outre-Mer. He was attached to the Ministry of Foreign Affairs between1963 and 1967 and, after the Eyadema takeover in 1967, he became head of the Pagouda Administrative District. In October 1968 he was named First Secretary at the Embassy of Togo in France; he served in Paris for two years, returning to administrative duties in Togo in 1970 as head of the Sotouboua Administrative District, but in 1972 he was again called to undertake diplomatic duties, this time as Ambassador to Zaire. He was repatriated in 1975 and briefly headed the Bafilo Administrative District before being named Togo's Ambassador to France. Upon his return from Paris in 1980, he joined Eyadema's cabinet as Minister of Labor and the Civil Service and in July 1985 was appointed Ambassador to Germany. With the liberalizations of 1990 he was recalled to Lomé and currently heads a division in the Ministry of Foreign Affairs.

NASSAR, PHILIPPE, 1916– . Lomé commerce and transport entrepreneur and former Deputy Treasurer of the CUT parliamentary party. Born in Lomé on March 3, 1916, Nassar was a successful business figure, with interests in a variety of commercial enterprises, and a strong supporter and contributor to the **Comité de l'Unité Togolaise**. He was elected to the National Assembly in 1961 and served there as Deputy Treasurer of the CUT parliamentary party until the 1963 coup d'état. He has also been a member of the Executive Committee of the Jeunesse de l'Unité Togolaise, President of the Executive Committee of the Tsévié district, and a member of Togo's Chamber of Commerce. Nassar is one of Togo's major economic figures.

NATCHABA, FOUMBARA OUATTARA. Former Director of President Eyadema's cabinet and cabinet minister. A northern administrator and Law Professor at the University of Benin, Natchaba replaced **Laclé** when the latter was appointed minister. Natchaba owed his high post to Eyadema's penchant to surround himself in his presidential office with northerners. Nevertheless, Natchaba fell from grace over a clouded incident and fled to Paris in 1981 for fear of his life. He was ultimately persuaded to return to Lomé and was given an administrative appointment in the Ministry of Interior. After the liberalizations of 1990 he became General Eyadema's personal advisor on legal matters. In September 1992 he was appointed RPT Minister of Foreign Affairs in the coalition under interim Prime Minister Koffigoh. He was retained in the same position in the next transitional government of 1993.

NATIONAL FORESTS/NATIONAL PARKS. Starting from colonial times but redefined and expanded since independence, several areas have been set aside as national forests and/or parks. These currently include the Foret de Togodo, north of Tokpli on both sides of the Guor river and hard against the Benin border; the Foret de la Fosse aux Lions, just southwest of Dapaong—a small national forest; the Foret de Fazao that links the Reserve de Koué from Bassar to Blitta, parallel to the Ghana border; and the Reserve de la Keran, along the western side of the north-south national highway axis from Naboulgou to Mango, between the Oti and Koumougou rivers. This is the largest park in

Togo. Several other small ones also exist but are sometimes not even marked on maps.

NATIONAL MOVEMENT FOR THE LIBERATION OF WESTERN TOGOLAND (TOLIMO). Former Togo-based, largely Ewe irredentist movement aimed at reversing the plebiscite of 1956 that gave Ghana parts of the former colony of Togo, and specifically the Volta region. TOLIMO first attained its notoriety when in 1972 it petitioned the OAU to help attain its goals, citing the fact that in Ghana the Ewe were among the poorer strata in the country, while in Togo they were the leaders of economic life. The movement, though banned in Ghana in 1975, received formal support from the Eyadema regime for some time. Eyadema even had several ministers specifically charged with liaising (i.e., controlling) the movement, both at home and in Ghana.

N'GAM-GAM (also N'GAM). Small, largely animist ethnic group. Of nonindigenous origin, the N'Gam-Gam reside in the northern areas of Togo, intermixed with the Chamba. Their numbers are estimated at around 25,000.

N'GUISSAN, KOMLAN (FRANCOIS), 1934– . Civil administrator. Born in Sansanné-Mango in 1934, N'Guissan was trained as a civilian administrator in France and assumed command over the administrative post of Kévé in May 1961. Shortly after, he was promoted to head the Bafilo circonscription. In 1963 he was sent to France to retrain as an accountant and, between 1965 and his recent retirement, he has been Deputy Director of Financial Services at the Banque Togolaise de Devéloppement.

NIAMTOUGOU. Small village north of Kara in mostly Kabré country. Formerly the administrative headquarters of a circonscription with the same name, since renamed the prefecture de Doufelgou. The area has a high density of population. In 1991 during the wide ranging debates in the National Conference about corruption, it was alleged that the small town's airport, built to serve General Eyadema's penchant for traveling in style, was not built at the cost of twelve but six billion CFAF, the difference ending up at Eyadema's disposal.

NIGERIAN BANKNOTES DISPUTE. On June 19, 1968, a DC-7 plane, registered in Paraguay and with Rhodesian bills of lading, on its way to Lisbon, Portugal, made a forced landing in Lomé. The plane was found to be carrying seven million pounds sterling in Nigerian currency for the Biafra government, and the funds were confiscated. After Nigerian and Biafran representations regarding the ownership and disposition of the currency, the funds were released to Nigeria in exchange for a ten percent "indemnity." (The Togolese government had threatened to recognize Biafra otherwise.) Though never acknowledged, this indemnity was used to finance the building of Eyadema's modernistic Presidential Palace.

NINTSE, SAMAROU. Entrepreneur. Nintsé completed his studies in France, following which he worked for nine years with the N.E.T. and, in 1974, branched off on his own. Setting up a construction company, he rapidly expanded his operations to become an important factor in the Lomé construction business. In 1980 he was cited as a prime example of the new breed of modern Togolese entrepreneurs.

NIOTO. The new name for IOTO, the former State-owned company producing cooking oil from ground seeds, privatized in 1987. Deficitory under State hands, once majority ownership (fifty-one percent equity) passed into French (CFDT) hands, the workforce was fully halved while production soared from the processing of 1,000 tons in 1987 to 340 tons a day in 1990. *See also* IOTO.

NOMENYO, SETH. Secretary General of the Evangelical Church of Togo. Of Mina origins, Nomenyo was educated locally before seeking further Theological studies in Cameroun and France. He was named Secretary General of the Church in 1961.

NORDDEUTSCHE MISSIONGESELLSCHAFT *see* BREMEN MISSIONARY SOCIETY.

NOTSE. Historically important Ewe town 100 kilometers north of Lomé and 67 kilometers from Atakpamé. Also one of the districts in the Plateaux region, until the June 1981 administration reorganization changed its name to the prefecture of Haho, though with headquarters still in Notsé. The name Notsé (changed in the mid-1970s from the colonial Nuatja) derives from the words Ihoua-tche ("I want to stay here under the tree"). The town was founded late in the seventeenth century by **Afotche**—from Afotchegnon ("we have made a good journey")—following the **Adja**-Ewe trek from **Tado**. Afotche's son was King **Agokoli**, whose arbitrary and cruel reign led to the major Adja-Ewe dispersal from Notsé, still celebrated throughout the region in the **Hogbetsotso** festival. The town (pronounced "Notsieis" by the Ewe) thus has a special role in Ewe traditions and lore and is also referred to in oral history as Amedzofe ("place of origin"), Glime ("in the walls"), Agbogbome ("in the gates"), etc. A large number of legends recount the Ewe dispersal in 1720, done in the middle of the night in order not to alert Agokoli to the desertion of a segment of his people. The Bé clan remained last, beating drums to cover the noise of the mass departure and then forming the rear guard to scatter millet over their tracks, which pigeons picked up, further obliterating signs of the exodus. (For this reason pigeon meat is still taboo among the Bé.) The clans went off in three directions: west (establishing the town of Ho, among others); south (to found Lomé, Agouevé, and Bagida), and northwest. Several years later another migration occurred after a bad drought. The new settlers (most of whom went south) were called **Ouatchi**—coming from Notsé—which acquired a pejorative sense.

NOUVELLE MARCHE, LA. The "New Road," name of **Togo-Presse** since 1979, when the Third Republic came into effect. "La Nouvelle Marche" has also been the rallying cry of the Eyadema regime, referring to his alleged non-ethnic approach, an alternative to the sterile infighting of the pro-1967 period. At its height the daily sold some 10,000 copies. Since the liberalizations of 1990 and the sprout of various other non-governmental papers, sales fell dramatically to around 2,000 copies, though the subsidized paper costs only 30 CFAF compared to the average 250 CFAF of the independent press.

NUATJA *see* NOTSE.

NYALA. Northern district renamed the prefecture of Nyala in the 1981 administrative reorganization of the country. Prior to this, the district was known as the circonscription de Tchamba. The headquarters of the prefecture remains the same, in the village of Tchamba. Nyala is in the Centrale region. It is in itself a new creation, formally set up as a separate district only in 1975.

NYATEPE COO, DJODJI AKOLY, 1942– . Academic. A Togolese born in Nigeria on May 19, 1942, Nyatepe-Coo was educated at the University of Paris in Sociology with specialization in Demography. He is a Professor of Sociology at the University of Benin in Lomé and is the author of a number of studies on African Demography.

N'ZARA. Name of Sansanné-Mango by the **Chokossi** founders of the Anufo kingdom, and conquerors of the town of Kundyuku, that was renamed N'zara.

O

OCAM and OCAMM *see* ORGANISATION COMMUNE AFRICAINE, MALGACHE ET MAURITIENNE.

OCAM VILLAGE. Elaborate housing complex built on the eastern approaches to Lomé for the 1972 Heads of State meeting of **OCAM**. The complex includes 16 double villas that can be transformed into 32 adjoining suites of international luxury class hotel status, with a total capacity of 216 rooms. Indeed, though used to house important international delegations, the OCAM Village has doubled as a hotel. In the 1970's this luxury complex alone consumed fully 25 percent of Lomé's electricity. The suites have been decorated by the well-known Togolese artist **Paul Ahyi** and others.

OFFICE DES PRODUITS AGRICOLES DU TOGO (OPAT). State purchasing and exporting monopoly for coffee, cocoa, cotton, peanuts, palm oil, karite, and other agricultural products. Established on June 22, 1964, OPAT was also given the function of stabilizing and controlling local prices, granting loans for agricultural projects, and conducting research on methods that could yield higher productivity. The group is supervised by the Ministry of Trade and Industry, and until 1973 its Secretary General was [Joseph] **Ogamo Bagnah**. OPAT essentially took over the functions performed previously by the Togolese Caisses de Stabilisation. Throughout the years, several crops have either been added or removed from its sphere of control, reflecting the need for either greater centralization or more specialized agencies. Affiliated organizations obliged to sell their produce to OPAT include the Société Togolaise du Coton, the several Unions de Coopératives (UNICOOPS) in the various prefectures, the Société Commerciale Industrielle et Agricole (SCIA), the Union des Sociétés de Commercialisation d'Achats de Produits Agricole de Togo (USCAPAT), and the Société Togolaise pour le Commerce des Produits Agricole (STCP).

OFFICE NATIONAL DE DEVELOPPEMENT ET EXPLOITATION DES FORESTS (ODEF). Specialized state agency set up on October 26, 1971, and operative since February 1973, under the Ministry of Rural Economy. ODEF is in charge of research, reforestation, development, exploitation, and export of Togo's timber resources. Headquartered in Lomé, and formerly under the directorship of Tosseh Gnrofoun, it is now headed by Koffi Agognoo.

OFFICE NATIONAL DES ABATTOIRS ET FRIGORIFIQUES (ONAF). State organization set up in September 1975 with funds from Togo's then booming phosphate exports, charged with centralizing and coordinating beef supplies and slaughterhouses in Togo. ONAF was one of the first of the deficitory state companies dissolved in 1984 in accord with the 1982 RPT edict that decimated the state sector.

OFFICE NATIONAL DES PECHES (ONP). State group set up to develop the Togolese fishing industry. There has always been a small but vibrant indigenous fishing industry in Togo, at various times organized into (ethnic) cooperatives. Their centralization and modernization is regarded by the government as of prime priority in order to augment the protein supplies of the country. ONP was headed by Akwetey Kuwadah.

OFFICE NATIONAL DES PRODUITS VIVRIERS (TOGOGRAIN). State company set up to market staple food products in Togo. Its activities are limited to maize, sorghum, millet, and rice. In order to stabilize prices, TOGOGRAIN purchases stocks of these grains at the time of harvest and stockpiles them in silos as a hedge against droughts or shortages. Until recently, under the leadership of Méatchi, audits of the company in 1982 showed extremely poor financial accounting procedures and evidence of embezzlement, for which Méatchi was arrested. The major scandal that erupted after these revelations did further damage to Togo's deficit-ridden state sector and added a boost for its privatization.

OFFICE NATIONAL DU DEVELOPPEMENT DE L'ELEVAGE (ONADEC). State group set up in 1976 to aid and develop Togolese stockbreeding and to serve as a conduit of supplies for ONAF.

OFFICE REGIONALE POUR LA POPULATION DES PRODUITS VIVIERS (ORPV). Series of state organizations set up in each prefecture replacing the **SORAD**s that previously performed much the same task. Two years later, under the ORPVs the "Green Revolution" commenced. *See* GREEN REVOLUTION; SORAD.

OFFICE TOGOLAIS DES PHOSPHATES (OTP). State agency created on January 10, 1974, to market Togo's phosphates after the nationalization of **COTOMIB**. Headed by Director General M'ba Kabessema under the general supervision of the Minister of Finance and the Economy, OTP is the key economic force in Togo in view of the importance of phosphate exports in the national economy. *See* PHOSPHATES.

OGMA YAGLA, WEN'SAA. Educator, graduate of Algiers University in the field in Public Administration. Ogma Yagla is an Instructor at the University of Benin, where he heads the division of Judicial and Administrative Studies. He has written several articles and books.

OGOU. New name for the former circonscription of Atakpamé, renamed in the 1981 administrative reorganization of the country. The headquarters of Agou remains in Atakpamé, also the seat of the region's administration.

OHIAMI, KOKOU CONSTANTIN, 1942– . Diplomat. Born on December 13, 1942 in Amou-Oblo and of Akposso origins, Ohiami studied at the University of Toulouse (1963–67) and at the University of Paris (1967–68), following which he was appointed Director of the Cultural and Personnel Division of the Foreign Ministry. In 1970 he became Deputy-Head of the Conferences section in the Ministry and between 1970 and 1972 he was Assistant Director of its Economic Division. In 1972 he was shifted to active diplomatic duties by an appointment to Togo's Mission in Geneva, Switzerland.

OHIN, ALEXANDRE JOHN, 1920– . Surgeon and diplomat. Born in Aného on March 20, 1920, Ohin studied at Dakar's School of Medicine, practiced in Togo for ten years (1943 to 1953), and then continued his studies at Washington University, New York's Academy of Medicine, and the University of California. He served as Resident Surgeon at the Washington University School of Medicine (1954–60) and later as Research Fellow at New York's Albert Einstein College of Medicine (1960–61), before returning to Lomé to become Chief Surgeon of Togo's National Hospital (1961–67). A member of Sylvanus Olympio's **Comité de l'Unité Togolaise**, Dr. Ohin was involved in the 1966 mass upheaval against the successor regime of Nicolas Grunitzky—*see* COUP (ATTEMPTED) OF 1966—and was briefly imprisoned after the coup failed. After the 1967 coup, he served on the **Comité de Reconciliation Nationale** with responsibility for the health portfolio, and in June 1967 was appointed Ambassador to the United States, the United Nations, and Canada. He served as Vice President of the twenty-third General Assembly of the United Nations and relinquished his diplomatic duties in 1971, returning to his medical post in Lomé. Since 1967 Dr. Ohin has also been a member of the Expert Advisory Board on Cancer of the World Health Organization and a regular guest at the National Cancer Institute in Bethesda, Maryland. He has written several books on cancer and on surgical metabolism.

OHIN, JACOB. Togolese painter whose pioneering work and assistance to budding painters has created a new generation of artists in Togo.

OLYMPIO, BONITO HERBERT, 1933–1994. One of Sylvanus Olympio's sons. Bonito Olympio was born on April 1, 1933 and after starting his schooling in Togo completed it at Achimota College (Accra) and later was sent by his father to the Imperial College (London) to study engineering. He left Imperial College in 1955 to join his father's company, Unilever, first in London, later in Accra as sales manager. His entrepreneurial talent brought him to the attention of Enrico Mattei who appointed him managing director of Agip in Togo and Benin. After his father's assassination Bonito went to Guinea where he worked for some time with USAID. At the time allegedly the most important financial contributor to the several plots aimed at unseating Eyadema, he was arrested and spent some time in jail in both Conakry and Cotonou. In May 1969 he was expelled from Ghana (where he had gone to reside with his mother), and set up residence in Paris and Abidjan, though he was to return to Accra several years later where he was eventually to die. In August 1979 the Eyadema regime sentenced him to death in absentia (together with his brother Gilchrist) for his role in the 1977 attempted coup. An urbane bon-vivant Bonito Olympio suffered a mild heart attack in December 1993, and died of the same cause on August 25, 1994. His funeral was attended by the Vice President of Ghana and condolences were received from several heads of state.

OLYMPIO, ELPIDO, 1940– . Architect. One of Sylvanus Olympio's sons. Born in Lomé on August 5, 1940 and educated locally and at Achimota College (Ghana, 1952–60), Princeton (1960–65), and Cornell universities (1965–67) Olympio married Marie, daughter of Ivory Coast's President Houphouet-Boigny, though they later divorced. Olympio is still a resident of Abidjan, where he has a flourishing practice.

OLYMPIO, GILCHRIST, 1936– . One of Sylvanus Olympio's sons and prime seeker of revenge against his murderer, General Eyadema. Trained in Britain in Economics and a businessman based in Paris, Olympio was involved in several attempts to unseat the Eyadema regime. In 1977 he was a prime financier of a mercenary plot that had to be aborted, and in 1983 and again in 1987 he was again implicated in plots to import assassins to Lomé to kill Eyadema, for which he was twice sentenced to death in absentia. Forced to leave France (that was supportive of Eyadema) Olympio—who in 1977 in Paris had set up the Mouvement Togolaise pour la Democratie (MTP) with the support of his brothers and members of the De Souza family—relocated to London where he was a part time lecturer at the London School of Economics.

During the liberalization of the 1990's Olympio returned to Togo after twenty-five years of exile to participate in the National Conference and was greeted by several thousand supporters. His first speech before the Conference electrified the audience; in it he called for a new agenda for Togo and not for revenge against Eyadema. The latter's ouster was, however, assumed, since the National Conference stripped Eyadema of all executive powers and barred him from running for office again. Olympio then set up a political organization to further his goals. At the conference he threw his support behind **Koffigoh**, assuring the latter's election as interim Prime Minister, a post supposedly for only one year until new elections were held. His insistence that Eyadema vacate the Presidential Palace at all costs led to attempts on his life by military units loyal to Eyadema, one of which—in the midst of an electoral campaign in the northern Assoli prefecture on May 5, 1992—led to his motorcade being assaulted (by a unit commanded by Eyadema's son) and Olympio being seriously wounded and evacuated to Paris where he spent six months under treatment.

In 1993 Olympio, the most popular and powerful politician of Togo, was excluded by Eyadema from contesting the August 1993 Presidential elections, on the grounds that Olympio had not properly tendered the necessary medical certificate attesting to his good health, and this led to an electoral boycott of several other southern leaders who had considered contesting the elections. The result was that Eyadema's "victory" of a huge majority of the small, largely northern turnout has not been recognized as placing Togo among the new democracies of Africa. Since then, Olympio has been behind a number of more violent attacks against Eyadema, infiltrating men and armaments across the Ghanaian border. Though widely supported among many Ewe, he is not France's choice, since he is regarded as too independent-minded, with Edem Kodjo, also an Ewe but with very little mass support, being France's choice. Olympio and Kodjo are not on good terms, largely because Olympio regards Kodjo as an Eyadema collaborationist and partly due to intra-Ewe cleavages represented by the two individuals.

OLYMPIO, LUCIEN. Lawyer. As an Attorney, Olympio, one of Sylvanus Olympio's sons, served as General Eyadema's envoy to **Noe Kutuklui**—Olympio's brother-in-law—to invite the latter to return from exile in Ghana in 1967 after the coup d'etat of that year. Olympio served as Attorney General to the Supreme Court between 1966 and 1970. In 1970 he was downgraded to Technical Counselor at the Ministry of Civil Service after he expressed, together with other lawyers, dissatisfaction with the manner in which the plotters of the August 1970 conspiracy were being tried. Though the other lawyers were later reinstated to their former positions, Olympio was not, and he left the country for Paris shortly after.

OLYMPIO, PEDRO, 1898–1969. Founder and leader of the **Parti Togolais du Progrès** and, after his expulsion from the latter, of the **Mouve-**

ment Populaire Togolais and former Ambassador to West Germany. Born in Lomé on May 28, 1898, Dr. Olympio was educated locally, in Steyl (Netherlands), and in Germany, following which he completed his medical studies in Munich, Hamburg, and Paris, returning to Lomé to open a private clinic and to practice surgery. Sylvanus Olympio's cousin, Pedro Olympio linked up with Nicolas Grunitzky in 1946 to form Togo's second political party (after the Comité de l'Unité Togolaise), the pro-French and French-supported Parti Togolais du Progrès. The party was composed mostly of French officials, citizens, and evolués and was favored by the local administration over Sylvanus Olympio's CUT. From 1951 to 1955 the party suffered a major schism in its leadership over the PTP's conservative stance and loss of electoral support, a schism that resulted first in the expulsion from the party of Secretary General Grunitzky and then his comeback and the expulsion of Dr. Olympio. In 1955 Olympio set up a new party, the MPT, but the party fared poorly at the polls, declined rapidly in importance, and was banned, as were other parties, after the imposition of one party rule in 1962. Dr. Olympio himself became a representative (of Africa) on the United Nations Economic and Social Council in 1958, and between 1964 and 1968 he served as Togo's ambassador to West Germany.

OLYMPIO, SYLVANUS EPIPHANIO, 1902–1963. Former President of Togo, founding member of the **Comité de l'Unité Togolaise** and nationalist leader. Born in Lomé on September 6, 1902 to an influential **Brazilian** family (*see* DA SILVA, FRANCISCO OLYMPIO). Olympio was educated locally, at the University of Vienna, and at the London School of Economics. Returning to Lomé in 1926, he joined the then largest commercial firm, the United Africa Company (UAC), and served with it in Nigeria (1926 to 1928), Gold Coast (1928), and Togo (1928 to 1938), becoming its General Manager for Togo and a prosperous merchant himself. A founding member of the pro-French **Cercle des Amitiés Françaises** and later the CUT, Olympio was imprisoned in 1942 by the local Vichy regime (in Djougou, Benin) and only returned to Togo after de Gaulle's rise to power. In 1946 he led his young party to victory at the polls for the Assemblée Representative and became the Assembly's President (1946–52). His involvement in the pan-Ewe unification movement and links with the All-Ewe Conference in the Gold Coast and British Togoland and his various petitions to the United Nations against the local French administration brought him into a collision course with France in the late 1940's. The local administration engineered his relocation to the Paris branch of the UAC and, when he refused the "promotion," convicted him of contravening currency regulations in 1954, imposing both a fine ($25,000) and a prohibition from running for elective office. Simultaneously with the crackdown on the CUT and the harassment of its leaders, the French administration actively encouraged the formation of more pliable parties and alternate political strata, leading to the CUT boycott of all elections until 1958 and the rise of Olympio's major rival, Nicolas Grunitzky. In 1958 the United Nations-supervised elections put an end to the **Autonomous Republic** administration of Grunitzky and brought Olympio and the CUT to power. Olympio became Prime Minister (1958–61), and, after constitutional revisions, President (1961–63). In 1959 he was also elected Mayor of Lomé. Disillusioned by the 1956 plebiscite in British Togo—which resulted in the latter's merger with the Gold Coast—Olympio pressed for the separate independence of French Togo, which occurred in 1960. After independence, his overly conservative and paternalistic policies alienated various groups in the country. By 1959 the more militant **Juvento**—once the CUT's youth wing—had declared its autonomy and become a separate party. Northern leaders chaffed at the total lack of attention their regions were receiving, merchants in Lomé grew antagonistic over the closure of the border with Ghana (*see* GHANA-TOGO FRICTION), the cocoa/coffee producers of the Kloto area (both Akposso and Ewe) grew discontented with the tax levied on their crop by the fiscally hard-pressed regime in Lomé, and Catholics in urban areas were incensed by Olympio's clash with the Archbishop and his seizure of several issues of the local Catholic journal. From 1961 to 1962 Olympio intensified his drive against organized political opposition to his administration. Political leaders were imprisoned for alleged plots, a political coalition that was coalescing to compete in the elections of 1961 was disqualified (for alleged failure to post the necessary deposits), and, in 1962, all parties except the CUT were formally banned. In 1962 Olympio's stress on budget balancing and austerity brought him into conflict with the recently demobilized veterans of France's colonial armies. The latter petitioned to be integrated into an enlarged Togolese army, a request Olympio rejected on the grounds that Togo neither had the need for a bigger army nor the funds to subsidize such a luxury. The veterans' aspirations to continue their military careers coalesced with ambitions within the existing NCO and officer corps for faster promotion and enhanced status within an enlarged force, resulting in the 1963 assault on Olympio's residence. Olympio met his death, at the hands of Sergeant (later General) Eyadema and a small group of veterans, in what was in essence cold-blooded murder. The self-acknowledged assassin was Eyadema. Following the collapse of the regime, all opposition leaders returned to Lomé or were freed from prison, and Nicolas Grunitzky assumed the presidency with Antoine Méatchi as Vice President. A cabinet and National Assembly were formed out of a four-cornered coalition of the formerly banned parties and a segment of the CUT (renamed PUT) that was willing to accept the changed political scene. Organized opposition to the results of the 1963 coup d'etat, and to the integration into the armed forces of the men that had assassinated Olympio, coalesced around **Noe Kutuklui,** a former Olympio lieutenant, who masterminded, from Cotonou, the early plots to unseat both the Grunitzky (1963–67) and Eyadema (1967+) regimes. Events in the 1970s and 1980s proved that Olympio's assassination would not be forgotten or forgiven: two of Olympio's sons and members of the powerful Brazilian elite in self-exile have been at the core of several attempts to overthrow Eyadema, and since 1990 one, **Gilchrist Olympio,** has directly attempted to challenge him electorally. Sylvanus Olympio's memory was formally rehabilitated in 1990 and, indeed, more people observed the January 1991 anniversary of his murder than participated in the government-orchestrated celebrations of Eyadema's seizure of power.

OMBRI, PANA, 1932– . Former Minister of the Civil Service. A Kabré born in Kouméa in 1932, Ombri was educated locally and worked as a schoolteacher between 1952 and 1959. In 1960 he became Administrative Secretary at the Ministry of Interior and shortly after Head Administrator for the districts of Lomé, Kara, and Atakpamé (1960–63). After the collapse of the Olympio regime, Ombri was brought into the Grunitzky cabinet as Minister of Civil Service, Labor, and Social Affairs, a position he held until late 1966. Since 1968 he has served as Fiscal and Program Director at the Ministry of Commerce, Industry, and Tourism and in other technical and administrative positions. Until recently attached to the Ministry of Foreign Affairs, he is currently retired.

OPPOSITION GROUPS, 1967–1990. The main opposition groups to the Eyadema regime during the period 1967–1990 (when the era of multi-partyism was inaugurated) were movements set up by Togo's Brazilian families, who refused to accept the Eyadema "usurption" of power and refused to forget Sylvanus Olympio's cold-blooded murder. Most of the original politicians of 1963, who for some time had connived in this plotting, rapidly fell by the wayside, some in retirement, others having made peace with the regime, and still others living in exile in West Africa or in Paris. Organized opposition to the Eyadema regime centered around the Mouvement Togolaise pour la Démocratie (MTP) of the Olympio sons and the Front National de Liberation (FNLT) of former Lieutenant Colonel **Merlaud Lawson,** both based in Paris. Later, in the mid-1980s a newer, ideological, opposition party was established abroad—the Communist Party of Togo. For opposition groups since the liberalization of parties in Togo *see* POLITICAL PARTIES.

ORGANISATION COMMUNE AFRICAINE, MALGACHE ET MAU-
RITIENNE (OCAM). A grouping of most of Francophone Africa, later
joined by Mauritius, for purposes of economic, social, and cultural cooperation. Indirect successor to the Brazzaville Group, the UAM, and
the OAMCE, OCAM's most successful venture to date has been the creation of Air Afrique, the multinational airline of French Africa, as well
as a joint telecommunications system and cooperation on joint technical colleges. Since 1970 the organization (and Air Afrique) has suffered
attrition as several states have resigned their membership or curtailed
their participation. Paradoxically, it has been since 1970 that Togo began to play a more active role in OCAM, including hosting the 1972
Heads of State meeting. *See also* OCAM VILLAGE.

ORGANISATION TOGOLAISE DES TRAVAILLEURS DEMOC-
RATIQUES (OTTD). New, popular Trotskyite trade union organization under the charismatic leadership of Claude Ameganvi. The
OTTD rose on the ashes of Eyadema's enforced trade union unity
once political liberalization reached Togo in 1991.

OSSEYI, JEAN-ALEXANDRE, 1935–1971. Police inspector and one
of the main defendants in the 1970 conspiracy trial. Born on April 22,
1935 in Atakpamé, Osseyi was an early member of the CUT party and
in August 1960 was appointed Regional Secretary of Nyékonakpoe.
In January 1962 he was brought into the secretariat of Minister of Interior **Theophile Mally** as an attaché, a position he occupied until the
1963 coup d'etat. Following the coup, he reverted to normal police duties until arrested in his home in August 1970, together with the anti-
Eyadema plotters. *See* COUP (ATTEMPTED) OF 1970. Osseyi was
the main defendant at the subsequent trial and was given a stiff prison
sentence. He died in 1971 while in prison, secretly executed.

OTI. Known until the 1981 administrative reorganization of Togo as the
circonscription de Mango. The new prefecture gets its name from the
Oti river. Sansanné-Mango remains its administrative headquarters.

OUATCHI. Ewe ethnic group estimated in 1992 as numbering roughly
250,000 people, residing mostly in the vicinity of Aného and Tabligbo. Their name means "from Nuatja"; they migrated from that town
(now Notsé) not at the time of the original major **Adja**-Ewe dispersal
in 1720 but some time later during a time of major droughts. (*See*
NOTSE; AGOKOLI; HOGBETSOTSO FESTIVAL.) Their late migration from Notsé has given them a bad name and in contemporary
times "Ouatchi" has acquired a pejorative connotation of backward-
ness among the more developed and sophisticated coastal **Mina** and

Ewe populations. Their dialect (Ouatchi or Watyi) is quite similar to **Anlo-Evegbé** and is also spoken in Atakpamé and in the Grand Popo-Athiemé regions of Benin. Most Ouatchi are animist, though some have recently been converted to Christianity.

P

PAGOUDA. Small town near the Bénin border in Kabré country and formerly the center of an administrative circonscription of the same name. In the 1981 reorganization of the country, the name of the district was changed to Prefecture de la Binah; the prefecture was also detached from the Centrale region and made part of a large La Kara region.

PALIME. Bustling capital of the Kloto prefecture, renamed Kpalimé in 1972. *See* KPALIME.

PALIME CONGRESS, 1971 *see* KPALIME CONGRESS, 1971.

PALM PRODUCTS. Palm plantations and the production of both palm oil and palm by-products are not as fully developed in Togo as in neighboring countries, especially Benin. Moreover, with the coming of age of Togo's phosphate industry, the economic importance of palm products declined drastically. The administration tried to revive, develop, and centralize this branch of agricultural activity through the creation of the **Société Nationale pour le Devéloppement de la Palmeraie et les Huileries** but the effort was costly and ultimately deficitory.

PAN EWE MOVEMENT *see* ALL-EWE CONFERENCE.

PARASTATALS. Though formally espousing a free enterprise system, Togo erected a large number of State enterprises, especially in the aftermath of the phosphate mini boom of 1974. Most of these were grossly deficitory, opened the gates to crass corruption and embezzlement, and ultimately literally bankrupted the State. In 1987, by which date the privatization of the State sector had commenced, with Eyadema even declaring the goal of being the sole country in Africa without even one parastatal, there were thirty-three fully State-owned and twenty-five mixed economy companies in the country. *See also* STATE SECTOR and PRIVATIZATION.

PARATAO. One of the seven royal villages of the Kotokoli and, prior to the German conquest of the area, the Kotokoli seat of power. *See* KOTOKOLI.

PARC NATIONAL DE LA KERAN. National park formally established on June 19, 1973, though in reality only completed between 1977 and 1981, comprising 86,000 hectares of land south of the Kandé-Sansanné-Mango road and 27,000 hectares of hunting reserves contiguous with it. Though some of the scenery is lovely, there is simply not much wildlife in the park, which cannot compare in attractions to similar reserves in neighboring Burkina Faso and Benin. The creation of the park required the forced relocation from their lands of thousands of farmers, with racalcitrant individuals bombed from the air, their huts and fields burned and headmen imprisoned in **Sansanné-Mango.**

PARTI COMMUNISTE TOGOLAIS (PCT). Originally clandestine hard-line pro-Albanian party (Bainsite version of Albanian interpretation of Marxism-Leninism) established in exile in 1980 with links to counterpart parties in Benin, Burkina Faso, and Canada (obtaining from the latter both funds and printed material) with the goal of fomenting a national revolution. During the single party years of the Eyadema dictatorship the PCT was active among youth and distributed a large amount of leaflets acutely embarrassing to the regime and to Eyadema personally. Many of the abuses of human rights of the 1980s were detentions, tortures, and liquidations of youth suspected of links with the PCT or found with its leaflets in their possession. The party came out in the open in May 1991 with the political liberalizations of that year, but, apart from support within the **OTTD** union, it has not been very successful with the wider urban public, something that was viewed as surprising by observers in light of its significant inroads (when underground) among youth at the local university. The party is very indirectly the successor of the earlier **Parti de la Revolution Socialiste du Bénin** (PRSB).

PARTI D'ACTION POUR LE DEVELOPPEMENT (PAD). Opposition political party set up after the liberalizations of 1991, in alliance with the **CAR** coalition. *See also* POLITICAL PARTIES.

PARTI DE LA REVOLUTION SOCIALISTE DU BENIN (PRSB). Stillborn "parent" political party established in 1959 by two Béninois cousins, Louis Béhanzin (later Marxist instructor in Guinea and briefly in the early 1970s advisor to the militant Béninois military regime) and Theophile Paoletti, at the time Béninois trade union leader. The PRSB drew inspiration from the neo-Marxist Parti Africain d'Indépendence in Senegal and was supposed to operate in Togo and Benin. In Togo, its branch, even less active than in Benin, was the Parti Socialiste Révolutionnaire du Togo (PSRT). Its ideological plank included immediate independence, socialist economic policies, and militant pan-Africanism. Though it appealed to some students and intellectuals, especially in Benin, the PRSB has had no impact whatsoever upon either Togolese or Béninois politics. In the 1980s, a more radical version of the PRSB was founded, when Radio Albania announced the establishment of the Parti Communiste Togolaise. *See also* POLITICAL PARTIES.

PARTI DE L'UNITE TOGOLAISE (PUT). New name of Sylvanus Olympio's **Comité de l'Unité Togolaise**. Though the new name was adopted as early as 1961, the party was still widely known as the CUT until the 1963 coup. *See also* POLITICAL PARTIES.

PARTI DEMOCRATIQUE DU RENOUVEAU (PDR). Opposition political party set up after the liberalizations of 1991 by Zarifou Ayéva, a former Minister under General Eyadema, to garner the generally solid Kotokoli vote around Sokodé, its prime base. *See also* POLITICAL PARTIES.

PARTI DES DEMOCRATES POUR L'UNITE (PDU). Opposition political party set up after the liberalizations of 1991, in May, by **Savi de Tové**. The party did not succeed in garnering much political support. *See also* POLITICAL PARTIES.

PARTI POPULAIRE POUR LA DEMOCRATIE ET LE DEVELOPPEMENT DU TOGO (PPDD). Opposition political party set up in 1989. *See also* POLITICAL PARTIES.

PARTI PROGRESSISTE TOGOLAIS (PPT). Militant opposition political party set up in May 1991 after the liberalizations of that year. *See also* POLITICAL PARTIES.

PARTI SOCIAL-DEMOCRATE (PSD). New opposition political party set up in May 1991 following the liberalizations of that year, aiming at a redistribution of wealth and moderate Democratic Socialist policies. *See also* POLITICAL PARTIES.

PARTI SOCIALISTE REVOLUTIONNAIRE DU TOGO (PSRT). Togolese, largely inactive, branch of the radical **Parti de la Révolution Socialiste du Bénin**. *See also* POLITICAL PARTIES.

PARTI TOGOLAIS DU PROGRES (PTP). Togo's second political party after Sylvanus Olympio's **Comité de l'Unité Togolaise**. Founded in 1946 by Dr. Pedro Olympio and Nicolas Grunitzky (both related to

Sylvanus Olympio) and also having as leading members such politicians as Dr. **Ajavon, Fousseni Mama, Georges Apedo-Amah, Derman Ayeva,** Frederic Brunner, and others. The PTP was essentially a conservative pro-French association of traditional northern notables and southern civil servants and évolués with a sprinkling of French citizens, heavily supported by the local French administration against the CUT and its nationalist and pan-Ewe platforms. The PTP fared poorly at the beginning, with Grunitzky polling only twenty-five percent in his race for a seat in the French National Assembly in 1946 against the candidacy of Dr. **Akou,** who ran with CUT support. From 1951 to 1955 the party was rent by major leadership schisms. Grunitzky, who in 1951 was deserted by large blocs of voters in his own home districts, was first expelled; then, making a comeback, he expelled the rival faction headed by Dr. Pedro Olympio, which set up the **Mouvement Populaire Togolais**. Since Grunitzky had won his second contest against Akou in 1951 and had a source of support in the French National Assembly and among the local French administration, he emerged as the main leader of the PTP.

The party dominated the Togolese political scene in the early and mid-1950s, relying upon French support and established tactical alliances with the nascent northern **Union des Chefs et des Populations du Nord**. The above formation was dislodged from power following the 1958 United Nations-sponsored elections: the PTP barely campaigned in the latter election, sure of its electoral alliance of chiefs and notables, but obtained only a fifth of the votes cast for the CUT. The 1958 defeat brought down the premiership and government of Nicolas Grunitzky and catapulted Sylvanus Olympio and the CUT to power. In October 1959 the badly shattered PTP and UCPN merged to form the **Union Democratique des Peuples Togolais** under the leadership of Grunitzky, **Antoine Méatchi**, and several other northern leaders. As the CUT began to hound and harass opposition parties (prior to their ban in 1962), Grunitzky left the country and renounced political activities, leaving the UDPT to fall under the control of Méatchi. Following the 1963 coup d'état, the exiled leadership of both the former PTP and the UCPN coalesced to revive the UDPT, which became the dominant party of the Second Republic (1963–67). *See also* POLITICAL PARTIES.

PARTITION *see* FRENCH ADMINISTRATION; LEAGUE OF NATIONS MANDATE.

PASSAH, SETH. Former Mayor of Tsévié and early PUT militant. Born in 1910 in Tsévié, Passah served as Chef-de-Canton under the French colonial administration. After independence, Passah, an early PUT militant, was elected Mayor of Tsévié, serving until the 1963 coup d'état. He is currently retired from public life.

PATAKIDEO, AHI. Journalist. Patakideo was the author of a series of underground tracts attacking General Eyadema for abuse of power, corruption, and human rights violations. He was arrested in 1978 and detained without trial until 1991.

PATASSE, KPANLON. Director General of Customs of Togo.

PATSOH, KOUMLAN FELIX, 1934– . Journalist. Born in Chra on April 14, 1934, Patsoh was educated locally and later obtained a diploma in Journalism from the Ecole Supériéur de Journalisme in Paris. He has worked as Editor of *Togo-Républicain* (1957–58) and the information *Bulletin* of the Togolese government (1958–59), as well as serving as Chief Editor of *Togo-Presse* between 1962 and 1963 and General Director of the Establissement National des Editions between 1963 and 1969. He is still involved in Journalism in Lomé.

PEDA. Small ethnic sliver found mostly in the south, nearly exclusively in their home village of Pedah-Condji in the district of Aného.

PEDANOU, GABRIEL DOUJI. Senior foreign ministry official. Pedanou has served in a variety of capacities, including Director of Economic Affairs and Technical Assistance (1967), Chargé d'Affairs at the Togolese Embassy in Lagos (1967–68), Director of Economic Affairs and Technical Assistance again (1969–72), and, since 1973, has been attached to one of the specialized groups of the United Nations.

PEDANOU, MACAIRE KWASI, 1934– . International administrator. Born on April 10, 1934 in Lomé, Pedanou was educated at home following which he proceeded to obtain his first degree at the University of Toulouse (1955–59). In 1960 he joined the Ministry of Foreign Affairs as Director of the Division of Political Affairs and International Organizations and in 1961 moved to the United Nations where he served as a Political Affairs Officer at the Department of Political and Security Council Affairs until 1965. He was then for one year Executive Secretary of the Organization of African Unity United Nations office before reverting back to his old duties at the United Nations (1967–68), following which he was reassigned to a variety of other duties within the organization.

PERE, DAOUKO. RPT militant and former Minister of Labor and Civil Service. Pere joined the cabinet in February 1990, continuing to hold his RPT Politburo portfolio as General Delegate for Youth. After the political upheavals of 1991 he lost his cabinet seat.

"PERSONAL UNION" WITH DAHOMEY *see* FRENCH ADMINIS-
TRATION.

PERSONALITY CULT. Starting rather "modestly" in the early 1970s and
rapidly reaching grotesque proportions (until somewhat restrained by
negative world opinion in the mid-1980s and completely arrested with
multi-partyism in 1992), the Eyadema Personality Cult has been visible
everywhere in Togo. Giant pictures of "Le Guide" appeared all over the
country, mamie dresses depicting Eyadema's portrait were nearly de
rigueur in many circles; his larger-than-life busts and monuments were
erected in many centers, and the press constantly referred to the "Guide
de la Nation," "Le Fondateur-President du RPT," "Le General," and the
"Savior of the Common Man." The Personality Cult paradoxically commenced early in the 1970s as a modest effort on the part of Eyadema—
a northerner and a military usurper—to drum up support for his rule.
Later inspired and aided by North Korean advisors, the Personality Cult
became a stifling aspect of contemporary Togolese life. In 1977, a three-
and-one-half ton statue of Eyadema (sculpted in North Korea) was
erected in downtown Lomé, at the height of the perennial adulation of
Eyadema. (The latter was mutilated and removed with the liberalization
in 1991.)

At the same time, Eyadema began to withdraw into a cocoon of relatives and northerners, sycophants, and fortune seekers. In the 1980s,
for example, a half-brother commanded the presidential guard (Lieutenant Donou), a son (Etienne Gnassingbé) began his career in command of an elite unit of the army, a cousin served as Minister of Higher
Education (Aissah Agbetro), an old crony (Yaya Malou) headed the
police college, his nephew (Agbetifa) was appointed minister, as was
an old school teacher from his home village, Pya.

PETIT POPO *see* ANEHO.

PEUL *see* FULANI.

PHOSPHATES. Togo's principal export since the mid-1960s and the
country's major industry and employer. First detected in 1927 and "re-
discovered" in 1952, Togo's calcium-phosphate deposits are mostly
found and quarried northeast of **Lac Togo** in Hahotoe and Dagbati, to
be transported to the coast at Kpémé where the ore is loaded onto ships
for export. France is Togo's main phosphate client. Deposits are estimated at fifty million tons, though figures have been revised upward
over the years, with Togo currently ranked fifth globally in terms of
phosphate production after the United States, USSR, Morocco, and
Tunisia. (New phosphate resources were discovered in the north of the

country in the 1990s, but to tap them costly infrastructure would have to be erected.)

In 1954 an international consortium was formed to develop the mines and facilities in the south that were renamed the Compagnie Togolaise des Mines du Bénin (CTMB, or COTOMIB) in 1957. (*See also* CO-TOMIB.) State participation went up from 19.5 percent to 35 percent by November 1972 and soon after to 50 percent. The mines were fully nationalized early in 1974 after General Eyadema's claim that COTOMIB officials, fearful of impending nationalization, had conspired to assassinate him. (*See* EYADEMA'S PLANE CRASHES.) In 1973 the company had 1,100 workers, and exports amounted to 6.3 million CFA francs. A major surge in world prices for phosphates in 1974 quintupled Togo's earnings from phosphate exports to 34,532 million CFA francs that year, but prices dropped abruptly in 1975, causing major fiscal shortfalls on a regime that had banked that prices would remain high.

In order to garner higher profits, Togo erected a state phosphate marketing organization (*see* OTP) in 1974, and COTOMIB's productive capacity has been expanded since nationalization, with a fifth line (of lower grade ore) coming into production in 1980, raising capacity to over four million tons a year. Moreover, in 1984 a feasibility study was carried out that supported the opening up of the Dagbati phosphate deposits (near existing mines) and the erection of a phosphoric acid factory and fertilizer plant (at a cost of $500 million) with a capacity of 1,000 tons of phosphoric acid. Early expectations of a phosphate-led transformation of the country were thwarted, however, since phosphate prices have generally remained stagnant, even going down. In 1988, for example, phosphates accounted (at 36.5 billion CFAF) for 26.5% of exports, while in 1991 (before the social upheavals that lowered production, making comparisons impossible) phosphate exports brought in 35.6 billion CFAF accounting for 24.7% of Togo's exports.

PIC D'AGOU. Name of Togo's second merchant marine cargo ship. Purchased in 1980, it joined the *Hodo,* flagship of the Société Nationale Maritime.

PISANG, ATABANAM PETCHETHOU, 1938– . Senior civil administrator. Born in 1938 and educated locally, including at the Ecole Nationale d'Administration, Pissang's first appointment was in 1963, when he joined the Ministry of Civil Service as a cabinet attaché. He served in that post until 1965. In 1969 he became head of Administration of the Sokodé Administrative Council, and between 1975 and 1976 he was comptroller of Public Expenditures at the Togolese Treasury. In 1980 he was appointed to Kara as head of Administration and Personnel of the North-Togo project.

PLACCA, BOEVI JOSEPH, 1926– . Psychologist, civil and international administrator, and employment specialist. Born on December 4, 1926 in Porto Seguro and educated at home and in Cote d'Ivoire, Placca proceeded to France to study in Versailles and at the Sorbonne, emerging with both Teaching degrees and a Psychology degree in 1955. He then spent one year in Turin, Italy in specialized studies before becoming Director of Togo's Employment Service in 1956 and in 1964 head of Togo's Employment Planning Services. In 1970 he became Technical Adviser to the Minister of Planning and Development, and in 1974 he was appointed to the Employment Development section of the Addis Ababa-based Economic Commission for Africa where he stayed until his recent retirement. Placca is a former Vice President of the African Psychology Association.

PLATEAUX. Region of Togo with administrative headquarters in **Atak-pamé**, subdivided into the **circonscriptions** (i.e., districts) of Atak-pamé, Akposso, Notsé, and Kloto. The region encompasses a territory of 20,430 square kilometers and a population of 700,000, composed of **Ouatchi, Ewe, Ana, Akposso,** and **Kabré** immigrants from the north. The region has some of the more fertile land in Togo, is the center of Togo's cocoa/coffee producing plantations, and is the most advanced socio-economically after the Maritime. Cotton and peanuts are also grown in several areas of the Plateaux, though production levels are low. The region is well connected with the north via all weather roads and to the south by the railroad and several paved roads. In the June 1981 administrative reorganization, the region was subdivided into five prefectures: Ogou (ex-Atakpamé), Haho (ex-Nuatja), Kloto (ex-Kluoto), Wawa, and Amou (ex-Akposso).

PLEBISCITE OF 1956. The 1956 plebiscite was held in the British Trusteeship of Togoland at the suggestion of the Visiting Mission of the Trusteeship Council (1955), after Britain's announcement that following the impending independence of the Gold Coast she could not continue administering British Togoland. (The British administered the Trusteeship Territory from the Gold Coast.) In the plebiscite all adults were given two choices: independence as a region within Ghana or continued trusteeship status, pending a later decision regarding the disposition of the territory. The Visiting Mission divided the region into four "zones" along linguistic and ethnic criteria, but the Trusteeship Council rejected the recommendation that each zone decide its own future separately, though later, in 1958, the formula was used for a similar plebiscite in northern and southern British Cameroons. France resisted efforts to have her conduct a similar plebiscite, holding instead the **Referendum of 1956** that led to the creation of the **Au-**

tonomous Republic of Togo. The 1956 plebiscite resulted in 93,095 votes for merger with the Gold Coast and independence within Ghana and 67,492 votes against that course of action. In the northern regions of British Togoland, where pro-unification desires were strongest on the part of the ethnic elements artificially separated by the Gold Coast-British Togo border, among the **Dagomba** for example, the pro-unificationist vote was solid: 49,119 for and 12,707 against. In the south, among Ewe and other ethnic groups, the vote was 43,976 for unification and 54,785 against. On the basis of the combined vote of the entire territory, British Togoland merged with the Gold Coast and became a region of Ghana, contrary to the desires of a significant percentage of the Ewe and related ethnic groups that had hoped for unification within a larger Ewe state. Since then, successive Togolese governments and leaders have periodically voiced irredentist claims, as have Ewe groups in Ghana. In the late 1970's, for example, the Eyadema regime sponsored a remarkable press campaign to support its demand that the results of the 1956 plebiscite be put aside, and close contacts have always been maintained with irredentist groups in Ghana, which have received financial support from Togo.

PLIYA, JEAN, 1931– . One of neighboring Benin's foremost authors and former minor political ideologue, currently established in Togo as an educator. Born in Djougou (Benin) to a chiefly Fon family on July 13, 1931, Pliya studied locally and in Ivory Coast, Senegal, and France, training as a teacher. He has taught at Lycée Coulibaly in Porto Novo (Benin) and at Benin's national university. In the 1960s he published his widely acclaimed *Kondo, Le Requin* and *L'Arbre Fetiche,* the latter bringing him the highly coveted Grand Prix de la Nouvelle Africaine. From 1959 to 1960 he was briefly co-founder of a militant Béninois party, and between 1961 and 1965 he served as Benin's Director of National Education, Deputy to the National Assembly, and Secretary of State for Information and Tourism. Following the coup d'état of 1965 in Benin, Pliya worked mostly abroad in France, and later in Togo as Professor of Geography at the Université du Bénin in Lomé, where he still teaches.

POLITICAL PARTIES. [Note: for additional information on all parties mentioned below, see the individual entries under their names] The history and evolution of the Togolese party system, that has not been linked, except in a few instances and then only superficially, with Francophone Africa's interterritorial movements such as the RDA, MSA, or CA, can be divided chronologically.

　(1) 1945 to 1961: A multiplicity of parties existed on the Togolese scene, with a tug-of-war between the CUT and the other formations but

especially with the PTP (see below); (2) 1961 to 1963: For about 18 months until Olympio's murder in the 1963 coup d'etat the CUT was the only party within a uniparty system, that developed an increasingly harsh side to it; (3) 1963 to 1967: A multi-party system formally existed during the Grunitzky-Méatchi regime until General Eyadema's second coup d'etat of 1967. The four main parties shared power in an equally divided National Assembly, with representatives in the cabinet; (4) 1967 to 1969: During the first two years of the regime of General Eyadema, parties were banned, but the imminent return to civilian politics and the withdrawal of the army were continuously touted; (5) 1969 to 1991: Eyadema, following constant stage-managed mass petitions to remain in office, began an attempt to legitimize his rule through the construction of a single "national" movement in which all political elements were represented, the RPT, while abroad opposition movements are set up; and (6) the post-1991 era, in which Eyadema is forced to concede multi-partyism, with as many as sixty-six political parties emerging, most cooperating in two broad coalitions in opposition to the still existing RPT.

Togo's principal political parties, prior to the creation of Eyadema's political machine (the Rassemblement du Peuple Togolais) (see 10 below), were as follows:

(1) *Comité de l'Unité Togolaise* (CUT). An outgrowth of the French-sponsored sociocultural **Cercle des Amitiés Françaises**, also known as Unité Togolaise and, after 1961, officially as the Parti de l'Unité Togolaise, though the new name became increasingly used only after the 1963 coup d'etat. Established in 1941 as an essentially pan-Ewe movement, the CUT garnered most of the Ewe and Mina intelligentsia—and obtained much support from the center of the country as well—to become Africa's first nationalist movement and Togo's political party par excellence. Its domination over Togolese politics lasted between 1946 and 1951, following which the French administration, for some time fearful of the party's pan-Ewe aspirations and alleged "pro-British" stances, engineered the creation, entrenchment, and electoral success of alternate conservative, pro-French, and docile political formations such as the PTP and the UCPN. The CUT boycotted the 1951 elections and was in the political wilderness until the 1958 United Nations-supervised elections in which the party scored a smashing victory against all the other parties and formed the government that was to lead Togo to independence. In 1959 the CUT's more militant and pan-Africanist youth wing, Juvento, seceded and ran as a separate party. After independence, the CUT began to harass sources of opposition, and in 1962 Togo officially became a uniparty state. (By mid-1961 all parties except for the CUT had been "disqualified" from competing in the elections of that

year.) Following the 1963 coup d'etat, one wing of the CUT (now PUT) joined the successor Grunitzky-Méatchi four-cornered electoral coalition, while the more radical wing, refusing to accept the return of the PTP-UCPN politicians so roundly trounced in 1958, rejected co-operation and engaged in a variety of subversive activities that punctuated the four years of the Grunitzky presidency with rhythmic regularity. The Lomé upheaval of 1966—*see* COUP (ATTEMPTED) OF 1966—itself linked to a major cabinet crisis (see MEATCHI-MAMA CRISIS), led several weeks later to the 1967 coup and the ban of all political parties.

(2) *Juvento.* Also known as Mouvement de la Jeunesse Togolaise and as Juventos Togo. Juvento was originally the militant CUT youth wing, differing with Sylvanus Olympio and other CUT leaders on a variety of positions. The party had, in the late 1950s and early 1960s, a pan-Africanist and socialist coloration that led it to break with the CUT and emerge as a separate party in 1959. In 1961 the party formed an opportunistic alliance with the conservative UDPT (called the Mouvement Nationaliste Togolais-Juvento, see below) but the electoral alliance was disqualified by the increasingly oppressive CUT administration, and the party was disbanded with the establishment of a one party (CUT) system in 1962. Following the 1963 coup d'etat the Juvento party was resurrected, and it participated in the four-cornered electoral alliance that ruled Togo between 1963 and 1967. After the 1967 coup, Juvento and all other parties were banned.

(3) *Parti Togolais du Progrès* (PTP). Togo's second oldest party, established in 1946 by Nicolas Grunitzky and Dr. Pedro Olympio both of whom were related to Sylvanus Olympio, leader of the Comité de l'Unité Togolaise (see 1 above). The PTP—strongly supported by the local French administration against the CUT—was essentially a conservative alliance of pro-French notables, chiefs, civil servants and evolués. From 1951 to 1955, the party suffered a series of leadership schisms that resulted first in the expulsion of Grunitzky and later (1955) his ascendance and the expulsion of Pedro Olympio (who then formed the Mouvement Populaire Togolais, see 4 below). Aided by the French administration and allied with the northern Union des Chefs et des Populations du Nord (see 5 below), the PTP formed or participated in the governments until 1958. In that year, the United Nations-supervised elections brought about the dramatic electoral victory of the CUT and the collapse of the Grunitzky administration. Totally shattered by the 1958 results, the PTP never recovered; the party merged with the equally defeated UCPN to form the Union Démocratique des Peuples Togolais (see 6 below), which was shortly afterward banned as Olympio established his uniparty state in Togo.

(4) *Mouvement Populaire Togolais* (MPT). Founded by Dr. Pedro

Olympio after his expulsion from the leadership hierarchy of the Parti Togolais du Progrès (see 3 above). The MPT was not very successful at the polls and suffered from an attrition of leadership; it was banned in 1961 when Sylvanus Olympio established a CUT one party state. Resurrected after the 1963 coup d'etat, under **Samuel Aquereburu's** leadership (Pedro Olympio had assumed diplomatic duties), the MPT participated in the four-cornered coalition that ruled Togo between 1963 and 1967. In 1967 the party, and all others, was banned in the aftermath of the 1967 coup.

(5) *Union des Chefs et des Populations du Nord* (UCPN). French-aided northern conservative alliance of chiefs/notables set up in opposition to the dominance of political life by southern elites and parties. The UCPN was founded in 1951 and was allied to Grunitzky's PTP party with which it merged in October 1959 (following the shattering comeback of Sylvanus Olympio's CUT) to form the Union Démocratique des Peuples Togolais (see 6 below).

(6) *Union Démocratique des Peuples Togolais* (UDPT). Established in October 1959 as a merger of the electorally mauled and disintegrating Parti Togolais du Progrès (see 3 above) and its former ally, the Union des Chefs et des Populations du Nord (see 5 above), following the collapse of the Grunitzky **Autonomous Republic** administration and the rise to power of the CUT. The UDPT formed a tactical electoral alliance in 1961 to compete against the CUT in that year's election, but the formation was disqualified on spurious grounds and shortly afterward all parties except the CUT were abolished. Nicolas Grunitzky, former leader of the UDPT who had left Togo for Cote d'Ivoire, returned to Lomé in the aftermath of the 1963 coup d'etat and the re-establishment of competitive politics and wrenched the leadership of the party from **Antoine Méatchi**, who had stayed in Togo until his 1961 arrest and escape from the police. The two established a very unstable executive branch and formed a government coalition that included representatives of the other three major Togolese parties, the MTP, Juvento, and a "collaborationist" part of the PUT, (ex-CUT). The coalition remained in power until the collapse of the Second Republic in 1967, which was due to continuous friction between Méatchi and Grunitzky and, in part, to opposition to the leadership on the part of the masses in the southern urban centers. Following the 1967 coup all political parties were banned.

Apart from the above six major political parties of the pre-1967 era, the following minor parties or electoral formations should be noted:

(7) The *Parti de la Révolution Socialiste du Bénin* (PRSB). Stillborn radical political party founded in 1959 with nuclei in Benin and Togo.

(8) *Mouvement Nationaliste Togolaise-Juvento*. Brief 1961 tactical

electoral alliance of Juvento and the UDPT to compete against the CUT in the 1961 elections. The formation was disqualified as the CUT moved to impose a one party state.

(9) *Liste Nationale de l'Unité et Réconciliation.* Official name of the unified electoral list of the four-cornered political alliance of the PUT, Juvento, MPT, and UDPT for the 1963 election following the coup e'état that resulted in Olympio's assassination. The parties divided equally the seats in the National Assembly, and their representatives sat in the cabinet of Nicolas Grunitzky (1963–1967). The coalition collapsed after the 1967 coup and the individual parties were all banned.

In 1969 a new "national" single party was set up by General Eyadema, who had decided to remain in office and needed legitimation:

(10) The *Rassemblement du Peuples Togolais* (RPT). Highly decentralized for much of its existence, the party has been barely active in several regions (even in Kabré areas), though it boasted an increasingly large membership. Governed by a collegiate Political Bureau (that replaced a short-lived experiment under a Secretary General and several Deputies), the RPT established ancillary organs such as a youth wing and a women's branch. Holding Congresses in various parts of the country, the RPT was nominally the ultimate source of authority in Togo, though it has always been under the control of General Eyadema and his closest associates, and in any case could never debate issues let alone adopt positions contrary to those of Eyadema. The RPT acquired special status in 1979 when the Togolese regime formally constitutionalized itself. Though by the mid-1980s the RPT appeared less lifeless than in the 1970s, its activity was largely sporadic and carried out by sycophants (including many opportunistic Ewe, whose presence was touted by Eyadema as attesting to the RPT's national character) and other favor-seekers aware that links to the RPT hierarchy could unlock doors. The RPT survived the 1991 democratization intact (though originally banned by the **National Conference**) but is now clearly a solidly northern party and more specifically a Kabré one.

In the late 1970s and early 1980s, a number of opposition parties were established abroad, vowing to oust the usurper Eyadema. Among these three parties stand out:

(11) the *Mouvement Togolaise Pour la Démocratie* (MTD). A Paris-based political vehicle for the Olympio-De Souza and other **Brazilians'** interests, headed by Gilchrist Olympio (one of President Olympio's sons), who became in the 1980's Eyadema's most implacable foe, and supporter of increasingly violent efforts to topple the dictatorship in Lomé. At Eyadema's demand the movement was

proscribed by Paris, and Olympio had to relocate to London in 1981, where it became largely moribund. After the 1991 liberalization in Togo Olympio's formation changed names—see post-1991 parties below.

(12) *Front National de Liberation du Togo* (FNLT). Also Paris-based, though with nuclei in West Africa where it had supporters, the FNLT supported efforts at ousting Eyadema by force, though it has been largely moribund, or its activities have been coordinated with the MTD. The FNLT was set up by former Lieutenant Colonel Merlaud Lawson, of the Brazilian **Lawson family**, shortly after he fled the country.

(13) The *Parti Communiste Togolais* (PCT). At the time a clandestine Trotskyite party (currently operating in the open in Lomé), receiving assistance from Trotskyite sources in Canada, whose foundation was originally reported by Radio Albania, and intermittently viewed as Albanian-led. The party stood for a total restruction of Togolese society and not merely the replacement of Eyadema. Until legalized in 1991 the party was primarily active in distributing inflammatory anti-Eyadema leaflets and embarrassing details about the regime. Especially active amongst youth in urban centers, and with several active cells at the local University (including students and faculty), many of the human rights abuses perpetrated by Eyadema were related to the regime's harsh treatment of actual or suspected PCT members, since mere possession of its literature was grounds for torture and possible death in prison.

In 1990 global pressures, and in 1991 domestic upheaval, forced Eyadema to seek to ride out the democratization storm by legalizing all political formations and inviting back all opposition elements (many sentenced to death in absentia) to participate in the **National Conference**. The result was a large number of new parties, most emerging in May 1991, and various multi-party coalitions were formed. Since some of the "parties" were in reality single member power vehicles not to be heard of again, or later mergers with larger coalitions, only the most important formations will be noted. A few additional ones, however, are briefly listed under their names in the dictionary.

The *RPT*, that is not a "new" party (see 10 above), needs to be mentioned here, because of its changed nature. (It actually also changed its name briefly.) After the National Conference and a prolonged total strike in the south failed to dislodge General Eyadema—who emerged supreme through heavy-handed brutalization of the interim government and society in the south—the much postponed 1994 legislative elections were held with the participation of the originally-banned RPT. After considerable intimidation in the non-Kabré north (it has little support in the south) the RPT emerged the country's second largest party. It is now clearly a regional party of the Kabré, led by old-timer Eyadema stalwarts and with only a small layer of its former southern collaborators. The RPT's platform is simple—to keep Eyadema in power and to retain control of all ministries that might affect the military or the Kabré people, since fears of southern retribution for decades of northern brutalization (starting with Olympio's 1963 murder) run high.

The new parties (individually listed) that emerged after 1991 coalesced into three relatively stable electoral alliances. These are (a) the *Union des Forces Démocratiques* (UFD) comprising inter alia of the *Convention Démocratique des Peuples Africaines* (CDPA, headed by Gnininvi), the *Union Togolaise pour la Démocratie* (UTD, headed by Kodjo), the *Parti Démocratique de Rénouveau* (PDR, led by Ayéva), and a few leftist political slivers. This alliance—referred to at times as Eyadema's "moderate" opposition but in reality the pragmatic opportunists—is currently (1994) in office in the governing coalition with Eyadema's RPT, under Prime Minister Edem Kodjo. (b) The *Union des Forces du Changement* (UFC, led by Gilchrist Olympio)—sometimes referred to as Eyadema's "hard" opposition, that boycotted the 1994 elections—includes inter alia Olympio's own *Mouvement Togolaise Pour la Démocratie* (MTD), the *Unité Togolaise pour la Réconstruction* (UTR), *Alliance Togolais des Démocrates* (ATD), and the *Parti des Démocrates pour l'Unité* (PDU). (c) the *Comité d'Action pour le Rénouveau* (CAR, led by Yao Agboyibor) that is Togo's largest party and is also supported by the *Parti de l'Action pour le Développement* (PAD).

The parties noted above include specifically:

(14) the *Parti Démocratique du Rénouveau* (PDR) set up in May 1991 by **Zarifou Ayéva,** a businessman and former Minister under Eyadema. As his name attests Ayéva is of the Kotokoli chiefly family based in Sokodé with strong support in the Tchaoudjo district (200 miles north of Lomé), which is the Kotokoli heartland. The PDR joined with the CDPA of Gnininvi, the UTD of Kodjo, and some smaller leftist parties to form the UFD coalition in the National Conference that was pitched against the two main southern alliances headed by Olympio and Agboyibor (see below).

(15) Gilchrist Olympio's resurrected MTD party (see above) that formed a broad alliance with the UTR (headed by Mankouby), the ATD of Ife, and the PDU of de Tové, called the *Union des Forces du Changement* (UFC).

(16) The *Union Togolaise pour la Démocratie* (UTD) set up in May 1991 by Edem Kodjo, a Ewe from the Kpalimé area and a former Eyadema supporter and current Prime Minister. (The division of the

Ewe vote between Kodjo and Olympio—that has its roots in intra-Ewe competitions as much as in Kpalimé's memories of excess taxation on their coffee-cocoa crops by Gilchrist Olympio's father—and the two leaders' inability to join hands in general were major reasons why Eyadema was able to claw his way to power in 1993.) The UTD is essentially the party of the Kpalimé Ewe solidly ranked behind Kodjo, who has been in the broad UFD alliance (see above) of the Kotokoli grouping north of Kpalimé under Ayéva's PDR and the more radical CDPA of Gnininvi and other small leftist parties. Within the context of Togolese ethnic voting, the UTD cannot but be a small party, and it secured less than ten percent of the seats (seven) in the 1994 legislative elections but emerged in a pivotal role when Kodjo was appointed Prime Minister.

(17) The *Comité d'Action pour le Rénouveau,* actually a close alliance of several southern formations headed by **Yao Agboyibor** with the support of the PAD (see below) party as well, emerged in the legislative elections as the largest party in Togo with thirty-six seats. (For that reason the CAR was *not* invited to form the government but rather the minority UTD and its allied groups that could be more easily manipulated by Eyadema.

The smaller groups that need noting include (18) the *Parti de l'Action pour le Développement* (PAD) that is independent of, but supportive of Agboyibor's CAR alliance; (19) the *Parti des Démocrates pour l'Unité* (PDU) set up in May 1991 by Savi de Tové (cooperating closely with Olympio in the UFC coalition [see 15]), a small party reflecting primarily **Brazilian** interests that, despite de Tové's pretensions, has minimal public support; (20) the *Unité Togolaise pour la Réconstruction* (UTR), set up in May 1991 and headed by **Hospice Coco**, a close associate of Sylvanus Olympio and the sole surviving member of the original executive body of the CUT (see above). In 1992 leadership of this party moved to Bawa Mankouby (a Moba from the Far North) and the party has been a member of Gilchrist Olympio's UFC grouping (see 16 above); (21) the *Convention Démocratique des Peuples Africaines* (CDPA), a small radical party headed by the ambitious **Gnininvi** who joined forces with Edem Kodjo to form the 1994 government; (22) the *Alliance de Démocrates pour la République* (ADR); (23) the *Alliance Togolais des Démocrates* (ATD) set up in May 1991 and headed by Adani Ife, aligned with Gilchrist Olympio; (24) the *Social-Liberal Togolaise* (SOLITO) a social-democrat party under Yao Atikpo formerly known as (25) the *Parti Social-Démocrate* (PSD) set up originally in May 1991 and (26) the radical *Parti Socialiste Révolutionnaire du Togo* (PSRT) the epistemologically reborn PCT (see above); the *Unité Togolaise pour la Justice* (UTJ) that is in alliance with the RPT and (27) the *Alliance de Démocrates pour la Développement* (ADD) that changed

names in 1992, set up by **Tchabaroue Gogue**; and the (28) *Parti Socialiste Pan-Africaine* (PSP) headed by Francis Agbobli, that joined
with other small radical groupings to form the (29) *Groupe Social Pan-
Africaine* (GSPA), all the latter being small localized formations. Two
late-comers include (30) the *Comité Togolaise de Résistance* (CTR), a
"liberation" front set up in exile in Paris in December 1992 by Isidore
Lajo, calling for Eyadema's ouster to come before anything else, and
(31) *Mouvement Nationaliste pour l'Unité* (MNU) set up also in 1992,
by Koffitsé Adzouko with a similar platform. Additional parties were
formed: according to one account as many as sixty-six such groups
emerged in Togo.

POLO, AREGBA. Minister of Justice, representing the RPT. Appointed
to the third interim Koffigoh cabinet in September 1992, Polo was retained in his post in 1993 for another term of office.

POLO, KPAROU ANDRE-MARIE, 1929– . Former PUT militant.
Born in Kandé in 1929 and trained as a nurse, Polo was an early delegate to the Togolese Legislative Assembly, being elected on the PUT
ticket in 1952. He served on the assembly until the 1963 coup (except
for the period 1955–58) and was the PUT parliamentary party Deputy
Treasurer. Polo is currently retired.

PORT AUTONOME DE LOME. Lomé's booming deep water port. On
July 9, 1963, a West German-Togolese treaty was signed for the construction of a new deep water port immediately east of the center of
Lomé that would also serve landlocked Burkina Faso. The project—
negotiated by former President Olympio—was at the time Germany's
biggest capital commitment in Africa and an indication of a desire to
assist her former **Musterkolonie**. Lomé's original wharf traced its origins to the German colonial era, though a new one had been constructed in 1928. The latter rapidly became inadequate, and negotia-
tions had commenced for the erection of a major joint Togo-Benin
port in **Agoué**, midway between Cotonou and Lomé but in Béninois
territory. Benin, however, obtained a French commitment to build up
Cotonou's port and, shortly afterward, Togo sought out West German
funds for her own port in Lomé. The port and duty-free zone were
completed in 1968 and have been a major boost to trade. Imports rose
between 1968 and 1972 from 189,641 to 300,000 tons, straining the
400,000 ton capacity of the installations, leading to a major expansion
of the facilities in the late 1970s. In 1978, for example, 808 vessels of
3.3 million gross tons called at Lomé, unloading 1.12 million tons of
goods and loading in turn 326,000 tons.
    By 1981, existing facilities were again under strain as more and

more transit traffic for the inland states (Burkina Faso, Niger) chose Lomé as their preferred port. A virtual doubling of the capacity of the port was completed in the mid-1980s, but further expansion is already envisaged as Togolese exports/imports have expanded even as transit traffic has increased above expectations. Niger, for example, has more than tripled its traffic via Lomé, while Burkina Faso has announced its intention to increase the tonnage of its goods using the port. Even Mali imports some 3,000 tons via Lomé, since this overland route is 400 kilometers shorter (and easier) than via Abidjan. The long social turmoil in the 1990s, aimed at dislodging General Eyadema, played havoc, however, with the Port's activities, as union strikes and a drop in economic activity plagued the country.

PORTO SEGURO *see* LAC TOGO.

PRESENCE CHRETIENNE. Fortnightly Catholic newspaper published in Lomé since 1960, with a circulation of 3,000. During the Olympio era, issues of the publication were confiscated by the police after a clash between Olympio and Archbishop Robert Casimir Dosseh.

PRESIDENCE, PALAIS DE LA. In contrast to most Francophone states, Togo lagged behind in the construction of a new official residence for its chief executive. For fiscal reasons, the stately but old German colonial headquarters served, until 1969, as the presidential residence during the administrations of both Olympio and Grunitzky. A new modernistic building began to be constructed in 1969 and was completed in time for Togo's tenth anniversary of independence (1970). Allegedly built with funds obtained from Nigeria (*see* NIGERIAN BANKNOTES DISPUTE), the low profile building is near the waterfront, centered on a 5,000 square meter plot. Designed by the Frenchman Jean Cyr, the structure was built at a cost of 500 million CFA francs. Paradoxically, General Eyadema prefers, for security reasons, to sleep in his modest villa in the Tokoin military camp in the northern part of the town, and only since 1979 has he come to use the palace even intermittently as his official residence.

PRESIDENTIAL ELECTIONS, 1993 *see* ELECTIONS, 1993–94.

PRESIDENTIAL GUARD. General Eyadema's main power prop within the armed forces and personal force of repression against society. A 1,200 man elite corps, much of it **Kabré** with many of the personnel recruited not only from General Eyadema's home village of Pya but from his neighborhood quarter of Pya-bas. Entrusted with guarding the presidency, the guard, heavily armed with Israeli weapons, was originally trained by North Korean officers. At the head of the guard is an Eyadema second cousin, Colonel Ayi Donou Gnassingbe. The Guard has been implicated in a string of individual murders and mass brutalities as far back as 1980 and was involved, inter alia, in the **Bé Lagoon massacres** and the assault on **Gilchrist Olympio**'s motorcade in 1992.

PRINDSENSTEEN. Danish fort built in Keta on the coast (currently in Ghana, midway between Accra and Lomé) in 1784. The fort funnelled the slave trade from the hinterland and helped radiate Danish influence along the coast. The fort was ceded to Britain in 1850.

PRIVATIZATION. The drive to privatize the country's State sector commenced in the mid-1980s as the deficits piled up by the mismanaged and plundered state companies began to exert a major fiscal drag on the economy. At the time Togo had thirty-three publicly owned enterprises and twenty-five mixed economy companies in which the government possessed a share in equity, down from the original seventy-three of the early 1980s. Efforts to sell off much of the State sector were difficult, for the prices offered by foreign entrepreneurs—often for risky enterprises, hitherto poorly run—were low, while other enterprises could not find a buyer. Ten companies, finding no buyers, no matter what the price, were actually closed down and dismantled.

The best examples of state enterprises closed down due to mismanagement to metamorphose later under private ownership as profitable, are the former Société Nationale de Sidurergie (SNS) that was profitable from its first month (under an American entrepreneur) and Nioto—the former **IOTO** cooking oil company—that under French majority control saw soaring production and profits after nearly halving the workforce. State enterprises recently privatized include Soprolait (milk production and distribution) purchased by a Danish company, Industrie Togolaise des Plastiques (fifty-eight percent of shares purchased by a German-Dutch-Danish group), the Industrie Togolaise des Textiles (ITT) at Dadja and the Société Togolaise de Textiles (Togotex) at Kara, now operating as Togotex International, bought by a Chinese entrepreneur from Hong Kong. Also restructured were SOTOMA, SOTEXMA, and **STH**. Another twenty-five companies are in different stages of closure, privatization and/or restructuring, including Togoroute; the Office du Disque; Société des Salines; Société des Detergents du Togo; the Société de Galvanisations des Toles (SOTOTOLES); and the Société Togolaise de Confection (Sotcon). *See also* PARASTATALS; STATE SECTOR.

PROTESTANTS. Large scale Protestant missionary efforts in Togo began at an early date. Partly because of this, fully half of Togo's intellectuals, especially the **Mina** elite from the Aného area, are currently Protestant, despite the fact that contemporary figures indicate that only three percent of the population considers itself Protestant as opposed to sixteen percent that profess Catholicism and five percent Islam. Moreover, the establishment in Aného of a Methodist university (the cornerstone of which was laid on January 20, 1970) attests to the vitality of Protestant sentiments among one section of the coastal elements, notwithstanding the much more intensive Catholic effort in the country in recent decades. There are around 170 Protestant missionary centers in Togo, with 250 personnel. Four main organizations have proselytized:

(1) The Norddeutsche Missiongesellschaft (or Bremen Missionary Society): First major Protestant society to undertake consistent missionizing in Togo. (But *see also* MORAVIAN BROTHERS.) Approximately 100 pastors were sent to the Gold Coast-Togo coastal areas before official German colonization of Togo, fully half of them perishing from various tropical diseases. For a long time, their base was Aného, where other orders were also established. Despite the withdrawal of the society after the German loss of the colony, many Protestants still called themselves "Brema" up to the 1940s. Missionary efforts were concentrated in the south, and only in 1912 was the north opened to proselytizing. The Society was joined in its efforts by the Basle Missionary Society, which commenced activities in the Gold Coast in 1827, spreading from there to the Akwapim hills and into German Togo.

(2) The Eglise Evangélique du Togo: Following the expulsion of German missionaries from Togo in the aftermath of the First World War, neither British nor French orders were able to staff the vacated Protestant centers. Consequently, in both British and French Togo the Protestant churches became autonomous, staffed by indigenous elements. They underwent several changes in nomenclature, and in 1957 the French Togo church renamed itself the Eglise Evangélique du Togo. The church is an extremely vigorous one and has aggressively expanded its efforts among youth and into the north. In 1960 it had twenty-eight pastors and baptized 15,688 children. It also counted as members fully 20,000 of the country's 37,000 Protestants and operated some 50 schools (three quarters of them in the Ewe areas of Kloto) with 8,382 pupils. The church has also had a major part in revitalizing the **Evegbe** language, having a vitality in Ewe areas unrivalled by any other sect/religion.

(3) The Methodist Church: The oldest major Protestant church still operating in Togo. Established in Aného in the mid-nineteenth century and originally assisted by the local **Lawson family** there, the Methodist Church suffered heavy attrition in membership with the rise of the

Prophet Harris Movement in the Ivory Coast. It still has serious support among the **Mina** of Aného, a fact that encouraged it to erect a Methodist university there in 1970. Just prior to independence, the church operated three schools and counted 3,447 converts (with many not officially registered) and was served by five pastors and other auxiliary staff.

(4) The Assembly of God: American missionary society that first established itself in Upper Volta (now Burkina Faso) and Dahomey in the interwar years and then moved into Sansanné-Mango (1950) and, in 1951, to Bassari (now Bassar) in north Togo. At independence the Assembly of God counted 1,000 converts, mostly **Moba** and related northern ethnic groups. *See also* the individual entries.

PROTTEN, JACOB, 1708?–1769. Early missionary in the Gold Coast-Togo coastal regions. Born in **Christiansborg** to a Danish soldier and a princess of the Aného chiefly family, Protten was enrolled at the school for mulattos established in the fort in 1722 by Army Chaplain Elias Svane. In 1727 Protten was brought to Copenhagen where he met Count Zinzendorf, founder of the **Moravian Brothers**, who assured Protten's education and sent him back to Africa in 1737 (together with a European missionary who promptly succumbed to disease) to proselytize in the Gold Coast-Togo area. After several efforts in the Aného area, Protten fell afoul of Dutch Governor Hartog when he suggested a school for mulattos at El Mina. He was imprisoned until April 1739, following which he taught children of local notables, undertook missionary efforts without the support of the Moravian Brothers (1757–61, 1764–69), married in Europe, and tried to spur attention to the need for more missionaries in Africa.

PYA. General Eyadema's home village. A small, undistinguished, and inconsequential village twelve kilometers from Kara (ex-Lama Kara), Pya acquired fame, recognition, and massive largess—water, electricity, roads, school improvements, funds for churches—as side benefits from Eyadema's rise to power. In 1976 the structure of an old Protestant church was transformed into a temple for all faiths, refurbished with mosaics and imported tiles, all in honor of Eyadema. Many of Eyadema's childhood friends, a few of his primary school teachers, and most youth in the quarter where he was born (Pya-bas) have obtained jobs in Lomé, in the latter instance in the Presidential Guard.

Q

QUADJOVIE, CHRISTOPHE, 1928– . Former Cabinet Director and senior civil servant. Born on April 26, 1928 in Badougbé and trained abroad as a physician. Dr. Quadjovie served as Cabinet Director of the

Ministry of Public Health between 1967 and 1970, before rejoining the staff of the Lomé Hospital. He is currently in retirement.

QUADJOVIE, SEMEHO, 1934– . Former Director General of Editogo. Born in Lomé on December 26, 1934 and educated locally, Quadjovie worked as a teacher in Ivory Coast between 1954 and 1958 and at home (1959–61). In 1961 he won a prize that secured him entry to study journalism at the University of Strasbourg. He returned to Lomé in 1965 and joined Editogo with specific responsibilities over *Togo-Presse,* the daily newspaper of Editogo. After moving up to the newspaper's editorial board, Quadjovie became Editor in Chief in 1967 and Director General of Editogo in 1975. He is currently retired.

QUAM-DESSOU XIII, ATA. Traditional King (chief) of Aného between 1922 and 1977 (when he died). Head of the Adjigo clan in competition with the Lawson clan, each historically claiming original arrival in the area and hence the right to be Superior Chiefs of Aného. In 1961, with the concurrence of the major leaders of both clans, the actual title was abolished.

QUAM-DESSOU, MESSAN KOFFI (HUBERT) KPONTON. Better known as **Hubert Koffi Mensah Kponton**.

QUARTIER ADMINISTRATIF. Administrative center of Lomé, stretching from the coastal road inland to the Olympio Netime quarter that borders the lagoon in the north. Most of the major urban renewal of the 1970s has been in this strip of land.

QUASHIE, LEONIDAS. A lawyer by training, Quashie served as interim Minister of Justice in President Grunitzky's cabinet during the last few weeks of the latter's administration. After the demotion of **Lucien Olympio** in 1970, Quashie was appointed Procurer (Attorney) General to the Supreme Court of Togo but reverted to private practice a short time later.

R

RADIO DIFFUSION TELEVISION DE LA NOUVELLE MARCHE (RTNM). State television system established in July 1975 at a cost (at that time) of 600 million CFAF, for the barely 2,000 TV sets in the country.

RADIO TOGO or RADIO LOME or RADIO DE LA NOUVELLE MARCHE. Names under which Togo's state radio has been known.

Established in 1953, the station transmits in French and several local dialects. The country had 50,000 radio sets in 1972; 75,000 in 1983; and around 120,000 in 1992.

RAILROADS *see* CHEMIN DE FER DU TOGO (CFT).

RANDOLPH, EMILE MARC, 1940– . Diplomat. Born in Aného on April 25, 1940. A graduate of IHEOM in Paris, Randolph commenced his career in the foreign ministry with an appointment as head of Economics and Technical Cooperation Programs in 1963. In 1968 he was transferred to Bruxelles as Counsellor at the Togolese Embassy to the EEC; in 1973 he was shifted to Paris in a similar capacity.

RASSEMBLEMENT DES JEUNES TOGOLAIS. Former, not overly active, youth wing of the **Parti Togolais du Progrès** political party.

RASSEMBLEMENT DU PEUPLE TOGOLAIS (RPT). General Eyadema's political vehicle and between 1969 and 1991 Togo's single political party. Founded in 1969 after preliminary caucuses in Kpalimé (in August) and in Kara and a constituent congress in November in Lomé. Prior to the latter assembly, the RPT was referred to as the Mouvement du Regroupement National (MRN). The RPT was originally established as a "national" (i.e., non-ethnic) movement with General Eyadema as President, **Edem Kodjo** as Secretary General, along with **Benoit Bedou, Henri Dogo,** and **Jacques Togbé** as Kodjo's Deputies. The latter positions were all abolished in 1971, and a Political Bureau and Central Committee were established, largely out of Kabré apprehensions that under the vigorous drive of Secretary General Kodjo the party was really becoming "national" and might become overly independent and an alternate source of political power not beholden to Eyadema. The party's motto was "La Nouvelle Marché" (or sometimes, "Le New Deal"), although its original planks were rather vague, primarily referring to the need to mobilize and unite all ethnic groups in the country. The creation of the RPT was very much an effort in the direction of legitimating Eyadema's rule. The latter had ruled until 1969 with virtually no legitimating structures, despite promises of an early return to civilian rule and the half-hearted gesture of setting up a Constitutional Committee whose recommended constitutional draft was not adopted. Indeed, one of the first major pronouncements of the RPT was that the "constitutionalization" of the regime was not yet opportune in light of existing ethnic cleavages that, allegedly, were the reason for the 1967 coup d'etat; the party instead recommended the continuation of the Eyadema regime and set the groundwork that led to the popular plebiscite that confirmed Eyadema in power.

The RPT's statutes called for a Congress at least every three years. Ten were indeed held, including those in Kpalimé, Lomé, and Kara. A women's section (*see* UNION NATIONALE DES FEMMES DU TOGO) and a youth wing (*see* UNION NATIONALE DE LA JEUNESSE TOGOLAISE) were set up in the period 1971–1973, both tightly under the control of the RPT and heavily staffed by either loyal Eyadema supporters or relatives of the latter's principal political lieutenants. The party and its ancillary organizations were headquartered in the imposing **Maison du Peuple** in Lomé until the social upheavals of 1991, when in June the National Conference renamed the latter Maison de l'Unité and the RPT was dissolved. (It survived, just as Eyadema was to bounce back to power.) RPT membership drives have always been low-key but relatively successful affairs (in the south) with Togo's urban **revendeuses**, who were supportive of the regime, and a major pressure group that the RPT has not dared to antagonize. Until the mid-1980s the party was nevertheless highly decentralized; in some districts (especially in the north where its function of mobilizing support for the regime is superfluous), it was essentially lifeless, while in the south its considerable opportunistic membership simply avoided meetings in order not to be overly tainted by association with what was recognized as in essence a northern party. In urban areas, where membership may lead to tangible rewards, activities are more visible.

In May 1978 membership (and the paying of dues) became compulsory for all government employees, but this has failed to revitalize the moribund party, while the membership dues have met only a small part of the fiscal needs of the voracious party hierarchy. Earlier, in 1976, the RPT Congress had passed several administrative changes to make the party even more beholden to Eyadema, with all members of the smaller Politburo (nine instead of fifteen) and Central Committee (twenty-two) becoming personal appointees of the president. Militancy was declared as the criteria for all promotion within the party and civil service, and nonparticipation in RPT activities was for the first time equated with disloyalty. This created much sycophancy and a phalanx of yes men, hiding corruption and inefficiency that finally emerged into the limelight in the late 1970s.

Increasingly since 1978 the issue of corruption has dominated RPT debates. The economy, in shambles as many of the post-1975 State companies were in a state of collapse, further drained the scarce fiscal resources of the country. By 1981, the situation was catastrophic. A series of purges at the highest levels of the party toppled key figures of the past, former Eyadema lieutenants of long standing. In 1982 it was also announced that much of the State sector would be denationalized if private buyers could be found. A long list of such companies scheduled for dismantling was published, though the process of closing down companies, selling them off, or restructuring them has been a very long, drawn out one. (*See* STATE COMPANIES; PRIVATIZATION.)

The convening of the National Conference marked an end of an era for the RPT. Many Southerners and other non-Kabré collaborators deserted the RPT to publicly castigate the party, regime, and Eyadema and to set up their own political vehicles. The party itself was briefly banned and evicted from its headquarters—until November 1991 when a coup attempt by the loyalist army brought about a rescindment of the edict. Though the Convention stripped Eyadema of most executive powers in 1992, he was able to force interim Prime Minister Koffigoh to set up a coalition government with his RPT (with the latter securing six of the eighteen ministries, including the most important). In the 1993–94 Presidential and Parliamentary elections—using heavy doses of brute intimidation that drove out opposition political parties from the North and Presidential contenders who boycotted the elections—Eyadema was "reelected," while the RPT emerged as the country's second largest political party. The party is, however, clearly a Northern and, more specifically, a Kabré party.

RASSEMBLEMENT DU PEUPLE TOGOLAIS (RPT) CONGRESS (SIXTH), DECEMBER 3, 1982. Important RPT Congress convened in Lomé with a specific mandate to examine Togo's crumbling State sector that was dragging the state to national bankruptcy. A favorite sinecure posting for former high officials since the 1970s, the State sector had become bloated, eminently unprofitable, and corruption-ridden. The RPT decided at its meeting to immediately dissolve several companies (including Sotexma, Togofruit, Salinto, the Regie Municipale de Transports Urbain, CNPSE, Compagnie du Bénin, and others) and place several others on strict probation, ordering their dissolution unless they turned in profits within three months. One state company, Togoroute, was denationalized and contracted to private interests. Most of the RPT recommendations were not followed through with until years later. *See* STATE COMPANIES; PARASTATALS; PRIVATIZATION.

REFERENDUM OF 1956 (FRENCH TOGOLAND). In October 1956, the French administration in Togo held a referendum over the issue of whether Togo was to remain a United Nations Trusteeship Territory or become an **Autonomous Republic** within the **French Union**. Fearing the pan-Africanist appeal of Nkrumah's neighboring Ghana and the pan-Ewe sentiments rife on both sides of the Ghana-Togo border, the French administration "assisted" in the victory of the Autonomous

Republic option, with Nicolas Grunitzky emerging as the leader of the republic. Sixty percent of Lomé's voters (and thirty percent in the entire south) did not vote, many heeding the CUT appeal for a boycott on the grounds that the referendum was not being supervised by the United Nations and that its results would be falsified. In 1958 France was forced to allow United Nations-supervised elections (on April 27) in which Nicolas Grunitzky was solidly defeated and Sylvanus Olympio's CUT party won twenty-nine of the forty-six seats of the National Assembly.

REFERENDUM OF 1992. The referendum of September 27, 1992 was on the issue of a return to a multi-party civilian rule and a new constitution. All the political parties campaigned for a yes vote, and 98.11% of the people ratified a return to civilian rule and the new constitution. The latter set up a semi-Presidential system with a separation of powers and a Head of State elected for five years.

REGIE MUNICIPALE DES TRANSPORTS URBAINS. State transport company operating in Lomé. Facing constant fiscal losses and administrative chaos, the company was officially closed down as part of the 1982 RPT Congress decision on the fate of the State sector.

REGIE TOGOLAISE DES TABACS (TOGOTABAC). State organ set up in 1978 with sole authority over the import and distribution of tobacco products in the country.

REGIMENT INTER-ARME TOGOLAIS (RIAT). Elite ultra-loyalist, mostly northern, rapid intervention force, part of General Eyadema's bulwark against opposition. The highly mobile and well-armed force is barracked in Lomé.

REGIONS. Post-independence administrative units into which Togo is divided. There were four such regions originally: **Maritime, Plateaux, Centrale,** and **Savanes**; a fifth "economic" region was set up in 1967, **La Kara**, later greatly expanded and transformed into a fifth full-fledged political division. The regions are subdivided into prefectures. *See also* ADMINISTRATIVE ORGANIZATION.

RELIGION. The estimated religious breakdown of the Togolese population stands at seventy-five percent animist, ten percent Muslim and fifteen percent Christian; the latter figure is composed of twelve percent Catholics and three percent Protestants. The Muslim population is, as elsewhere in Black Africa, no doubt underestimated, while the Christian affiliation estimates may be somewhat inflated. The most exact and reliable religious estimates are those from 1960, no longer of much use. They did enumerate, however, 260,000 Christians (215,000 Catholics and 45,000 Protestants, 40,000 of the latter belonging to the **Eglise Evangélique du Togo**). All other figures are estimates, such as those of 1974 that are extrapolations from the 1960 data—400,000 Catholics, 75,000 Protestants, and 170,000 Muslims, with the rest of the population animist. *See also* PROTESTANTS; ISLAM; CATH-OLICISM.

RESERVE DE LA KERAN. A national reserve along the western side of Togo's north-south road axis, north of Naboulgouto Mango, and between the Oti and Kamougou rivers. It is the largest such park in Togo.

REVENDEUSES. Retail merchants, mostly women, that constitute fully one third of Togo's working population and are a prime economic power in Lomé. Many of Lomé's revendeuses are extremely prosper-ous, involved in long distance import-export, the profitable smuggling activities between Ghana and Togo, and in the retail textile trade. Eyadema has gone out of his way to appease and assure Lomé's reven-deuses of the government's intentions not to change the country's lib-eral import-export code, thus cultivating the political support of this extremely important and influential interest group.

S

SAFIOU, MOHAMED (EL HADJ). Religious leader and first President of the **Union Musulmane du Togo**. A former Deputy to the National Assembly and its Vice President, Safiou had fallen out with President Olympio and been imprisoned in the far north at the time of the 1963 coup d'état. A Kotokoli Muslim with a significant following, he was appointed head of the nascent UMT in 1963, at the suggestion of **Fousseni Mama**. Safiou came under attack for his quasi-dictatorial leadership traits and was ousted in a bitter internal upheaval in 1970. Since then Safiou has been retired from the union, engaging in teach-ing and various religious activities.

SAGBO, KODJO. Minister of Interior since May 1994 in the RPT-UDT coalition government headed by Edem Kodjo.

SALAMI, ABDOULAYE, 1935– . Trade unionist and former Secretary General of the **Union Nationale des Travailleurs Togolais**. Born in Bassar in 1935 to a Nigerian **Yoruba** father and a Togolese mother, Salami was educated locally (in Sokodé and Lomé) and in France, where he studied Telecommunications. Immediately after his return to Togo, Salami joined trade union activities, becoming Secretary General of the Postal and Telecommunications Workers' Union. A very popular figure among unionists, Salami presented his candidacy for the leadership of Togo's main trade union, the UNTT, and in 1968 at the age of 33 he defeated the incumbent, Innocent Toovi, becoming Secretary General of the union. A former opponent of the Eyadema regime, Salami was denied entry into Togo when he tried to attend the Sixth Congress of the union in Lomé in May 1968; only the threat of a paralyzing general strike made the government change its mind and relent. He was definitively deported out of the country in the 1970's— after being arrested and tortured by the regime—on the grounds that he was Nigerian. For much of the 1970s Salami was involved in wider unionist activities, mostly abroad. An implacable foe of Eyadema, Eyadema's secret service tried to kidnap him from Ghana in 1977, but were not successful.

SALAMI, AMOUSSA, 1938– . Former Minister of Equipment, Public Works, and Housing. Born in September 18, 1938, in Mango and educated in Lomé and at the University of Dakar in Physical Education, Salami proceeded to study for a degree in Civil Aeronautical Engineering at the School of Aviation of Toulouse (1966–68). Upon his return home, he was promptly appointed Director of Aviation (1970–77), and in 1977 he joined the cabinet. Later, Salami was injured in a car crash and dropped from the cabinet (mid-1968). He has been a division head within the ministry since.

SALINES DU TOGO see SOCIETE DE SALINES DU TOGO.

SAMA, KOFFI. Former Minister of Youth, Sports, and Culture. Prior to this appointment to the cabinet in May 1979, Sama—by training a teacher—had been head of a division in the Ministry of Education. In the December 1979 elections, he was elected Deputy to the National Assembly. Sama is of Kotokoli origins. He left the cabinet in 1984.

SAMARI, ISSA (EL HADJ). Influential Lomé trader and entrepreneur. Of Kotokoli origins, Samari owns extensive property in Togo (including several movie theaters in Sokodé, Kpalimé, Kara, and Dapaong), numerous buildings, and a trucking fleet that is involved in both internal and external trade.

SAMAROU, ISSA ALASSANI. Political leader and former cabinet minister. First joining the cabinet of the interim government of Prime Minister Koffigoh on September 1991 as Minister of Industry and State Corporations, Samarou was retained through the latter's third interim government. Samarou, who is a leader of the Parti d'Action pour le Développement (PAD), was dropped from the cabinet in February 1993.

SANI, ABDOULAYE, 1888–1970. One of the most famous Chokossi imams of Sansanné-Mango, under whose leadership the Chokossi solidified their Muslim affiliation. Raised and educated in a Koranic school, Sani was a trader for many years, traveling to Benin, Burkina Faso, and Ghana before settling down as a Koranic teacher in Sansanné-Mango in 1921. He acquired great renown as a devout Muslim and in 1929 was elevated to the imamship that he was to occupy for the next forty-one years. Sani was extremely active as a Muslim proselytizer, spreading the faith to neighboring ethnic groups as well as serving as a cultural anchor for the Chokossi, who were undergoing major socioeconomic change at the time.

SANKAREDJA, MARTIN, 1922– . Former Minister of Education. Of **Moba** origins, Sankaredja was born in Dapaong in the north and worked as a teacher at a local Catholic mission. A member of Sylvanus Olympio's Comité de l'Unité Togolaise, Sankaredja was appointed Minister of Education in May 1959 and held that position for four years until the coup d'état of 1963. After the coup, he became Director of the **SORAD** branch in the Savanes region and, following the 1967 coup, he was briefly the First President of the Conseil Economique et Social, relinquishing the post to Gervais Kodjo in October 1968, though remaining a member. Following this, Sankaredja had been out of the public limelight, involved in teaching and commerce until his retirement.

SANSANNE-MANGO. Northern Togolese town (estimated population, over 13,500, making it Togo's ninth largest), administrative capital of the **Savanes** region and of the Mango district, renamed the prefecture of Oti in June 1981. Capital of the pre-colonial **Chokossi** kingdom, the town's name comes from the **Hausa** words for "war camp" (Sansanni) and the Mande name for the **Anno**, founders of the town and kingdom around 1765. The actual inhabitants, the Chokossi, call the town and region N'zara, and their chiefs claim descent from the ruling Kong clan in Cote d'Ivoire. Most of Togo's Chokossi are found in the Oti prefecture, where the Anoufou dialect and Muslim religion are widely prevalent. Since the kingdom straddled the kola nut routes and was in close contact with Hausaland to the east, there is an important Hausa element in Sansanné-Mango.

SANTOS, ANANI IGNATIO, 1912– . Former Minister of Justice and leader of the **Juvento** party. Of **Brazilian**-Ewe origins, Santos was born in Aného on February 3, 1912 and was educated locally and at the University of Paris (on one of France's first scholarships to Togolese), where he obtained a Law degree, thus becoming one of Francophone Africa's first lawyers. (His Ph.D. thesis, defended in 1943, was on the possibility of France's assimilation policy's solving Africa's problems.) Santos gained a great deal of fame for his defense of the leaders of the bloody 1947 uprising in Madagascar (and similar individuals and events), and he appeared before the United Nations in 1954 and 1957 to plead for the independence of Togo. An early member of Olympio's **Comité de l'Unité Togolaise** and the leader of the latter's more militant Juvento youth wing, Santos was elected to the Chambre de Deputés in 1958 and shortly after became Olympio's Minister of Justice, Transport, and Commerce (May 1958–June 1959). In June 1959 he resigned from the cabinet and led Juvento out of the CUT, becoming one of Olympio's sharpest critics. In April 1961 — as the CUT began cracking down on all sources of opposition — Santos forged an alliance between the Juvento and the northern parties in the country (*see* MOUVEMENT NATIONALISTE TOGOLAIS-JUVENTO), which was disqualified from competing against the CUT in that year's elections. Shortly thereafter Togo became a de facto one party state, and Santos and all other opposition leaders were imprisoned under harsh conditions in **Sansanné-Mango** in the far north. Released after the 1963 coup d'état and called to participate in the post-coup Grunitzky four-cornered coalition, Santos was prevented from assuming a political role because of his broken health, though his party joined the coalition. Abroad for some time after the 1963 coup, Santos was appointed to the **Comité Constitutionnel** following the 1967 military takeover by General Eyadema. Long not involved in politics, Santos resides in Lomé, where he still practices law.

SANTOS, MICHEL ADJAI, 1930– . Former international journalist. Born in Lomé on May 7, 1930 and educated at the Catholic Mission School in Lomé and at a Lycée in Dakar, Senegal, Santos acquired his higher education at the University of Paris (1956–59), obtaining also additional degrees/ diplomas in Paris. He served as Program Producer for the Voice of America in Paris between 1962 and 1965 and later (1965–67) as Program Producer for the Voice of America in Liberia. Between 1967 and 1970 he served in a similar capacity with the Voice of Germany, when he was appointed Information Officer with the United Nations Economic Commission for Africa based in Addis Ababa.

SANVEE, KOUAO (STEPHEN) (MAJOR). Former Commander of the Second Battalion of the Togolese armed forces. Of Mina origins and linked to the influential Brazilian clans, Sanvée was a Lieutenant and head of the General Services Administration of the armed forces in 1971. In 1974 he was promoted to Captain and two years later to Major. In 1977 he was involved in the anti-Eyadema mercenary plot. Arrested and severely tortured at the time, he has been in ill health since. Although sentenced to death for his role in the conspiracy, his sentence was commuted to life imprisonment, and in 1985 he was pardoned.

SARAKAWA MAUSOLEUM. Part of the Eyadema **Personality Cult**, the small Sarakawa village, in the La Kara region, is the site of the January 24, 1974 crash of General Eyadema's plane. Allegedly a conspiracy by French expatriate interests fearful of impending nationalization of the coastal phosphate works (an act that came in retaliation for their alleged attempt to liquidate Eyadema), Eyadema's alleged miraculous escape from the crash landing is commemorated in Sarakawa. A virtual shrine for RPT and/or Kabré members, a monument has been erected in the exact spot of the crash (including parts of the original plane as well), and RPT youth and militants periodically trek to the site to swear allegiance to the goals of the party. The village is otherwise known for its sacrifices and dances in the rainy season in honor of its founder priestess.

SAVANES. Northern region with administrative headquarters in **Sansanné-Mango** and encompassing the prefectures of Oti and Tone (prior to 1981 known as Mango and Dapango). The region covers 8,130 square kilometers and, prior to the 1967 creation of the economic region of **La Kara**, stretched even further south. The population of the Savanes is estimated at 350,000, composed mostly of **Lamba, Chokossi, Kabré, Fulani**, and other groups, including Mossi from Burkina Faso. The main cash crops are cotton and peanuts.

SAVI DE TOVE, BIBI YAO (BRUNO JOHN EMMANUEL), 1922– . Administrator and diplomat. Born in Lomé on August 17, 1922, Savi de Tové was educated locally and at the Ecole William Ponty in Dakar, after which he joined the colonial administration to serve in postings in Togo (1943–52), with the Guinean Treasury (1952), in Senegal (1952–58), and in Mali (1958–67), where he was Inspector of Finances. Returning to Togo in 1967, Savi de Tové was appointed Ambassador to West Germany and Ambassador to Ghana in 1976. In February 1978 he returned to Lomé to become Minister of Justice in Eyadema's cabinet but was dropped in March 1980 to become a Technical Consultant in the Ministry of Foreign Affairs until his recent retirement.

SAVI DE TOVE, JONATHAN, 1895–1971. One of Togo's towering personalities. Born in Tové (near Tsévié) to an influential family on August 15, 1895, Savi de Tové started his adult life as a lawyer's clerk in Cameroun, then under German rule. He eventually became German Governor Ebermayer's personal secretary and accompanied him to Rio Muni, Fernando Poo, and later to Spain where he worked in the German Embassy in Madrid. After a trip to Germany (in 1918), Savi de Tové returned to Togo to become an instructor of languages and later School Director of the Protestant mission in Togo (1920–28). He was the principal assistant of Diedrich Westermann, the famous linguist, in the compilation and codification of the Evegbé grammar, having first met him in Barcelona, Spain. In 1928 Savi de Tové became Secretary of the Lomé **Conseil de Notables**, and in 1934 he was one of the first appointments to Lomé's Municipal Council. Already an extremely influential and well-off merchant, his official standing and pro-French sentiments focused popular resentments upon him that burst out during the Lomé disturbances of 1933 (*see* LOME INCIDENTS OF 1933) and resulted in the burning of his house. In 1936 Savi de Tové became head of the Press and Information Services of the colonial administration (under Governor Montagne), a position he held until 1941 when he was the cofounder and Secretary General of the **Comité de l'Unité Togolaise**. Following World War II, Savi de Tové was elected to Togo's first Assembly and continued serving as Deputy for seventeen years until the 1963 coup d'etat; he was President of the Assembly between 1958 and 1963. In 1947 he also became a councilor of the **French Union** in Paris (1947–53). A strong pan-Ewe nationalist, Savi de Tové cooperated with **Daniel Chapman** and the latter's **All-Ewe Conference** and *Ewe Newsletter*. Also an expert on various African and European languages (including French, German, Spanish, and English), Savi de Tové served as editor of both *Le Guide de Togo* and the influential *Unité Togolaise,* while retaining his position as Professor of Linguistics. He concluded his career in diplomacy. In 1961 he served as Vice President of the Inter-Parliamentary Conference in Strasbourg and, between 1961 and 1964, as Ambassador to West Germany. During the Grunitzky presidency, Savi de Tové was mostly locked out of power and positions of influence. Early in 1971 he was appointed President of the Association Togolaise d'Echanges Culturelles avec l'Etranger, but he died the same year, in Lomé.

SAVI DE TOVE, KWASSI (JEAN-LUCIEN). Opposition leader. Savi de Tové, a member of the famous southern family, has consistently been an opponent of General Eyadema and was jailed in 1979 for nine years for a conspiracy against Eyadema. On his release he went to France. In May 1991, with the liberalizations in Lomé, he returned to set up a political party, the Parti de Démocrates pour l'Unité (PDU), aligned with **Gilchrist Olympio**. In March 1993 he was selected by a segment of the opposition parties (organized as COD-2) as their candidate for the Prime Ministership instead of Koffigoh, by this time regarded in the south as a collaborationist. In the 1994 parliamentary elections, Savi de Tové did not even qualify to run for election in the second round in his own district.

SCHUPPUIS, KODJO-ELLOM (WILLIAM), 1938– . Diplomat and Ambassador of Togo to the United States. Born on June 10, 1938 in Aného, Schuppuis was educated locally and in Douala, Cameroun. He continued his studies in Law and Political Science at the University of Paris until 1969. Returning to Togo, he first served as Deputy of the Administrative Department of the Foreign Ministry (1970–72), following which he was appointed First Councillor at Togo's Mission to the United Nations. In 1977 he was reassigned to Brussels as Togolese Ambassador to the EEC, and in July 1983 he was appointed Ambassador to the United States, remaining in that post through 1992.

SCHUTZGEBIET TOGO. German for Togo Protectorate, official name during the German colonial era.

SEASONAL WORKERS *see* MIGRANT LABOR.

SEMA, AROUNA, 1937– . Agricultural engineer and administrator. Born in Bafilo on June 22, 1937, Sema served as head of the Cooperative Studies Office (1962–64), Deputy Director of Agricultural Services in Lomé (1964–65), and Acting Director of the same service (1965–67), before becoming Director of the Agricultural Credit Bank in June 1967, a position he still holds.

SEVOR, KOSSI ANDRE, 1916– . Former influential member of CUT. Born in Aflao-Adidogomé on April 20, 1916, Sevor was an early CUT militant, Secretary of the national headquarters of the CUT party, and Vice President of the Council of the Circonscription of Lomé. In April 1961 Sevor was also elected Deputy to the National Assembly, serving until the 1963 coup d'etat. Throughout this period, he had also been Administrator in Charge of Loans at the Lomé SPAR. After the 1963 coup, Sevor retired from politics, and in 1976 he went into retirement.

SEYBOU FOFONA, HARIMIAOU (EL HADJ), 1892–1976. Religious leader and educator. Born in Chamba of a Guinean grandfather who married into Chamba royalty, Seybou Fofona fell under the influence of the **Tidjaniya** sect and consequently began to travel extensively in Africa and the Middle East. He undertook six years of intensive religious studies in Beirut, Lebanon and then moved and settled down in Sokoto, Nigeria, Mauritania, and Morocco. Later he also traveled to India, Italy, Turkey, and British Palestine. At home, he became Imam of the Lomé Hausa community as well as leader of the Hausa of Kandi, North Benin, where he maintained a Koranic school. Seybou Fofona died in Kandi on January 6, 1976.

SHIARI *see* FETISHISTS.

SIDI TOURE, DJIBRILLA, 1928–1973. Surgeon and former Ambassador to France. Born in Sokodé and of Kotokoli origins, Sidi Touré studied Medicine and Surgery abroad and, upon his return to Togo, became Resident Surgeon at Sokodé's hospital and Municipal Councilor of Sokodé. In September 1965 he interrupted his medical career to become Togo's Ambassador to France and the European Economic Community, positions he held until March 1968. He died several years later in 1973.

SIMILSI *see* FULANI.

SIMTEKPEATI, MICHEL, 1927– . Educator, diplomat, and former cabinet minister. Born in 1927 in Patatoukou, Simtekpeati studied Political Science and Languages, graduating with a doctorate. He first taught at various schools in Ghana (1948–52) and Liberia (also 1948–52), and served for two years in an administrative position with the French Embassy in Monrovia (1957–59). After completing his studies in Paris, Simtekpeati taught English at a lycée in Munster (1964–65), served the next two years with the Liberian Foreign Ministry, and was appointed head of the Organization of African Unity's Social Affairs Section (1966–68), with headquarters in Addis Ababa. In 1968 Simtekpeati was appointed Togo's Ambassador to Ghana, following which he became Technical Councilor at the Foreign Ministry. In mid-1975 he was brought into the cabinet as Minister of Youth and Sports but was reassigned to technical duties in the Foreign Ministry in 1978. After teaching a few years in Northern Togo, he retired.

SIO RIVER DAM. Inaugurated in January 1980 after two years of construction, the dam, ten kilometers west of Tsévié, irrigates 660 hectares of land, making it suitable for rice cultivation. Part of the Chinese effort in Togo, the dam's construction cost 5,000 million CFAF. Its construction involved some 360 Togolese workers and 61 Chinese technicians.

SIVOMEY, MARIE, 1923– . Former Mayor of Lomé. Born in Aného on July 3, 1923 with the maiden name of Gbikpi, Mrs. Sivomey was educated locally and in Porto Novo, Benin. She then entered the colonial administration and served first in Togo and then in Burkina Faso (1953–58), returning to Togo in 1959. Between 1959 and 1964 she continued working in the higher echelons of the civil service, but in 1964 she was purged (on political grounds) from her post as Principal Administrative Secretary of the Direction des Finances. Following the 1967 coup d'etat, she made a comeback and was personally appointed Mayor of Lomé by General Eyadema. An able administrator, Mrs. Sivomey has also been Togo's Delegate to the United Nations General Assembly's sixteenth and seventeenth sessions. In mid-1974 she was dropped from Lomé's mayoralty and appointed to an administrative position in the Ministry of Interior.

SLAVE COAST. Geographic stretch of the coast of West Africa which historically large numbers of slave ships visited to purchase slaves from native middlemen. The "Coast" is conventionally defined as the region between the Volta River (in Ghana) and Lagos (Nigeria) or in effect the mostly coastal regions controlled by the **Adja** or **Ewe** people, whose principal kingdoms were Ouidah, Allada, and Dahomey, all currently in Benin.

SMUGGLING. A major problem in many African states, the illegal transfer of crops and luxury goods across state borders, smuggling is a sign of (a) the permanence of traditional pre-colonial trade routes and commercial networks, (b) weak control over their territorial boundaries by African states, and (c) the enhanced profit motive in a situation where borders separate countries with radically different import/export policies and taxation systems. While traditional patterns of trade have continued in Togo, smuggling activities have been greatly encouraged by neighboring Ghana's consistently strict import policies and high import tariffs alongside Togo's extremely liberal policies. Consequently, large quantities of Ghanaian crops are smuggled into Togo and exchanged for low-priced European imports (watches, liquor, cigarettes, etc.), which are then smuggled back to Ghana where they fetch high prices. The principal commodities smuggled into Togo are coffee and cocoa, and it is estimated that as much as one third of Togo's exports of these items to third countries are actually of Ghanaian origin. Despite efforts on the part of Ghana and half-hearted moves on the part of Togo to stop the illicit trade, smuggling activities continue with native pirogues leaving daily from Lomé's beaches for the run to Keta, in Ghana. Most of the trade is in the hands of Ewe on both sides of the border, with the active connivance of the Ghanaian and Togolese border patrols. One estimate of the turnover is fifteen million. An indication of how lucrative this illicit trade is, is the fact that in 1979 the Ghanaian producer price for cocoa stood at five cedis while in Togo it was 6,000 CFAF, convertible in the black market into 300 cedis; if the 6,000 CFAF were reimported into Ghana in the form of smuggled goods from Togo, they could bring in locally as much as 450 cedis, ninety times the original 5 cedi investment. At the same time, the Ghanaian cedi, officially pegged in Accra at 214 CFAF, could be bought in Lomé in 1979 for less than 35 CFAF.

SOCIETE AGRICOLE TOGOLAISE-ARABE-LIBYENNE (SATAL). Joint company set up in Togo in 1978 with Togolese and Libyan capital (1.4 million CFAF equally shared), aimed at agricultural development and especially the setting up of experimental farms and the production, processing, and marketing of agricultural goods.

SOCIETE CEREKEM EXOTIC TOGO. Private agro-industrial complex set up in 1987 in Adétikopé and with offices in Lomé, capitalized at 400 million CFAF, cultivating and processing aromatic plants. It employs 400 workers.

SOCIETE DES CIMENTS DU TOGO (CIMTOGO) *see* CIMENTS DU TOGO.

SOCIETE DES PRODUITS LAITIERS DU TOGO (SOPROLAIT). Originally a small State company producing milk products for the Togolese and neighboring markets. Set up in 1981 with a capacity of producing 360 tons of cheese annually, SOPROLAIT was sold off to Danish interests in 1985 as part of the privatization drive.

SOCIETE DES SALINES DU TOGO (SALINTO). Former State-owned company mining Togo's salt deposits. In 1981 the company produced 600 tons of salt, selling its entire product on the local market. The company has been both deficit-ridden and inherently unprofitable, despite several major infusions of capital. Keen competition from both foreign and local suppliers and inefficient operations at the plant made SALINTO a constant money loser. The company closed down in 1983, after the RPT Congress edict to eliminate unprofitable companies from the State sector, and after a prolonged search for someone to purchase the company, it was privatized in 1987.

SOCIETE GENERALE DES MOULINS DU TOGO (SGMT). Joint company and the only grinding plant in Togo. It has a monopoly over supplies to local bakers, importing its grains/wheats from abroad. Set up in 1971 with forty-five percent Togolese state capital and fifty-five percent foreign private funds, total capital investments have been 750 million CFAF. The company has the capacity to produce 120 tons per hour, and recent annual production has been around 20,000 tons.

SOCIETE GENERALE DU GOLFE DE GUINEE-TOGO (SGG-TOGO). Import-export and transport company founded in Lomé in 1969 with 2,745 million CFAF capitalization. Its 1991 turnover was 13,315 million CFAF, and it employs 402 workers.

SOCIETE INDUSTRIELLE DE PREPARATIONS ALIMENTAIRES (SIPAL). Joint confectionary company set up on April 23, 1975, with an initial modest capitalization of five million CFAF, later increased to twenty-two million (1977). It is a partnership of Togolese, Burkinabe, and French investors, producing confectionery from wholly imported raw materials. Later renamed LUDO—its trade name—current production is around 800 tons per year.

LA SOCIETE JAZZAR. Perfume producing company. Despite very strong competition from Nigerian manufacturers (that dominate the market) and from foreign imports, the Jazzar enterprise has been profitable and completely controls the Togolese market for perfumes and fragrances. Created in 1973 with French and Togolese capital (amounting to sixty-six million CFAF by 1978), the company employs sixty workers and has a turnover of around 200 million CFAF.

SOCIETE NATIONALE DE COMMERCE (SONACOM). Former State agency established on November 29, 1972 to replace the **Société Togolaise d'Exportation et d'Importation** with 2,000 million CFAF capitalization. SONACOM had a total monopoly over the sale of certain basic staples within Togo, expanded progressively to cover all food and industrial products. Its Director General, operating under the Minister of Commerce, was first Germain Choukroun and later **Maurice Assor**. SONACOM's monopoly over certain products was abolished in December 1988, and its activities came under greater scrutiny when it was revealed at the 1991 National Conference that the company had become a major conduit for illegal transactions on behalf of General Eyadema. It now has a French Director General.

SOCIETE NATIONALE DE DEVELOPPEMENT (SONAD). Main executive arm of the National Development Plan. Each region in Togo has a regional SONAD charged with locally executing portions of the plan relevant to the region and submitting suggestions of development projects to be included in the next plan.

SOCIETE NATIONALE DE SIDERURGIE (SNS). Former State-owned steel factory. Located in the Port of Lomé, the SNS's founding stone was laid on January 13, 1977 to commemorate the economic independence of Togo. The plant commenced operations exactly two years later but immediately encountered major technical problems and being utterly uneconomic to operate had to be shut down for three months. Scheduled to produce 20,000 tons of steel yearly, with plans to expand production by 1984 to 80,000 tons (via a second branch at Bandjeli, site of local iron ore deposits), the factory worked at less than thirty-seven percent capacity. Inefficient, it piled up monumental deficits and was closed down in 1982. Its flagship role as leader of the "heavy industry" sector of Togo gained it a reprieve in 1983, and it was allowed to reopen conditionally, subject to rectifying its balance sheet. It was incapable of doing so, working at 25 percent of capacity, and was closed down again. Its twelve ton electrical steel making furnace, for example, was too costly to operate all along, it being cheaper by far to import steel billets for the rolling mill than to produce them locally.

The company became the first major one to be privatized when it was leased in 1984 for ten years at $250,000 a year to an American entrepreneur (John Moore), who reopened the plant with only 140 of its original 300 workers and immediately turned a profit. It is currently called the Société Togolaise de Siderurgie. John Moore has in the meantime expressed interest in other distressed plants in Togo and in neighboring Benin's similar inoperative steel mills.

SOCIETE NATIONALE DE TRANSPORTS ROUTIERS (TOGO-ROUTE). Originally a mixed economy company involved in long distance trucking. Set up in Lomé in 1976 with 250 million CFAF capital (60 percent from the State, the rest from abroad) the company was privatized in 1986, becoming a private enterprise under the sole name of Togoroute.

SOCIETE TOGOLAISE DE NAVIGATION MARITIME (SOTONAM). Lomé-based shipping company in which the state originally has a controlling (51 percent) interest. Capitalized at 100 million CFAF, the company purchased its first vessel in 1978 (the *M.S. Hodo* container ship) and in 1980 received its second vessel (the *M.S. Pic d'Agou*). The company serves a variety of ports but concentrates its shipping activities on the Rouen (France)-Lomé route. The company was privatized in 1987.

SOCIETE NATIONALE D'INVESTISSEMENT ET FOND ANNEXES (SNIT & FA). State organ established in mid-1972 with 300 million CFAF capital (later, 500 million) for the purpose of encouraging foreign investments in Togolese enterprises and industry.

SOCIETE NATIONALE POUR LA RENOVATION ET LE DEVEL-OPPEMENT DE LA CACAOYERE ET DE LA CAFEIERRE TO-GOLAISES (SRCC). State agency created on June 14, 1973, in charge of modernizing Togo's agricultural crops—coffee and cocoa. Among the specific tasks of the SRCC are the regeneration of 10,500 hectares of plantations and the planting of new crops on a further 29,000 hectares. By 1978 it had rehabilitated 15,000 hectares of cocoa land. It employs some 480 workers and is assisted by the French IRCC and IRAT.

SOCIETE NATIONALE POUR LE DEVELOPPEMENT DE LA CUL-TURE FRUITIERE (TOGOFRUIT). Better known as Togofruit.

SOCIETE NATIONALE POUR LE DEVELOPPEMENT DE LA PAL-MERAIE ET LES HUILERIES (SONAPH). Successor to the Société Togolaise d'Extraction de Palme (SOTEHPA). Established in 1968 with an initial capital of 160 million CFA francs (increased to 1,320 million by 1983) and headquartered in Lomé, SONAPH was originally charged with implementing the palm development plan of 1968. The first stage of the latter—planting 3,000 hectares of new palm trees in the Tsévié area—was completed in 1973. Since then, the company has launched several other replanting projects encompassing 1,700 hectares by 1976 and a further 5,200 in 1977, as part of the **Green Revolution**, in an effort to develop Togo's palm oil and palm by product capacities which lag behind neighboring countries. SONAPH also runs the Alokoégbé oil mills and in 1978 constructed a second mill at Agbou. It employs 245 permanent workers. SONAPH was restructured in 1989 as a mixed economy venture.

SOCIETE OUEST AFRICAINE D'ENTREPRISE MARITIMES DU TOGO (SOAEM-TOGO). Small, coastal shipping company and forwarding agents. Founded in 1959 with eighty-four million CFAF of local capital.

SOCIETE SUCRIERE DE LA REGION CENTRALE (SSRC). Joint company set up on December 16, 1977 with 100 million CFAF in local capital and with German participation. Headquartered in Sokodé, it is charged with tending extensive sugar plantations in the area and producing some 300,000 tons of cane sugar and 35,000 tons of processed sugar. The SSRC was initially administered for five years by the French Somdina company.

SOCIETE TOGOLAISE DE BOISSONS (STB). Former State enterprise established in 1970 to produce soft drinks and other beverages.

By 1981 STB had invested 350 million CFAF and had a turnover of 3,000 million CFAF. As part of its activities, STB also distributed products of the Brasserie du Togo. STB operates in Lomé and employs 149 workers. The company was privatized and streamlined under French management in 1990, and the State now has only a 25 percent equity.

SOCIETE TOGOLAISE DE L'HOTELLERIE (STH). Former State organ that owned most large hotels in Togo. Set up as part of a massive expansion of tourist facilities in Togo in the 1970's aimed at satisfying a significant tourist boom. By 1980 the boom had ended, causing acute fiscal squeezes on STH. By 1982 Togo had 4,000 international class hotel beds, 1,400 in Lomé, and some hotels of rather stunning architectural grace. Among the latter, one could mention the ultra-luxurious, thirty-story $100 million "2 Fevrier Hotel" in the center of the capital (reputed the most luxurious in all of Africa but a white elephant otherwise) and the Hotel Sarakawa that was designed by a Camerounian architect to resemble the famous plane crash from which Eyadema escaped unhurt in 1974. STH signed management contracts with foreign hotel groups, thus assuring efficient management of the buildings. Only the old (but in the 1960's, the pride of Lomé) Hotel du Bénin is directly managed by the STH. The company was privatized in 1990.

SOCIETE TOGOLAISE DE MARBRERIE ET DE MATERIAUX (SO-TOMA). Mixed economy enterprise founded in 1968 with headquarters in Lomé and initial capitalization of 350 million CFA francs, two thirds of which is state capital and the rest that of an Italian company. SO-TOMA exploits the marble and dolomite deposits in Gnaoulou, 150 kilometers northwest of Lomé and Pagola, that have an estimated twenty million tons of reserves. The company also produces bricks and ceramics. Its turnover has been over 200 million CFAF. It employs 350 workers and had an initial capacity of 25,000 tons yearly, augmented to 50,000 tons. Between 1968 and 1975 the State took a controlling stake in the company that went bankrupt. The company was privatized and restructured in 1986 in cooperation with the company Norcem, Togo's share was reduced to 39 percent, and it was renamed the Nouvelle Société Togolaise de Marbrerie et de Materiaux (NOUVELLE-SOTOMA).

SOCIETE TOGOLAISE DE PROMOTION POUR LE DEVELOPPE-MENT (TOGOPROM). State organ based in Lomé and capitalized with 200 million CFAF, charged with identifying areas of need in the developmental drive of the country and satisfying the investment needs of these areas. The company was involved in the urban renewal of downtown Lomé after the forced relocation of the city's **zongo** opened up valuable urban space.

SOCIETE TOGOLAISE DE SIDERURGIE (STS). Successor to the **Société Nationale de Siderurgie**, the first Togolese state enterprise to be privatized. Leased for ten years to an American entrepreneur (John Moore) in 1984 for a rent of $250,000 a year and capitalized at 700 million CFAF, the STS produces 8,000 tons of reinforced bars for the Mali, Niger, and Burkinabe markets, some 2,000 to 2,500 tons of scrap iron for Spain per quarter, and has a turnover of four million dollars. The new management has been profitable from its first month of operations, having cut the labor force by fifty percent and switched to production of various coils from local scrap material. In the late 1980's Moore was in the process of bidding for a similar steel mill in neighboring bankrupt Benin and in trying to acquire two other former Togolese State enterprises.

SOCIETE TOGOLAISE DE STOCKAGE DE LOME (STSL). Capitalized at 300 million CFAF, later increased to 4,000 million, STSL is owned by Shell, includes the old refinery facilities of **STH**, and is used for stockpiling purposes.

SOCIETE TOGOLAISE DES ATTAPULGITES ET BENTONITE (STAB). Mixed economy company chartered in 1981 and operational in 1984. Capitalized at 500 million CFAF, it exploits (through the open pit method) the large bentonite and attapulgite deposits found in Avéta, some 30 kilometers from Lomé. The company includes Swiss financial interests.

SOCIETE TOGOLAISE DES HYDROCARBURES (STH). Former state body controlling Togo's oil refinery that processes oil imported from Nigeria, Ghana, and Libya. The refinery was inaugurated on January 12, 1978 and was hailed as a symbol of Togo's coming of age industrially. It has a capacity of one million tons and the ability to satisfy the processed oil needs of the entire region. Capitalized at 4,000 million CFAF (60 percent Togolese, 40 percent Libyan) the facilities were to be supplied by tankers of up to 80,000 tons in weight. Togo's hopes to break into the global oil monopoly were, however, dashed. The refinery lost massive amounts of money yearly, while operating at 25 percent capacity with few customers abroad. Even neighboring Nigeria imports processed oil from Curacao and elsewhere around the globe rather than from Lomé, 200 kilometers away, whose oil is too expensive. In 1982 the new refinery was reduced to the demeaning task of selling on the Rotterdam spot market where there are no fixed, long term contracts. The plant, operating much below capacity, was scheduled for closure or privatization in 1982 in order to eliminate the massive drain on State fiscal resources. It was finally privatized in 1985 and taken over by Shell for stockpiling (not refining) purposes, under the name of Société Togolaise de Stockage de Lomé (STSL).

SOCIETE TOGOLAISE DES PRODUITS DU MER (SOTOPRO-MER). Joint company set up with French interests in July 1978 to develop a small fishing fleet and a fish processing center.

SOCIETE TOGOLAISE D'EXPLOITATION DE MATERIEL FRUIT-IERE (SOTEXMA). Mixed economy company with thirty percent state participation in equity. Set up on March 3, 1978, with capitalization of 250 million CFAF, to administer all agricultural support services, including agricultural works, feeder road construction, and maintenance of farm vehicles. The company had 32 bulldozers at its disposal, 300 tractors, 120 trucks, and 1,500 other farm vehicles. It is decentralized throughout the entire country, maintaining depots in every prefecture. The company was a prime target for dissolution at the 1982 **RPT Congress** due to the massive losses accruing from its operations and was finally taken over in 1987 by the French group Gamag.

SOCIETE TOGOLAISE D'EXPORTATION ET D'IMPORTATION (SOTEXIM). State trading organization in existence between 1961, when it was founded, and 1972 when it was replaced by **SONACOM**. SOTEXIM exercised a total monopoly over the import and export of a selected list of goods and their sale within Togo.

SOCIETE TOGOLAISE D'EXTRACTION D'HUILE DE PALME (SOTEHPA) *see* SOCIETE NATIONALE POUR LE DEVELOPPE-MENT DE LA PALMERAIE ET LES HUILERIES.

SOCIETE TOGOLAISE DU COTON (SOTOCO). State company founded in March 1972 with 200 million CFAF capital (augmented to 2.2 billion) under the direction of the Ministry of Rural Economy. The company, with headquarters in Atakpamé, was created to counter peasant dissatisfaction with facilities previously offered them by the state, leading to major disaffection with cotton production following the 1972 drought. SOTOCO was entrusted with some of the activities previously handled by **OPAT**, specifically with developing new private and state cotton plantations and assisting in the planting and harvesting of existing plantations, with the aim of doubling the cotton harvest by 1976 (from 12,000 tons in 1974). SOTOCO opened much new acreage to cotton cultivation in the 1980's and set up a new ginning factory in Kara in 1981 with a capacity of 24,000 tons of cotton. A new ginnery, with the assistance of the French CFDT was also opened in Notsé in 1984, and Togo's 1989 overall cotton production zoomed up to 86,000 tons. Yields per hectare in the north and center of the country remain, however, low (824 and 948 kilograms respectively.)

SOCIETE TOGOLAISE ET DANOISE SAVONS (SOTODAS). Formerly a State enterprise, and since 1987 a joint Togo-Denmark soap and detergent manufacturing company, forty percent owned by the Danish Domo Kemi company and capitalized at 205 million CFAF. Despite efficiencies introduced following the privatization of the State company, SOTODAS is incapable of competing price-wise with Nigerian imports since the latter's huge market allows for lower costs.

SOCIETE TOGOLO-ARABE-LIBYENNE DE PECHE (STALPECHE). Joint Togolese-Libyan fishing enterprise, established in 1977 with three million in capital, put up equally by the two states. The company was part of the several joint enterprises set up under an agreement of technical cooperation signed by Libya in exchange for the ouster of Israeli influence in the country. The company produces roughly 1,000 tons of fish a year.

SOCIETES INDIGENES DE PREVOYANCE (SIP). Predecessors of the Societés (Publiques) d'Action Rurale, (which in turn preceded the **Sociétés Regionales de Développement et d'Amenagement**, created in 1965). The SIP structures, of which there were several, were set up during the colonial era to unite in a quasi-cooperative manner the agricultural activities and marketing of the produce of Togo's peasants. Coordination was lodged in a Fonds Commune des Sociétés de Prévoyances. In 1958 the SIP were given greater flexibility and new functions and were renamed Sociétés Mutuelles Rurales Togolaises, which, with independence, were again renamed Sociétés Publiques d'Action Rurale but became more popularly known as Sociétés d'Action Rurale.

SOCIETES MUTUELLES RURALES TOGOLAISES (SMRT). Quasi-cooperative agricultural organs that replaced the previous **Sociétés Indigènes de Prévoyance** in 1958. With independence, the SMRT were renamed **Sociétés Publiques d'Action Rurale** and in 1965 became the contemporary **Sociétés Regionales de Développement et d'Amenagement**.

SOCIETES PUBLIQUES D'ACTION RURALE (SPAR). Successors of the **Sociétés Mutuelles Rurales Togolaises** and immediate predecessors of the contemporary **Sociétés Regionales de Développement et d'Amenagement**. The SPAR were public groups aimed at spurring agricultural development and quasi-cooperative harvesting and marketing. They were replaced by the contemporary SORAD because of their general lethargy, poor leadership, and hazy goals.

SOCIETES REGIONALES DE DEVELOPPEMENT ET D'AMENAGEMENT (SORAD). Regional development organizations established in 1965 in each of Togo's regions. Their predecessors were the pre-independence **Sociétés Indigènes de Prévoyance** and the post-independence **Sociétés Publiques d'Action Rurale**. The SORAD were quasi-public organs, specifically called for by the First Five-Year Plan (1966–70), with administrative and fiscal autonomy under the general supervision of the Ministry of Rural Economy. Expected to become fiscally solvent, each regional SORAD was originally set up with six million CFA francs capital. Their purpose was to spur agricultural modernization, supply credit to farmers, develop cooperatives, open new roads and markets, and, in general, to coordinate and execute all regional development plans called for in the national Five-Year plans. Each SORAD was subdivided into sections responsible for each circonscription, though some of these sections were much more active than others. The record of the SORAD has been mixed; most did not become fiscally solvent and all have from the outset lacked trained cadres and funds. Moreover, only a few regions actually benefited from the activities of the SORAD (La Kara being a prominent example), and there has been poor coordination among the regional bodies. The SORADs were replaced in 1975 by the **ORPV** structures.

SOKODE. Rapidly growing northern town of 60,000 (1994 estimate), Togo's second in size after Lomé. Sokodé is the administrative center of the Centrale region and the Sokodé district. (The district's name was changed in 1981 to the prefecture of Tchaoudjo.) In the precolonial era, Sokodé was an important trading center and juncture of various caravan trails. (*See* CARAVAN ROUTES.) The Sokodé region is inhabited by the **Kotokoli**, and their paramount chief (Ayéva) resides in the Dedaure quarter of the town. Sokodé is by far Togo's most Muslim city. The name of the town comes from the **Dendi** word "to close," from the Kotokoli practice of barring routes leading into town. Sokodé has in the past twenty years greatly expanded in size, overtaking and surpassing **Kpalimé** in the south, which used to be the second largest town in Togo. Statistics indicate that in the last ten years the city grew from 45,000 to 60,000; in 1953 it was but an overgrown village of 5,000.

SOLIDARITY TAX. Tax, levied on all salaries in the public and private sector effective January 1, 1983. Amounting to a five percent levy, it is similar to the tax imposed during the Olympio years, much hated and contributing to the disenchantment of much of the population. The tax was made necessary by the increasing economic morass so evident in the 1980s in Togo.

SOMBA. Known also as the Tamberma, the Somba are an ethnic group (in reality, three quite disparate groups) found in the Atakora mountains in northwestern Benin and in adjoining areas of Togo, including in the vicinity of Sansanné-Mango. Their main concentration is in the Kandé area with scattered groups also found in Sokodé and Dapaong. Extensively studied in the past, the Somba number 59,000 in Benin and 20,000 in Togo. Frobenius referred to them as Africa's "castle" peasants (in German, "burgbauern"), a reference to their unique two-storied domiciles (sombatata or **tekyete**) and individualistic pattern of life.

SOMBATATA *see* TEKYETE.

SOTOUBOUA. Large prefecture in the Centrale region with headquarters in the town of the same name, spanning the entire western half of the region and including the important town of Blitta. Prior to the June 1981 administrative reorganization. Sotouboua was a circonscription with the same borders. The area encompasses some 85,000 people; the town of Sotouboua is 55 kilometers southwest of Sokodé.

SOUWA. Colorful traditional celebration of the harvest among the **Kotokoli.**

SOVINTO. Company created in 1964 to bottle wines and produce soft drinks not manufactured by other companies in Lomé. SOVINTO also distributes products of the Brasserie du Togo. Wines are imported from Spain and France and rebottled locally. SOVINTO's turnover quintupled between 1973 and 1978.

STANISLAS, BAMOUNI SOMOLOU. Leader of the ADR party. Stanislas joined the third interim government of Prime Minister **Koffigoh** in September 1992 as Minister of Technical Education and Professional Training and was retained in the same spot in the fourth interim cabinet of 1993.

STATE SECTOR. Togo's State sector, mostly deficitory and mismanaged, was one main reason for the economic decline in the 1980s. Starting with the 1974 one-year boom in state revenues (*see* PHOSPHATES) the government began a major expansion of the number of enterprises either fully or partly under State ownership. By 1982 it was clear that their deficits were a major drag on the economy and could no longer be sustained: Eyadema paradoxically noted at that year's RPT Congress his impression that the state was "investing only to make losses" (*West Africa*, May 18, 1987) and that this was no longer acceptable. Despite an effort to close down or sell off much of the State sector, this was a slow process since several enterprises were in unprofitable areas. However, as the experience of both **NIOTO** and the **Société Nationale de Siderurgie** point out, money-losing companies can be easily turned around given proper management. In 1987, Togo still had thirty-three companies under full State ownership and twenty-five in which the State had part ownership. Fully twenty-five of these are currently in various stages of liquidation, privatization, or restructuring with foreign capital. *See also* PRIVATIZATION; PARASTATALS.

STREBLER, JOSEPH. Former Archbishop of Lomé. Born in Strasbourg in 1892, Strebler came to Togo from the Gold Coast, and his proselytizing activities in the north resulted in the creation of a separate vicarage centered around Sokodé under his charge (1937). Fluent in several dialects, Strebler expanded the missionary effort among the Moba and other northern ethnic groups in the 1940's. In 1945 he became Bishop of Lomé (replacing Cessou) and in 1956 Archbishop of Lomé. During the Olympio presidency (1960–63), Strebler clashed with Sylvanus Olympio a number of times, and the Church's journal was banned on at least two occasions. (*See* PRESENCE CHRETIENNE.) In 1962 Strebler left Togo, turning over the leadership of the Church to the native-born **Robert Casimir Dosseh**.

SURETE NATIONALE. The official Togolese security service that monitors potential sources of subversion. Distrusted by Eyadema, some of the Sûrété's activities were duplicated by ancillary organizations set up by and attached to the presidency. (*See* the two BRIGADES structures.)

SYNDICAT DES COMMERCANTS IMPORTATEURS DE LA REPUBLIQUE TOGOLAISE (SCIMPEXTO). Organization of the country's import and export traders under Kodjo Kenzler.

SYNDICAT DES ENSEIGNANTS PROTESTANTS DU TOGO (SEPT). Small trade union of Protestant teachers in Togo under Secretary General Michel Kodjo. In 1973 the union was forced to merge into the single national union federation, the **Confederation Nationale des Travailleurs du Togo.**

SYNDICATS DES ENTREPRENEURS DE TRAVAUX PUBLICS, BATIMENTS ET MINES DU TOGO. Employers association headed by Tabligbo Clarence Olympio. It groups together most of the large builders of Togo.

T

TABLIGBO. Agricultural circonscription (district) in the Maritime region with administrative headquarters in the town of the same name that is Togo's twelfth largest with 5,600 people. It is the site of the important CIMAO plant. The district has a population of 85,000 with one sixth of these within the town and its suburbs. The town of Tabligbo is 47 kilometers from Aného. In the June 1981 administrative reorganization of the country, the district's name was changed to the Prefecture of Yoto, though its headquarters and the name of the town remained unchanged.

TADO. Historically important group of small villages (some in ruins) on the east side of the **Mono River,** 72 kilometers from Atakpamé. According to tradition, a small earth house in Tado Adjatché (or Tado-Adja), the oldest village, contains a jar with the skulls of the ancient kings of the Adja-Ewe. Tado is regarded as the area where the **Adja** settled after their trek from Kétou (currently in Benin.) Later they moved from Tado to **Notsé**—one branch swinging into Benin—and starting dispersing again in 1720, mostly to the south. The area is therefore the traditional point of origin of both the Adja population of Benin and of the Ewe of Togo.

TAMBERMA. Ethnic group found in Togo and in Benin, better known in both as the **Somba.** Tamberma is the corruption of the word Betammariba.

TANDJOUARE. Formerly a poste administratif in the extreme northwest of Togo, Tandjouaré was reclassified as a sous prefecture in the 1981 administrative reorganization of the country. Its role as a small but vibrant regional marketing center assisted in this upgrading of status. Tandjouaré is part of the Tone prefecture. The village of Tandjouaré, seat of the sous prefecture, is southwest of Dapaong.

TAY, AMEWUSIKA ALPHONSE KWADZO, 1942– . Administrator. Born in Agou on November 15, 1942, Tay was educated locally and at a lycée in France before going to study Engineering (1959–64) followed by Commerce (1967–71) in Paris. He then joined the Togolese civil service as Chief Administrative Officer and head of the Division of Surveys and Planning (1971–73) and then (1973–75) Deputy Director of the Department of Education Planning, and Cultural Advisor and Principal Officer to the Secretary General of the World Festival of Black Arts and Culture in Lagos (1975–77). In 1977 he was appointed Director of the Department of Conferences at the latter's Dakar headquarters, where he currently serves.

TCHA-GOUNI, ATI ATCHA, 1953– . Economist. Born in 1953 and educated in France in Economics, on his return to Lomé Tcha-Gouni became Deputy Head of Regional Coordination in the Department of Regional Planning. He is the author of several books on agrarian planning and development.

TCHALLA, PITANG. Director of Togo's national radio since mid-1987. Prior to that, Tchalla had been editor-in-chief of Television Togolaise.

TCHALLI, PAUL, 1947– . Long a key cabinet minister. Tchalli was Eyadema's Minister of Commerce and Transport for five years until March 1987, when he was briefly dropped from the cabinet and appointed Director General of **OPAT,** Togo's Phosphate Authority. He was brought back into the cabinet as Minister of Rural Development later that year and was finally dropped from the cabinet in February 1990.

TCHAMA, CHRISTOPHE (COLONEL). Little-known Lamba senior officer from Kandé. Though not part of the inner circle in the armed forces, Tchama was the third ranking officer in the Army in the late 1970s. As head of the Commando Battalion, he ranked in protocol listings ahead of Major **Adewui** and Major **Kongo.** He had not served in any senior political or administrative capacity and in 1977 was allegedly liquidated after disagreeing with General Eyadema's ethnic policies.

TCHAMBA. Circonscription created in 1975 out of the Centrale region to cater to the specific cultural and administrative needs of the populations east of Sokodé along the Benin border. The Tchaoudjo headquarters of the district is in the town of the same name. In the 1981 administrative reorganization of Togo, Tchamba's name was changed to

Nyala, and the district became a prefecture. The headquarters remains in the village under its old name of Tchamba. For the ethnic group (also Tchamba) *see* BASSARI.

TCHAMDJA, POBOZU, 1949– . Economist. Born in 1949 and educated in France in Banking and Economics, Tchammdja joined the Banque Ouest Africaine de Développement branch in Lomé as a Financial Analyst and in due course became head of its Department of Administrative and Social Affairs.

TCHANILE, MARC M. Curator of the Musée National du Togo.

TCHAOUDJO. New name for the former circonscription of Sokodé, the key district in the Centrale region. Headquarters of the prefecture remains in the town of Sokodé, Togo's second largest urban unit. *See also* SOKODE. The core of the Kotokoli ethnic group resides within this prefecture.

TCHAPTIKPI, OURO BANGNA. Minister of Rural Planning between May 1981 and 1984. Prior to his integration into the cabinet, Tchaptikpi had been a civil administrator whose last post had been in the Lomé urban administration. As his name, "Ouro," signifies, Tchaptikpi comes from the Sokodé royal lineage.

TCHEKOSSI *see* CHOKOSSI.

TCHOKOURA, NATCHABA. Current Superior Chief of the northern Chokossi.

TCHOUKOU. Millet beer, a very popular beverage especially among the rural population of North Togo.

TEKYETE. Known also as Sombatata, these are the unique two-storied domiciles ("castles") of the **Somba.** Usually twelve to fourteen feet high, with a diameter of thirty feet, the lower section is for stables and storage and the upper section provides living quarters for the extended family. The granaries are turret-like protrusions. There is usually also a shrine near the entrance to the house, honoring the clan's lineage founder and its place of origin. Widely photographed by tourists, the Somba now routinely—and very aggressively—demand payment for the privilege.

TELEVISION TOGOLAISE. Togo initiated television broadcasts in September 1973 with daily twenty-one-hour programming. The extremely small audience and poor sales of television sets resulted in 1974 in a forty-percent slash of prices of TV sets. For technical reasons broadcasts could only be seen within a fifteen kilometer radius of Lomé. With the infusion of state funds in the 1970's, improvements were initiated, and by 1982 broadcasts could be seen in most parts of the country. The number of sets has only slowly gone up to 7,000. Transmissions—amplified by three stations—are beamed in French and in the country's three main languages. The Director General of the Television Togolaise has been for long Solitoko Esso, followed by Pitang Tchalla.

TEM. Language of the Kotokoli.

TEMBA *see* KOTOKOLI.

TEMEDJA CAMP. Military camp near Atakpamé, one of the most notorious detention and torture centers under General Eyadema.

TEO *see* BOKONOU.

TEPE, KOFFI (COLONEL), 1947–1993. A former Minister of Interior and Deputy Chief of Staff of the Togolese armed forces, Tépé died during the March 25, 1993 assault on General Eyadema's compound in the Tokoin barracks. The brains behind the daring assault to eliminate Eyadema, Tépé personally killed **General Amegie** when the latter, captured, refused to join the rebels. He was then attacked by surrounding troops and beaten to death.

TERRITORIAL REORGANIZATION, 1981 *see* ADMINISTRATIVE ORGANIZATION.

TEVI, JEAN *see* TEVI-BENISSAN, TETE.

TEVI-BENISSAN, TETE (JEAN). Former Minister of Finance, Economy, and Planning. Born in Aného of Mina origins, Tevi-Benissan became President Grunitzky's head of the Programs Division in the Ministry of Finance and the Economy in 1964. In August 1968 he was shifted to Director of Customs, and exactly one year later he was brought into General Eyadema's cabinet as Minister of Finance, Economy, and Planning. In a 1973 cabinet reshuffle, Tevi-Benissan moved to head the Ministry of Commerce and Industry. In March 1975 he was dropped from the cabinet, later to be reintegrated into it as Minister of Finance and the Economy. Seen as close to Eyadema, he was regarded in several circles as vital for the recovery of the Togolese economy. Nevertheless, in September 1984 he was dropped from the cabinet and fled the country under charges of corruption in a large (twenty million dollars) foreign-financed road improvement project. Tevi-Benissan was to claim from Paris that he was made a scapegoat for the fiscal irregularities of others, including Eyadema himself.

THOMPSON DOSSOU, RUDOLPHE MESSAN, 1894–1965. Civil administrator. Born in Aného on November 30, 1894 and educated under German colonial rule as an Accountant, Thompson Dossou served as Lomé's Municipal Councillor between 1959 and 1963 and was concurrently CUT Deputy to the National Assembly (1961–63). A longtime Accountant and Administrator with the Caisse de Compensation des Prestations Familiales, Thompson Dossou died shortly after the 1963 coup.

THOMPSON TRENOU, ADJOAVI (Mrs.), 1921– . Defense Counsel with the Lomé court. Born in Tsévié on October 1921 of Ewe origins, Mrs. Thompson Trenou studied locally in Benin and Senegal, becoming an Instructor of Music and Physical Education. She then switched fields and studied Economics in Paris and in Rabat, Morocco, returning home to serve in quick succession as Secretary General of the Togo Representative Assembly (1950–52), bilingual (English/French) Secretary for World Health Organization's Africa headquarters (1952–54), Secretary General of the Grand Council of French West Africa (1956–59) and, between 1959 and 1972, Secretary General of the Chamber of Commerce. Completing her Law degree at the University of Abidjan (1972–73), Mrs. Thompson Trenou assumed duties as Defense Counsel with the Lomé Lower Court. A prolific author, she has written extensively on the condition of women in Africa.

TIDJANIYA. Dominant Islamic sect in Togo. Introduced in Chamba areas by Mallam Aboubaker from Segou, Mali, some time before the German occupation of the territory, it rapidly became the dominant sect of Togolese Islam. Aboubaker himself returned to Mali after twelve years of proselytizing in Togo, but his work was continued by **El Hadj Harimiao Seybou Fofona** who gave the sect its greatest drive towards supremacy in the country. *See also* ISLAM.

TIGOUE, VICTOR, 1936– . Diplomat. Born in Lomé on September 12, 1936, Tigoué received a Law degree abroad before joining the Togolese civil service. Technical Counselor at the Ministry of Interior during the last year of Sylvanus Olympio's administration (1962–63), Tigoué was dispatched to France after the 1963 coup d'état to serve at the Togolese Embassy with the rank of First Councilor. In October

1966 he was named Deputy Representative to the European Economic Community in Brussels, and in 1968 he was transferred back to Lomé to head the Political Division of the Foreign Ministry (eventually becoming its Secretary General), following which he was appointed Togo's representative to **OCAM** based in Bangui, Central African Republic. He is currently retired.

TOGBE, JACQUES DABRA, 1930– . Former Ambassador to the United Nations, educator, and lawyer. Born in Akloa in the Akposso circonscription on May 3, 1930, Togbé was educated in Lomé, Porto Novo, and in Ouidah's seminary (both in Benin), following which he studied at the University of Montpellier and at the Institut des Hautes Etudes d'Outre Mer, obtaining a Law degree with specialization in Labor Law. Initially head of the Labor Inspection Services (1965–68), Togbé became Director General of Labor and Social Security in 1968. A member of the **Rassemblement du Peuple Togolais** from its inception, Togbé was the party's Deputy Secretary General for two years prior to the abolition of the post and later was a member of the party's Political Bureau (1969–1971). A delegate to the International Labor Organization (1964–65) and Professor of Labor Law and Social Security at the Ecole Nationale d'Administration Togolaise in Lomé (1965–1972), Togbé was appointed permanent Representative to the United Nations in April 1972. He served in that post until 1977, when he was recalled to Lomé and placed on trial for embezzlement of embassy funds. He was sentenced to ten years' imprisonment. Released in 1984, he relocated to Paris.

TOGBLAKOPE. Relocation site of the Lomé **zongo.** At the time the original zongo was a slum, a veritable eyesore in downtown Lomé. It was razed to the ground, and the entire population relocated to the new zongo some eighteen kilometers north of Lomé. The distance from the capital is a major hardship for much of the population who, as in other zongo, are traders who must now commute a total of thirty-six kilometers daily on foot.

TOGO AIRWAYS. Small expatriate-controlled (German) civil transport company, founded in 1975 in Lomé with some 8.5 million CFAF capital. The airline operates charter cargo flights within Togo.

TOGO-DIALOGUE. Monthly cultural publication issued by Editogo, with a section of poetry, book reviews, oral, and modern literature.

TOGO EN MARCHE. Publication issued by the Ministry of Information and published by Editogo. Produced since 1962 and currently having a circulation of 10,000, *Togo en Marche* includes articles in French and Ewe on social, economic, and political matters.

TOGO PROTECTORATE TREATY: BAGUIDA, JULY 5, 1884. Treaty between the German Consul General Dr. **Gustav Nachtigal** and Chief Mlapa III of the village of Togo that formed the basis of the establishment of the German colony of Togo. For the entire text see the introduction.

TOGOBUND *see* BUND DER DEUTSCHEN TOGOLANDER.

TOGODO. The Togodo National Forest is located north of Tokpli on both sides of the Guor river to the Benin border.

TOGOFRUIT. Parastatal organization set up in November 1971 under the Ministry of Rural Development to assist in the diversification of Togo's agricultural produce and specifically to assist in the cultivation and marketing of locally grown fruits. Despite several well-conceived projects (including a cashew nut program with Italian assistance), Togofruit has always been an uneconomical enterprise, and it was finally disbanded in 1983 as part of the drive against the deficit-ridden state sector.

TOGOGRAIN. Popular name for the **Office Nationale des Produits Vivriers (ONPV).**

TOGO-PRESSE *see* LA NOUVELLE MARCHE.

TOGOROUTE *see* SOCIETE NATIONALE DE TRANSPORTS ROUTIERS.

TOGOTEX *see* COMPAGNIE TOGOLAISE DES TEXTILES.

TOGOVILLE (or TOGO). Name of a small lagoon village (whose population has gone up to 5,000) where, on July 4, 1884 Dr. **Gustav Nachtigal** signed a treaty of protection with Chief Mlapa III that became the key document sanctioning the absorption of the entire area into the new German colony of Togo, called after the name of the village. A descendant of Mlapa is Chief of the village that is also an important animist site. Other descendants are found in a Lomé quarter.

TOKOIN. Lomé suburb in which are located the international airport, Army headquarters, barracks of the First Infantry Battalion (within which General Eyadema resides), and the Université du Bénin.

TOLIMO *see* NATIONAL MOVEMENT FOR THE LIBERATION OF WESTERN TOGOLAND.

TONE. Northern prefecture known until the 1981 administrative reorganization of Togo as the circonscription de Dapango (later Dapaong). Its headquarters remains in the town of Dapaong. *See also* DAPAONG.

TORDJO, ALFRED KWAMI, 1944– . Academic and briefly cabinet minister. A Professor of Law at the University of Benin, Tordjo was integrated into the first interim government of Prime Minister Koffigoh as Minister of Justice between September 26, 1991 and September 1992.

TOSSOU, KOMLAN, 1939– . Former banker. Born in 1939 in Cotonou, Benin and educated in Porto Novo and Grenoble (France), where he obtained a doctorate in Economics. Tossou taught for a few years in France (1968–72) before joining the Banque Nationale de Paris. He was appointed Director General of the Togolese Bank for Commerce and Industry in 1976 but relocated to Paris in 1981.

TOULEASSI, KOKOU (PASTOR). Pastor of the Evangelical Church of Togo. Touléassi, General Eyadema's brother-in-law, acquired notoriety in March 1990 when he was elected in an irregular manner by the forty-sixth synod of the Church as the new Moderator of the 113 pastors. He replaced Pastor Agbi-Awumé, who was unacceptable to Eyadema, having refused to echo government positions on several occasions. In the first (secret) ballot, notwithstanding pressure behind Touléassi's candidacy, Agbi-Awumé received the highest vote. Asked to withdraw his candidacy that was splitting the Church, Agbi-Awumé complied but in the second secret vote Touléassi still could obtain only 54 votes. Despite standing rules requiring an absolute majority (fifty-seven votes), Touléassi was declared elected.

TOURISM. Though relatively small in absolute numbers, both the number of tourists coming to Togo and revenue accruing to Togo from tourist expenditures are significant. Indeed, in the late 1970s tourism became the third highest foreign currency earner after exports of phosphates and coffee. Though Togo has less to offer the tourist than, say, neighboring Benin, tourism has been constantly on the rise. This has been due to two factors. First, proximity to Accra (two hours overland on a very scenic road) has meant that Togo has benefited from the spillover of the tourist traffic to her more attractive neighbor; second, in contrast to the stringent austerity in Ghana and the Marxist curtain blanketing Benin until 1990, Togo has been able to offer an easygoing way of life, attractive and modern tourist facilities, an open economy that makes tourist purchases easy, and some of the very same attractions that appeal to visitors to West Africa. The worldwide recession notwithstanding, in 1979 twice as many tourists came to Togo as in 1974, for a grand total of 100,000 (twice that of neighboring Benin in that year), dramatically increasing to 143,000 tourists in 1982, followed by a downswing, accelerated in the 1990s due to the three years of social turmoil in the country.

Togo's attractions are modest. Apart from the scenic coastal strip (duplicated on either side in Ghana and Benin), the hinterland is not particularly remarkable. Nor does Togo have (as both Ghana and Benin do, as well as Nigeria) a rich historical heritage or architectural depository, since kingdoms were not highly developed in this region. In the far north, the La Kara region and the Somba areas are very appealing, but again, their counterparts in Benin are of equal attraction.

The biggest of Lomé new hotels is the 400 room "2 Fevrier Hotel" followed by the Hotel Sarakawa, Hotel de la Paix, and the older Le Bénin, Tropicana, and Miramar. In the hinterland an extensive drive to provide facilities for tourists brought about the erection of a series of new, though small, establishments, making travel easy and convenient. Some 4,600 million CFAF flowed into Togo in 1981 from tourism, rising and stabilizing at 6,500 million in the mid-1980s. Occupancy rates declined in the 1980s, however, to forty-two percent from an earlier high of sixty-one percent, and the average stay of a tourist declined to 2.6 days from a previous 3.5 days, in part due to the deterrent of the high cost of Lomé's ultra-luxury hotels.

TOWNS *see* URBAN CENTERS.

TRADE UNIONS. In January 1973 all trade unions were merged into the single trade union federation, the **Confédération Nationale des Travailleurs du Togo** that in 1989 had 70,000 members in three federations—public labor, parastatal labor, and private sector labor. Prior to that date, Togo had several trade unions, including the most important: (1) **Union Nationale des Travailleurs Togolais,** with 15,000 members and by far Togo's biggest union federation (the UNTT had twenty-two different unions affiliated to it), its secretary general was Seth Bassah; (2) **Confédération Syndicale des Travailleurs du Togo,** a small (600 member) Catholic trade union affiliated internationally with the **Confédération Africaine des Travailleurs Croyants;** and (3) **Syndicat des Enseignants Protestants du Togo,** an even smaller union of Togo's Protestant teaching personnel.

With the liberalization of 1990, trade union unity was thrown into a situation of flux. Many local unions seceded—spearheaded by **Claude Ameganvi's Organisation Togolaise des Travailleurs.** The CNTT retained most unions, however, by adopting a confrontational stance against the regime and Eyadema and today still encompasses some eighty percent of organized labor.

TRANSITIONAL GOVERNMENTS, 1990–1993. As an aftermath of the National Conference a one year transitional government was envisaged to usher in a new constitution, presidential, and legislative elections. The process was prolonged, however, by Eyadema, his loyalist armed forces, and disarray in the opposition forces, so that three transitional governments, each headed by Prime Minister Koffigoh, for one year were necessary. At the end of the third such government—in which by brute force a "national unity" coalition with the RPT was forced upon Koffigoh—parliamentary elections took place and General Eyadema (who was "re-elected" President via fraud and intimidation) appointed **Edem Kodjo** as the new Prime Minister of Togo. *See also* HAUT CONSEIL DE LA REPUBLIQUE.

TRENOU, RODOLPHE, 1917– . Former President Sylvanus Olympio's indispensable Chef du Cabinet and former Secretary of State for Information and the Press. Born in Aného on June 2, 1917, Trenou was educated locally and at the prestigious Ecole William Ponty in Dakar, Senegal, following which he completed medical studies at Dakar University and in Paris. He worked as a physician in Lomé, Sansanné-Mango, Bassar, and Aného, and, as an early member of the **Comité de l'Unité Togolaise,** was elected to Togo's Assembly as a delegate from Sokodé in 1946, becoming Secretary General of the Assemblée Représentative. During the mid-fifties, Trenou was abroad as an intern and physician in Congo-Brazzaville, Cote d'Ivoire, Senegal, and France, returning to Lomé upon Olympio's assumption of power in 1958. He served as Olympio's Cabinet Director (1958–62) and in January 1962 was named Secretary of State for Information and the Press. At the time of the 1963 coup d'état, he was one of two ministers not caught in the dragnet for Olympio's cabinet and stayed abroad practicing medicine. He returned to Lomé in 1984, where he operated a private medical clinic until his retirement.

TSEVIE. Agricultural prefecture (district) in the Maritime region with administrative headquarters in the town with the same name. The district has a population of 198,000—over 17,000 of whom live in the town, which is thirty-five kilometers from Lomé. Tsévié, Togo's eighth largest urban concentration, traces its name to one of the Ewe clans that migrated from Notsé during the great dispersal at the beginning of the eighteenth century. The region is in the center of extensively cultivated palm plantations and has a palm oil mill. The name of the district was changed in June 1981 to the prefecture of Zio; the headquarters and name of Tsévié remained unchanged, however.

TYOKOSSI *see* CHOKOSSI.

U

UNION DEMOCRATIQUE DES PEUPLES TOGOLAIS (UDPT). October 1959 merger of the **Parti Togolais du Progrès** of Nicolas Grunitzky and the **Union des Chefs et des Populations du Nord,** both in the process of disintegration following the 1958 United Nations-supervised elections that toppled the Autonomous Republic of Grunitzky and brought to power the **CUT** of Sylvanus Olympio. In March 1961 the CUT declared a one party system and, by the end of the year, all parties, including the UDPT, were dissolved. Following the 1963 coup d'état, the party was resurrected under Nicolas Grunitzky (who returned from self-imposed exile) and **Antoine Méatchi.** The UDPT joined with Togo's other three major political formations in an electoral coalition that divided the National Assembly's seats in equal numbers, forming the parliament during the Grunitzky administration. Following the 1967 coup, all parties were dissolved. *See also* MEATCHI-MAMA CRISIS.

UNION DES CHEFS ET DES POPULATIONS DU NORD (UCPN). French-supported conservative northern political alliance of traditional elements and notables established in 1951 to break the political dominance of southern and Ewe-led political parties. Its leaders were the Kotokoli Derman Ayéva and Fousseni Mama (before the latter switched his support to Grunitzky); other traditional leaders were the **Uro** of the Bassari; Nabiema Tabi, chief of the **Chokossi;** and Oudine, leader of the Konkomba. The party initially allied itself with the **PTP** of Nicolas Grunitzky and Dr. **Pedro Olympio** and, after the internal PTP schism that led to the creation of the **MPT,** supported Grunitzky over Pedro Olympio. Following the 1958 United Nations-sponsored elections that brought to power Sylvanus Olympio and the latter's **CUT,** the UCPN rapidly disintegrated and in 1959 merged with its old ally, the PTP, to form the **Union Démocratique des Peuples Togolais.**

UNION ELECTRIQUE COLONIALE (UNELCO). Colonial era electricity installations in Togo that were transferred in 1965 to State ownership under the **Compagnie Electrique du Togo.** The sole hydroelectric station at the time was at Kpéme, inaugurated in 1963, and relying on electricity from Ghana.

UNION MONETAIRE OUEST AFRICAIN. French West Africa's monetary union. *See* CFAF; FRANC ZONE.

UNION MUSULMANE DU TOGO (UMT). Association of Togo's Muslim leaders. Successor since 1963 of the **Association de la Jeunesse Musulmane du Togo.** The UMT only began to operate in earnest a decade later, as a result of which Togolese Islam received a major boost, especially in the educational field. The first UMT leadership included **Fousseni Mama,** a minister who was instrumental in setting up the UMT and later stepped in to heal the schism that tore the association apart. Mama was Councillor, with **Belly El Fouti** as Treasurer, **Kassim Mensah** as Secretary General, and El Hadj Safiou (Mama's cousin and an ex-deputy to the National Assembly, imprisoned by President Olympio in the far north of Togo) as President.

The UMT suffered numerous splits and was beset by chronic strife. In 1970 the leadership of Safiou was challenged, and he was overthrown on charges of quasi-dictatorial rule. It took the personal intervention of President Eyadema and all the persuasive powers of Fousseni Mama (untarnished by the strife) to attain a modicum of stability in the association. In May 1970 Mama was appointed President, with Mensah and **Namoro Karamoko** as Vice Presidents. In 1972 Mama stepped down, and Mensah was named his successor but rapidly fell afoul of the membership. In 1976 a new President, Halilou Adam, was selected with Karamoko as Second Vice President and Mama Zendjina as First Vice President. Both Fousseni Mama and Kassim Mensah were designated as "honorary members" of the ruling council. *See also* ISLAM.

UNION NATIONALE DE LA JEUNESSE TOGOLAISE (UNJT). Until 1990 the country's unified youth movement into which all existing movements were consolidated in 1972.

UNION NATIONALE DES CHEFS TRADITIONNELS DU TOGO (UNCTT). National Union of Togo's traditional leaders. In one form or another, the union has been in existence since President Olympio's days and is today largely apolitical. Members receive a stipend that has varied over the years and was once curtailed (under Olympio), causing much antagonism. President Eyadema in particular has cultivated the leaders of the UNCTT, realizing that they form an important source of political support.

UNION NATIONALE DES ETUDIANTS TOGOLAIS (UNETO). Student association that was disbanded in October 1977, when it was discovered that it was involved in anti-Eyadema activities. To replace it, the regime set up another organization, MONESTO.

UNION NATIONALE DES FEMMES DU TOGO (UNFT). The women's section of the **Rassemblement du Peuple Togolais,** Togo's single political movement. Established in a constituent congress in Lomé March 28 through 29, 1972, all existing women's organizations were merged into the UNFT. Among UNFT's former Executive Presidents/Vice Presidents have been Mrs. Giselle Djondo, Mrs. Amédorne, and Mrs. Joséphine Méatchi. The wives of the Togolese establishment serve on the council in various capacities. With the liberalizations of 1990, the UNFT monopoly was challenged by the erection of an anti-Eyadema Collectif d'Associations des Femmes (CAF) that rapidly became the largest women's association in Togo.

UNION NATIONALE DES TRAVAILLEURS TOGOLAIS (UNTT). Until the January 1973 creation of a single trade union confederation (*see* CONFEDERATION NATIONALE DES TRAVAILLEURS DU TOGO), the UNTT was Togo's biggest trade union. Founded in 1946, the UNTT had 15,000 members and 22 affiliated unions under the secretary generalship (1972) of Seth Bassah. Most members were government workers and employees of the private sector. During the presidency of Sylvanus Olympio, organized labor was one of the bulwarks of the regime (despite the austerity of his administration that resulted in periodic friction), and after the rise to power of Grunitzky in 1963 the UNTT lashed out on several occasions against the conservative policies of the regime. The UNTT's former leaders included **Innocent Toovi** and **Abdoulaye Salami.**

UNION TOGOLAISE DE BANQUE (UTB). Commercial bank established in 1964 with 2,000 million CFAF in capital and with headquarters in Lomé. The bank has branches in Atakpamé, Sokodé, Kara, Kpalimé, and Aného. The state has a thirty-five percent share in the equity, with the other partners being Crédit Lyonaise (thirty five percent), Deutsche Bank (eighteen percent), and the Banca Commerciale Italiana (twelve percent). The Director General of the UTB is Michel Callier.

UNION TOGOLAISE POUR LA DEMOCRATIE (UTD). New political party set up by **Edem Kodjo** in May 1991 with its strength in the Ewe areas of the Kpalimé area.

UNION TOGOLAISE POUR LA RENOUVEAU (UTR). Political party set up in May 1991 and headed by Dr. Marc Atipidé, aligned with Gilchrist Olympio. Atipidé was killed in the Army ambush of the Olympio motorcade (of which he was a part) on May 5, 1992.

UNITE TOGOLAISE (UT). Popular abbreviation of the **Comité de l'Unité Togolaise (CUT)** and its successor, **Parti de l'Unité Togolaise.** Also the name of the influential party newspaper edited by CUT Secretary General **Jonathan Savi de Tové.**

UNITED NATIONS TRUSTEESHIP *see* FRENCH ADMINISTRATION.

UNIVERSITE DU BENIN. Founded on September 11, 1970 as an autonomous national university after the collapse that year of the former joint Togo-Bénin Institut d'Enseignement Supérieure du Bénin, which had operated with a Humanities section in Lomé and a Science section in Porto Novo. The new university, on the Atakpamé road in Lomé's northern suburbs, commenced with schools of Law and Economics, Medicine, Social Sciences, and Letters, and an Institute of Technology, expanded to ten schools by 1974. A school of Medicine and a university hospital have since been added. Its Director was Dr. Gabriel Johnson, a former Togolese Professor of Biology at Abidjan University. Shortly after it was set up, the university had 1,800 students and 150 instructors (1973), rapidly increasing to 4,500 students and 427 instructors in 1983. In 1990 the university enrolled 9,000 students and had 533 instructors.

URBAN CENTERS. As elsewhere in Africa, Togo's rapid urbanization—a phenomena of the postindependence era—has not been an even process. Aného, barely a thirty-minute drive from Lomé, has seen its population growth stagnate for decades, progressively siipping in urban rankings, while the capital, a minor fishing village when Aného had been an internationally known commercial center, has developed in leaps and bounds. Attracting a huge influx from the countryside (including thousands of northerners coming to benefit from the "patronage" of their northern leader, Eyadema), Lomé's population spurted to 229,400 in 1977, over 300,000 in 1983, and an estimated 450,000 in 1993. Only thirty-five years ago, Lomé had been a small administrative center of 80,000.

There are significant difficulties in ranking Togo's urban centers. Virtually every set of reputable statistics is in contradiction with each other. One of the most authoritative reference works did not even include Kara (ex-Lama Kara), the booming Kabré center of over 25,000, in its 1982 edition, though it listed the southern Tabligbo, an overgrown village of 5,000, and such paradoxes continue to this day. Also, some centers are widely known as being much larger than dated census material indicates: the best example is Kara, still normally listed as having a population of 25,000, but which other sources note was in the 1990s competing with Sokodé (60,000) for second rank. The following tabulation, based on official Togolese estimates, should thus be regarded only as indicative of size.

1. Lomé	450,000
2. Sokodé	60,000
3. Kpalimé	35,000
4. Atakpamé	30,000
5. Kara	25,000
6. Aného	24,000
7. Bassari	18,000
8. Tsévié	17,000
9. Mango	13,500
10. Bafilo	12,000
11. Dapaong	7,000
12. Tabligbo	5,600

URO. Title of the paramount chief of the **Kotokoli,** whose residence is in the Dedaure quarter of Sokodé in northern Togo.

URO ISSIFOU. Fourteenth **Uro** of the Kotokoli of Sokodé, ascending the throne in 1949. *See* AYEVA, ISSIFOU, URO OF THE KOTOKOLI.

URO JOBO II. The first **Uro** of the Kotokoli to convert to Islam. Although Uro Jobo III converted to Christianity after the death of Uro Jobo II, the Kotokoli rapidly became Islamized.

V

VEHICLES. The urban and interurban communications system of Togo is clogged with vehicles, far beyond the numbers originally envisaged when the roads and streets were laid out. A direct result of the prosperity of mercantile interests in the country, it has suggested (and partly implemented) that all streets in Lomé be converted into one-way thoroughfares. Motor vehicle registrations have been increasing at the rate of ten percent annually. The most recent figures show 29,654 cars in 1991 compared to 21,733 in 1979 and 13,104 trucks compared to 10,998 in 1979. By contrast, the number of trucks in Togo in 1973 stood at only 2,573.

VIDEROT, TOUSSAINT MENSAH. One of Togo's best-known poets.

VILLAGE DU BENIN. Originally created in 1968 for other purposes, the Village du Bénin acts as a cultural and training center and has become Togo's leading specialized French language schools. Found in the outskirts of Lomé, it currently offers a wide variety of courses of varying lengths, often bilingual, with the financial support of France, Canada, and several international organizations such as the Commonwealth Fund for Technical Cooperation. A one-year course in French Language and Culture is its most popular. Some eighty percent of its students tend to be from Nigeria, seeking for diplomatic, advanced study, or other purposes to master the French language. Its director was long Koffi Abalo Ogoubi, who happened to be also a member of the National Assembly and a linguist educated in France, who was assisted by Professor N. Tidjani-Serpos of the University of Benin.

VO. One of five prefectures in the Maritime region, with administrative headquarters in the town of Vogan. The prefecture had been previously known as the circonscription of Vogan until changed in the 1981 administrative reorganization of Togo. *See also* VOGAN.

VODUN. Various ancestral and spirit cults, deities, and **fetishes,** encompassing cosmological beliefs and myths. Once the powers of the vodun have been proven effective, they become venerated and worshipped. Many such beliefs and practices have come to Togo from Ashanti areas, and there has also been a very strong **Yoruba** influence. The beliefs have also been exported via the slave trade to the islands of the Caribbean and to Brazil. The cults are still very well established in southern Togo and in non-Muslim areas in the north. The Ewe in the south have an estimated 5,000 divinities, the principal ones being Mahou and Lissa, the female and male original progenitors. It is speculated that Lissa may be a deformation of the Yoruba Orisha, corresponding to the sun, while Mahou symbolizes the moon.

VOGAN. Agricultural district in the Maritime region with administrative headquarters in the town of the same name, which is 23 kilometers from Lomé. The population of the district stands at 170,000 and, within its boundaries, is found Hahotoé, the center of Togo's phosphate mines. In the administrative reorganization of the country in 1981, the name of the district was changed to the prefecture of Vo, though the name of the town remained unchanged.

VOIX DE LA RENOVATION NATIONALE. Official name for Radio Togo. Previously known as the Voix du Nouveau Marché, and after the liberalizations of 1991, as Voix du Togo.

VOUDUN. Ancient Ewe quarter of Atakpamé settled by a clan that did not follow the standard **Adja**-Ewe route from **Tado** to **Nuatja** (now Notsé).

VOULE-FRITITI, KOFFI AGBENYAGIN, 1934– . Formerly known as Marcel Voulé-Fritz. Former Minister of Youth, Sports, and Culture. An Ewe born in Kayès, and educated for a teaching career, Voulé-Frititi completed an IHEOM degree in Paris and became the Director of the cabinet of the Minister of Interior. He later served in rapid succession as Technical Consultant to the Minister of National Education and Director of the **INARES** and in 1966 head of the Department of Planning of Education, a post he held for eleven years. In January 1977 he was brought into Eyadema's cabinet, serving for the next four years until June 1981. A member of the RPT Politburo, he was dropped from the leadership strata in 1983 and completely purged from his other duties on the grounds of "inefficiency." During his tenure in the Eyadema cabinet Voulé-Frititi had been charged with liaising with **TOLIMO.** He is currently retired.

VOULE-FRITZ, MARCEL *see* VOULE-FRITITI, KOFFI AGBENYAGIN.

VOVOR, VALENTIN MAWUPE, 1925– . Surgeon, former Minister of Health, and former President of the Supreme Court. Born on October 29, 1925, in Agomé-Koussountou, Vovor was educated in Kpalimé's Catholic mission, the elitist Ecole William Ponty in Dakar, Senegal, Dakar's School of Medicine, and at the Universities of Montpellier and Dijon. He specialized in Surgery and Gynecology and returned to Togo in 1957 to join the National Hospital Center. In 1961 he became head of the Surgical Clinic of Dakar's Faculty of Medicine, and in 1962 he was appointed Chief Physician of the Kpalimé Medical Subdivision and head of the Office of Studies at the Ministry of Health (1962–63) and Director of the Nursing School of Togo (1962–63). Well-known abroad through his seventy-odd scientific papers and books, the essentially apolitical Vovor was appointed Minister of Health following the 1963 coup d'état, holding the position until January 1966, when he became Director of Togo's Midwives School. A member of the **Rassemblement du Peuple Togolais** and its Political Bureau, Dr. Vovor was appointed President of the Supreme Court in 1972. In 1974 he stepped down from this position and reverted back to his medical and teaching duties in Lomé. In 1979 he was appointed Director of Medical Education at the University of Benin, a position he held until his retirement.

W

WALLAH, KOFFI. Former Minister of Rural Development between 1984 and 1988. Wallah replaced the powerful Kodjoulou Dogo in September 1982 as Minister of Planning and Administrative Reform. Prior to this, he had been Minister of Commerce and Transport. In December 1979 he was also elected Deputy to the National Assembly. Wallah, who is indirectly related to General Eyadema, is of Kabré ethnicity. He was dropped from the cabinet in December 1988 and reverted to administrative duties in the parastatal sector.

WALLAH, SINZING AYI AKAWELOU, (COLONEL). Formerly the Kabré commander of the Second Military District of Kara, Wallah—who is General Eyadema's brother-in-law—was the first Kabré to graduate from the elite St. Cyr military staff college in France. In March, when **Colonel Assih** was purged due to gross corruption, Wallah, then a Major, replaced him.

WANGARA. Name given in north Togo to "strangers' " quarters in urban centers. Also known as **zongo** or maro.

WASUNGU, PASCAL BAGNINGUSAMA ARFA, 1937– . Sociologist and international administrator. Born in Baga-Niamtougou in north Togo on September 8, 1937 and educated locally at the Ouidah (Benin) Seminary and in Brussels Institut de Travail where he obtained inter alia certification as a Labor Inspector (1963–67), Wasungu also studied at Brussels Free University and at the Catholic University of Louvain, specializing in the Social Sciences (1966–68). He then proceeded to the Sorbonne and other Parisian institutes, completing a Ph.D. in Sociology at EHESC (1976). He has occupied a variety of positions: before his advanced studies, he was a teacher at the Sokodé Catholic Mission and later a civil servant in the Ministry of Social Affairs and Civil Service. In Paris he taught in the University of Paris's Department of Anthropology (1968) and was a Sociologist attached to the Renault vehicle factories (1970–71). He then joined the Economic Commission for Africa as Associate Social Affairs Officer (1972–1980) and has since resided in Paris as a Financial Advisor with SA Georges Maurer.

WATYI *see* OUATCHI.

WAWA. Prefecture, formerly known as the circonscription de Badou, and renamed in the 1981 administrative reorganization of Togo. Its headquarters remains in the important market center of Badou. Wawa was originally carved out of the larger circonscription of Akposso, largely to separate the Akposso ethnic group from the non-Akposso in a region that has been the scene of much unrest.

WESTERMANN, DIEDRICH, 1875–1957. World-renowned and foremost linguist of Southern Togolese dialects. Born on June 24, 1875 in Baden, a small village near Bremen, Germany, of humble peasant stock, Westermann became a missionary at the age of twenty and was eventually sent to German Togo. There he displayed his remarkable aptitude for linguistics and wrote the standard dictionary of Ewe and several other seminal tracts. He made major contributions to the linguistic study of at least a dozen other coastal and interior languages in his barely four years in Togo, works that have withstood the test of time and remain seminal studies to this day. He later served in Liberia, Sudan, and Spain. In his work he was assisted by **Jonathan Savi de Tové** while in Spain. Between 1925 and 1930, Westermann also served as Director of the International African Institute in London.

Y

YANGA. Small ethnic sliver of no more than 8,000 people found in the extreme north of Togo in the Dapaong area. Some members have recently migrated as far south as Notsé. Most have converted to Islam in recent decades.

YANNINIM, BITOKOTIPOU. Cabinet minister during General Eyadema last few years of absolute power in Togo. An administrator from north Togo, Yanninim was Minister of Labor and the Civil Service between 1987 and February 1990 when he replaced General Amegée in one of the latter's portfolios as Minister of Justice. With the liberalizations of 1991 he lost his sensitive post.

YEKE-YEKE *see* ADOSSA.

YEMTIA, MAGBENGA BISSAM, 1953– . Economist. Born in 1953 in Sion, Yemtia completed his education in Togo in Atakpamé, following which he went to the local University of Benin obtaining a Master's degree in Developmental Economics and obtained further specialization in Tourist Economics at the University of Aix-Marseille in France. He is currently head of the Human Resources Division and a Developmental Economist at the Ministry of the Plan in Lomé.

YENDI. Capital of the **Dagomba** people, formerly part of German Togo and later of British Togoland, now in Ghana. *See* DAGOMBA.

YORUBA. An ethnic group found mostly in southwestern Nigeria and numbering over five million. Also found in such neighboring countries as Benin, Cameroun, Togo, and in small trading communities throughout western Africa. In Togo, the Yoruba **Ana** ethnic group resides in Atakpamé and its vicinity and is regarded as the most western extension of the Yoruba people. They are highly Islamized, and no estimates of their numbers exist. Apart from the Ana, there are several small Yoruba trading communities in the country's big cities, especially in Lomé.

YOTO. The former circonscription of Tabligbo, renamed in the June 1981 administrative reorganization of Togo. One of five prefectures in the Maritime region, it retains as its capital the town of Tabligbo.

YOUSSIF, AHMED, 1946– . Director of the Lomé Medersa, educator, and religious leader. Born in 1946 in Kpalimé of a Hausa father and a Yoruba mother, Youssif studied locally in a Koranic school and was later sent to study in a similar center in Djougou, Benin. He returned to Lomé and taught in the newly opened **Medersa,** becoming its Director in 1976. Youssif has traveled extensively, including to Libya and the Soviet Union.

YWASSA, LEONARD BAGUILMA, 1926– . Former Minister of Rural Economy, prominent member of the UDPT party and Ambassador to France. Born on December 1, 1926 in Koka near Niamtougou in the far north, Ywassa was trained as an Agricultural Engineer at the Agricultural College of Nancy (France) and at other institutes of Agriculture. In 1953 he returned to Togo to become Deputy Chief of the Aného district and Director of the Glidji experimental farm (1953–55). He later headed a similar project in Kandé and in Barkoissi (1955–56), serving also as head of Agricultural Services in Sansanné-Mango. As a prominent member of Nicolas Grunitzky's **Union Démocratique des Population Togolaises,** in August 1956 Ywassa was appointed Minister of Education, Civil Service, Labor, and Social Affairs, holding these positions until Grunitzky's government was ousted, following the United Nations-sponsored elections of 1958. A member of the opposition to the successor **CUT** regime of Sylvanus Olympio and a Deputy from Niamtougou (1958–61), Ywassa rose to become Secretary General of the UDPT in 1960, shortly before the party was banned by the CUT and Togo became a one party state. In 1962 he became Deputy Director of Inspections at several agricultural pilot centers, and with Nicolas Grunitzky's return to power after the 1963 coup d'état, Ywassa was promoted to Director of Agriculture (1963–66). In the last weeks of Grunitzky's government Ywassa was brought into the cabinet as Minister of Rural Economy, but he lost the post after the coup of 1967. Between 1967 and 1968, he served as technical counselor to **SORAD** and Director of the Tové Agricultural Farm. In March 1968 he was appointed Ambassador to France, Great Britain, and the European Economic Community. Somewhat later he was reassigned to the Ministry of Rural Economy, where he served as deputy director until his retirement in 1986.

Z

ZINSOU, SENOUVO. World-famous Togolese dramatologist. Zinsou founded a theatrical group in Sokodé in 1968 and in 1972 won the coveted African Grand Prix for his *On Joue la Comedie,* which allowed him to complete a Master's in Fine Arts in France. A very talented dramatical author who has written several popular plays, he again won an inter-African prize in 1984 for his *La Tortue qui Chante.* He is employed in the Ministry of Culture and was a member of the transitional Haut Conseil de la République.

ZIO. The former circonscription de Tsévié as renamed in the 1981 administrative reorganization of Togo in 1981. Its headquarters remains the town of Tsévié. *See also* TSEVIE.

ZONE FRANCHE DE TRANSFORMATION POUR L'EXPLOITATION (ZFTE). Duty-free ("offshore") manufacturing zone established in 1990 in the port of Lomé area, intended to revitalize the Togolese economy. By 1991—when the massive societal turmoil in the country set back all developmental projects—fifteen manufacturing companies had relocated to the Zone, investing fifty-six billion CFAF and employing 879 Togolese and 39 expatriates.

ZONES D'AMENAGEMENT AGRICOLE PLANIFIE (ZAAP). Structures set up in April 1978 to assist in better land use, the collectivization of agriculture, and the organization of more collectives.

ZONGO. Name in much of West Africa, and in Togo, referring to "strangers' " commercial quarters in urban centers, at times used specifically to refer to Hausa quarters. The original zongo of Lomé, founded in 1884 when Lomé was a small village, was a sprawling slum on prime downtown land by 1970 and was razed to the ground in 1977, and its population was forcibly relocated to Togblakodé, eighteen kilometers north of the town, where the new zongo was created. (Each original resident was given a plot of land and 200,000 CFAF indemnity.) At the time it included a community of 12,000 people, 7,000 Nigerian (4,000 Hausa, 2,000 Yoruba, and 1,000 Fulani) as well as some 3,000 Djerma from Niger and about 500 each Kotokoli, Dagomba, Mossi, and Mende. Many of the original traders did not relocate to the new zongo but moved to other zongo, feeling (correctly) that its distance from downtown Lomé and "modern character" would detract from prospects of trade. As a result the ethnic composition of the traders has changed, and the quarter is now composed of 49 percent Hausa, followed by ten percent Songhay, and five percent Fulani.

The term zongo comes from the original caravan encampments in the vicinity of urban centers and water supplies that were specifically reserved for the use of foreign transient traders passing by. Virtually every important commercial entrepot in Togo has a zongo, for a total of forty-five.

Appendix: Tables

Table 1: Demography, 1980 Census.

Region	District	Population	Density per square kilometer
Maritime	Golfe	447,806	163
	Lac	137,855	193
	Vo	150,575	201
	Yoto	100,682	81
	Zio	203,323	61
		1,040,241	
Plateaux	Amou	78,125	39
	Haho	110,768	30
	Kloto	186,778	67
	Ogou	165,143	27
	Wawa	109,579	44
		650,393	
Centrale	Sotouboua	131,637	18
	Tchamba	44,810	14
	Tchaoudjo	96,691	38
		273,138	
La Kara	Assoli	32,425	35
	Bassar	115,934	19
	Binah	50,081	108
	Dougelfou	59,331	53
	Keran	44,844	41
	Kozah	121,036	72
		426,651	
Savanes	Oti	77,803	21
	Tone	251,341	52
		329,144	
Total		2,719,567	48

Note: More recent census figures not available. With an annual growth rate of 3.3%, the population of Togo was by the mid-1990s some 50% higher.

Table 2: Ethnic Breakdown. 1980 Estimates.

Group	Estimated % of population
1. Ewe cluster: Ewe, Ouatchi, Mina, Fon, Adja, etc.	44%
2. Kabré cluster: Kabré, Losso, Lamba, Tamberma, Moosi, Logba	27%
3. Moba cluster: Moba, Konkomba	6%
4. Kotokoli cluster: Kotokoli, Bassari, Tchamba	6%
5. Central Togo cluster: Akposso, Bassila	4%
6. Gurma	4%
7. Yoruba cluster: Nago, Ana	3%
8. Hausa, Fulani	2%
9. Others	4%

Table 3: Togolese Budgets: Intermittent Years.

Year	Budget (in million CFAF)
1973	17.3
1975	30.5
1977	55.2
1979	64.8
1981	70.7
1983	75.4
1985	80.1
1987	89.6
1989	92.4
1991	92.4
1993	72.0

Table 4: Foreign Trade, 1959–1992

Year	Imports	Exports	Balance of Trade	Exports as % of Imports
1959	3,747	4,348	+601	116.0%
1960	6,452	3,588	−2,864	55.6
1961	6,476	4,615	−1,861	71.2
1962	6,724	4,239	−2,485	63.0
1963	7,166	4,509	−2,657	62.9
1964	10,286	7,448	−2,838	72.4
1965	11,100	7,184	−3,916	65.3
1966	11,668	8,872	−2,796	76.0
1967	11,133	7,894	−3,239	70.9
1968	11,623	9,549	−2,074	82.1
1969	14,572	11,477	−3,095	78.7
1970	17,928	15,176	−2,752	84.6
1971	19,455	13,627	−5,828	70.0
1972	21,381	12,659	−8,722	59.2
1973	22,388	13,755	−8,633	61.4
1974	28,612	45,174	+18,562	157.9
1975	32,270	26,962	−10,308	72.3
1976	44,420	24,914	−19,506	56.1
1977	69,834	39,115	−30,719	56.0
1978	100,898	54,238	−46,660	53.8
1979	110,208	46,432	−63,776	42.1
1980	116,357	71,285	−45,072	61.3
1981	117,769	57,469	−61,528	48.8
1982	128,354	58,173	−70,181	45.3
1983	108,141	61,921	−46,220	57.3
1984	118,460	83,588	−34,872	70.6
1985	129,406	85,380	−44,026	66.0
1986	107,963	70,551	−37,432	65.3
1987	127,308	73,212	−54,096	57.5
1988	106,310	126,204	−19,894	84.2
1989	131,600	121,829	− 9,771	92.5
1990	136,633	107,641	−28,992	78.7
1991	135,802	114,500	−21,312	84.3
1992	173,922	147,710	−26,212	84.9

Figures in millions CFAF.

Table 5: Gross Domestic Product, 1989: Sectoral Origins.

Sector	Percentage of GDP
Agriculture	33.9
Retail trade, hotels	21.7
Manufacturing	8.6
Mining	8.0
Government	8.0
Transport	6.5
Construction	3.2
Electricity, water	2.8
Other Services	7.3

Table 6: Production of Main Consumption Crops: 1987, 1991

Crop	1987	1991
Cassava	355	504
Yams	360	433
Maize	172	236
Millet/sorghum	168	176
Rice	23	33

In 1,000 tons.

Table 7: Production of Main Cash Crops: 1986, 1991

Crop	1986	1991
Cotton	79,066	100,247
Coffee	11,372	9,653
Cocoa	12,585	7,278
Karite	4,468	6,396

In 1,000 tons

Table 8: Recent Levels of Phosphate Exports/Earnings

	1988	1990	1992
Exports/tons	2,867	2,309	1,990
Receipts/CFAF	41,329	27,160	20,464

Exports in 1,000 tons; receipts in million CFAF

Table 9: External Debt: 1986, 1991.

| 1986 | 1,069 |
| 1991 | 1,356 |

In million US dollars

Table 10: Imports/Exports: Main Trading Partners, 1986, 1991.

Exports to:	1986	1991	Imports from:	1986	1991
France	19.5	8.0	France	27.4	21.2
Canada	1.8	9.0	Hong Kong	2.0	8.3
Spain	1.5	6.1	Netherlands	8.7	6.6
India	2.7	5.8	Thailand	4.0	4.8
Italy	5.6	4.8	Germany	8.9	4.5

As percentages of total trading value.

Table 11: Exports/Imports: Main Commodities, Selected Years.

	1979	1981	1983	1985	1987
Exports, f.o.b.					
Phosphates	21,620	28,139	26,002	42,815	33,554
Cotton	837	4,419	4,871	11,638	8,619
Cocoa	7,295	8,227	5,526	6,837	8,344
Coffee	6,256	5,418	4,871	11,891	9,255
Cement, clinker	743	6,325	13,237	1,214	2,640
Karite	244	479	729	3,311	148
Petroleum products	5,268	908	784	1,304	8
Palm products	379	814	336	—	24
Imports, c.i.f.					
Foodstuffs	11,098	16,787	21,816	21,939	18,551
Drinks, tobacco	5,233	13,222	10,366	7,253	6,690
Fuel	20,169	9,885	10,191	8,893	9,335
Raw materials	12,425	6,079	1,803	2,475	1,553
Machinery	24,939	15,602	20,052	24,344	34,624
Other industrials	13,098	33,291	42,666	62,773	54,554

In million CFAF.

Bibliography

Introductory Note

As is true for much of Francophone Africa, most of the literature on Togo is in the French language. Because of the country's pre-World War I status as a German colony, there also exists a significant amount of material in German on the history of the German penetration of the hinterland, and also reflecting continuing German academic interest in the development of their former colony.

The literature in English includes early material on the deliberations regarding the future of the two Togoland trusteeships in the aftermath of World War II (mostly United Nations documentation) and more recent material, mostly scholarly articles, chapters in books not exclusively devoted to Togo, and a variety of brief reports on contemporary developments. Only recently did the first monograph on Togo appear in English (by Knoll, 1974, on the German era). Though English language material on Togo has recently been much augmented, including two monographs (one a memoir of a Peace Corps volunteer) today, fully thirty-five years after independence there is still not a single comprehensive academic work exclusively on Togo, no matter what field. Thus, whatever one's specific interests, any serious research must automatically rely heavily on non-English sources.

The bibliography that follows, though extensive, is not all-inclusive and stresses, in particular, the Social Sciences and History. It lists most of the English language sources available and a representative sample of the most easily accessible or important material in French and other European languages. Though Togolese publications are quite difficult to obtain in the United States, many are first rate, and hence the most important of these (that are available in several African Studies' Centers and at the Library of Congress) are included. By contrast the bulk of the briefer and/or more ephemeral material (primarily from news weeklies), that was included in previous editions of this *Dictionary,* has been dropped for reasons of space. (Readers interested in this material should refer to the second edition.)

For researchers and other readers who must rely primarily on English sources, the following are especially suggested: for the pre-colonial era along the Ghana-Nigeria coast, Newbury's (1961) study is unrivaled; for the early colonial period see the articles by Amenumey (1969), Cardinall (1926, 1927), Darkoh (1967, 1968), and the dissertation (1963/4) and subsequent book by Knoll (1974). For the so-called Ewe "problem" prior to Togo's independence, the best items are Coleman's 1956 monograph, Amenumey's several works (1969, 1986, 1990), and Welch's chapters in his 1966 book. Most of the anthropological work on Togo is in French, as are sources on Togo's economy; Tait's articles—especially his 1961 chapter on the Konkomba in Ghana—are solid, as is the chapter on Togo in the International Monetary Fund's *Surveys of African Economies* (1970). Finally, post-independence events are surveyed by Kitchen (1963), Howe (1967), De Chardon (1970), and Decalo (1973), in individual chapters on Togo in the books by Thompson (1972) and Decalo (1976, 1990), in the weekly *West Africa* and monthly *Africa Research Bulletin* (both series), in the annuals of *Africa Contemporary Record,* until it stopped publication, and in the annual reports and quarterly country survey of the Economist Intelligence Unit. Most of the seminal material in English (and a sampling of the most important in other languages) is briefly reviewed and annotated in Decalo (1995).

The literature in French is much more extensive and wide-ranging. The best single volume on Togo remains the massive *Histoire du Togo,* written by the prolific Robert Cornevin. The book, twice updated, presents the best single work compendium of facts on Togo's ethnic groups, pre-colonial history, French administration, religion, and early political evolution. It contains only sparsely detailed data on the post-independence era, but such material is not lacking in French, including in Cornevin's other publications. He has also written a brief book on German colonization in Africa (1969), which can be read in conjunction with Attignon's (1972) study of the evolution of Togo from the Congress of Berlin to the Conference of Brazzaville (1944). Also of note are the studies of Froelich (1956), Luchaire (1957)—whose articles are really lengthy monographs—Pauvert (1960), and Brieux (1967) on the Ewe unificationist movement and Kratz's two part contribution on Togo's early decades under German rule. Other seminal historical works include that of Agbanon II (1991), d'Almeida (1982) on the period under Governor Bonnecarrere, and Gayibor's numerous fascinating studies (especially of 1983). These are but a sampling of a very rich body of historical analysis that exists in French.

For Togo's ethnic groups there is likewise a wealth of data, though some groups have been much more extensively studied than others. Works that should be especially noted are those by Cornevin (1962) on the Bassari—as well as his other shorter pieces—supplemented by the more recent excellent English articles by Barros (1986, 1988), Froelich's articles, the jointly written study by Froelich, Cornevin, and Alexandre on the "Populations du Nord Togo" (1963), and the articles by Alexandre, Agblemagnon, Bertho, and Blier (1981, about whom more later), Cordonnier's tour de force on the textile women traders of Lomé (1982), Kubik (1986, in German, about one of the towering patrons of art in Togo), Lucien-Brun, the excellent collection of articles on all coastal groups in de Medeiros (1984), the remarkably prolific Nieuwaal (who has seemingly single-handedly taken on the task of publicizing the northern Chokossi), Pauvert on the Kabré, and Riviere's and Surgy's numerous outstanding contributions on the Ewe.

For Togo's economy, the monthly compilations of reports and statistics by the Banque Centrale des Etats de l'Afrique de l'Ouest are simply indispensable, as well as the various reports by French governmental agencies and Togo's Haute Commissariat au Plan, some of which are listed in the "Economics" section of the bibliography. Toporowski (1988) provides (in English) a dissident note on the Structural Adjustment programs forced upon Togo. Also useful are Robert's early article (1965) on Togo's all important phosphates industry (which can be updated by the numerous briefer articles published since), Agier's studies on the economic activities in Lomé's zongo (1981, 1983), and Le Bris's on rural markets in Vo (especially his 1984 monograph).

There is no single book, even in French, dealing in detail with Togolese politics in the entire post-independence era. However, a large number of articles have been written on various aspects or periods of Togo's evolution, and in the past seven years a significant number of critical assessments on the Eyadema era have finally appeared. Among the early material, one can note Cornevin's twin articles on Togo's foreign affairs (1972) and army and military coups (1968). Also important are the annuals *Année Africaine* and *Année Politique Africaine* and the various articles that have appeared in *Le Mois en Afrique* and in the more recently appearing *Politique Africaine*. But starting with the mid-1980s a much more hard-nosed analysis has developed on Togo, both its early history (see Ajavon, 1989) and, especially, the Eyadema era of misrule. Among the truly outstanding contributions of this genre one can note the work of Toulabor. His *Le Togo sous Eyadema* (1986) is the single best source to de-mystify Eyadema's Cult of Personality; his earlier 1981 article on the use of derisory language in Togolese political discourse is pioneering, as is his lengthy chapter in the book jointly written with J. F. Bayart and A. Mbembe, *La Politique par le Bas* (1991).

An increasing number of doctoral dissertations (many in English) have been conducted on gender-related issues and on education in recent years, and these have been followed up by more easily available articles listed under Education. Riviere has published a large number of fascinating studies on Ewe religion (1978, 1980, 1990), as has Surgy (1979, 1983), with some of the work of these two authors to be found under

Anthropology. The richness and vibrance of Togolese literature, poetry, and (more recently) drama, is well-known and is attested to by the ever increasingly larger section on Literature in this *Dictionary*. One could note Blier's remarkable studies of Tamberma (or Somba) Art and Architecture, especially her 1987 tour-de-force that is a work of art in and of itself and is more on the symbiosis of space design with a society's culture and moral values.

Finally, for the prospective tourist or the first time visitor, there are now infinitely more sources to choose from, especially in English, notably the sections on the country in Crowther's *Africa on a Shoestring* (1989), Shuttles and Shuttles-Graham's *Fielding's Guide South of the Sahara* (1986), and Trillo and Hudgens's *West Africa: A Rough Guide* (1990). A much more comprehensive country guide has appeared recently, however, in French: Passot (1988). Jeune Afrique's *Togo* (1979), though dated, remains useful.

General Works

Afrique Occidentale Française. 2 vols. Paris: Encyclopédie Coloniale et Maritime, 1949.

Ansprenger, Franz. *Politik im Schwarzen Afrika.* Cologne: Westdeutscher Verlag, 1961.

Baumann, Hermann, and Diedrich Westermann. *Les Peuples et les Civilisations de l'Afrique.* Paris: Payot, 1957.

Bourges, Hervé, and Claude Wauthier. *Les 50 Afriques.* Paris: Le Seuil, 1979.

Brass, William. "The Demography of French-Speaking Territories." In *The Demography of Tropical Africa,* edited by A. J. Coale 342–439. Princeton, N.J.: Princeton University Press, 1968.

Chailley, Marcel. *Histoire de l'Afrique Occidentale Française.* Paris: Berger-Levrault, 1968.

Corbett, Edward M. *The French Presence in Black Africa.* Washington, D.C.: Black Orpheus Press, 1972.

Cornevin, Robert. *Histoire de l'Afrique des Origines à Nos Jours.* Paris: Payot, 1956.

———. *Histoire des Peuples de l'Afrique Noire.* Paris: Berger-Levrault, 1960.

Deloncle, Pierre. *L'Afrique Occidentale Française: Découverte, Pacification, Mise en Valeur.* Paris: Editions Ernest Leroux, 1934.

Désiré-Vuillemin, G. "Les capitales de l'Ouest-Africain." 2 vols. Paris: Service d'Etudes et de Recherches Pédagogiques pour les Pays en Développement, 1963.

Dossier Togo. Paris: Recontres Africaines, 1987.

Hardy, Georges. *La Politique Coloniale et le Partage de la Terre aux XIXe et XXe siècles.* Paris: Albion Michel, 1937.

Hodgkin, Thomas. *African Political Parties*. London: Penguin, 1961.
————, and Ruth Schachter. "French-Speaking West Africa in Transition." *International Conciliation*, no. 528 (May 1960), 375–436.
International Institute for Strategic Studies. *The Military Balance 1993–94*. London: International Institute for Strategic Studies, 1994.
Kimble, George H. T. *Tropical Africa*. New York: Twentieth Century Fund, 1960. 2 vols.
Lusignan, Guy de. *French-Speaking Africa Since Independence*. London: Pall Mall Press, 1969.
Martin, Gaston. *Histoire de l'Esclavage dans les Colonies Françaises* Paris: Presses Universitaires de France, 1948.
Mercier, Paul. *Cartes Ethno-Démographiques de l'Ouest Africain*. Dakar: IFAN, 1954.
Meyers Handbuch über Afrika. Mannheim: Bibliographisches Institut, 1962.
Monnet, A., ed. *La Mise en Valeur de l'A.O.F. et du Togo*. Casablanca, 1955.
Morgenthau, Ruth Schachter. *Political Parties in French-Speaking West Africa*. Oxford, England: Oxford University Press, 1964.
Mortimer, Edward. *France and the Africans 1944–1960: A Political History*. New York: Walker Co., 1969.
Packer, George. *The Village of Waiting*. New York: Vintage Books, 1988.
Robinson, Kenneth. *The Dilemmas of Trusteeship*. New York: Oxford University Press, 1964.
Southall, Aidan. *Social Change in Modern Africa*. London: Oxford University Press, 1962.
Spitz, Georges. *L'Ouest Africain Français*. Paris: Société d'Editions Géographiques, Maritimes et Coloniales, 1947.
Suret-Canale, Jean. *Afrique Noire: Occidentale et Centrale*. 2 vols. Paris: Editions Sociales, 1964 and 1968.
Tenaille, Franck. *Les 56 Afriques*. 2nd ed. Paris: Maspero, 1979.
Thompson, Virginia, and Richard Adloff. *French West Africa*. London: George Allen & Unwin, 1958.
Trimingham, John Spencer. *Islam in West Africa*. London: Oxford University Press, 1959.

Early (19th-Century) Historical/Exploration

Adams, John. *Remarks on the Country Extending from Cape Palmas to the River Congo*. 1823. Reprint, London: Frank Cass, 1966.
————. *Sketches Taken During Ten Voyages to Africa Between the Years 1786 and 1800*. London: Hurst, Robinson Co., 1822.
Bettencourt, Vasconcellos Corte Real do Canto, Vital de. *Descripçao Historica, Topographica e Ethnographica do Diçtricto de S. Joao*

Baptista d'Ajuda e do Reino de Dahomena Costa da Mina. Lisbon, 1869.

Bosman, Willem. *A New and Accurate Description of the Coast of Guinee.* London: J. Knapton, 1705.

Bouche, Pierre Bertrand. *Sept Ans en Afrique Occidentale; La Côte des Esclaves et le Dahomey.* Paris: Plon-Nourrit, 1885.

François, Kurt von. *Ohne Schuss Durch Dick und Dunn. Erste Erforschung des Togohinterlandes.* Esch-Waldems: Eigenverlag von Gotz, 1972.

Freeman, Thomas Birch. *Journal of Various Visits to the Kingdoms of Ashanti, Aku and Dahomi in Western Africa.*1844. Reprint, London: Cass, 1968.

Norregard, Georg. *Danish Settlements in West Africa (1658–1850).* Boston: Boston University Press, 1966.

Schnapper, Bernard. *La Politique et le Commerce Français dans le Golfe de Guinée de 1838 à 1871.* Paris: Mouton, 1961.

Snelgrave, William. *A Full Account of Some Parts of Guinea and the Slave Trade.* London: Knapton, 1734.

Zoller, Hugo. *Die Deutschen Besitzungen an der Westafrikanischen Kuste.* Berlin: W. Spemann, 1885.

German Colonial Era

Adick, Christel. *Bildung und Kolonialismus in Togo: Eine Studie zu den Entstehungszusammenhangen eines Europaisch Gepragten Bildung Wesens im Afrika am Beispiel Togos (1850–1914).* Basel: Beltz Verlag, 1981.

———. "Padagogische Idylle und Wirtschaftswunder im Deutschen Schutzgebiet Togo." *Die Dritte Welt,* vol. 5, no. 1 (1977): 27–46.

———. "Theorie und Analyse Kolonialer Lehrplane: Beispiele aus Deutsch-Togo." *Bildung und Erziehung* (Cologne), vol. 34, no. 4 (1985): 513–29.

Amenumey, D.E.K. "German Administration in Southern Togo." *Journal of African History,* vol. 10, no. 4 (1969): 623–639.

Arboussier, Henri d'. "La Conquete du Togoland: l'Action des Partisans Mossi." *Bulletin du Comité de l'Afrique Française,* April 1915.

Asmis, Rudolf. *Kalambra Na M'Putu: Koloniale Erfahrungen und Beobachtung.* Berlin: E. S. Mittler, 1942.

Avornyo, Raphael Quarshie. *Deutschland und Togo (1847–1987).* Frankfurt: Peter Lang, 1989.

Barbier, H. C. "L'Histoire Veçue: Sokodé, 1914. Les Allemands Evacuent le Nord-Togo." *Revue Français d'Histoire d'Outre Mer,* vol. 75. no. 1 (1988): 79–88.

Batson, Adolf. *African Intrigues.* Garden City, New York: Garden City Pub. Co., 1933.

Beazley, R. C. "Das Deutsche Kolonialreich, Gross-Britannien und der Vertrag von 1890." *Die Berliner Monatsschrift,* May 1930.

Brunschwig, Henry. *L'Expansion Allemande Outre-Mer du XVe siècle a Nos Jours.* Paris: Presses Universitaires de la France, 1957.

Buttner, R. "Ergebnisse der Forschungreisen von Togo 1890–1892." *Globus,* 1895.

———. "Expedition in das Anyangaland." *Mitteilungen fur Forschungreisenden und Gelehrten aus den Deutschen Schutzgebieten,* vol. 21, 1908.

———. "Togo." In *Das Uberseeische Deutschland.* Stuttgart: Union Deutsche Verlagsgesellschaft, 1911.

Cardinall, A. W. "The Story of the German Occupation of Togoland." *Gold Coast Review,* vol. 2 (1926): 192–207; vol. 3 (1927): 56–72.

Christaller, J. G. "Ein Reise in den Hinterländern von Togo." *Geographische Gesellschaft für Thuringen,* vol. 8 (1890): 106–133.

Cornevin, Robert. "La Dernière Période (1906–1914) de la Colonisation Allemande au Ruanda, Urundi, et Nord-Togo." *Problèmes Sociales Congolais,* vol. 83 (Dec. 1968): 3–22.

———. *Histoire de la Colonisation Allemande.* Paris: Presses Univesitaires de France, 1969.

———. "La Prise de Sansanné-Mango par l'Administrateur Pierre Duranthon, le 15 Août 1914." *France-Eurafrique,* no. 174 (June 1966): 42–44.

Crabtree, W. A. "Togoland." *African Society Journal,* vol. 14 (1915): 168–184.

Cridel, B. "Notes sur les Guerres Tribales et l'Arrivée des Allemands: d'Après le Récit de Madame Kpéso, de Lama-Kolidé." *Documents de Centre d'Etudes et de Recherches de Kara.* Piya (Togo), vol. 3 (1968): 20–22.

Czaplinski, Marek. "The German Colonial Civil Service: Image and Reality." *Africana Bulletin* (Warsaw), vol. 34 (1987): 107–119.

Darkoh, M. "Togoland Under the Germans: Thirty Years of Economic Development." *Nigerian Geographical Journal,* no. 10 (1967): 107–122; no. 11 (1968): 153–168.

Delavaud, Louis. *La Politique Coloniale de l'Allemagne.* Paris, 1887.

Deutsches Kolonial-Lexicon. 3 vols. Leipzig, 1920.

Diehn, Otto. "Kaufmannschaft und Deutsche Eingeborenenpolitik in Togo und Kamerun. Von der Jahrhundertwende bis zum Ausbruch des Weltkrieges." Thesis, Hamburg, 1956.

Epstein, K. "Erzberger and the German Colonial Scandals, 1905–1910." *English Historical Review,* vol. 74, no. 293 (1959): 637–663.

Fabri, F. *Der Deutsche-Englische Vertrag.* Köln, 1890.

"Français, Anglais et Allemands dans l'Arrière-pays du Dahomey." *Bulletin du Comité Afrique Française,* vol. 2 (1895).

France, *La Conquête du Cameroun et Togo*. Paris: Imprimerie Nationale, 1931.

François, Kurt von. "Bericht uber Seine Reise im Hinterland des Deutschen Schutzgebiets Togo." In *Mitteilungen fur Forschungreisenden und Gelehrten aus den Deutschen Schutzgebieten*. Vol. 1. Berlin: 1888. 87–9, 145–82.

———. *Ohne Schuss Durch Dick und Dünn*. Taunus, 1972.

———. "Voyage á Salaga et au Mossi." *Revue de Géographie* (Paris), no. 45 (1888).

Ganier, Geneviève. "Les Rivalités Franco-Anglaise et Franco-Allemande de 1894–98. Dernière Phase de la Course au Niger: La Mission Ganier dans le Haut Dahomey 1897–98." *Revue Française d'Historie d'Outre Mer,* vol. 49, no. 175 (1962): 181–261.

Ganslmayr, Herbert. *Gustav Nachtigal 1869–1969*. Bad Godesberg: Inter Nationes, 1969.

Gärtner, Karl. *Togo: Finanztechnische Studie über die Entwicklung des Schutzgebietes unter Deutscher Verwaltung*. Darmstadt: Erdmann Raabe, 1924.

Germany. Kolonialamst. *Deutsches Kolonialblatt Jahresbericht über die Entwickelung des Schutzgebietes Togo*. Annual.

———. ———. *Die Kolonialdeutschen aus Kamerun und Togo in Französischer Gefangenschaft*. Berlin, 1917.

———. ———. *Verhalten der Enlischen und der Unter Englischen Oberbefehl Stehenden Französischen Truppen een die Weisse Bevölkerun der Deutschen Schutzgebiete Kamerun und Togo*. Berlin, 1917.

Gifford, Prosser, and William Roger Louis, eds. *Britain and Germany in Africa: Imperial Rivalry and Colonial Rule*. New Haven: Yale University Press, 1967.

Gironcourt, G. de. "Les Conquêtes Franco-Anglaises en Afrique: Le Togo et le Cameroun." *Bulletin de la Société de Géographie et d'Etudes Coloniales de Marseilles,* vol. 40 (1917): 72–89.

Gorges, Edmund Howard. *The Great War in West Africa*. London: Hutchinson, 1930.

Goucher, Candice L. "The Impact of German Colonial Rule on the Forests of Togo." In *World Deforestation in the Twentieth Century,* edited by J. F. Richards and R. P. Tucker, 56–69. Durham, North Carolina: Duke University Press, 1988.

Grundemann, D. "Die Mission in den Deutschen Schutz Gebieten in Westafrika: Das Togo." *Deutsche Kolonialzeitung,* 1888.

"La Guerre dans les Possessions Allemandes; La Version Allemande." *Bulletin du Comité de l'Afrique Française,* 1915.

Haan, Leo de. "Die Kolonialentwicklung des Deutschen Schutzgebietes Togo in Raumlicher Perspektive." *Erkunde* (Bonn), vol. 37, no. 2 (1983): 127–37.

Haenicke, Alex, ed. *Das Buch der Deutschen Kolonien.* Leipzig: W. Goldmann, 1937.

Hassert, Kurt. *Deutschlands Kolonien.* Leipzig: Seele, 1910.

Henderson, W. O. *Studies in German Colonial History,* London: Frank Cass, 1962.

Henrici, Ernst. *Das Deutsche Togogebiet und Meine Afrikareise, 1887.* Leipzig: C. Reissner, 1888.

———. "Das Volksrecht der Epheneger und sein Verhältniss zur Deutschen Colonisation im Togogebiete." *Zeitschrift für Vergleichende Rechtswissenschaft,* vol. 11, no. 1 (1892): 131–153.

Henry, Yves. "Le Togo. Ce qu'il Vaut; Méthodes Allemandes de Colonisation." *Colonies et Marine,* vol. 2 (1918): 407–434.

Hupfeld, F. "Die Erschliessung des Kaburelandes in Nordtogo." *Globus,* vol. 77 (1990): 281–285, 305–307.

———. "Wirtschaftliche Grundlagen und Aussichten der Togokolonie." *Koloniale Monatsblätter,* vol. 15 (1913): 161–170, 236–247.

Kalous, Milan. "Some Correspondence Between the German Empire and Dahomey in 1882–1892." *Cahier d'Etudes Africaines,* no. 32 (1968): 635–641.

Klose, Heinrich. *Togo unter Deutscher Flagge.* Berlin: D. Reimer, 1899.

Knoll, Arthur J. "Togo Under German Administration 1884–1910," Ph.D. dissertation, Yale University, 1963/64.

———. *Togo Under Imperial Germany 1884–1914.* Stanford: The Hoover Institution, 1974.

Koert. "Das Kisenerzlager von Bangeli in Togo." *Mitteilungen für Forschungreisenden und Gelehrten aus den Deutschen Schutz gebieten,* vol. 14 (1906): 113–131.

Küas, Richard. *Togo—Erinnerungen.* Berlin: Vorhut-Verlag O. Shlegel, 1939.

Külz, Ludwig. *Blätter und Briefe eines Arztes aus dem Tropischen Deutschafrika.* Berlin: Süsserott, 1906.

Die Lage in Afrika: Unmittelbar vor und Nach dem Deutschen-Englischen Vertrag von Politischen Standpunkt aus Betrachtet. Dresden and Leipzig, 1890.

Langheld, Wilhelm. *Zwanzig Jahre in Deutschen Kolonien.* Berlin: Marine und Kolonial Verlag, 1909.

Lewin, Evans. *The Germans in Africa.* New York: Cassell, 1915.

Maier, Donna J. E. "Slave Labor and Wage Labor in German Africa." In *Germans in the Tropics,* edited by A. J. Knoll and L. H. Gann, 73–91. New York: Greenwood, 1987.

Markov, W., and P. Sebald. "The Treaty Between Germany and the Sultan of Gwandu." *Journal of the Historical Society of Nigeria,* vol. 4, no. 1 (1967): 141–153.

Martin, Camille. *Togo et Cameroun*. Paris: Comité de l'Afrique Française, 1916.

———. "Les Trente Années de Colonisation Allemande en Afrique (1884–1914)." *Bulletin du Comité de l'Afrique Française,* no. 1 (1915).

Metzger, O. F. *Die Forstwirtschaft im Schutzgebiet Togo*. Jena: G. Fischer, 1911.

Meyn, Matthias et al. *Der Aufban der Kolonialreiche*. Munich: Beek, 1987, 3 vol.

Moberly, Frederick James. *Military Operations: Togoland and the Cameroons*. London: H.M.S.O., 1931.

Nussbaum, Manfred. *Togo Eine Musterkolonie?* Berlin: Rutten-Loening, 1962.

Och, Helmut Wilhelm A. *Die Wirtschaftsgeographische Entwicklung der Früheren Deutschen Schutzgebiete Togo und Kamerun*. Königsberg, 1931.

Olurunfemi, A. "Trade and Politics and the German Occupation of Togoland, 1882–1884." *Africana Marburgensia,* no. 11 (1986): 48–70.

Preil, Friedrich. *Deutsch-Französische Waffenbruderschaft in Hinterlande von Togo und Dahome*. Leipzig: Ed. Engleman, 1909.

Roume, E. *Conquête des Colonies Allemandes*. Paris: Blond et Gray.

Schack, F. *Das Deutsche Kolonialrecht in seiner Entwicklung bis zum Weltkriege*. Hamburg, 1923.

Schnee, Heinrich, ed. *German Colonization, Past, Present, Future*. New York: Knopf, 1926.

Schnitt, Rochus. *West Afrika und Südsee*. Berlin, 1895.

Schramm, Percy Ernst. *Deutschland und Ubersee*. Braunschweig: Westermann, 1950.

Sebald, P. "The History of Togo and Capitalist Colonial Policy: the Treaty of July 1884." *African Studies,* 983: 155–171.

———. "Togo, 1884–1900." In *German Imperialism in Africa,* edited by H. Stoeckler, 83–93. London: C. Hurst, 1986.

———. "Togo, 1900–1914." In *German Imperialism in Africa,* edited by H. Stoeckler, 174–184. London: C. Hurst, 1986.

Simtaro, Dadja Haua-Kawa. "Le Togo 'Musterkolonie,' Souvenir de l'Allemagne dans la Société Togolaise." Thesis, University of Provence, 1982.

Soyaux, Herman. *Deutsche Arbeit in Afrika: Erfahrungen und Betrachtungen*. Leipzig, 1888.

Spieth, J. *Die Rechtsanschauungen der Togoneger und ihre Stellung zum Europäischen Gerichtswesen*. Bremen, 1908.

Steer, George Lowther. *Judgement on German Africa*. London: Hodder & Stoughton, 1939.

Taylor, A.J.P. *Germany's First Bid for Colonies*. London, 1938.

Togo und Kamerun. Eindrücke und Momentaufnahmen. Leipzig: Wilhelm Weicher, 1905.

Townsend, Mary Evelyn. *Origins of Modern German Colonialism, 1871–1885.* New York: Columbia University Press, 1921. Reprint, 1974.

―――. *The Rise and Fall of Germany's Colonial Empire.* New York: Columbia University Press, 1930.

Trierenberg, Georg (Lt.). *Togo: Die Aufrichtung der Deutschen Schutzherrschaft und die Erschliessung des Landes.* Berlin: E. S. Miller, 1914.

Vogt, August. *Westafrika in Vorkolonialer Zeit, Freuden und Leiden eines Bielefelder Kaufmannes vor 50 Jahren in Togo der Früheren Sklavenküste in den Jahren 1873–77.* Bielefeld, 1923.

Von Doering, Hans Georg. "Berlicht über eine Reise von Klein Popo nach Bismarckburg in Jahre 1893." *Mitteilungen für Forschungreisenden und Gelehrten aus den deutschen Schutzgebieten,* 1897.

Winkelmann, G. "Die Eingeborenenrechtspflege in Deutsch-Ostafrika, Kamerun und Togo unter deutscher Herrschaft." *Zeitschrift für Vergleichende Rechtswissenschaft,* vol. 53, no. 2 (1939): 189–221.

Wrigley, G. M. "The Military Campaign Against Germany's African Colonies." *Geographical Review,* vol. 5 (Jan. 1918): 44–65.

Zahn, Frederic M. *Der Westafrikanische Branntweinhandel.* Gütersloh, 1886.

Zech auf Neuhofen, Julius von. "Land und Leute an der Nordwestgrenze von Togo." *Mitteilungen für Forschungsreisenden und Gelehrten aus den deutschen Schutzgebieten,* vol. 17 (1904): 107–135.

―――. "Pays et Gens de la Frontière Nord-Ouest du Togo." *Etudes Dahoméennes,* no. 2 (1946).

―――. "Vermischte Notizen über Togo und des Togo Hinterland." *Mitteilungen für Forschungsreisenden und Gelehrten aus den deutschen Schutzgebieten,* vol. 11 (1898): 89–161.

Zimmerman, A. *Geschichte der deutschen Kolonialpolitik.* Berlin, 1914.

Zoeller, Hugo. *Die Deutschen Besitzungen an der Westafrikanischen Küste.* Berlin: W. Spemann, 1885.

―――. *Das Togoland und die Sklavenküste.* Berlin: W. Spemann, 1885.

League of Nations/United Nations Documents

"Assembly Approves Union with Gold Coast." *US State Department Bulletin,* vol. 36 (Jan. 21, 1957): 106–109.

"Council Commends Political Reforms." *UN Bulletin,* 13 (Aug. 15, 1952): 189–193.

"Efforts on Unification." *UN Bulletin,* 14 (Jan. 1, 1953): 11–20+.

France. *Agence de la France d'Outre-Mer. Cameroun et Togo sous Tutelle Française.* Rennes: Imprimerie Oberthur, 1952.

————. La Documentation Française. "L'Evolution Politique du Togo sous Tutelle Française." *Notes et Etudes Documentaires,* no. 2121 (Jan. 1956).

————. *Rapport Annuel du Gouvernement Français au Conseil de la Société des Nations sur l'Administration du Togo sous Mandat,* 1922–1938.

————. *Rapport du Gouvernement Français a l'Assemblée Générale des Nations Unies sur l'Administration du Togo placé sous la Tutelle de France.* Paris, 1947+ (annual).

————. "Le Togo sous Tutelle Britannique." *Notes et Etudes Documentaires,* no. 1760 (July 1953).

"French Togoland Gains Wider Autonomy." *UN Review,* vol. 4 (Oct. 1957): 28–31.

"French Togoland: Mission Finds Conflicting Political Views." *UN Bulletin,* 15 (June 1, 1953): 404–406.

"The Future of Togoland under French Administration: Report of the Trusteeship Council." *International Organization,* vol. 12 (1958): 162–164; vol. 13 (1959): 112–113.

Great Britain. Foreign Office. Historical Section. *Togoland,* H.M.S.O., 1920.

Luard, Evan. "The Trusteeship System." In *A History of the United Nations,* vol. 2, Evan Luard, 120–43. London: Macmillan, 1989.

"Progress in French Togoland." *UN Bulletin,* 11 (Aug. 15, 1951): 162–166.

"Report to UN—British Togoland." *International Organization,* vol. 6 (May 1952): 611; vol. 8 (May 1954): 249–251.

"Three Trust Territories Prepare for Independence." *UN Review,* vol. 6 (Sept. 1959): 19–21.

"Togo: New Effort to Solve Unification Problem." *UN Bulletin,* 12 (Jan. 15, 1952): 66–71.

"Togo: New Phase: Decision on Ewe Problem." *UN Bulletin,* 11 (Aug. 15, 1951): 177–182.

"Togoland Elections." *UN Review,* vol. 4 (April 1958): 5; vol. (June 1958): 43–45.

"Togoland: Plebiscite Soon." *UN Review,* vol. 2 (Feb. 1956): 14–25.

"Togoland under French Administration." *International Organization,* vol. 4 (1950): 469; vol. 6 (1952): 612; vol. 8 (1954): 251–252; vol. 9 (1955): 399–401; vol. 10 (1956): 446–452; vol. 11 (1957): 525–529; vol. 13 (1959): 622–623.

"Togoland under United Kingdom Administration." *International Organization,* vol. 4 (1950): 468–469; vol. 6 (1952): 611–612; vol. 8 (1954): 249–251; vol. 9 (1955): 401–402; vol. 11 (1957): 151–152.

"The Togoland Unification Problem and the Future of the Trust Territories of Togoland under United Kingdom Administration and Togoland under French Administration." *International Organization,* vol. 11 (1957): 153–155.

"The Togoland Unification Problem and the Future of the Trust Territory of Togoland under United Kingdom Administration." *International Organization,* vol. 10 (1956): 305–308.

United Kingdom. *Report by His Majesty's Government in the United Kingdom of Great Britain and Northern Ireland to the Trusteeship Council of the United Nations on the Administration of Togoland.* London, 1947–1955.

United Nations. Trusteeship Council. *The Ewe Problem: Joint Anglo-French Memorandum.* T/931, February 3, 1951.

———. ———. *"The Ewe Problem: Working Paper Prepared by the Secretariat.* T/L. 131, February 21, 1951.

———. ———. *The Future of the Trust Territory of Togoland under French Administration: Report of the Referendum Administrator on the Popular Consultation of 28 October 1956.* T/1292, December 8, 1956.

———. ———. *Report of the United Nations Commissioner for the Supervision of the Elections in Togoland under French Administration.* T/1392. June 21, 1958.

"Visiting Mission in French Togoland." *International Organization,* vol. 7 (August 1953): 400–402.

"Visiting Mission Recommends Plebiscite." *UN Review,* vol. 2 (December 1955): 33–37.

Historical

Adabra, Samuel Suka. "Les Autorités Traditionnelles et le Pouvoir Politique Moderne au Togo." Thesis, University of Paris, 1973.

Adotevi, Jon-Bosco Adovi. *Sacrilage à Mandali.* Yaoundé: Clé, 1982.

Aduayom, Messan Adimado. "Un Prélude au Nationalisme Togolais: la Révolte de Lomé." *Cahiers d'Etudes Africaines,* vol. 24, no. 1 (1984): 39–50.

Agbanon II. *Histoire de Petit Popo et du Royaume Guin.* Lomé: Haho, 1991.

Agblemagnon, Ferdinand N' Sougan. "Le Concept de Crise Appliqué a une Société Africaine: les Ewes." *Cahiers Internationaux de Sociologie,* vol. 23 (1957): 157–166.

Ahadji, A. *Relations Commerciales entre l'Allemagne et le Togo, 1680–1914.* Lomé: Université du Bénin, Institut National des Sciences de l'Education, 1984.

Ahianyo, Anani. *Histoire des Adangbé.* Lomé: Editions INRS, 1972.

Aithnard, Koukou M. *Aspects de la Politique Culturelle au Togo.* Paris, UNESCO, 1975.

————. "Transiert et Partage des Connaissances au Togo." In *Transformations Sociales et Dynamique Culturelle,* edited by P. H. Chombart de Lauwe, 121–26. Paris, CNRS, 1981.

Akakpo, Amouzouvi Maurice. "La Delimitation des Frontières Togolaises." In *Symposium Leo Frobenius,* 92–109. Cologne, UNESCO, 1980.

————. *Les Frontières Togolaises a Propos de l'Delimitation de 1927–1929.* Lomé: Université du Bénin, 1974.

————. "La Naissance du Togo." *Africa Zamani* (Yaoundé), no. 8/9 (Dec. 1978): 113–132.

————. "Le Togo de 1919 a 1929." *Annales de l'Ecole des Lettres* (Lomé), vol. 1 (1972): 57–66.

Akinjogbin, I. A. *Dahomey and Its Neighbors 1708–1818.* Cambridge, England: Cambridge University Press, 1967.

Aligwekwe, Iwuoha Edozie. "The Ewe and Togoland Problem: A Case Study in the Paradoxes and Problems of Political Transition in West Africa." Ph.D. Thesis, Ohio State University, 1960–61.

Almeida, Silivi Kokoe d', and Seti Y. G. Gbedemah. *Le Gouverneur Bonnecarrère au Togo.* Abidjan: Les Nouvelles Editions Africaines, 1982.

Almeida-Topor, Helene d'. "Les Populations Dahoméennes et le Recrutement Militaire Pendant la Première Guerre Mondiale." *Revue Française d'Histoire d'Outre-Mer,* vol. 60, no. 219 (1973): 196–241.

Amenumey, D.E.K. *The Ewe in Pre-Colonial Times: a Political History with Special Emphasis on the Anlo, Ge, and Krepi.* Accra: Sedco, 1986.

————. "The Ewe People and the Coming of European Rule 1850–1914." Thesis, London University, 1964.

————. *The Ewe Unification Movement. A Political History.* Legon (Ghana): Ghana University Press, 1990.

————. "The Extension of British Rule to Anlo (Southeast Ghana) 1850–1890." *Journal of African History,* vol. 9, no. 1 (1968): 99–117.

————. "The 1956 Plebiscite in Togoland under British Administration and Ewe Unification." *Universitas* (Accra), vol. 5, no. 2 (1976): 126–139.

————. "The Pre-1947 Background to the Ewe Unification Question." *Transactions of the Historical Society of Ghana,* vol. 10, (1969). 65–85.

Angoulvant, G. "Le Togo: Resultats, Acquis et Perspective d'Avenir." *Colonies et Marine,* vol. 4 (1920): 663–688.

Asare, Theodore O. *The Case for a Reunited Togoland.* New York, 1953.

Attignon, Hermann. "Lomé." *Revue Française d'Etudes Politiques Africaines,* no. 81 (1972): 49–57.

————. "Le Togo de Congrès de Berlin à la Conference de Brazzaville." *Revue Française d'Etudes Politiques Africaines,* no. 82 (Oct. 1972): 28–58.

Ayaché, Georges. *Si la Maison de Votre Voisin Brule.* Paris: Editions ABC, 1983.

Barbier, J. C. "L'Histoire Vécue. Sokodé, 1914: Les Allemands Evacuent le Nord-Togo." *Revue Française d'Histoire d'Outre-Mer,* vol. 75, no. 278 (1988): 79–88.

Barros, Philip de. "L'Archéologie et Préhistoire Togolaise." *Etudes Togolaises,* no. 23/26 (1983): 1–13.

Bening, R. Bugalo. "The Ghana-Togo Boundary." *Africa-Spectrum,* vol. 18, no. 2 (1983): 191–209.

Bergfeld, Ewald. *Die Franzosischen Mandatsgebiete Kamerun und Togo.* Griefswald: H. Adler, 1935.

Besson, Maurice. "Nos Deux 'Colonies à Mandat,' le Togo et le Cameroun." *Action Nationale,* vol. 12 (July 1920): 124–133.

Biarnes, P. *Les Français en Afrique Noire de Richelieu à Mitterand.* Paris: Armand Colin, 1987.

Bocco Yao, E. "Peuples et Nationalisme, les Partis Ewe et l'Eglise Evangélique du Togo." Thesis, University of Poitiers, 1982.

Bourret, Florence M. *The Gold Coast: A Survey of the Gold Coast and British Togoland, 1919–1951.* London: Oxford University Press, 1952.

————. "The Gold Coast and the British Mandate of Togoland, 1919–1939." Ph.D. Thesis, Stanford University, 1947.

Brieux, Jean-Jacques. "L'Affaire Ewe: Un Exemple du Role de l'ONU dans le Processus de Decolonisation." *Revue Française d'Etudes Politiques Africaines,* no. 21 (Sept. 1967): 102–121.

Brown, D. "Anglo-German Rivalry and Krepi Politics 1886–94." *Transactions of the Historical Society of Ghana,* vol. 15, no. 2 (1974).

Calvert, Albert Frederick. *Togoland.* London: T.W. Laurie, 1918.

Cameroun-Togo. Vol. 5 of *Encyclopedie de l'Afrique Française.* Paris: Editions de l'Union Française, 1951.

Chapman, D. A. *The Anlo Constitution: The Framework of the Constitution.* Achimota, Ghana: Achimota Press, 1944.

Chazelas, Victor. *Les Territoires Africains sous Mandat de la France: Cameroun et Togo.* Paris: Société d'Editions Geographiques, Maritimes et Coloniales, 1931.

Chudeau, R. "La Nouvelle Situation des Colonies Françaises Africaines Togo-Cameroun." *Geographie,* vol. 33, no. 2 (1920): 193–218.

Cohen, William B. *Rulers of Empire: The French Colonial Service in Africa.* Stanford, California: Hoover Institution Press, 1971.

Coleman, James S. *Togoland.* New York: Carnegie Endowment for International Peace, 1956.

Commissariat de la Republique Française au Togo. *Guide de la Colonisation au Togo*. Paris: Larose, 1924.

Cooke, James J. *New French Imperialism, 1880–1910*. Hamden, Connecticut: Archon Books, 1973.

Cornevin, Robert. "Evolution dans le Nord du Togo." *Sociologie,* vol. 4, no. 1 (1954): 59–66.

———. *Histoire du Togo*. Paris: Berger-Levrault, 1969.

———. "La Tension Franco-Anglaise durant la Deuxième Guerre Mondiale et la Naissance de la Question Évhé." *France-Eurafrique,* no. 170 (Feb. 1966): 35–40.

———. *Le Togo*. Paris: Presses Universitaires de France, 1973.

———. *Le Togo: des Origines à Nos Jours*. Paris: Académie des Sciences d'Outre-Mer, 1988.

———. *Le Togo, Nation-Pilote*. Paris: Nouvelles Editions Latines, 1963.

———. "Le Togo, 20e Anniversaire." *Afrique Contemporaine,* no. 142 (1987): 41–60.

Cowan, L. Gray. *Local Government in West Africa*. New York: Columbia University Press, 1958.

Crowder, Michael. *West Africa under Colonial Rule*. Evanston, Illinois: Northwestern University Press, 1968.

D'Arboussier, Henri. "La Conquete du Togoland: l'Action des Partisans Mossi." *Bulletin du Comité de l'Afrique Française,* vol. 25 (1915): 49–55.

Davies, Oliver. *The Old Stone Age Between the Volta and the Niger*. Dakar: Bulletin de l'IFAN, 1957.

Davis, Shelby Cullom. *Reservoirs of Men: A History of the Black Troops of French West Africa*. Westport, Connecticut: Negro Universities Press, 1970.

De Beauchene, Guy. "Prehistory and Archeology in Niger, Togo, Upper Volta, Dahomey and Ivory Coast." *West African Archeological Newsletter,* (Nov. 5, 1966): 6–8.

Deloncle, Pierre. *L'Afrique Occidentale Française: Decouverte, Pacification, Mise en Valeur*. Paris: Ernest Leroux, 1934.

Deval, Raymond. *Les Musulmans au Togo*. Paris: Academie des Sciences d'Outre Mer, 1981.

De Souza, Norberto Francisco. "Contribution à l'Histoire de la Famille de Souza." *Etudes Dahoméennes,* no. 13 (1955): 15–22.

Diel, Louise. *Die Kolonien Worten: Afrika im Umbruch*. Leipzig: P. List, 1939.

Dotsé, Theophile. "Dossier d'un Circonscription: Anécho." *Espoir de la Nation Togolaise,* no. 13 (May–June 1971): 10–15.

———, and Pierre Kamkpor, "Dossier d'un Circonscription: Kluoto." *Espoir de la Nation Togolaise,* no. 5–6 (April–May 1970): 11–19.

Ferjus, Samuel. "Le Mise en Valeur du Togo sous le Mandat Français." Ph.D. Thesis, University of Paris, 1976.

Fol, Jean Jacques. "Le Togo Pendant la Deuxième Guerre Mondiale." *Revue d'Histoire de la Deuxième Guerre Mondiale* (Paris), vol. 29, no. 115 (1979): 69–77.

Foltz, William Jay. *From French West Africa to the Mali Federation.* New Haven, Connecticut: Yale University Press, 1965.

François, Louis, and R. Mangin. *La France et les Territoires d'Outre-Mer.* Paris: Hachette, 1959.

Froelich, Jean Claude. *Cameroun-Togo: Territoires sous Tutelle.* Paris: Berger-Levrault, 1956.

Fuglestad, Finn. "Quelques Refléxions sur l'Histoire et les Institutions de l'Ancien Royaume du Dahomey et de ses Voisins." *Bulletin de l'IFAN,* vol. 39, no. 3 (July 1977): 493–517.

Full, August, *Funfzig Jahre Togo.* Berlin: D. Reimer, 1935.

Gayibor, Nicoué Lodjou. "Agokoli et la Dispersion de Notsé." In *Peuples du Golfe du Benin,* edited by François de Medeiros, 21–34. Paris: Karthala, 1984.

———. Ecologie et Histoire: les Origines de la Savane du Bénin." *Cahiers d'Etudes Africaines,* vol. 26, no. 1/2 (1986): 13–41.

———. "Elements de Polémologie en Pays Ewe." *Cultures et Developpement,* vol. 16, no. 3/4 (1984): 511–36.

———. *Foli Bébé ou l'Epopèe des Ga du Togo.* Dakar: NEA, 1983.

———. "Le Remodelage des Traditions Historiques: la Légende d'Agokoli, Roi de Notsé." In *Sources Orales de l'Histoire de l'Afrique,* edited by Claude-Hélène Perrot, 209–214. Paris: CNRS, 1989.

Gifford, Prosser, and William R. Louis. *France and Britain in Africa: Imperial Rivalry and Colonial Rule.* New Haven, Connecticut: Yale University Press, 1971.

Goody, Jack, and T. M. Mustapha "The Caravan Trade from Kano to Salaga." *Journal of the Historical Society of Nigeria,* vol. 3, no. 4 (June 1967): 611–616.

Goucher, Candice Lee. "The Iron Industry of Bassar, Togo," Ph.D. Thesis, Los Angeles: University of California, 1984.

Greene, Sandra. "Social Change in Eighteenth Century Anlo: the Role of Technology, Markets and Military Conflict." *Africa,* vol. 58 no. 1 (1988): 70–86.

Grove, Eric J. "The First Shots of the Great War: The Anglo-French Conquest of Togo, 1914." *Army Quarterly and Defence Journal* (London), vol. 106, no. 3 (1976): 308–323.

Grove, Jean M., and A. M. Johansen, "The Historical Geography of the Volta Delta During the Period of Danish Influence." *Bulletin d'lFAN,* vol. 30, no. 4 (Oct. 1968): 1374–1421.

Gu-Konu, E. Yema. "Une Pratique Foncière dans le Sud-Ouest du Togo." In *Espaces Disputés en Afrique Noire,* 174–189. Paris: Karthala, 1984.

Guernier Eugene, and Rene Briat, eds. *Cameroun-Togo.* Paris: Editions de l'Union Française, 1951.

Hodder, B. W. "The Ewe Problems, a Reassessment." In *Essays in Political Geography,* edited by C. A. Fisher, 271–283. London: Methuen, 1968.

Horner, George R. "Togo and Cameroons," *Current History,* vol. 34, no. 198 (Feb. 1958): 84–90.

Ita, J. M. "Frobenius in West African History." *Journal of African History,* vol. 13, no. 4 (1972): 673–688.

Kea, R. A. "Akwamu-Anlo Relations, c. 1750–1813." *Transactions of the Historical Society of Ghana,* vol. 10, (1969): 29–63.

Kratz, Achim. "Le Togo au Debut de Notre Siècle." *Revue Française d'Etudes Politiques Africaines,* no. 211–2 (Aug.–Sept. 1983): 144–165; no. 213–4 (Oct.–Nov. 1983): 125–142.

Kuevi, Dovi André. *Contribution a l'Histoire de Peuplement: Tradition, Histoire et Organisation de la Cité Chez les Akposso.* Lomé: INRS, 1972.

Kuevidjen, Ignace. "Le Problème de l'Internationalisation des Colonies et le Gestion de la France au Togo sous Tutelle Française." Thesis, University of Montpellier, 1953.

Kwakoumé, Henry. *Precis d'Histoire du Peuple Ewe.* Lomé: Mission Catholique, 1948.

Labouret, H., and P. River. *Le Royaume d'Ardra et Son Evangélisation au XVII Siècle.* Paris: Institut d'Ethnologie, 1929.

Laigret, Christian. "Ou en est le Togo sous le Mandat Français?" *Renseignements Coloniaux et Documents,* (April 1930): 213–226.

Luce, Edmond Pierre. *Le Referendum du Togo (28 Octobre 1956); L'Acte de Naissance d'une République Africaine Autonome.* Paris: Pedone, 1958.

Luchaire, François. "Le Togo Français de la Tutelle à l'Autonomie." *Revue Juridique et Politique de l'Union Française,* vol. 20, no. 1, (Jan.–Mar. 1957): 1–46; vol. 20, no. 3 (July–Sept. 1957): 501–587.

Martin, Gaston. *Histoire de l'Esclavage dans les Colonies Françaises.* Paris: Presses Universitaires de France, 1948.

Martonne, E. de. "La Delimitation du Togo 1927–1929." *Renseignements Coloniaux et Documents,* 1930: 136–151.

Maunry, R. "Etat Actuel de Nos Connaissances sur la Prehistoire du Dahomey et du Togo." *Etudes Dahoméennes,* no. 6 (1950): 5–11.

Medeiros, François de, ed. *Peuples du Golfe du Bénin.* Paris: Karthala, 1984.

Merle, Marcel. "Les Plebiscites Organisés par les Nations Unies." *Annuaire Français de Droit International,* 1961: 425–45.

Messavussu-Akué, Adokué. *Aperçu Historique du Togo*. Lomé: Imprimerie ATP, 1978.

Michel, Marc. "The Independence of Togo." In *Decolonization and African Independence*. edited by Gifford Prosser and William Roger Louis. New Haven, Connecticut: Yale University Press, 1988.

———. "Les Recrutements de Tirailleurs en AOF Pendant la Premiere Guerre Mondiale." *Revue Française d'Histoire d'Outre Mer*. vol. 60, no. 221 (1973): 644–660.

Moncharville, M. "L'Execution du Mandat au Togo et au Cameroun." *Revue Generale de Droit International Public,* vol. 2, no. 7 (1925): 58–78.

Mortimer, Edward. *France and the Africans 1944–1960*. London: Faber & Faber, 1969.

Newbury, Colin W. *The Western Slave Coast and Its Rulers: European Trade and Administration Among the Yoruba and Adja Speaking Peoples of Southwestern Nigeria, Southern Dahomey and Togo*. Oxford: Clarendon Press, 1961.

Paulin, Honore. *Cameroun-Togo*. Paris: L. Eyrolle, 1923.

Pauvert, Jean-Claude. "L'Evolution Politique des Ewe." *Cahiers d'Etudes Africaines,* no. 2 (May 1960): 161–192.

Pazzi, Roberto. "Aperçu sur l'Implantation Actuelle et les Migrations Anciennes des Peuples de l'Aire Culturelle Aja-Tado." In *Peuples du Golfe du Bénin,* edited by François de Medeiros, 11–21. Paris: Karthala, 1984.

Pechoux, Laurent. *Le Mandat Français sur le Togo*. Paris: Pedone, 1939.

Peppy, D. "La Republique Autonome du Togo Devant les Nations Unies." *Politique Etrangère,* vol. 22, no. 6 (1958): 671–690.

Person, Yves. "Les Grandes Compagnies Zarma au Dahomey et au Togo, 1875–1898: Regions de Djougou et de Sokodé." *Le Mois en Afrique,* vol. 16 (1982): 136–59; vol. 17 (1983): 127–44.

Pic, Joseph. "Justice Repressive Indigene au Togo." Thesis, University of Bourdeaux, 1936.

Quashie, Adjo M., and Ahloko M. Komlan. *Precis d'Histoire de l'Enseignement au Togo des Origines à 1975*. Lomé: University of Bénin, 1986.

Reclus, Elisee. *Cote des Esclaves*. Paris: Hachette et Cie., 1887.

Rouard le Card, Edgar. *Les Mandats Français sur Togoland et le Cameroun: Etude Juridique*. Paris: A. Pedone, 1924.

Ryder, Alan F. C. *Benin and the Europeans, 1485–1897*. London: Longmans, 1969.

Santos, Anani. *L'Option des Indigenes en Faveur de l'Application de la Loi Française (en AOF et au Togo)*. Paris: Maurice Lavergne, 1943.

Schwanold. "Prahistoriches aus Togo." *Zeitschrift fur Ethnologie,* vol. 35 (1913): 969–973.

Silla, Ousmane. "L'Afro-Bresilien dans sa Nation." *Bulletin d'IFAN.* vol. 31, no. 2 (April 1969): 531–573.

Simtaro, Dadja Halla-Kawa. "Le Togo 'Musterkolonie,' Souvenir de l'Allemagne dans la Société Togolaise." Thesis, University of Provence, 1982.

Spitz, Georges. *L'Ouest Afrique Français: A.O.F. et Togo.* Paris: Société d'Editions Géographiques, Maritimes et Coloniales, 1947.

Staudinger, Paul. "Uber Bronzeguss in Togo." *Zeitschrift fur Ethnologie,* vol. 41 (1909): 855–862.

Suret-Canale, Jean. *The Colonial Era in French West and Central Africa.* London: C. Hurst, 1970.

Toutée, R. *Du Dahomé au Sahara.* Paris: Armand Colin, 1899.

Verger, Pierre. "Les Cotes d'Afrique Occidentale entre Rio Volta et Rio Lagos (1535–1773)." *Journal de la Société des Africanistes,* vol. 38, no. 19 (1968): 35–58.

———. *Flux et Reflux de la Traite des Negres entre le Golfe du Bénin et Bahia de Todos los Santos du 17e au 19e Siécle.* Paris: Mouton, 1968.

———. "Retour des 'Bresiliens' au Golfe du Bénin au XlXe Siécle." *Etudes Dahoméennes,* no. 8 (Oct. 1966): 5–28.

Videgla, Michel W. "Quelques Aspects des Frontières Coloniales en Pays Aja, Ewé et Yoruba." In *Peuples du Golfe de Bénin,* edited by François de Medeiros, 103–26. Paris: Karthala, 1984.

Vignes, K. "Etude sur la Rivalité d'Influence entre les Puissances Européenes en Afrique Equatorial et Occidentale Depuis l'Acte General de Berlin Jusqu'au Seuil du XXe Siécle." *Revue Française d'Histoire d'Outre-Mer,* vol. 48, no. 1, (1961): 5–95.

Voule, Marcel Fritz. *Les Origines de l'Administration Publique Togolaise.* Lomé: INRS, 1969.

Welch, Claude E. "The Birth and Growth of Ewe Nationalism" and "Conflict over Self-Determination in Togoland." In *Dream of Unity, Pan Africanism and Political Unification in West Africa,* Claude E. Welch, 37–147. Ithaca, N.Y.: Cornell University Press, 1966.

Wilson, S. "Aperçu Historique sur les Peuples et Cultures dans le Golfe du Bénin: le Cas des 'Mina' d'Anécho." In *Peuples du Golfe du Bénin,* edited by François de Medeiros, 127–150. Paris: Karthala, 1984.

Wyllie, R. W. "Kponie and the Tado Stool: a Problem in the Interpretation of the Anlo Migration Tradition." *Anthropos,* vol. 72, no. 1/2 (1977): 119–128.

Zoeller, Hugo. *Le Togo en 1884.* Lomé: Editions HaHo, 1990.

Anthropology/Sociology

Abi, Kao. "Les Attitudes des Togolais à l'Egard de la Polygynie." Ph.D. Thesis, University of Bordeaux, 1988.

Acouetey, Theodore. "Unité ou Dualité de Statuts dans le Droit de la Famille au Togo." *Revue Juridique et Politique,* no. 1 (Jan.–Mar., 1967): 34–47.

Adabra, Samuel S. "Les Autorités Traditionnelles et le Pouvoir Politique Moderne au Togo." Ph.D. Thesis, Sorbonne University, 1973.

Adjéodah, Onuh S. "Pensée Togolaise." *Etudes Togolaises,* no. 27/30 (1984/85): 1–18.

Agbekponou, Kouèvi. "La Vocation Héreditaire de la Femme dans le Droit Positif Togolais des Successions." *Penant,* no. 798 (Oct.–Dec. 1988): 424–32.

Agbetiafa, Komla. *Les Ancétres et Nous: Analyse de la Pensée Religieuse des Bé de la Commune de Lomé.* Dakar: Les Nouvelles Editions Africaines, 1985.

Agblemagnon, Ferdinand N'Sougan. "Personne, Tradition et Culture en Afrique Noire." *Recherches et Debats de Centre Catholique des Intellectuels Français,* vol. 24 (Sept. 1958): 22–30.

———. "Research on Attitudes Toward the Togolese Women." *International Social Science Journal,* vol. 14, no. 1 (1962): 148–56.

———. *Sociologie des Sociétes Orales d'Afrique Noire: Les Eve du Sud-Togo.* Paris: Mouton, 1969.

Agier, M., and T. Lulle, "Elements d'Anthropologie des Lieux de Travail." *Anthropologie et Sociétés,* vol. 10, no. 1 (1986): 109–43.

Ahianyo-Akakpo, Anani. "L'Impact de la Migration sur la Sociale Villageoise: Approche Sociologique, Exemple Togo-Ghana." In *Modern Migrations in Western Africa,* edited by Samir Amin, 156–59. Oxford: Oxford University Press, 1974.

———. "Kososo: Une Forme de Mariage Traditionnel?" *Etudes Togolaises,* no. 1. (Jan.–Mar. 1971): 75–85.

Ahyi, Paul. "Die Schwigende Welt der Togoleischen Kunst und das Motiv der Schildkrote." *Afrika,* April 1960: 157–160.

———. "Sculptures en bois du Togo de 1894 à 1900." *Entente Africaine,* Nov. 1969: 66–67.

Aithnard, Kokou. "Transfert et Partage des Connaissances au Togo." In *Transformation Sociales et Dynamique Culturelle,* edited by P. H. Chombart de Lauwe, 121–126. Paris: CNRS, 1981.

Ajavon, Pierre-Lawoetry. "Un Certain Conception de la Mort Chez les Ge-Mina du Sud-Est Togo." *Anthropos,* vol. 85, no. 1/3 (1990): 182–87.

———."La Mort Chez les Guins du Sud Togo." Ph.D. Thesis, University of Bordeaux, 1980.

Akpakossi, Yawo. "Un Etudiant Togolais Enquete dans son Village." *Herodote* (Paris), vol. 9 (Jan.–Mar. 1978): 123–131.

Albenque, Alexandre, et al. "Cartes du Terroir d'Etyolo, Village Bassari." *Cahiers du Centre de Recherche Anthropologique,* vol. 3 (1965): 45–74.

Alexandre, Pierre. "Le Facteur Islamique dans l'Histoire d'un Etat du Moyen-Togo [Kotokoli]." *L'Afrique et l'Asie,* no. 65 (1964): 26–30.

———. "Organisation Politique des Kotokoli du Nord-Togo." *Cahiers d'Etudes Africaines,* vol. 14, nos. 2, 4 (1963): 228–274.

———. "The Political Institutions of the Kotokoli, a Tribe of Northern Togo." Thesis, University of London, 1959.

Amenumey, D.E.K. "Some Aspects of Ewe Machinery of Government with Special Reference to the Anlo Political System." *Ghana Journal of Sociology,* vol. 4, no. 2 (Oct. 1968): 100–108.

Antheume, Benoit. *Agbetiko, Terroir de la Basse Vallée de Mono.* Paris: ORSTOM, 1978.

———. "Centre Bloqué, Periphérie Liberée: le Terroir et Ses Marges. L'Exemple de Bena, Plateau Akposso, Centre-Ouest du Togo." In *Le Développement Rural en Question. Paysages, Espaces Ruraux, Systemes Agraires,* edited by C. Blanc-Bamard et al. Paris: ORSTOM, 1984.

———. "Des Hommes à la Rencontre des Arbres." *Cahiers d'ORSTOM,* vol. 18, no. 1 (1981–82). 47–62.

Antoine, Philippe, and Sidiki Coulbaly. *L'Insertion Urbaine des Migrants en Afrique.* Paris: ORSTOM, 1989.

Aperçu des Résultats d'Ensemble du Recensement Général de la Population et de l'Habitat au Togo de Novembre 1981. Lomé: Direction de la Statistique, 1981.

Armand, R. "Ethnologie des Differentes Races du Cercle de Sokodé." Lomé: Archives du Bureau des Affaires Politiques de Togo, 1930.

Armattoe, Raphael E. G. "Epe-Ekpe." *African Affairs,* 1951: 326–331.

Asmis, Rudolf. "Die Stammesrechte der Bezirke Misahohe, Anecho und Lomeland (Schutzgebiet-Togo)." *Zeitschrift fur Vergleichende Rechtswissenschaft,* vol. 26 (1911): 1–133.

———. "Die Stammesrechte des Bezirkes Atakpame (Schutzgebiet Togo)." *Zeitschrift fur Vergleichende Rechtswissenschaft,* vol. 25 (1910): 67–130.

———. "Die Stammesrechte des Bezirkes Sansane Mangu." *Zeitschrift fur Vergleichende Rechtswissenschaft.* vol. 27 (1912).

Assogba, M. L. "Perspectives de la Population Togolaise 1971–2006." Lomé: Unite de Recherche Démographique, 1984.

Attignon, Hermann. "Foundation du Village d'Agu-Nyogbo: Origine Evhé des Aguawo." *Documents de Centre d'Etudes et de Recherches de Kara* (Piya, Togo), vol. 3 (1968): 1–17.

———. "Lomé." *Revue Française d'Etudes Politiques Africaines,* no. 81, (Sept. 1972): 49–57.

Augé, M. "L'Anthropologie de la Maladie." *L'Homme,* vol. 26, no. 1–2 (1986): 81–87.

Ayissi, Theo Ahaligah Komi. *Medicine et 'Remedies Miracles' des Plantes de Chez Nous.* Lomé: Ayissi, 1989, 2 vol.

Barbier, J. C. "Les Lotissements et Leur Destin: l'Example de Sokodé au Togo." In *Actes du Colloque Internationale Stratégiques Urbaines dans les Pays en Voie de Développement,* edited by N. Haumont and A. Marie. Paris: Harmattan, 1987.

———. "Sokodé: un Plan d'Urbanisme Contesté." *Cités Africaines,* no. 2 (1985): 7–12.

Barros, Philip de. "Bassar: a Quantified, Chronologically Controlled Regional Approach to a Traditional Iron Production Center in West Africa." *Africa,* vol. 56. no. 2 (1986): 148–74.

———. "The Bassar: Large Scale Iron-Producers of the West African Savanna." Ph.D. Thesis, University of California, Los Angeles, 1985.

———. "Societal Repercussions of the Rise of Large-Scale Traditional Iron Production." *African Archeological Review,* vol. 6 (1988): 91–113.

Benoit, D., et al. "Structures des Ménages Dans les Populations Rurales du Sud-Togo." *Cahiers ORSTOM,* vol. 19, no. 3 (1983): 321–34.

Bernolles, Jacques. "Note Sur le Cycle Vegetatif et Humain des Danses en Pays Dompago." *Etudes Dahoméennes,* no. 3 (1964): 91–105.

Bertho, Jacques. "Le Gbadou Chez les Adja du Togo et du Dahomey." *Première Conference Internationale des Africanistes de l'Ouest; Comptes Rendus,* vol. 2 (1951): 331–350.

———. "La Parenté des Yoruba aux Peuplades de Dahomey et Togo." *Africa,* vol. 19, no. 2 (April 1949): 121–132.

———. "Races et Langues du Bas Dahomey et du Bas Togo." *Bulletin d'IFAN,* vol. 13, no. 4 (Oct. 1951): 1265–1271.

"Bibliographie Tchokossi." *Documents de Centre d'Etudes et de Recherches de Kara.* Lama Kara: 1968.

Binet, J. "Le Droit Foncier des Ewes de Tsévié." *Cahiers de l'Institut de Science Economique Appliquée,* Serie V, vol. 9, no. 166 (Oct. 1965): 101–118.

———. "Le Droit Successoral chez les Ewes." In *Etudes de Droit Africain et de Droit Malgache,* edited by Jean Poirier, 307–315. Paris: Cujas, 1965.

———. "Note sur le Droit Successoral Chez les Ewes de Tsévié." *Penant,* vol. 76, no. 710 (Jan.–Mar. 1966): 127–131.

Blier, S. "The Dance of Death: Notes on the Architecture and Staging of Tamberma Funeral Performances." *Anthropology and Aesthetics,* vol. 2 (1981): 107–43.

Boremanse, Didier. "The Tamberma of Togo." *Geographical Magazine,* vol. 51, no. 3 (1978): 196–200.

Brand, Roger-Bernard. "Les Hommes et les Plantes." *Genève-Afrique,* vol. 15, no. 1 (1976).

Breitkopf, P. E. "Beitrage zur Ethnographie der Kpando-Leute." *Anthropos,* vol. 22, no. 3/4 (May–Aug. 1927): 477–506.

Bris, Emil Le. *Les Marchés Ruraux dans la Circonscription de Vo*. Paris: Editions de l'ORSTOM, 1984.

―――. "Migration and the Decline of a Densely Populated Rural Area: the Case of Vo Koutime in South-East Togo." *African Perspectives* (Leiden), vol. 1 (1978): 109–23.

―――. "Suppression Démographique et Evolution Foncière: le Cas du Sud-Est du Togo." *African Perspectives* (Leiden), vol. 2 (1979): 109–23.

Brydon, Lynne. "Rice, Yams and Chiefs in Avatime." *Africa,* vol. 51, no. 2 (1981): 659–677.

Bunle, Henri. "Note sur la Démographie de la Population au Togo." *Metron,* vol. 10 (1932): 133–151.

Cardinall, Allan Wolsey. *Tales Told in Togoland to Which Is Added the Mythical and Traditional History by E. F. Tamakloe.* London: Oxford University Press, 1931.

Cartry, M. "La Calebasse de l'Excision en Pays Gourmantché." *Journal de la Société des Africanistes,* vol. 38, no. 2 (1968): 189–225.

Chardley, Francis. "Résurrection d'un Mort et Apparitions de Morts Chez les Ewe." *Anthropos,* vol. 46, no. 5/6 (Sept.–Dec. 1951): 1005–1006.

Cheneveau, R. "Pièrre de Tonnerre du pays Mina." *Notes Africaines,* no. 77 (Jan. 1958).

Christaller, Johann G. "Die Adelesprache in Togogebeit." *Zeitschrift fur Afrikanischen und Ozeanischen Sprachen,* vol. 1 (1895): 16–33.

Comhaire-Sylvain, Suzanne. *Femmes de Lomé.* Bandundu (Zaire): CEEBA, 1982.

Connen, Bernard. "Un Code de la Famille au Togo." *Penant,* no. 774 (Oct.–Dec. 1981): 5–22.

Contran, Nazareno P. *La Morte è una Cosa Antica.* Afanya (Togo): 1975.

―――. *Zobada il Fuoco Cattivo: Canti Populari del Togo Meridionale.* Afanya (Togo): 1975.

Cordonnier, Rita. *Femmes Africaines et Commerce: les Revendeuses de Tissu de la Ville de Lomé.* Paris: ORSTOM, 1982.

Cornevin, Robert. "A Propos des Cotokoli du Moyen-Togo." *Notes Africaines d'IFAN,* vol. 101 (Jan. 1964): 7–11.

―――. "A Propos des Masques de Laiton du Nord-Togo." *Notes Africaines d'IFAN,* vol. 101 (Jan. 1964): 12–18.

―――. "Avec le Lieutenant Plehn à la Recherche d'un Cercle du Moyen-Togo." *Etudes Dahoméennes,* no. 4 (1962): 43–60.

―――. *Les Bassari du Nord Togo.* Paris: Berger-Levrault, 1962.

―――. "Le Centre Urbain de Bassari." *Bulletin de l'IFAN,* 1957: 81–84.

―――. "Connaissance des Kabré Depuis Frobenius." *Monde non Chretien,* vol. 59/60 (July–Dec. 1961): 95–99.

————. "Contribution à l'Etude des Populations Parlant des Langues Gouang au Togo et au Dahomey." *Journal of African Languages,* vol. 3, no. 3 (1964): 226–230.

————. "Contribution à l'Histoire de la Chefferie Cotokoli." *Cahiers d'Etudes Africaines,* vol. 4, no. 3 (15) (1964): 456–460.

————. "Dynasties Tyokossi de Sansanné-Mango." *Annales de l'Ecole des Lettres* (Lomé), vol. 1 (1972): 9–24.

————. "Kilir, Logba and Lamba." *Journal of African History,* vol. 6 (1965): 23–27.

————. "Note à Propos du Canton de Kpessi." *Bulletin de l'Enseignement Supérieur du Bénin,* vol. 8 (Jan. 1969): 11–20.

————. "Note sur la Toponymie des Villages Konkomba de la Circonscription de Bassari." *Bulletin d'IFAN,* vol. 26, vol. 3/4 (July–Oct. 1964): 694–708.

————. "Notes sur le Cercle de Dapango (République du Togo), et l'Histoire de Ses Habitants." *Monde non Chrétien,* vol. 67 (July–Sept. 1963): 168–186.

————. "Structures Agraires et Systèmes de Culture en Pays Kabré." *Documents de Centre d'Etudes et de Recherches de Kara,* Piya (Togo), 1967: 37–48.

————. "Totemisme, Liens Communautaires et Coutumes Chez Quelques Groupes Ethniques, Togolais." *Etudes Dahoméennes,* no. 17 (1964): 9–34.

————, and B. Cridel. "Cuillette, Chasse, Peche et Alimentation en pays Kabré." *Documents de Centre d'Etudes et de Recherches de Kara,* Piya (Togo), 1968: 62–74.

————, and R. Verdier. "Etudes sur le Mariage Kabré." *Documents de Centre d'Etudes et de Recherches de Kara,* Piya (Togo), 1967: 61–111.

Crapuchet, S. "Femmes Villageoises de la Région des Plateaux." *Le Mois en Afrique.* no. 196/7 (March–April 1982): 79–80, 97–112.

Dadadzi, Veronique. "La Femme en Droit Coutumier Togolais, Son Role en Tant qu'epouse et Mère." *Revue Juridique et Politique,* Oct.–Dec. 1974: 801–807.

————. "La Femme Epouse et la Femme Mère au Togo." *Revue Juridique et Politique,* no. 4 (Oct.–Dec. 1974): 810–817.

"Dans Lomé, Ville Chrysalide." *Europe-France Outremer,* no. 502, (Nov. 1971): 17–20.

Daveau, S. "Activités et Structure Sociale de Palimé, Petite Ville du Togo." *Annales de Geographie,* no. 372 (Mar.–April 1960): 218–220.

Debrunner, Hans W. "Die Bowiri: Volkwerdung und Selbstbehauptung Eines Togo-Restvolkes." *Anthropos,* vol. 59, no 3/4 (1964): 597–633.

————. *Le Kabiyé.* Lomé: Institut de la Recherche Scientifique, 1976.

————. "Notes sur les Peuples Témoins du Togo: A Propos de Sites Montagneux Abandonnés." *Bulletin de l'Enseignement Supérieur du Bénin* (Lomé) no. 11: 54–79.

Delord, J. "L'Initiation des Kondona en Pays Cabrais," *Notes Africaines.* no. 39 (1948): 27–32.

Deniel, Raymond. *Femmes des Villes Africaines.* Abidjan: Inades, 1985.

Dipere, Fogote. "Le Nouveau Droit du Mariage au Togo." Ph.D. Thesis, University of Lille, 1989.

Djimangar, N. M. "Un Terroir Kabyé: Mandèla Nord Togo." Thesis, University of Benin, 1984.

Djobo, B. "La Dot Chez les Kotokoli de Sokodé." *Penant,* vol. 72, no. 693 (Sept.–Oct. 1962): 546–556.

Dresch, J. "Paysans Montagnards du Dahomey et du Cameroun: Les Vrais Paysans Noirs." *Bulletin de l'Association des Geographes Français,* nos. 222–223 (Jan.–Feb. 1952): 1–9.

Ducat, Marc. "La Reforme Foncière Togolaise." *Penant,* no. 749 (July–Sept. 1975): 291–308.

Dugast, Stéphan. "Déterminations Economiques Vesus Fondements Symboliques: la Chefferie de Bassar." *Cahiers d'Etudes Africaines,* vol. 28, no. 2 (1988): 265–80.

————. La Pince et le Soufflet: Deux Techniques de Forge Tradition-nelles au Nord-Togo." *Journal des Africanistes,* vol. 56, no. 2 (1986): 29–53.

Dupont, Véronique. *Dynamiques des Villes Secondaires et Processus Migratoires en Afrique de l'Ouest: Atakpamé, Kpalimé, Badou.* Paris: ORSTOM, 1986.

Dzobo, N. K. "Logical Demonology Among the Ewe in West Africa." *West African Journal of Education,* vol. 18, no. 3 (Oct. 1974): 239–242.

Elements pour une Strategie d'Emploi dans les Zones Rurales au Togo. Addis Ababa: ILO, 1983.

Ellis, A. B. *The Ewe-Speaking Peoples of the Slave Coast of West Africa.* London: Chapman and Hall, 1890.

Enjalbert, H. "Paysans Noirs, les Kabrés du Nord Togo." *Cahiers d'Outre Mer,* no. 34 (April–June 1956): 137–180.

Fiawood, D. K. "Some Reflections on Ewe Social Organization." In *Peuples du Golfe du Bénin,* edited by François de Medeiros, 221–34. Paris: Karthala, 1984.

Foli, Messanvi. *Detournement des Deniers au Togo.* Lomé: Institut National de la Recherche Scientifique, 1975.

France, Ministère des Finances et des Affaires Economiques. *Récensement Général de la Population du Togo 1958–1960.* Paris: Service de la Statistique Generale du Togo, 1960.

Francis, D. C., and J. R. Velasco. "Diffusion of Innovation in West Africa." *Journal of Asian and African Studies,* nos. 1–2, (Jan.–Apr. 1974): 67–76.

Friedlander, M. "Zur Frage der Klassenverhaltnisse der Ewe unter dem Einflussder Kolonisation." *Ethnographische-Archaologische Zeitschrift,* vol. 4, no. 2 (1963): 147–152.

Frobenius, Leo. *Das Unbekannte Afrika.* Munich: 1923.

———. "Les Paysans Kabré du Nord-Togo." *Le Monde non-Chretièn.* no. 59–60 (July–Dec. 1961): 101–172.

———. *Und Afrika Sprach: Unter den Unstraflichen Aethiopien,* vol. 3. Berlin: Vita, Deutsches Verlagshaus, 1913.

Froelich, J. C. "Catalogue des Scarifications en Usage Chez Certaines Populations du Dahomey et du Nord Togo." *Memoires d'IFAN,* no. 23 (1953): 253–264.

———. "Généralités sur les Kabré du Nord Togo." *Bulletin de l'IFAN,* (1949): 77–105.

———. "Le Kina et le Nwi des Konkomba." *Cahiers d'Etudes Africaines,* vol. 11 (1971): 308–374.

———. *Les Konkomba.* Dakar: Memoire d'IFAN, 1952.

———. "Les Konkomba du Nord-Togo." *Bulletin de l'IFAN,* no. 11 (1949).

———. "Le Paysan Noir et le Defi Moderne." *Civilisations,* vol. 19, no. 4 (1969): 452–465.

———. "Les Sociétés d'Initiation Chez les Moba et les Gourma du Nord Togo." *Journal de la Société des Africanistes,* vol. 19, (1949): 99–142.

———. *La Tribu Konkomba du Nord Togo.* Dakar: IFAN, 1954.

———, and P. Alexandre. "Histoire Traditionnelle des Kotokoli et des Bi-Tchambi du Nord-Togo." *Bulletin de l'IFAN,* vol. 22(B), no. 1/2, (Jan.–April 1960): 211–275.

———, and Robert Cornevin. *Populations du Nord-Togo.* Paris: Presses Universitaires de France, 1963.

Gbikpi-Benissan, Date Fodio. "La Chefferie Dans la Nation Contemporaine: la Chefferie en Pays Bassari, Akposso et Mina." Ph.D. Thesis, University of Paris, 1985.

Gessain, Monique. "A Propos de l'Evolution Actuelle des Femmes Coniagui et Bassari." *Journal de la Société des Africanistes,* vol. 34, no. 2 (1964): 255–276.

———. "Etude Socio-Démographique du Mariage Chez les Coniagui et Bassari." *Cahiers du Centre de Recherches Anthropologiques,* vol. 2 (1963): 123–222.

———. *Les Migrations des Coniagui et Bassari.* Paris: Société des Africanistes, 1967.

Gessain, Robert, et al. "Groupes d'Heptoglobine et de Transferrine et Groupes Gm des Coniagui et des Bassari." *Cahiers du Centre de Recherches Anthropologiques,* vol. 3 (1965): 19–22.

Gibbal, Jean-Marie. "Loin de Mango: les Tiokossi de Lomé." *Cahiers d'Etudes Africaines,* vol. 21, no. 81/83 (1981): 25–51.

Gluck, Julius. "Die Gelbgusse des Ali Amonikoyi." *Jahrbuch des Linden-Museums,* 1951: 27–71.

Gouellain, Réné. "Recherches Anthropologiques et Theatre Akposso." *Documents du CERK:* 110–117.

Greene, Sandra E. "The Anlo-Ewe: Their Economy, Society and External Relations in the Eighteenth Century." Ph.D. Dissertation, Northwestern University, 1981.

Gu-Konu, E. Y. "Tradition et Modernité." Thesis, University of Paris, 1983.

Haselberger, Herta. "Die Wandmalerei der Afrikanischen Neger." *Zeitschrift fur Ethnologie,* vol. 82 (1957): 209–237.

———. "Quelques Cas d'Evolution du Decor Mural en Afrique Occidentale." *Notes Africaines,* no. 101 (1964): 14–26.

Hetzel, Wolfgang. "Est-Mono: Die Kabré Und ihr Neues Siedlungsgebiet in Mitteltogo." *Wurzburger Geographische Arbeiter,* vol. 12 (1964): 45–80.

Houenassou, K. D. "Méthodes d'Elaboration des Données Primaires." In *Seminar on Research on African Women.* Dakar: Aaword, 1983.

Houndedoke, Zokia. "La Femme Ewe du Sud du Togo." Ph.D. Thesis, University of Limoges, 1989.

Kling, E., and R. Buttner. "Ergebnisse der Forschungsreisen im Hinterlands von Togo." *Mittheilungen aus den Deutschen Schutzgebieten,* vol. 6 (1893): 103–161.

Klose, H. "Das Bassarivolk." *Globus,* vol. 33, no. 20 (May 20, 1903): 309–341.

———. "Religiose Anschauungen und Mennschenofer in Togo." *Globus,* no. 81 (1902): 187–94.

———. "Wohnstatten und Huttenbau in Togogebiet." *Globus,* no. 84 (1903): 165–173, 184–192.

Kohler, J. "Das Togorecht." *Zeitschrift fur Vergleichende Rechtswissenschaft,* vol. 27, no. 1 (1912): 134–141.

Konu, Emmanuel. *La Population Togolaise, 1967.* Lomé: Institut National de la Recherche Togolaise, 1967.

———. "Notes Sur les Résultats Provisoires de Recensement Général de la Population Togolaise en 1970." *Annales de l'Ecole des Lettres* (Lomé), vol. 1: 25–36.

Kouassigan, Guy-Adjété. *L'Homme et la Terre: Droits Fonciers Coutumiers et Droit de Propriété en Afrique Occidentaie.* Paris: ORSTOM, 1966.

Kreamer, Christine Muller. "The Art and Ritual of the Moba of Northern Togo." Ph.D. Thesis, Indiana University Press, 1988.

Kubik, Gerhard. "Hubert Kponton, Erfinder, Kunstler und Bergrunde Eines Ethnographischen Privatmuseums in Lomé, Togo." *Archiv fur Volkerkunde* (Vienna), vol. 40 (1986): 157–171.

Kuczynski, Robert R. *The Cameroons and Togoland: A Demographic Study*. London: Oxford University Press, 1939.

Kuevi, Andre Dovi. "Les Akposso N'ont Pas Tourjours Eté un Peuple de Montagne." *Etudes Togolaises,* no. 1 (1971): 33–38.

———. "Traditions, Histoire et Organisation dans la Cité Chez les Akposso." *Institut National de la Recherche Scientifique,* Lomé, 1970.

Kumekpor, Tom K. *Rural Women and Attitudes to Family Planning, Contraceptive Practice and Abortion in Southern Togo*. Legon (Ghana): University of Ghana, Department of Sociology, 1970.

———, and S. I. Looky. "External Migration in Togo." In *Modern Migration in Western Africa,* edited by Samir Amin, 358–70. Oxford: Oxford University Press, 1974.

Kurchoff, D. "Das Kunstliche Wegenetz in Togo." *Globus,* vol. 88, (1905): 137–139.

Lallemand, Suzanne. "Pratiques de Maternage Chez les Kotokoli du Togo et les Mossi de Haute Volta." *Journal de Africanistes,* vol. 51, no. 1/2 (1981): 43–70.

———. "Sur Deux Contes Kotokoli et un Conte de Grimme." *Notes et Documents Voltaiques,* vol. 1, no. 4 (July–Sept. 1968): 3–12.

———, and H. Aboudou Issifou. "Un Rite Agraire Chez les Kotokoli du Nord Togo: La Fete Sinda." *Journal de la Société des Africanistes,* vol. 37, no. 1 (1967): 73–85.

Larson, T. J., and D. W. Gentile. "Intertribal Integration in a Lomé Compound." *South African Journal of Ethnology,* vol. 10 no. (1987): 68–72.

Le Bris, E. "Migration and the Decline of a Densely Populated Rural Area: The Case of the Vo Koutime in Southeast Togo." *African Perspectives* (Leiden), no. 1 (1978): 109–126.

———, André Quesnel, and Patrice Vimard. "Essai d'Enquete Scientifique dans une Région à Forte Pression Démographique." *Cahiers d'ORSTOM,* vol. 14, no 4 (1977): 383–408.

Levi, P., and M. Pilon, *Enquete Socio-Démographique Chez les Moba-Gurma (Nord-Togo)*. Paris: ORSTOM, 1988.

Locoh, Thérèse. *Fécondité et Famille en Afrique de l'Ouest: le Togo Méridional Contemporain*. Paris: Presses Universitaires de France, 1984.

———. "La Nuptialité au Togo. Evolution Entre 1961 et 1970." *Population,* vol. 31, no. 2 (March–Apr. 1976): 379–98.

———, and M. Janssens. *La Population Togolaise d'Hier à Demain*. Lomé: Unite de Recherche Démographique, 1984.

————, et al. "L'Espacement des Naissances au Sud-Est Togo." In *Childspacing in Africa: Tradition and Change,* edited by R. Lestaghe and H. Page. London: Academic Press, 1981.

————, et al. "Mariage et Nuptialité au Togo." *Etudes Togolaises de Population* Lomé: 1983. 2 vol.

Lopez-Escartin, N. *Données de Base Sur la Population Togolaise.* Paris: Centre Français sur la Population et le Développement, 1991.

Lucien-Brun, Bernard. *La Colonisation des Terres Neuves du Centre-Togo par les Kabré et les Losso.* Paris: ORSTOM, 1974.

————. "Coup d'Oeil sur l'Expansion Kabré." *Documents de Centre d'Etudes et de Recherches de Kara,* Piya (Togo), 1967: 56–60.

————, and Anne-Marie Pillet-Schwartz, *Les Migrations Rurales des Kabyé et des Losso.* Paris: ORSTOM, 1987.

Madjri, Dovi J. *Vogan: Etude Socio-Economique.* Lomé: Editions Centre Social Vogan, 1973.

Mamattah, Charles. *The Ewes of West Africa.* Accra: Volta Research Publications, 1979.

Manoukian, Madeline. *The Ewe-Speaking Peoples of Togoland and the Gold Coast.* London: International African Institute, 1952.

Marguerat, Yves. *L'Armature Urbaine du Togo.* Paris: ORSTOM, 1985.

Martinelli, Bruno. "Pour une Anthropologie de la Pluralité Technique: Le Cas de la Culture de l'Igname au Sud-Togo." *Cultures et Developpement,* vol. 13, no. 4 (1981): 633–659.

Maupon, Bernard. *Le Géomancies à l'Ancienne Cote des Esclaves.* Paris: Institut d'Ethnologie, 1943.

Maurice, A. "Les Chateaux Somba." *Tropiques,* vol. 55, no. 395 (May 1957): 59–66.

Medeiros, François de, ed. *Peuples du Golfe du Bénin.* Paris: Karthala, 1984.

Mercier, Paul. "L'Habitat et l'Occupation de la Terre Chez les Somba." *Bulletin de l'IFAN,* 1953: 798–817.

————. "L'Habitation à Etage dans l'Atakora." *Etudes Dahoméennes,* no. 11 (1951): 29–86.

————. "Mouvement du Population dans les Traditions des Betammaribé." *Etudes Dahoméennes,* no. 1 (1947).

————. "Notice sur le Péuplement Yoruba au Dahomey-Togo." *Etudes Dahoméennes,* no. 4 (1950): 29–40.

————. "Remarques sur la Signification du 'Tribalisme' Actuel en Afrique Noire." *Cahiers Internationaux de Sociologie,* vol. 31, (1961): 61–80.

————. *Tradition-Changement-Histoire: Les 'Somba' du Dahomey Septentrional.* Paris: Anthropos, 1968.

Merlo, Christian. "Statuettes of the Abiku Cult." *African Arts,* no. 8 (Summer 1975): 30–35.

Mignot, Alain. "La Justice Traditionnelle, une Justice Parallele." *Penant,* vol. 92, no. 775 (1982): 5–30.

———. "Les Mariages Coutumiéres et le Droit Togolais de la Famille." *Revue Juridique et Politique,* no. 3 (Sept. 1984): 756–774.

———. "Mobilité Conjugale et Divorce en Milieu Rural au Sud-Est du Togo." *Penant,* vol. 91, no. 771 (1981): 23–64.

———. *La Terre et le Pouvoir Chez les Guin du Sud-Est du Togo.* Paris: Publications de la Sorbonne, 1985.

Mohr, Richard. "Beobachtungen und Erkundigungen zur Soziologie und Religion der Naudeba in Nord-Togo." *Ethnologica,* N.F. 2 (1960): 297–322.

———. "Das Yamsfest bei den Ewe von Aloi (Togo)." *Anthropos,* Vol. 57, no. 1/2 (1962): 177–182.

———. "Reisenotizen aus Bassari." *Paideuma,* vol. 10, no. 1, (1964): 39–51.

Moussy, Bernadette. "Des Jardins d'Enfants au Togo et au Tchad." *Les Carnets de l'Enfance,* No. 21 (Jan.–Mar. 1973): 63–75.

Muller, Julius Otto. "I Contratti di Allevamento Tra i Pastori Foulbet nel Togo." *Rivisto Economico Agraria,* vol. 25, no. 1 (1970): 137–157.

———. *Probleme der Auftrags-Rinderhaltung durch Fulbe-Hirten in Westafrika.* Berlin: Springer-Verlag, 1967.

———. *Probleme der Flugtrags-Rinderhaltung durch Fulbe-Hirten,* Berlin: Springer-Verlag, 1967.

Nieuwaal, E. A. B. van Rouveroy van. *Changing Views About the Restitution of Marriage Payments Among the Tyokossi of Northern Togo.* Leyden: Afrika Studiecentrum, 1974.

———. "Chef Coutumiér: un Métier Difficile." *Politique Africaine.* no. 27 (1987): 13–31.

———. "Droit Moderne et Droit Coutumier au Togo." *Penant,* no. 747 (Jan.–March 1975): 5–18.

———. *Essai Sur Quelques Aspects du Droit Matrimonial des Tyokossi: Règlement d'un Litige à la Cour du Chef Supérieur de Sansanné-Mango (Nord-Togo).* Leyden: Afrika Studiecentrum, 1973.

———. "Etat et Pouvoir néo-Traditionnel en Afrique: Position Ambigué du Chef Coutumière face à l'Etat Africaine." *Droit et Cultures.* no. 15 (1988): 71–113.

———. *Mbambim: Un Chef de Famille d'Ayikpéré (Nord Togo).* Leiden: Afrika Studiecentrum, 1972; 1982.

———. "The Plot of the Sophisticated Son-in-Law Disparity." *Kroniek van Afrika,* 1975: 47–58.

———. "The Plot of the Sophisticated Son-in-Law: Old and New Ways of Establishing Rights over Land in N'zara, Northern Togo." In *Anthropology of Law in the Netherlands: Essays on Legal Pluralism,* edited by K. von Benda-Beckmann and F. Strijbosch. Dordrecht: Foris Publications, 1986.

————. *Sherea: Justice du Chef Superieur à N'zara, Sansanné-Mango.* Leiden: Afrika Studiecentrum, 1975.

————. "Sorcéllerie et Justice Coutumière dans une Société Togolaise: Une Quantité Negligeable?" *Penant,* vol. 99, no. 801 (Aug.–Dec. 1989): 433–453.

————. "Terre au Nord-Togo: Quelques Aspects sur la Relations Anufo-Ngam en Matière Foncière." *African Perspectives,* no. 1 (1979): 139–151.

————, and Elsa van Nieuwaal. *A la Recherche de la Justice: Quelques Aspects du Droit Matrimoniale des Anufon à Mango.* Leiden: Afrika Studiecentrum, 1976.

————, and ————. *Tri Anufo, Un Coup d'Oeil sur la Société des Anufon au Nord Togo.* The Hague: Mouton, 1976.

————, and ————. "To Claim or Not to Claim: Changing Views about the Restitution of Marriage Prestations Among the Anufon in Northern Togo." In *Law and the Family in Africa,* edited by S. Roberts, 94–114. The Hague: Mouton, 1977.

Nooteboom, C. "Somba, Kasteelbewoners in West-Afrika." *Mededelingen van Afrika Instituut,* vol. 17, no. 1 (1963): 20–23.

Norris, Edward, and Peter Heine. "Genealogical Manipulations and Social Identity in Sansanne Mango." *Bulletin of the School of Oriental and African Studies,* vol. 45, no. 1 (1982): 118–137.

Nukunya, G. K. *Kinship and Marriage Among the Anlo Ewe.* London: Athlone Press, 1969.

Nyassogbo, Kwami. "Juxtaposition de Deux Pratiques Foncières et de Deux Fromes Architecturales dans une Ville Secondaire au Togo, Atakpamé." In *Actes du Colloque International Strategies Urbaines dans les Pays en Voie de Développement,* edited by N. Haumont and A. Marie, 112–128. Paris: Harmattan, 1987.

————. "L'Urbanisation et Son Evolution au Togo." *Les Cahiers d'Outre Mer,* no. 146 (April–June 1984): 135–158.

Nyatepe-Coo, A. "La Fete du Pé-Ekpé." *Etudes Togolaises,* no. 23/26: 21–31.

Olympio, Lucien. "La Condition Juridique de l'Enfant en Togo et Son Evolution." *Revue Juridique et Politique,* vol. 20 (Jan.–Mar. 1966): 85–95.

————. "Justice Coutumière et Ordre Public au Togo." *Penant,* No. 735 (Jan.–Mar. 1972): 104–108.

Painter, C. "The Guang and West African Historical Reconstruction." *Ghana Notes and Queries,* vol. 9 (Nov. 1966): 58–66.

Patokideou, Honoré K. *Les Civilisations Patriarcales des Kabré Face aux Programmes Modernes de Développement Economique et Social.* Lomé: Editogo, 1970. Also, Thesis, University of Abidjan, 1970.

Pauvert, Jean-Claude. *L'Ancienne Colonisation Kabré et Ses Possibilités d'Expansion dans l'Est Mono.* Lomé: ORSTOM, 1955.

————. *Etude démographique du pays Kabré.* Lomé: ORSTOM, 1955.

————. *L'Etude des Migrations au Togo.* Lomé: ORSTOM, 1956.

————. "Migrations et Droit Foncier au Togo." *Cahiers de L'Institut de Science Economique Appliquée,* Serie V (9), no. 166 (Oct. 1965): 69–89.

Pawlik, J. "La Mort, Experience d'un Peuple. Etude des Rites Funeraires des Bassar du Nord-Togo." Thesis, University of Paris, 1988.

Pazzi, Roberto. "Culte de Mort Chez le Peuple Mina (Sud-Togo)." *Cahiers des Religions Africaines,* vol. 2, no. 4 (July 1968): 249–260.

————. "La Donna Sposa [Mina]." *Nigrizia,* vol. 87, no. 7/8, (July–Aug. 1969): 31.

Person, Y. "Brève Note Sur les Logba et Leurs Classes d'Age." *Etudes Dahoméennes,* no. 17: 35–49.

————. "Note Sur les Nyantruku." *Etudes Dahoméennes,* no. 16 (1957).

————. "Notes Sur les Baseda." *Etudes Dahoméennes,* no. 15 (1956).

————. "Première Esquisse du Peuple Biyobé." *Bulletin de l'IFAN,* vol. 17, no. 3–4 (July 1955), p. 141–150.

Pfennig, Ursula. "Zur Arbeitsbelastung von Frauen im Landlichen Bereich Togos." *Bulletin of the International Committee on Urgent Anthropological and Ethnological Research* (Vienna), no. 28/29 (1986–87): 77–89.

Pignan, Pidalani. *Initiations Africaines et Pédagogie de la Foi: Le Mariage Chrétien et la Mariage Traditionnel Kabiyé à la Lumière de l'Enseignement du Councile Vatican II.* Paris: Sogico, 1987.

Pillet-Schwartz, Anne-Marie. "Amenagement de l'Espace et Mouvements de Populations au Togo: l'Exemple du Pays Kabyé." *Cahiers d'Etudes Africaines,* vol. 26, no. 3 (1986): 317–332.

————. *Le Migrations Rurales des Kabyé et des Losso.* Lomé: ORSTOM, 1984.

Piot, Charles Daniel. "Fathers and Sons: Domestic Production, Conflict, and Social Forms Among the Kabré." *Research in Economic Anthropology,* col. 10 (1988): 269–285.

————. "Production, Exchange and Symbolic Forms Among the Kabré." Ph.D. Thesis, University of Virginia, 1986.

Placea, Dovi, and K. Sossah. "L'Espacement des Naissances: Les Problèmes de Nutritions au Togo." *Etudes Togolaises,* no. 27/30 (1984/5): 17–51.

Pontie, Danielle. "Les Moba de Lomé." *Cahiers d'Etudes Africaines,* vol. 21, no. 81/3 (1981): 53–65.

Prost, André. *Mi Gangan.* Dakar: University of Dakar, Linguistic Documents No. 81, 1947.

————. "Notes sur les Boussansé." *Bulletin de l'IFAN,* 1945: 47–53.

————. "Notes sur le Naudem du Togo: Rapports Entre le Naudem et le Morè." *Bulletin de l'IFAN,* vol. 28(B), no. 1/2 (Jan.–April 1966): 433–469.

Puig, François. *Etudes Sur les Coutumes des Cabrais.* Toulouse: Imprimerie Toulousaine Lion et Fils, 1934.

Reisner, Gena. "Three Ceremonies in Togo." *The Drama Review,* vol. 25, no. 4 (Winter 1981): 51–8.

Rey-Hulman, Diana. "Les Bilinguismes Littéraires, Signification Sociale de la Litterature Orale Chez les Tyokossi." Ph.D. Thesis, Sorbonne, Paris, 1976.

Riviere, Claude. "Deuil et Veuvage Chez les Evé du Togo." *Anthropos,* vol. 77, no. 3/4 (1982): 461–474.

————. "La Divorce Chez les Evé." *Revue Française d'Etudes Politiques Africaines,* no. 203/4 (Dec. 1982–Jan. 1983): 118–128.

————. "Dzo et la Pratique Magique Chez les Evé du Togo." *Cultures et Développement,* vol. 2, no. 11 (1979): 193–218.

————. "La Gemelleite Chez les Evé du Togo." *Cultures et Développement,* vol. 12, no. 1 (1980): 81–122.

————. "La Grosseusse Chez les Evé du Togo." *Le Mois en Afrique,* no. 227/228 (1984–85): 120–132.

————. "La Naissance Chez les Evé du Togo." *Journal des Africanistes,* vol. 51, no. 1/2 (1981): 71–95.

————. "Rites du Mariage Chez les Evé du Togo." *Anthropos,* vol. 79, no. 4/6 (1984): 377–395.

————. *"Union et Procréation en Afrique: Rites de Vie Chez les Evé du Togo."* Paris: Harmattan, 1990.

Roulon, P. "La Conception Gbaya'Bodoe du Temps." *Systèmes de Pensée en Afrique,* vol. 7 (1984): 11–44.

Russell, Sharon Stanton, et al. *International Migration and Development in Subsaharan Africa,* vol. 2: Washington, D.C.: World Bank Discussion Papers, 1990.

Salaun. "Etude sur les Somba." *Compte Rendu de l'Academie des Sciences Coloniales,* March 1947.

Sauvaget, Claude. *Boua, Village de Kondé, un Terroir Kabiyé.* Paris: ORSTOM, 1981.

Schicho, W. "Traditional Basis for Modern Political Institutions in the Kabré-occupied Districts of Lama-Kara and Pagouda, Northern Togo." *Review of Ethnology,* vol. 3, no. 7 (1971): 53–56.

Schilling, Claud. "Tamberma." *Globus,* no. 89 (1906): 261–274.

Schlettwein, A. "Kodifikation des Eingeborenenrechts, in Togo." *Zeitschrift fur Vergleichende Rechtswissenschaft,* vol. 43, no. (1927): 248–252.

Schonhaerl. *Volkskundisches aus Togo.* Leipzig: 1909.

Sergent, Bernard. "Les Clans de Tami: Pour Une Nouvelle Approche De

L'Histoire Africaine De L'Histoire Africain." *Mondes et Cultures,* vol. 47, no. 2 (1989): 199–228.

Sicre, C. *Monographie du Cercle de Sokodé.* Kara: Centre d'Etudes et de Récherches, 1972.

Smend, von. "Eine Reise Durch die Nordostecke von Togo." *Globus,* no. 92 (1907): 245–250, 265–269.

Spies, Carl. "Zum Kultus und Zauberglauben der Evheer." *Baessler Archiv,* no. 1 (1910): 223–226.

Spieth, J. *Die Ewe Stamme; Material zur Kunde des Ewe-Volkes in Deutsch-Togo.* Berlin: Dietrich Reimer, 1906.

———. *Die Eweer: Schilderung von Land und Leuten in Deutsch-Togo.* Bremen, 1906.

Sprigge, R. G. S. "Eweland's Adangbe: An Enquiry into an Oral Tradition." *Transactions of the Historical Society of Ghana,* vol. 10 (1969): 87–128.

———. "A Note from Ewe-land's Adangbe: Notes and Queries." *Ghana Notes,* vol. 10 (Dec. 1968): 23–28.

Staudinger, Paul. "Uber Bronzeguss in Togo." *Zeitschrift fur Ethnologie,* no. 1 (1909): 855–862.

Steemers, J. C. S. "The Okra Traditions Among the Guangs of the Volta Basin." *Ghana Bulletin of Theology,* vol. 2, no. 9/10 (Dec. 1965–June 1966): 1–11.

Stillman, David George. "Population-Related Policy: A Framework for Analysis with Examination of Two Cases: Togo and Ghana." Ph.D. Dissertation, Duke University, 1974.

Surgy, Albert de. "Les Ceremonies de Purification des Mauvais Projets Chez les Mwaba-Gurma du Nord-Togo." *Systèmes de Pensée en Afrique Noire,* no. 4 (1979): 9–76.

———. "Le Culte des Ancestres en Pays Evhé." *Systèmes de Pensée en Afrique Noire,* no. 1 (1975): 105–128.

———. "Le Deuil du Conjoint en Pays Evhé." *Systèmes de Pensée en Afrique Noire,* no. 9 (1986): 105–33.

———. *De l'Universalité d'Une Forme Africaine de Sacrifice.* Paris: CNRS, 1988.

———. *Géomancie et le Culte d'Afa Chez les Evhé.* Paris: Publications Orientales de France, 1981.

———. "Les Libations dans la Sacrifice Mwaba-Gurma." *Systèmes de Pensée en Afrique Noire,* no. 5 (1981): 127–136.

Szwark, Marian. *Proverbes et Traditions des Bassars du Nord Togo.* St. Augustin: Hans Volker, 1981.

Tait, David. "The Family, Household and Minor Lineage of the Konkomba." *Africa,* vol. 26 (1956): 219–249, 332–342.

———. ed. *The Konkomba of Northern Ghana.* London: Oxford University Press, 1961.

————. "The Political System of the Konkomba." In *Cultures and Societies of Africa*, edited by Simon and Phoebe Ottenberg, 271–283. New York: Random House, 1963.

————. "The Role of the Diviner in Konkomba Society." *Man,* 1952: 167–178.

————. "The Territorial Pattern and Lineage System of Konkomba." In *Tribes Without Rulers*, edited by John Middleton and David Tait, 167–202. London: Routledge & Kegan Paul, 1958.

Tamakloe, M. D. *A Brief History of the Dagomba People.* Accra: Gold Coast Printing Office, 1931.

Tchabi, M., and R. Verdier. "Fondation du Village de Kpana." *Documents de Centre d'Etudes et de Récherches de Kara,* (Piya: Togo), vol. 3 (1968): 23–26.

Tchagbalé, Zakari, and Suzanne Lallemand. *Toi et le Ciel, Vous et la Terre: Contes Paillards Tam du Togo.* Paris: SELAF, 1982.

Togo. Service de la Statistique Générale. *Enquete Démographique 1961—Resultats Definitifs.* Lomé: 1965.

————. ————. *Etude Demographique au Pays Kabré, 1957.* Paris: Servant-Crouzet, 1960.

Tossou, Kossi J. "Ehe und Eheabschlus in der Tradition der Ewe." *Zeitschrift fur Missionswissenschaft und Religionswissenschaft* (Munster), vol. 73, no. 2 (1989): 109–125.

Toulabor, C. M. "L'Enonciation du Pouvoir et de la Richesse Chez les Jeunes de Lomé." *Revue Française de Science Politique* (June 1985): 446–58.

Tscha-Tokey, J. *Migration et Développement: Le Cas de Kabyé et Losso au Togo.* Yaoundé, Cameroun: International School of Journalism, 1975.

————. "Le Mode D'Attribution de la Terre dans les Sociétés Pre-Capitalistes d'Afrique Comme Système de Blockage à L'Accumulation du Capital au Développement." *African Perspectives,* no. (1979): 127–38.

Vajda, L. "Leo Frobenius Heute." *Zeitschrift fur Ethnologie,* vol. 98, no. 1 (1973): 19–29.

Van Dyck, C. "An Analytic Study of the Folktales of Selected Peoples of West Africa." Ph.D. Thesis, Oxford University, 1966–67.

Verdier, Paul. "Structure et Imaginaire Dans Le Conte Togolais." Ph.D. Thesis, University of Grenoble, 1970, 3 vols.

Verdier, Raymond. "Le Mariage dans la Pensée Kabré." *Revue Juridique et Politique,* vol. 22, no. 1 (Jan.–March 1968): 157–162.

————. *Le Pays Kabyé, Cité de Dieux, Cité des Hommes.* Paris: Karthala, 1982.

————. "Notes sur la Canicide Chez les Kabiyé du Nord Togo." *Systémes de Pensée en Afrique Noire,* no. 1 (1975): 129–136.

Verdon, Michel. "Political Sovereignty, Village Reproduction and Legends of Origin," *Africa,* vol. 51, no. 1 (1981): 465–76.

―――. "The Structure of Titled Offices Among the Abutia Ewe." *Africa,* vol. 49, no. 2 (1979): 159–171.

Vermot-Mangold, R. *Die Rolle der Frau bei den Kabre in Nord Togo.* Basel: Ethnologisches Seminar fur Volker-Kunde, 1977.

Vignikin, Kokou. "Production, Fécondité et Migration en Milieu Agricole: Les Cas du Sud-Est Togo." Thesis, University of Montreal, 1987.

Von Seefried. "Beitrage zur Geschichte des Mangovolkes in Togo." *Zeitschrift fur Ethnologie,* vol. 45, no. 3 (1913): 421–435.

Ward, B. "Some Notes on Migration from Togoland." *African Affairs,* vol. 49 (1950): 129–135.

Wassungu, Pascal. "Classes D'Age et Initiations Chez les Nawdeba." In *Classes et Associations D'Age en Afrique de l'Ouest,* edited by Denise Paulme. Paris: Plon, 1971.

Welsch, R. P. "Les Tyokossi du Togo Nord." *Notes Africaines,* no. 47 (July 1950): 77–78.

Westermann, Diedrich. *Die Glidyi-Ewe in Togo.* Berlin: Walter de Gruyter, 1935.

Wezin, K. *La Puissance et l'Etérnité.* Lomé: Akpagnon, 1985.

Witte, Ant. "Beitrage zur Ethnographie von Togo Westafrika." *Anthropos,* vol. 14/15, no. 4/6 (July–Dec. 1919–1920): 981–1001.

―――. "Der 'Konigseid' in Kpandu und Bei Einigen Benachbarten Ewe-Stammen." *Anthropos,* vol. 3 (1908): 426–430.

―――. "Der Zwillingskult Bei den Ewe-Negern." *Anthropos,* vol. 24, no. 5/6 (Sept.–Dec. 1929): 943–951.

Wulker, Gabriele. *Togo: Tradition und Entwicklung.* Stuttgart: E. Klett, 1966.

Zachariah, K. C., and N. K. Nair. "Togo: External and Internal Migration." In *Demographic Aspects of Migration in West Africa,* vol. 2, T1–63. Washington D.C.: World Bank Staff Working Papers No. 415, 1980.

Zech, Graf von. "Aus dem Schutz Gebiete Togo." *Mittheilungen aus den Deutschen Schutzgebieten,* no. 11 (1898): 89–161.

―――. "Pays et Populations de la Frontiére Nord-Ouest du Togo." *Etudes Dahoméennes,* no. 2 (1949): 9–11.

Zwernemann, Jurgen. "Leo Frobenius et la Recherche Scientifique sur les Civilisations Africaines." *Notes et Documents Voltaiques,* vol. 2, no. 3 (April–June 1969): 27–42.

―――. *Magische Vorstellungen der Gurma Nord-Togo.* Lisbon: 1974.

―――. "Un Masque de Laiton Provenant du Togo au Linden Museum à Stuttgard." *Notes Africaines d'IFAN,* vol. 101 (Jan. 1964): 11–13.

―――. "Mundliche Uberlieferungen zur Geschichte der Moba." *Afrika und Ubersee,* vol. 60, no. 1/2 (1977): 86–116.

————. "Personennamen der Moba." *Afrika und Ubersee,* 1972: 245–258.

————. "La Querelle Pour L'Enfant Pas Encore Né: Une Legende Historique des Gurunsi et Ses Paralléles." *Notes Africaines,* vol. 101 (Jan. 1964): 26–27.

Politics and International Relations

Adabra, Samuel Suka. "Les Autorités Traditionnelles et le Pouvoir Politique Moderne au Togo." Thesis, University of Paris, 1973.

————. "Le Controle De L'Etat sur les Institutions Territoriales au Togo." Thesis, University of Saint-Naur, 1977.

Afua, Akjemado. "Etude Comparative de Deux Régimes Militaires: Cas du Bénin et du Togo." Thesis, University of Paris, 1988.

Agbekponou, Kouévi. "La Determination de la Loi Applicable au Divorce International et le Nouveau Code Togolais de la Famille." *Penant,* vol. 93, no. 781/2 (Aug–Dec. 1983): 283–305.

————. "La Vocation Héréditaire de la Femme dans la Droit Positif Togolais des Successions." *Penant,* vol. 98, no. 798 (1988): 421–452.

Agblemagnon, Ferdinand N'Sougan. "Conflits de Passage et Sociologie des Jeunes Etats Africains: Le Cas du Togo." *Civilisations,* vol. 18, no. 2 (1968): 232–246.

————. "Masses et Elites en Afrique Noire: Le Cas du Togo." In *The New Elites of Tropical Africa,* edited by P. C. Lloyd, 118–125. London: Oxford University Press, 1966.

————. "Mythe et Realité de la Classe Sociale en Afrique Noire: Le Cas du Togo." *Cahiers Internationaux de Sociologie,* vol. 12, no. 38 (Jan.–June 1965): 155–168.

Agbodan, Mavor Tety. "La Coopération Germano-Togolaise Depuis 1960." *Le Mois en Afrique,* vol. 21, no. 235/6 (Aug.–Sept. 1985): 52–63.

Agbodjan, Combevi. *Institutions Politiques et Organisation Administrative du Togo.* Lomé: Haho, 1983.

Aithnard, K. M. *Aspects de la Politique Culturelle du Togo.* Paris: UNESCO, 1975.

Ajavon, A. "Le Togo dans les Relations Internationales." Ph.D. Thesis, University of Paris, 1976.

Ajavon, Robert. *Naissance d'un Etat Africain, le Togo, Territoire Pilote. Lumière et Ombre (1951–1958).* Lomé: Nouvelles Editions Africaines, 1989.

Alassounouma, Boumbera. "La Reconversion des Mentalités et les Problèmes de l'Unité Nationale." *Etudes Togolaises,* vol. 15/18, (Dec. 1981): 7–15.

Aleandre, Sylvine. *La République Autonome du Togo: De la Fiction à la Realité.* Paris, 1957.

Aliewekwe, Iwuoka. "The Togoland Problem: A Case Study in the Paradoxes and Problems of Political Transition in West Africa." Ph.D. Thesis, Ohio State University, 1960.

Amega, Atsu Koffi. *Condition de Validition du Mariage et Legitimation des Enfants.* Leiden: Afrika Studiecentrum, 1974.

———. "L'Evolution du Droit en Afrique." *Présence Africaine,* Special Issue 39, 1971.

———. "Les Mecanismes Juridiques de la Protection des Droits de la Personne au Togo." *Revue Juridique et Politique,* (Jan.–Mar. 1982): 250–256.

Amenumey, D.E.K. "The 1956 Plebisicite in Togoland under British Administration and Ewe Unification." *Universitae* (Legon, Ghana), vol. 5, no. 2 (May–Nov. 1976): 126–140.

Apati-Bassah, A. "Role des Préfets et Chefs de Régions au Togo." *Revue Juridique et Politique.* vol. 36, no. 2 (June 1982): 797–810.

Austin, Dennis. "The Coup in Togo." *The World Today,* February 1963: 56–60.

———. "The Uncertain Frontier: Ghana-Togo." *Journal of Modern African Studies,* vol. 1, no. 2 (1963): 139–145.

———. "Die Autonome Republik Togo." *Zeitschrift fur Auslandisches Offentliches Recht und Volkerrecht,* vol. 18, no. 2 (Dec. 1957): 287–317.

Awesso, B.A. "Entre Israel et le Togo: Une Experience de Coopération entre Deux Etats Petits et Jeunes." *Espoir de la Nation Togolaise,* (Lomé) no. 5–6 (April–May 1970): 24–34.

Ayache, Georges. *Si la Maison de Votre Voisin Brule . . . Eyadema et la Politique Extérièure du Togo.* Paris: ABC, 1983.

Bachelet, Michel. *Lomé, Capitale du Togo.* Paris: Delroisse, 1977.

Bail, Réné. *Forces Armées Togolaises.* Paris: ABC, 1977.

Barbier, Jean-Claude. "Jalons pour une Sociologie Electorale du Togo, 1958–1985." *Politique Africaine,* no. 27 (1987): 6–18.

———. "Sokodé, Capitale Administrative, ou le Destin d'une Hégémonie au Nord-Togo." *Revue Française d'Administration Publique,* vol. 42 (June 1987): 353–364.

Bawa, I.B. *Togoland Must Unite.* Lomé: 1978.

Bening, Bagulo R. "The Ghana-Togo Boundary 1914–1982." *Afrika Spectrum,* no. 18 (1983): 191–209.

Blanchet, A. "Le Voyage du President Georges Pompidou en Haute Volta et au Togo." *Comptes Rendus Trimestriels des Séances de l'Academie des Sciences d'Outre-Mer,* vol. 32, no. 3/4 (1972): 529–542.

Blaublomme, Bernard. "Traditionalisme et Réalités Politiques. Les Ewé du Togo Sud et le Problème de l'Opposition du Nord et du Sud." Thesis, Aix-en-Provence, 1970.

Bonin, A. A. *Le Togo du Sergent en Général.* Paris: Lescaret, 1983.

Brown, David. "Borderland Politics in Ghana: the National Liberation Movement in Western Togoland." *Journal of Modern African Studies,* vol. 18, no. 4 (1980): 575–609.

———. "Sieges and Scapegoats: Politics of Pluralism in Ghana and Togo." *Civilisations,* no. 2 (1983): 71–112.

Codo, Léon C. *Le Bénin dans le Rapport Ouest-Africains. Strategie d'Insertion, Bilateralisme Sous-Régional, et Engagements Régionaux.* Bordeaux: CEAN, 1987.

Conac, Gérard, ed. *Les Institutions Administratives des Etats Francophones d'Afrique Noire.* Paris: Economica, 1979.

Connen, Bernard. "Le Code Penal Togolais." *Revue de Droit des Pays d'Afrique,* no. 773 (July-Sept. 1981): 5–15.

———. "Un Code de la Famille au Togo." *Penant,* vol. 91, no. 774 (1981): 5–22.

Constantin, François. "Togo." In *Année Africaine 1971.* Paris: Pedone, 1972+

———, and C. Coulon. "Des Casernes au Chancellaries." *Canadian Institute of African Studies,* no. 1 (1975): 17–49.

"Constitution de la Republique Togolaise." *Afrique Contemporaine,* no. 108, Mar.–April (1980): 19–23.

Constitution 1963. Lomé: Editogo, 1963.

Cornevin, Robert. "Les Elections à l'Assemblée Togolaise." *Encyclopedie Mensuelle de l'Afrique,* July 1958: 3–7.

———. "Evolution dans le Nord du Togo." *Sociologus,* vol. 4, no. 1 (1954): 54–62.

———. "Les Militaires au Dahomey et au Togo." *Revue Française d'Etudes Politiques Africaines,* Dec. 1968: 65–84.

———. "La Politique Extérieure du Togo." *Revue Française d'Etudes Politiques Africaines,* no. 82 (Oct. 1972): 59–71.

———. "Le Togo Independant." *Europe-France-Outre-Mer,* no. 364 (Mar. 1960): 16–27.

Creppy, N. "Le Role de l'Armée dans la Vie Togolaise." Thesis, Paris University, 1978.

Creppy, R. K. "La Nationalité Togolaise." *Revue Juridique et Politique* (Oct.–Dec. 1971): 577–586.

Da Costa. "The Dictator's Duet." *Africa Report.* (Nov.–Dec. 1993): 61–5.

Decalo, Samuel. "Military Rule in Togo." *Pula: Journal of African Affairs* (Gaborone), no. 2 (Summer 1979): 13–17.

———. "The Politics of Military Rule in Togo." *Geneve-Afrique,* vol. 12, no. 2 (1973): 62–96.

———. "Togo." In *The Oxford Companion to the World,* 151–6. New York: Oxford University Press, 1993.

———. "Togo: Benevolent Rule in a Military State." In *Coups and Military Rule in Africa: Essays on Military Style,* 89–127. New Haven, Connecticut: Yale University Press, 1976.

————. "Togo: Stability and Stagnation under a Military Brokerage." In *Coups and Military Rule in Africa: Motivations and Constraints,* 111–163. New Haven, Connecticut: Yale University Press, 1990.

De Chardon, Theophile. "Togo's Liberal General." *Africa Report,* vol. 15, no. 1 (Jan. 1970): 8–10.

Decottignies, Roger. "La Condition des Personnes au Togo et au Cameroun." *Annales Africaines* (Dakar), no. 6 (1957): 7–52.

Decraene, Philippe. "Togo: Entre Francophones." *Revue Française d'Etudes Politiques Africaines,* no. 23 (Nov. 1967): 15–16.

————. "Togo: Un Regain de Prestige Pour le Général Eyadema." *Revue Française d'Etudes Politiques Africaines,* no. 77 (May 1972): 11–13.

Djabie, Cyrille. "La Section Feminine du R. P. T. est Née: C'est l'UNFT." *Espoir de la Nation Togolaise* (Lomé), no. 19 (May–June 1972): 18–22.

Djondo, Gervais Koffi. "Le Conseil Economique et Social du Goto." *Nations Nouvelles,* no. 20 (June 1969): 15–22.

Dogbé, Y. E. *Le Rénouveau Démocratique au Togo.* Paris: Akpagnon, 1989.

"Droits de l'Homme au Togo." *Politique Africaine.* no. 21 (Dec. 1985): 110–13.

Duanenyo, S. "La Révolution Verte: Discours et Financement." *Politique Africaine,* no. 27 (Oct. 1987): 31–36.

Ducat, Marc. "La Reforme Foncière Togolaise." *Penant,* no. 749, July–Sept. 1975: 291–308.

Ekué, G. "Le Parti Unique au Togo." Ph.D. Thesis, Aix-en-Provence, 1974.

Everett, Richard. "Eyadema's Nightmare," *Africa Report* (Nov.–Dec. 1986): 14–17.

"Eyadema: 15 Ans de Pouvoir." *Europe-Outre-mer,* Special issue, no. 620–1 (Sept.–Oct. 1981).

Felli, Do. "Les Pratiques Foncières Face à l'Urbanisation dans la Région Maritime du Togo." In *Espaces Disputés en Afrique Noire,* 41–49. Paris: Karthala, 1987.

Ferrand, C. *La Presse au Togo, 1911–1966.* Lomé: 1968.

Feuillet, Claude. *Le Togo 'En Général': La Longue Marche de Général Eyadema.* Paris: ABC, 1976.

Foli, Messanvi-Leone. "L'Organisation Judiciaire du Togo en Matière Civile." *Revue Juridique et Politique,* no. 2 (April–June 1975); 222–251.

Folly, Linus Koué. "Eyadema's Flat-Footed Opponents." *West Africa* (3 May 1993): 728–9.

France. La Documentation Française. "Constitution de la République Togolaise (Mai 1963)," in "Les Nouvelles Constitutions Africaines." *Notes et Etudes Documentaires,* no. 3175 (1965).

————. ————. "Constitution du 14 Avril 1961," in "Les Constitutions des Républiques Africaines et Malgache d'Expression Française." *Notes et Etudes Documentaires,* no. 2995 (May 30, 1963): 57–62.

————. ————. "L'Organisation Judiciare en AOF, en AEF, au Togo et au Cameroun." *Notes et Etudes Documentaires,* no. 1947 (1954).

————. ————. "La République du Togo." *Notes et Etudes Documentaires,* no. 2706 (Oct. 5, 1960).

————. ————. "Le Togo." *Notes et Etudes Documentaires,* no. 1193–94 (1949).

————. ————. "Le Togo." *Notes et Etudes Documentaires,* no. 3531 (Oct. 31, 1968) [by Tessier du Cros].

————. ————. "Situation de la Presse dans les Etats de l'Union Africaine et Malgache, en Guinée, au Mali, au Togo." *Notes et Etudes Documentaires,* 1963 [by J. Gras].

Froelich, Jean Claude. "Escale au Togo (Mars 1970)." *Revue de Défense Nationale,* vol. 26 (Aug.–Sept. 1970): 1299.

———— "Togo." In *Année Africaine.* Paris: Pedone, 1967 +.

Golan, Tamar. "The Council of the Entente." Ph.D. Thesis, Columbia University, New York, 1980.

Gonidec, P. F. "L'Evolution de la République Autonome du Togo." *Annuaire Français de Droit International,* vol. 3 (1957): 627–638.

————. "La République du Togo." *Penant,* Mar.–April 1958: 474–491.

Guillaneuf, Raymond. *La Presse au Togo, 1911–66.* Paris: C. Lermont Ferraud, 1968.

Heilbrunn, John R. "The Social Origins of the National Conferences in Benin and Togo." *Journal of Modern African Studies,* June 1993: 277–299.

Hirschhoff, Paula M. "The Privatization Drive." *Africa Report.* July–Aug. 1986: 89–95.

Histoire de Togo: Il était une Fois . . . Eyadema. Tournai, Belgium: ABC & Casterman, 1976.

Hodges, Tony. "Eyadema's Unchallenged Rule." *Africa Report,* July–Aug. 1977: 61–64.

Howe, Russell Warren. "Togo: Four Years of Military Rule." *Africa Report,* May 1967: 6–12.

Hughes, Anthony J. "Gnassingbe Eyadema, President of the Republic of Togo." *Africa Report,* July–Aug. 1982: 24–27.

Jones, Edward A. "Togo, West Africa—An Appraisal by an Afro-American." *Phylon,* no. 22 (Fall 1961): 234–240.

Kakayé, N. "L'Administration Local Togolaise et Ses Problemes." Thesis, University of Paris, 1978.

Kelly, C. "Response in Togo to the Expulsions from Nigeria." *Disasters,* vol. 7, no. 3 (1983): 187–90.

Kitchen, Helen. "Filling the Togo Vacuum." *Africa Report,* vol. 8 (Feb. 1963): 7–10.

Kitissou, M. L. "L'Armée et le Pouvoir Politique au Togo." Thesis, Bordeaux University, 1976.

Kodjo, Mensah. "Elements pour une Sociologie Politique de la Vie Togolaise." Thesis, Paris University, 1967.

Leclerq, Claude. "La Constitution Togolaise du 13 Janvier 1980." *Revue Juridique et Politique,* vol. 34, no. 4 (Dec. 1980): 817–824.

Le Cornec, Jacques. "Le Statut du Togo." Ph.D. Thesis, University of Paris, 1957.

Lee, A., and A. Astrow. "In Search of Friends." *Africa Report,* vol. 32, no. 2 (1987): 51–53.

Lewis, William H. "Togo: Africa's New Pressure Point." *Africa Report.* April 1960.

"Livre Blanc sur la Réunification du Togo." *Revue Française d'Etudes Politiques Africaines,* no. 121 (1976): 21–57.

Mademba, Samba. "Les Institutions Municipales en Afrique Occidentale Française au Togo et au Cameroun." Ph.D. Thesis, University of Paris, 1957.

Madjri, John Dovi. "Audience et Impact d'un Media Rural Africain: le Journal *Game Su* au Togo." *Communication et Information,* vol. 2, no. 1 (1977): 127–34.

Maldonado, C. "The Underdogs of the Urban Economy Join Forces." *International Labour Review,* vol. 128, no. 1 (1989): 65–84.

Mangeart, Remi. *Paysans Africains: Des Africains s'Unissent pour Ameliorer Leurs Villages au Togo.* Paris: Harmattan, 1984.

Manouan, A. "L'Evolution du Conseil de l'Entente." *Penant,* nos. 746/747/748 (Oct.–Jan. 1974): 447–497; (Jan.–Mar. 1975): 19–92; (April–June 1975): 211–236.

Marguerat, Yves. "Etat et Organisation Territoriale du Togo." *Afrique Contemporaine,* vol. 27, no. 145 (1988): 47–54.

———. "Logiques et Pratiques des Acteurs Foncièrs à Lomé." In *Actes du Colloque Internationale Strategies Urbaines dans les Pays en Voie de Développement,* edited by N. Haumont and A. Marie, 74–85. Paris: Harmattan, 1987.

Martinelli, B. "La Production des Outils Agricoles en Pays Bassar." In *Les Instruments Oratoires en Afrique Noire: La Fonction de la Signe,* edited by J. Peltre-Wurtz. Paris: ORSTOM, 1985.

Massina, Palouki, "Plaidoyer pour le Fonctionnement de la Juridiction." *Penant,* no. 804 (Oct.–Dec. 1990): 403–421.

Mayemba, Focanem. "Quelques Aspects du Code Togolais de la Famille." *Penant,* no. 791 (July–Oct. 1986): 228–256.

Mazza, Olympio. "Les Problémes Militaires en Afrique Noire." CHEAM Memoire no. 4398, 1972.

Meissonnier, Georges. "Analyse de la Legislation Africaine en Matière de Droit des Sociétés." *Revue Juridique et Politique,* no. 3 (July–Sept. 1976): 331–375.

Merlet, Luois. "Domaine Réservé: La Protection de la Faune." *Politique Africaine,* no. 27 (1987): 55–66.

Michel, M. "The Independence of Togo." In *Decolonization and African Independence,* edited by P. Gifford and W. R. Louis. New Haven, Connecticut: Yale University Press, 1988.

———. "Le Togo dans les Rélations Internationales au Lendemain de la Guerre: Prodrome de la Décolonisation ou 'Petite Mésentente Cordiale'?" In *Les Chemins de la Décolonisations de l'Empire Colonial Français,* edited by C. R. Ageron. Paris: CNRS, 1986.

Mignot, Alain. "La Justice Traditionnelle, une Justice Parallèle." *Penant,* no. 775 (Jan.–Mar. 1982): 5–30.

———. "Les Rélations entre la France et le Togo en Matière de Securité Sociale." *Penant,* no. 758 (Oct.–Dec. 1977): 450–485.

Milcent, E. "Tribalisme et Vie Politique dans les Etats du Bénin: Togo et l'Ombre d'Olympio." *Revue Française d'Etudes Politique Africaine,* no. 18 (June 1967).

Natchaba, Ouattara Fambare. "Bilan de la Ière Législature de la 3ème République Togolaise." *Revue Juridique et Politique.* vol. 39, no. 3–4 (1985): 860–70.

———. "L'Evolution de l'Administration Territoriale du Togo." Thesis, University of Poitiers, 1973.

———. "L'Unité du Syndicalisme Togolais." *Penant,* vol. 92, no. 777/78 (1982): 32–72.

Nieuwaal, E.A.B. van Rouveroy van. "Chieftainship in Northern Togo." *Verfassung und Recht in Ubersee,* vol. 3, no. 2 (1980): 115–121.

———. "La Justice Coutumière dans le Nord Togo." *Penant,* no. 751 (Jan.–Mar. 1976): 35–70.

Nomedji, Nicolas. "Les Partis Politiques au Togo et au Cameroun." Thesis, Poitiers University, 1966.

Olympio, Sylvanus. "African Problems and the Cold War." *Foreign Affairs,* vol. 40 (1961): 50–57.

Owona, Joseph. "Le Constitution de la IIIème République Togolaise — l'Institutionalisation du RPT." *Revue Jurdique et Politique,* no. 3 (July–Sept. 1980): 716–729.

Pana, Ewihn-Liba. "Les Limites Sectorielles de l'Experience Togolaise de Vingt and de 'Planification'." *Africa Development,* vol. 14, no. 3 (1989): 63–77.

Pauvert, Jean-Claude. "L'Evolution Politique des Ewe." *Cahiers d'Etudes Africaines,* no. 2 (May 1960): 161–92.

Peloux, Alain. "Les Rélations Ghaneo-Togolaises, Jusqu'en Fevrier 1965." Thesis, University of Paris, 1967.

Placca, Jean-Baptiste Dossé. "Is Togo Television Yours or Mine?" *Index on Censorship,* vol. 13, no. 5 (1984): 21–24.

Pocanam, Meyela. "Quelques Aspects du Code Togolais de la Famille." *Penant,* vol. 46, no. 791 (1986): 228–256.

"Pompidou en Haute Volta et au Togo." *Revue Française d'Etudes Politique Africaines,* no. 84 (Dec. 1972): 5–8.

Praetor, Africanus. "La Fin d'une Idylle." *L'Afrique et l'Asie,* no. 3 (1958): 16–22.

"President Eyadema Parle de la Jeunesse." *Bingo,* no. 432 (Jan. 1989): 8–13.

Prouzet, Michel. *La République du Togo.* Paris: Berger-Levrault, 1976.

Quashie, Leonidas. "La Commune Togolaise." *Revue Juridique et Politique,* no. 2 (April–June 1968): 397–406.

Rauss, R. "Les Disparités Régionales en Togo." *Globe* (Geneva), no. 117 (1977): 57–70.

"République Togolaise." *Europe-France-Outre-mer,* annual June Special Issue, 1960–1987.

Riou, Lucien. *Répertoire de Legislation Togolaise.* Lomé: Editogo, 1965.

Schramm, Josef. *Togo.* Bonn: K. Schroeder, 1959.

Segbeaya, Louis. "L'Organisation Judiciaire du Togo en Matière Civile." *Revue Juridique et Politique,* no. 4 (Oct.–Dec. 1969): 605–612.

Soglo, Christian Komi. "Les Hesitations au Togo." In *Les Nouvelles Constitutions Africaines: La Transition Démocratique,* edited by Henry Roussillon, 163–172. Toulouse: IEP, 1992.

Taton, Robert. "Le Général Eyadema Plébiscité." *Europe-Outre-mer,* no. 56 (Sept. 1979): 7–12.

"Tentation de Coup d'Etat au Togo." *Afrique Contemporaine,* no. 141 (Jan.–Mar. 1987): 57–8.

Thibault, Jean. "Togo—Affirmation de l'Autorité du Général Eyadema." In *L'Année Politique Africaine 1972,* edited by Pierre Biarnes, et al. 1170–1173. Dakar: Société Africaine d'Edition, 1973.

———. "Togo—Entre 'Francophone' et 'Anglophones'." In *L'Année Politique Africaine 1973,* edited by Pierre Biarnes, et al. 1167–1171. Dakar: Société Africaine d'Edition, 1974.

Thompson, Virginia. *West Africa's Council of the Entente.* Ithaca, New York: Cornell University Press, 1972.

Togo. Conference Nationale Souverain. *Resolutions, Declaration et Appel.* Lomé: 1991.

"Togo." *Europe Outre-mer,* Special Issue March–April 1978; Special Issue March 1982; Special Issue February 1986; and April–May 1987.

Togo. Paris: Editions Delroisse, 1971.

Togo. Buhl-Baden: Verlag Konkordia, 1961.

"Togo." In *Academic Freedom and Human Rights Abuses in Africa.* New York: Human Rights Watch, 1991.

"Togo." In *Africa,* edited by Sean Moroney, 543–550. New York: Facts on File, 1989.

"Togo." In *Africa South of the Sahara 1971+.* London: Europa Publications Ltd., 1971+

"Togo." In *African Contemporary Record 68/69+,* edited by Colin Legum. New York: Africana Pub. Corp., 1969–1991.

"Togo." In *Année Africaine 1969+.* Paris: Pedone, 1971+.

"Togo." In *L'Année Politique Africaine 1970+,* edited by Pierre Biarnes, et al. Dakar: Société Africaine d'Edition, 1970+.

"Togo." In *Black Africa: A Comparative Handbook,* edited by Donald G. Morrison, et al. New York: The Free Press, 1972, 1990.

"Togo." In *Constitutions of Nations,* edited by Amos J. Peaslee, 890–905. The Hague, Mouton, 1965, 5th ed.

"Togo Aujourd'hui." Special issue of *Sentiers,* no. 62 (1969).

"Togo Authentique." Special Issue of *Politique Africaine,* March 1987.

"Togo: Le Complot de Me. Kutuklui." *Revue Française d'Etudes Politiques Africaines,* no. 58 (Oct. 1970): 10–11.

"Togo and Dahomey: The Kutuklui Affair." *Africa Confidential,* vol. 12, no. 25 (Dec. 21, 1971): 4–5.

"Togo: Eyadema, Quinze Ans de Pouvoir." *Europe Outre-mer,* no. 620–1 (Sept.–Oct. 1981): 5–35.

"Togo: Game, Set and Match." *Africa Confidential* (Dece. 6, 1991): 4–6.

"Togo: Leaders at Daggers Drawn." *Africa Confidential* (20 Nov. 1992): 4–5.

"Togo: Une Nouvelle Etape." *Europe-Outre-mer,* no. 596 (Sept. 1979): 3–12.

Togo: Political Imprisonment and Torture. London: Amnesty International, 1986.

"Togo: Priorité au Développement Integral." *Europe-Outre-mer,* special issue, no. 594 (July 1979).

"Togo, West Africa: An Appraisal." *Phylon,* vol. 22 (Fall 1961): 234–240.

Toulabor, Comi M. "L'Art du Faible." In *Le Politique par le Bas.* 107–45. J. F. Bayart, A. Mbembe, and C. Toulabor. Paris: Karthala, 1992.

———. "Dix Ans de 'Démocratisation' au Togo: Les Faussaires de la Démocratie." In *Année Africaine 1989,* 287–310. Paris: Pedone, 1989.

———. "Jeu de Mots, Jeu de Vilains: Lexique de la Derision Politique au Togo." *Politique Africaine,* 1, 3 (Sept. 1981): 55–71.

———. *Le Togo sous Eyadema.* Paris: Karthala, 1986.

Touval, Saadia. "Ghana and Togo." In *The Boundary Politics of Independent Africa,* 203–211. Cambridge, Massachusetts: Harvard University Press, 1972.

Traska, T. M. "Togo: Africa in Miniature." *Travel,* no. 158 (Aug. 1982): 33–38.

Verdier, Raymond. "Le Deuxième Congres Statuaire du R.P.T." In *L'Evolution Recente du Pouvoir en Afrique Noire,* 153–161. Bordeaux, CEAN, 1977.

———. "La Formation Juridique au Togo." In *La Formation Juridique en Afrique Noire,* A. Bockel, et al. Bruxelles: Bruglant, 1979.

———. "La R.P.T." *Revue Française d'Etudes Politiques Africains.* no. 745 (Jan. 1978): 86–97.

La Verité sur les Complots Contre le Peuple Togolais et son Guide. Paris: ABC, 1980.

Voule-Fritz, Marcel. "La Fonction Publique du Togo. Origine. Evolution. Perspectives." Thesis, University of Paris, 1966.

Yagla, Wen'Saa Ogma. *L'Edification de la Nation Togolaise: Naissance d'une Conscience Nationale dans un Pays Africain.* Paris: Harmattan, 1978.

Zatzfpine, Alexandre. "L'Evolution du Droit de la Nationalité des Républiques Francophones d'Afrique et de Madagascar." *Penant,* no. 748 (April–June 1975): 147–201; no. 749 (July–Sept. 1975): 346–380.

Ziemer, Klaus. "Togo." In *Demokratisierung in Westafrika.* Munich: Ferdinand Schoningh, 1984.

Economics

Aboki, Comlan R. "Essai de Formulation d'une Problématique de Développement à Partir de l'Etude de la Formulation Sociale Kuma." Ph.D. Thesis, University René Descartes, 1973.

Aduayom, Messou Adimado, and Ayéle Kponton. "Place des Revendeuses de Tissus dans l'Economie Togolaise." In *Entreprises et Entrepreneurs d'Afrique Noire,* 385–400. Paris: Ediafric.

Agbemegnan, J. "Le Commerce Extérieur du Togo." *Revue de la Société d'Etudes et d'Expansion,* no. 212 (Sept.–Oct. 1964): 617–623.

Agbobli, Edo Kodjo. *Les Moyens Financières du Développement au Togo.* Lomé: Editions du Togo, 1978.

Agier, Michel. *Commerce et Sociabilité: Les Negoçiants Soudanais du Quartier Zongo de Lomé.* Paris: ORSTOM, 1983.

———. "Etrangers, Logeurs et Patrons: l'Improvisation Sociale Chez les Commerçants Soudanais de Lomé." *Cahiers d'Etudes Africaines,* no. 81/3 (1981): 251–265.

"Agriculture: Une Action Dynamique." *Europe-Outremer,* no. 620–1, (Sept.–Oct. 1981): 21–25.

Akakpo-Ahianyo, Anani Kuma. "L'Exploitation du Palmier à Huile." Paris: Institute des Hautes Etudes de Droit Rural et d'Economie Agricole, 1962.

Alibert, Jacques. *Le Guide Bancaire du Togo.* Paris: EDITM, 1988.

———. "La Privatisation des Enterprises Publiques en Afrique Noire Francophone." *Afrique Contemporaine* (July–Sep. 1987): 35–50.

"L'Allegmagne et l'Afrique." *Marches Tropicaux et Mediterranéens,* Special issue, no. 1040 (Oct. 16, 1965): 2471–2506.

Allsopp, W.H.L. "Establishing a Fisheries Industry in Togo." *Nigerian Field,* vol. 32, no. 1 (Jan. 1967): 33–37.

Almeyda de Stemper, G. "The Role of Credit in Development Projects: The Credit Union Movement in Togo." *African Review of Money, Finance and Banking,* no. 1 (1987): 27–44.

Amin, Samir. *L'Afrique de l'Ouest Bloquée: L'Economie Politique de la Colonisation, 1880–1970.* Paris: Editions de Minuit, 1971.

Anheier, Helmut K. "Private Voluntary Organizations, Networks and Development in Africa—Nigeria, Senegal and Togo." Ph.D. Thesis, Yale University, 1986.

Annuaire des Statistiques du Commerce Extérieur du Togo. Lomé: Ministére des Finances, 1969.

Anson-Meyer, Monique. "Activités d'Exportation de Produits Primaires et Développement Economique: l'Example du Togo." *Mondes et Développement,* no. 29–30 (1980): 163–169.

———. "Les Illusions de l'Autosuffisance Alimentaires: Bénin, Ghana, Nigeria, Togo." *Mondes et Développement,* vol. 11, no. 41–2 (1983): 51–79.

Antheume, Benoit. *Agbetiko: Terroir de la Basse Vallée du Mono.* Paris: ORSTOM, 1978.

———. "La Palmerie du Mono: Approche Géographique." *Cahiers d'Etudes Africaines,* no. 47 (1972): 458–484.

"Aperçus Economiques sur le Togo." *Bulletin de l'Afrique Noire,* no. 1040 (March 1980): 20072–82; no. 1147 (July 1982): 6–9.

Apithy, Sourou Migan. "A Propos du Port Commun Togo-Dahomey." *France-Outre-mer,* no. 297–8 (Sept. 1954): 16–20.

Aquereburu, S. "Le Port du Lomé." *Europe-France-Outre-mer,* no. 432 (Jan. 1966): 36–38.

Assogba, M. et al. "Intégration de la Population dans la Planification du Développement Socio-Economique. Lomé: University of Bénin, Unité de Recherche Démographique, 1986.

Atayi, Emmanuel Ayikoe. "Perceived Incentives and Disincentives as Related to Adoption of Agricultural Innovations: The Case of Small Farmers in Aného District, Togo." Ph.D. Thesis, Cornell University, 1979.

L'Atlas du Togo. Paris: Editions Jeune Afrique, 1978.

Ayawo, Hellegbo. "La Politique Agricole au Togo." Ph.D. Dissertation, University of Paris, 1981.

Ayina, Egboni. "Pagnes et Politique." *Politique Africaine,* no. 27 (1987): 47–54.

Banque Africaine de Développement. "Etude des Possibilités de Coopération Economique Entre le Ghana, la Cote d'Ivoire, la Haute

Volta, le Niger, le Dahomey et le Togo." Paris, 1970, 3 vols. Mimeograph.

Banque Centrale d'Afrique de l'Ouest. "Accords de Coopération Economique Entre la République Française et la République Togolaise 10 Juillet 1963," no. 106 (May 1964).

———. "L'Activité Industrielle au Togo." *Notes d'Information,* no. 293, April 1981.

———. "L'Agriculture au Togo en 1982." *L'Economie Ouest Africaine,* no. 316 (May 1983).

———. "Aperçu sur le 'Secteur Public' de l'Economie Togolaise." *L'Economie Ouest Africaine,* no. 177 (Oct. 1970).

———. "Balance des Paiements Extérièurs du Togo, 1978." *L'Economie Ouest Africaine,* no. 305 (April 1982).

———. "Balance des Paiements Exterièurs du Togo." *L'Economie Ouest Africaine,* annually.

———. "La Balance des Paiements du Togo: Années 1965–1967." *L'Economie Ouest Africaine,* no. 164 (July 1969).

———. "Chronologie Economique et Politique." *L'Economie Ouest Africaine,* quarterly.

———. "Le Commerce Exterièur du Togo." *L'Economie Ouest Africaine,* annually.

———. "Conjecture Economique Togolaise." *L'Economie Ouest Africaine,* annually.

———. "Les Echanges Exterièures du Togo en 1974: Evolution du Commerce Exterièur du Togo de 1950 a 1974." *L'Economie Ouest Africaine,* no. 234 (Dec. 1975).

———. "Estimation de la Population du Togo au Lér Janvier 1968." *Bulletin de Statistique,* no. 1 (1968).

———. "Indicateurs Togolais" and "Togo: Statistiques," three times annually.

———. "Togo: Chronologie Economiques et Politiques," three times annually.

———. "Togo: Comptes Economiques," three times annually.

Banque Ouest Africaine de Dévellopement. *3ème plan de Développement Economique et Social du Togo (1976–1980).* Lomé: 1983.

Barry, A. J. *Coordination et Efficacité de l'Aide.* Paris: OCDE, 1988.

Batsche, Christophe. "Le Togo et la Crise: Contrastes Régionaux et Dependance Accrué." *Revue Française d'Historie d'Outre Mer,* vol. 63, no. 3–4 (1976): 590–600.

Baudin, P. "Pathologie de la Canne à Sucre au Dahomey et Togo." *L'Agriconomie Tropicale,* no. 8–9 (Aug.–Sept. 1964): 747–755.

Bebléadzi, Atsou. "La Controle Financier et la Legislation Financéere Togolaise," Lomé: INRS, 1976.

Benoit, Daniel, and Pierre Levi. "Structures des Menages dans les Populations Rurales du sud Togo." *Cahiers d'ORSTOM,* vol. 3, no. 19 (1983): 321–333.

Bergeron, Ivan. "Privatization through Leasing: The Togo Steel Case." In *Privatization and Control of State-owned Enterprises,* edited by Ramamurti Ravi and Raymond Vernon, 153–78. Washington: The World Bank, 1991.

Bernard, Paul. *Perspectives de Péches Maritimes au Togo.* Paris: SCET Cooperation, 1969.

Blanc, M. "L'Assainissement de la Lagune de Lomé." *Industries et Travaux d'Outre Mer,* no. 254 (Jan. 1975): 33–40.

Bouffel, Marc. *Une Action de Développment à Dzogbegan.* Abidjan: Institut Africain pour le Développement Economique et Sociale, 1967.

Bovet, David, and Unnevehr, Laurian. *Agricultural Pricing in Togo.* Washington: The World Bank, 1981.

Buhler, Peter. "The Volta Region of Ghana: Economic Change in Togoland, 1850–1914." Ph.D. Thesis, University of California/San Diego, 1975.

Catrisse, Benolt. "Les Mines." *Afrique Industrie,* no. 259 (Aug. 1982): 32–48.

————. "Le Textile." *Afrique Industrie,* no. 178 (Feb. 1979): 34–81.

Checchi and Co. *A Development Company for Togo: Economic Growth in a Small Market.* Washington, D.C.: 1963.

Les 500 Produits Cles du Marché Africain. Paris: Ediafric, 1974, 1977.

Communauté Economique Européenne. République Togolaise. *Plan de Développement Economique et Social 1966–70.* 2 vols. Paris: Société d'Etudes pour le Développement Economique et Social, 1965.

Comptes nationaux du Togo. Lomé: Ministère des Finance, 1983.

Contribution aux Etudes Ethnobotaniques et Floristiques au Togo. Paris: ACCT, 1987.

Cordonnier, Rita. "Les Commerçants Ouest-Africains Entre Marchés Formels et Informel." *Cahiers de Sociologie Economiques et Culturelles,* no. 5 (1986): 115–136.

————. *Femmes Africaines et Commerce: Les Revendéuses de Tissu de la Ville de Lomé.* Paris: Harmattan, 1987.

Cornevin, Robert. Evolution des Modèles Agricoles Chez les Kabyé et Losso du Togo dans Leur Canton d'Origine et dans Les Terres de Colonisation. Paris: Dessain et Toltra, 1983.

————. "La Mise en Valeur de l'Est-Mono (Togo)." *Encyclopedie Mensuelle d'Outre-Mer,* no. 65 (Jan. 1956): 21–27.

————. "Togo 1987." *Marchés Tropicaux et Méditerranéens.* no. 2148 (Jan. 9 1987): 57–73.

————. "Togo: 20ème Anniversaire." *Afrique Contemporaine,* no. 142, 1987.

Cotton Development Programs in Burkina Faso, Cote d'Ivoire and Togo. Washington: The World Bank, 1988.

Crise Economique et Perspective de l'Emploi dans une Economique Ouverte: Le Cas du Togo. Addis Ababa: ILO, 1985.

Cuevas, Carlos E. "Togo." In *Rural Finance Profiles in African Countries,* edited by Mario Masini, 209–306. Milan: Finafrica, 1990.

Dadson, R. B., and C. Brooks. "Responses of Bambara Groundnut to Applied Nitrogen in Southern Togo." *Tropical Agriculture,* vol. 66 no. 2 (1989): 169–175.

"Dahomey, Niger, Togo: Le Decollage Economique est Commencé." *Moniteur du Commerce International,* no. 1083 (Aug. 26, 1971): 3387–3401.

Decraene, Philippe. "Togo: Eviction des Privés du Secteur Minier." *Revue Française d'Etudes Politique Africaines,* no. 98 (Feb. 1974): 15–16.

Demol, E., et al. "Lomé's Informal Industrial Sector." In *Industry and Accumulation in Africa,* Martin Fransman, 372–84. London: Heinemann, 1982.

Derrien, Jean-Maurice. *Conditions de Travail et Sous-Développement: Les Industries Agro-Alimentaires au Senegal et au Togo.* Paris: CNRS, 1981.

De Surgy, Albert. *La Péche Traditionnelle sur le Littoral Evhé et Mina (de l'Embouchure de la Volta au Dahomey).* Paris: Groupe de Chercheurs Africanistes, 1966.

"Le Deuxiéme Plan Quinquennal du Togo (1971–75)." *Industries et Travaux d'Outre Mer,* no. 211 (June 1971): 445–451.

"Le Développement Minièr de l'Afrique Francophone." *Europe-France-Outre-mer,* no. 411 (Apr. 1964): 9–53.

Didier, Jean. "L'Economie Togolaise." *Revue Française d'Etudes Politique Africaines,* no. 82 (Oct. 1972): 72–79.

"La Diversification du Secteur Industriel du Togo est en Bonne Voie." *Industries et Travaux d'Outre Mer,* no. 211 (June 1971): 471–474.

Doe, Lubin Kobla. "A Simple Macroeconomic Model of Togo." Ph.D. Thesis, University of Arizona, 1979.

Doku, M. K. "Economics, Foreign Aid and Foreign Policy." Ph.D. Thesis, Claremont College, 1972.

"Dossier Togo." *Afrique Industrie,* vol 138 no. 1, (May 1973): 34–73.

Duanenyo, S. "La Révolution Verte: Discourse et Financment." *Politique Africaine.* no. 27 (1987): 31–36.

Dupré, George. "Aspects Techniques et Sociaux de l'Agriculture en Pays Bassari." *Cahiers du Centre de Récherches Anthropologiques,* vol. 3 (1965): 75–159.

Dzobegan, A. *Togo: Une Action de Développement.* Lomé: INADES, 1967.

Economic Commission for Africa. *Le Role des Sociétés Transnationales dans l'Economie Togolaise.* Addis Ababa: 1984.

Economie des Pays d'Afrique Noire: Paris: Ediafric, 1979.

"Effectifs et Masses de Salaires dans le Secteur Privé." *Bulletin de Statistique* (Lomé), no. 9 (1967): 1–19.

Egbeto, K. I., and A. Bender. "La Limitation des Risques dans la Pratique des Crédits Traditionnels en Afrique Noire: Quelques Réflexions sur la Base de l'Experience Togolaise." *Genève-Afrique,* vol. 26, no. 2 (1988): 29–46.

"L'Entreprises Industrielles Togolaises." In *Enterprises et Entrepreneurs d'Afrique Noire,* 493–506. Paris: Ediafric.

"Etude sur les Agents du Secteur Public en Mars 1967." *Bulletin de Statistique* (Lomé), no. 1 (1968): 1–11.

Evaluation de l'Impact Economique et Social des Programmes de Développement Contonnier. Washington: The World Bank, 1988.

Everett, R. "Privatization: A Case Study of the Société Togolaise de Siderurgie." *Africa Report,* vol. 32, no. 6 (1987): 59–61.

Fair, Denis. "The Poorest of West Africa—Benin, Togo, Ghana and Cote d'Ivoire." *Africa Insight* (Pretoria), vol. 19, no. 4 (1989): 241–7.

Finance, Echanges et Monnaie des Pays d'Afrique Noire. Paris: Ediafric, 1975.

Francis, David George. "Individual Characteristics and Structural Effects as Predictors of Adoption of Improved Agricultural Practices in Togo." Ph.D. Thesis, Cornell University, 1971.

———. "Population Statistics and Response to Rural Development Activities in Togo." *Journal of Rural Economics and Development* (Ibadan), vol. 10, no. 1 (September 1976): 21–28.

———, and Velasco, J. R. "Diffusion of Innovation in West Africa: A New Look at the Western Model." *Journal of Asian and African Studies,* Jan.–Apr. 1974: 67–76.

Francophone West Africa: Business Opportunities. London: Metra Consulting Group, 1982.

Fuller, Susan. "Cornflake Syndrome: Scorning of Local Foods." *Atlantic,* vol. 217 (May 1966): 110–112.

Funk, E., et al. *Incentive Policy Concept and Principles with an Application to Small-Scale Enterprises in Togo.* Paris: Laboratoire de Récherches en Economie Appliquée, 1988.

Gartner, Karl. *Togo: Finanztechnische Studie uber die Entwicklung des Deutscher Verwaltung.* Darmstadt: E. Raabe, 1924.

Gerardin, Hubert. *La Zone Franc.* 2 vol. Paris: Harmattan, 1989.

Gerster, Richard. "How to Ruin a Country: The Case of Togo." *IFDA Dossiers* (Nyon), no. 71 (1989): 25–36.

Gibert, Charles. *Etude d'une Reforme des Structures de la SONADEF.* Paris: 1963.

Goussault, Y., and G. Delprat Dulphy. "L'Animation des Communautés de Base en Afrique. Au Maroc, au Togo, au Senegal la Commune est la Cellule de Base." *Développement et Civilisations,* no. 2 (June 1960): 39–47.

Gozo, K. M. *Effets de la Recession sur l'Economie Togolaise.* Addis Ababa: ILO, 1985.

Gribelin, Pierre, and Georges Beal-Rainaldi. "Trente Ans d'Aide Française à la Production Africaine et Malgache de Café." *Bulletin de Liaison et d'Information de l'Administration Centrale,* no. 25 (Feb.–April 1964): 31–41.

Hallard, J. N. "Une Action de Développement Integrée dans le Nord Togo (1967–68)." *Agronomie Tropicale,* no. 5 (May 1969): 463–504.

Hauser, A. "Problèmes poses par l'Evaluation du Nombre des Chomèurs en Milieu Urbain Africain." *Manpower and Unemployment Research in Africa* (Montreal), vol. 6, no. 1 (1973): 11–22.

————. *Rapport d'Enquete sur les Travailleurs d'une Industrie Extractive au Togo.* Paris: ORSTOM, 1974.

Hegba, Jean. "La Place de l'Afrique dans la Politique des Investissements Privés Allemands à l'Etranger." *Revue Française d'Etudes Politiques Africaines,* Apr. 1971: 36–65.

Hetzel, Wolfgang. *Studien zur Geographie des Handels in Togo und Dahomey.* Cologne: 1974.

Hirschhoff, P. M. "The Privatization Drive." *Africa Report* vol. 31, no. 4 (1986): 89–92.

Houngues, Kouami E. "Planning Process of Public Enterprises in Togo." Thesis, California State University, 1983.

International Labor Office. *La Planification de la Main-d'Ouvre.* Addis Ababa: 1985.

————. *Rapport au Gouvernement de la République du Togo sur les Conditions de Développement du Mouvement Cooperatif au Togo.* Geneva: 1960.

————. *Rapport au Gouvernement de la République du Togo sur l'Organisation du Credit Rural et Cooperatif.* Geneva: ILO, 1969.

————. *Rapport au Gouvernement de la République du Togo sur la Situation de l'Emploi et l'Organisation du Service dans le Main d'Ouevre.* Geneva, 1960.

————. *Rapport au Gouvernement de la République du Togo sur la Situation et les Possibilités de Creation et d'Organisation de l'Artisanat Togolais.* Geneva: ILO, 1968.

Johnson-Romauld, Francis. "L'Experience des Pharmacies d'Etat en République Togolaise." *Coopération et Développement,* no. 38 (Nov.–Dec. 1971): 39–44.

————. "Togopharma et le Problème Médicament au Togo." *Afrique Contemporaine,* vol. 20, no. 116 (1981): 13–16.

Josch, Peter, and Siegfried Moslein. *Togo: Bilder, Eindrucke, Probleme, Oberfranken, Bezirkjugendring.* 1965.

Kagbara, Bassabi. *La Securité Sociale au Togo et l'Economie Nationale.* Lomé: INARES, 1976.

Kirk, M. "Technological Innovations and Changes in Agrarian Structures: The Diffusion of Animal Traction in Cameroon and Togo." *Quarterly Journal of International Agriculture,* vol. 27, no. 1 (1988): 52–63.

Kirsch, M. "Le Travail des Femmes dans les Etats Membres de la Communauté: La République du Togo et l'Etat Sous-Tutelle du Cameroun." *Industries et Travaux d'Outre Mer,* vol. 69 (Aug. 1959): 572–575.

Kjellstrom, Sven B. *Institutional Development and Technical Assistance in Macroeconomic Policy Formulation: A Case Study of Togo.* Washington: The World Bank, 1986.

Kodjovi, Nukunu. "Le Mouvement Cooperative d'Epargne-Credit du Togo." *Communautés,* no. 77 (1986): 68–85.

Konu, E. *La Cooperative Agricole d'Agu-Nyogbo ou Quelques Problèmes du Développement Rural au Togo.* Lomé: Institut d'Enseignement Supériéur du Bénin, 1969.

Kouévi, Ayi Foly. "Effets de Structure et de Termes de l'Echange sur le Deséquilibre du Commerce Exterièure et la Croissance Intense du Togo 1921–1960. Etude Complementaire sur l'Evolution Recente 1960–1967." Ph.D. Thesis, University of Paris, 1969.

Kouloun, T. "Agriculture et Aménagement Rural au Togo: Le Kabyé du Nord-Togo." Thesis, University of Clermont-Ferrand, 1985.

Kpeglo-Womas, Adjoa Hélène. "Evaluation des Besoins en formation des Travailleurs Sociaux de la Région Africaine: Le Cas du Togo." Thesis, University of Laval, 1981.

Kroker, Detlef. *Innovatives Handeln und Motivation.* Saarbrucken: Breitenbrach, 1977.

Kumekpor, Tom K., and Sylvere Issifou Looky. "External Migration in Togo." In *Modern Migrations in Western Africa,,* edited by Samir Amin. London: Oxford University Press, 1974.

Kwobie, Ayenam. "An Economic Analysis of the Farmer Resettlement Project in Northern Togo." Thesis, University of West Virginia, 1982.

Lançon, F. "Centres Urbaines Secondaires et Commercialisation des Produits Vivriers au Togo." *Economie Rurale,* no. 190 (1989): 33–39.

Lawrence, Antoine. "De l'Assistance Technique des Nations-Unis et les Objectifs des Plans de Développement des Pays Africaines." 2 vol. Thesis, University of Paris, 1973.

Le Bris, Emile. *Les Marchés Ruraux dans la Circonscription de Vo.* Paris: ORSTOM, 1984.

————. *Les Migrations Agricoles Internes dans le Sud-Est du Togo.* Paris: Maspero, 1979.

————. "Une Politique de Développement Rural dans le Sud-Est du Togo: L'Operation Regeneration des Terres de Barre." *Cahiers de l'ORSTOM,* vol. 44, no. 22 (1977): 171–198.

————. "Supression Démographique et Evolution Foncière: Le Cas du Sud-Est du Togo." *African Perspectives,* no. 1 (1979): 105–25.

Le Coq. A. *Carte Pédologique et Carte des Capacités Agronomiques des Sols: Région de Bassar.* Paris: ORSTOM, 1986.

Le Hegarat, Guy. "La Comptabilité Nationale; L'Exemple du Togo." *Développement et Civilisations,* no. 8 (Dec. 1961).

Leplaideur, A., et al. *Atlas Agro-Economique de la Région Sud-Ouest Togo.* Montpellier: CIRAD, 1986.

Le Roy, P. "Du Marchandage à la Marchandise de la Communication à l'Echange—l'Example du Togo." *Tiers Monde,* vol. 25, no. 100 (Oct.–Dec. 1984): 893–899.

Locoh, Thérèse. *La Participation des Femmes à la Vie Economique en Milieu Rural: Le Cas du Sud-Est Togo.* Lomé: Université de Bénin, Unité de Récherche Démographique, 1979.

————, and Marc Pilon. *Les Unions au Togo en 1988: Permanences et Changements.* Lomé: Université de Bénin, Unité de Récherche Démographique, 1988.

Maier, D. J. E. "Colonial Distortion of the Volta River Salt Trade." *African Economic History,* vol. 15 (1986): 13–37.

Maldonado, C. "The Underdogs of the Urban Economy Join Forces: Results of an ILO program in Mali, Rwanda and Togo." *International Labour Review,* vol. 128, no. 1 (1989): 65–85.

Mangeard, Rémi. *Paysans Africains s'Unissent pour améliorer leur Village au Togo.* Paris: Harmattan, 1984.

"Le Marché Togolais." *Marchés Tropicaux et Mediterranéens,* no. 1308 (Dec. 5, 1970): 3455–3528.

Marchés Nouveaux: Togo. Paris: Editions Jeune Afrique, 1981.

Marquette, J. "Evaluation de l'Effet du l'Arachide Comme Précédent Cultural au Togo." *Agronomie Tropicale,* vol. 41, no. 3/4 (1986): 231–41.

————. "Maintien et Améliorer des Rendements du Mais sur les Terres de Barre dans le Sud du Togo." *Agronomie Tropicale,* vol. 41, no. 2 (1986): 132–148.

Martinelli, B. "Pour une Anthropologie de la Pluralité Technique; le Cas de la Culture de l'Igname au Sud Togo." *Culture et Développement,* no. 4 (1981): 633–659.

Metra Consulting. *Francophone West Africa: Business Opportunities in the 1980's.* London: Metra, 1982.

Mignot, A. "Les Relations Entre la France et al Togo en Matière de Securité Sociale." *Penant*, no. 758 (Oct. 1977): 450–485.

Mijoux, Claude. "Les Desillusions du Phosphate." *Revue Française d'Etudes Politiques Africains*, no. 264 (Oct. 1977): 13–16.

Müller, J. O. *Etudes Sociologiques pour le Plan Quinquennal du Développement 1966–1970 de la République Togolaise.* Göttingen: Institut für Ausländische Landwirtschaft, n.d.

————. *Problèmes d'élevage Contractuel des Bovins par les Pasteurs Foulbé (Peulh) en Afrique Occidentale.* Munich: IFO Institute, 1967.

————. *Probleme der Auftrags-Rinderhaltung durch Fulbe-Hirten (Peul) in Westafrika: Motivationen und Meinungen im Hunblick auf die Entwicklung der Bäuerlichen Viehwirtschaft am Beispiel der Ewe und Andere Stämme in Togo.* Berlin: Springer, 1967.

Naigeon, Chritophe. "La Pèche sur la Cote Ouest." *Afrique Agriculture*, no. 47 (July 1979): 22–48.

Nalouara, Douti. "Le Système Coopèratif, un Instrument de Développement Economique et Social pour le Monde Rural Togolais." Thesis, Sherbrooke University, 1985.

Nankani, H. "Togo: Techniques of Privatization." In *Techniques of Privatization of State-Owned Enterprises,* vol. 2, 137–146. Washington: The World Bank, 1988.

Natchaba, O. F. "L'Unité du Syndicalisme Togolais." *Penant*, no. 777–8 (July–Dec. 1982): 32–72.

Nicolas, B. *Opération de Mise en Valeur Agricole dans la Vallée de la Kara.* Bruxelles: CEE, 1984.

Niqueux, Germaine. "La Situation Alimentaire au Togo." Thesis, University of Paris, 1984.

Norris, Edward Graham. "The Hausa Kola Trade through Togo, 1899–1912. Some Quantifications." *Paideuma* vol. 30 (1984): 161–184.

O'Brien, Louis P. "The Togo Rural Water Sanitation Development Project in the Context of Community Hand-Pump Maintenance." Thesis, University of California, Los Angeles, 1986.

Pana, Ewihn-Liba. "Les Limites Sectorielles de l'Experience Togolaise de Vingt Ans de 'Planification': Agriculture 1966–85." *Afrique et Développement*, vol. 14, no. 3 (1989): 63–79.

Payson, Michael M. "The Management of Economic Development in the Republic of Togo." In *Managing Economic Development in Africa*, 227–236. Cambridge, Massachusetts: MIT Press, 1963.

"Les Pharmacies d'Etat du Togo ou l'Experience du Togopharma." *Nations Nouvelles*, no. 18 (Dec. 1968): 17–23.

Pillet-Schwartz, Anne-Marie. "Aménagement de l'Espace et Mouvement de Population au Togo: L'Exemple du Pays Kabyé." *Cahiers d'Etudes Africaines*, vol. 26, no. 3 (1986): 317–31.

————. "Togo: Suffit-il d'Etre Kabyé pour Acceder au Développement." *Politique Africaine*, no. 32 (Dec. 1988): 85–90.

Pointel, J. G. "Essai et Enquete sur Greniers à Mais Togolais." *Agronomie Tropicale*, no. 8 (Aug. 1969): 709–718.

Pradeilles, Jean-Claude, et al. "L'Organisation Corporative des Chauffeurs de Taxis Collectifs à Bamako et Lomé." *Afrique Contemporaine*, no. 158 (Apr.–June 1991): 4–13.

"Le Premier Plan, 1966–1970." *Europe-France-Outre-mer*, no. 432 (Jan. 1966): 24–27.

"Premier Plan Quinquennal: Bilan Positif; Deuxième Plan: 76 Milliards d'Investissements." *Europe-France-Outre-mer*, no. 502 (Nov. 1971): 34–38.

Quesnel, A., and P. Vimard. "Système de Production et Dynamique de Populations en Economie de Plantations—Le Plateau de Dayes." *Cahiers des Sciences Humaines*, vol. 23, no. 3–4 (1989): 483–503.

Raunet, M. "Contribution à l'Etude Pedo-Agronomique des 'Terres de Barres' du Dahomey et du Togo." *Agronomie Tropicale*, no. 11 (Nov. 1973): 104–109.

Reithinger, Anthon. *Togo als Wirtschaftspartner*. Cologne: Bundesstelle für Aussenhandelsinformation, 1965.

Répertoire des Industries et Activités du Togo. Abidjan: Service d'Etudes Economiques de Cote d'Ivoire, 1982.

Rey, Pierre Philippe. *Les Formes de la Decomposition des Sociétés Pre-Capitalistes au Togo-Nord et la Mecanisme des Migrations Vers les Zones de Capitalisme Agraire*. Paris: Maspero, 1976.

Robert, Max. "La Mise en Valeur des Phosphates du Togo." *Annales des Mines*, Mar. 1965: 11–34.

Roudit, Philippe. "Aspects du Développement Récent de l'Economie Togolaise." *Les Cahiers d'Outre-Mer*, vol 31, no. 124 (Oct.–Dec. 1978): 359–374.

Sauvaget, Claude. *Boua, Village de Koudé: Un Terroir Kabyé*. Paris: ORSTOM, 1981.

Schwartz, Alfred. *Elements pour une Etude de l'Emploi au Togo à l'Horizon du Quatrième Plan Quinquennal 1981–5*. Paris: ORSTOM, 1982.

————. *Evolution de l'Emploi dans les Entreprises Togolaises du Secteur Moderne de 1979 à 1982*. Paris: ORSTOM, 1982.

————. *Le Paysans et al Culture du Coton au Togo*. Paris: ORSTOM, 1985.

————. "Révolution Verte et Autosuffisance Alimentaire au Togo." *Politique Africaine*, no. 36 (1989): 97–107.

Sicre (Captain). "L'Artisanat, l'Industrie et le Commerce dans le Cercle de Sokode." *Documents de Centre d'Etudes et de Récherches de Kara*, Piya (Togo), 1968: 224–236.

Sociétés et Fournisseurs d'Afrique Noire: Guide Economique Ediafric. Paris: Ediafric, 1985.

Sokal, R. "Etude de Micro-Centrales Hydroélectriques au Togo et au Bénin." *Academie Royale des Science d'Outre-Mer* (Bruxelles), vol. 32, no. 3 (1986): 479–97.

Steinholtz, Manfred. "Togo: West Africa's Middleman in a Pinch." *Africa Report* (July–Aug. 1985): 29–31.

Surgy, Albert de. *Géomancie et le Culte d'Afa Chez les Evhé.* Paris: Publications Orientalistes de France, 1981.

——— *La Pèche Traditionnelle sur le Littoral Evhé et Mina.* Paris: Groupe de Chercheurs Africanistes, 1966.

Togo. *Inventaire Economique du Togo, 1964.* Lomé: Service de la Statistique Générale, 1965.

———. *Plan de Développement Economique et Social, 1966–1970.* 10 vols. Lomé: 1966.

———. Haut Commissariat au Plan. *Annuaire Retrospectif du Commerce Special du Togo 1937–1964.* Lomé: 1966.

———. ———. *Code des Investissements du Togo.* Lomé: 1965.

———. ———. *Inventaire Economique du Togo 1965.* Lomé: 1966– (annual).

———. Ministère des Finances, de l'Economie et du Plan. *Annuaire Statistique—Années 1966–1969.* Lomé: 1971.

———. ———. *Annuaire Statistique du Togo.* Lomé, annual.

"Togo." *Africa Contemporary Record.* New York: Africana, 1975–1991.

"Togo." *Année Africaine.* Paris: Pedone, 1967+

"Togo." In *L'Economie Africaine.* Dakar: Société Africain d'Edition (annual).

"Togo." In *Momento de Economie Africaine.* Paris: Ediafric, 1966 (annual).

"Togo." In *Surveys of African Economies,* vol. 3, 613–688. Washington, D.C.: International Monetary Fund, 1970.

"Togo Authentique." *Politique Africaine,* Special Issue no. 27 (1987).

"Togo: De Réels Progrès Economiques Dans Tous Les Domaines." *Europe-France-Outre-mer,* no. 495 (April 1970): 36–40.

"Togo: Decennie de la Paix." *Europe-France-Outre-mer,* Special issue, no. 502 (Nov. 1971).

"Togo: Decennie de la Révolution Economique et Sociale." *Europe-Outre-mer,* Special Issue no. 578–9 (Mar.–Apr. 1978).

"Togo: Modest Aims Produce Rapid Growth." *Africa Report,* vol. 17, no. 8 (Sept.–Oct. 1972): 38–39.

"Togo: Priorité au Développement Integral." *Europe-Outre-mer,* no. 594 (July 1979): 11–60.

Toporowski, Jan. "Togo: A Structural Adjustment That Destabilizes Economic Growth." *IDA Bulletin* (Brighton), vol. 19, no. 1 (1988): 17–23.

Tun Wai, U., E. L. Bornemann, M. M. Martin, and P. E. Berthe. "The Economy of Togo." *IMF Staff Papers,* vol. 12, no. 3 (Nov. 1965): 406–469.

United Nations. Economic Commission for Africa. *The Cooperative Movement in Africa.* New York, 1962.

United States. Bureau of Labor Statistics. Office of Foreign Labor and Trade. *Labor Conditions in Republic of Togo.* Washington, D.C.: 1966.

United States. Department of Interior. Bureau of Mines. *Mineral Industry of Togo.* Washington, D.C.: 1965.

Uzureau and Servant. *Les Mutuelles de l'Est Mono.* Paris: SEDES, 1968.

Vignikin, K. "Production, Fécondité et Migration en Milieu Agricole: Le Cas du Sud-Est Togo." Thesis, University of Montreal, 1986.

Weigel, Jean Yves. " 'Nanas' et Pecheurs du Port de Lomé." *Politique Africaine,* no. 27 (Oct. 1987): 37–46.

"Women's Participation in Development." In *Women and Economic Development,* edited by Kate Young, 171–208. Paris: UNESCO, 1986.

Wuffli, Peter A. "Karl Rohrback: Praktische Entwicklungshufe in Togo." *Schweizer Monatsheft für Politik, Wirtschaft, Kultur,* (Zurich), vol. 62. no. 2 (Feb. 1980): 107–112.

Wulker, Gabriele. *Togo: Tradition und Entwicklung.* Stuttgart: E. Klett, 1966.

Wyllie, Robert W. "Migrant Anlo Fishing Companies and Socio-political Change: A Comparative Study." *Africa,* vol. 39, no. 4 (Oct. 1969): 396–410.

La Zone Franc et l'Afrique. Paris: Ediafric, 1977.

Education

Actes du Second Séminaire sur les Questions de Population dans l'Enseignement des 2e et 3e Degrés au Togo. Lomé: Université de Bénin, Unité de Récherche Démographique, 1983.

Actes du Troisième Séminaire sur les Questions de Population dans l'Enseignement des 2e et 3e degrés au Togo. Lomé: Université de Bénin, Unité de Récherche Démographique, 1984.

Adick, Christel. *Bildung und Kolonial issues in Togo: eine Studie zù den Entstehung Zusammenhangen eines Europaisch Gepragten Bildung-Swesens in Africa.* Basel: Beltz Weinhelm, 1981.

Agbloyoe-Koumagio, A. "La Scolarisation des Filles au Togo." Thesis, University of Montreal, 1984.

Akakpo, A. "The Intersection of Education, Culture and Communications in Africa: The Togolese Experience." *Educafrica,* no. 11 (1984): 138–146.

Atignon, Koffi. "Reform of the Educational System of Togo." In *Educational Reforms and Innovations in Africa,* 38–47. Paris: UNESCO, 1978.

Biraimah, Karen Coffyn. "The Impact of Gender-Differentiated Education on Third World Women's Expectations: A Togolese Case Study." Ph.D. Thesis, SUNY/Buffalo, 1982.

―――. "The Impact of Western Schools on Girls Expectations: A Togolese Case." *Comparative Education Review,* vol. 24, no. 2, pt. 2 (June 1980): 196–208.

Cheser, David Wayne. "Effects of Age, Sex and Cultural Habitat on the Development of Piagetian Spatial Concepts Among Rural and Urban Children from Togo." Ph.D. Thesis, George Peabody College for Teachers, 1978.

Comhaire-Sylvain, S. "L'Instruction des Filles à Lomé." *Problèmes Sociaux Congolais,* no. 82 (Sept. 1968): 93–122.

Devauges, Roland. *Conceptions et Attitudes des Eleves Togolais au Lendemain de l'Independance (1961), à l'Egard de Leur Avenir Personnel.* Paris: ORSTOM, 1973.

Djassoa, G. "Educational Guidance and Students' Personal Satisfactions." *Journal of Negro Education,* vol. 53, no. 4 (1984): 481–90.

Dogbé, Yves Emmanuel. "La Crise de l'Education." Thesis, University of Benin, 1975.

Ehlan, Dogbevi Badagbo. *Mana ou Jeu d'Education Sanitaire.* Lomé: Publications Ehlan, 1977.

L'Enfance et al Jeunesse dans le Développement National du Togo. Paris: SEDES, 1966.

Floriani, Estelle. "Qui à Peur de la Philosophe?" *Politique Africain,* vol. 27 (1987): 67–72.

Fontvieille, J. *Togo, Les Bibliothèques: Enquetes et Propositions de Développement.* Paris: UNESCO, 1977.

Gbégnon, Amévi Gbedefé. "Education and Modernization in Togo Since Independence." Thesis, University of Southern California, 1988.

Hein, Charles. "Adult Literacy and Adult Language Preference for the Language of Instruction and Mass Media in Selected Adult Populations in Southern Togo." Ph.D. Thesis, University of Wisconsin, 1975.

Houenassou, Kayissou L. *Dualisme de l'Education dans les Pays de la Cote de Bénin.* Lomé: INRS, 1973.

Houenassou-Houangne, K. "Intégration de la Jeune Fille aux Institutions Educatives du Togo." *Aaword in Nairobi 1985.* Dakar: Aaword, 1986.

Kogoe, Akrima Ayadete. "Assessment of School Effectiveness and Professional Needs of School Administrators in the Republic of Togo." Ph.D. Thesis, Southern Illinois University at Carbondale, 1981.

―――. "Perceived Administrative Needs of School Executives in Togo." *Comparative Education,* vol. 22, no. 2 (1986): 149–158.

Komlan, Ahlonko. "Les Politiques Scolaires au Togo: 1960–1982." Thesis, University of Geneva, 1982.

Lange, Marie-France. "Diderot au Certificat d'Etude Togolais." *Politique Africaine,* no. 33 (1989).

———. "La Refus de l'Ecole: Pouvir d'une Société Civile Bloquée." *Politique Africaine,* vol 27 (1987): 74–86.

Locoh, T., and F. B. Dovi-Sodemekou. *Evolution de la Scolarisation au Togo vue à Travers les Statistiques Scolaires 1971–1984.* Lomé: Université de Bénin, Unité de Récherche Démographique, 1986.

Moussy, Bernadette. "Des Jardins d'Enfants au Togo et au Tchad." *Les Carnets de l'Enfance,* no. 21 (Jan.–Mar. 1973): 63–75.

Packham, E. "The Planning of an Adult Literacy Project." *Community Development Journal,* vol. 3, no. 1 (Jan. 1968): 22–28.

Statistiques Scolaires. Lomé: Direction Général de la Planification de l'Education, 1987.

Takassi, I. *Le Français Ecrit des Eleves Bassari.* Abidjan: Institut de Linguistique Appliquée, 1971.

Togo. Ministère de l'Education Nationale. *La Reforme de l'Enseignement au Togo.* Lomé: 1975.

———. ———. *La fille et l'école.* Lomé, 1973.

"Togo." In *The Educated African,* edited by Helen Kitchen, 513–518. New York: Praeger, 1962.

"Togo." In *Educational Systems of Africa,* Martena Sasnett and Inez Sepmeyer, 729–737. Berkeley: University of California, 1987.

"Togo: Educational Developments." In *International Yearbook of Education.* New York: UNESCO, 1961+.

Toulabor, C. M. "La Violence à l'Ecole: Le Cas d'un Village au Togo." *Politique Africaine,* vol. 2, no. 7 (Sept. 1982): 43–49.

Ward, Ted. "Cognitive Processes and Learning." *Comparative Education Review,* vol. 17, no. 1 (Feb. 1973): 1–10.

Science

Adabra, Agbalenyo Kossi. "L'Action Sanitaire au Togo." Ph.D. Thesis, University of Paris, 1979.

Adjanohoun, E. J., et al. *Médicine Traditionnelle et Pharmacopée.* Paris: ACCT, 1986.

Agbo, K., and M. Deniau. "Anguillulosphermie Rebelle au Traitement." *Bulletin de la Société de Pathologie Exotique et de ses Filiales,* vol. 80, no. 2 (1987): 271–273.

Aicard, Pierre. "Le Precambrien du Togo et du Nord-Ouest du Dahomey." Ph.D. Thesis, University of Nancy, 1953.

Aku, Afitier. "Contribution à l'Etude des Problèmes Posés par la Mortinalité et al Mortalité Infantile du Togo." Ph.D. Thesis, University of Toulouse, 1952.

Amegée, Yawo Emmanuel. *Les Onchocerchoses Bovines en Afrique.* Paris: Agence de Cooperation Culturelle et Technique, 1980.

Amorin, Julio-Kodzo. "Panorama de l'Evolution de la Pathologie au Togo sous Tutelle Française de 1934 a 1954." Thesis, University of Paris, 1958.

Ancelin, Rene. "Les Animaux Domestiques au Togo." Ph.D. Thesis, University of Paris, 1926.

Attignon, Hermann. *Géographie du Togo.* Lomé: 1961.

Aubreville, A. "Les Forets du Togo et du Dahomey." *Bulletin du Comité d'Etudes Historiques et Scientifiques de l'AOF,* vol. 20, no. 1–2 (1937): 1–112.

Awissi, Dayoka. "Contribution à l'Etude de l'Etiologie des Gastro-Entérites Humaines au Togo." Thesis, University of Quebec, 1981.

Bernard. "Le Cocotiers dans le Golfe du Bénin." *Etudes Dahoméennes.* no. 1 (1949): 20–46.

Breman, J. G. et al. "Single-dose Chloroquine Therapy for Children in Togo." *American Journal of Tropical Medicine and Hygiene,* vol. 36, no. 3 (1987): 469–73.

Bürg, Georg. *Die Nutzbaren Minerallagerstätten von Kamerun und Togo.* Berlin: W. de Gruyter, 1943.

Capepetta, H., and M. Traverse. "Une Riche Faune de Selaciens dans le Bassin de Phosphate de Kpogame-Hahotoe." *Geobios,* vol. 21, no. 3 (1988): 359–65.

Castaing, C., et al. "Les Umies Quessiques et la Zone de Cissaillement Crystal du Sud-Togo." *Journal of African Earth Sciences,* vol. 7, no. 5/6 (1988): 821–28.

Cheka, R. A. and A. M. Denke. "Anthropophily, Zoophily and Roles in Onchocerciasis Transmission." *Tropical Medicine and Parasitology,* vol. 39, no. 2 (1988): 123–27.

Cheneveau, R. "Pièrres de Tonnerre du Pays Mina." *Notes Africaines,* no. 77 (Jan. 1958): 11–15.

Church, R. J. Harrison. *West Africa,* chapter 24. London: Longmans, 1968.

Denke, A. M. "The Prevalence of Onchocerca in Cattle in Northern Togo in 1979." *Tropical Medicine and Parasitology,* vol. 37, no. 1 (1986): 46–48.

Dipoy-Camet, J., et al. "Epidémiologie des Teignes du Cuir Chevelu au Togo." *Bulletin de la Société de Pathologie Exotique et de ses Filiales,* vol. 81, no. 3 (1988): 299–310.

Doh, A., et al. "Facteurs Etiologiques du Goitre au Togo." In *Les Manutations dans les Pays du Tiers Monde,* edited by D. Lemonnier and Y. Ingenbleek, 403–412. Paris: INSEM, 1986.

Fishpool, L.D.C., and G. P. Popov. "The Grasshopper Faunas of the Savannahs of Mali, Niger, Benin and Togo." *Bulletin d'IFAN,* vol. 43, no. 3/4 (1981).

Food and Agriculture Organization. *Contribution aux Etudes pour la Mise en Valeur de la Région Maritime et de la Région des Savanes.* Rome: 1967.

————. *Données Hydrologiques Concernant la Région Maritime et des Savanes* [by Bouchardeau, Colombani, Roche and Feat]. Rome: 1967.

————. *Etudes Pédohydrologiques au Togo*. Rome: 1967.

————. *FAO Africa Survey*. Rome: 1961.

————. *Les Sols de la Région Maritime et de la Région des Savanes* [by Millette and Vieillefon]. Rome: 1963.

Garbonnel, G., and A. K. Johnson "Les Ostracodes Paléogènes du Togo." *Geobios*, vol. 22, no. 4 (1989): 409–443.

Gbary, A. R., et al. "Emergence du Paludisme Chloroquinorésistent en Afrique de l'Ouest: Cas de Sokodé." *Tropical Medicine and Parasitology*, vol. 39, no. 2 (1988): 142–44.

Guilcher, André. "La Région Cotière du Bas-Dahomey Occidentale: Etude de Géographie Physique et Humaine Appliquée." *Bulletin IFAN*, vol. 21, no. 3–4 (July–Oct. 1959): 357–418.

Johnson-Romauld, Faadji. "Togopharma et le Problème du Medicament au Togo." *Afrique Contemporaine*, no. 116 (July–Aug. 1981): 13–16.

Klerx, J., and J. Michot. *Géologie Africaine*. Tervuren: Musée Royal de L'Afrique Centrale, 1984.

Koulekey, Cornellie Kodjo. "Modèles Mathematiques de Précipitation Application à l'Etude Régionale de la Pluviométrie au Togo." Thesis, University of Laval, 1978.

Kouriatchy. "Contribution à l'Etude Géologique du Togo." *Bulletin du Comité d'Etudes Historiques et Scientifiques de l'AOF* (Oct.–Dec. 1933): 493–630.

————. *Géologie de Territories du Togo*. Paris: Larose, 1934.

Kpodar, Kangni-Simon, "La Lepre au Togo." Ph.D. Thesis, University of Paris, 1950.

Leveque, André. *Pedogenese sur la Soile Granitogneissique du Togo*. Paris: ORSTOM, 1979.

Locoh, Thérèse. "La Répartition par Sexe des Enfants Hospitalisés à Lomé." *Population*, vol. 42, no. 3 (1987): 549–57.

Metzger O. F. *Unsere alte Kolonie Togo*. Neudamm: J. Neumann, 1941.

Meyer, Hans Heinrich J., ed. *Das deutsche Kolonialreich*, vol. 2: *Togo, Südwestafrika, Schutz Gebiete in der Südsee und Kiautchougebiet*. Leipzig: Verlag des Bibliographischen Instituts, 1910.

Meyer, Martin. *Die Entwicklung des Medizinalwasens in der Republik Togo*. Pattensen: Horst Wellm, 1987.

Niort, Paul L. *Esquisse Géologique du Togo*. Lomé: Direction des Ecoles Evangéliques du Togo, 1965.

Poss, R., and G. Rossi. "Systèmes de Versants et Evolution Morphopédologique au Nord-Togo." *Zeitschrift fur Geomorphologie*, vol. 31, no. 1 (1987): 21–43.

Raunet, M. "Contribution à l'Etude pédoagronomique des 'Terres de Barre' du Dahomey et du Togo." *Agronomie Tropicale*, no. 11 (Nov. 1973): 1049–1069.

Robertson, T. "The Geology of Western Togoland." Ph.D. Thesis, London University, 1925.

Rossi, G. "L'Evolution Bioclimatique Actuelle de la Région des Plateaux Sud-Ouest du Togo." *Revue de Géomorphologie,* vol. 33, no. 2 (1984): 57–72.

Seeliger, H. P. R. *Togo und seine Bewohner: Entwicklungshilfe aus der Sicht des Hygienikers.* Wurzburg: Verlag der Physik-Med Gesselschaft, 1976.

Slanski, Maurice. *Contributions à l'Etude Géologique du Bassin Sedimentaire Cotièr du Dahomey et du Togo.* Paris: Editions Techniques, 1963.

Tchamie, Thiou. "Contributions à l'Etude des Savanes du Togo Central." Thesis, University of Bordeaux, 1988.

Teuscher, T., et al. "Absence of Diabetes in a Rural West African Population with a High Carbohydrate/Cassava Diet." *Lancet,* no. 8536 (1987): 765–68.

———, and P. Baillod. "Alimentation en Milieu Rural au Togo." In *Les Manutations dans les Pays du Tiers Monde,* edited by D. Lemonnier and Y. Ingenbleek, 157–162. Paris: INSEM, 1986).

Vimard, Patrice. "Tendances et Facteurs de la Mortalité dans l'Enfance sur le Plateau de Dayes, Sud-Ouest Togo." *Cahiers ORSTOM,* vol. 20, no. 2 (1984): 185–206.

Religion

Adjakly, Edoh. *Pratique de la Tradition Religieuse et Reproduction Sociale Chez les Guen/Mina du Sud-Est du Togo.* Geneva: Institut Universitaire d'Etudes du Développement, 1985.

Agbley, Seth. "The Origin of Idols [Ewe beliefs]." *Ghana Bulletin of Theology,* vol. 1, no. 7 (Dec. 1959): 3–11.

Aguessy, Honorat. "Convergences Religieuses dans les Sociétés Aja, Ewé et Yoruba sur la Cote du Bénin." In *Peuples du Cote de Bénin,* edited by François de Medeiros. Paris: Karthala, 1984.

Akakpo, Amouzouvi Maurice. *Des Origines du Christianisme en Afrique et son Expansion au XIXe siècle.* Lomé: Universite du Bénin, 1973.

Amouzou, M. "La Fonction Sociale de la Religion et la Sociologie de la Connaissance chez les Dirigeants Religieux—Etude de Cas: les Bé du Togo." *Etudes Togolaises.* vol. 23/26 (1983): 33–61.

"Arbeitberichte aus Togo." In *Mission-Entwicklung Partnerschaft Jahrbuch 1970 der Norddeutschen Missions Gesellschaft.* Bremen: 1970.

Azam, P. "Au Togo, l'Islam Devant la Foret." *Memories de CHEAM,* no. 888 (1948).

Bartels, F. L. *The Roots of Ghana Methodism.* London: Cambridge University Press, 1965.

BIBLIOGRAPHY • 365

Boucher, R. *A Travers les Missions du Togo et du Dahomey*. Paris: Librairie P. Tequi, 1926.

Carre, Olivier. *L'Islam et l'Etat dans le Monde d'Aujourdhui*. Paris: Presses Universitaires de France, 1982.

Chesi, Gert. *Voudou*. Paris: Arthaud, 1980.

Contran, Nazarene P. *Il Figlo di Avatse e la Preghiera Pioggia a Dzabi Automatico Testi Vodu*. Afanya, Togo: 1975.

Contran, Neno. "Chi a Come Lui? Nomi Teofori in Togo." *Nigrizia* (Verona), vol. 98, no. 10 (June 1980): 38–41.

Cornevin, Robert. "Lorsque les Missionaires Protestants du Bale Avaient des Vues sur Dapango." *Bulletin de l'Institut de l'Enseignement Superieur de Bénin*, no. 14 (Oct.–Nov. 1970).

David, David C. "Strategies of Minority Survival: The Case of the Gambaga Imams." *Journal of the Institute of Muslim Minority Affairs*, vol. 7, no. 1 (1986): 232–246.

Debrunner, Hans W. "Gottheit und Urmensch bei den Togo Restovoken." *Anthropos*, vol. 63/64, no. 3/4 (1968/69): 549–560.

———, and D. M. Barton. *The Church Between Colonial Powers: A Study of the Church in Togo*. London: Lutterworth Press, 1965.

Delval, Raymond. *Les Musulmans au Togo*. Paris: L'Academie des Sciences d'Outremer, 1979.

———. "Les Musulmans au Togo." *L'Afrique et l'Asie Modernes*, no. 100 (1974): 4–21.

Depaoli, Pio. "Intervistiamo un Feticista Togolese." *Nigrizia,* vol. 85, no. 3 (March 1967): 20–21.

Depeursinge, André. *Agbé-Yéyé*. Lausanne: Editions du Soc, 1966.

De Surgy, A. *La Divination par les Huit Cordolettes Chez les Mwaba Gurma*. Paris: Harmattan, 1983.

Ellingworth, P. "Methodism on the Slave Coast; 1842–1870." *Society for African Church History Bulletin*, vol. 2, no. 3 (1967): 239–248.

Faure, Jean. *Togo, Champ de Missions*. Paris: Société des Missions Evangéliques, 1948.

Fies, K. "Das Fetischdorf Arhegame und seine Bewohner auf dem Aguberge in Deutsch-Togo." *Globus*, vol. 80 (1901): 377–384.

Froelich, Jean-Claude. "Problèmes Actuels de l'Islam en Afrique Noire." *Communautés et Continents*, vol. 26 (April–June 1965): 35–47.

Gaba, C. R. "The Idea of a Supreme Being Among the Anlo People of Ghana." *Journal of Religion in Africa*, vol. 2, no. 1 (1969): 64–79.

Garnier, Christine. *Le Fetichisme en Afrique Noire*. Paris: Payot, 1951.

Grau, Eugene Emil. "The Evangelical Presbyterian Church of Ghana and Togo." Ph.D. Thesis, The Hartford Seminary Foundation, 1964.

Grunder, Horst. *Christliche Mission und Deutscher Imperialismus (1884–1914)*. Paderborn: Schoningh, 1982.

Guillon, F. "L'Islam au Dahomey et au Togo." *Memoires de CHEAM,* no. 948 (1948).

Houenassou-Houangbé, L., et al. "Les Gestionnaires du Monde: Vodu et Tro Chez les Evhé du Togo." *Etudes Togolaises,* no. 15–18 (Dec. 1981), 49–101.

Huber, Hugo. "Das Totenritual einer Ewe-Gruppe des Südöstlichen Ghana." *Ethnos,* vol. 30 (1965): 79–104.

Johnson, Gabriel Kwaoui. "'Mawu' ou 'Dieu' Chez les Ge-Mina du Bas Togo par le Patronyme." *Etudes Togolaises,* vol. 1, no. 1 (Dec. 1965): 74–87.

Larson, Thomas J. "Kabiye Fetish Religion: A Comparative Study." *Anthropos,* vol. 79, no. 1/3 (1984): 39–46.

Lasisi, R. O. "Religious Freedom Under International Mandate: The Study of French Togo Muslims—1922 to World War II." *Journal of Muslim Minority Affairs* (London), vol. 8, no. 1 (1987): 144–155.

Lohse, Wulf. "Ein Orakelbrett von den Ewe." *Mittelungen Musee für Volkerkunde Hamburg,* no. 8 (1978): 85–88.

Lucien, Frare. "A Propos du Culte des Ancetres au Togo." *Bulletin de l'Enseignement Superièur de Bénin,* vol. 7 (Oct.–Nov. 1968): 105–120; (Jan. 1969): 63–87.

Maiwald, Jürgen. *Noch Herrschen Fetisch und Phantom.* Erlangen: Verlag der Evangelische Lutheranmission, 1971.

Martin, B. G. "Les Tidjanis et Leurs Adversaires: Développements Récents de l'Islam au Ghana et au Togo." In *Les Ordres Mystiques dans l'Islam,* edited by A. Popovic and G. Veinstein. Paris: EHESS, 1986.

Maupoil, Bernard. *La Géomanie à l'Ancienne Cote des Esclaves.* Paris: Institut d'Ethnologie, 1943.

Merlo, Christian. "Synthèse de l'Activité Fetichiste aux Bas Togo et Dahomey." *Bulletin de l'IFAN,* vol. 12, no. 4 (Oct. 1950).

Meynier, O. *De Dakar au Dahomey Pays des Feticheurs et des Palmes.* Algiers: Ancienne Imprimerie Victor Heintz, 1937.

Milum, John. *Thomas Birch Freeman: Missionary Pioneer to Ashanti, Dahomey and Egba,* London, 1881.

Müller, Franz. "Die Religionen Togos in Einzeldarstellungen." *Anthropos,* vol. 1 (1906): 509–520; vol. 2 (1907): 201–210; vol. 3 (1908): 272–279.

Müller, Gustav. *Geschichte der Ewe Mission.* Bremen: 1904.

Müller, Karl. *Geschichte der Katholischen Kirche in Togo.* Kaldenkirchen: Steyler Verlagsbuchhandlung, 1958.

———. *Histoire de l'Eglise Catholique au Togo (1892–1967).* Lomé: Bon Pasteur, 1968.

Nelle, Albrecht. *Aufbruch von Gótterberg.* Stuttgart. Evangelische Missions Verlag, 1968.

———. *Nicht Sterben, Sondern Leben.* Bremen: Verlag der Norddeutschen Missionsgesellschaft, 1969.

Nieuwaal-Baereads, E. A. van Rouveroy, and E.A.B. van Rouveroy van Nieuwaal. "Het Mogalijke in Verzoening Bij de Anufon in Noord Togo." *Sociologische Gids,* vol. 28, no. 4 (July–Aug. 1981): 305–326.

Nomenyo, Seth. "Un Exemple d'Etude, Après Bangkok: Eglise Evangélique du Togo." *Flambeau,* vol. 40 (Nov. 1973): 207–216.

———. *Muslims in Mango.* Leiden: Afrikia Studiecentrum, 1986.

———. *La Notion de Dieu Createur dans les Croyances Traditionelles des Ewe du Sud-Togo.* Piya: Centre d'Etudes et de Recherches de la Kara, 1967.

———. *Tout l'Evangile à Tout Homme.* Yaoundé: CLE Press, 1967.

Nukunya, G. K. " 'Afa' Divination in Anlo: A Preliminary Report." *Research Review,* vol. 5, no. 2 (1969): 9–26.

———. "The Yewe Cult Among Southern Ewe-Speaking People of Ghana." *Ghana Journal of Sociology,* vol. 5, no. 1 (Feb. 1969): 1–7.

Palau-Marti, Monserrat. *Le Roi-Dieu au Bénin, Sud-Togo, Dahomey, Nigeria Occidentale.* Paris: Berger-Levrault, 1964.

Parrinder, Geoffrey. "Theistic Beliefs of the Yoruba and Ewe Peoples of West Africa." In *African Ideas of God,* edited by Edwin W. Smith, 224–240. London: Edinburgh House Press, 1950.

———. *West African Religions; Illustrated from the Beliefs and Practices of the Yoruba, Ewe, Akan and Kindred Peoples.* London: Epworth Press, 1949.

Pawlik, Jacek Jan. *Expérience Sociale de la Mort: Etude des Rites Funéraire des Bassar du Nord Togo.* Fribourg: Editions Universitaires de Fribourg, 1990.

Pazzi, Roberto. "Concezioni Religiose del Popolo Mino." *Nigrizia,* vol. 87, no. 1 (Jan. 1969): 18–23.

———. "Essai sur la Conception Religieuse du Peuple Mina (sud Togo)." *Bulletin de Enseignement Superièur du Bénin,* vol. 7 (Oct.–Nov. 1968): 87–103.

———. "Il Magico Mondo Dei Mina." *Nigrizia,* vol. 85, no. 11 (Nov. 1967): 8–12.

"Prayer in Anlo Religion." *Orita: Ibadan Journal of Religious Studies,* vol. 2, no. 2 (Dec. 1968): 71–78.

Ramsauer, R. E. "Fortschritte auf dem Wege zur Kirchlichen Reife in West Afrika." *Jahrbuch 1967–68 der Norddeutschen Missionsgesellschaft,* 1968: 68–85.

Richter, Julius, ed. *Das Buch der Deutschen Weltmission.* Gotha: L. Klotz, 1935.

Rivière, Claude. *Anthropologie Religieuse des Evhé au Togo.* Paris: Nouvelles Editions Africaines, 1978.

———. "Dzo et la Pratique Magique chez les Evé du Togo." *Cultures et Développement,* vol. 11, no. 2 (1979): 193–218.

————. "Mawu, l'Insurpassable Chez les Ewe du Togo." *Anthropos*, vol. 74, no. 1/2 (1979): 25–39.

————. "La Sorcellerie au Sud-Togo." *Ethnopsychologie*, vol. 35, no. 4 (Oct.–Dec. 1980): 63–84.

————. *Union et Procréation en Afrique: Rites de la Vie Chez Les Evé du Togo*. Paris: Harmattan, 1990.

Rivinius, Karl J. "Akten zur Katholischen Togo-Mission." *Neue Zeitung fur Missionswissenschift* (Schoneck), vol. 30, no. 3 (1979): 171–191.

"Sacrifice in Anlo Religion." *Ghana Bulletin of Theology*, vol. 3, no. 5 (Dec. 1968): 13–19.

Schlunk, Martin. *Die Evangelische Ewe-Kirche in Süd-Togo*. no. 35. Bremen: Bremer Missionsschriften, 1912.

————. *Die Norddeutsche Mission in Togo*. 2 vols. Bremen: Verlag der Norddeutschen Missionsgesellschaft, 1910–1912.

Sidza, Seti. "Islam au Togo." *Bulletin on Islam and Christian-Muslim Relations in Africa* (Birmingham), vol. 7, no. 1 (1989): 1–12; vol. 7, no. 2 (1989): 1–26.

Sossah, Kounoutcho. *Panorama Sociologique des Sectes Religieuses au Togo*. Lomé: Institut National de la Recherche Scientifique, 1976.

Spieth, Jacob. *Die Religion der Eweer in Sud-Togo*, Leipzig: 1911.

————. *50 Jahre Missionsarbeit in Ho*. Bremen: 1910.

Streibler, J. "L'Eglise Catholique du Togo." *AOF Magazine*, no. 15 (Aug. 1956).

Surgy, Albert de. "Les Cérémonies de Purification des Mauvais Projets Prénataux Chez les Mwaba-Gurma du Nord-Togo." *Systèmes de Pensée en Afrique Noire*, vol. 3 (1979): 9–75.

————. "La Deuil du Conjoint." *Systèmes de Pensée en Afrique Noire*, vol. 9 (1986): 105–134.

————. *La Divination par les Huit Cordelettes Chez les Mwaba-Gurma*. Paris: Harmattan 1983.

————. "Examen Critique de la Notion de Fétiche à Partir du Cas Evhé." *Systèmes de Pensée en Afrique Noire*, vol. 8 (1985): 263–304.

————. "Les Libations et le Role de la Presentratrice d'Eau Enfarinée dans le Sacrifice Mwaba-Gurma." *Systèmes de Pensée en Afrique Noire*, vol. 5 (1981): 127–154.

————"L'Objet du Sacrifice Moba." In *Ethnologues: Hommages à Marcel Griaule*, edited by Solange Ganay, et al., 391–413. Paris: Harmattan, 1984.

————. "Objet et Fonction Humanisante de la Mort Selon les Mwaba." *Anthropos*, vol. 79, no. 1/3 (1984): 129–143.

————. "La Sacrifice à la Lumière des Conceptions Mwaba-Gurma et Evhé." *Anthropos*, vol. 84, no. 1/3 (1989): 63–80.

————. *La Système Religieux des Evhé*. Paris: Harmattan, 1988.

Trautman, Réné. *La Divination à la Cote des Esclaves et a Madagascar*. Dakar: Memoires de l'IFAN, no. 1, 1939.

Trimua Ekom, Dake. *Naissance et Développement de l'Eglise Evangélique au Togo 1847–1980.* Strasbourg: University of Human Sciences, 1983.

Torre, Inès de la. *Le Vodu en Afrique de l'Ouest.* Paris: Harmattan, 1991.

Toulabor, Comi M. "Mgr. Dosseh, Archéveque de Lomé." *Politique Africaine,* no. 35 (1989): 68–76.

United States. Joint Publications Research Service. "Cult of the God of Thunder in Southern Togo" [by Mario Piotti]. In *Translations on Africa,* no. 429 (Sept. 8, 1966): 47–53.

Verger, Pierre. *Dieux d'Afrique: Culte des Orishas et Vodouns à l'Ancienne Cote des Esclaves en Afrique à Bahia, la Baie de Tous les Saints au Bresil.* Paris: P. Hartmann, 1954.

———. *Notes sur le Culte des Orisa et Vodun á Bahia, la Baie de Tous les Saints, au Bresil et a l'Ancienne Cote des Esclaves en Afrique.* Dakar: Memoires de l'IFAN, no. 51, 1957.

Viering, Erich. *Mission in Afrika ist Nicht Zu Ende.* Bad Salzuflen: Editions M.B.K., 1963.

———. *Togo Singt Ein Neues Lied.* Erlangen: Verlag der Evangelische Lutheramission, 1969.

Voran, Gemeinsam. *Annuaire 1974 de la Mission de l'Allemagne du Nord.* Bremen, 1975.

Wasungu, Pascal. "Idee de 'Sambande-Dieu' des Nawdeba." *Ethnopsychologie,* vol. 31, no. 2 (Sept. 1976): 171–179.

Wiegrabe, Paul. *Befreit zum Dienst.* Bremen: Verlag der Norddeutschen Missionsgesellschaft, 1970.

———. *Gott Spricht auch Ewe.* Bremen: Verlag der Norddeutschen Missionsgesellschaft, 1970.

———. *Soll's Uns Hart Ergehen.* Bremen: Verlag der Norddeutschen Missionsgesellschaft, 1970.

Wood-Lane, Paul. *La Missionnaire Freeman et les Debuts de la Mission Protestante au Dahomey-Togo.* Porto Novo, 1942.

Wülker, Gabriele. *Togo: Tradition und Entwicklung.* Stuttgart: Ernst Klett, 1966.

Literature

Adali-Mority, G. "Eve Poetry." *Ikyeame,* vol. 1, no. 1 (Jan. 1961): 49–52.

Adinyira, F. K. *Tartuif.* Accra: B.G.L., 1975.

Adotevi, Adovi John-Bosco. *Sacrilège à Mandali.* Yaoundé: CLE, 1982.

Adzomada, Jacques Kofi. *Ewe-Français Nyag Medegbale.* Lomé: Institut National de la Récherche, 1976.

———. *Repertoire et Resumes en Français des Ouvrages Ewe.* Lomé: Editogo, 1970.

Afaafia, S. I., ed. *Ku le Xome.* Accra: B. G. L., 1976.

Agawu, V. Kofi. "Tone and Tune: The Evidence for Northern Ewe Music." *Africa,* vol. 58, no. 2 (1988): 126–46.

———. "Variation Procedures in Northern Ewe Song." *Ethnomusicology,* vol. 34, no. 2 (1990): 221–244.

Agbetiafa, Komla, and Yao Nambou. *Contes au Togo.* Paris: CLE Internationale, 1980.

Agbleame, Simon A. "La Théatre dans la Litterature Ewe." In *Peuples de la Cote du Golfe de Bénin,* edited by François de Medeiros, 191–200. Paris: Karthala, 1984.

Agbotzinsou, Semuwo. "La Naissance du Theatre Togolaise Moderne." *Culture Française,* Special issue, 1984.

Ajavon, Henri. "Datchi, l'Esclave Marronne." *France-Eurafrique,* no. 168 (Dec. 1965): 36–41.

Akakpo, Thypamm Paul. "Poèmes et Contes d'Afrique." *Cercle de la Poésie et de la Peinture* (Paris), no. 25–6 (1958): 1–31.

———. *Rythme et Cadence d'une Coeur Noire.* Lomé: Imprimerie Moderne, 1959.

Akakpo-Ahianyo, Anani K. *Au Hazard de la Vie, du Monde à l'Autre.* Paris: Nouvelles Editions Africaines, 1983.

Akotey, K. *Ku di na wo.* Accra: B. G. L., 1974.

Akpatsi, R. S. *Ameadeke Memya.* Accra: B. G. L., 1974.

Aladji, Victor. *Akossivana Mon Amour.* Yaoundé: CLE, 1972.

———. *L'Equilibriste.* Yaoundé: Editions CLE, 1972.

———. *La Voix de l'Ombre.* Lomé: Haho, 1985.

Alapini, Julien. *Les Dahoméns et Togolais au Centenaire des Apparitions.* Avignon: Aubanel, 1959.

Almeida, Modeste d', and Gilbert Lacle. *Kateyoule, l'Etudiant Noir.* Lomé: Editions de la Lagune, 1965.

Amegbleame, Simon. "La Fiction Narrative dans la Production Litteraire Ewe." *Africa,* vol. 50 (1980): 24–36.

———. *Le Livre Ewe: Essai de Bibliographie.* Bordeaux: Centre d'Etude d'Afrique Noire, 1976.

———. *Sociologie des Sociétés Orales d'Afrique Noire: Les Evé du Sud-Togo.* Paris: Mouton, 1969.

Amela, Hilla-Laobe. *Odes Lyriques.* Paris: Akpagnon, 1983.

Amuzu-Kpeglo, A. *Xexeame Do Atsye.* Accra: B. G. L., 1975.

Ananou, David. *Anaphores Nouvelles.* Paris: Edition du Cerf, 1970.

———. *Le Fils du Fetiche.* Paris: Nouvelles Editions Latines, 1955.

Atsou, Julien. *L'Abomination de la Desolation.* Paris: La Pensée Universelle, 1980.

———. *Agokoli: Cruante ou Devoir.* Paris: CLE 1977.

Ayeke, K. *Asitsu Ateawo.* Accra: B.G.L., 1975.

———. *Hiebiabia.* Accra: B.G.L., 1974.

Bidi Setsoafia, H. K. *Togbui Kpeglo II.* Accra: B.G.L., 1975.

Blake, Susan Louise. *Letters from Togo.* Iowa City: University of Iowa Press, 1991.

Brench, A. C. *The Novelist's Inheritance in French Africa: Writers from Senegal to Cameroun.* London: Oxford University Press, 1967.

Byll, Cataria J. B. *L'Hote des Drance Suivi de une Pensée pour la Veuve.* Lomé: Akpagnon, 1983.

Cherchari, Amar. *Reception de la Litterature Africaine d'Expression Française jusqu'en 1970.* Paris: Editions Silex, 1982.

Contran, Nazareno P. *La Morte a una Cosa Antica.* Afanya, Togo: 1975.

———. *Zobada il Fuoco Cattivo. Canti Populari del Togo Meridionale.* Afanya, Togo: 1975.

Cornevin, Robert. "Felix Couchoro (1900–1968), Premier Romancier Régionaliste Africain." *France-Eurafrique,* no. 196 (June 1968): 74–76.

———. "Les 'Romans Togolais' de Werner von Rentzell." *France-Eurafrique,* no. 207 (June 1969): 42–43.

Couchoro, Felix. *Accussée, Levez Vous.* Lomé: Togo-Presse, 1967.

———. *Amour de Feticheuse.* Ouidah: Almeida, 1941.

———. *Amour de Feticheuse au Togo.* Lomé: Togo-Presse, 1967.

———. *Bea et Marilou.* Lomé: Togo-Presse, 1963.

———. *Les Caprices du Destin.* Lomé: Togo-Presse, 1966.

———. *Crouzet, Henri. Aziza de Niamkoko.* Paris: Presses de la Cité 1959.

———. *D'Aklakou a El Mina.* Lomé: Togo-Presse, 1970.

———. *Le Dix Plaies de l'Afrique.* Lomé: Togo-Presse, 1968.

———. *Le Dot, Plaie Sociale.* Lomé: Togo-Presse, 1966.

———. *Drame d'Amour à Anécho.* Ouidah: Almeida, 1950.

———. *L'Esclave.* Ouidah: Almeida, 1930. Reprint, Paris: Akpagnon, 1984.

———. *Fille de Nationaliste.* Lomé: Togo-Presse, 1969.

———. *Gangsters et Policiers.* Lomé: Togo-Presse, 1967.

———. *Les Gents sont Mechants, Ici Bas Tout se Plaie.* Lomé: Togo-Presse, 1968.

———. *L'Héritage, Cette Peste, ou Les Secrets d'Eléonore.* Lomé: Editogo, 1963.

———. *L'Homme à la Mercedes-Benz.* Lomé: Togo-Presse, 1963.

———. *Max Mensah.* Lomé: Togo-Presse, 1962.

———. *Le Passe Ressurgit.* Lomé: Togo-Presse, 1966.

———. *Pauvre Alexandrine.* Lomé: Togo-Presse, 1964.

———. *Le Secret de Ramanou.* Lomé: Togo-Presse, 1968.

———. *Les Secrets d'Eleonore.* Lomé: Togo-Presse, 1963.

———. *Sinistre d'Abidjan.* Lomé: Togo-Presse, 1965.

Cridel, B. "Contes Kabré." *Documents du CERK* (1968): 156–74.

————. "Le Gendes, Proverbes er Devinette Kabré." *Documents du CERK* (1968): 256–62.

Dabla, Amevi. "Pour l'Eclosion d'une Litterature Togolaise Populaire." *Afrique Nouvelle,* July 3–9, 1985: 12–13.

Depeursinge, André. *Agbe-Yeye: Croquis du Togo.* Lausanne: Editions du Soc, 1966.

De Saivre, D. "Entretien avec Senouco Agbota Zinsou, Auteur Togolais." *Recherche, Pédagogie et Culture,* vol. 57 (1982): 71–5.

Djeguema, Koffi. *Introduction à une Etude du Profane et du Sacré dans La Litterature Orale Traditionnelle Ife.* Paris: Creteil, 1980.

Dogbé, Yves-Emmanuel. *Affres!* Porto Novo: Rapidex, 1966.

————. *Anthologie de la Poesie Togolaise.* Paris, Akpagnon, 1980.

————. *Contes et Legendes du Togo.* Paris: Akpagnon, 1981.

————. *Le Devin Amour.* Paris: Oswald, 1976.

————. *Fables Africaines.* Paris: Akpagnon-ACCT, 1979.

————. *Fables Africaines, Precedées de la Puissance des Mots.* Paris: Harmattan, 1978.

————. *Flammé Bleme.* Paris: Editions de la Revue Moderne, 1969.

————. *Gedichten Van Yves Emmanuel Dogbé.* Utrecht, 1987.

————. *L'Incarceré.* Paris: Akpagnon-ACCT, 1979.

————. *Morne Soliloque.* Paris: Akpagnon, 1982.

————. *La Victime.* Paris: Akpagnon-ACCT, 1979.

Dogbeh-David, Richard. "L'Offrande aux Ancetres (dans une Famille Houédah du Bas Togo)." *France-Eurafrique,* no. 166 (Oct. 1965): 29–32.

Dunton, Chris. "Appraisal of a Pioneer." *West Africa,* July 4, 1988: 1208.

Dzobo, N. K. *African Proverbs: Guide to Conduct.* Accra: University of Cape Coast, 1973.

Ebia, Bassari. *Lexique Français-Kabiyé-Evé.* Lomé: Institut National de la Récherche, 1976.

Egblewogbe, E. Y. *Games and Songs as Education Media: A Case Study Among the Ewe of Ghana.* Accra: Ghana Publishing Corporation, 1975.

Elaho, Raymond O. "Literature et Politique: L'Incacere de Yves-Manuel Dogbé." *Peuple Noirs—Peuple Africaines,* vol. 20 (1981): 133–47.

————. "Une Lecture de 'Morne soliloque," d'Yves-Emmanuel Dogbe." *Présence Africaine,* no. 144 (1987): 103–108.

En Savior plus sur la Litterature Togolaise. Paris: Institute Nationale des Sciences de l'Education, 1987.

Fiawoo, F. Kwasi. *Toko Atolia.* London: Longman's, 1962.

Garnier, Christine. *Va-t'en avec les Tiens!* Paris: B. Grosset, 1951.

————. *Les Voleurs de Morts.* Paris: Editions du Temps, 1958.

Ghan. A., et al. *Semences Nouvelles.* Lomé: Haho, 1986.

Gouellain, René. "Récherche Anthropologique et Théatre Akposso." *Documents de Centre d'Etudes et de Recherches de Kara,* Piya (Togo), vol. 3 (1968): 27–34.

Guenou, Julien. *Le Bonheur à l'Arrache.* Paris: Africa Media International, 1983.

Guillaneuf, Raymond. "La Presse au Togo (1911–1966)." Thesis, University of Dakar, 1967.

Herzberger-Fofona, Pierrette. *Ecrivains, Africains et Identités Culturelles Entretiens.* Tubinger: Stauffenberg, 1989.

Huannou, Adrien. *Essai sur L'Escalve, Roman de Felix Couchoro.* Paris: AM, 1987.

Inawissi, Naye Theophile. *Les Grands Jours.* Paris: Editions Akpagnon, 1983.

Ketoglo, A. *Petit Recueil de Chants et Rythmes Populaires Togolais.* Lomé: Ministère de l'Education Nationale, 1974.

Klutse, L. *Akpalm fe hawo.* Accra: B.G.L., 1974.

Koffi, Koffi. *Experience de Ma Jeunesse.* Lomé: Editions, 1982.

Kpomassie, Tete-Michel. *L'Africain du Groenland.* Paris: Flammarion, 1980.

Kuakavi, K. M. *Les Racines du Mal Négre.* Lomé: Haho, 1985.

Kwasimunka, G.W.K. *Evegbé-Daganawo.* Accra: B.G.L., 1973.

———. *Henewe fe gbe.* Accra: B.G.L., 1975.

Lebel, A. Roland. *L'Afrique Occidentale dans la Litterature Française Depuis 1870.* Paris: Larose, 1925.

Le Boul, P., and P. Verdier. "Une Expression Litteraire: La Conte Togolais." *Bulletin de l'Enseignement Supérièur du Bénin,* no. 1 (Jan. 1967): 9–34.

———. "Les Personnages dans le Conte Togolais." *Bulletin de L'Enseignement Supérièur du Bénin,* no. 3–6, Nov. 1967–June 1968.

Lecharbonnier, Bernard. "Introduction à la Litterature Negroafricaine d'Expression Française." *Française dans le Monde,* vol. 12, no. 94 (Jan.–Feb. 1973): 6–10.

La Litterature Africaine Francophone. Lausanne: Bibliotheque Cantonale et Universitaire, 1991.

Madjri, Dovi J. *Sociologie de la Litterature Togolaise.* Lomé: Direction des Affaires Culturelles, 1975.

Magnier, Bernard. "Senouvo Agbota Zinsou: De Lomé à Limoges." *Notre Librairie,* vol. 102 (July–Aug. 1990): 61–3.

Michael, Colette Verger. "Entretien avec Yves Emmanuel Dogbe." *Contemporary French Civilization,* vol. 7, no. 2 (Winter 1983): 211–16.

Midiohouan, Guy Ossito, and C. A. Amoura. "Entre la Résignation et le Refus: Les Ecrivains Togolais d'Expression Française sous le Régime Eyadema." *Géneve-Afrique,* vol. 29, no. 1 (1991): 53–70.

Mongoya, Segnon K. *L'Ecoute du Sage*. Lomé: ACCT, 1982.

Motte, S. A. *Mia Denyigba*. Accra: B.G.L., 1976.

Nicole, Jacques. "Downstepped Low Tone in Nawdm." *Journal of African Language and Literature* (Dordrecht), vol. 2, no. 2 (Oct. 1980): 133–139.

Nyomi, C.K. *Nunyata Enelia*. Accra: B.G.L., 1975.

Obianim, James S. *Amegbetoa alo Agbezuge fe mutinya*. London: Macmillan, 1949.

———. *Pmegbetoa ou les Aventures d'Agbezuge*. Paris: Karthala, 1990.

Oloukpona-Yinnon, Adjai. "L'Arbre de la Connaissance: Le Roman de la Conquete du Togo Allemand." *Komparatistische Hefte,* vol. 12 (1985): 91–105.

Ouro-Djobo, Mamah Fousseni Abby-Alphah. *La Culture Traditionnelle et la Litterature Oral des Tem*. Stuttgart: Franz Steiner, 1984.

Prilop, G. *Contes et Mythes du Togo*. Lomé: Haho, 1985.

Rentzell, Werner von. *Die Fahrt des Ave Cornelius*. Hamburg: Alster Verlag, 1921.

———. *Die Heisse Not*. Hamburg: Alster Verlag, 1922.

———. *Unvergessenes Land*. Hamburg: Alster Verlag, 1922.

Rey-Human, Diana. "Pratiques Langagiares et Formes Litteraires." *Journal of the Anthropological Society of Oxford,* vol. 13, no. 1 (1982): 1–13.

Rey-Hulman, Diana. "La Vie Ephemere d'un Conteur Public à Sansanné-Mango." *Cahiers de Litterature Orale,* vol. 11 (1982): 182–5.

Ricard, Alain. *L'Invention du Théatre: Le Théatre et le Comédiens en Afrique Noire*. Lausanne: L'Age d'Homme, 1986.

———. *Naissance du Roman Africain: Félix Couchoro*. Paris: Présence Africaine, 1987.

———. "Une Pays des Tortues Qui Chantent: Melanges Pour Jacques Scherer." In *Dramaturgies: Langages dramatiques,* edited by Jacqueline de Jomaron, 99–103. Paris: Nizet, 1986.

———. "Reflexions sur le Théatre à Lomé." *Récherche, Pedagogie et Culture,* vol. 57 (1982): 63–70.

———. "Du Romancier au Feuilletoniste: Les Limites de l'Ecriture de Félix Couchoro." *Récherche, Pedagogie, Culture,* vol. 57 (1982): 47–56.

Riez, Janos, and Alain Ricard. *Le Champ Littéraire Togolaise*. Bayreuth: Echard Breitinger, 1991.

Salami, Sabit Adegboyega. "Félix Couchoro." *Black Orpheus* (Lagos), vol. 4, no. 2 (1982): 33–45.

———. "L'Héritage de la Technique du Conte Africain dans l'Oeuvre de Félix Couchoro." Thesis, University of Sherbrooke, 1979.

Sellin, Eric. "Letter from West and Central Africa." *World Literature Today,* vol. 58, no. 1 (Winter 1984): 42–5.

Stephenson, E. *Terres Brulées.* Lomé: Akpagnon, 1984.

Sypol, Francis. *Qui Donc est Mon Prochain?* Paris: Promotion et Edition, 1966.

Szwark, Marian. *Proverbes et Traditions des Bassars du Nord Togo.* St. Augustin: Hans Volker und Kulturen, 1981.

Tchagbale, Zakari, and Suzanne Lallemand. *Toi et la Ciel: Vous et la Terre: Contes Paillars Tem du Togo.* Paris: SELAF, 1982.

Trautman, Réné. *La Littérature Populaire à la Côte des Esclaves.* Paris: Institut d'Ethnologie, 1927.

Typamm, Paul Akakpo. *Rythmes et Cadences.* Paris: Editions Akpagnon, 1981.

Van Dyke, C. "An Analytical Study of the Folktales of Selected Peoples of West Africa." Thesis, Oxford University, 1967.

Verdier, Jean. "Structures et Imaginaire dans le Conte Togolais." Thesis, Grenoble University, 1970.

Verdier, Paul. "Contes Togolais. Corpus des Contes." Thesis, Grenoble University, 1971.

————. "Une Tentative d'Approche des Problèmes Littéraires Posés par le Conte Togolais." *Bulletin de Enseignement Supérièur du Bénin,* vol. 7 (Oct.–Nov. 1968): 19–43. Also in *Documents de Centre d'E-tudes et de Récherches de Kara,* Piya (Togo), vol. 3 (1968): 39–55.

————, et al. "Colloque sur La Littérature et Les Traditions Orales Togolaises." *Documents de Centre d'Etudes et de Récherches de Kara,* Piya (Togo), 1968.

Viderot Mensah, Toussaint. *Courage, Si Tu Veux Vivre et t'Epanouir, Fils de la Grande Afrique.* Monte Carlo: Regain, 1960.

————. *Pour Toi, Nègre, Mon Frère.* Monte Carlo: Regain, 1960.

Vignondé, Jean-Norbert. "Autour de 'L'Esclave' de Félix Couchoro." *Research in African Literature,* vol. 16, no. 4 (1985): 556–63.

————. "Les Precurseurs: Félix Couchouro, Paul Hazoumé." *Notre Librairie,* vol. 69 (1989): 33–40.

Werk, Jan Kees van de. "Publishing and Literature in Togo." *The African Book Publishing Record,* vol. 11, no. 1 (1985): 201–204.

Wiegrabe, P. "Neuere Literatur in Ewe." *Afrika und Übersee,* vol. 44, no. 2 (Nov. 1960): 132–135.

Wilkinson, Jane. "Kofi Anyidoho: An Ewe Poet Between Tradition and Change." *Africa* (Rome). vol. 43, no. 4 (Dec. 1988): 543–73.

Zinsou, Senouvo Agbota. "Aux Sources de la Creation." *Notre Librairie,* vol. 98 (July–Sept. 1989): 22–25.

————. *Le Club, Piece de Théatre.* Lomé: Haho, 1984.

————. "La Naissance du Théatre Togolaise Moderne." *Culture Française,* vol. 3–4, no. 1 (1982/3): 49–57.

————. *On Jou la Comédie.* Lomé: Haho, 1984.

————. "Le Théatre et la Bible: La Katata Togolaise et le Syncretisme Culturel." Thesis, University of Bordeaux, 1989.
Zwernemann, Jurgen. *Erzahlungen aus der Westafrikannischer Savanne.* Stuttgart: Steiner, 1985.

Linguistics

Abbott, Mary, and Monica Cox. *Collected Field Reports on the Phonology of Bassari.* Legon: Institute of African Studies, University of Ghana, 1966.
Agbadza, Kokou Sénamé. "Pour une Approchment Nouvelle des Prétendus "Adverbes" Evé." *Afrique et Langage,* vol. 19, no. 1 (1983): 32–51.
Agudze-Vioka, B. "Caracteristiques des Proverbes Ewe." *Documents de Centre d'Etudes et de Recherches de Kara,* Piya (Togo), vol. 3.
Ansre, Gilbert. "Reduplication in Ewe." *Journal of African Language,* vol. 2, no. 2 (1963): 128–132.
————. *The Tonal Structure of Ewe.* Hartford, Connecticut.: Hartford Seminary Foundation, 1961.
Bertho, Jacques. "Les Dialectes du Moyen Togo." *Bulletin de l'IFAN,* vol. 14, no. 3 (1952): 1046–1107.
————. "Langues Voltaiques du Togo-Nord et du Dahomey-Nord." *Notes Africaines,* Oct. 1949: 124.
————. "Parenté de la Langue Yoruba de la Nigeria du Sud et la Langue Adja de la Région Cotière du Dahomey et du Togo." *Notes Africaines,* no. 35 (July 1947): 10–11.
Boethus, Hélène. "Basic Mood in Ife." *Journal of West African Languages,* vol. 17, no. 2 (1987): 43–70.
Bole-Richard, Remy. *Systématique Phonologique et Grammaticale d'un Parler Ewe: Le Gen-Mina du Sud Togo et Sud Bénin.* Paris: Harmattan, 1983.
Brungard, R. *Grammaire et Dictionnaire Kabré.* Notre Dame de la Providence: Polyglotte, 1937.
Bürgi, F. "Sammlung von Ewe-Sprichworten." *Archiv für Anthropologie,* vol. 13 (1914): 415–450.
Calvet, Louis-Jean. *Les Langues de Marchés en Afrique,* Paris: Didier Erudition, 1992.
Capo, Hounkpati C. "Elements of Ewe-Gen-Aja-Fon Dialectology." In *Peuples du Cote de la Golfe du Bénin,* edited by François de Medeiros, 167–178. Paris: Karthala, 1984.
————. "Le Gbe est une Langue Unique." *Africa* (London), vol. 53, no. 2 (1983): 47–57.
————. *Renaissance du Gbe: Reflèxions Critiques et Constructions sur l'Evé, le Fon, le Gen, l'Aja, le Gun.* Hamburg: Buske, 1988.
Christaller, J. G. "Die Adelesprache im Togogebiet." *Zeitschrift für Afrikanische und Ozeanische Sprachen,* vol. 1 (1895): 16–23.

Clements, G. N. "Four Tones from Three: The Extra-High Tone in Anlo Ewe." In *Language and Linguistic Problems in Africa,* edited by P.F. Kotey and H. Der-Houssikian, 168–181. Columbia, Maryland: The Hornbeam Press, 1977.

Cornevin, Robert. "Note au Sujet de la Carte Linguistique du Togo." *Bulletin de Enseignement Supérièur du Bénin,* vol. 7 (Oct.–Nov. 1968): 14–18.

Crunden, Sheila. "Une Comparaison Entre les Systèmes Phonologiques du Kabiyé, de l'Ewé et du Bassar." *Etudes Togolaises,* no. 1518 (Dec. 1981): 102–116.

Dalby, David, and P.E.H. Hair. "A Further Note on the Mina Vocabulary of 1479–80." *Journal of West African Languages,* vol. 5, no. 2 (1968): 129–131.

Debrunner, Hans W. "Vergessene Sprachen und Tricksprachen bei den Togorestvölkern." *Afrika und Übersee,* vol. 46, no. 1/2 (Dec. 1962): 109–118.

Delord, Jacques. "Le Kaure de la Polyglotta Africana et la Kabré d'Aujourd'hui." *African Language Review,* vol. 7 (1968): 114–39.

———. *Morphologie Abregèe du Kabré.* Dakar: IFAN, 1964.

———. "Les Mots-Voyageurs [Kabré]." In *Wort und Religion/Kalima na Dini,* edited by H. J. Greschat, 133–138. Stuttgart: Evangelische Missionsverlag, 1969.

———. "Nasale Préposée dans les Noms Kabré." *Bulletin de l'IFAN,* vol. 28(B), no. 1/2 (Jan.–April 1966): 476–480.

———. "Sur le Kabré du Togo, Jeux de Tons." *Bulletin de l'IFAN,* vol. 30 (Jan. 1968): 256–268.

———. "La Transcription du Kabré." *Documents de Centre d'Etudes et de Récherches de Kara,* Piya (Togo), vol. 3 (1968): 58–60.

Der-Houssikian, Haig. "Togo's Choice." In *The Linguistic Connection,* edited by Jean Casagrande. Lanham, Maryland: University Press of America, 1983.

Duthie, A. S., and R. K. Vlaardingerbroek. *Bibliography of the Gba.* Basel: Basler Afrika Bibliographeien, 1981.

Ebia, Bassari, *Lexique Français-Kabiyé-Ewé.* Paris: Slosen, 1968.

Gasser, Marcel. "The Use of Completive and Incompletive Aspect of Nawdm Narrative Discourse." *Journal of West African Languages,* vol. 18, no. 1 (1988): 73–88.

Gayibor, N. L. "Elements de Polemologie en Pays Ewé." *Cultures et Développement,* no. 3–4 (1984): 511–36.

Hair, P.E.H. "A Note on de la Fosse's 'Mina' Vocabulary of 1479–80." *Journal of West African Languages,* vol. 3, no. 1 (Jan. 1966): 55–57.

Härrter, G. "Aus der Volkslitteratur Evheer in Togo." *Zeitschrift für Afrikanische und Ozeanische Sprachen,* vol. 6 (1902).

Heine, Berndt. "The Allocation of Loan-Words within the Nominal Class Systems of Some Togo Remnant Languages." *Journal of African Languages,* vol. 7, no. 2 (1968): 130–139.

─────. *Die Verbreitung und Gliederund der Togo Restsprachen*. Berlin: Reimer, 1968.

Hintze, Ursula. *Kwasprachen und der Sprachen der Togorestvölker*. Berlin: Akademie Verlag, 1959.

Jacobs, G. "The Structure of the Verbal Clause in Bimoba." *Journal of West African Languages*, vol. 3, no. 1 (Jan. 1966): 47–53.

Johnson, Gabriel Kwaoui. *Anécho-Ewe/Ge-Mina; Mina Basic Course*. Bloomington: University of Indiana, African Studies Program, 1967.

─────. "Le Cauri Chez les Ge (Guin) Mina du Bas-Togo." *Notes Africaines d'IFAN*, vol. 53 (Jan. 1952): 20–21.

─────. "Morphologie des Nominaux dans la Langue Ge ou Gegbe (Minapopo) du bas Togo." *Etudes Togolaises*, vol. 1, no. 1 (Dec. 1965): 51–61.

─────. "Numeration en Langue Ge ou Gegbe-Mina-Popo du Bas Togo." *Etudes Togolaises*, vol. 1, no. 1 (Dec. 1965): 88–105.

─────. "Un Problème de Terminologie: Le Mot Ewe/Eve du Bas Togo dans la Classification des Langues Negro-Africaines." *Etudes Togolaises*, vol. 1, no. 1 (Dec. 1965): 38–50.

─────. "Sur la Patronymie Ge ou Guin (Mina) et Ewe du Bas-Togo." *Notes Africaines d'IFAN*, vol. 47 (July 1950): 97–98.

Kohler. *Worterbuch des Ewesprache*. Berlin, 1954.

Kozelka, Paul Robert. "The Development of National Languages: A Case Study of Language Planning in Togo." Thesis, Stanford University, 1984.

Krass, A. C. *A Dictionary of the Chokosi Language*. Legon: University of Ghana, Institute of African Studies, 1970.

Kropp, M. E. "The Adampe and Anfue Dialects of Ewe in the Polyglotta Africana." *Sierra Leone Language Review*, vol. 5 (1966): 116–121.

─────. *Ga, Adangme and Ewe (Lomé) with English Gloss*. Legon: University of Ghana, Institute of African Studies, 1966.

Lafage, Suzanne. "Contribution à un Inventaire Chronologique des Ouvrages Entiérement ou Partiellement en Langue Ewé." *Annales de l'Université d'Abidjan*, vol. 7, no. 1 (1974): 169–204.

─────. "Le Dictionnaire des Particularités du Français au Togo et au Dahomey." *Annales de l'Université d'Abidjan*, vol. 9, no. 1 (1976): 131–141.

─────. "Facteurs de Differenciation Entre le Français d'Afrique." *Cahiers Ivoiriens de Récherche Linguistique* (Abidjan), no. 1 (April 1977): 1–49.

Lavergne de Tressan, M. de. *Inventaire Linguistique de l'AOF et du Togo*. Dakar: IFAN, 1953.

Lebikaza, Kéziè L. "L'Alternance Consmantique et le Problème de l'Interaction Entre Traits Segmentaux et Suprasegmentaux en Kabyé." *Afrikanistische Arbeitspapiere* (Cologne), vol. 19 (1989): 147–163.

Manessy, G. "La Classification Nominale en Proto-Guang." *Afrikanistische Arbeitspapiere* (Cologne), vol. 9 (1987): 5–49.

―――. "Le Français d'Afrique Noire." *Langue Française,* no. 37 (Feb. 1978): 91–105.

Mukarovksy, Hans G. "Zur Struktur des Ewe." In *Wort und Religion/ Kalima Na Dini,* edited by H. A. Greschat, 107–126. Stuttgart: Evangelischer Missionsverlag, 1969.

Muller, F. "Beitrag zur Kenntnis der Tem-Sprache (Nord-Togo)." *Mitteilungen des Seminars fur Orientalische Sprachen,* vol. 8, (1905): 251–286.

―――. "Ein Beitrag zur Kenntnis der Akasele (Tsamba)-Sprache." *Anthropos,* vol. 1 (1906): 787–803.

Ourso, Mèterwa A, "Critères de Distribution des Affixes en Lama." *Journal of West African Languages,* vol. 19, no. 1 (1989): 35–56.

―――. "Root Control Underspecification and ATR Harmony." *Studies in Linguistic Sciences,* vol. 18, no. 2 (1988): 111–127.

Paaluki, M. Tetveehaki. *La Kabiyé Standard.* Lomé: Imprimerie de L'Alphabetisation, 1981.

Painter, Colin. *Linguistic Field Notes from Banda.* Accra: Institute of African Studies of the University of Ghana, 1966.

Potekey, F. K., and D. A. Chapman. *Ewe Spelling.* Achimota, Ghana: Achimota Press, 1944.

Prost, André. "Les Classes Nominales en Bassari-Tobote." *Journal of African Languages,* vol. 2 (1963): 210–217.

―――. *Le Lamba, Dialecte des Lambadu Kandé au Togo.* Dakar: IFAN, 1964.

―――. *Li Tamari, Documents Linguistiques.* University of Dakar, Dakar, 1983.

―――. *Li-tamari, Langue des Tamberma du Togo.* Dakar: IFAN, 1964.

―――. *Le Moba.* University of Dakar, Documents Linguistiques, no. 11 (1967).

―――. "Notes Sur le Naudem du Togo: Rapports Entre le Naudem et le Moré." *Bulletin de l'IFAN,* vol. 28, no. 1/2 (1966): 433–469.

―――. "Vocabulaires Comparés des Langues de l'Atakora." *Bulletin de l'IFAN,* vol. 34, no. 2 (1972): 299–392; vol. 34, no. 3 (1972): 617–682; vol. 35, no. 2 (1973): 712–758; vol. 35, no. 3 (1973): 712–758; vol. 35, no. 4 (1973): 903–996; vol. 36, no. 3 (1974): 628–659; vol. 37, no. 2 (1975): 412–448.

―――. "Vocabulaires Comparés de Quatre Langues Voltaiques du Togo." *Bulletin de l'IFAN,* vol. 26 (B), no. 1/2 (Jan.–April 1964): 212–257.

Rapp, E. L. "Die Adangme-Ga Mundart von Ajotime in Togo." *Afrika,* vol. 2 (1943): 4–58.

Rey-Hulman, Diana. *Les Biligualismes Littéraires: Signification Sociale de la Littérature Orale Chez les Tyokossi,* 3 vol. Paris: Slisen, 1965.

Ricard, Alain. "Les Parisiens du Concert: Discours Metisse ou Discours Dominé?" *Politique Africaine,* vol. 2, no. 5 (Feb. 1982): 35–46.

Rouget, Gilbert. "Un Chromatisme Africain." *L'Homme,* vol. 1, no. 3 (Sept.–Dec. 1961): 32–46.

Rusch, Gunther. *Die Verhindererte Mitsprache: Aspeckte zur Sprachpolitik in Ghana, Togo, und Obervolta.* Hamburg: Institut für Afrika-Kunde, 1984.

Sallée, Pierre. "Improvisation et/ou Information: Sur Trois Exemples de Polyphones Africaines." In *L'Improvisation dans les Musiques de Tradition Orale,* Bernard Lortat-Jacob. Paris: SELAF, 1987.

Schlegel, J. B. *Schlussel zur Ewe-Sprache.* Stuttgart: Steinkopf, 1857.

Schober, R. "Die Semantische Gestalt des Ewe." *Anthropos,* vol. 28, no. 5/6 (1933): 621–632.

Seidel, A. *Togo-Sprachen.* Leipzig: Koch, 1904.

Sprigge, R.G.S. *Tone in the Adangbe Dialect of Ewe.* Legon: University of Ghana, Institute of African Studies, 1967.

Steele, Mary, and Gretchen Weed. *Collected Field Reports on the Phonology of Konkomba.* Legon: University of Ghana, Institute of African Studies, 1966.

Takassi, I. *Le Français Ecrit des Elèves Bassari (Togo).* Abidjan: Institut de la Linguistique Appliquée, 1971.

Tersis, Nicole. *Essai pour une Phonologie du Gurma Parlé à Kpana, Nord Togo.* Liege: Université de Liège, 1972.

Tetveehaki. *La Kabiyé standard.* Lomé: Imprimerie de l'Alphabétisation, 1981.

Trotter, D. *A Grammatical Guide and Numerous Idioms and Phrases for Beginners in the Ewe Dialect.* London: Harrison & Sons, 1921.

Westermann, Diedrich. *Die Ewe-Sprache in Togo: Eine praktische Einfuhrung.* Berlin: De Gruyter, 1961.

———. *Die Sprache der Guang in Togo und auf der Goldkuste und funf andere Togosprachen.* Nendelen (Liechtenstein): Kraus, 1974. (Reprint of 1922 edition published by D. Reimer in Berlin.)

———. "Drei Dialekte des Tem in Togo: Cala, Delo und Bago nach Aufnahmen von Mischlich." *Mitteilungen des Seminars fur Orientalische Sprachen,* vol. 36 (1933): 7–33.

———. *Gbesela Yeye or English-Ewe dictionary.* Berlin: Reimer 1910, 1922, 1930.

———. *Grammatik der Ewe-Sprache.* Berlin: D. Reimer, 1907 & 1957.

———. *A Study of the Ewe Language.* London: Oxford University Press, 1930.

———. "Die Togo Restvolker unde ihre Sprachen." *Tribus,* 1956: 63–68.

———. *Worterbuch der Ewe-Sprache.* Berlin: 1905.

———, and Margaret Bryan. *The Languages of West Africa.* New York: Oxford University Press, 1952.

Witte, Ant. "Sprichworter der Ewhe-neger, Ge-Dialekt, Togoland." *Anthropos,* vol. 12/13, no. 1/2 (1917/1918): 58–83.

Zech auf Neuhofen, Julius von. "Vermischte Notizen uber Togo und das Togo Hinterland." *Mitteilungen aus den Deutschen Schutzgebeiten,* vol. 2 (1898).

Zima, Petr. "Research in the Territorial and Social Stratification of African Languages." *Zeitschrift fur Phonetik,* vol. 28, no. 3–4 (1975): 311–323.

Yu, Ella Ozier. "Theoretical Aspects of Noun Classes in Lama (Togo)." Thesis, University of Illinois, 1991.

Art

Adler, Peter, and Nicholas Barnard. *African Majesty: The Textile Art of the Ashanti and the Ewe.* London: Thames & Hudson, 1992.

Agawu, V. Kofi. "Tone and Tune: The Evidence for Northern Ewe Music." *Africa,* vol. 58, no. 2 (1988): 127–46.

Aithnard, K. M. *Aspects of Cultural Policy in Togo.* Paris: UNESCO, 1972.

Akam, Noble, and Alain Ricard, eds. *Mister Tameklor, Suivi de Francis-le-Parisien.* Paris: SELAF, 1981.

Allain, Richard. "Concours et Concert: Théatre Populaire et Théatre Scolaire au Togo." *Revue d'Histoire du Théatre,* vol. 27, no. 1 (1975): 44–86.

———. "Hubert Ogunde à Lomé." *Revue d'Histoire du Théatre,* vol. 27, no. 1 (1975): 26–30.

Anku, William Oscar. "Procedures in African Drumming: A Study of Akan/Ewe Traditions and African Drumming in Pittsburgh." Thesis, University of Pittsburgh, 1988.

Anquetal, Jacques. *L'Artisanat Createur au Togo.* Paris: Agence de Coopération Culturelle et Technique, 1980.

Apedo-Amah, Togoata. "Le Concert-Party: Une Pedagogie pour les Apprimés." *Peuples Noirs-Peuples Africains,* vol. 8, no. 44 (1985): 61–72.

Benot-Latour, B. "L'Artisanat Togolais." *Afrique Literaire et Artistique,* vol. 30 (Nov. 1973): 40–42.

Blier, Suzanne Preston. *The Anatomy of Architecture: Ontology and Metaphor in Betammaliba Architectural Expression.* Cambridge: Cambridge University Press, 1987.

———. "Antelopes and Anvils: Tamberma Works of Iron." *African Arts,* vol. 17, no. 3 (May 1984): 58–63.

———. "Architecture of the Tamberma." Thesis, Columbia University, 1981.

———. "Houses Are Human: Architectural Self-Images of Africa's Tamberma." *Society of Architectural History Journal,* vol. 42, no. 4 (1983): 371–82.

————. "Moral Architecture: Beauty and Ethics in Batammaliba Design." In *Dwelling, Settlements, and Tradition,* edited by Jean-Paul Bourdier and Nezer Alsayyad, 335–56. New York: Lanham, 1989.

Contran, Nazareno P. *Zobada: Il Fuoco Cattovo, Canti Populari del Togo.* Afanya, Togo: 1975.

Cudoe, Dzagbe. "Ewe Sculpture in the Linden-Museum." *Tribus,* no. 18 (Aug. 1969): 49–72.

Darbois, Dominique, and V. Vasut. *Afrika Tanzt.* Prague: Artia, 1963.

Fagg, William Buller. *Yoruba Sculpture of West Africa.* New York: Knopf, 1982.

Fassassi, Masudi Alabi. *L'Architecture en Afrique Noire: Cosmoarchitecture.* Paris: Maspero, 1978.

Fiagbedzi, N. "Notes on Membranophones of the Anglo-Ewe." *Institute of African Studies Research Review* (University of Ghana), vol. 8, no. 1 (1971): 90–96.

Fischer, Eberhard. "Die Gelbgussmaske des Ali Amonikoyi (aus Togo) im Museum fur Volkerkunde in Basel." *Tribus,* vol. 15 (Aug. 1966): 89–95.

Gilbert, Michelle V. "Ewe Funerary Sculpture." *African Arts,* vol. 14, no. 4. (Aug. 1981): 44–46.

————. "Mystical Protection Among the Anlo Ewe." *African Arts,* vol. 15, no. 4 (Aug. 1982): 60–66.

Hardy, Georges. *L'Art Negre: L'Art Animiste des Noirs d'Afrique.* Paris: Laurens, 1972.

Haselberger, Herta. "Le Décor Grave chez les Boussansé." *Notes Africaines d'IFAN,* vol. 105 (Jan. 1965): 26–31.

————. "Wandmalerie, Gravierter und Modellierter Wandschmuck in den Savannen von Togo und Obervolta." *Archives Internationales d'Ethnographioe,* vol. 49, no. 2 (1960): 201–224.

————, and Thurston Shaw. "Au Sujet des Masques de Laiton au Togo." *Notes Africaines d'IFAN,* vol. 104 (Oct. 1964).

Ketoglo, A. *Petit Recueil de Chants et Rythmes Populaires Togolais.* Lomé: Institut Pédagogique Nationale du Ministère, 1974.

Kreamer, Christine Mullen. "The Art and Ritual of the Moba of Northern Togo." Thesis, Indiana University, 1986.

————. "Moba Shrine Figures." *African Arts,* vol. 20, no. 2 (Feb. 1987): 52–57.

Kuakavi, K. M. *Les Racines du Mal Nègre.* Lomé: Haho, 1985.

Kubik, G. "Hubert Kponton, Erfinder, Kunstler und Bergrynder eines Ethnographischen Privatmuseums in Lomé." *Archive fur Volkerkunde,* vol. 90 (1986): 157–171.

Lawson, Clement Boevi. "Peinture: Un Jeune Specialiste du Dessin sur Tissu." *Espoir de la Nation Togolaise,* no. 5–6 (April–May 1970): 42–43.

Locke, David Lawrence. *A Collection of Atsiagbeko Songs: 1975–1977.* Legon (Ghana): Institute of African Studies, 1980.

———. "The Music of the Atsiagbeko." Thesis, Wesleyan University, 1979.

"Le Peintre Emmanuel Dabla." *Espoir de la Nation Togolaise,* no. 13 (May–June 1971): 49–51.

Renne, Elisha. "The Thierry Collection of Hausa Artifacts at the Field Museum." *African Arts,* vol. 19, no. 4 (Aug. 1986): 54–8.

Witte, Ant. "Lieder und Gesange der Ewhe-Neger (Ge-Dialekt)." *Anthropos,* vol. 1, no. 1/4 (1906): 65–81, 194–209.

Tourism

Afrique Occidentale. *Guide Poche-Voyage.* Paris: Marcus, 1984.

Akoueté, Laure. "Aperçu Touristique sur la Région de Kluoto." *Espoire de la Nation Togolaise,* no. 5–6 (April–May 1970).

Bachelet, Michel. *Lomé, Capitale du Togo.* Paris: Delroisse, 1974.

Banque Centrale des Etats de l'Afrique de l'Ouest. "Le Développement Touristique au Togo," no. 213 (Jan. 1974).

Benot, Latour B. "Le 'Village du Bénin': Une Création Originale à Vocations Multiples." *Afrique Litteraire et Artistique,* vol. 30 (Nov. 1973): 43–46.

Blumenthal, Susan. "Togo." In *Bright Continent: A Shoestring Guide to Subsaharan Africa,* 242–260. New York: Anchor Books, 1974.

Boone, Sylvia Ardyne. "Togo." In *West African Travels: A Guide To People and Places,* 289–308. New York: Random House, 1974.

Brydon, David. *Africa Overland: A Route and Planning Guide.* Brentford: Roger Lascelles, 1991.

Catrisse, Benolt. "Hotellerie et Tourisme." *Afrique Industrie,* no. 203 (Mar. 1980): 42–69.

"Forest Elephants of Togo." *African Wildlife* (Cape Town), vol. 46, no. 2 (March–Apr. 1993): 71–75.

Glaser, Sylvie. *Guide du Voyageur en Afrique de l'Ouest.* Paris: Ediafric, 1984.

Gosset, Pierre, and Renée Gosset. *L'Afrique, les Africains,* vol. 1. Paris: R. Julliard, 1958.

Harrington, R. "The Republic of Togo, West Africa." *Travel,* June 3, 1970: 71–73.

Harris, Elizabeth. *Ghana: A Travel Guide. Supplementary Notes on Togo.* Flushing, N.Y.: Aburi Press, 1976.

Naasou, Kohou. "Le Togo Mise sur le Tourisme." *Europe-Outre-mer,* no. 594 (July 1979): 21–25.

Passot, B. *Togo, Les Hommes et Leur Milieu. Guide Pratique.* Paris: Harmattan, 1988.

Pecos. "Now Starring at the Rex Cinema Lomé!" *Africa Report,* vol. 18, no. 4 (July–Aug. 1973): 43–44.

Piraux, Maurice. *Le Togo Aujourd'hui.* Paris: Jeune Afrique, 1978.

"La Politique Touristique." *Europe-Outre-mer,* Mar.–Apr. 1978: 53–56.

Rake, Allen, ed. *Travellers Guide to West Africa.* London: IC Publishers, 1988.

"Rendez-vous à Lomé." *Europe-France-Outre-mer,* no. 514 (Nov. 1972): 40–42.

Togo. Information Service. *Togo 1962 Handbook.* Paris: Diloutremer, 1962.

Togo. Paris: Jeune Afrique, 1979.

Togo. Boulogne: Delroisse, 1979.

"Togo." *Europe-France-Outremer,* no. 380–381 (July–Aug. 1961); no. 387 (May 1962).

"Togo." In *Africa A to Z,* Robert S. Kane. Garden City, New York: Doubleday, 1961.

"Togo." In *Africa on a Shoestring,* Geoff Crowther, 195–204. Hawthorne (Australia): Lonely Planet Publishers, 1989.

"Togo." In *Fielding's Guide South of the Sahara,* Sherry A. Shuttles and B. Shuttles-Graham, 156–184. New York: Fielding Travel Books, 1986.

"Togo." In *Guide de Voyageur: l'Afrique de l'Ouest,* 261–70. Paris: Ediafric, 1984.

"Togo." In *Guid'Ouest Africain.* Paris: Diloutremer. Annual, 1948+.

"Togo." In *Le Moniteur du Tourisme Africain.* Dakar: Société Africain d'Edition, 1971 [annual].

"Togo." In *West Africa: The Rough Guide,* Richard Trillo and Jim Hudgens. London: Harrap-Columbus, 1990.

"Togo." In *West Africa: A Survival Kit,* Alex Newton, 425–448. Berkeley, California: The Lonely Planet, 1988.

"Togo." In *UTA Travel Guide to Western and Central Africa,* 343–58. Paris: UTA French Airlines, Tourism Department, 1989.

Le Togo Aujourd'hui. Paris: Editions Jeune Afrique, 1876.

"Togo's Empty Beds." *West Africa,* Jan. 3, 1983: 25–26.

"Togo Goes Gently." *West Africa,* May 24, 1982: 1381–1382.

"Togo: Tourisme, l'Afrique en Raccourci." *Europe-Outre-mer,* no. 620–1 (Sept.–Oct. 1981), special supplement.

Waibel, Leo. *Vom Urwald zur Wuste; Natur und Lebensbilder aus Westafrika.* Breslau: F. Hirt, 1928.

Sources and Bibliographies

Adzomada, Jacques Kofi. Répertoire et Résumé en Français des Ouvrages Ewe. Lomé: Imprimerie Editogo, 1970.

Africa Research Bulletin. Series A: Political, Social and Cultural. Series B: Economic, Financial and Technical. Exeter, England: 1963+ [monthly].

Africa South of the Sahara. London: Europa Publications, 1971 [annual].

Africa South of the Sahara: Index to Periodical Literature: Washington, D.C.: Library of Congress, 1985 (3rd suppl.).

Africa Yearbook and Who's Who. 2 vols. London: Africa Journal Ltd., 1976. Second edition, 1989.

Afrique. Annual publication of *Jeune Afrique* (Paris and Tunis).

Afrique Contemporaine. Paris, quarterly.

L'Afrique Noire de A à Z. Paris: Ediafric, 1971.

Afrique Nouvelle. Dakar.

Akakpo, Amouzouvi. *Les Frontières Togolaises, Les Modifications de 1927–9.* Lomé: Faculty of Letters and Humanities, 1979.

Année Africaine. Paris: Pedone, 1963–.

Année Politique Africaine. Dakar: Société Africaine d'Edition, 1966–.

Annuaire d'Afrique Noire. Paris: Ediafric, annual.

Annuaire Economique Officiel. Paris: ABC, 1983.

Asamani, J. O. *Index Africanus: Catalogue of Articles in Western Languages published from 1885 to 1965.* Stanford, California: Hoover Institution Press, 1975.

Ballantyne, James, and Andrew Roberts. *Africa: A Handbook of Film and Video Resources.* London: British Film and Video Council, 1986.

Banque Centrale des Etats de l'Afrique de l'Ouest. "Indicateurs Economiques Togolaises." Paris.

Bederman, Sanford H. *Africa: A Bibliography of Geography and Related Disciplines.* Atlanta: Georgia State University, 1974.

Biarnes, Pierre, et al. *L'Economie Africaine.* Dakar: Société Africaine d'Edition, annual.

Bibliographie des Travaux en Langues Française sur l'Afrique au Sud du Sahara. Paris: CARDAN, 1982.

Bibliographie Rétrospective du Togo 1950–1970. Lomé. Bibliotheque Nationale, 1975.

"Bibliographie sur la Litterature Orale au Togo." *Documents de Centre d'Etudes et de Recherches de Kara,* Piya (Togo), 1968: 272–275.

"Bibliographie Tchocossi." *Documents de Centre d'Etudes et de Recherches de Kara,* Piya (Togo), 1968: 271.

Blackhurst, Hector, ed. *Africa Bibliography.* Manchester: Manchester University Press, annual.

Blake, David, and Carole Travis. *Periodicals from Africa.* Boston: G. K. Hall & Co., 1984.

Bogaert, Jozef. *Sciences Humaines en Afrique Noire: Guide Bibliographique (1945–1965).* Brussels: Centre Documentation Economique et Sociale Africaine, 1966.

Brasseur, P., and J. F. Maurel. *Les Sources Bibliographies de l'Afrique de l'Ouest et de l'Afrique Equatoriale d'Expression Française*. Dakar: Bibliotheque de l'Université, 1970.

Bridgman, Jon, and David E. Clarke. *German Africa: A Select and Annotated Bibliography*. Stanford: Hoover Institution, 1965.

Carson, P. *Materials for West African History in French Archives*. London: Athlone Press, 1968.

Chauveau, J. P., and F. Verdeaux, eds. *Bibliographie sur les Communautés de Pecheurs de l'Ouest*. Cotonou: DIPA, 1989.

Chronologie Politique Africaine. Paris: Fondation Nationale des Sciences Politiques, Centre d'Etudes des Relations Internationales, 1960–1970 [bi-monthly].

Conover, H. F. *Official Publications of French West Africa 1946–1958*. Washington, D.C.: Library of Congress, 1960.

Cornevin, Robert. "Bibliographie." In his *Histoire du Togo*. Paris: Berger Levrault, 1962.

Country Profiles: Togo, Benin. London: The Economist Intelligence Unit, 1986–.

Country Reports. Togo, Niger, Benin, Burkina. London: The Economist Intelligence Unit, 1986–.

Cyrot, Catherine. *Togo 1990. Series Reference Bibliographie*. Paris: IBISCUS, 1991.

Decalo, Samuel. *Togo*. Oxford and Santa Barbara: Clio Press, 1995.

Deutsche Afrika-Gesellschaft. *Afrika-Bibliographie: Verzeichnis des Wissenschaftlichen Schrifttums in Deutscher Sprache aus dem Jahre 1964*. Bonn.

Dictionary of African Biography. 2nd ed. London: Melrose Press, 1971.

Directory of African Experts, 1989. Paris: United Nations Economic Commission for Africa, 1989.

Dossier Togo. Paris: Recontres Africaines, 1987.

Duic, Walter Z. *Africa Administration*, vol. 1, 845–904. Munich: Verlag Dokumentation, 1978.

L'Economie des Pays d'Afrique Noire. Paris: Ediafric, 1982.

Les Elites Africaines 1970–71. Paris: Ediafric, 1971.

Etudes Togolaises. Lomé: University of Benin, 1971.

Europe-France-Outre-mer. Paris, monthly.

Gaignebet, Wanda. *Inventaire de Thèses Africanistes de Langue Française*. Paris: Cardan, 1977.

———. *Répertoire des Thèses Africanistes Françaises*. Paris: CARDAN, 1982.

———. *Répertoire des Thèses africanistes Françaises 1988–89*. Paris: CARDAN, 1991.

Gorman, G. E., and M. M. Mahoney. *Guide to Current National Bibliographies in the Third World*. Munich: Hans Zell, 1983.

Hertefelt, Marcel d', and Anne-Marie Bouttiaux-Ndiaye. *Bibliographie de l'Afrique Sud-Sahariénne: Sciences Humaines et Sociales 1986–87.* Tervuren: Musée Royal de l'Afrique Centrale, 1990.

Hintz, V. *Bibliographie der Kwa-Sprachen und der Sprachen der Togo-Restvolker.* Berlin, 1969.

Hommes et Destins. 4 vols. Paris: Academie des Sciences d' Outremer, 1977+.

Hoover Institution. *U.S. and Canadian Publications and Theses on Africa, 1961–1966.* Stanford, California: Hoover Institution Press.

International African Institute. *Africa* [bibliography section]. 1929– [quarterly].

Jahn, Janheinz, et al. *Who's Who in African Literature.* Tubingen: Horst Erdmann Verlag, 1972.

Jakande, L.K., ed. *West Africa Annual.* Lagos: John West Publications.

Jeune Afrique. Paris and Tunis [weekly].

Johnson, G. Wesley, "The Archival System of Former French West Africa." *African Studies Bulletin,* vol. 8, no. 1 (April 1965): 48–58.

Joucla, E. *Bibliographie de l'Afrique Occidentale Française.* Paris: Société d'Editions Geographiques, Maritimes et Coloniales, 1937.

Journal Officiel de la République Togolaise. Lomé, 1956–[semimonthly].

Journal Officiel du Territoire du Togo Place Sous le Mandat de la France. Lomé, 1920–26 [monthly]; 1927–56 [semi-monthly].

Kohler, Jochen. *Deutsche Dissertationen uber Afrika: Ein Verzeichnis für die Jahre 1918–1959.* Bonn: K. Schroeder fur Deutsche Afrika-Gesselschaft, 1962.

Kouassi, Kwam. "Documents et Travaux Inédits E.S.A.C.J.-E.S.T.E.G." *Annales de l'Université de Bénin,* vol. 2, no. 1 (1978): 153–66.

Lafage, S. "Contribution à un Inventaire Chronologique des Ouvrages Entièrement ou Partiellement en Langue Ewé." *Annales de l'Université d'Abidjan,* vol. 7, no. 1 (1974): 169–204.

Lafond, Mireille. *Recueil des Thèses Africanistes, 1967–84.* Paris: Centre d'Etudes Juridiques et Comparitives, 1984.

Lauer, Joseph, et al. *American and Canadian Doctoral Dissertations and Masters Theses on Africa 1974–1987.* Atlanta, Georgia: Crossroads Press, 1989.

Legum, Colin, ed. *Africa Contemporary Record.* London: Rex Collins, 1968–1990.

Lipschutz, Marc R., and R. Kent Rasmussen. *Dictionary of African Historical Biography.* Berkeley: University of California Press, 1986.

Lordereau, Paulette. *Littératures Africaines à la Bibliotheque Nationale 1920–1972.* Paris: Bibliotheque Nationale, 1991.

———. *Littératures Africaines à la Bibliotheque Nationale 1972–1983.* Paris: Bibliotheque Nationale, 1991.

Madjri, Dovi J. *Sociologie de la Littérature Togolaise.* Lomé: Direction des Affaires Culturelles, 1975.

Martineau, Alfred, et al. *Bibliographie d'Histoire Coloniale 1900–1930.* Paris: Société de l'Histoire des Colonies Française, 1932.

Mauny, R. "Contribution à la Bibliographie de l'Histoire de l'Afrique Noire des Origines à 1850." *Bulletin de l'IFAN,* vol. 28, no. 3/4 (July–Oct. 1966): 927–965.

Milner, Toby. *The Business Traveller's Handbook.* London: Michael Joseph, 1982.

Le Mois en Afrique: Revue Française d'Etudes Politiques Africaines. Paris, monthly and/or quarterly, to 1989.

Momento de l'Economie Africaine. Paris, Ediafric, 1966–1987 [annual].

Noel, Danielle, and Michélle Santraille. *Contribution à la Bibliographie du Togo: Inventaire Bibliographique d'Archives, de Services Administratifs et de Bibliothéques de Lomé.* Lomé: Direction d'Etudes et de la Plan, 1971.

Nomenyo, A. "Bibliographie démographique du Togo." In *Analyse Régionale du Recensement de 1970.* Mensah L. Assogba and Thérèse Locoh, et al. Lomé: Université de Lomé, Unité de Recherches Démographique, 1983.

Panofsky, A. E. *A Bibliography of Africana.* London, 1975.

Personalites Publiques de l'Afrique de l'Ouest. Paris: Ediafric, 1968.

Peter, J. *Annuaire des Etats d'Afrique Noire—Gouvernements et Cabinets Ministeriels des Républiques d'Expression Française.* Paris: Ediafric, 1961.

Rake, Alan. *Africa's Top 300.* New York: Africa File, 1990.

Récherches en Sciences Humaines de l'ORSTOM au Togo: Bibliographie 1946–83. Lomé: ORSTOM, 1983.

Répertoire Bibliographique, 4 vol. Lomé: Ministère du Plan et des Mines, 1988.

Répertoire des Centres de Documentation et Bibliotheques. Abidjan: Conseil de l'Entente, Service de Documentation, 1980.

Répertoire des Enseignants et Chercheurs Africains. Montreal: Association des Universités Partiellement ou Entièrement de Langue Française, 1984.

Répertoire des Memoires Soutenus à l'Ecole des Lettres et Deposés à la Bibliotheque Universitaire, 1978–1985. Lomé: University of Bénin Library, 1987.

Répertoire des Pouvoirs Public Africains. Paris: Ediafric, 1975.

Répertoire des Thèses Africanistes Françaises 1982–83. Paris: CEA-CARDAN, 1986.

Revue des Marchés et Mediterranéens. Paris [weekly].

Rydings, H. A. *The Bibliographies of West Africa.* Ibadan: Ibadan University Press, 1961.

Scheven, Yvette. *Bibliographies for African Studies 1970–1986.* London: Hans Zell, 1988.

Schmidt, Nancy J. *Subsaharan African Films and Filmakers: A Preliminary Bibliography.* Bloomington: Indiana University African Studies Program, 1986.

Segal, Ronald. *Political Africa.* London: Stevens & Sons, 1961.

Shaw, Thomas McDonald. "A Bibliography of Art and Architecture in Togo." *Africana Journal,* vol. 8, no. 2 (1977): 131–135.

Sims, Michael, and Alfred Kagan. *American and Canadian Doctoral Dissertations and Master's Theses on Africa 1886–1974.* Waltham, Massachusetts: African Studies Association, 1976.

Sociétés et Fournisseurs d'Afrique Noire. Paris: Ediafric, annual.

Standing Conference on Library Materials on Africa. *United Kingdom Publications and Theses on Africa.* Cambridge, England: Heffer, 1963.

Sternberg, Ilse, and Patricia M. Larby, eds. *African Studies.* London: SCOLMA, 1986.

Stewart, John, *African States and Rulers.* Jefferson, North Carolina: MacFarland, 1989.

Ternaux-Compans, Henri. *Bibliothèque Asiatique et Africaine ou Catalogue des Ouvrages Relatifs à l'Asie et à l'Afrique, Qui ont Paru Depuis la Découverte de l'Imprimerie Jusqu'en 1700.* Amsterdam: B.H. Gruner, 1968. Reprint of 1841 Paris edition.

Togo. Service de l'Information. *L'Annuaire du Togo.* Lomé, annual.

"Togo." In *African Biographies,* vol. 4. Bonn-Bad Godesberg: Research Institute of the Friedrich-Ebert Stiftung, 1967. Updated Nov. 1974.

"Togo." In *Who's Who in Africa,* John Dickie and Alan Rake, 521–525. London: African Development, 1973.

"Togo in 1980–85." Washington, D.C., Embassy of Togo, 1979?

Togo 1990, Références Bibliographiques. Paris: Ministère de la Cooperation et du Développement, 1990.

United Nations. Economic Commission for Africa. *Foreign Trade Statistics of Africa.* Series A: Direction of Trade. New York, May 1962+.

———. *Foreign Trade Statistics of Africa.* Series B: Trade by Commodity. New York, 1960–[semiannual].

U.S. Office of Geography. *Togo: Official Standard Names Approved by the US Board on Geographic Names.* Washington, D.C., 1966.

Vignes, Jacques, ed. *Annuaire de l'Afrique et du Moyen Orient.* Paris. 1982.

West Africa. London [weekly].

Westermann, Diedrich, and M. A. Bryan. *Handbook of African Languages. Part 1: Languages of West Africa.* London: Dawsons, 1970.

Wieschhoff, Heinrich A. *Anthropological Biography of Africa.* New Haven, Connecticut: American Oriental Society, 1948.

Wiseman, John A. *Political Leaders in Black Africa*. Aldershot: Edward Elgar, 1991.

Witherell, Julian. *Africana Resources and Collections*. Metuchen, New Jersey: Scarecrow Press, 1989.

—————. *French-Speaking West Africa: A Guide to Official Publications*, 130–141. Washington, D.C.: Library of Congress, 1967.

—————. *Official Publications of the French Equatorial Africa, French Camerouns and Togo, 1949–58*. Washington, D.C.: Library of Congress, 1964.

Yaranga, Zofia. *Bibliographie des Travaux en Langue Française sur l'Afrique au Sud du Sahara*. Paris: Centre d'Etudes Africaines, 3 vol. 1981, 1985, 1989.

Zielnica, K. *Bibliographie der Ewe in West-Afrika*. Vienne: Institut Volder Kde Universitat, 1976.

La Zone Franc en Afrique. Paris: Ediafric, 1981.